THE ENCYCLOPEDIA OF CODENAMES OF WORLD WAR II

THE ENCYCLOPEDIA OF CODENAMES OF WORLD WAR II

Christopher Chant

Routledge & Kegan Paul
London

for Clarinda

First published in 1986 by
Routledge & Kegan Paul Ltd
11 New Fetter Lane, London EC4P 4EE

Set in 9/10 pt Linotron Baskerville
by Input Typesetting Ltd, London
and printed in Great Britain
by T. J. Press (Padstow) Ltd, Padstow, Cornwall

© *Christopher Chant 1986*

No part of this book may be reproduced in
any form without permission from the publisher
except for the quotation of brief passages
in criticism

British Library Cataloguing in Publication Data

Chant, Christopher
The encyclopedia of codenames of
World War II.
1. World War, 1939-1945—Campaign—
Code words
I. Title
940.54'1   D743

ISBN 0-7102-0718-2

CONTENTS

Introduction   vii
The Encyclopedia of Codenames of World War II   1

INTRODUCTION

'Operations . . . ought not to be described by code-words which imply a boastful and over-confident sentiment . . . which are calculated to invest the plan with an air of despondency. . . . They ought not to be names of frivolous character. . . . They should not be ordinary words. . . . Names of living people should be avoided.'

Prime Minister Churchill to General Sir Hastings Ismay (August 1943)

A codename is one selected by those party to the concept as a method of imparting a meaning different from the conventional one, and is designed as an aid to security of information. Codenames were an important feature of World War II, serving as a type of mental shorthand for those in the know, and obfuscating the issue for those not in the know. Thus operations, plans, locations and personalities could be disguised from the enemy (who sought to garner information either directly by the use of their own intelligence services or indirectly through the indiscretions of those who had come into possession of information to which they had no right) while the codeword was itself an adequate mental trigger for those concerned with the planning and implementation of the operation in question. Such codenames were used from the highest levels, in the planning of grand strategic moves affecting the conduct of the whole war, to the lowest command echelons, in the conduct of small-scale tactical operations. At the one level the codename might be valid for months or even years, while at the other it would maintain its currency for only a short period, measured most probably in hours rather than days.

This dictionary is designed as an aid to those interested in the higher command levels of World War II, and is intended not so much as a complete listing (which would be virtually impossible) but as a summary of the more important strategic and operational codenames, together with a sample of other codenames designed to provide a small insight into more obscure operations such as the infiltration of agents into occupied Europe and the tactical use of special airborne forces. The core of the work is thus a fairly

Introduction

large but none the less eclectic selection of operational codenames, and my aim has been to provide the reader with a summary of the concept embodied in the selected codenames. In the case of planning and strategic concepts, the rationale has been to provide the context in which the codename arose, was used and was developed either into implementation or ultimate abandonment. In the case of operational codenames, the rationale has been to provide a summary of the operation: its aims, the forces involved, the commanders, the geographical and time frames in which it happened, and the results.

The *Codenames of World War II* has been a subject of enduring fascination to me, and I hope that the reader will find it of equal interest and stimulation. I am conscious that so monumental a task of selection and appreciation must reflect my own bias, but I feel that it has been fair to the parties concerned, and hope that the reader will agree. I remain candidly open to suggestions for modification and expansion, and will gratefully consider any opinions which readers may proffer.

Christopher Chant
Swayfield,
Grantham,
Lincolnshire, UK.
October 1985

A

A Japanese naval counteroffensive (19/20 June 1944) planned after the US capture of the Marshall Islands between 20 November 1943 and 23 February 1944, the Japanese high command having appreciated that the next forward move would take the Americans to the Marianas Islands on the Japanese home islands' strategic doorstep and thus able to strike at Japan, Iwo Jima, the Ryukyus (Okinawa) and Formosa, so severing the Japanese maritime links to the Philippines, South-East Asia and all their raw materials. Operation 'A' called for the American invasion force off the Marianas (in the event the 5th Amphibious Force supported by Task Force 58) to be attacked by powerful surface forces moving in from the south-west, where they were based close to vital oil supplies.

Under the command of Vice Admiral Ozawa, the 1st Mobile Fleet from Tawitawi was supported by Vice Admiral Ugaki's Southern Force from Batjan, the two forces rendezvousing east of the Philippines on 16 June 1944, one day after the US forces landed on Saipan in the Marianas. The rendezvous gave Ozawa a fleet of 5 fleet and 5 light aircraft-carriers (carrying only very poor aircrew and obsolescent aircraft), 5 battleships, 11 heavy and 2 light cruisers, and 28 destroyers; Vice Admiral Mitscher's TF58 comprised 7 heavy and 8 light aircraft-carriers (with experienced aircrew and modern aircraft), 7 battleships, 8 heavy and 13 light cruisers, and 69 destroyers. The Japanese plan became apparent to Mitscher after the Japanese rendezvous was spotted by US patrol submarines, and the scene was thus set for the climactic Battle of the Philippine Sea (otherwise 'The Great Marianas Turkey Shoot') on 19/20 June 1944, which resulted in the utter decimation of the Japanese carrier strength, especially in the Imperial Japanese Navy's last reserve of combat-experienced aircrew. Ozawa launched a first air strike early on 19 June, but the radar-warned Americans intercepted this initial wave 50 miles short of the US force, shooting down more than 200 Japanese aircraft. US submarines had meanwhile attacked Ozawa's force, torpedoing the carriers *Taiho* and *Shokaku*, both of which sank. The Japanese second strike, launched at 14.00, was intercepted on its way to Guam and again the Japanese aircraft were decimated, some 100 aircraft being lost. Thus Ozawa had by the end of the first day lost 2 carriers and more than 300 aircraft, whereas the Americans' losses were some 35 aircraft and slight damage to one battleship.

It was now the turn of the Americans, and Mitscher launched his aircraft from 16.24 on 20 June as TF58 pursued the Japanese fleet that was withdrawing to the north-west to refuel. The American strike sank two tankers and the carrier *Hiyo*, damaged the carriers *Zuikaku*, *Junyo* and *Chiyoda* and the heavy cruiser *Maya*, and destroyed another 65 Japanese aircraft, for the loss of 20 of their own aircraft. It was night by the time the American aircraft headed for their parent carriers, which Mitscher ordered to turn on their lights as an aid to the pilots. Nevertheless some 80 US aircraft ran out of fuel and ditched, most of their crews being saved. Operation 'A' and the resultant Battle of the Philippine Sea may thus be seen as marking the end of the Imperial Japanese Navy's air arm as an effective weapon.

A.B. Designation (together with a numeral) of Allied convoys plying the route across the Indian Ocean from Aden to Bombay; the start date of the A.B. convoys was November 1942.

ABC-1 Military agreements reached by the Allies at the Washington Conference (January/March 1941), embodied in the catchphrase 'Germany first' that characterized the Allies' determination that Nazi Germany was the primary enemy, and that all major efforts should be devoted to the defeat of Germany before significant forces were allocated for anything but holding operations against the Japanese.

ABC-2 Designation of the air agreement reached by the British and Americans at the Washington Conference (January/March 1941). The plan established that the US would develop a 54-group air force for hemisphere defence while preparing for the development of a 100-group air force for offensive operations, but that until such time as the USA entered the war, primary allocation of aircraft from new production capacity would go to the UK, and then be split evenly between the UK and USA after the latter's entry into the war.

ABC-4 Designation of the overall strategy agreed by the Allies in the 'Arcadia' Conference (December 1941); this established that in 1942 the Allies would tighten the ring round Germany with blockade, bombardment and secondary-theatre operations, specifically in the Mediterranean.

ABDA Designation of the combined Australian, British, Dutch and American command structure established by the Washington Conference (January/March 1941) to co-ordinate Allied defence against Japanese aggression in South-East Asia and the East Indies.

Abel Airborne operation by the French 3ème Regiment Colonial des Parachutistes to harass the German retreat through France (27 August/6 September 1944).

Abercrombie Canadian raid on Hardelot in northern France (22 April 1942) as part of the operational and tactical build-up for the 'reconnaissance in force' against Dieppe by the 2nd Canadian Division in August 1942 (Operation 'Jubilee').

Aberdeen (i) British 8th Army offensive against the forces of the Deutsches Afrika Korps trapped in the area known as 'The Cauldron' (5/6 June 1942) during the Battle of Gazala.
(ii) Fly-in airstrip for the British 14th Long-Range Penetration Brigade (23/24 March 1944) during the 2nd Chindit Expedition behind the Japanese lines in Burma.

Abigail Ultimately abortive plan for a major raid by forces of RAF Bomber Command on a German city (December 1940).

Abigail Rachel First British area bombing raid of the war, planned as the start of 'Abigail' (in response to the devastating German bomber attack on Coventry) with 235 aircraft against Bremen, Düsseldorf or Mannheim. In the event the raid was undertaken (16/17 December 1940) by 134 Vickers Wellington, Armstrong Whitworth Whitley and Handley Page Hampden bombers (of which only 103 bombed) against Mannheim.

Abwehrschlacht (defensive battle) Alternative designation for Operation 'Herbstnebel'.

Accolade Allied plans for an operation to capture the Dodecanese Islands in the Aegean Sea from the Germans after the capitulation of Italy in September 1943, the object being the possible opening of communication with western Turkey through the port of Izmir to aid that country in the event of an invasion by German forces.

Achse (axis) (i) German plan to support the offensive by Italian forces in Libya towards the Suez Canal, rendered fruitless by the failure of Marshal Graziani's offensive (September 1941).

(ii) German seizure of key points and installations in Italy (and of Italian positions in southern France, the Balkans and the Aegean) after the Italian armistice with the Allies on 9 September 1943. The Germans also planned to take the whole Italian fleet, but this part of the operation was frustrated by the fact that the major surface units of the Italian fleet were already on their way from La Spezia and other Italian mainland naval bases to Malta as part of the armistice agreement with the Allies.

Acid British task force for Operation 'Husky'.

Acrobat Plan for the British 8th Army to advance into Tripolitania from Cyrenaica after the successful conclusion anticipated for Operation 'Crusader' (January 1942).

Adele (Adelie) Headquarters of the German Oberkommando der Wehrmacht (PKW) in Potsdam.

Adler (eagle) **(i)** German mopping-up operation on the Dalmatian coast and in the Adriatic islands after the implementation of Operation 'Achse' (ii), and designed to secure these important base areas from seizure by the Allies or by the communist partisan forces commanded by Marshal Tito.
(ii) German operation against Soviet partisans operating in the region of Chechivichi in the USSR (20 July/7 August 1942).

Adlerangriff (eagle attack) Designation of the all-out attack by the Luftwaffe against the southern portion of the UK (August/September 1940), known to the British as the Battle of Britain. The battle was designed by the German air force with strategic objectives, the intention being to eliminate the main fighting strength of the RAF (by flying bomber attacks against coastal convoys, radar stations and fighter airfields to tempt up the British defences on tactical terms advantageous to the German fighters, which would then eliminate an RAF fighter strength that had been woefully underestimated by Luftwaffe intelligence, as had production and repair rates) as a prelude to the intended German airborne and seaborne invasion known as Operation 'Seelöwe'.

The failure of Operation 'Adlerangriff', as a result of Reichsmarschall Hermann Goering's overambitious plans for what was essentially a tactical air arm, speiled the postponement and ultimately the cancellation of 'Seelöwe', and this played a decisive part in the outcome of the war. Hitler was an avowed opponent of the concept of war on two fronts, but the failure of Germany's plans against the UK meant that unless the proposed invasion of the USSR (Operation 'Barbarossa') was postponed, Germany would indeed be faced with two powerful opponents at the same time. With hindsight it is possible to see that the failure of 'Adlerangriff' was perhaps inevitable, for the Germans were attempting to achieve a strategic result with an air force designed specifically for the tactical support of the German army. Though useful results were achieved as long as tactical commanders were left in control of operations, the decision by Hermann Goering to tie his fighters to close escort of the bombers (which were being severely mauled by British fighters) meant that the fighters were just as vulnerable as the bombers, increasing losses at a time when the British forces were at the limit of their endurance. To cap it all, the Germans then decided to switch their forces away from the destruction of RAF airfields and fighters to the destruction of London, a politically motivated decision which gave the British fighters both a breathing space and just the targets they had been trained to tackle.

Adlerhorst (eyrie) Hitler's headquarters at Bad Neuheim for Operation 'Herbstnebel' (10 December 1944/15 January 1945).

Adlertag (eagle day) German codename for the launch date of Operation 'Adlerangriff', originally set for 10 August 1940 but postponed for weather reasons to 13 August 1940.

Admiral Q Allied priority message code for President Franklin D. Roosevelt.

Aerial Smaller-scale counterpart to Operation 'Dynamo' and designed to remove by sea all British troops in north-west France, largely from the ports of Cherbourg, St Malo, Brest, St Nazaire and La Pallice (16/24 June 1940). Admiral Sir William James, the Commander-in-Chief Portsmouth, was controller of the evacuations from Cherbourg and St Malo, while the others came under the command of Admiral Sir M. Dunbar-Nasmith, Commander-in-Chief Western Approaches. At Cherbourg some 30,630 men of the 52nd Division and Norman Force were lifted between 16 and 18 June; at St Malo 21,474 men of the 1st Canadian Division and other units were picked up between 16 and 18 June; at Brest some 32,584 soldiers and airmen were rescued between 17 and 18 June; at St Nazaire the total was 57,235 troops (including a number from Nantes) evacuated between 16 and 20 June; and at La Pallice 2,303 British and a large number of Polish troops were brought out between 17 and 20 June. Another 19,000 or so troops, most of them Polish, were lifted from ports in the southern half of the French Atlantic coast. At the same time it was decided to evacuate as many as possible from the Channel Islands, and between 19 and 24 June some 22,656 British citizens were removed from these islands, which must inevitably fall to the Germans after the capture of France.

Afloc Designation of the Allied supply route across Africa used to deliver vehicles from ports in West Africa to the operational theatres in the Western Desert, East Africa and the Middle East.

Agent Allied priority message codename for Prime Minister Winston S. Churchill.

Agreement British combined assault (overland and amphibious) on the Axis supply base of Tobruk (13/14 September 1942), designed to harass the German and Italian lines of communication and supply during the build-up to the 2nd Battle of El Alamein. The raid was not a resounding success, and led the Axis forces to use second- rather than first-line units to garrison key staging areas.

Aïda Axis forces' advance into Egypt after the fall of Tobruk (26 June/1 July 1942), designed to clear the British and Common- wealth forces from Egypt, but leading in fact to the 1st Battle of El Alamein. Generalfeld- marschall Erwin Rommel's intention was to exploit the disarray of the British and Commonwealth forces in the aftermath of the Battle of Gazala despite the weakness of his own forces (particularly the German forma- tions), but the Axis effort was too much for their fuel supplies and other physical resources at a time when the British 8th Army was beginning finally to find its feet under an energetic and capable commander, General Sir Claude Auchinleck.

Airborne Cigar British airborne device to jam the German night-fighter control frequencies.

A.K.D. Designation (together with a numerical suffix) of Allied convoys plying the East African coastal route from Aden via Kilindini to Durban. These convoys were instituted in September 1943 and replaced all earlier southbound East African coastal convoys.

Alabaster Convoy carrying British forces for the occupation of Iceland (17/18 May 1940), at the time thought to be under the threat of German occupation with dire results to the British convoy routes across the North Atlantic.

AL Japanese naval operation (3/7 June 1942) at the same time as Operations 'AOB' and 'AQ' to seize the islands of Kiska and Attu in the Aleutians group. The object of Operation 'AL', as part of the diversionary effort in the Imperial Navy's ultimately over- complex Midway operation in June 1942, was to shield the occupation forces but also to strike against the US base at Dutch Harbor on Unalaska Island to cause as much damage as possible and to draw in major US Navy surface combatants from the south, away from the Midway operations. Operation 'AL' involved Vice Admiral Boshiro Hosogaya's Northern Force (2 light aircraft-carriers, 7 cruisers and 12 destroyers including the units of Rear Admiral Kakuji Kakuta's 2nd Carrier Striking Force, which was to provide air cover for the landings and the main strike force against American naval intervention) and was generally successful in attaining its occupation objectives, though it failed to draw in American naval forces as Admiral Chester W. Nimitz, US Commander-in-Chief Pacific, knew Operation 'AL' to be a diversion.

Alacrity Entry of British forces into the Azores after the agreement of neutral Portugal (8 October 1943). This move, long desired by Winston Churchill, had the double advantage of denying this key base to the Germans should they overrun the Iberian peninsula, and also providing the Allies with bases for long-range patrol aircraft and short-range escort ships so desperately needed to cover the mid-Atlantic gap in which the German U-boats were proving so successful.

Alamo Codename for the US 6th Army in South-West Pacific Area operations.

Alarich (Alaric) Earlier version of Operation 'Achse' (ii).

Albacore Ultimately abortive plan for the Chinese forces based in northern India (after the retreat from Burma in 1942) to invade and recapture northern Burma in 1943 as part of the Allied effort to reopen land communications with Generalissimo Chiang Kai-shek's Chinese Nationalist forces.

Albert Linie (Albert line) German defensive line in Italy to the north of Perugia. The line ran to each side of Lake Trasimeno, and was designed as a subsidiary position to check the Allies as they moved forward to the important 'Gotisch Linie' defences farther north. Lieutenant General Mark Clark's US 5th Army and Lieutenant General Sir Oliver Leese's British 8th Army both moved through the 'Albert Linie' defences in the second half of June 1944 and pushed on to the north against the forces of General Joachim Lemelsen's German 14th Army and Generaloberst Heinrich von Vietinghoff-Scheel's German 10th Army.

Album Leaf Improved version of 'Oboe'.

Alpenveilchen (cyclamen) German reinforcement plan for the Italian forces in Albania (spring 1941), where they were being severely handled by a determined Greek counteroffensive.

Alpha (i) Beach between Toulon and Marseilles for Operation 'Dragoon'.
(ii) US plan to halt the Japanese 'ICHI' offensive towards Kunming and Chungking in China (November 1944).

Alsos Allied intelligence mission to determine the nature and progress of German research into atomic weapons development.

Altona German support operation for Operation 'Hamburg' to prevent Soviet partisans from escaping to the south (December 1942).

Aluminium British commando intelligence mission operating in Czechoslovakia.

Amherst Airborne operation by the 2ème and 3ème Regiments Coloniaux des Parachutistes to disrupt German rear-area communications in the region of Apeldoorn in the Netherlands (7/8 April 1945).

Anakim British plan for a seaborne invasion of lower Burma in the spring of 1943 with the object of recapturing Rangoon and making possible an advance up the Irrawaddy river. The plan was conceived as one-third of an overall scheme for the recapture of Burma, the other two parts being Operations 'Cannibal' and 'Ravenous'. The scheme was ultimately abortive as the British and Indian forces in the theatre were wholly incapable of launching sustained offensive operations. The Japanese launched a number of spoiling attacks, and the amphibious capability needed for Operations 'Anakim' and 'Cannibal' were absorbed by Allied operations of higher priority in other theatres.

Anchorage US plan for a landing in Hansa Bay in New Guinea during April 1944.

Andalusien (Andalusia) German ocean rendezvous in the south Atlantic north of Tristan da Cunha where warships and raiders could resupply from waiting supply vessels to increase their endurance.

5

ANFA US Operations Division code for the Allied conference at Casablanca.

Anklet British plan for a landing in Norway during 1941.

Anna German cable address of the Oberkommando des Heeres (OKH).

Anthropoid Czech commando mission to assassinate Reinhard Heydrich, the Reichsprotektor of Bohemia and Moravia (27 May 1942).

Antimon (antimony) German codename for war supplies delivered to Romania.

Anton (Anthony) Alternative designation for Operation 'Attila'.

Anvil Under this codename the Allies planned the invasion of southern France that was to complement the northern effort codenamed Operation 'Overlord'. The primary objective of the invasion was to free the ports of Marseilles and Toulon and so make possible another Allied (US and Free French) advance against the Germans in western Europe, in this instance up the Rhône river and into southern Germany. For the actual assault the codename was altered to 'Dragoon'.

AOB Japanese seizure of Kiska Island in the Aleutians group as part of the Japanese Operation 'AL' (7 June 1943).

Aphrodite US project to use obsolete Boeing B-17 bombers as remotely-controlled bombs; the aircraft were stripped of equipment and packed with explosive, and then taken off and flown towards the target by a two-man crew whose members baled out just before reaching the edge of friendly territory, the bomber then being radio-controlled towards the target, which was hit in a steep dive to cause maximum destruction. Only a few test flights were undertaken.

Apostle I Allied plan for a return to Norway after the Allied invasion of the European mainland. The operation was in fact implemented only on 10 May 1945, two days after the surrender of German forces.

Apostle II Allied plan for a return to Norway in the event that the German forces in the country surrendered while the rest of the German army continued to fight in mainland Europe.

Apple Airborne raid by the 1st Parachute Commando of the Chinese Nationalist army to cut the Japanese lines of communication near Kai-ping (12 July 1945).

AQ Japanese seizure of Attu Island in the Aleutians group as part of the Japanese Operation 'AL' (5 June 1942).

Aquila Allied codename for the headquarters of the US 10th Air Force in New Delhi for operations emanating from the Indian subcontinent.

Arcadia Codename for the Washington Conference between Prime Minister Churchill and President Roosevelt (22 December 1941/14 January 1942), in which the decision was taken to develop the British concept for Operation 'Gymnast' into an Anglo-American 'Super Gymnast' that eventually matured as Operation 'Torch' for implementation towards the end of 1942. Another major decision of the 'Arcadia' Conference was the establishment of the ABDA and ANZAC command structures for the better containment of Japan's expansion into South-East Asia and the South-West Pacific. Command of ABDA was entrusted to General Sir Archibald Wavell, who accepted the task on 3 January 1942 and then established his headquarters at Bandoeng in the western half of Java. The ANZAC command was entrusted to Admiral Chester W. Nimitz, Commander-in-Chief Pacific with his headquarters at Pearl Harbor in the Hawaiian Islands, with local commanded exercised by another US Navy officer, Vice Admiral H. F. Leary.

Archery British commando raid against German installations and other installations on the Lofoten Islands in the Vestfjord area and on Vaagso and Maaloy Islands off the

Norwegian coast just to the south of Stadtlandet (21 December 1941/1 January 1942). The raid was planned as a two-pronged affair to capitalize on the growing strength, expertise and success of British combined operations capabilities during 1941, the intention being that a major (repeat) raid on the Lofoten Islands in the Vestfjord region should be mounted with the Vaagso operation as a subsidiary thrust to draw the Germans' attentions away from the northern region just before the descent of the main force. The Vaagso part of Operation 'Archery' was commanded by Rear Admiral H. M. Burrough in the cruiser *Kenya*, which with four destroyers escorted the assault ships carrying the landing forces. In conjunction with a UK-launched bombing attack, the warships silenced the coastal batteries on Vaagso and allowed the troops to get ashore without difficulty for the destruction of German facilities.

The force pulled out on 28 December having achieved all their objectives and having sunk 5 merchantmen, 2 trawlers and 1 tug of some 16,000 tons total displacement under the cover of RAF Coastal Command aircraft operating effectively from bases in norther Scotland. However, the Lofoten part of Operation 'Archery' was not as successful. This half of the scheme was entrusted to Rear Admiral L. H. K. Hamilton in the cruiser *Arethusa*, which with 8 destroyers and 2 Norwegian corvettes escorted 2 assault ships. The operation got off to a sorry start when one of the assault ships had to return to Scapa with engine trouble, forcing Hamilton to scale down the basic plan he was tasked to fulfil. Two coasters were captured and a number of landings made, but on receiving information that German fighter and bomber forces were moving north to deal with his force, which was operating beyond the range of fighter cover from the UK, Hamilton decided to withdraw. It was Operation 'Archery' that finally confirmed Hitler in his opinion that the British were determined to make a major assault on Norway, an opinion that compelled the German leader to station over-large garrison forces in the country to the detriment of the German war effort elsewhere.

Argent French Force 136 airborne mission to aid Laotian resistance fighters against the Japanese near Phou Loi (10 July 1945).

Arena Plan schemed by the Allied 1st Airborne Army for an air assault by three corps east of Paderborn in the spring of 1945 as a means of breaking through to the heart of Germany through the creation of an airhead of the type that had failed so unfortunately at Arnhem in September 1944.

Argonaut Codename for the meetings held in Malta (30 January/2 February 1945) and at Yalta (4/11 February 1945). The first was a summit meeting of the Allies' military leaders designed to finalize arrangements for the closing stages of the wars against Germany and Japan, while the latter was altogether more significant as the 'big three' (namely Prime Minister Churchill, President Roosevelt and Premier Stalin) agreed on the three Allies' post-war spheres of influence, especially in Europe, and the fact that the USSR would come into the war against Japan in August 1945 in return for the Kurile Island group, the whole of Sakhalin Island and a dominant position in Manchuria.

Argument Major air offensive by the US 8th and 15th Air Forces against German fighter strength and production (20/26 February 1944). While the bombers blasted the major production centres in Germany and occupied Europe, causing a good deal of disruption, the escorting fighters were able to tackle the German fighters that rose to challenge the American maximum effort. For the loss of 244 bombers and 33 fighters, the Americans destroyed substantial numbers of German fighters, though the real importance of the battle lay not so much with causing German losses, but on forcing the Germans to use irreplaceable fuel supplies and suffering the loss of yet more experienced pilots at a time when the German flying schools were wholly unable to make good such losses with adequately trained replacements.

Arno Linie (Arno line) German defensive line to the north of Florence in Italy.

A.S. Designation (together with a numerical suffix) for military sealift convoys plying from the USA to Freetown, Sierra Leone, and inaugurated in March 1942.

ASH Designation of pod-mounted ship-detection radar that could be fitted to Allied anti-shipping aircraft.

Ashcan Detention camp for high-ranking German officials after the end of the war.

Aspidistra Secret radio station established in the UK by the Allies to broadcast messages and information to occupied European countries.

Aspirin British jamming countermeasures to the German 'Knickebein' blind-bombing system used in the night Blitz of 1940.

Astonia Operation in which the British I Corps of the Canadian 1st Army (21st Army Group) established a bridgehead over the River Seine downstream of Rouen to capture the major port of Le Havre (12 September 1944), though by this time other Allied forces had pushed through to take the more significant harbour facilities at Antwerp, which were also closer to the front.

A.T. Designation of military convoys ferrying troops across the North Atlantic from the USA to the UK in giant liners converted as troopships. Instituted in January 1942, the A.T. convoy route was generally plied by singleton liners, which relied on their speed and size for protection against the attentions of the German U-boats.

Atlantic British and Canadian holding operation by the 21st Army Group in Normandy (June 1944).

Atlas Codename of the personal train used by Adolf Hitler.

Attika (Attica) Attempt by the German Army Group 'A' to break out south of Rostov through the defences of the Caucasus Front to take the Black Sea port of Tuapse (23 September/18 November 1942). The German assault was spearheaded by two corps of Generaloberst Richard Ruoff's 17th Army with the aid of the 11th Army, and was finally checked just short of Tuapse by the Soviet 18th and 56th Armies.

Attila German plan for the occupation of Vichy France in the event of increasing French support for the Allies. The actual occupation was undertaken (11/17 November 1942) after the Allied landing in French North-West Africa in Operation 'Torch', and resulted in the scuttling by their crews of most French warships in the naval base at Toulon.

Aufbau Ost (deployment east) Overall German plan for the gradual shift eastwards of troops into Poland in preparation for Operation 'Barbarossa'. Undertaken during the first half of 1941, the operation was implemented with great care lest the sudden appearance of greatly increased number of men, *matériel* and war supplies should alarm the Soviets. The secrecy of the movement was made the more important as German aircraft were overflying the western parts of the USSR on essential tactical and operational reconnaissance missions.

Augsburg Codename for a delay in the German plans for a major offensive against Western Europe in 1939; in the event these plans were never fully implemented as the German planners devoted their efforts to the altogether more ambitious scheme for Operation 'Gelb' in May 1940, making inspired operational use of the 'impassable' Ardennes region to descend on an Allied weak spot.

Augsburg A German E-boat attack on coastal shipping off Eastbourne (February 1941). Such attacks on British mercantile shipping off the south and east coasts had been undertaken with relative impunity from the summer of 1940, the E-boats generally laying mines but sometimes engaging larger targets with torpedoes. The effectiveness (but not the intensity) of this German campaign declined with the widespread adoption of the motor gunboat (MGB) by British coastal flotillas, though the Germans feared destroyers and aircraft more than the MGBs, which engaged in occasional actions with the E-boats but more generally disrupted their nocturnal activities.

Augsburg B German E-boat attack on coastal shipping off Eastbourne (March 1941).

Ausladung (unloading) Advance by the Division von Manteuffel towards Djebel Abiod in Tunisia as part of Operation 'Ochsenkopf' (26 February/19 March 1943).

Ausserordenliche Befriedigungsaktion (foreign order befriending action) German plan for the liquidation of Poland's intelligentsia as part of the programme to bring the Poles into total moral and economic subservience to the German Reich by eliminating all those with any leadership capability. The programme was first undertaken by SS and Gestapo squads operating on a local basis, but was then absorbed into the concentration camp system.

Avalanche Designation for the first Allied landing on mainland Italy, undertake by the US 5th Army under Lieutenant General Mark Clark from 03.30 on 9 September 1943 in the Bay of Salerno. The landings went in just over three hours after the announcement of the armistice between the Allies and Italy (in fact signed on 3 September), and put Lieutenant General Sir Richard McCreery's British X Corps (46th and 56th Divisions supported by US Rangers and British Commandos) ashore in spots between Amalfi in the north and the mouth of the River Sele in the south as the left-flank formation, and Major General Ernest W. Dawley's US VI Corps (36th Division with the 45th Division as floating reserve) in a single large beach-head between the mouth of the Sele and Agropoli in the south as the right-flank formation. After some desperate fighting against extemporized battle groups of Generaloberst Heinrich von Vietinghoff-Scheel's German 10th Army, the Allies managed to consolidate their initial four lodgements into a single beach-head by 12 September, the day on which the beach-head was nearly severed into two segments by a powerful German counteroffensive (centred on the 16th and 26th Panzer Divisions) after some heavy and extremely accurate shelling from the hills surrounding the Allied landing areas. Initial Allied reinforcements arrived on 10 September (45th Division) and on 13/14 September (US 82nd Airborne Division), allowing the consolidation of the beach-head by 18 September in preparation for a break-out to link up with the advance units of the British 8th Army advancing from the south through Calabria. The link-up of the two forces was effected at Auletta on 19 September.

Avonmouth Designation of the original plan for an Allied landing at Narvik to support Norwegian forces in the event of a German invasion of Norway. This reflected in particular the British fears of the effect on the Allies' strategic position should Germany secure Norway's lengthy coastline, allowing them year-round export capability for Swedish iron ore, and protected egress for their U-boats and surface vessels into the Norwegian Sea and hence the Denmark Strait and the North Atlantic, with potentially disastrous effects on Allied convoys plying across the North Atlantic with desperately needed war *matériel* from the USA.

Axiom Designation of the high-level mission despatched by the South-East Asia Command to London and Washington to urge the rapid implementation of Operation 'Culverin' (February 1944).

Aztec Airborne operations by the Office of Strategic Services to aid Italian partisans north of Venice (13 October 1944 and 26 December 1944).

B

B.A. Designation (together with a numerical suffix) of Allied convoys instituted in May 1941 from Bombay to any of the ports in the Red Sea, but notably Aden.

Backbone Allied contingency plan for a seaborne landing in Spanish Morocco during Operation 'Torch' in late 1942. The scheme was abandoned as adding additional logistic and strategic complexity to no real purpose, and as raising the possibility of a Spanish entry into the war on the side of the Axis powers, with consequent threat principally to Gibraltar.

Backbone II Plan for a US counter to any Spanish reaction to the implementation of Operation 'Backbone'. This operation was rendered superfluous by the politically motivated but militarily sensible abandonment of Operation 'Backbone'.

Backhander Designation of the landing by the US 7th and 1st Marine Divisions on Cape Gloucester at the extreme western end of New Britain in the Bismarck Archipelago (26 December 1943). This was an initial step in the western component of the 'Elkton' plan agreed in April 1943 to cut off and isolate at the eastern end of New Britain and in New Ireland the Japanese 8th Area Army, which would be left 'to wither on the vine' for the rest of the war as the Allies pushed on towards the Japanese home islands. In tactical and operational terms, the assault on Cape Gloucester might have been considered superfluous to General Douglas MacArthur's plans, but the operation provided the forces of the South-West Pacific Area with an important airfield (from 1 January 1944) for support of further operations up the coast of New Guinea towards Saidor and Madang and points farther to the north-west.

Bagration Designation of one of the Red Army's greatest strategic offensives of World War II (23 June/29 August 1944), designed to liberate Belorussia from the German yoke, to destroy as much as possible of the German Army Group 'Centre' and to pave the way for the Soviet invasion of Poland. Schemed by the *Stavka* (Soviet high command) under the personal supervision of Stalin (supreme commander) and Marshal of the Soviet Union Georgi Zhukov (deputy supreme commander), the latter being entrusted with operational command of the offensive, Operation 'Bagration' co-ordinated the efforts of General I. Kh. Bagramyan's 1st Baltic Front (10th Guards, 3rd Shock, 22nd, 4th Shock, 6th Guards and 43rd Armies), General I. D. Chernyakovsky's 3rd Belorussian Front (39th, 5th Guards Tank, 5th, 11th Guards and 31st Armies), General G. F. Zakharov's 2nd Belorussian Front (33rd, 49th and 50th Armies) and Marshal of the Soviet Union K. K. Rokossovsky's 1st Belorussian Front (3rd, 48th, 65th, 28th, 61st, 70th, 47th, 8th Guards, 2nd Tank and 69th Armies).

Facing these powerful and well-equipped forces, under able leadership and riding the moral wave of previous successful campaigns, the Germans mustered the overextended 16th, 3rd Panzer, 4th, 9th and 2nd Armies of Army Groups 'North' and 'Centre' (commanded respectively by Generaloberst Georg Lindemann and Generalfeldmarschall Ernst Busch), which Hitler had ordered to stand fast without thought of retreat to shorter and more defensible lines farther to the west. The German defence was further hampered by a severe outbreak of partisan activity in the rear areas of Army Group 'Centre', which almost completely severed the group's lines of communication as the Soviets launched their offensive on a 350-mile front on 23 June 1944 under an umbrella of almost total air superiority and a local artillery density of 400 pieces per mile. The Soviet offensive drove on remorselessly until 29 August 1944, and it is estimated that Army Group 'Centre' lost 25 of its 33 divisions cut off and annihilated in pockets at places such as Vitebsk, Minsk, Bobruysk, Vilnyus and Brest-Litovsk. The Soviets claimed 400,000 German dead and 15,000 captured, together with 2,000 tanks, 10,000 pieces of artillery and 57,000 motor vehicles destroyed or captured. The German defeat was enormous beyond description, and led to the immediate replacement of Busch by Generalfeldmarschall Walter Model. Model finally managed to check Zhukov's thrust just outside the gates of Warsaw, but only because the Soviets had far outreached their own lines of communication.

As a partner offensive to the Belorussian offensive, the Soviets also launched a massive drive to clear the Germans out of southern Poland, and to destroy as much as possible of Army Group 'North Ukraine'. Led by Marshal Ivan Konev, the Soviet forces of the 1st and 4th Ukrainian Fronts comprised the 3rd Guards, 1st Guards Tank, 13th, 60th, 3rd Guards Tank, 4th Tank, 38th, 1st Guards and 18th Armies to assault the German 4th and 1st Panzer Armies, as well as the Hungarian 1st Army, of Model's Army Group 'North Ukraine'. The Ukrainian fronts' offensive was unleashed on 13 July and smashed through the southern portion of Poland, isolating and then destroying substantial portions of Army Group 'North Ukraine', to reach the upper Vistula by 29 August. By this time the woefully depleted Army Group 'North Ukraine' had been redesignated Army Group 'A', which came under the command of Generaloberst Josef Harpe during August 1944. In just over two months the Soviets had pushed forward some 450 miles to the very limits of their lines of communication, and dealt a mortal blow to the German armies on the Eastern Front, especially as the 1st Baltic Front in the north of the sector had reached the outskirts of Riga and thus cut off most of Army Group 'North' in Estonia and Latvia.

Bamboo British scheme to take the Kra Isthmus in southern Thailand and so cut off the Japanese forces in Malaya from all sources of supply and reinforcement (March 1945), so easing the eventual task of reconquering Malaya.

BAN Defensive scheme devised by the Japanese Burma Area Army headquarters for the area around Mandalay and Meiktila in central Burma (December 1943/March 1944). Known in essence to the British, this Operation 'BAN' resulted in the development of Operation 'Capital' into Operation 'Extended Capital' to cut off and destroy the Japanese forces in the area of Mandalay and Meiktila.

Bär (bear) (i) Axis plan for the co-operation of the Italian army with the Germans forces to crush any determined resistance by the French in Alsace (April 1940).
(ii) German 7th Army offensive in Alsace (15/25 June 1940), the southern counterpart to 'Tiger' (i).

Barbara Linie (Barbara line) German defensive line between the Volturno and Garigliano rivers, west of the Monti del Matese in southern central Italy, breached by the British X and US V Corps of the US 5th Army in October 1943 after the dire tribulations of forcing a passage of the Volturno on their way to the Gustav Line and the climactic battle at Monte Cassino.

Barbarity Operation to reinforce the Greek air force fighting the Italians with RAF fighter and bomber squadrons (December 1940). This diversion of strength from the Western Desert, followed by others in the early months of 1941, had unfortunate results for the British and Commonwealth forces operating against the Italian forces based in Libya.

11

Barbarossa German strategic offensive against the USSR, launched at 03.00 on 22 June 1941 with almost total tactical surprise and under a comprehensive umbrella of Luftwaffe fighter, ground-attack and bomber aircraft.

Hitler's conviction that the USSR must be conquered by Germany had its origins in the German leader's far past, when he became convinced that communism was an evil that must be extirpated completely, together with the nation which had brought it to practical fruition in the early twentieth century. Quite apart from this overtly political determination, Hitler also saw the USSR as being peopled by Slavic 'subhumans' whose destruction would free this vast land (with all its agricultural and raw materials potential) as *Lebensraum* (living area) for the Aryan master race. Yet Hitler was aware of the dangers with which such a campaign bristled, and the total disaster to which Charles XII of Sweden and Napoleon I of France had come in their campaigns against this monolithic state. He was also aware of the dangers inherent in the waging of war on two fronts, and had averred that he would never fall into this trap. But with the stalemating of the war with the recalcitrant UK at the end of 1940, Hitler decided that he would now deal with the USSR in a rapid campaign of Panzer movement to encircle the Soviet forces, which would then be annihilated by the German infantry formations as the Panzer forces swept on to the next victory.

Hitler appreciated that the USSR's forces were vast (and could call on relatively limitless reserves of raw manpower), and for this reason had seen fit to placate Stalin (in the so-called Ribbentrop-Molotov Pact of August 1939) with offers of *matériel* aid and half of Poland if the USSR would stand idly by while Germany undertook its campaigns in Poland and against the Western European nations should this latter prove necessary. But by 1941 Hitler was convinced that his substantial (and, perhaps more importantly, battle-experienced) forces, with a good proportion of Panzer and motorized formations, could comprehensively defeat the Soviet armies, which the German intelligence apparatus revealed to be demoralized after the political purges of the late 1930s, lacking in tactical expertise (as demonstrated by the USSR's reverses against Finland in the 'Winter War' of 1939/1940), and equipped with obsolescent weapons. Hitler foresaw that he could deploy against the USSR some 145 of his 205 divisions, including 19 Panzer divisions and 12 motorized divisions, though the bulk of the German forces would still have to rely on horse transport for this fast and extensive campaign, which the army high command anticipated might be over in 10 weeks. Hitler too was confident that the campaign would be completed in short order, for he could easily have bolstered the forces in the East by another 10 divisions drawn from the 38 in the West and the 12 in Norway. To face these German armies the Soviets could call on about 12,000,000 men under arms or available as reserves for a strength of some 160 infantry divisions, 30 cavalry divisions and about 35 armoured or motorized brigades. In armoured and aircraft strengths the Germans were quantitatively inferior but qualitatively superior, though the German planners failed to appreciate that the Soviets had new tank and combat aircraft types under final development and would be able to produce these new and highly capable types in vast numbers and in short order.

Hitler had ordered the Oberkommando des Heeres, the army high command, to begin planning for an invasion of the USSR as early as 21 July 1940, and the German plans had since that time gone through a lengthy development phase. However they were never fully completed, especially with regard to the ultimate stop line envisaged for the offensive, which glibly (and fatally) assumed that Soviet resistance would end once the three largest cities west of the Ural Mountains (Moscow, Leningrad and Kiev) had fallen to the Germans, together with the Soviets' main industrial areas. Planning without any real strategic object in mind, the OKH first came up with a plan for a two-part major offensive directed by Army Group 'North' at Moscow via Smolensk and by Army Group 'South' at Kiev, with Kharkov as a follow-on target. These major thrusts would be covered by two subsidiary flanking offensives, that in the north directed at Leningrad, and that in the south directed from Bulgaria at Kiev through the Ukrainian agricultural heartlands. It was anticipated that the northern main force would then drive south from Moscow to link up with the southern thrust at Kharkov for an offensive to the River Volga at Stalingrad. War games revealed deficiencies in this scheme, which was thus altered to place greater emphasis on the northern thrusts, in which a weakened Army Group 'North' would take the Baltic States and Leningrad and a new but stronger Army Group 'Centre' would take Moscow before exploiting east and north towards the Volga and Archangel respectively. Army Group 'South' would have a strengthened flank in the south Ukraine and would concentrate on Kiev, only then exploiting eastwards to Kharkov and Stalingrad.

In December 1940 Hitler reviewed the revised OKH plan and approved it in principal, though he insisted that Leningrad should be the major target in the north, and that after taking Smolensk en route to Moscow, part of the forces allocated to Army Group 'Centre' should be detached to aid Army Group 'North' against Leningrad. After the fall of Moscow Army Group 'Centre' would now not exploit to the east, but only to the north with the objective of taking Archangel so that the German armies would arrive at an undefined stop line running basically south from Archangel to Moscow, the River Don, and Rostov at the mouth of the Don on the Sea of Azov.

Operation 'Barbarossa' finally emerged therefore as a triple-pronged offensive designed to take the three major cities before the onset of winter, and to destroy or capture the bulk of the Soviets' field armies (now estimated at 155 divisions, but in fact 230 with 170 of these within operational distance of the western theatre) by the use of large-scale enveloping movements. Thus the 26 divisions (including three Panzer) of Generalfeldmarschall Wilhelm Ritter von Leeb's Army Group 'North' would be supported by Luftflotte I in its drive through the 24 divisions (including four tank) of General F. I. Kuznetsov's North-West Front to take the Baltic states and seize Leningrad. The 51 divisions (including 9 Panzer) of Generalfeldmarschall Fedor von Bock's Army Group 'Centre' would be supported by Luftflotte II in its thrust towards Minsk, Smolensk and ultimately Moscow through the 38 divisions (including 8 tank) of General D. G. Pavlov's West Front. And the 59 divisions (including 5 Panzer, 14 Romanian and 2 Hungarian) of Generalfeldmarschall Gerd von Rundstedt's Army Group 'South' would have the considerable weight of Luftflotte IV for geographically the largest task, that of taking Lvov and Kiev after disposing of the defence found by the 56 divisions (including 16 tank) of General M. P. Kirponos's South-West Front and the 16 divisions (including 4 tank) of General I. V. Tyulenev's South Front. The main weight of the German forces was composed of Army Groups 'North' and 'Centre' to the North of the Pripet Marshes that divided the German offensive, and it was expected that the more determined resistance would be found in this massive sector, though the main weight of the Soviet defences was in fact located to the south of the Pripet Marshes to defend the vital agricultural and industrial regions of the Ukraine.

The campaign opened with devastating attacks by the Luftwaffe on Soviet front-line airfields, in which the Soviets are conservatively estimated to have lost some 2,000 aircraft during 22 June. Thereafter the Red air force was able to put up only token resistance, and the German ground forces forged ahead spearheaded by the *Panzergruppen*, which achieved several huge encirclements of Soviet ground forces, and then pushed on once the infantry had assumed the task of defeating the trapped forces. By 30 September the Germans were deep in European Russia, with their leading units on a line running roughly north/south on a line from Leningrad to Melitopol (just north of the Sea of Azov) via Novgorod, Kholm, Smolensk, Bryansk, Poltava and Zaporozhye. But here Hitler intervened, for though the progress of Army Groups 'North' and 'Centre' was satisfactory, that of Army Group 'South' was not, and the German dictator thus diverted the 2nd Army and the 2nd Panzergruppe from Army Group 'Centre' to aid Army Group 'South' in its drive towards the lower reaches of the Donets river. This enabled Army Group 'South' to speed its progress, but on the other hand slowed Army Group 'Centre' just as Soviet resistance in front of Moscow and Leningrad was affecting Army Groups 'Centre' and 'North' respectively.

Coupled with the three-week delay forced on Operation 'Barbarossa' by Hitler's decision to overrun the Balkans (Operation 'Marita') before turning on the USSR, this was sufficient to spell failure for Operation 'Barbarossa'. Leningrad never fell, the Germans were checked just before Moscow, and then winter arrived, catching the Germans totally unprepared. So while the German army and air force had scored staggering tactical and even operational successes over the Soviet armed forces, they had failed in their primary strategic objectives, and as the Soviets still had manpower to spare, and had evacuated their industrial base to safety east of the Urals, the Germans were finally faced with a long and ultimately impossible task in the USSR.

Barclay Allied plan to induce a German reinforcement of southern France and the Balkans at the expense of northern France and the Low Countries in preparation for Operation 'Overlord' during the spring of 1944. Carefully contrived hints of major invasion in the Mediterranean were leaked, but the Germans diverted little strength from the primary regions.

Barium British commando intelligence mission in Czechoslovakia.

Bark British task force in Operation 'Husky'.

Barker Airborne operation by the French 2ème Regiment Colonial des Parachutistes to harass the retreat of the German Army Group 'B' through northern France in the region of Salornaye (13 August 1944).

Barracuda Allied plan for a combined airborne and amphibious assault on Naples in the autumn of 1943. No detailed plans were evolved for the operation, which presupposed a collapse by the Italian armed forces, and the whole notion was cancelled on 27 July 1943.

Barrister British and Free French operation against Dakar in French West Africa (23/25 September 1940). The object was for the Free French Force M under General de Gaulle to sail from the UK (31 August) with Royal Navy escort and refuel in Freetown, Sierra Leone, before moving north to take Dakar against passive Vichy resistance, but in the event the Vichy forces resisted strongly and a three-day naval bombardment by the Royal Navy failed to quell the defence, leading to the cancellation of the operation and so putting off the chances of bringing French West Africa into the Allied fold.

Battleaxe British offensive (15/17 June 1941) in the Western Desert designed by General Sir Archibald Wavell to pin the Axis forces in front of Sollum while a combined infantry and armoured force swung northwest round the Germans' and Italians' desert flank to take the Hafid Ridge and so open the way for a drive to relieve the garrison in beleaguered Tobruk. The offensive was made possible by the arrival in Alexandria on 12 May of the 'Tiger' convoy through the Mediterranean with 238 tanks, giving the British forces a useful armoured superiority at a time when General Erwin Rommel's forces were exhausted by an advance that had taken them to the end of overextended lines of communication. Rommel had in fact been forbidden to essay further advance, and had therefore halted in good defensive positions behind dug-in 88-mm Flak guns, which were to prove phenomenal tank-killers during Operation 'Battleaxe'. Wavell's plan was for part of the 4th Indian Division to tackle the Halfaya Pass position frontally while the rest of the division and the 4th Armoured Brigade swung past the German position at Point 206 to engage the strongpoint at Fort Capuzzo as an inner flank guard for the 7th Armoured Brigade, which was to strike deeper through the desert and take Hafid Ridge, controlled by the German defensive strongpoint on its Point 208. The attack was committed on 15 June, and though no progress was made at Halfaya, Point 206 and Fort Capuzzo fell during the day while the 7th Armoured Division established itself on Hafid Ridge.

Tactically as astute as ever, Rommel was content to let the British make these initial advances, which helped to disperse the main units over an extensive area, while he moved forward the 8.Panzerregiment to cover the Fort Capuzzo and Sollum area and the 4th Light Division in a wide flank movement (outside the 7th Armoured Brigade's advance) to take the British in rear near Sidi Omar and Sidi Suleiman. Heavy fighting followed on 16 June (the 7th Armoured Brigade losing almost all its tanks in battle or to mechanical failure) before Wavell realized the hazard of his forces on 17 June with the arrival of the 5th Light Division in Sidi Omar and Sidi Suleiman. The 4th Armoured Brigade could not move to shield the 7th Armoured Brigade's left flank because of the pressure exerted by the 8.Panzerregiment, and the British fell rapidly back, allowing Rommel to relieve the Axis position at Halfaya in the evening of 17 June.

Batty Developed version of 'Aphrodite'.

Baus Au US Army plan for a guerrilla defence of the Visayan Island area in the Philippines in the event of a successful Japanese onslaught on the islands (1941). In the event guerrilla operations on an extensive scale did much to undermine Japan's garrison in the islands in the period from 1942 to the US invasion in 1944.

Baytown Designation of the first Allied landing made in mainland Italy, when formations of the British 8th Army under General Sir Bernard Montgomery crossed the Straits of Messina to land near Reggio di Calabria at 04.30 on 3 September 1943. This was just a few hours after the implementation of the armistice signed between the Allies and the Italian government of Mareschale Ugo Cavallero formed after the overthrow of Benito Mussolini on 24 July, though the armistice was not declared openly until the US/British landings in the Gulf of Salerno (Operation 'Avalanche') six days later.

The actual 'Baytown' landings were undertaken (from north to south) by the 17th Brigade and the 13th Brigade (British 5th Division) and the 3rd Canadian Brigade (1st Canadian Division) of Lieutenant General Sir Miles Dempsey's XIII Corps, which would then cross in force, the object being to pressure the German 29th Panzergrenadier Division with a British advance along the north coast of Calabria and a Canadian advance along the south coast in an effort to draw in German reserves from the north, thus facilitating the task of the 'Avalanche' landing. Generalfeldmarschall Albert Kesselring was not taken in by the Allied deception, and kept the bulk of his strength in the area of Salerno, where he correctly felt the main Allied blow would fall.

Bazaar US plan to provide the USSR with air support in Siberia (with aircraft ferried from Alaska) in the event of a Japanese invasion of the eastern USSR (1943).

Bearskin Yugoslav partisan interdiction campaign against German road and rail communications north through Slovenia (May 1944). The object of the campaign was to prevent German forces from being moved from the Balkans in anticipation of the Allied landings in north-south Europe during Operation 'Overlord'.

Beaver US VII Corps landing operation training exercise in the UK in preparation for the 'Utah' Beach part of Operation 'Overlord'.

Beethoven Original German designation of the weapon later known as 'Mistel'.

Bellicose Designation of the RAF's first 'shuttle bombing' raid: the outward flight (20/21 June 1943) involved an attack on Friedrichshafen by bombers en route to Algeria, while the return flight (24/25 June) included a raid on the Italian naval base at La Spezia by the bombers as they returned to the UK.

Beneficiary Plan for an Allied break-out from the Normandy lodgement area after Operation 'Overlord' by means of a combined airborne and amphibious descent on St Malo to expose the right flank of the German 7th Army's defences (summer 1944).

Benito British codename for the German 'Y-Gerät' blind-bombing system.

Benjamin British codename for a device to jam the German 'Y-Gerät' blind-bombing system.

Benson Airborne intelligence operation by the Belgian Independent Parachute Company, SAS, near Estrée St Denis in France (27 August 1944).

Beowulf Invasion and reduction of the Soviet-held islands of Dago and Osel in the Gulf of Riga by elements of the German 18th Army (14 September/21 October 1941) as part of Operation 'Barbarossa'. These islands would have posed a threat to the left flank of Generalfeldmarschall Wilhelm Ritter von Leeb's Army Group 'North' if left in Soviet hands, and also dominated the entrance to the Gulf of Finland and its seaward approaches to the city of Leningrad. Realizing the hopelessness of their position at the throat of the Gulf of Finland after the fall of the two islands, the Soviets evacuated their garrison in the Finnish port of Hanko on 3 December 1941, after it had been under Finnish siege since 29 June.

Berbang Airborne operation by the Belgian Independent Parachute Company, SAS, to cut German communications near Burbuy in Belgium (2/9 September 1944).

Berghof (mountain house) Hitler's headquarters in Obersalzberg.

Berlin Raiding cruise into the north and central Atlantic by the German battlecruisers *Gneisenau* and *Scharnhorst* (23 January/22 March 1941). During the course of the cruise, which ended when the ships put into the Brittany port of Brest, the two ships undertook several actions that resulted in the sinking of 22 merchant ships of 115,622 gross registered tons.

Bernhard (i) German plan to drop very skilfully forged £5 notes over the UK in an effort to disrupt the British wartime economy. (ii) Alternative designation for 'Reinhard'. (iii) German ground-to-air communication system.

Bestrafung (punishment) Luftwaffe terror offensive (6/9 April 1941) against the Yugoslav capital, Belgrade, to break the back of Yugoslav resistance to the Germans invasion, and to 'punish' the Yugoslavs for the coup that ousted the pro-Axis regency and so produced their 'defection' from the Axis.

Beta US plan to take Hong Kong and Canton with Chinese and US forces in southern China (August/September 1945). The object of the plan was thus to recapture from the Japanese 6th Area Army the regions seized by Japanese forces in Operation 'ICHI' (April 1944/May 1945) and drive a land wedge between the Japanese forces in northern China and those in the extreme south of China and in South-East Asia (Burma, Malaya, Thailand and Indo-China) at a time when the disruption of Japan's maritime lines of communications by the US Navy's submarine and air forces was almost total.

Bettelstab (beggar's staff) Plan for an offensive by the XXVI Corps of the German 18th Army against the Soviet Coastal Command occupying the bridgehead around Oranienbaum on the southern side of the Gulf of Finland to the west of Leningrad and covering the major naval base on the island of Kronstadt (February/July 1942).

Bibber Allied plan for the occupation of Thailand in the light of Japan's imminent collapse (August 1945).

Bigot Security portion of the overall Operation 'Neptune' procedure.

Bigot Dragoon Airborne drop as part of Operation 'Dragoon'.

Big Scheme Polish resistance movement plan for a national rising against the Germans to coincide with the arrival of Soviet forces from the east (summer 1944). The result of the plan was 'Burza', the national rising in Warsaw, which was started in the expectation of Soviet help from the east bank of the River Vistula at the end of Operation 'Bagration'. For political and logistical reasons the Soviets were unwilling and/or unable to furnish useful material support to the pro-Western forces in the city, and in a campaign of ruthless devastation the Germans were able to use SS forces to put down the rising without Soviet hindrance.

Big Week Concentrated Allied (especially US) air strikes against German aircraft production centres (20/26 February 1944). The object of the offensive was to destroy as much as possible of German fighter production capability and, more importantly, to entice the German fighter arm into the air in large numbers so that its strength in men and machines could be decimated by the Allied fighters escorting the bombers. In the event, German fighter production was damaged only slightly (as a result of the programme of decentralized production already under way), though Germany's losses of experienced fighter pilots proved more damaging.

Bingo US bomber attacks on electricity-producing plants supplying the railway system over the Brenner Pass (November 1944). The object of the short campaign was to obstruct as decisively as possible the main reinforcement route for the German forces in Italy from secure regions in Austria.

Bioscope British commando liaison mission to the resistance forces in Czechoslovakia.

Birch Allied codename for Christmas Island.

Birdcage Allied leaflet drops to prisoner of war camps in South-East Asia (August 1945) to tell the inmates of the end of the war and to instruct them on procedures until Allied land forces arrived to liberate the camps and take into custody the elements of the Japanese armed forces in charge of the camps.

Birke (birch) Evacuation of the German forces from Finland (September 1944) after the collapse of Finnish resistance in the face of massive attacks by the Soviet Karelian Front (under Marshal K. A. Meretskov) on three fronts (the 32nd Army north of Lake Onega, the 7th Army between Lakes Onega and Ladoga, and the 21st, 23rd and 59th Armies west of Lake Ladoga) in southern Finland.

The armistice imposed on Finland demanded co-operation in removing Finland's erstwhile allies, the Germans, but in the north the Soviets had to mount a large campaign by the 14th Army to drive the German 20th Mountain Army (under Generaloberst Lothar Rendulic) out of the northern USSR and across northern Finland into the Kirkenes region of Norway between 7 and 29 October 1944.

Birkhahn (black cock) German plan for the evacuation of forces from Norway (1945), in the event never implemented.

Biting British assault on the German radar station at Bruneval near Le Havre in northern France (27 February 1942). The attack force of the 2nd Battalion, the Parachute Regiment, was parachuted in, and the object of the raid was to seize key components of the radar equipment for analysis in the UK after an evacuation by sea in craft of the coastal forces.

Bivouac British commando liaison mission to the resistance forces in Czechoslovakia.

Black Original and unrefined version of 'Barrister'.

Blacklist Plan devised by the staff of General Douglas MacArthur for the occupation of the Japanese home islands after the surrender of the Japanese empire.

Black Pit Term for the mid-Atlantic 'air gap' beyond the reach of land-based aircraft operating from North America, the UK and even Iceland, where U-boats could operate with opposition only from surface units of the Allied navies until the introduction of escort carriers and their small air complements turned the tide against the German submariners.

Blackpool Fly-in strip and 'block' between Hopin and Taungni on the rail line between Indaw and Mogaung in northern Burma. This was one of the key points after the launching of Major General Orde Wingate's 2nd Chindit Expedition (March

1944) to harass the Japanese 15th Army in general, with a particular task of aiding the Chinese and US forces commanded by Lieutenant General Joseph W. Stilwell in advancing through the Hukawng valley to capture the strategically vital town of Myitkyina.

Blackstone Portion of the US Western Task Force that landed at Safi in Operation 'Torch'.

Blau (blue) Luftwaffe contingency plan for air operations against the UK in the event of war between Germany and the UK in 1938 after the annexation of Czechoslovakia. The German success at the Munich Conference in September 1938 rendered the plan superfluous.

Blau I (blue I) Northern portion of the German summer offensive of 1942 in the USSR. In this drive (28 June/7 July 1942) the northern part of Generalfeldmarschall Fedor von Bock's Army Group 'South' advanced from the region just east of Kursk to the line of the River Don between Livny and Rossosh, taking the vital city of Voronezh against the forces of the Soviet South-West Front. Commanded by Generaloberst M. Freiherr von Weichs, this offensive by the German 2nd Army and 4th Panzerarmee provided the necessary left-flank protection for the 'Donets Corridor' through which the 6th Army advanced to Stalingrad. When Army Group 'South' was divided on 9 July into Army Groups 'A' and 'B', von Weichs was given command of Army Group 'B' on 13 July.

Blau II (blue II) Second component of the German summer offensive of 1942 in the USSR, consisting of an offensive launched by the reinforced German 6th Army (Generaloberst Friedrich Paulus) of Army Group 'South' along the 'Donets Corridor' to the west of the River Don to take Stalingrad at the apex of the great westward bend of the River Volga. The offensive (28 June/22 July 1942) was launched with great success, and the ineffectual opposition of the Soviet South-West Front (under Lieutenant General F. Ya. Kostenko) led to its dissolution into the Voronezh Front (7 July) and Stalingrad Front (12 July) under General F. I. Golikov and Marshal of the Soviet Union S. K. Timoshenko respectively. Starting from Kharkov, the 6th Army reached its first objective on the eastward bend of the River Don at Kachalinskaya by 22 July.

Blau III (blue III) Third component of the German summer offensive of 1942 in the USSR, undertaken by Generalfeldmarschall Wilhelm List's Army Group 'A', formed from the southern component of Army Group 'South' on 7 July. Operation 'Blau III' used the 1st Panzerarmee and the 17th Army in a drive (7/22 July 1942) between Izyum on the River Donets and Taganrog on the Sea of Azov to provide a right flank for the 6th Army's advance through the 'Donets Corridor' towards Stalingrad, the object being to take the area as far south as the River Don between Tsimlyansky and Rostov. So successful was Army Group 'A' that the scope of its offensive was extended to a drive into the Caucasus, with the objects of taking the oilfields at Maikop, Grozny and Baku (the last on the Caspian Sea) and the port of Batumi close to the Turkish frontier. Great progress was made, but the exhausted Army Group 'A' was halted along the line of the River Terek by 18 November 1942 by strong resistance from the Caucasus and Trans-Caucasus Fronts despite the arrival of the German 11th Army over the Straits of Kerch from the Crimea and the main strength of the 4th Panzerarmee diverted from Army Group 'B' in a decisive weakening of that army group's offensive.

Blaue Linie (blue line) German defensive line in the lower Alps of northern Italy (1945).

Blaufuchs (blue fox) Drive by German XXXVI Corps, part of Generaloberst Nikolaus von Falkenhorst's AOK Norwegen, in the Salla area of central Finland (June 1941) to retake areas taken by the Soviets in 1940 and then to push forward with the aim of cutting the rail lines between Leningrad and Murmansk on the White Sea between Kandalaksha and Loukhi. The offensive succeeded in its primary aim, but failed to penetrate far into the USSR.

Bleacher Allied codename for Tongatapu in the Tonga island group.

Blei (lead) Alternative designation for 'Antimon'.

Blissful Invasion of Choiseul in the central Solomons (28 October 1943) by the US Marine 2nd Parachute Battalion. Landed at Voza, the battalion was successfully intended to create a major diversion in preparation for the major landings on Bougainville farther north up the Solomons chain. The battalion was withdrawn on 3 November, two days after the implementation of the Bougainville landings in Operation 'Cherryblossom', after firmly convincing the Japanese that the Americans were undertaking a full-scale invasion of the island.

Blitz (lightning) Plan by the German opposition to Hitler to assassinate the German leader in an aeroplane crash (March 1943).

Blitzableiter (lightning conductor) German study group investigating the opportunities for bacteriological warfare, a field in which the Germans held a considerable lead over the Allies, but were fearful to implement because of propaganda and 'leaks' about Allied capabilities.

Blitz Week Semi-official US designation of the US 8th Air Force's most intensive offensive campaign up to that time (24/30 July 1943). Planned by Major General Ira C. Eaker, the 'Blitz Week' launched major raids against targets in Norway (24 July), Hamburg and Kiel (25 July), Hamburg and Hannover (26 July), Kassel and Oschersleben (28 July), Kiel and Warnemunde (29 July), and Kassel (30 July). Some 1,672 sorties were flown, and the Americans lost 88 bombers over Germany plus many more written off in the UK after heavy battle damage. It was convincing evidence that VIII Bomber Command was not yet ready for deep-penetration raids over Germany without powerful escort fighter protection.

Blockbuster Drive to the Rhine by the Canadian II Corps (part of Lieutenant General Sir Henry Crerar's Canadian 1st Army) as part of Operation 'Veritable' (7 February/7 March 1945).

Blot British air operation complementary to 'Circus' and 'Rhubarb' sweeps, and designed to tackle peripheral targets in occupied Europe (1941 onwards).

Blucher (i) German 11th Army crossing of the Straits of Kerch from the eastern tip of the Crimea into the Kuban region (July 1942) as support for the 17th Army's effort to take the oilfields of Maikop and the port of Batumi on the Black Sea coast near the frontier with Turkey against the defences of the Soviet Caucasus Front. The 11th Army in fact managed to penetrate south along the coast only as far as Novorossiysk.
(ii) Counterattack by the 3rd Panzerarmee to halt a Soviet breakthrough in the region of Rzhev (August/September 1942); the Soviet drive was launched by the West and Kalinin Fronts against the weakened forces of Army Group 'Centre'.

Blueberry Airborne operation by the Chinese 2nd Parachute Commando to cut the Japanese lines of communication near Chakiang (27 July 1945).

Bluebottle Royal Navy rescue of escaped prisoners of war from a beach near Perpignan in south-west France (13 September 1942).

Bluecoat British capture of Mont Pinçon in Normandy (30 July 1944).

Bluie Allied codename for Greenland, which had US air bases at 'Bluie East' and 'Bluie West'.

Blume I (bloom I) German codename for the reporting of any Allied landing on the north coast of France.

Blume II (bloom II) German codename for the reporting of any Allied landing on the Mediterranean coast of France.

Bobcat US Navy refuelling centre for the Pacific Fleet in the Society Islands.

Bodenplatte (baseplate) Germany's last air offensive of the war (1 January 1945) with the aim of supporting Operation 'Herbstnebel'. All available fighter and bomber aircraft, aircrews and fuel were combined for this decisive stroke against Allied airfields in north-west Europe, though in the event few Allied aircraft were lost (these being replaced immediately from stocks) as a result of the weather and the ineptitude of Germany's mostly inexperienced aircrew. German losses were devastating, and irreplaceable fuel was expended to no real advantage.

Bodyguard Allied deception plan to shield Operation 'Overlord' from penetration by German intelligence.

Bodyline Allied codename for German secret weapon production centres, which were thus identified and attacked by bomber forces (autumn 1944).

Bolero Allied cover name for the movement of massive US ground forces across the Atlantic to the UK in preparation for the opening of a 'second front' in north-west Europe.

Bombardon Designation of a floating steel breakwater in the 'Mulberry' assembly.

Bonus British plan for an amphibious operation against the Vichy-held island of Madagascar in the Indian Ocean (1941).

Boomerang Air attack by the XX Bomber Command (US 20th Air Force) against the Japanese-operated oilfields and their associated installations near Palembang at the southern end of Sumatra in the Dutch East Indies (10 August 1944).

Boozer British radar-detection device designed to assess the ability of German 'Würzburg' fire-control radar to detect small targets such as de Havilland Mosquito bombers.

Boston Allied codename for Abau-Mullins harbour in south-east New Guinea.

Bowery Combined British and American operation to deliver 64 Supermarine Spitfire fighters to Malta (9 May 1942). The aircraft were flown off the carriers *Eagle* and *Wasp* some 700 miles from Malta, and the lessons from the disaster after Operation 'Calendar' had been carefully learned, all the arriving fighters being immediately refuelled or put into bomb-proof shelters. At the same time the British fast minelayer *Welshman* ran through to the island with 340 tons of supplies.

Bracelet Designation of the visit by Prime Minister Winston Churchill to North Africa (August 1941).

Braddock Air supply of explosives and other munitions to resistance forces in occupied Europe.

Braid Cover name for General George C. Marshall, the US Army chief-of-staff and chairman of the Joint Chiefs-of-Staff Committee.

Brandenburg Designation of a special commando unit in German service, being specially trained for operations behind the Allied front line, sometimes in Allied uniform and with Allied vehicles.

Brassard French landings to retake the island of Elba (17/19 June 1944).

Braun (brown) Axis operation to establish and reinforce a major defensive beach-head area in northern Tunisia (November 1942), a move deemed imperative after the success of the British 8th Army in the Western Desert and the establishment of major Allied forces in north-west Africa after Operation 'Torch'. The object of this combined German and Italian move was to maintain an Axis presence in North Africa and so tie down Allied forces which could otherwise have been deployed for the forthcoming invasion of the European mainland. The operation cost the Axis powers dearly in shipping and transport aircraft.

Braunschweig (Brunswick) Extension of Operation 'Blau III', designed to take the

11th and 17th Armies and 1st Panzerarmee of Generalfeldmarschall Wilhelm List's Army Group 'A' from the line of the River Don into the region of the Caucasus to take the oilfields at Maikop, Grozny and Baku (9 July/18 November 1942). The offensive ultimately failed as a result of the overextension of German lines of communications and the sterling defence of the Soviet North Caucasus and Trans-Caucasus Fronts (commanded by Marshal of the Soviet Union S. M. Budenny and General I. V. Tyulenev respectively), and had the result of causing Hitler on 17 July to divert the 4th Panzerarmee from the drive on Stalingrad to support Army Group 'A'. This reinforcement could not produce the desired result, and also helped to condemn the 6th Army to its period of trial in Stalingrad during the following winter.

Breastplate Allied concept for an amphibious assault on Sousse in Tunisia from Malta (November 1942) as a means of opening up the Axis defence in North Africa in conjunction with the advances by the Allies from the West (1st Army) and from the east (8th Army). The plan was rendered superfluous by the general success of the Allied armies closing in on the Axis beachhead in Tunisia.

Brevity British offensive against the Axis positions in the Halfaya Pass (15/17 May 1941), seized by the Germans on 25 April 1941. The situation in the region had stabilized as both sides build up their strengths and consolidated after a headlong German advance and British retreat. Operation 'Brevity' was planned as a precursor to Operation 'Battleaxe' to take the tactically vital pass. Under the command of Brigadier 'Strafer' Gott a British force was to undertake a triple offensive, with the Coast Group securing Halfaya Pass and the town of Sollum, the 22nd Guards Brigade Group swinging inland to co-operate in the Halfaya operation and take Fort Capuzzo, and the 7th Armoured Brigade Group striking yet farther inland towards Sidi Azeiz to shield the left flank of the operation.

Halfaya Pass and Fort Capuzzo were taken by the British after severe fighting, but Rommel feared that the operation presaged the imminent arrival of a major British offensive and counterattacked with the 54th Light Infantry Regiment and the 8.Panzerregiment (to bolster Sollum's defences) and the 2/5.Panzerregiment (to retake Fort Capuzzo). The Germans retook Fort Capuzzo after a strenuous fight, and then discovered that the 7th Armoured Brigade Group had fallen back to Halfaya Pass, which the 54th Light Infantry Regiment and 8.Panzerregiment took in a classic pincer attack on 27 May, forcing the British to retire to their start line.

Brewer US amphibious assault on the Admiralty Islands in the Bismarck Archipelago (29 February/25 March 1944), one of the two final offensives of the 'Elkton' plan to cut off the Japanese 8th Area Army in New Britain and New Ireland and so leave them to 'wither on the vine' for the rest of the war. The attack began as a reconnaissance in force of Los Negros in the Admiralties by part of the US 1st Cavalry Division, it thereupon being decided to exploit the situation by the committal of two whole divisions (Major General William Rupertus' 1st Marine Division and Major General William C. Chase's 1st Cavalry Division) so that by 25 March Los Negros and Manus islands had been taken, together with the useful airfield at Lorengau, to bottle up the Japanese escape route to the east-north-east. This route towards other Japanese positions was closed on 20 March when the 4th Marine Division landed unopposed on Emirau and Mussau islands in the St Matthias group, the effect being to trap General Imamura's 8th Area Army on New Ireland and the eastern end of New Britain, and the 17th Army on Bougainville, where it was hotly engaged with Major General Oscar Griswold's US XIII Corps in the jungles of Bougainville farther down the chain of the Solomon Islands.

Bridford Royal Navy operation to pick up vital war supplies (ball bearings, rare metals, etc.) from Sweden by the use of specially adapted motor gunboats (26/31 October 1943, and on various other dates up to March 1944).

Brimstone Allied plan to use Lieutenant General Mark Clark's US 5th Army take the

Italian island of Sardinia in the autumn of 1944, by that time behind the Allied left flank in Italy. The plan was not pursued as the German forces on the island were considered impotent to make any significant impact on Allied operations. The capture of the island had been envisaged first during the planning for the Italian campaign, an alternative to the campaign eventually undertaken (through Sicily and into southern Italy) being a 'left-hook' advance from Tunisia straight north into Sardinia before a double debouchment into northern Italy and, via Corsica, into southern France. The option was not pursued as the alternative offered safer maritime lines of communication and also provided the chance to draw German forces farther from the Normandy region.

Operation 'Brimstone' would have used substantial Allied forces, in the shape of the US VI Corps (1st Armored, 34th Infantry and 36th Infantry Divisions), the British V Corps (1st and 4th or 56th Divisions) and, in army reserve, the US 82nd Airborne Division, but the whole plan was cancelled on 20 July 1943 after the success of Operation 'Husky' made the Sardinian adventure superfluous.

Brisk British plan to take the Portuguese Azores (1940/1941) to provide air and naval bases for the closing of the 'Atlantic gap' in which German U-boats could operate with little threat of British air attack.

Broadway Fly-in strip to the west of the River Irrawaddy between Myitkyina and Bhamo in northern Burma. This was the site for the aerial delivery (5 March 1944) of the 77th Long-Range Penetration Brigade (followed by the 111th Long-Range Penetration Brigade) during Major General Orde Wingate's 2nd Chindit Expedition. In a classic exercise of fighting and marching, the 77th LRP Brigade operated to considerable effect behind the lines of the Japanese 15th Army and then, though utterly exhausted, co-operated with the US 5307th Provisional Regiment ('Merrill's Marauders') in the captures of Mogaung (26 June) and of Myitkyina (4 August) before evacuation to India.

Bromide British VHF jamming counter-measures to the German 'X-Gerät' blind-bombing system.

Bronze British commando liaison mission to the local resistance movement in Czechoslovakia.

Brückenschlag (bridge blow) Offensive by Generaloberst Georg von Küchler's Army Group 'North' to relieve the German II Corps cut off in the Demyansk pocket (21 March/21 April 1942). Encircled by the 11th, 34th and 3rd Shock Armies of Colonel General P. A. Kurochkin's North-West Front, General W. Graf von Brockdorff-Ahlefeldt's seven divisions held out with the aid of extensive air resupply until the special strike force of five divisions under Generalleutnant Walter von Seydlitz-Kurzbach opened a 'land bridge' to the pocket, which Hitler had all along considered an offensive fortress rather than a defensive pocket. The forces trapped in the Demyansk pocket had been ably supplied by the Luftwaffe, and it was this ability for ground forces to be supplied from the air that persuaded Hitler that any German formation cut off behind the Soviet lines could be nourished with food, ammunition, fuel and other essential supplies, an erroneous assessment that led to the destruction of the 6th Army at Stalingrad, and to the loss of other such formations encircled by the increasingly powerful Soviet forces, whose improving tactical air forces could decimate the German transport units that were running out of adequate freight aircraft.

Brushwood That portion of the US Western Task Force which landed near Fedala during Operation 'Torch'.

Brutus Airborne operation by the Belgian Independent Parachute Company, SAS, to aid a local resistance unit near Mulet in Belgium (5/9 September 1944).

B.T. Designation (together with a numerical suffix) of the Allied maritime convoy route from Sydney (New South Wales) to the USA, and inaugurated in January 1942.

BU Plan by Lieutenant General Renya

Mutaguchi's 15th Army for a Japanese offensive (May 1943) to cross the River Chindwin south of Homalin to take the hills between the Rivers Yu and Chindwin as a protective barrier for the Japanese in the light of experience with the 1st Chindit Expedition during February and March 1943. Mutaguchi anticipated that such a move could be completed before the onset of the 1943 monsoon to provide protection and also the springboard for a major offensive towards India in the dry season of 1944.

Buccaneer British plan for the recapture of the Andaman Islands (spring 1944). The plan could not be implemented for lack of landing craft, which were needed more urgently for the Pacific and European campaigns, despite the fact that the recapture of the Andamans would have deprived the Japanese of the important airfield at Port Blair, and also provided the Allies with an effective base for the strangulation of Japan's maritime lines of communication between the Malayan peninsula and Burma at a time when Japanese rail communications and other overland transport capabilities were wholly incapable of meeting the demands of Japan's forces in Burma.

Büffel (buffalo) German evacuation of the Rzhev salient (February 1943). Here the German 9th Army of Generalfeldmarschall Günther von Kluge's Army Group 'Centre' was nearly encircled by elements of the Soviet West and Kalinin Fronts (commanded by General I. S. Konev and Lieutenant General M. A. Purkaev respectively), which had attacked westward at the end of July 1943. Hitler's acquiescence in this retreat to the line of the River Mius was strategically sound, but forced on the German leader against his will by Generalfeldmarschalle von Manstein and von Kluge, further exacerbating the relations between Hitler and his senior commanders on the Eastern Front.

Bugle Allied air offensive to interdict communications in the Ruhr and between the Ruhr and the rest of Germany (February 1945) in preparation for the advance of the 21st Army Group (Canadian 1st, British 2nd and US 9th Armies) under Field-Marshal Viscount Montgomery from the line of the River Maas in 7 February 1945. The implementation of Operation 'Bugle' did much to ensure that the bulk of the German 5th Panzerarmee and 15th Army were trapped in the Ruhr when the leading echelons of the US 1st Army (12th Army Group) and of the 9th Army met at Lippstadt at the beginning of April 1945.

Buick Mass supply drop to the French maquis (1 August 1944) in preparation for the wide-sweeping exploitation of the breakout of Allied land forces from the Normandy beach-head at the end of July in Operation 'Cobra'.

Bulbasket Airborne raid by the 1st SAS Regiment on Chateauroux (6 June 1944).

Bulldozer British plan for an amphibious assault on Akyab in Burma (spring 1944) using the 36th Division and the 50th Parachute Brigade. The operation was cancelled for a variety of reasons, including the need for the required transport aircraft for the containment of the Japanese offensive in the Imphal and Kohima regions.

Bullfrog British plan to retake Akyab Island (March 1943) in Burma using two brigades of the 36th Indian Division and three brigades of the British 2nd Division. The object of the offensive was to remove the threat posed to Chittagong by Japanese forces operating from Akyab, and to provide the Allied air forces with advanced air bases from which they could interdict Japanese lines of communication deep in southern Burma and so materially improve the chances of the Allies' land campaigns in central and northern Burma.

Bumper British and Canadian exercise in the Chiltern Hills (autumn 1941).

Bunghole Allied intelligence mission infiltrated into Czechoslovakia (27 February 1944).

Bunyon Airborne raid by the Belgian Independent Parachute Company, SAS, on

Burlesque

German rear-area installations near the Foret de Senonches (2 August 1944).

Burlesque Allied codename for Roi atoll in the Kwajalein group.

Burza Uprising in Poland by the Polish Home Army under Lieutenant General Tadeusz Bor-Komarowski (1 August 1944) in anticipation of the arrival of Soviet troops to help them at the end of Operation 'Bagration'. However, the Soviets had reached the limits of their lines of communication and were exhausted after this magnificent summer offensive of 1944, and were ordered by Stalin to halt just over the River Vistula from the uprising, giving German SS formations a free hand to crush the uprising despite material aid dropped by Allied aircraft operating from the UK and Italy. Quite apart from the military necessity of pausing his armies, Stalin saw his halt order as a golden opportunity to cause the destruction of the pro-Western Home Army in preparation for the inauguration of a pro-Soviet regime in Poland.

In moderately heavy fighting the Home Army managed to take most of Warsaw by 4 August, though the progress of the Polish effort was hampered by lack of heavy weapons and ammunition, resulting in an inability to consolidate into one defensive whole the three enclaves they secured in the city; the Germans launched their major counterattack on 10 August, and by 14 August the Home Army had been divided into six enclaves. The fighting increased extraordinarily in bitterness during the following two months of attritional warfare and starvation amongst the Poles, and the rising ended with Bor-Komarowski's surrender on 5 October, by which time the front line of General K. K. Rokossovsky's 1st Belorussian Front was only a few hundred yards distant from the last Polish pocket, on the eastern bank of the Vistula.

Button Allied codename for Espiritu Santo in the New Hebrides group.

Buttress British plan for an invasion of southern Italy in the Gulf of Goia during the autumn of 1943. This was one of many contingency plans evolved by temporarily uncommitted formation headquarters of General Dwight D. Eisenhower's Allied Forces in North Africa command at the behest of General George C. Marshall. Operation 'Buttress' was the responsibility of the British X Corps under Lieutenant General Sir Brian Horrocks, which was not involved in the Sicilian campaign and thus available for a major landing in the 'toe' of Italy. Operation 'Buttress' was to put ashore in the Gulf of Goia the British 7th Armoured, 46th and 56th Divisions for an advance along the northern shore of the 'toe', supported after about one month (necessary for the reassembly of the theatre's limited amphibious forces) by Operation 'Goblet' to be undertaken at Crotone on the 'ball' of the Italian foot by Lieutenant General C. Alfrey's British V Corps.

These plans were laid in the light of unknown Axis defensive capabilities, though these were assumed to be strong. However, after the successful launch of Operation 'Husky' and the revelation that the Axis defence was not as powerful as had been feared, the caution that had characterized the planning for Operation 'Buttress' was overtaken by enthusiasm. It was eventually decided, however, that X Corps (now commanded by Lieutenant General Sir Richard McCreery) would be loaded with a view to participation in Operation 'Avalanche' as a possible alternative to Operation 'Buttress'. With the success of Operation 'Baytown', Operation 'Buttress' was cancelled on 4 September and X Corps allocated definitely to Operation 'Avalanche'.

Byproduct Allied codename for the Trobriand Islands.

C Indian Ocean raid by the Japanese 1st Carrier Fleet and 2nd Expeditionary Fleet (1/9 April 1942) from an advanced base in Sulawesi with 5 aircraft-carriers (veterans of Pearl Harbor) and 4 battleships plus powerful escorts, all under the command of Vice Admiral Chuichi Nagumo. The British feared an invasion of Ceylon, but the Japanese did not have the troops or transports needed for such an undertaking, and instead confined themselves to a raid designed to disrupt British defence plans in the theatre, based on six infantry brigades and the Eastern Fleet commanded by Admiral Sir James Somerville and including 5 battleships (4 of them old) and 3 aircraft-carriers (one of them old).

When the Japanese blow fell the British Force A, consisting of the more modern elements, was refuelling at Addu Atoll in the Maldive Islands, and 100 Japanese aircraft were able to bomb Colombo on the morning of 5 April, followed by 50 more during the afternoon. During that day two British cruisers were sunk, and on 9 April the old carrier *Hermes* was also sunk before the Japanese retired, a detached force operating in the Bay of Bengal having in the meantime sunk 23 ships of 112,000 gross registered tons. It was a further humiliating defeat for the British by the Japanese, who nevertheless failed to capitalize further on the disruption they had caused as their ships were in urgent need of overhaul.

Cabaret Royal Navy attempt to bring out from Sweden blockade runners with vital war supplies such as ball bearings, rare metals etc (4/6 February 1943).

Cabrank RAF system of operating fighter-bombers for close support of the Allied ground forces in 1944 onwards. The squadrons tasked with close support orbited above the battlefield, and were called down by RAF forward liaison officers operating with the ground forces as and when required. The whole system operated with commendable speed and precision, the fighter-bombers being able to tackle targets in close proximity to friendly ground forces within minutes of demand.

Cactus Allied codename for Guadalcanal in the Solomon Islands.

Cadillac Allied mass supply drop to the French maquis (14 July 1944).

Caesar Linie (Caesar line) German defensive line in Italy, running from a point just north of Anzio on the Tyrrhenian Sea across the Apennines via Valmontone, Avezzano and Popoli to Pescara on the Adriatic coast. The main Allied target defended on this line by the 10th and 14th Armies of Generalfeldmarschall Albert Kesselring's Army Group 'C' was Rome. The line was breached by the US 5th Army at the end of May 1944, but instead of swinging east to encircle the 10th Army, which was pinned by the British 8th Army, Lieutenant General Mark Clark opted instead to advance unopposed on the city of Rome, which was entered on 4 June.

Caiman Plan for the support of the French maquis with a specifically constructed operation (June 1944).

25

Cairo Three Cover designation of the Tehran Conference (28/30 November 1943) between President Roosevelt, Prime Minister Churchill and Premier Stalin. This was a conference to decide on the Allies' priorities after the successful invasion of Italy, and the conclusions reached were the abandonment of Operation 'Buccaneer', the application of increased pressure in Italy (up to a proposed stop line between Livorno and Rimini) to prevent the Germans from withdrawing forces that could then be sent to the Eastern Front, the timing of Operation 'Overlord' moved to the beginning of June 1944 so that it would coincide with the opening of the Soviets' summer offensive of that year, and the launching of Operation 'Anvil' (later Operation 'Dragoon') in conjunction with Operation 'Overlord' to pin as many German forces in France as possible. Preliminary agreement was also reached between 'the big three' on the partition of post-war Europe into spheres of influence that would greatly enhance the political, economic and military strength of the USSR.

Calcium British commando intelligence mission to the Czech resistance.

Calendar Combined British and American operation to deliver 47 Supermarine Spitfire fighters to Malta (20 April 1942). The aircraft were flown off the carrier *Wasp* some 700 miles from Malta, and reached the island safely only to be caught on the ground by a carefully planned Axis air attack before they had been put into sheltered revetments or been refuelled.

Caliban Airborne operation by the Belgian Independent Parachute Company, SAS, to cut the rail lines near Peere in Belgium (5 September 1944).

Caliph Allied plan to take the French port of Bordeaux in the Bay of Biscay (June/July 1944) with amphibious forces diverted from the Mediterranean theatre.

Camel Landing beach in the Marseilles/St Raphael/Toulon area during Operation 'Dragoon'.

Camouflage Allied codename for Namur Atoll in the Kwajalein group.

Cannibal British offensive designed to recapture Akyab in Burma (1 January/25 May 1943) after the overland advance by the 14th Indian Division from Chittagong via Cox's Bazar to the 'Tunnels' line between Maungdaw and Buthidaung. The advance by Major General W. L. Lloyd's division then moved slowly down the Mayu peninsula towards Donbaik and Mayu Point at the tip of the peninsula across the River Mayu from the northern side of Akyab, whose valuable airfield and other installations were reinforced from February 1943 onwards by the Japanese 55th Division from the Prome area. However, the British advance had been slow and hesitant, and was thus checked in front of Donbaik by the end of January, allowing Major General T. Koga to complete his preparations and then go over to the offensive on 4 March, pushing the 47th and 55th Indian Brigades back north up the Mayu peninsula with direct and outflanking attacks. By 25 May the 14th Indian Division was back along a line just south of Bawli Bazar. Operation 'Cannibal' had been designed along limited lines to provide small-scale successes that would show that the Japanese could be defeated, but in fact had just the opposite effect as thorough preparation and training had yet again been worsted by the ability of the Japanese to improvise in defence and then extemporise a rapid counteroffensive.

Cannonshot Attack by the 1st Canadian Division across the River IJssel near Deventer (11 April 1945).

Canvas Offensive by British forces in Kenya (11th and 12th African Divisions and the 1st South African Division, commanded by Lieutenant General Sir Alan Cunningham) to take Italian Somaliland and push forward into Abyssinia (10 February/March 1941). These forces occupied Kismayu in Italian Somaliland on 16 February and pushed forward to take Mogadishu, the capital, by 25 February, and then launched a double advance up the River Juba from Kismayu and up the River Shibeli from

Mogadishu towards Negelli and Jijiga in Abyssinia, taken on 21 and 17 March respectively.

Capital British 14th Army plan for an advance across the River Chindwin in northern Burma, in co-operation with the Chinese forces commanded by Lieutenant General J. Stilwell, to take Mandalay (summer 1944). The plan was overtaken by Operation 'Extended Capital', a more ambitious offensive designed to make use of Japanese exhaustion after the Imphal and Kohima battles.

Capri German plan for a counteroffensive by Axis forces to retake Medenine (spring 1943) and so halt the westward advance of the British 8th Army for a link-up with the 1st Army in Tunisia, paving the way for a resurgence of Axis fortunes in the Western Desert.

Carbonado Revised version of 'Beta'.

Car Development of the 'Highball' weapon.

Cardinal Airborne operation by units of the Office of Strategic Services to rescue Allied prisoners of war held by the Japanese at Mukden in Manchukuo (Manchuria) at the time of Japan's collapse (15 August 1945).

Cargo (i) Allied codename for President Franklin D. Roosevelt.
(ii) Allied amphibious exercise in preparation for Operation 'Overlord'.

Carpet British and American radar jammer designed for use against German 'Würzburg' fire-control radar.

Carpetbagger Allied air operations ferrying messages and *matériel* to agents in occupied Europe.

Cartwheel Northern component of the final 'Elkton' plan (26 April 1943) whereby the forces of Vice Admiral William Halsey's South Pacific Area were to co-operate with those of General Douglas MacArthur's South-West Pacific Area in a double advance to seal off the Japanese 8th Area Army in New Britain and New Ireland. The 'Cartwheel' portion of the campaign involved an advance north-west up the chain of the Solomon Islands against the forces of Lieutenant General Hyatutake's Japanese 17th Army (operational command passing to the South-West Pacific Area between Choiseul and Bougainville) before a wide outflanking descent on the St Matthias group (March 1944) north-west of Kavieng in New Britain to seal off the 8th Area Army's possible route for escape or even reinforcement. The Japanese forces thus isolated were to be left undisturbed for the rest of the war.

Case 3 Early version of Operation 'Talisman'.

Castor Developed version of 'Aphrodite'.

Cat US and Canadian codename for countermeasures against German acoustic-homing torpedoes, and known to the British as 'Foxer'.

Catapult Attack by Force H of the Royal Navy on the French naval base at Mers el Kebir near Oran in Algeria (3 July 1940). At the time of her collapse to the Germans in June 1940, France had a major naval strength of 6 battleships and 2 battle-cruisers, with another battleship nearing completion, though at the time of the French armistice with Germany 3 of the battleships were in British ports (two in the UK and one at Alexandria). However, the British were alarmed at the prospect of the other units (2 battleships and 2 battle-cruisers at Mers el Kebir, the nearly completed *Richelieu* at Dakar and the half-completed *Jean Bart* at Casablanca) falling into German hands, and on 27 June decided on a preemptive strike against Mers el Kebir to prevent these ships from returning to French mainland ports if the French would not surrender them.

Commanded by Vice Admiral Sir James Somerville, the Gibraltar-based Force H comprised the battle-cruiser *Hood*, 2 battleships, one aircraft-carrier and supporting units, and arrived on 3 July off Mers el Kebir, where Admiral Gensoul refused even to reply to the British ultimatum to join the British,

Catchpole

or to demilitarize his ships, or to scuttle his ships. With the expiry of the British ultimatum and the obvious preparations of the French for sea, Somerville reluctantly gave the order to open fire. Within a few minutes the battleship *Bretagne* had blown up, the battleship *Provence* had been beached, the battle-cruiser *Dunkerque* had been crippled, and the battle-cruiser *Strasbourg* had escaped, eventually reaching Toulon. The *Richelieu* was attacked by British naval torpedo bombers on 8 July and severely damaged.

Catchpole Seizure of Eniwetok Atoll (17/23 February 1944) as the final element of the US capture of the Marshall Islands using the reserve forces that had not been needed for the capture of Kwajalein in Operation 'Flintlock'. Under the overall control of Admiral Chester W. Nimitz's Pacific Ocean Areas, the US 5th Fleet (Vice Admiral Raymond Spruance) and 5th Amphibious Force (Rear Admiral Richmond K. Turner) were responsible for the entire campaign to retake the island groups of the central Pacific with the support of Major General Willis H. Hale's US 7th Air Force operating out of the Ellice Islands. The amphibious forces assigned to the campaign were the US Marine Corps and US Army formations of V Amphibious Corps commanded by Major General 'Howling Mad' Smith.

For the seizure of Eniwetok Atoll the invasion sailed right into the lagoon of the atoll, and made three separate landings. First (17/19 February) two battalions of the 22nd Marine Regiment and the 106th Regimental Combat Team of the 27th Infantry Division secured Engebi island against minimal opposition. Second (19/21 February) one battalion of the 22nd Marine Regiment and two battalions of the 106th Regimental Combat Team secured Eniwetok island against fiercely determined resistance. And third (22/23 February) three battalions of the 22nd Marine Regiment secured Parry island again in the face of strenuous defence. All 2,000 defenders of Eniwetok Atoll were killed, but the completion of this campaign opened the way for the US advance to the Marianas. Total US casualties in Operation 'Catchpole' were 195 dead and 521 wounded in comparison with Japanese losses of 2,677 dead out of a garrison of 2,741. The Japanese garrisons on the atolls of Wotje, Maloelap, Mille and Jaluit were thus isolated, finally surrendering on 2 September 1945.

Catherine British plans for naval operations in the Baltic to halt the Swedish iron ore trade with Germany (April/May 1940). The concept was rightly dropped as being totally risky in the face of overwhelming German air superiority and the real chance of bringing Sweden into the war on the side of Germany.

Causeway US plan to invade Formosa (1945), ultimately deemed unnecessary as better opportunities were offered by a direct assault on the Japanese home islands (Operations 'Olympic' and 'Coronet'). The object of Operation 'Causeway' would have been to provide Allied (especially US) forces with a springboard for operations against the Japanese in China.

C.D. Designation of East African coastal convoys (together with a numerical suffix) plying from Cape Town to Durban in South Africa, and inaugurated in November 1942 ending in September 1943.

C.E. Designation of British coastal convoys (together with a numerical suffix) plying from St Helen's on the Isle of Wight to Southend, and inaugurated in September 1940.

Cellophane Allied amphibious exercise in preparation for Operation 'Overlord'.

Cent US task force and its beach in Operation 'Husky'.

Cerberus Designation of the dash up the English Channel (11/13 February 1942) by the German battle-cruisers *Scharnhorst* and *Gneisenau* with the heavy cruiser *Prinz Eugen*, all of which had arrived in the Breton port of Brest after commerce-raiding cruises into the Atlantic and which had since endured a protracted series of British bombing raids. Though Grossadmiral Erich Raeder was convinced that the ships should be left at Brest for further raids into the Atlantic, Hitler demanded that they be brought home to

Germany as insurance against the British invasion of Norway that he thought inevitable, and it was decided that a high-speed dash under massive fighter protection offered the best chance of breaking through the inevitable British attacks.

The squadron sailed at 22.45 on 11 February, and caught the British completely off balance, so that it was not until 11.30 on 12 February that the German squadron was positively identified and marked for attack. By this time the German units were off Boulogne, and managed to fight right through determined but unco-ordinated British air and surface attacks to reach Wilhelmshaven (*Scharnhorst*) and Brunsbüttel (*Gneisenau* and *Prinz Eugen*) on the morning of 13 February. The *Gneisenau* was slightly damaged after hitting one mine, but the *Scharnhorst* was more seriously affected by striking two mines. British aircraft losses were heavy as a result of the ships' massive AA armaments and the superb fighter escort provided by the Luftwaffe.

C.F. Designation of British ocean homeward convoys (together with a numerical suffix) plying from Cape Town via West Africa to the UK, and inaugurated in May 1941.

C.G. Designation of Allied North-West African convoys (together with a numerical suffix) plying from Casablanca to Gibraltar, and inaugurated in January 1943; these were originally F.T. convoys.

Chain Home British medium-range air-warning radar network.

Chain Home Low British short-range low-level air-warning radar network.

Champion (i) Original version of Operation 'Capital' (1943).
(ii) The decisions reached at the 'Trident' conference at Washington in May 1943, notably to concentrate on the prosecution of the war against Germany as the first priority while containing Japan; to obtain bases in the Azores as a means of combating the U-boat threat; to build up the bomber campaign against Germany from the UK; to undertake as soon as practical a cross-Channel invasion of north-west France; to increase pressure on Italy and eliminate her from the war; to undertake the bombing of the Romanian oilfields at Ploesti in order to deprive Germany of her most important oil resources; to concentrate Allied efforts in Burma on the development of the air and land links with China; to capture Akyab and Ramree Islands off the Burmese coast; in the Pacific to pursue a two-pronged advance against the Japanese from New Guinea and through the Central Pacific by means of the capture of the rest of New Guinea, the Solomons and the Bismarck Archipelago and of the Marshall and Caroline Islands while intensifying the pace of air operations in and from China; and to aid the USSR however possible.

Channel Stop Daylight aircraft patrols by the RAF to prevent the movement of German light shipping and coastal convoys in the English Channel.

Character British plan to raise and use levies of the Karen hill tribes to harass and cut Japanese lines of communication in northern Burma (1944/1945).

Chariot British combined naval and commando assault on the German naval base at St Nazaire (28 March 1942). This French base contained the only Atlantic drydock capable of accepting the Germans' only surviving modern battleship (*Tirpitz*), and its destruction would therefore seriously hamper the German deployment of this unit to the Atlantic on commerce-raiding cruises. The plan was basically simple, and involved the ramming of the Normandie dock's seaward gate by the ex-US destroyer *Buchanan*, which was loaded with explosives timed to detonate after the ship's skeleton crew had been evacuated (together with the covering commando parties) in a flotilla of motor gunboats. The whole operation was fraught with difficulty and in the end frustratingly confused, leading to the abandonment of large numbers of commandos, but succeeded in putting the Normandie dock out of action for the rest of the war when the *Buchanan* blew up during the morning after the raid.

Charnwood Air support scheme for Operation 'Goodwood'.

Chastise Designation of the attack (16/17 May 1943) by Avro Lancaster bombers led by Wing Commander Guy Gibson against the Möhne, Eder and Sorpe dams controlling the water level in the Ruhr area. Using special 'bouncing bombs' developed by Dr Barnes Wallis of Vickers, the raid succeeded in breaching two of the dams, causing considerable damage, though not the devastation that had been anticipated.

Chastity Allied plan to place an artificial harbour such as 'Mulberry' in Quiberon Bay to support operations in Brittany.

Chattanooga Choo-Choo Offensive by fighter-bombers of the British 2nd Tactical Air Force and US 9th Air Force (21/28 May 1944) against German locomotives and rolling stock in northern Europe. The object of the offensive was to reduce the quantities of such equipment available to the Germans as a means of reinforcing their armies in north-west France once Operation 'Overlord' had been launched.

Chaucer Airborne operation by the Belgian Independent Parachute Company, SAS, against German rear-area installations near Condreceau (9 August 1944).

Cheerful Offensive by Général Jean de Lattre de Tassigny's French 1st Army (20 January/9 February 1945) against General Siegfried Rasp's German 19th Army trapped in the Colmar pocket in central France. With a total of eight infantry and four armoured divisions, the French I and II Corps (commanded by Général de Corps d'Armée Marie-Emile Béthouart and Général de Corps d'Armée G. de Monsabert) were tasked with the elimination of Generalleutnant Helmuth Thumm's LXI Corps and Generalleutnant Erich Abraham's LXIII Corps, which between them mustered seven poor infantry or mountain divisions and one Panzer brigade. The battle was extremely hard fought, and ended only on the 20th day after the loss of 1,600 French and 540 American dead plus 8,585 and 2,670 wounded.

Even so, the Germans managed to pull back relatively intact over the Upper Rhine, leaving behind some 22,000 men to become prisoners of war.

Cherryblossom Final operation in the eastern portion of the 'Elkton' plan, namely the establishment of a substantial US beach-head at Empress Augusta Bay on Bougainville in the Solomon Islands (1 November 1943). The object of the landings was to sever and isolate the Japanese forces on the island, who were already concentrated in the northern and southern ends, and to provide the US forces with an airfield from which the Japanese bastion at Rabaul could be brought under attack.

Under the overall control of Lieutenant General Alexander A. Vandegrift's I Amphibious Corps of Vice Admiral William F. Halsey's South Pacific Area, Major General Allen H. Turnage's US 3rd Marine Division landed in the almost undefended area around Cape Torokina and soon established a viable lodgement against increasingly strenuous opposition from elements of Lieutenant General Harukichi Hyakutake's 17th Army, initially the Japanese 23rd Infantry Regiment and the Japanese 17th Division, the latter being brought in by sea from Rabaul on 7 November and virtually destroyed by 8 November. Hyakutake could call upon some 60,000 men (40,000 from the army and another 20,000 naval troops), but by the end of 1943 the American beach-head had been reinforced by the 37th Division of the US Army, which had started to land on 8 November, allowing the inland extension of the lodgement to make possible the establishment of three airfields and a major naval base at Empress Augusta Bay.

At the beginning of 1944 the US Army's Americal Division replaced the 3rd Marine Division, allowing command to pass to Major General Oscar Griswold's XIV Corps. Hyakutake threw in his last assault on 9 March 1944 under the direst of climatic and geographical conditions, and by the time XIV Corps crushed this effort on 31 March the Japanese had lost 6,000 of the 15,000 men committed. The US divisions of XIV Corps were later replaced by Australian units, who kept the Japanese in check for the rest of the war without undue effort.

Chesterfield Offensive by the Canadian I Corps of Lieutenant General Sir Oliver Leese's British 8th Army to breach the 'Führer-Senger' Line at Pontecorvo just west of Monte Cassino (22 May 1944). This opened the right flank of Army Group 'C' commanded by Generalfeldmarschall Albert Kesselring, but Lieutenant General Mark Clark, commanding the US 5th Army, preferred the political coup of capturing Rome to the military advantage of possibly trapping the bulk of Generaloberst Heinrich von Vietinghoff-Scheel's German 10th Army against the 8th Army.

Chestnut Airborne operations (13 July 1943) in support of General Sir Bernard Montgomery's British 8th Army in Sicily after the landings in Operation 'Husky', notably the capture of the Primasole bridge on the east coast road between Syracuse and Catania.

Chilli Allied air operations undertaken at night (January 1945) to prevent U-boats breaking out into the Atlantic from German bases.

Choker I Allied 1st Airborne Army plan for an airborne operation to breach the 'Siegfried' line defences near Saarbrücken (December 1944).

Choker II Allied 1st Airborne Army plan for an airborne crossing of the River Rhine near Mainz (spring 1945) to create a bridgehead that could be rapidly reinforced to split Army Groups 'B' and 'G' (commanded by Generalfeldmarschall Walter Model and Generaloberst Johannes Blaskowitz respectively) and so trap German forces in a pocket between Koblenz and Frankfurt-am-Main.

Chop Line marking the division of British and US areas of command in the Atlantic.

Chowringee Fly-in strip for Morrisforce, east of the River Irrawaddy in a bend of the River Schweli for Major General Orde Wingate's 2nd Chindit Expedition (5 March 1944). The strip was abandoned on 10 March.

Chronicle Capture of Woodlark and Trobriand Islands (30 June 1943) to protect the right flank of the advance by General Douglas MacArthur's South-West Pacific Area forces in the western component of the 'Elkton' plan. Moving by sea from the Allied base in Milne Bay at the extreme south-east tip of New Guinea, part of the US 158th Infantry Regiment took Trobriand Island while the 112th Cavalry Regiment seized Woodlark Island, these two successes completing Allied domination of the Solomon Sea.

Chuckle Offensive by Lieutenant General E. L. M. Burns' Canadian I Corps of Lieutenant General Sir Richard McCreery's British 8th Army across the Fiumi Uniti river towards Ravenna in northern Italy (December 1944).

Cigar Allied jamming of German night-fighter radio frequencies as an aid to the bomber streams of RAF Bomber Command.

Circus Designation of daylight bombing raids by RAF light and medium bombers of No. 2 Group, Bomber Command, against targets in occupied Europe, the object being to inflict damage on these targets, but more importantly to lure German fighters up against the escorting British fighters, and so cause high levels of attrition in the strength of the *Jagdgeschwader* left in north-west Europe from spring 1941 onwards.

Clarion Major Allied bombing offensive designed to destroy German communications and morale (22 February 1945).

Clausewitz Alternative designation of Operation 'Blau III', part of the German summer offensive of 1942 in the southern USSR.

Claymore Designation of the UK's first major commando raid of World War II, directed against German-controlled targets in the Lofoten Islands off the northern coast of Norway (4 March 1941). On 1 March some

31

500 commandos sailed in two converted cross-Channel ferries from Scapa Flow under the command of Brigadier J. C. Haydon, the escort being found by five destroyers. The landings were unopposed, men of No. 3 Commando going ashore at Stamsund on Vest Vaago and Henningvaer, and men of No. 4 Commando at Stolvaer and Brettesnes on Ost Vaago. Opposition was encountered after the landings, but the raid was a complete success, some 200 German prisoners being taken, the fish oil factories totally destroyed, the factory ship *Hamburg* sunk together with a number of smaller vessels, and 300 Norwegian volunteers for the Allied forces picked up. In overall terms, the raid validated the concept of commando raids against targets on the long coastline of German-occupied Europe, and did much to improve British morale at a time of considerable military gloom.

Cleanser Offensive by the Canadian 5th Armoured Division of Lieutenant General Sir Henry Crerar's Canadian 1st Army to the IJsselmeer (15 April 1945).

Cleanslate Final move in the US campaign to retake Guadalcanal for the Allies, assault battalions from the US 43rd Infantry Division on Guadalcanal taking Pavuvu and Banika in the Russell Islands (21 February 1943). The capture of these two islands closed off the southern end of New Georgia Sound to the Japanese and thus helped to seal Guadalcanal from any possible Japanese counteroffensive, while also opening the way for further advance up the chain of the Solomon Islands once an airfield and naval facilities had been built on each of the two islands. Despite the comparative ease of this task, the move served notice on the Japanese that the Americans were not exhausted by the rigours of the Guadalcanal campaign, and were prepared to harry the Japanese 17th Army up the length of the Solomons chain.

Clinch Plan for a landing in Thailand as an alternative to Operation 'Bamboo', but conceived as being undertaken to the north of the Kra Isthmus and opening the way for the establishment of major Allied land forces in South-East Asia for an offensive south into Malaya or east through Thailand into Indo-China.

Clipper Offensive undertaken by Lieutenant General Sir Brian Horrocks' XXX Corps of General Sir Miles Dempsey's British 2nd Army to eliminate the Geilenkirchen salient (8/15 December 1945), which jutted dangerously forward to the west of the River Roer at the junction of Field Marshal Viscount Montgomery's 21st Army Group and General Omar Bradley's 12th Army Group.

Cloak British cover scheme to explain the presence of IV Corps in the Myittha valley (December 1943/January 1944).

Clydeside Fly-in strip for Major General Orde Wingate's 2nd Chindit Expedition (March 1944).

C.M. Designation of military convoys (together with a numerical suffix) plying from the Cape of Good Hope or Durban via Kilindini to the Red Sea ports, and inaugurated in June 1940.

Coat Designation of a reinforcement operation (7/9 November 1940) for the Mediterranean Fleet based at Alexandria under Admiral Sir Andrew Cunningham. The reinforcement consisted of the battleship *Barham*, the cruisers *Berwick* and *Glasgow* and three destroyers from the Home Fleet in British waters, and these departed from Gibraltar on 7 November, escorted by Force H and reinforcing Malta en route with guns and men carried on the warships. The one unfortunate result of this successful operation lay in the fact that it convinced the British naval authorities, in the Mediterranean and at home, that east/west convoys could with relative impunity be passed through the Mediterranean to reinforce the British forces in Egypt, which subsequent events were to disprove at great cost to the British.

Cobra Designation of the Allied break-out from the Normandy beach-head (24/31 July 1944). The operation was undertaken just to the west of St Lô on the western side of the

Cotentin peninsula, where Generalleutnant von Choltitz's LXXXIV Corps of Generaloberst Paul Hausser's German 7th Army faced two corps of Lieutenant General Omar Bradley's US 1st Army. These two corps were Major General Lawton J. Collins's US VII Corps and Major General Troy Middleton's US VIII Corps, the major part being entrusted to VII Corps on the Left.

The offensive was opened by a massive 'carpet bombing' of the German positions to the west of St Lô by Allied bombing. The Americans then poured through the gap torn in the German defences to their immediate front and exploited to the south, with Major General Corlett's US XIX Corps holding the inland shoulder of the breakthrough against the determined counterattacks of the German II Parachute Corps under Generalleutnant Eugen Meindl.

The Germans could not stem the American tide, which by the end of the month had swept past Avranches and opened the way for the US 3rd Army under Lieutenant General George S. Patton to sweep south and then east into the heart of France. The Normandy lodgement thus turned into a full-scale drive through central France, and though great credit must be given to the US forces who achieved the breakout, it should not be forgotten that the task was facilitated by the actions of the British 2nd and Canadian 1st Armies in the Caen area to the east, where their determined thrusts had served to draw the main weight of the German defence away from the US breakout region.

Cockade Designation of Allied diversionary schemes to pin down German forces in the West (1943) and so prevent their movement to the Eastern Front, where the Germans were in dire need of reinforcement against the full flood of Soviet offensives.

Cockpit Raid by the Fleet Air Arm and surface units of the Royal Navy on Sabang Island off the northern tip of Sumatra (25 July 1945). The raid was executed by 2 aircraft-carriers, 3 battleships, 7 cruisers and 10 destroyers of the Eastern Fleet under Admiral Sir James Somerville, and caused considerable damage to the port and oil installations, largely as a result of naval gunfire.

Cold Comfort Airborne operations by the 3rd Squadron, 2nd SAS, to aid Italian partisans in the neighbourhood of Verona (17 and 25 February 1945).

Collar Sequel to Operation 'Coat', in this instance the first attempt to pass a maritime convoy from Gibraltar to Malta and Alexandria (25/28 November 1940) with vitally needed supplies. Three fast merchantmen (2 for Malta and 1 for Alexandria) and 2 cruisers plus 4 corvettes were escorted by Vice Admiral Sir James Somerville's Force H to a point south of Sardinia, where elements of Admiral Sir Andrew Cunningham's Mediterranean Fleet would take over. All went well until 27 November, before Force H and the Mediterranean Fleet had met, when an Italian force of 2 battleships (*Vittorio Veneto* and *Guilio Cesare*), 7 heavy cruisers and 16 destroyers was sent to intercept the British force. Somerville realized that though he was heavily outnumbered and outgunned, his best course was to engage the Italians and give the merchantmen a chance to get away. An inconclusive running engagement followed before the Italian commander decided on a tactical withdrawal in the face of 'superior' numbers. Little damage was caused on either side, but Somerville's object of ensuring the merchantmen's safe passage was amply fulfilled.

Colonel Warden Allied codename for Prime Minister Winston Churchill.

Colorado Allied codename for the island of Crete in the eastern Mediterranean.

Colossus British airborne operation undertaken by 38 paratroops against the Tragino Viaduct in southern Italy (10 February 1941). This was the first British airborne operation of the war, and was certainly an overambitious target, for though the viaduct was attacked, the damage was negligible and soon repaired, while the raiding party failed to escape.

Comet British plan to seize crossing points

over the Lower Rhine river near Arnhem with airborne troops (7 September 1944) and so speed the advance of Lieutenant General Sir Miles Dempsey's British 2nd Army towards the northern part of the Netherlands and into the north German plain. The plan was evolved into the definitive Operation 'Market'.

Compass Offensive by Major General Richard O'Connor's Western Desert Force against the Italians in Egypt and Libya (6 December 1940/9 February 1941). Having accepted the Italians' initial cautious advance into Egypt, as far as Sidi Barrani in September 1940, the British prepared a careful offensive with limited manpower and few tanks to oust the Italians, who had dug themselves into a series of interlocking fortified camps.

The advance of the Western Desert Force (7th Armoured Division, 4th Indian Division and the New Zealand Division) started on 6 December with a probe into the 70-mile no man's land separating the British and Lieutenant General Annibale Bergonzoli's Italian XXIII Corps. With their armour operating on the desert flank and their infantry closer to the coast and its road system, the British rapidly routed the Italians under Mareschale Rudolfo Graziani and pushed on deep into Libya, the only delay being occasioned by General Sir Archibald Wavell's need to replace the 4th Indian Division (needed in the Sudan) with the 6th Australian Division.

The Western Desert Force (redesignated the British XIII Corps on 10 January 1941) took Sidi Barrani on 10 December, Tobruk on 22 January, Derna on 30 January and finally El Agheila on 9 February. The Italians had lost the equivalent of eight divisions and large quantities of *matériel*, and the British were at the absolute limit of their communications, exhausted and already warned that forces would have to be diverted from the Western Desert to bolster Greece. Though a classic of its type, the British offensive thus suffered ultimately from a diversion of strength needed for follow-on operations, and at the same time spurred the Italians to request German aid, which materialized in the form of Generalleutnant Erwin Rommel's Deutsches Afrika Korps.

Conclave Deception scheme to shield the left flank of the final advance of General Sir William Slim's 14th Army down the Rivers Irrawaddy and Sittang towards Rangoon (April 1945).

Cooney Airborne raids by parties of the French 3ème Regiment des Chasseurs Parachutistes to disrupt German communications in the Vannes region (7 June 1944).

Cope Designation of British bombing raids in which 'Oboe' was used successfully.

Cork Patrol scheme for British maritime reconnaissance aircraft to detect and destroy German U-boats in the Western Approaches to the English Channel.

Corkscrew Amphibious operation to capture Pantelleria (11 June 1943). The island was seen by Benito Mussolini as an Italian counterpart to the British bastion of Malta, and had by mid-1943 been heavily fortified and provisioned with a garrison of 12,000 men of the Brigata Mista Pantelleria under the overall command of Generale Alfredo Guzzoni's 6th Army in Sicily. The island was devastated by a week-long Allied bombing campaign before the landings, and the defenders were totally stupefied when men of Major General W. Clutterbuck's British 1st Division began to come ashore after being transported from Sfax and Sousse, the Italians immediately surrendering. The capitulation of Pantelleria was followed by those of Lampedusa and the other Italian islands to the south of Sicily on 12 June. The neutralization of Lampedusa was essential for the planned Allied landings in Sicily, for the island lay athwart the only practical approach routes from Tunisia.

Corncob (i) Allied bombing campaign against the bridges on the Rivers Adige and Brenta (20/23 April 1945) to cut the lines of retreat for the German 10th and 14th Armies pulling back respectively towards the Brenner Pass and Venice in front of the US 5th and British 8th Armies.

(ii) Designation of the blockships used in 'Gooseberry'.

Corona The broadcasting by German-speaking Allied controllers of false information to German night-fighter crews, so diverting them from the bomber streams coming in to devastate German cities.

Coronet Amphibious operation planned by the Americans to capitalize on the confusion caused by Operation 'Olympic'. Tentatively scheduled for 1 March 1946, Operation 'Coronet' was to use a large proportion of US forces transferred to the Pacific theatre after the end of hostilities in Europe, and would put ashore two US armies, one on each side of Tokyo on Honshu island, after the seizure of the Izu Shoto offshore island group. Sagami Bay, to the west of Yokohama, was the landing area designated for General Robert L. Eichelberger's US 8th Army (Lieutenant General F. C. Sibert's US X Corps with three infantry divisions, Lieutenant General Oscar Griswold's US XIV Corps with three infantry divisions and Lieutenant General Alvem C. Gillem's US XIII Corps with two armoured divisions), while Kujikurihama Beach to the east of Tokyo was assigned to General Courtney H. Hodges's US 1st Army (Lieutenant Roy S. Geiger's US III Amphibious Corps with three marine divisions and Lieutenant General John R. Hodges' US XXIV Corps with three infantry divisions).

The plan was for the armoured forces to isolate Tokyo from the rest of Japan by pushing inland to the Kanto Plain for the seizure of Kumugaya and Kogo, while the infantry took Yokohama, Tokyo and the Boso peninsula. The Americans expected the operation to be extremely costly in manpower, and were highly relieved that they did not have to implement the plan, which envisaged an inland exploitation and link-up with the forces involved in the earlier Operation 'Olympic' before the four US armies swept on to crush all Japanese resistance.

Cottage Reoccupation of Kiska island in the Aleutians by a combined US and Canadian force (15 August 1943). The move had been presaged by the occupation of Amchitka, only 60 miles from Kiska, by the Americans on 12 January 1943, this island providing the US forces with an adequate forward harbour and land suitable for the construction of a forward airstrip. However, the US forces leapfrogged Kiska, the main Japanese garrison in the Aleutian Islands, to land on Attu.

The Japanese defence was in the hands of some 2,500 men, and 11,000 men of the US Army took until 29 May to reduce the garrison, in the process taking only 28 prisoners. The Japanese high command cited the futility of trying to hold Kiska in this revised strategic situation, and sensibly decided to evacuate the garrison. The first evacuation attempt, on 26 May 1943, resulted in the loss of 7 of the 13 'I' class submarines involved, and it was therefore decided to attempt a surface vessel evacuation under cover of the area's notoriously foggy conditions. The flotilla left Paramushiro on 21 July and slipped into Kiska Harbor on 28 July, in 55 minutes lifting all 5,183 Japanese on the island before returning to Paramushiro. The Americans were wholly unaware of the evacuation, and a force of 35,000 men was landed on 15 August, deciding that the island had been abandoned after a two-day sweep had failed to reveal any defenders.

Crossword Allied designation given to a German approach via Italian intermediaries for a surrender of the German forces in Italy (1945).

Countenance British and Indian operations in Persia and the Persian Gulf (25/28 August 1941) to protect the vital oil installations in the region, to protect the supply route to the southern USSR (in conjunction with Soviet forces) and to deter German plans for anti-British risings in the Middle East. Under the overall control of General Sir Archibald Wavell in India, the operation used the forces of Lieutenant General E. P. Quinlan in Iraq for a rapid and successful campaign. The 8th Indian Division took the southern oilfield region, the Royal Navy and units of the Indian and Australian navies seized Axis shipping in the region's ports, and Shahabad in the north of Persia was taken by

Cricket

the 10th Indian Division aided by the British 9th and 2nd Indian Armoured Brigades. Only the most limited resistance was encountered, and on 28 August the Persian government fell and the Shah abdicated in favour of his son. British and Soviet troops entered Tehran on 17 September and set about improving communications in the country as a means of moving supplies to the USSR.

Cricket Designation of the Combined Chiefs-of-Staff conference held in Malta (30 January/2 February 1945) to prepare military decisions before the beginning of the Yalta Conference between 'the big three'. The results of the conference fixed the immediate priorities of the Allied forces in western and southern Europe, with emphasis on the early termination of the main campaign in Germany by refusal to dilute forces for peripheral operations in Italy and the Balkans except where absolutely necessary for reasons of post-war stability.

Crimson Designation of the ferry route for aircraft through Canada.

Cromwell British codeword to be used to signal any German invasion of the British Isles.

Crossbow British intelligence and photo-reconnaissance campaign to learn about the development of German secret weapons at Peenemünde, and then destroy the means of producing and launching such weapons (1943/1944).

Crumpet I Air offensive planned by the US 15th Air Force for attacks on German troop concentrations in the area of Rimini in northern Italy (September 1944).

Crumpet II Actual air offensive by the US 15th Air Force against German troop concentrations in the area of Rimini in northern Italy (14 September 1944).

Crusader Designation of the major Western Desert offensive (18 November 1941/6 January 1942) undertaken by Lieutenant General Sir Alan Cunningham's 8th Army, under the overall control of General Sir Claude Auchinleck, to relieve Tobruk, which had been under Axis siege since early April 1941. The failure of the 'Battleaxe' offensive had spurred Prime Minister Churchill to insist on General Sir Archibald Wavell's replacement by Auchinleck, who was under strict orders to launch a major offensive as rapidly as possible. Auchinleck devised a bold scheme for XIII Corps to use its 4th Indian Division to pin the Axis forces between Halfaya Pass and Sidi Omar, while its New Zealand Division hooked round Sidi Omar to the south before striking north against Fort Capuzzo and Sollum on the coast, and for XXX Corps to strike yet farther to the south before turning north-west to engage the Axis armoured formations in the region of Gabr Saleh and then pushing on to the relief of the 70th Division bottled up in Tobruk by the Italian XXI Corps supported by the German 15th Panzer and 90th Light Divisions.

The part played by XIII Corps went according to plan, and so too did the first moves by XXX Corps. However, on the corps' left flank the 22nd Armoured Brigade and 1st South African Division were checked at Bir el Gubi by the Italian 'Ariete' Division, while on its right flank the 4th Armoured division was handled roughly by the 21st Panzer Division moving south from the Trigh Capuzzo. Thus in the centre only the 7th Armoured Brigade and the 7th Armoured Support Group pushed through towards Tobruk, reaching Sidi Rezegh just outside the Axis perimeter on 19 November.

At this stage General Erwin Rommel thought the British offensive to be a reconnaissance in force, and it was Generalleutnant Ludwig Crüwell, commanding the two Panzer divisions of the Deutsches Afrika Korps, who first appreciated the significance of the British offensive and responded accordingly, moving the 15th and 21st Panzer Divisions towards Sidi Azeiz on 19 November to prevent what he imagined to be the main British strength (in fact the New Zealand Division) from reaching Bardia. However, once the importance of the armoured move in the southern desert had become clear, Crüwell shifted his focus to the triangle between Gabr Saleh, Sidi Rezegh and Sidi Azeiz where the 4th Armoured Brigade was operating. Here Rommel intervened and, as the 22nd Armoured Brigade was being shifted north to the assistance of the 4th Armoured Brigade, ordered Crüwell to move from Gabr Saleh towards Sidi Rezegh, which he did with the 4th and 22nd Armoured Brigades in pursuit.

The 70th Division was now breaking out of Tobruk to link up with the 7th Armoured Brigade, which became embroiled in a major action with Crüwell's forces before being able to help the 70th Division. Heavy and confused fighting followed in the next few days as the New Zealand Division reached the Via Balbia coast road and began to advance westwards along it towards Tobruk. XXX Corps was now concentrated in the area south-east of Sidi Rezegh, and Rommel conceived on 24 February the notion of a 'dash to the wire' along the Egyptian/Libyan frontier to relieve the Axis forces holding out against XIII Corps and to cut the British lines of communication. Thus the 15th and 21st Panzer Divisions headed off to the east, reaching Halfaya Pass on 25 November, but then hearing that the New Zealanders were about to relieve Tobruk and threaten the Axis lines of communication. So on 26 November the 15th and 21st Panzer Divisions moved off from Bardia at about the time that the New Zealand and 70th Divisions met at El Duda.

The Italian 'Trieste' Division had severed the link by 1 December, but by then Rommel's forces were exhausted and again threatened from the Bir el Gubi area by a refreshed XXX Corps. Rommel decided on a strategic withdrawal to El Agheila, which he reached on 31 December 1941. The weary British pursued, reaching Rommel's new positions on 6 January 1942. Tobruk was relieved properly on 10 December 1941, and other major towns to fall into British hands were Derna, Barce, Benghazi and Agedabia. There now followed a lull as both sides recouped, the Axis having lost 38,000 men and 300 tanks to the British losses of 18,000 men and 275 tanks.

Crush Allied codename for the United States of America.

Crystal Allied codename for meteorological stations in northern Canada.

C.T. Designation of military convoys (together with a numerical suffix) plying from the UK to North America, and inaugurated in August 1941.

C.U. Designation of ocean homeward tanker convoys (together with a numerical suffix) plying from the Caribbean to the UK, and inaugurated in February 1943.

Cudgel British 14th Army land offensive in the Arakan region of Burma planned for the spring of 1944 originally in concert with Operation 'Bullfrog' and to be followed by Operation 'Bulldozer', but in fact undertaken on its own. The offensive was the responsibility of Lieutenant General A. F. P. Christison's XV Corps from a start line between Bawli Bazar and Goppe Bazar at the end of December 1943, Major General H. R. Briggs's 5th Indian Division advancing from Bawli Bazar towards Maungdaw, and Major General F. W. Messervy's 7th Indian Division pushing south from Goppe Bazar towards Buthidaung, with Major General C. G. Woolner's 81st West African Division in reserve. The Japanese were at this time planning the offensive to take Imphal in the north, and the British offensive played into their hands, Lieutenant General T. Hanaya's 55th Division planning a counterstroke in the Arakan to pin the British forces. By 3 February 1944, the date on which the Japanese Operation 'HA' was launched, the 55th Division had halted the 5th Indian Division at Wabyin, Maungdaw and Razabil, and the 7th Indian Division at Letwedet, Kyaukyit and Awlanbyin, the two divisions being connected across the British front by the Nyakyedauk pass and river, centred on the so-called 'Admin Box' at Sinzweya. Thus was the scene set for Operation 'HA'.

Culverin British plan for an amphibious assault against the northern end of Sumatra (dry season 1944/1945), presupposing the capture of the Andaman and Nicobar Islands. Such a move was eventually ruled out as needing forces three times larger than those already required for planned Burma operations, at a time when all amphibious transport was in short supply because of operations in the Pacific, the Mediterranean and the

C.W.

English Channel. Had the 'Culverin' operation gone ahead and succeeded, it would have opened the way for an attack to the Isthmus of Kra for an advance on Bangkok, and for an attack south along the Strait of Malacca with a view to recapturing Malaya and/or Singapore.

C.W. Designation of UK coastal convoys (together with a numerical suffix) plying from Southend to St Helen's (Isle of Wight), and inaugurated in September 1940.

C.X. Designation of Indian Ocean convoys (together with a numerical suffix) plying between Colombo (Ceylon) and the Maldives and Chagos Island groups, and inaugurated in April 1943.

Cycle Operation undertaken to evacuate British troops from Le Havre (10/13 June 1940) during the collapse of France. The evacuation was under the command of Admiral Sir William James, Commander-in-Chief Portsmouth, and moved some 11,059 British troops, nearly 9,000 of them at Cherbourg out of immediate danger.

Cyclone Conquest of Numfoor Island towards the western end of New Guinea by the US Army's 168th Infantry Regiment, under the control of General Douglas MacArthur's South-West Pacific Area (2 July 1944). US losses were 63, and those of the Japanese 2,328.

D

D-Day Popular name for the operation known properly as 'Overlord'.

Dampfhammer (steam hammer) Alternative designation of Operation 'Blau III', the southward extension of the Germans' summer offensive of 1942 into the Caucasus.

DAN Japanese operation devised by Lieutenant General M. Kawabe's Burma Area Army for Lieutenant General M. Honda's 33rd Army (2nd, 18th, 49th, and 56th Divisions) to keep the Burma Road closed and to regain the strategic initiative on the Salween front (3/15 September 1944). The offensive was designed to drive east from Lungling astride the Burma Road to push back the Chinese and relieve the Japanese garrisons at Pingka, Lameng and Tengchung. The 33rd Army's offensive was spoiled by increased Chinese pressure from the middle of August.

Danzig German codeword to proceed with the attack planned on the West (November 1939) but not implemented.

Day Ranger Day intruder missions by de Havilland Mosquito fighter-bomber aircraft of the RAF over Germany and occupied Europe to disrupt German activities, attack targets of opportunity, and draw up German fighters in circumstances where the defence was at a tactical disadvantage.

D.C. Designation of South African coastal convoys (together with a numerical suffix) plying between Durban and Cape town, inaugurated in December 1942 and terminated in September 1943.

Deadlight British operation to sink German U-boats surrendered at the end of hostilities.

Decker British pyrotechnic device, designed for air-dropping on German crops.

Deficient Advance of the 10th Indian Division (June/July 1941) from Haditha in Iraq to Aleppo in Syria as part of the Allied reduction of the Vichy territories of Lebanon and Syria.

Delta Mopping-up operation in western Greece (May 1941) by elements of Generalfeldmarschall Wilhelm List's German 12th Army after the successful implementation of Operation 'Marita'.

Demon Evacuation of British and Allied forces from Greece (24/30 April 1941) at the end of the Axis conquest of the country. As the port of Piraeus had been destroyed by the explosion of the munitions ship *Clan Fraser* (which also sank 10 ships in the harbour), the evacuation had to be made from 8 out of a possible 20 small ports by an extemporized force (6 cruisers, 19 destroyers, 3 escorts, 6 landing craft and 3 'Glen' class transports) under the command of Vice Admiral H. D. Pridham-Wippell. Some 50,732 men were evacuated, most of them to Crete, but the British forces had been forced to abandon all their heavy weapons, equipment and aircraft, while the evacuation force lost 4 ships and

39

Derange

many others were damaged, several of them most severely.

Derange Companion operation to 'Enclose II' (April 1943). In the course of these two operations 52 U-boat sightings were made, but the 28 attacks that followed were instrumental in securing only one U-boat sinking.

Derfflinger German plan for the 9th and 16th Armies of Generaloberst Georg von Küchler's Army Group 'North' to take Ostashkov (summer 1942).

Derry Airborne operation by the French 2ème Regiment des Chasseurs Parachutistes to protect bridges near Finisterre (5 August 1944) against demolition as General Wilhelm Fahrmbacher's XXV Corps of the German 7th Army pulled back into the Brittany ports under pressure from the US VIII and XX Corps.

Dexterity Amphibious assault of the 126th Infantry Regiment of the US 32nd Infantry Division against Lieutenant General Hatazo Adachi's Japanese 18th Army bastion at Saidor in New Guinea (2 January 1944). This operation cost the Americans 55 dead and the Japanese 1,275 dead, and was conceived as one of the series of combined operations (including Yalau Plantation by two US battalions on 5 March and Madang on 24 April) against Japanese strongholds along the northern coast of New Guinea as General Douglas MacArthur's South-West Pacific Area's left flank of the 'Elkton' plan offensive. Between September 1943 and April 1944, the US and Australian forces in New Guinea cleared the main Japanese-held area of the Huon peninsula, the Markham and Ramu valleys to the south of the Finisterre and Saruwaged mountain ranges, and the coastal areas to the north of these ranges, in the process destroying the equivalent of a whole army and setting the scene for MacArthur's bold 'leapfrog' campaign of seven more combined operations to take the Allied forces to Sansapor at the extreme western tip of the huge island by the end of July 1944, this in turn opening the way for MacArthur's long-promised return to the Philippines.

Diadem Spring offensive of 1944 devised by General Sir Harold Alexander's 15th Army Group headquarters for the Allied capture of Rome in the early summer of 1944 (11 May/4 June in the event) after the breakthrough being sought at Monte Cassino. In essence the plan called for a rapid penetration of the 'Gustav' Line at Cassino and a joint exploitation northwards by Lieutenant General Oliver Leese's British 8th Army (up the Liri valley as far as Sora and up the Sacco valley as far as Valmontone) and by Lieutenant General Mark Clark's US 5th Army along the coast to link up (in the event on 25 May just north of Latina) with the US VI Corps that would break out from the Anzio beach-head and strengthen the 5th Army for the final push on Rome through the defences of Generaloberst Eberhard von Mackensen's 14th Army.

Dickens Airborne operations by the French 2ème Regiment des Chasseurs Parachutistes to cut German rail communications near the Forêt de l'Absie (15 and 29 July 1944).

Dime US 1st Division task force for the landings near Gela on Sicily during Operation 'Husky'.

Diminish Allied codename for Finschhafen in New Guinea.

Dingson Airborne raid by the French 3ème Regiment des Chasseurs Parachutistes near Lilleran to establish a base behind the German lines (6 June 1944).

Diver Allied air attacks on the German V-1 launch sites in northern France and along the Belgian coast (spring and summer 1944).

Dixie US observation team with the Chinese communist forces of Mao Tsedung during the intermittent campaign against the Japanese.

Disclaim British Force 133 airborne liaison mission drop near Sarajevo (5 February 1942) to link up with Yugoslav resistance forces.

D.K.A. Designation of East African coastal convoys (together with a numerical suffix) plying the route from Durban via Kilindini to Aden, and inaugurated in September 1943 to replace all previous convoys northward-bound along the coast of East Africa.

Domino British jamming device for use against the German 'Y-Gerät' blind-bombing system.

Donnerkeil (thunderbolt) **(i)** Luftwaffe air support for Operation 'Cerberus'.
(ii) German operation against Soviet partisans between Trudy and the River Obdol (21 March/2 April 1943).

Donnerschlag (thunderclap) Plan for the German forces trapped in Stalingrad under the command of Generaloberst Friedrich Paulus (6th Army and part of 4th Panzerarmee) to break out of the encircling forces of the Soviet Stalingrad Front to link up with the advanced elements of Generalfeldmarschall Erich von Manstein's Army Group 'Don' trying to break through to the city (December 1942). The plan was expressly vetoed by Hitler, who refused to consider even the possibility of losing Stalingrad, but instead considered it an offensive fortress embedded in the Soviets' rear.

Doomsday Allied liberation of Norway (May 1945) after the German surrender.

Dortmund Alternative for 'Barbarossa'.

Dove Airborne operation near Oraguignan by the US 1st Provisional Airborne Division (15 August 1944) in support of Operation 'Dragoon'. The division dropped in the rear of the main beach landing areas, and later linked up with the US 36th Infantry Division (VI Corps of the US 7th Army) after ensuring that the inland road between Cannes and the Marseilles area was available to the advancing Americans without demolitions by the retreating Germans of Generalleutnant Friedrich Wiese's 19th Army.

Downfall Overall designation of US plans for the defeat of Japan.

Dracula British combined operation (1/3 May 1945) to secure the capture of Rangoon before Lieutenant General H. Kimura's Burma Area Army could organise a last-ditch defence as its formations fell back down the valleys of the Rivers Irrawaddy and Sittang before IV and XXXIII Corps of Lieutenant General Sir William Slim's 14th Army. The operation started on 1 May with the airborne capture of Elephant Point on the seaward side of Rangoon between the estuaries of the Rivers Rangoon and Irrawaddy by the 2/3rd Gurkha Parachute Battalion of the 50th Parachute Brigade, ensuring that no Japanese artillery could impede the entry into the Rangoon estuary of the transport force bringing in the 26th Indian Division on 2 May. However, by the time that the seaborne force was approaching Rangoon, it had become clear that the Japanese had abandoned the Burmese capital, which was occupied on 3 May.

Dragoon Allied landing in the south of France, originally schemed as Operation 'Anvil' to coincide with Operation 'Overlord' in the north of France. The plan never had the wholehearted support of a powerful British school of thought, which thought that the Allied forces in Italy should be massively reinforced to make possible a decisive thrust northwards through Italy and into Austria and southern Germany, in the process rendering both 'Anvil' and possibly 'Overlord' superfluous. The Americans were set completely against this reasoning, emphasizing that the major Allied blow should be struck directly against the enemy's main strength in Europe, a move which also provided short lines of communication (across the English Channel) and direct access to Germany without intervening mountain chains, etc. The 'Overlord' school carried the day, and with it decided to implement 'Anvil', now renamed 'Dragoon' with forces pulled out of the Italian campaign and supported by French units brought over from North Africa.

In strategic terms the 'Dragoon' landings were nugatory, as they could not be concerted with 'Overlord' for lack of adequate amphibious transport capability, as they detracted from the diversionary campaign in

Italy, and as they could not make an effective contribution to the Western European campaign until the Franco-American forces had pushed up the line of the River Rhône as far north as Dijon. Moreover, the anticipated success of 'Overlord' and its exploitation eastwards towards Germany meant that the German forces in south and south-western France (Generaloberst Johannes Blaskowitz's Army Group 'G' comprising the 19th Army with 11 divisions, including 2 Panzer and 5 forming or refitting, and the 1st Army with 6 divisions, including 5 forming or refitting) would have had to be pulled back to avoid being cut off.

American pressure secured the implementation of 'Dragoon' by Lieutenant General Alexander M. Patch's US 7th Army from Naples, reinforced by Général Jean de Lattre de Tassigny's French II Corps from North African ports. Operation 'Anvil' was in fact launched some 10 weeks later than 'Overlord', the landings (15 August 1944) being made between Cannes and Hyères by Major General Lucian K. Truscott's US VI Corps (from left to right the 3rd, 45th and 36th Infantry Divisions) flanked by French commando units. The landings started at 08.00 against minimal opposition, and by nightfall some 94,000 men and 11,000 vehicles had come ashore to exploit the successes of the airborne landing behind the beaches to press ahead towards Marseilles and the Rhône (3rd and 45th Infantry Divisions), and north towards the Route Napoleon and Grenoble (36th Infantry Division). On 16 August the French II Corps (1st Armoured Division, 1st Division, 3rd Algerian Division and 9th Colonial Division) came ashore and passed through VI Corps on the Marseilles road.

By 28 August the Allied forces had taken Toulon and Marseilles (47,000 prisoners) and secured the area between Nice and Avignon as far north as an arc running from Briançon via Grenoble to Montelimar, in the process destroying General Friedrich Wiese's German 19th Army as an effective fighting force, largely with air and artillery strikes as the Germans streamed north to link up with Generalleutnant Helmuth von de Chevallerie's 1st Army evacuating south-western France and making for the Belfort Gap. The 7th Army moved rapidly in pursuit, reaching Lyons on 3 September and Besançon on 7 September. On 12 September elements of the French II Corps met the leading echelons of the French 2nd Armoured Division from Lieutenant General George S. Patton's US 3rd Army at Châtillon-sur-Seine, and the northern and southern invasions joined forces. The French II Corps became the French 1st Army, and with the 7th Army became the US 6th Army Group under Lieutenant General Jacob Devers.

Drake Build-up of the Boeing B–29 Superfortress strength in China for the inauguration of the strategic bombing campaign against the Japanese home islands (1944). The launch of this campaign showed that despite the massive efforts of the Chinese in building new bases as far forward as possible, Chinese-controlled China was too far from Japan for the bombers to be able to inflict decisive blows from this theatre.

Draufgänger (daredevil) German operation against Montenegrin partisans (1944).

Draufgänger I (daredevil I) German operation against Soviet partisans in the Borisov-Lepel area in support of Operation 'Kottbus' (26 April/10 May 1943).

Draufgänger II (daredevil II) German operation against Soviet partisans in the Borisov-Lepel area (26 April/10 May 1943).

Drygoods Supply build-up on the island of Guadalcanal in the Solomons in preparation for operations against New Georgia (February 1943).

Dschingis Khan Linie (Genghis Khan line) German defence line in Italy, running between Bologna and Lake Comacchio in northern Italy, and designed to check the Allied advance against General Traugott Herr's German 10th Army on the southern approaches to Austria. Defended by I Parachute Corps and LXXVI Panzer Corps, the line was breached in a concerted offensive (8/23 April 1945) by General Sir Richard McCreery's British 8th Army (V and XIII Corps).

Duck Series of three exercises (January/February 1944) by the US V Corps in the UK as part of its preparations for Operation 'Overlord'.

Dunhill Airborne operations by the 2nd SAS to harass the German retreat in the Fougeray area (2, 3 and 5 August 1944).

Dunn Allied air evacuation of wounded from Yugoslavia to Italy (25/26 March 1945).

Düppel German codename for 'Window'.

Dynamo Operation to evacuate as many British and Allied troops as possible from the pocket on the Franco-Belgian north coast between Dunkirk and De Panne (26 May/4 June 1940) during the collapse of France. In this pocket were trapped the British Expeditionary Force and elements of the French 1st Army, pressured on the east by Generaloberst Fedor von Bock's Army Group 'B' and on the west by Generaloberst Gerd von Rundstedt's Army Group 'A' after the German forces had split the Allied armies into two by reaching the sea at Noyelles at the mouth of the River Somme on 20 May. Thereafter increasing Panzer pressure was exerted on the Allied forces to the north of the German corridor as the German infantry divisions consolidated along the line of the Somme. The Germans' strategic plan was to eliminate the Allied forces in the north before turning their attention to the French armies in the south, but Hitler was worried about the dangers of committing his strategic armour to the wet terrain of northern France, and readily accepted the offer of Hermann Goering that his Luftwaffe could crush the Allied forces while the army merely contained them.

Thus was set the scene for Operation 'Dynamo', the evacuation that was expected to lift some 45,000 men in 2 days, but in the event saved 338,226 men in 9 days at the cost of 72 vessels (including 9 destroyers and torpedo boats) lost to enemy action, 163 more (most of them small craft) lost to other causes and 45 British vessels damaged. The utmost credit for the evacuation must go to its organizers (Vice Admiral B. H. Ramsay and Captain W. G. Tennant), the courageous crews of the vessels involved, the steadfast men on the beaches, and the pilots of RAF Fighter Command. These last were much vilified at the time for failing to make a greater impression on the Luftwaffe, but in fact played a decisive part, destroying some 179 German aircraft over the beaches for the loss of 106 of their own number, and without this intervention it is clear that the Luftwaffe's bombers would have taken a far higher toll of the Allied ships lying off the beaches to pick up full loads of soldiers.

E

Eagle Allied codename for General Mark Clark.

Early Window Designation of 'Window' raids by de Havilland Mosquito aircraft of RAF Bomber Command in advance of major air raids.

E.C. Designation of UK coastal convoys (together with a numerical suffix) plying from Southend to Loch Ewe, Oban and the Clyde as a replacement for the E.N. convoys. The E.C. convoys were inaugurated on 31 March 1941 and ended on 28 October 1941.

Eclipse (i) Plan by the Allied 1st Airborne Army for a two-corps airborne descent on Berlin (spring 1945). The plan was vetoed by, amongst other factors, the Allied decision at the Yalta Conference to leave the reduction of Berlin to the Soviet forces.
(ii) Overall designation of the plans drawn up or considered by the Allies for the treatment of Germany after the end of the war.

Edelweiss The part of Operation 'Blau III' designed to capture Baku and its oilfields on the Caspian Sea during the German summer offensive of 1942. The task was entrusted to Generalfeldmarschall Wilhelm List's Army Group 'A', which allocated this strategic objective to Generaloberst Ewald von Kleist's 1st Panzerarmee (3 Panzer, 2 motorized, 4 infantry and 1 Slovak divisions, but only 400 tanks). The scene was thus set for great strategic and operational divergences, for while Army Group 'B' struck east towards Stalingrad, Army Group 'A' was moving on a southward axis, with Generaloberst Richard Ruoff's Gruppe Ruoff directed south-west towards the Strait of Kerch and the Black Sea coast between Novorossiysk and Batumi, and with its 1st Panzerarmee directed south-east towards Baku and the Caspian Sea, powerfully defended by the Trans-Caucasus Front of General I. V. Tyulenev. In the event Operation 'Edelweiss' could get no farther than the Caucasus mountains, being halted along the line from Mount Elbrus to Mozdok on the River Terek by 18 November 1942.

Effective US plan for the seizure of objectives in the Black Forest area of Germany by airborne assault in front of the US 7th Army (spring 1945) to aid the push by the US 6th Army Group through SS Oberstgruppenführer Paul Hausser's Army Group 'G' into southern Germany and to Munich.

Eiche (oak) German rescue of the deposed Italian leader Benito Mussolini (autumn 1943). Two basic plans were prepared, one calling for an airborne operation should Mussolini be kept in mainland Italy, and the other requiring a naval assault in the event of Mussolini being imprisoned on an offshore island. In the event the Italian ex-dictator was imprisoned in a mountain hotel in the Gran Sasso, from which he was rescued (12 September 1943) in a daring raid by the German commando leader Otto Skorzeny.

Eilbote (express messenger) Attack by various battle groups of the 334th Division and the 10th Panzer Division (all part of Generaloberst Jürgen von Arnim's 5th Panzerarmee) in northern Tunisia (18/24

January 1943). The object of this local offensive was to restore the position jeopardized by the retreat of the Italian Superga Division north of Kairouan, opening the possibility of an Allied thrust to the sea between Enfidaville and Sousse to cut the lines of communications between Tunis/Bizerta and the German forces retreating before the British 8th Army. The offensive was fought in the Fondouk pass area and was highly fragmented, but by its end the Germans had secured improved positions in the Djebel Mansour/Djebel Bou Kril/Djebel Bou Dabousse/Djebel er Rihana sector.

Eisbär (polar bear) **(i)** Capture of the island of Kos in the Aegean Sea by German airborne and amphibious attack (4 October 1943). In the aftermath of the Italian armistice of 9 September 1943 the island had been occupied by some 1,200 British troops, taking over from the erstwhile garrison of 4,000 Italians, but these British forces were unable to hold the island against a determined German airborne and seaborne assault under complete air superiority.
(ii) A series of three offensives by the Germans against Soviet partisans operating in the area of Bryansk and Dimitriev (January/February 1943). In this sector the Germans were planning to build up Generaloberst Walter Model's 9th Army in preparation for Operation 'Zitadelle', and the Soviet disruptive attacks played their part in hampering German preparations and also in keeping the Soviet high command informed as to the reinforcements reaching German front-line units in the area.

Eisenhammer (iron hammer) German air offensive against Soviet munitions factories and power plants (November 1944), using 'Mistel' composite attack aircraft for greater range and accuracy.

Eisstoss (ice pick) Air offensive by Luftflotte I against the Soviet Baltic Fleet (March/April 1942).

Elbe Earlier version of 'Augsburg'.

Elch (elk) German reinforcements for Norway (April 1942) at a time when Hitler was convinced that Norway was a decisive point in Allied (especially British) plans for the prosecution of the war against Germany. This fixation on the part of the German leader was also reflected in his insistence that Operation 'Cerberus' be implemented as a means of bolstering German naval strength in this theatre.

Elephant Offensive by the Canadian 4th Armoured Division (General Sir Henry Crerar's Canadian 1st Army) to the Kapelsche Veer (26/31 January 1945).

Elkton A series of three plans originated by the Americans for the conduct of operations against the Japanese in the south-west Pacific. The final plan (adopted on 26 April 1943) called for a double offensive against Lieutenant General H. Imamura's Japanese 8th Area Army, with its headquarters at Rabaul on the north-eastern tip of New Britain in the Bismarck Archipelago, with General Douglas MacArthur's combined US and Australian forces (South-West Pacific Area) responsible for a north-westward advance up the coast of New Guinea to defeat Lieutenant General Hatazo Adachi's 18th Army, and Vice Admiral William Halsey's US forces (South Pacific Area) responsible for the north-westward advance along the line of the Solomon Islands against the forces of Lieutenant General Harukichi Hyakutake's 17th Army. These two advances would meet at the northern end of the Bismarck Archipelago (Admiralty and St Matthias island groups respectively) in the first half of 1944 after isolating on New Britain and New Ireland the remnants of the 8th Area Army, which would then be left to 'wither on the vine' as MacArthur's reinforced army struck our along the northern coast of New Guinea towards an invasion and reconquest of the Philippines later in 1944.

E.N. Designation of British coastal convoys (together with a numerical suffix) plying between Methil and the Clyde (later changed to Loch Ewe), and inaugurated in August 1940.

Enclose I Second all-out air operation by No. 19 Group, RAF Coastal Command, against German U-boats in the Bay of Biscay (20/28 March 1943). Fifteen attacks were made in the course of 28 sightings, but only 1 U-boat was sunk.

Enclose II Successor to Operation 'Enclose I', undertaken in conjunction with Operation 'Derange' (April 1943).

End Run Operation by the survivors of the US 5307th Provisional Regiment ('Merrill's Marauders') and the Chinese 30th and 38th Divisions against Myitkyina in northern Burma, whose garrison from Lieutenant General H. Tanaka's Japanese 18th Division was thought by Lieutenant General Joseph W. Stilwell to pose a threat to the new supply road being built to China from Ledo. After an extremely difficult approach march, launched by the Chinese Army in India (22nd, 30th and 38th Divisions) in October 1943 and seriously checked by the Japanese 18th Division in the Hukawng Valley, the advance of Stilwell's forces was speeded by the arrival of Brigadier General Frank Merrill's US 5307th Composite Regiment at Sharawga on 21 February 1944, allowing a change in tactics to Chinese pinning attacks and American outflanking attacks. Aided by a diversion in Japanese strength to deal with the 2nd Chindit Expedition, the US and Chinese forces closed in on Myitkyina from the north (5307th Regiment and the 30th Division from Ritpong) during May, but were unable to wrest Myitkyina from a determined defence. Another attempt was made by the tired forces in late July, after the 22nd and 38th Divisions had advanced from the west, facilitated by the fact that the totally exhausted 77th Long-Range Penetration Brigade of the Chindits had taken Mogaung on 26 June. The Japanese now realized that Myitkyina was no longer tenable, and pulled out on 3 August, allowing the Allies to enter the town on the following day.

Enterprise Forward move of the US strategic air forces in China (1944) in anticipation of the arrival of Boeing B-29 Superfortress bombers for the start of a strategic bombing campaign against the Japanese home islands. Large bases were built for the bombers at Nanning, Liuchow, Kweilin, Lingling, Hengyang, Suichuan, Chihkiang, Laohokow and Ankang, and the threat was deemed sufficiently great by the Japanese for them to launch Operation 'ICHI' to take these areas as a means of denying the American bombers bases within range of Japan.

Epilogue Return of the British garrisons in the Far East to peacetime establishment (1945/1946) by the repatriation of wartime units for demobilization.

Epsom Major offensive by the newly-arrived British VIII Corps of Lieutenant General Sir Richard O'Connor towards Evrecy, south of Caen (26 June/1 July 1944) as a preventive strike against the arrival of German armour reinforcements. The corps numbered some 60,000 men and 600 tanks in its 11th Armoured, 15th and 43rd Divisions, and was flanked on its left by the Canadian II Corps and on its right by XXX Corps. The object of the strike was to skirt round the west of Caen, where the British forces had found considerable difficulty in using tanks, to drive south across the Caen-Bayeux road and then to the Fosse de l'Odon before turning south-east to Bretteville-sur-Laize some 10 miles south of Caen, having taken Carpiquet airfield and opened the way for the capture of Caen. The opposition was found by the experienced 9th, 10th and 12th SS Panzer Divisions, and VIII Corps was unable to make any but the slowest progress, resulting in tactical failure, though the River Orne was crossed and Hill 112 taken to drive a salient into the German defence west of Caen.

Erna Airborne raid in Estonia (9 July 1941) by the Brandenburg special intelligence unit.

Erntefest I (harvest home I) German operation against Soviet partisan forces to the west of Ossipovichi (18/27 January 1943).

Erntefest II (harvest home II) German operation against Soviet partisan forces to the west of the Minsk-Slutsk road (28 January/9 February 1943).

Eruption Plan by the Allied 1st Airborne Army to seize the Kiel Canal in northern Germany (summer 1945).

Esigenza C.3 (plan C.3) Italian plan for a combined operation to capture the British island bastion of Malta (1942). The island was proving at this time to be a severe thorn in the side of the Axis convoys plying between southern Italy and North Africa with reinforcements and supplies for the units fighting the British in the Western Desert.

E.T. Designation of North African coastal convoys (together with a numerical suffix) plying from North African ports to Gibraltar, and inaugurated in November 1942 after the successful implementation of Operation 'Torch'.

Eureka (i) Allied codename for the Tehran Conference (28/30 November 1943) between 'the big three', namely President Franklin Roosevelt of the USA, Premier Josef Stalin of the USSR and Prime Minister Winston Churchill of the UK. The conference was deemed necessary to assess the situation in the war after the termination of hostilities with Italy and given the potentially decisive nature of events on the Eastern Front and in the war against Japan. In the purely military sphere, it was decided to abandon Operation 'Buccaneer'; to increase pressure on the Germans in Italy as a means of preventing the despatch of reinforcements to the Eastern Front; to time Operation 'Overlord' to coincide with the Soviet summer offensive of 1944; and to launch Operation 'Anvil' (later 'Dragoon') at the same time as 'Overlord'. Wide-ranging political accords were also reached (though these were revized and finalized at the Yalta Conference) with regard to the post-war redrawing of Poland's frontiers, the treatment of Germany and Austria, and the establishment of spheres of influence.
(ii) British radio navigation aid for bombers.

Excelsior Allied codename for the Philippine Islands.

Excess British fast convoy operation in the Mediterranean (6/11 January 1941) intended to send three ships to Piraeus and one to Malta, all loaded with desperately needed supplies. The convoy was seen as being decisively important, and involved much of the Royal Navy's strength in the Mediterranean. The convoy was itself escorted by 1 cruiser and 4 destroyers as it left Gibraltar, with longer-range escort provided by Vice Admiral Sir James Somerville's Force H consisting of 1 battleship, 1 battle-cruiser, 1 aircraft-carrier, 1 cruiser and 7 destroyers. At the other end of the Mediterranean Admiral Sir Andrew Cunningham decided to use the opportunity to send (with an escort of 2 battleships, 1 aircraft-carrier and other units of his Mediterranean Fleet) 2 cruisers and 2 destroyers loaded with troops from Alexandria to Malta, together with 2 merchantmen, while 8 empty merchantmen made the dash from Malta to Alexandria. The whole exercise called for excellent timing for the correct rendezvous hand-overs to be made, but suffered from the fact that the Luftwaffe was now operational in the Mediterranean in the form of X Fliegerkorps, an experienced anti-shipping formation. In the event the convoy achieved its primary objectives of getting through the reinforcements and supplies, but only at the cost of severe damage to the carrier *Illustrious* and the cruiser *Gloucester*, the loss of the cruiser *Southampton*, and heavy bombing of Malta while emergency repairs were made to the *Illustrious* before she slipped back to Alexandria on 23/25 January 1941.

Exodus British air operation (26 April/7 May 1945) to ferry liberated prisoners of war home to the UK from airfields in the region of Brussels. The operation involved 469 flights by aircraft of Nos 1, 5, 6 and 8 Groups of RAF Bomber Command, in the course of which some 75,000 POWs were repatriated.

Exporter Designation of the British campaign to take Syria from Vichy French control (8 June/14 July 1941) as a time when there were serious Allied fears of Vichy movement into the Axis camp, and greater knowledge of German efforts to undermine the British presence in the Middle East. The plan underwent a number of modifications as troop movements dictated, but remained in essence a strong thrust (by the 7th Australian Division, the 1st Cavalry Division, the 5th

Indian Brigade Group, and the Free French Legentilhomme Brigade) from Palestine under the command of General Sir Henry Maitland Wilson against the two divisions commanded by Général Henri Dentz. Given the strength and vigour of the Vichy forces, the campaign perforce proceeded slowly, with Damascus falling on 21 June and Homs on 9 July. Forces from Iraq moved into the eastern part of Syria to prevent the outbreak of fighting in these semi-desert areas, and the campaign ended only after heavy casualties on both sides and an armistice which put Lebanon and Syria under the Free French command of Général Georges Catroux.

Extended Capital British offensive (19 November 1944/30 March 1945) in central Burma developed from the 'Capital' plan but extended to include the capture of Meiktila in addition to Mandalay, the object being to cut the main escape route to the south of Lieutenant General Shihachi Katamura's Japanese 15th Army and Lieutenant General M. Honda's Japanese 33rd Army (both part of Lieutenant General Hoyotaro Kimura's Burma Area Army). This offensive by Lieutenant General Sir William Slim's 14th Army was a logical successor to the events after the Japanese failure to take Imphal and Kohima, in which the 15th Army had been pressed back through the Kabaw Valley to the River Chindwin. Kimura appreciated that the British, probably with support from Lieutenant General Joseph Stilwell's Northern Combat Area Command (Chinese forces), would break into central Burma with Mandalay as their objective, and so used the summer and autumn of 1944 to rebuild his shattered forces with a view to drawing the 14th Army into the Mandalay area and then inflicting a crushing defeat on them, which would have been a possibility had the British adopted 'Capital' rather than 'Extended Capital'.

The campaign began with the successful capture of three bridgeheads across the Chindwin (Lieutenant General Sir Geoffrey Scoones's IV Corps at Sittaung, and Lieutenant General Sir Montague Stopford's XXXIII Corps at Mawlaik and Kalewa), all the bridgeheads being secured by 4 December. Slim was aware of Kimura's plans for a decisive battle north of Mandalay, and secretly switched IV Corps (now under the command of Lieutenant General F. W. Messervy) to the south of XXXIII Corps, leaving the 19th Indian Division at Sittaung as a decoy. Setting off from Kalemyo on the Chindwin, IV Corps headed south behind the cover of the Pondaung Range with its 7th and 17th Indian Divisions plus the 28th East African Brigade to erupt behind the Japanese front on the River Irrawaddy below Mandalay, capture Pakokku and secure a bridgehead over the Irrawaddy at Nyaungu.

Confirmation of Slim's appreciation of Kimura's intentions came on 11 January 1945, when the decoy 19th Indian Division met very severe resistance as it established bridgeheads across the Irrawaddy north of Mandalay at Singu and Thabeikkyin. At the same time XXXIII Corps was making little effort to hide its progress from Kalewa down the Chindwin towards Monywa, and to Shwebo north of Mandalay. XXXIII Corps began to cross the Irrawaddy just to the west of Mandalay at Ngazun on 12 February, and again met fierce resistance. However, when IV Corps threw its bridgehead across the Irrawaddy at Nyaungu on 14 February it met virtually no resistance, all Japanese attention and manpower being focussed farther north. The trap was now sprung, and as the Japanese began to stream south IV Corps swept out of its bridgehead on 21 February with the 7th and 17th Indian Divisions and the 255th Independent Tank Brigade to seize the road and rail nexus at Meiktila on 3 March (with the aid of the 9th and 99th Brigades of the 5th Indian Division, which had been flown into Thabuktong), trapping the 15th and 33rd Armies.

On 26 February the 19th Indian Division moved out of its bridgeheads north of Mandalay and headed south, taking Mandalay on 20 March in conjunction with elements of the British 2nd Division, which advanced from the bridgehead at Ngazun on 8 March as the 20th Indian Division from the same bridgehead towards Myotha and Kyaukse, which fell on 30 March. From 5 March the 17th Indian Division had been trapped in Meiktila by the attacks of three Japanese divisions, but held out until the fall

Extended Capital

of Mandalay enabled Slim to send in a relief force, compelling the Japanese to fall back on 29 March. The whole of Operation 'Extended Capital' had been an enormous British success, and ousted the Japanese from central Burma.

F

Fabian Airborne intelligence operation by the Special Air Service Regiment near Nykerk in the Netherlands (15 September 1944).

Fabius Series of six final rehearsal exercises for the US V Corps in preparation for Operation 'Overlord'.

Fabre Airborne operation by the French Force 136 to aid the Laotian resistance against the Japanese near Vientiane (21 January 1945).

Fairfield Headquarters of General D. Eisenhower near Carthage in North Africa (spring 1943) for the planning of Italian operations.

Fairfield Rear Alternative headquarters of General Eisenhower near Sidi Athman (spring 1943).

Falke (hawk) **(i)** Plan for Generalfeldmarschall Erich von Manstein's Army Group 'South' to undertake a relatively small enveloping operation to the east of Kharkov (summer 1943). The plan was abandoned in favour of the complete 'Zitadelle' offensive.
(ii) German codeword for any Allied landing in central or northern Norway.

Fallreep (gangway) Designation of the break-out by the forces of General W. Graf von Brockdorff-Ahlefeldt's German II Corps from the Demyansk pocket (21 April 1942) to meet the forces advancing to their relief in Operation 'Brückenschlag'.

Fall River Allied codename for Milne Bay at the eastern end of New Guinea.

Fanfare Generic name for Allied operations in the Mediterranean theatre.

Fantan Allied codename for the Fiji Islands.

Federal Allied codename for Gela in Sicily.

Felix German plan to take Gibraltar and close the Straits of Gibraltar to British shipping (late 1940). This plan presupposed the support of Spain, and was designed as a combined operation under the overall command of Generalfeldmarschall Walther von Reichenau. With the support of the Luftwaffe's crack VIII Fliegerkorps, the German force of two Panzer divisions, three infantry divisions and XLIX Mountain Corps would advance along the line Irun to Seville via Burgos and attack the British fortress from the landward side with the aid of superheavy tracked artillery before the mountain corps put in the final offensive. General Franco gave Spain's qualified approval to the scheme as the fall of the UK seemed imminent, demanding in return Oran and the French zone of Morocco.

Felix-Heinrich Definitive version of Operation 'Felix' (autumn 1941).

Felsennest (castle on a crag) Hitler's headquarters in the Wintereifel (10 May/6 June 1940) for the German campaign against France and the Low Countries.

Ferkel (suckling pig) Designation of the special forces allocated to the 2nd Panzergruppe (later the 2nd Panzerarmee) in the opening stages of Operation 'Barbarossa'.

Feuersee (fire sea) German plan for a large-scale attack on British bomber streams returning from Germany. The plan was devised as a means of countering British electronic countermeasures, the German fighters concentrating off the English coast and then flying south so that they would inevitably intercept the bomber stream before undertaking visual attacks.

Feuerstein (flint) German plan for the defence of the Alpine passes into Austria after the Italian armistice with the Allies (autumn 1943).

Feuerzauber (fire magic) Early version of 'Nordlicht'.

Fido British fog-dispersal system designed to allow returning bombers to land safely at night. The word was an acronym for Fog Investigation Dispersal Operation.

Finance Headquarters of General Dwight D. Eisenhower in Malta for the beginning of the Sicilian and Italian campaign (summer 1943).

Firebash Designation of low-level incendiary raids on German targets (especially airfields and communication centres) by de Havilland Mosquito light bombers carrying drop tanks filled with napalm.

Firebrand Plan for Free French forces under the command of Général Henri Giraud to invade Corsica (1943) after the occupation of southern Italy and the establishment of airfields in the Rome area to provide fighter cover. In the event the plan was unnecessary, for with the revelation that the Italians were defecting from the Axis camp, the Germans on 8 September implemented their own plan to evacuate all German forces on Sardinia to Corsica, which was then to be held by the Brigade Reichsführer-SS, elements of the 15th Panzergrenadier Division and substantial Flak units under the command of Generalleutnant Fridolin von Senger und Etterlin. However, on 12 September Hitler decided that Corsica too should be abandoned, the German forces being concentrated round Bastia for the sealift to Livorno and Piombino in Italy, and to the island of Elba. French forces landed on the island on 25 September from 2 cruisers, 2 destroyers and 1 submarine to harry the Germans in conjunction with the 20,000 men of local resistance units, some 6,400 French troops being put ashore by 27 September, but by 3 October the Germans had successfully pulled out 21,100 men by air and a further 6,250 men plus 1,200 prisoners of war by sea, in the process losing 55 transport aircraft and 17,000 tons of shipping.

Firepump Airborne operation by the 153rd Gurkha Parachute Battalion to prepare a landing strip near Fort Hertz in northern Burma (13 August 1942).

Fischfang (fish trap) German counter-offensive against the Anzio beach-head (3/19 February 1944). Three major counterattacks were undertaken, mostly by elements of the 29th Panzergrenadier Division and the 'Hermann Goering' Panzer Division under the control of General Eberhard von Mackensen's German 14th Army. The first (3/4 February) pinched off the salient extended by Major General John P. Lucas's US VI Corps up the road from Anzio towards Albano, the second (7/9 February) pushed back the Allies in the region of the Aprilia Factory, and the third (16/19 February) drove the Allies from the area of the Aprilia Factory back towards the sea. Though not decisive in driving the VI Corps out of its beach-head, these attacks stabilized the Anzio position to the Germans' benefit, leaving the beach-head as little more than an impotent spot on the German flank.

Fischreiher (heron) Extension of Operation 'Blau II' (22 July/18 November 1942), taking Generaloberst Friedrich Paulus's German 6th Army (18 German divisions in five corps, together with part of Generaloberst Hermann Hoth's 4th Panzerarmee) across the River Don to Stalingrad on the great western bend of the River Volga. In strategic terms this was an enormous blunder, for whereas the task originally entrusted to Generalfeldmarschall Maximilian Freiherr von Weichs' Army Group 'B', namely the establishment of a defensive front along the Don, was subsidiary to the southward offensive thrust of Generalfeldmarschall Wilhelm List's Army Group 'A', it had now become a strategic offensive in its own right, diverging at 90 degrees from the drive of Army Group 'A', which was also increased radically in scope. The forces controlled by Paulus for Operation 'Fischreiher' were modest for the task envisaged, and the Soviets had shown their determination not to lose Stalingrad by the formation, on 12 July under Marshal of the Soviet Union S. K. Timoshenko, of the Stalingrad Front.

Stalingrad was defended (from north to south) by the 66th, 4th Tank, 62nd, 1st Tank, 64th, 51st and 57th Armies within three defensive perimeters, the outermost brushing the Don some 30 miles or more from the city proper. The Germans came up against the first line on 17 August, and were thereafter embroiled in a ghastly battle without quarter. In the north General Gustav von Wietersheim's XIV Panzer Corps managed to break through on 22 August and reach the Volga north of the city a day later, while in the east General W. Freiherr von Langermann und Erlenkamp's XXIV Panzer Corps and the XLVIII Panzer Corps of the 4th Panzerarmee slowly pushed forward to breach the second defence line on 31 August and the third line on 12 September. Thereafter it was increasingly bitter urban fighting against the 62nd and 64th Armies until the Germans reached their offensive limit on 18 November. After that the 6th Army and the 4th Panzerarmee were on the defensive as their lines of communication to the rest of Army Group 'B' were cut by the surprise pincer offensive by General N. F. Vatutin's South-West Front and General A. I. Eremenko's Stalingrad Front, whose forces met in the Germans' rear on the River Karpovka between Kalach and Sovetskiy on 23 November.

Five Islands US task force for the defence of South Pacific ferry bases.

Fivesome Inter-Allied agreement on the co-ordination of operations in the South-West Pacific Area under the overall command of General Douglas MacArthur.

Flambo Allied HQ advanced administrative echelon in Naples (October 1943) for the planning of the campaign in Italy.

Flaschenhals (bottleneck) The corridor to Schlüsselburg on the southern shore of Lake Ladoga to the east of Leningrad held by the German 18th Army to divide Leningrad from the rest of the USSR. The Soviets planned to eliminate this corridor and restore land communications with the starving city in August 1942 with a concerted effort by the Neva Task Force and 55th Army of General L. A. Govorov's Leningrad Front, and the 8th, 2nd Shock and 54th Armies of General K. A. Meretskov's Volkhov Front, which would cut through the corridor at its neck and also near Lake Ladoga. The battle raged from 19 August to the end of September 1942, and totally failed as did the companion effort by the Leningrad Front's 42nd Army to link up with the Coastal Command in the Oranienbaum beach-head to the west of Leningrad on the south of the Gulf of Finland. A narrow supply corridor to the city of Leningrad was finally opened between 11 and 18 January 1943, when the forces of the Leningrad Front's 67th Army and the Volkhov Front's 2nd Shock Army met north of Sinyavino.

Flashpoint Operation of Lieutenant General William H. Simpson's US 9th Army within the overall Operation 'Plunder' by Field Marshal Viscount Montgomery's Allied 21st Army Group (24/28 March 1945). Designed as the right flank of the Allied offensive to secure a northern bridgehead over the River Rhine, Operation 'Flashpoint' was entrusted to Major General John B. Anderson's US XVI Corps, which was tasked with pushing its US 30th Infantry Division across the river between Wesel and Mollen in the northern sector of the corps' front, and the US 79th Infantry Division across the river between Mollen and Walsum in the southern half of the corps' front. The defence of this sector was in the hands of the German 180th Division of General Erich Straube's LXXXVI Corps and (in the extreme south) of the Hamburg Division of General Erich Abraham's LXIII Corps, both part of General Alfred Schlemm's 1st Parachute Army within Generaloberst Johannes

Blaskowitz's Army Group 'H'. By the end of 24 March the US XVI Corps had crossed the Rhine in five places, the 30th and 79th Infantry Divisions then securing a consolidated bridgehead between Wesel and Dinslaken so that the corps' reserves (the US 8th Armored, US 35th Infantry and US 75th Infantry Divisions) could move up for the exploitation, which reached Dorsten by 28 March.

Flax Allied air offensive to disrupt the Axis airbridge between Tunisia and Sicily (5 April 1943), many German and Italian transport aircraft being shot down for negligible losses to the Allied fighters.

Flensburg German radar device to enable night-fighters to home on the 'Monica' tail radars of British bombers.

Flintlock US amphibious operation to take the southern portion of the Marshall Islands (30 January/4 February 1944) after the capture of the Gilbert Islands to the south during November 1943 had provided the bases necessary for this next step towards Japan, and to threaten the main base of the Imperial Japanese Navy's Combined Fleet at Truk in the Caroline Islands to the west. Entrusted with the implementation of Operation 'Flintlock' was Vice Admiral Richard K. Turner's 5th Amphibious Force with Vice Admiral Marc A. Mitscher's Fast Carrier Task Force sweeping ahead of it to eliminate Japanese air strength on the Marshall Islands. Majuro Atoll was seized on 30 January as a preliminary, and then Operation 'Flintlock' proper descended on the massive Kwajalein Atoll in 1 February, with Major General Harry Schmidt's 4th Marine Division landing its 23rd and 24th Marine Regiments on Roi and Namur at the northern end of the lagoon, and Major General Charles H. Corlett's 7th Infantry Division landing its 32nd and 184th Infantry Regiments on Kwajalein. The fighting lasted for four days, and the Americans lost 372 killed and 1,582 wounded out of 42,000 men involved, while the Japanese lost 7,870 out of 8,000 men including their commander, Rear Admiral Akiyama. As the battle did not require the 5th Amphibious Force's reserves, these were used for Operation 'Catchpole' which took Eniwetok Atoll and so completed the American seizure of the Marshall Islands.

Flower British low-level night intruder mission by de Havilland Mosquitoes over German airfields (1944/1945).

F.N. Designation of British coastal convoys (together with a numerical suffix) plying from Southend to Methil, and inaugurated in September 1939.

Forager US campaign (15 June/10 August 1944) to take the Marianas Islands, some 1,000 miles to the north-west of the Marshall Islands and ideally located as a strategic stepping stone for a Pacific Ocean Areas offensive towards the Japanese home islands. It was also fully appreciated that these substantial islands would provide adequate bases for the fleets of Boeing B-29 Superfortress heavy bombers to be deployed by the US 20th Air Force. The islands already contained relatively small Japanese airfields, but US planners were convinced that three huge air base complexes could be built to provide a platform from which the US bombers could destroy Japan's cities and war-making potential, possibly removing the need for US forces to invade the Japanese home islands, which all agreed would be an exceptionally costly undertaking. For these reasons, therefore, the successful implementation of Operation 'Forager' was vital to US interests, and powerful forces were assembled for the task, entrusted to Admiral Raymond Spruance's 5th Fleet under the overall command and strategic control of Admiral Chester W. Nimitz's Pacific Ocean Areas command, which was in charge of the east/west thrust designed to take US Navy and US Marine Corps forces (with US Army formations under command) across the central Pacific towards a goal Nimitz envisaged as Formosa and then possibly the coast of mainland China.

Spruance assembled his command in the lagoon of Eniwetok Atoll, and all was prepared for Vice Admiral Richmond K. Turner's Joint Expeditionary Force to assault the islands with the 127,000 men of Lieutenant General Holland M. Smith's V

Forager

Amphibious Corps after the defences had been softened up by air strikes from the carriers of Vice Admiral Marc A. Mitscher's Task Force 58, which destroyed some 200 Japanese aircraft and sank 12 cargo ships. The American plan was for an initial landing on Saipan by a Northern Troops and Landing Force under Smith's personal command and comprising Major General Thomas E. Watson's 2nd Marine Division and Major General Harry Schmidt's 45th Marine Division, with Major General R. Smith's 27th Infantry Division as floating reserve. US intelligence estimated that the defence force available on Saipan to Admiral Chuichi Nagumo (commander of the Central Pacific Area Fleet) and Lieutenant General Hideyoshi Obata (commander of the 31st Army) amounted to some 20,000 men, though the actuality was 25,470 soldiers plus 6,160 sailors and naval troops.

The campaign began with a feint on Saipan's west coast during 15 June, followed by the landing of the 2nd Marine and 4th Marine Divisions on eight beaches to the south of Garapan. The landings ran into immediate resistance, and the 27th Infantry Division had to be committed on 17 June, just to the south of the 4th Marine Division. Thereafter the fighting went increasingly the Americans' way, though Japanese resistance did not end until 9 July, at Marpi Point on the extreme northern tip of the island, by which time the dead amounted to 3,126 US and 27,000 Japanese including Nagumo and Lieutenant General Yoshitsugu Saito, the latter commanding in the absence of Obata on an inspection tour in the Palau Islands at the time of the US invasion.

The next step was the descent on Guam by the Southern Troops and Landing Forces under the immediate command of Major General Roy S. Geiger's III Amphibious Corps and consisting of Major General Allen H. Turnage's 3rd Marine Division and Brigadier General Lemuel C. Shepherd's 1st Provisional Marine Brigade as the assault force with Major General Andrew D. Bruce's 77th Infantry Division as floating reserve. The Japanese garrison was commanded by Lieutenant General Takeshi Takeshina, who had 13,000 men plus 5,500 sailors and naval troops under the command of Captain Yutaka Sugimoto. Also on the island was Obata, who had returned from the Palau Islands to Guam on hearing of the US invasion of Saipan.

The campaign began on 21 July with the landing of the 3rd Marine Division at Asan and of the 1st Provisional Marine Brigade at Agat, both on the western side of the island. Yet again the Japanese resistance was fanatical, and the 77th Infantry Division had to be committed in support of the 1st Provisional Marine Brigade as the US forces drove slowly north up the island to end all resistance at Mount Machanao on 10 August. Both Obata and Takeshina were numbered amongst the dead, which amounted to 1,919 US and some 17,300 Japanese. Over the next years, it should be noted, Japanese survivors continued to attack the Americans, and as recently as 1972 a Japanese soldier surrendered himself.

The final campaign within Operation 'Forager' was the assault on Tinian, just to the south of Saipan, which was one of the reasons why the Saipan assault force was used for the Tinian operation. Holland Smith had been elevated to Commanding General, Fleet Marine Force, Pacific Fleet, and command of V Amphibious Corps had gone to Schmidt, Major General Clifton B. Cates assuming control of the 4th Marine Division. The Japanese garrison on Tinian amounted to 4,700 soldiers plus 4,110 sailors and naval troops commanded respectively by Colonel Kaishi Ogata and Captain Goichi Oya under the overall direction of Vice Admiral Kakuji Lakuda. The campaign began with a feint by the 2nd Marine Division towards the south of the island on 24 July, followed by the landing of the 4th Marine Division in the extreme north later in the day. The beachhead was expanded by the arrival of the 2nd Marine Division on the following day, and the usual pattern of Japanese resistance emerged, the island being deemed secure on 1 August after the failure of a final Japanese counterattack in the south of the island. This time the death toll was 290 Americans and 6,050 Japanese. The Marianas had fallen, and American engineers moved onto each island as soon as they could for the monumental task of carving out the huge runways needed for the B-29s.

Forearm Allied codename for Kavieng in New Ireland.

Forelle (trout) Overall designation of either of two German defensive plans to be implemented in the event of any Allied landings in the Aegean Sea, especially after the armistice with Italy, which occupied Rhodes and the Dodecanese Islands.

Fortitude Final version of 'Bodyguard'.

Fortune (i) Designation of the Allied headquarters in Algiers (spring 1943) for the planning of the Sicilian and Italian campaigns.
(ii) Naval operation in support of Operation 'Overlord'.

Fox Final amphibious exercise in the UK by the US V Corps in preparation for Operation 'Overlord'.

Foxer British codename for countermeasures system against German acoustic-homing torpedoes.

Frantic Overall designation of shuttle bombing raids by US heavy bombers of the 8th and 15th Air Forces operating between the UK, Italy and the USSR (1944).

Frantic Joe First raid in the 'Frantic' series (2 June 1944).

Franz German operation against Soviet partisans operating in the area of Pirurov-Most and Kolejna (7/11 January 1943).

Freedom (i) Allied codename for their headquarters in Algiers (spring 1943).
(ii) Operation by the US Army Air Forces to recover US prisoners of war incarcerated in Bulgaria (1945).

Freischütz (marksman) (i) Operation undertaken by the German Army Group 'Centre' against Soviet partisans operating the area north of Bryansk (May/June 1943). Operating from air-supplied bases deep in the inaccessible Pripet Marshes and comparable regions, the Soviet partisan forces had by mid-1943 become a very great thorn in the side of the Germans, constantly cutting rail and road lines of communication, and threatening vital installations such as bridges, telephone communication centres, supply dumps and the like. This forced the Germans to use large numbers of security troops in their rear areas, and also at times to detach front-line formations for the thankless and ultimately fruitless task of securing lines of communication and dumps when the partisan operations were beginning to affect the conduct of operations. At times too the activities of these increasingly well-led and well-armed partisan forces warranted specific attention from front-line troops in an effort to stabilize the position against the partisans. Before Operation 'Zitadelle', for example, the partisans were making it difficult for the German forces to concentrate their forces and bring them up to strength with men, *matériel* and supplies, warranting the use of first-line formations for operations such as 'Freischütz'. It was all to little avail, however, for the partisans could melt into the fastnesses that contained their bases, emerging later to resume their activities.
(ii) German plan for the occupation of the island of Vis (Lissa) to the south-west of Split in the aftermath of the Italian armistice (September 1943). The island was not in fact taken by the Germans, giving the Allies the chance to occupy it with a Commando operation in January 1944 and then establish it as a forward base for the coastal forces harrying German shipping in the Adriatic. An advanced air base was also developed on the island to serve the needs of tactical aircraft operating in support of the Yugoslav partisans and against tactical targets of opportunity in the western Balkans. The Germans at this stage reappreciated the significance of the island and resurrected their design for an occupation, in January gathering the men and vessels necessary for the invasion. However, so overwhelming was the Allied air and naval superiority in these confined waters that by April 1944 the Germans had again abandoned the idea of taking Vis.

Freshman Successful British Commando attack (19/20 November 1942) on the Norwegian facility in which the Germans were making heavy water for their atomic research programme.

Freya German early-warning radar system.

Fridericus I Reduction of the Izyum salient by the German Gruppe von Kleist (17/29 May 1942) under the command of Generaloberst Ewald von Kleist as a preliminary tidying move before the implementation of the German summer offensive of 1942. This salient had been driven into the line held by Generalfeldmarschall Fedor von Bock's Army Group 'South' by an offensive launched on 18 January 1942 by the 6th, 57th and 9th Armies of Lieutenant General F. Ya. Kostenko's South-West Front as part of a Soviet plan for the South-West and South Fronts to drive west across the River Donets between Balakleya in the north and Artemovsk in the south before wheeling south to reach the coast of the Sea of Azov at Melitopol and so to trap the German forces in the area. The advance did not go as the Soviets had planned, however, for the South Front was halted on its start lines and the South-West Front was checked on 31 January, after the creation of a substantial salient into the German lines, by the German 6th and 17th Armies, supported by General Eberhard von Mackensen's Gruppe von Mackensen, which turned back a breakout by the 57th Army.

It was this salient that was eliminated by Operation 'Fridericus I' after the Soviets had resumed their own offensive on 12 May in an effort to break out once more as the 6th Army and Group Bobrin struck westward (towards Krasnograd on the main rail line south-west of the city of Kharkov), supported to the north by the 38th and 28th Armies. These advances were checked in the north by the German 6th Army, opening the possibility for Gruppe von Kleist (comprising 2 Panzer divisions, 1 motorised division and 12 infantry divisions of the 1st Panzerarmee and the 17th Army) to strike into the left flank of the salient northwards towards Izyum, in an effort to cut off the 57th and 9th Armies as well as the 6th Army and Group Bobrin. Izyum fell on 18 May and the Soviet armies fell back in disarray, so that by the time that the German offensive ended along the line of the River Oskol the Soviets had lost 214,000 prisoners and 1,200 tanks to the Germans' 20,000 men. Much of the credit for 'Fridericus I' was given by the German propaganda machine to Generaloberst Friedrich Paulus of the 6th Army, paving the way for the trust placed in this commander to compound the German disaster at Stalingrad in the following campaign.

Fridericus II Companion offensive to Operation 'Wilhelm' and a logical successor to Operation 'Fridericus I', undertaken by the 1st Panzerarmee and part of the 6th Army (22/26 June 1942) as a preliminary to the German campaign of summer 1942 to clear the Soviet 9th and 38th Armies from the area of Kupyansk, in the course of the offensive securing a bridgehead over the River Oskol. Advancing from a point south-east of Kharkov, the Germans pushed the Soviets back without difficulty, securing some 40,000 prisoners in the process, and completed the virtual destruction of Lieutenant General F. Ya. Kostenko's South-West Front as an effective formation.

Fritz (i) German planning exercise leading towards the development of Operation 'Barbarossa'.
(ii) Headquarters of the Oberkommando des Heeres near Angerburg in East Prussia.

Frugal Designation of special air-mail flights by de Havilland Mosquitoes from the UK to the USSR, Italy and Egypt during the Moscow Conference (9/23 October 1944).

Frühlingserwachen (spring awakening) Germany's last offensive of the war, a massive and desperate effort to restore the position on the south-eastern approaches to Vienna with a counteroffensive against the Soviet 3rd Ukrainian Front (6/15 March 1945). While the German generals were against the whole plan, Hitler insisted on its implementation as the springboard to eventual victory in south-east Europe, for he imagined that the triumphant success of Operation 'Frühlingserwachen', wiping out the 3rd Ukrainian Front between the Rivers Danube and Drava on each side of Lake Balaton, would open the way for the recapture of Budapest and

Hungary, restoring to Germany the Hungarian oilfields that had until very recently supplied more than three-quarters of the oil available to the Third Reich.

Execution of this monstrously foolhardy plan was entrusted to General Otto Wöhler's Army Group 'South', whose 6th Army and 6th SS Panzerarmee (commanded respectively by General Hermann Balck and SS Oberstgruppenführer Sepp Dietrich, and numbering 10 Panzer and 5 infantry divisions) were to advance in the north from the line between Lakes Valencei and Balaton towards the Danube between Dunapentele and Mohacs, and whose 2nd Panzerarmee (commanded by General Maximilian de Angelis and consisting of 4 infantry divisions) was to push forward from south of Lake Balaton eastward towards the Danube. A subsidiary role was allocated to Generaloberst Alexander Löhr's Army Group 'E', which was to launch 3 divisions north-east across the Drava to take Mohacs. Facing this understrength and poorly-supplied force was the full strength of Marshal of the Soviet Union F. I. Tolbukhin's 3rd Ukrainian Front, a battle-hardened force (comprising the Soviet 4th Guards, 9th Guards, 27th, 26th and 57th Armies) of 37 rifle divisions, 2 tank corps, 1 mechanized corps and 1 cavalry corps, supported on its southern flank by the Bulgarian 1st Army of six rifle divisions and the Yugoslav 3rd Army.

Slight impressions were made in the Soviet lines, but the Germans were soon checked by the strength of the forces facing them, their own lack of equipment and fuel, and the appallingly muddy conditions prevalent in the spring thaw. Thereafter the Soviets were able to resume their own plans, advancing over the rest of Hungary to push into eastern Austria. Vienna fell to the 3rd Ukrainian Front on 14 April.

Frühlingsfest (spring feast) German operation against Soviet partisans operating in the area of Lepel, undertaken (16 April/10 May 1944) in support of Operation 'Regenschauer'.

Frühlingswind (spring breeze) Part of a complex operation devised by Generalfeldmarschall Erwin Rommel to extricate the German forces in danger of being trapped between Gabès and Sousse in Tunisia by the advances of Lieutenant General K. A. N. Anderson's Allied 1st and General Sir Bernard Montgomery's British 8th Armies of General the Hon. Sir Harold Alexander's 18th Army Group (14/22 February 1943). Rommel's plan was that the German armoured and motorized forces should strike hard at the 1st Army to break through between Lieutenant General Lloyd R. Fredendall's US II corps and Général de Corps d'Armée L. M. Koeltz's French XIX Corps in the region of the Kasserine Pass, pressing on to Tebessa and the coast near Bône if possible. The major problem with this plan was that there was no overall commander, for Rommel as commander of Army Group 'Africa' would control Operation 'Morgenluft', the half of the scheme allocated to the Deutsches Afrika Korps, while Generaloberst Jürgen von Arnim would control Operation 'Frühlingswind', the part of the scheme allocated to the 5th Panzerarmee, and while Rommel wanted a decisive stroke to repair the fortunes of the Axis in North Africa, von Arnim was more concerned with the winning of better defensive positions for his 5th Panzerarmee. However, the scheme went ahead on 14 February with the advance of von Arnim's 10th and 21st Panzer Divisions, the former pushing west from Faid towards Sbeitla, and the latter north-west from Maknassy towards Sbeitla via Bir el Hafey and Sidi Bou Zid. All went well, and substantial US forces were cut off in the Djebel Ksaira and Djebel Lessouda regions as the Germans pushed on to Sbeitla, which fell on 18 February despite the efforts of Major General Orlando Ward's US 1st Armored Division.

Now the plan began to go astray, for while Rommel urged a concerted thrust by his DAK forces of Operation 'Morgenluft' and von Arnim's two Panzer divisions from Kasserine (which fell to the Germans on 18 February) north-west to Tebéssa, von Arnim demurred and detached his 10th Panzer Division north towards Fondouk to secure adequate defence positions on the army's right flank. The 10th Panzer Division was then recalled, and a triple German thrust developed as the DAK pushed through the

Kasserine Pass in a diversionary thrust towards Tebéssa (checked with heavy casualties by the US 1st Armored Division), the 10th Panzer Division headed for Le Kef (now designated as the Germans' primary objective) via Thala, and the 21st Panzer Division struck out towards Le Kef via Sbiba. Alexander, the Allied deputy commander-in-chief under General Dwight D. Eisenhower, had assumed responsibility for this threatening situation and despatched Major General D. F. Keightley's British 6th Armoured Division of Lieutenant General C. W. Allfrey's British V Corps to bolster Thala (26th Armoured Brigade) and Sbiba (1st Guards Brigade). Heavy fighting developed in these two places as the Germans strove to break through, and on 22 February Rommel called a halt to his offensive and pulled back to better defensive positions. Kasserine was retaken on 25 February, but the whole offensive had cost the Allies 10,000 casualties (6,500 of them to the US II Corps) to the Germans' 2,000, a clear indication yet again of Rommel's tactical expertise.

FS Japanese plan to take New Caledonia, the Fiji Islands and the Samoa Islands, adopted (1942) in favour of a scheme to invade and conquer Australia. The Australian venture was proposed by the Imperial Japanese Navy as it was clear that the US forces would use Australia as a springboard for sustained operations against Japanese interests in the Central Pacific and South-East Asia, but was vetoed as impossible by the Imperial Japanese Army. The army and the navy concurred that Operation 'FS' was a feasible alternative, as more limited resources would be required for the operation, which would provide air and naval bases for the interdiction of Allied maritime lines of communication across the South Pacific. The scheme was not favoured by Admiral Isoroku Yamamoto, commander-in-chief of the Combined Fleet, who favoured instead the destruction of the US Navy's Pacific Fleet offered by his Midway operations, and the operation was ultimately made impossible by the success of the US counteroffensive in the Solomons, where the Japanese loss of Guadalcanal spelled the end of Japanese expansion in this direction after the Japanese had taken Nauru and Ocean Islands (25/26 August 1942), the planned springboards for Operation 'FS'.

F.S. Designation of UK coastal convoys (together with a numerical suffix) plying from Methil to Southend, and inaugurated in September 1939.

F.T. Designation of central Atlantic convoys (together with a numerical suffix) plying from Freetown (Sierra Leone) to Trinidad, and inaugurated in July 1943.

Führer-Senger Linie (Führer-Senger line) Designation of the German defence line just north of the 'Gustav Linie' position centred on Cassino along the Rivers Rapido and Garigliano. The 'Führer-Senger Linie' positions were roughly parallel with those of the 'Gustav Linie' between Atina in the mountains and Terracina on the coast, but were comprehensively breached on 22 May 1944 as Lieutenant General Mark Clark's US 5th Army swept forward from Cassino with Major General Geoffrey T. Keyes's US II Corps, Général de Corps d'Armée Juin's French Expeditionary Corps and Major General S. C. Kirkman's British XIII Corps, supplemented by Lieutenant General H. D. G. Crerar's I Canadian Corps.

Fuller British plans for naval and air forces to sink any major German warships trying to break north-east through the English Channel from Brest to Germany. The plans failed utterly as proved by the success of Operation 'Cerberus'.

Full House Overall designation of the tactical support furnished by the US 9th Air Force in Operation 'Overlord'.

Fusilade Capture of Dieppe (1 September 1944) by the 2nd Canadian Division of the Canadian II Corps of General Sir Henry Crerar's Canadian 1st Army.

Fustian Airborne mission in Sicily (13/14 July 1943) as part of Operation 'Husky'. This operation involved two brigades of Major General G. F. Hopkinson's British 1st Airborne Division, which were tasked to fly from the El Djem region in Tunisia to land north of Augusta in order to take the crossing over the River Mulinello and to take the northern suburbs of Augusta (1st Parachute Brigade) and to land astride the River Simeto and then to take and hold the Primasole bridge (Brigadier Gerald Lathbury's 2nd Parachute Brigade) as a means of speeding the advance of Lieutenant General M. C. Dempsey's British XIII Corps (part of General Sir Bernard Montgomery's British 8th Army) from Augusta to Catania along the eastern coast of Sicily. The airborne landings went well, but the advance of Major General S. C. Kirkman's 50th Division was too slow for the British armoured and infantry ground forces to relieve the 1st Parachute Brigade before the Germans had taken back the bridge. This was later retaken, but the delay meant that Catania fell only on 5 August rather than 13 July as Montgomery had hoped, as the main weight of the 8th Army's advance was shifted inland to Lieutenant General Sir Oliver Leese's British XXX Corps. This meant that instead of the British armour pouring through the plain of Catania to cut off the Axis forces in the west of the island, the Germans and Italians were able to undertake an effective evacuation of the island through Messina.

G

Gaff Airborne raid by the Belgian Independent Parachute Company, SAS, and by the 1st and 2nd SAS against German petrol dumps south of Rouen (25 July 1944). The Germans were acutely short of petrol by the middle of 1944, and the Allies fully appreciated that any diminution of the supplies reaching front-line units would have tactical effects highly beneficial to the Allies, so great efforts were made to bomb German oil production facilities, to bomb or otherwise cut the transport routes over which the oil derivatives reached the front, and to destroy dumps and the like.

Gain Airborne operation by D Squadron, 1st SAS, to cut rail communications in the Orléans region (16 June 1944) as German forces from other parts of France were beginning to reach the Normandy area in substantial numbers.

Galahad Overall designation of the US long-range penetration force operating in northern Burma with the Chinese forces of Lieutenant General Joseph W. Stilwell. The best-known of these was the 5307th Provisional Regiment, otherwise known as 'Merrill's Marauders' for their first commander, Brigadier General Frank D. Merrill; the unit was later commanded by Lieutenant Colonel C. N. Hunter.

Galia Airborne operation by the 3rd Squadron, 2nd SAS, to aid Italian partisans near Rossano (27 December 1944).

Galvanic First step in the drive across the central Pacific by the US forces controlled by Admiral Chester W. Nimitz's Pacific Ocean Areas, namely the capture of the Gilbert Islands (20/28 November 1943). US recruitment, training and industrial expansion had permitted a vast growth in the forces available for Pacific operations during the first nine months of 1943, and these land, sea and air assets were first concentrated at Pearl Harbor and elsewhere in the Hawaiian Islands before being despatched to forward bases in places such as Fiji and the New Hebrides for final training, as the organization for massive offensive moves over considerable distances was readied in the forms of Vice Admiral Raymond Spruance's 5th Fleet (7 battleships, 8 aircraft-carriers, 7 heavy and 3 light cruisers, and some 34 destroyers), Rear Admiral Richmond K. Turner's 5th Amphibious Force, Major General Holland M. Smith's V Amphibious Corps (100,000 men) and, in the Ellice Islands, the growing strength of Major General Willis H. Hale's 7th Air Force. The naval and marine assets had previously been Vice Admiral William Halsey's 3rd Fleet for the operations in the Solomons.

The overall scheme for Nimitz's advance was a careful but massive push in a series of steps, each step consisting of an island group, leading westwards across the Pacific towards Formosa and the mainland of China before a final concentration of US effort (General Douglas MacArthur's South-West Pacific Area and Nimitz's Pacific Ocean Areas) against the Japanese home islands. The first step was the Gilbert Islands, a wide-flung group of atolls at the edge of the Japanese defensive perimeter established by July 1942. Operation 'Galvanic' was schemed by Turner

60

and Smith as a two-part operation, with a Northern Attack Force to tackle Makin and a Southern Attack Force for Tarawa. Intelligence had confirmed that Makin was by far the softer of the two objectives, but the command team opted to capture Makin first with the Northern Task Force as any Japanese riposte (by air from the Marianas Islands or by sea from the Japanese Combined Fleet's base at Truk in the Caroline Islands) would reach Makin first. The force thus allocated to the capture of Makin was the 165th Infantry Regiment of Major General Ralph C. Smith's 27th Infantry Division, and this reduced Makin's garrison (300 troops and 400 labourers) in four methodical but uncomplicated days between 20 and 23 November.

However, Tarawa was an altogether tougher nut for Rear Admiral Harry W. Hill's Southern Attack Force built round Major General Julian C. Smith's 2nd Marine Division, for the island of Betio that formed the centrepiece of the Japanese defence had been fortified with great vigour and skill by the 4,700 men commanded by Rear Admiral Keichi Shibasaki. The result was some of the bitterest fighting of the war between 20 and 23 November, when the island of Betio was declared secure. Of the 18,600 men available to the 2nd Marine Division on 20 November, 990 had been killed and 2,391 wounded, while the Japanese survivors (all wounded) amounted to 1 officer and 16 men, plus 129 Korean labourers. Of the three other main islands in the Tarawa Atoll, Bairiki was taken on 21 November, Buariko on 27 November and Naa on 28 November. The campaign was completed by the seizure of Apamama against negligible resistance by a single company of US Marines. The Tarawa operation came as a considerable shock to the US forces and public, confirming how costly would be the advance to Japan's eventual defeat.

Gangway Allied plan for an unopposed landing in Naples during the autumn of 1943 with the support of the government of capitulated Italy. The plan was cancelled on 27 July 1943 before any order of battle or detailed plans had been formulated, but together with the similar Operation 'Barracuda' depended on a rapid overland advance by Allied forces to seize this vital port so that substantial reinforcements could be sealifted into the theatre for a major advance northwards before the Germans could recover their wits after the supposedly unexpected armistice with Italy.

Garden British XXX Corps part in the combined airborne/land offensive designed to secure the Allies a bridgehead over the Lower Rhine at Arnhem (17/20 September 1940). While the airborne plan consisted of parachute drops and gliderborne landings by formations of Lieutenant General F. A. M. Browning's British I Airborne Corps to seize the bridges over the Wilhelmina and Zuit Willemsvaart Canals at Zon and Veghel respectively (US 101st Airborne Division), over the River Maas at Grave and over the River Waal at Nijmegen (US 82nd Airborne Division) and over the Neder Rijn (Lower Rhine) at Arnhem (British 1st Airborne Division), the task facing the three divisions (Guards Armoured, 43rd and 50th) of Lieutenant General Sir Brian Horrocks's XXX Corps was to push forward from its bridgehead over the Meuse-Escaut Canal with the task of relieving the airborne forces, pushing on over the intact bridges and exploiting northwards towards the Zuider Zee. It was 64 miles from XXX Corps's start line to Arnhem, and Allied planners anticipated that XXX Corps, with the Guards Armoured Division in the lead, might reach the Zuider Zee (30 miles farther on from Arnhem) anywhere between two and five days after the start of the offensive on 17 September.

What the Allied planners had not adequately considered was that XXX Corps would have to advance a considerable distance over a single road, where the loss of even one leading tank would cause considerable delay. Moreover, the German defence was far stronger than anticipated, for under the overall control of Generalfeldmarschall Walter Model's Army Group 'B' was the newly established 1st Parachute Army of Generaloberst Kurt Student, and though this was finding it difficult to get itself established in the area to the north of the Meuse-Escaut Canal, the German situation was eased by the presence just north of the Meuse-Escaut Canal of the remnants of three veteran

Gardening

divisions under the command of Generalleutnant Kurt Chill, and in the Arnhem area of the recuperating but none the less capable 9th and 10th SS Panzer Divisions of SS Gruppenführer Willi Bittrich's II SS Panzer Corps.

At first all went well for XXX Corps, which suffered losses but broke through to relieve the US 101st Airborne Division in the afternoon of 18 September and the US 82nd Airborne Division at Grave in the early morning of 19 September, thereafter joining forces with the 82nd Airborne to take the bridge at Nijmegen on 20 September. This date is indicative of the delay now entering the land advance, which was faced with ever strengthening resistance from the hastily regrouped Germans and now had 6 miles to cover before it could relieve the 1st Airborne Division. This was in dire straits at Arnhem, being compressed into a small bridgehead in Oosterbeek just to the west of Arnhem proper, with the 2nd Battalion, The Parachute Regiment, cut off on the vital bridge and forced to surrender on 21 September. The pocket occupied by the bulk of the 1st Airborne Division held out until 26 September and then capitulated with the loss of 7,000 men, though another 2,200 had managed to break out across the Rhine to reach the leading elements of XXX Corps on the south bank of the river.

Gardening Overall designation of the aerial minelaying policy adopted by the British to hinder the movement of German naval and mercantile shipping in European waters. Such minelaying was usually undertaken at night by bombers.

Gasper Allied force to protect the Tinsukia/Nazira lines of communication in Assam (April 1944).

G.A.T. Designation of Caribbean convoys (together with a numerical suffix) plying between Guantanamo (Cuba) and Trinidad, and inaugurated in August 1942 having been W.A.T. when started in July 1942.

Gauntlet Canadian commando raid on Spitsbergen (3 September 1941). The origins of the idea lay with the need to offer visible support to the Soviets after the beginning of Operation 'Barbarossa', and thought was in the short term given to the establishment of British naval and air forces at Murmansk, a wing of Hawker Hurricane fighters in fact operating in the area for a short time in November 1941. But Murmansk was too distant for reliable support from the UK, and it was suggested that British naval and air forces could profitably operate from Spitsbergen. This proposal was rightly rejected as impractical once the Germans had reinforced their forces in northern Norway, but two reconnaissances of the island by Rear Admiral Sir Philip Vian bore fruit in the suggestion that the coal installations on the island could be destroyed to the detriment of the German war effort. The force sailed on 19 August from Scapa Flow, and the mainly Canadian commando forces were put ashore unopposed on Spitsbergen, where they burned all stocks of coal and captured three colliers in the harbour. The Norwegians and Soviets on the island were evacuated, and while the transports headed straight home, Vian took his escort warships in towards the Norwegian coast, meeting a troop convoy on the approaches to Portangerfjord. Vian's ships sank the training cruiser *Bremse*, but the two troopships she was escorting managed to slip away. Vian's force returned to Scapa Flow on 10 September.

G.C. Designation of North-West African coastal convoys (together with a numerical suffix) plying between Gibraltar and Casablanca, and inaugurated in November 1942 after the success of Operation 'Torch' with the original designation T.F.

Gee British radio navigation aid.

Gelb (yellow) German plan for the invasion of the Low Countries and France (1939). This plan was not implemented, as Hitler hoped to persuade the UK and France that he had completed his territorial plans with the conquest of Poland, and as the German high command advised caution, so giving Generalleutnant Erich von Manstein time to institute the sweeping reform of the plan that led to the climactic German success of 1940.

The original Operation 'Gelb', as planned

by Generaloberst Walther von Brauchitsch and General Franz Halder, was in essence an updated version of the 'Schlieffen' Plan of World War I, using a total of 102 divisions (including 9 Panzer and 6 motorized), with emphasis again placed on a strong right wing to sweep through Belgium into France north of the River Somme to take Boulogne and Dunkirk with a view to making as difficult as possible the sea communications between France and the UK. On the German right flank was thus to be Generaloberst Fedor von Bock's Army Group 'B' reinforced to 43 divisions for a westward thrust north and south of Liège, with central forces comprising Generaloberst Walther von Reichenau's 6th Army (containing 5 Panzer divisions) to move on Ghent and Generaloberst Günther von Kluge's 4th Army (containing 4 Panzer divisions) to move on Thuin on the River Sambre, cover for this main offensive strength being provided in the north by General Georg von Küchler's 18th Army (objective Antwerp) and in the south by General Maximilian Freiherr von Weichs' 2nd Army (objective Givet). Farther to the south would operate two more major formations, namely Generaloberst Gerd von Rundstedt's 22-division Army Group 'A' which would operate on a front between Laon and Longwy with General Wilhelm List's 12th Army and General Ernst Busch's 16th Army, and Generaloberst Wilhelm Ritter von Leeb's 18-division Army Group 'C' which would operate defensively on a front between Longwy and the Swiss frontier with the 1st and 7th Armies. Nineteen divisions, including two motorized divisions, would be held by the Oberkommando des Heeres as a general reserve.

This plan was orthodox in the extreme, and the French 'Dyle' Plan was schemed to counter just such an offensive. Hitler accepted this plan on 29 October 1939, and the only modification made in the short term was the inclusion of the Netherlands as a country to be conquered. The plan originally called for the 18th and 6th Armies to cross the 'Maastricht appendix' of the Netherlands en route to their objectives in Belgium, it being hoped that the Dutch would not enter the war for this 'small' violation of their territorial integrity. However, Hermann Goering feared that as a result the Dutch might accede to British pressure for the forward basing of British bombers on Dutch airfields, and it was decided to extend the scheme northward to include the Netherlands proper.

By the beginning of November Hitler was beginning to have doubts about the wisdom of leaving Army Group 'A' so weak, and demanded that the XIX Panzer Corps (2 Panzer divisions, 1 motorized division and 2 SS motorized regiments) under General Heinz Guderian should be shifted to Army Group 'A' in order that they could drive through the Ardennes to take Sedan on the River Meuse as an offensive bridgehead for armoured operations in the centre should the armoured thrust in the north fail. Von Manstein, chief-of-staff of Army Group 'A', was already thinking along similar lines, but his plans had proceeded no further than OKH, and it was only after Hitler's intervention that the scene was set for the full-scale evolution of von Manstein's magnificent Operation 'Sichelschnitt'.

General Collingwood Allied codename for King George VI.

Georg Plan devised by Generalfeldmarschall Wilhelm Ritter von Leeb's Army Group 'North' for the reduction of Leningrad (autumn 1941). Great importance was attached by the Germans to the elimination of Leningrad, which had been the cradle of the Russian Revolution and was now one of the country's primary industrial and population centres. The planners appreciated that Army Group 'North' was too weak for the military capture of the city, and therefore planned to keep Leningrad under artillery bombardment (from 1 September 1941) while the rest of the city was invested for a siege which was expected to starve it out within a few weeks. By 25 September the city was cut off from the rest of the USSR when the Germans reached the Gulf of Finland to the west of the city and Schlüsselburg on the southern shore of Lake Ladoga to the east of the city, while the Finnish IV Corps held the Karelian Isthmus to the north of Leningrad, which was defended by the Soviet 23rd Army (Karelian sector) and the 42nd and 55th

Geranium

Armies (southern sector) of Lieutenant General M. M. Popov's Leningrad Front.

The city had food for about one month, and widespread starvation was apparent by October, some 11,000 citizens dying of it in November despite the use of barges to ferry in supplies from Lednevo to Osinovets across Lake Ladoga. By 9 November the Germans had taken Tikhvin to the east of Leningrad and thus cut the road and rail links to Lednevo, forcing the Soviets to use small ships to take across food from Novaya Ladoga until thin ice closed the lake by the middle of the month. Matters for the Soviets improved on 6 December with the opening of the 'Lifeline Road' from a railhead at Zaborie to Novaya Ladoga via Karpino, and on 9 December, when Soviet forces retook Tikhvin and pushed the Germans back to the line of the River Volkhov, allowing the original rail line to Lednovo to be used once more, increasing the flow of supplies that could be carried across the thick ice in lorries from Lednovo to Osinovets for further movement to Leningrad by rail. It was a desperate time for the people of Leningrad (3,700 people died of starvation on 25 December 1941, the day on which bread rations were increased for the first time in the siege), but the worst had been weathered and the Germans could not starve out the city.

Geranium British air mining zone in the waters off Swinemunde in north Germany.

Gertrud (i) Joint German and Bulgarian contingency plan for an invasion of Turkey should that country come into the war on the side of the Allies.
(ii) Luftwaffe air campaign waged with bombers against Soviet electricity production centres (1942/1943).

G-H British radar blind bombing equipment.

Giant I Allied plan for an airborne crossing (by Major General Matthew B. Ridgway's US 82nd Airborne Division) of the River Volturno (September 1943), to prevent German reinforcements from moving south through the Campanion plain to counterattack the Allied forces landing at Salerno in Operation 'Avalanche'. It was also appreciated that the Allies' conventional crossing of the river in the following month might at the time offer great difficulties as the river would be in autumn spate and the Germans would likely have destroyed all the bridges across it. The plan was thus cancelled. In the event, on the third day after resuming the offensive on 12 October, Lieutenant General Mark Clark's US 5th Army managed to get its British X and US VI Corps across this formidable barrier and into the approaches of the yet more formidable 'Gustav Linie' defences, namely the 'Barbara Linie' positions.

Giant II Allied plan to airland Major General Matthew B. Ridgway's US 82nd Airborne Division near Rome (8 September 1943) just before the announcement of Italy's armistice with the Allies, to help safeguard the Italian royal family and government from the retribution of the German forces who were known to be prepared for such an Italian defection from the Axis camp. Support for the 82nd Airborne Division was to have been provided by the Italians, who were to eliminate German anti-aircraft positions in Rome, light marker fires at the drop zones and provide sufficient transport to move the division into Rome.

Giant III and **Giant IV** Allied plans to expand the US 5th Army's Salerno beachhead with a mass drop by the US 82nd Airborne Division from Sicily (September 1943). In the even this would have been too risky, and instead elements of the division were dropped on 13/14 September as reinforcements into that part of the beachhead held by the 36th Infantry Division of Major General Ernest J. Dawley's US VI Corps, which was hard pressed by major counterattacks from the German 16th Panzer Division and 29th Panzergrenadier Division.

Gibbon Transfer of the Italian fleet to British control as one of the terms of the armistice with Italy. The operation was carried out successfully (9/10 September 1943), the Italian force (the battleships *Roma*, *Vittorio Veneto* and *Italia* accompanied by 6 cruisers and 8 destroyers) setting sail from La Spezia at 03.00 on 9 September to rendezvous with a detachment of Force H off Bône later on the same day. En route the squadron was attacked by German bombers, which used radio-controlled glide bombs to sink the *Roma* (together with the commander-in-chief, Admiral Carlo Bergamini) and damage the *Italia*. The rendezvous was thus made on 10 September, the Italian force being escorted into Malta, which was also the destination for other Italian naval units including the battleships *Andrea Doria* and *Caio Duilio* plus 2 cruisers from Taranto (arrived in Malta on 9 September) and the battleship *Guilio Cesare* from Taranto (arrived in Malta on 13 September). Other naval forces surrendered at different bases, and at the same time 101 Italian merchantmen were surrendered, while another 168 were scuttled to avoid seizure by the Germans.

Gilbey   Overall designation of nocturnal anti-shipping strikes by aircraft of RAF Coastal Command vectored in to their targets by radar-equipped Vickers Wellington reconnaissance aircraft.

Gisela   (i) German plans to seize the ports along the north coast of Spain (October 1942/spring 1943).
(ii) Hitler's advanced headquarters near Giessen.

Gisella   German night-fighter operation (3/4 March 1945) in which some 200 aircraft were insinuated into the streams of British bombers returning to the UK from raids on Kamen and the Dortmund-Ems Canal. The German fighters shot down 20 bombers, losing 3 of their own number in accidents.

Gizo   German operation against Soviet partisans operating just to the south of the Pripet Marshes (March 1943) as they posed a severe threat to the German build-up before Operation 'Zitadelle', which German commanders knew to be Germany's last chance to regain the strategic initiative against the Soviets.

G.K.   Designation of Caribbean convoys (together with a numerical suffix) plying from Guantanamo (Cuba) to Key West, and inaugurated in September 1942.

Glimmer   Part of the Allied deception plan for Operation 'Overlord', together with the similar 'Taxable' (6 June 1944). 'Glimmer' was an air operation in the Straits of Dover, designed to persuade the Germans that an invasion force was crossing to the Boulogne area of the Pas-de-Calais.

Globetrotter   US 6th Infantry Division landing at Sansapor at the western tip of New Guinea (30 July 1944). The operation cost the Americans 2 dead and the Japanese 374 dead, and marked the end of General Douglas MacArthur's brilliantly conceived campaign along the coast of northern New Guinea. Experienced and highly skilled forces made possible a magnificent series of combined operations in which land, sea and air forces co-operated perfectly to identify key points in the Japanese defences for sudden assault and overwhelming. By the time the Sansapor operation had been undertaken, MacArthur was well advanced in his planning for the steps that would now take his forces back to the Philippines confident that there was no realistic threat to his rear in New Guinea, for though the Japanese 18th Army still had some 120,000 men under arms in this vast island, the Japanese forces were so scattered and demoralized that they could not offer any type of cohesive threat to the Allies as they were pressured constantly by Australian and US forces dedicated to the task.

Glucinium   British commando intelligence mission in Czechoslovakia.

G.M.   Designation of military convoys (together with a numerical suffix) plying from Gibraltar to Malta, and inaugurated in July 1941.

G.N.   Designation of US coastal convoys (together with a numerical suffix) plying from Guantanamo (Cuba) to New York, and inaugurated in August 1942.

Gnat   British codename for German acoustic-homing torpedoes.

Gneisenau Linie   (Gneisenau line) Alternative of the 'Grün Linie' position.

Goalpost That portion of the US Western Task Force which landed at Mehdia during Operation 'Torch'.

Goblet British plan for a landing at Crotone (on the 'sole' of Italy's 'foot') if the advance through Calabria by the 1st Canadian Division of the British XIII Corps were stalled for any reason (September 1943). This plan was schemed at the instigation of General George C. Marshall, US Army chief-of-staff, and the detailed planning was allocated by General Dwight D. Eisenhower to Lieutenant General C. W. Allfrey's British V Corps, which could call on the British 1st, 4th and 78th Divisions and the US 82nd Airborne Division. The landing was designed to aid the advance of the British XIII Corps and to provide fighter bases for the support of further offensive moves in southern Italy, but was cancelled on 4 September.

Gold Assault beach for the British XXX Corps in Operation 'Overlord', running from the junction point with I Corps' 'Juno' beach at La Rivière westwards to Arromanches, and defended by the 726th and 915th Infantry Regiments of the 716th Infantry Division of General Behlendorff's LXXXIV Corps of Generaloberst Friedrich Dollmann's German 7th Army.

Goldflake Transfer of Canadian formations from the British 8th Army in Italy to the Canadian 1st Army in the Low Countries (spring 1945).

Gomorrah Allied air offensive designed to destroy the important North German port of Hamburg (24 July/3 August 1943). This campaign by RAF Bomber command and the US 8th Air Force totally destroyed large portions of the city with self-sustaining firestorms created by incendiaries and feeding on the city's timbered buildings, and suffered few losses thanks to the use for the first time of 'Window' to fill German radar screens with millions of echoes in which those of the bombers could not be distinguished.

Gondola First all-out air operation by No. 19 Group, RAF Coastal Command, against German U-boats in the Bay of Biscay (4/16 February 1943). Eight attacks were made in the course of 19 sightings, but only one U-boat was sunk.

Goodtime Seizure of Treasury Island in the Solomon Islands by the New Zealand 8th Brigade Group (27 October 1943). In conjunction with Operation 'Blissful', Operation 'Goodtime' served to distract the attention of the Japanese 17th Army command from the island of Choiseul, which was in fact the next major target for the forces of Vice Admiral William Halsey's South Pacific Area forces as it contained six important airfields which had been bombed enough to destroy Japanese aircraft but not to ruin the facilities.

Goodwood (i) Operation by Lieutenant General J. T. Crocker's British I Corps to the east of Caen (18/21 July 1944) with the object of pinning German forces in the area to facilitate the capture of Caen and to ease the task of the US VII Corps due to break out of the Normandy beach-head area on 24 July. Though the corps suffered quite heavily in its offensive (supported by the British I Corps and Canadian II Corps of Lieutenant General Sir Miles Dempsey's British 2nd Army), it attained its major objectives. The plan called for I Corps to move up through the British VIII Corps in the area of Ste Honorine to the east of half-captured Caen, and then launch its powerful armoured forces (Guards Armoured Division, 7th Armoured Division and 11th Armoured Division) through the junction of the German I SS Panzer Corps and LXXXVI Corps of the 5th Panzerarmee.

The offensive was launched under an extraordinarily severe artillery barrage and with the benefit of massive bomber support, and smashed through the German first line of defence, the Luftwaffe's 16th Field Division, without difficulty. However it then began to run into more capable opposition from massed anti-tank guns and rocket-launchers as German armoured forces began to stream into the area in the form of the 1st and 12th SS Panzer Divisions, which checked I Corps by the evening of 20 July. The offensive had none the less achieved its objectives in strategic terms, and the support of the British I Corps and Canadian II Corps had allowed a general improvement in the Allied position round Caen as I Corps' 3rd Division moved south-east to Troarn, the 3rd Canadian Division with the support of the 51st (Highland) Division took Caen completely by 18 July, and the 2nd Canadian Division took advantage of the removal of the 1st SS Panzer Division from the area to the west of Caen to deal roughly with the remaining 272nd Infantry Division and advance as far as St André. Longer-term effects were the removal of the 2nd SS Panzer Division from the region of St Lô (site of the planned 'Cobra' breakout) to Caen, for Generalfeldmarschall Günther von Kluge of Panzergruppe 'West' felt that there was now severe danger of a British eruption from Caen towards Falaise, which would trap a large portion of the German forces in Normandy and Brittany.

(ii) Fleet Air Arm offensive against the German battleship *Tirpitz* in the Altenfjord of northern Norway (22/29 August 1944). The three fleet carriers *Formidable*, *Furious* and *Indefatigable*, supported by the light carriers *Nabob* and *Trumpeter*, flew four missions (two on 22 August, one on 24 August and one on 29 August), the 242 sorties achieving two ineffective bomb hits for the loss of 10 fighters and 1 Fairey Barracuda strike aircraft.

Gooseberry Breakwater for 'Mulberry', made of sunken ships.

Gotenkopf (Goth's head) Designation of the beach-head held by General E. Jaenecke's German 17th Army in the Kuban over the Strait of Kerch from the Crimea (late March/9 October 1943). This beach-head had been formed by the compression of Army Group 'A' forces into this region by the successful winter offensive of 1942/1943 undertaken by the Soviet Trans-Caucasus, North Caucasus and Stalingrad Fronts to eliminate the German forces south of the River Don. Hitler insisted that the beach-head be held at all costs as a springboard for renewed offensives into the Caucasus, but his ambitions were entirely overcome by the Soviet summer offensive of 1943, which threatened to cut off the German forces in the Crimea and the Kuban. The 17th Army was being pressured from 9 September by an offensive by General I. E. Petrov's North Caucasus Front, and by 9 October the last remnants of the 17th Army had been evacuated at the insistence of Generalfeldmarschall Ewald von Kleist's Army Group 'A', commanding in the southern USSR.

Gotisch Linie (Gothic line) German defence line in Italy, running north-west to south-east across northern Italy from La Spezia on the Tyrrhenian Sea to Pesaro on the Adriatic Sea. The Germans expected much of this formidably constructed line, but in the event the Allies managed to penetrate it without undue difficulty. First to punch through was Lieutenant General Sir Oliver Leese's British 8th Army, which approached the line in August 1944. Leese thought the inland sectors easier to overcome than the maritime section, and he was proved right when Lieutenant General E. L. M. Burns's Canadian I Corps and Lieutenant General Sir Charles Keightley's British V Corps broke through between Osteria Nuova and Montecalvo on 29 August, advancing rapidly to the dire battles on the Gemmano and Coriano Ridges in the middle of September. Lieutenant General Mark Clark's US 5th Army (US II and IV Corps, and the British XIII Corps) had a harder time pushing through the 'Gotisch Linie' positions, and then wore itself out in desperate attempts to reach Bologna before the arrival of winter weather.

Gotz von Berlichingen Extension of Operation 'Eisstoss' (April 1942).

Governor Diversionary sweep by Royal Navy units off the coast of Norway (26/29 July 1943).

Granite Overall designation of the plans devised by Admiral Chester W. Nimitz's Pacific Ocean Areas command (1944) for a terminal offensive against Japan directed not against Japan's main bastions and the home islands themselves, but rather against the weak points (in a line stretching from the Marianas Islands to China via Formosa and the Ryukyu island group). Nimitz and his staff felt that such a scheme would avoid the inevitable bloodbaths of tackling the Japanese main forces directly, and would achieve the

Grapefruit

same result by severing the Japanese empire into two parts, with Japan proper in the north isolated with its great population but without the oil, food and raw materials it was drawing from China and South-East Asia, and the Japanese forces in the main areas of the 'Greater East Asia Co-Prosperity Sphere' cut off from reinforcement and resupply, and thus likely to fall victim to limited Allied offensives within a short period. For a number of reasons, many of them strategically strong, the 'Granite' plan was far superior to the counterplan offered by General Douglas MacArthur's South-West Pacific Area command (a northward drive from New Guinea to liberate the Philippines and then to invade Japan). However, in their meetings with President Franklin Roosevelt and his staff, MacArthur emerged as the more dominant personality and so carried the day for his plan, leading to the abandonment of 'Granite' despite its promise of lower (but certainly not low) casualties through the exploitation of Japan's weaknesses where MacArthur's plan triumphed over Japan's strengths.

Grapefruit Final offensive by Lieutenant General Lucian K. Truscott's US 5th Army in Italy (13 April/6 May 1945). Undertaken to the west of Bologna, the offensive was aided by the start five days earlier of the British 8th Army's offensive, which drew German forces to the east in anticipation of Allied amphibious operations directed against Venice and German communications with Austria. Under Major Generals Geoffrey T. Keyes and Walter Crittenberger respectively, the US II and IV Corps drove decisively through General Joachim Lemelsen's German 14th Army, reaching the valley of the River Po on 20 April and forcing the Germans, despite the injection of their last reserves, to fall back in total disarray (and without their heavy equipment) to the north bank of the Po regardless of Hitler's specific instructions to the contrary. The divisions of the 5th Army fanned out into northern and north-western Italy (taking Milan and Turin on 2 May) to meet French troops advancing from Italy and US troops advancing from Austria on 6 May. This was four days after the surrender of the German Army Group 'C' in Italy had come into effect after the signature of Generaloberst Heinrich von Vietinghoff-Scheel on 29 April.

Gray Allied plan to take the Azores Islands (1941/1942) as part of an overall scheme to seize the Atlantic islands of Spain and Portugal in the event that these two countries should waver towards the Axis cause. There was a very real fear in the Allied camp that Germany would quickly seize the islands for itself should Spain and Portugal veer towards the Axis, providing German maritime patrol aircraft and submarines with ideal bases for more devastating attacks on Allied shipping. The Azores were handily placed for control of the sea routes across the North Atlantic, while Madeira and the Canary Islands could back the Azores to interdict Allied supply lines and invasion convoys heading for North-West Africa for the planned Operation 'Torch', and the Cape Verde Islands dominated the convoy routes round the west coast of Africa along which passed all reinforcements for the Middle East, India, South-East Asia and Australasia.

Green (i) US contingency plans for war with Mexico (1940).
(ii) Plan by the Special Operations Executive for operations by French maquis forces against German rail communications in northern France in support of Operation 'Overlord'.

Greenlight Special ammunition deliveries for the support of Operation 'Overlord'.

Greif (griffon) (i) German operation against Soviet partisans operating in the area of Orsha and Vitebsk (14/20 August 1942) and so threatening the lines of communication for Army Group 'Centre' along the 'Moscow Highway' running from Brest-Litovsk on the Polish frontier through Minsk to Smolensk.
(ii) German use of commando troops in US uniforms and Transport in Operation 'Herbstnebel' to disrupt the US areas and so prevent reinforcements and supplies reaching the units of Lieutenant General Courtney H. Hodges's US 1st Army most in need of them.

Grenade Advance by Lieutenant General

Alexander M. Patch's US 7th Army to the Upper Rhine as part of the advance of Lieutenant General Jacob Devers's US 6th Army Group (7 February/28 March 1945). This was part of the vast offensive by the Allied 21st, 12th and 6th Army Groups after the defeat of the German Ardennes push (Operation 'Herbstnebel') to secure the moral and operational advantages of advancing across the Rhine into the 'heart-land' of Germany. At the time of 'Herbstnebel' the Canadian 1st Army in the north and the French 1st Army in the south had reached the Rhine, but the 'Siegfried Linie' defences and the need to deal with 'Herbstnebel' had prevented the British 2nd, US 9th, US 1st, US 3rd and US 7th Armies from reaching this great river barrier between Nijmegen and Haguénau. The 7th Army was deployed at the southern end of this line, with its XXI, XV and VI Corps stretched out between Saarbrucken and the Rhine southeast of Haguénau (where it joined with the French 1st Army) facing the formations of General Hermann Foertsch's 1st Army of SS Oberstgruppenführer Paul Hausser's Army Group 'G'. At first only slow progress was made, but the success of the XX Corps of Lieutenant General George S. Patton's 3rd Army to the north, pressing on past Kaiserslautern towards Ludwigshafen and Mannheim on the Rhine threatened the 1st Army's left flank and caused Foertsch to pull back on 21 March, allowing the 7th Army to reach the Rhine along its whole army frontage by 28 March. The offensive was capped by the crossing of the Rhine by XV Corps at Worms on 26 March, allowing a break-out towards Darmstadt.

Gripfast British plan for an advance to the River Chindwin in Burma (spring 1944) as a modification of the 'Tarzan' plan.

Grog Airborne operation by the French 3ème Regiment des Chasseurs Parachutistes to establish liaison with the French maquis units in the region of Persquen (11 July 1944).

Grosskraftwerk Nordwest (north-west power station) Overall designation of the sites from which V-2 missiles were launched against the UK (1944/1945).

Groundsheet Minelaying operation by units of the Royal Navy off the coast of Norway (February 1945).

Grubworm Air transfer of the Chinese Army in India from Assam to China (5 December 1944/5 January 1945).

Grün (green) (i) German plan for an invasion of Czechoslovakia as part of a two-front war (1935/1937).
(ii) German occupation of Czechoslovakia (March 1939).

Grün Linie (green line) German defence line in the Apennine mountains of central Italy to cover the valley of the River Po, and also known as the 'Gotisch Linie'. These positions ran north-west to south-east across Italy from La Spezia on the Tyrrhenian Sea to Pesaro on the Adriatic Sea. The Germans expected much of this formidably constructed and powerfully defended strategic defence line, along which they could muster a total of 26 divisions against the Allies' 20 divisions, but in the event the Allies managed to penetrate it without undue difficulty and casualties.

First to punch through was Lieutenant General Sir Oliver Leese's British 8th Army, which had some 10 divisions allocated to the Canadian I Corps, the Polish II Corps, the British V Corps and the British X Corps, with one more division in army reserve. These forces approached the 'Grün Linie' positions in August 1944, and Leese considered that his formations would find it easier to drive through in the inland sector than along the coast, and he was proved right when Lieutenant General E. L. M. Burns's Canadian I Corps and Lieutenant General Sir Charles Keightley's British V Corps broke through between Osteria Nuova and Montecalvo on 29 August, advancing through the junction of General Valentin Feuerstein's LI Gebirgskorps and General Traugott Herr's LXXVI Panzer Corps of Generaloberst Heinrich von Vietinghoff-Scheel's German 10th Army, advancing rapidly to the dire battles of the Gemmano and Coriano Ridges in the middle of September.

Lieutenant General Mark Clark's US 5th Army (9 divisions in the British XIII Corps, the US II Corps and the US IV Corps) had a harder time pushing through the 'Grün Linie' positions in the sector held by the two corps (I Parachute Corps and XIV Panzer Corps) of General Joachim Lemelsen's German 14th Army, and then wore itself out in desperate attempts to reach Bologna before the arrival of winter and the end of the useful campaigning season.

In the end the line stabilized temporarily on 15 January 1945 with the 8th Army firmly through the 'Grün Linie' positions and halted along the line of the River Senio, and the 5th Army checked along a less well defined line from Firenzuola in the Apennines via Vergato on the southern side of the Po valley to the Tyrrhenian coast between Livorno and La Spezia. A small portion of the 'Grün Linie' positions along the Tyrrhenian coast was still in German hands at this time, which both sides used to recuperate before the arrival of spring and the next campaigning season. In the command sector, Clark succeeded Field Marshal the Hon. Sir Harold Alexander as commander-in-chief of the Allied 15th Army Group on the latter's elevation to Supreme Allied Commander in the Mediterranean, while Lieutenant General Lucian K. Truscott assumed command of the 5th Army and Lieutenant General Sir Richard McCreery took over as commander of the 8th Army.

Grünspecht (green woodpecker) German offensive by the 2nd Panzerarmee against Soviet partisans operating in the area south of Bryansk (summer 1942).

G.T.X. Designation of Mediterranean convoys (together with a numerical suffix) plying from Gibraltar via Tripoli to Egypt, and inaugurated in May 1943.

G.U. Designation of military ocean convoys (together with a numerical suffix) plying from North-West Africa to the USA, and inaugurated in November 1942 after the implementation of Operation 'Torch'.

Gunner British plan for a landing near Brest in western Brittany (November 1942). The scheme was considered as a means of placating US enthusiasms for an operation across the English Channel as soon as possible after the arrival of substantial US forces in the UK (Operation 'Bolero'), but the British were generally unenthusiastic given their experience with the disaster at Dieppe (Operation 'Jubilee') and sensibly wished to husband resources so that a massive strength could be built up for a definitive return to the continent as the major Allied blow against German strength in the West. Other schemes of this period envisaged descents on Cherbourg, the Channel Islands, other French ports and even Norway, but all were sensibly shelved in favour of Operation 'Overlord'.

Gunnerside Airborne operation by the Norwegian Company Linge near Lake Skryken in Norway to reinforce 'Swallow' (16 February 1943).

Gunther German operation against Soviet partisans operating in the area of Manily (2/7 July 1943). At this time the Germans were heavily involved in Operation 'Zitadelle' around Kursk, and were very worried about the threat to their rear-area communications posed by a severe resurgence of Soviet partisan activities, inspired to this very end by the Soviet high command in Moscow.

Gustav Linie (Gustav line) Most difficult of the German defensive lines in Italy, stretching right across the country from the Tyrrhenian coast at the mouth of the River Garigliano between Gaeta and Mondragone, and running up the line of the Garigliano and Rapido rivers past Cassino into the Apennine mountains before descending to the plain on the eastern side of the country in the region of Casoli, and then paralleling the line of the River Sangro just to its north to arrive on the Adriatic Sea between Fossacesia and San Vito. The defence of this line, which added formidably designed and constructed human elements to natural difficulties, was entrusted to Generaloberst Heinrich von Vietinghoff-Scheel's German 10th Army, which deployed General Hans Hube's XIV Panzer Corps (3 infantry and 2 Panzergrenadier divisions) on the Tyrrhenian side and General Traugott Herr's LXXVI Panzer Corps (1 airborne, 1 infantry and 2 Panzergrenadier divisions) on the Adriatic side. The former was intended to halt the 5 infantry divisions (2 British, 2

US and 1 French colonial divisions) of Lieutenant General Richard McCreery's British X and Major General John P. Lucas's US VI Corps of Lieutenant General Mark Clark's US 5th Army, and the latter had the task of checking the 5 divisions (2 British, 1 Indian, 1 Canadian and 1 New Zealand) of Lieutenant General Sir Oliver Leese's British XIII and Lieutenant General C. W. Allfrey's British V Corps of General Sir Bernard Montgomery's British 8th Army. Along the whole of the 'Gustav Linie' defences, the Germans could deploy 18 divisions (with another 3 forming) to the Allies' 13 divisions, which together with the natural and man-made strengths of their positions gave them a decided edge.

The western end of the 'Gustav Linie' defences was stronger than the eastern end, and here the Anglo-American forces were faced by immense difficulties of approach over rain-swollen rivers and the 'Barbara Linie' and 'Bernhard Linie' preliminary defence positions before they could approach the bastion represented by the Germans' positions in the mountains on each side of the River Liri and around Monte Cassino. The 5th Army attacked on 20 November 1943 and suffered appalling losses for the rest of the year before being halted some 5 miles from the 'Gustav Linie' positions to the south of the Rapido. At the other end of the line the British 8th Army was enjoying greater success, for Montgomery reinforced his right wing with two divisions pulled out of the left wing and forced the Sangro on 15 November, then closing in rapidly on the sector of the 'Gustav Linie' between Lanciano and the sea. Here the British V Corps broke through the defence line and pushed forward to take Ortona on 27 December.

The offensive continued until 15 January 1944, and by this time the sector of the 'Gustav Linie' between Casoli and the sea had been penetrated by the 2nd New Zealand Division, the 5th Division, the 1st Canadian Division and the 78th Division, with the 8th Indian Division following close behind them in the centre of this sector. On the western end of the line the ghastly Cassino battles raged until May 1944 before the Allies broke through the 'Gustav Linie' between Valvori in the mountains and Minturno on the coast against a reinforced defence now undertaken in the inland sector by General Valentin Feuerstein's LI Gebirgskorps and in the coastal sector by Generalleutnant Fridolin von Senger und Etterlin's XIV Panzer Corps. The battle began to open as the 5th Army approached the 'Gustav Linie' positions along the lower Garigliano at the beginning of 1944, though farther inland in was still held up in front of the 'Bernhard Linie' outlying positions in front of the Rapido.

The landing at Anzio was about to happen, and General the Hon. Sir Harold Alexander (commander-in-chief of the Allied 15th Army Group) ordered a full-scale offensive against the German positions on the western end of the 'Gustav Linie', confidently expecting that this pressure, in combination with that to be exerted by the US VI Corps at Anzio in January, would force Generalfeldmarschall Albert Kesselring (commander-in-chief of the German Army Group 'C') to order a withdrawal from the 'Gustav Linie' in the western sector. The Allies struggled to reach the Rapido and the 'Gustav Linie' proper, but finally the US VI Corps (now commanded by Major General Lucian K. Truscott) and supported by Général de Corps d'Armée Alphonse Juin's French Expeditionary Corps, reached the line and made it possible for Alexander's offensive to begin on 17 January with probing attacks that took the British 5th and 56th Divisions (of the British X Corps) through the outlying positions of the 'Gustav Linie' close to the coast at Minturno and Castelforte respectively.

Inland the offensive began on 20 January with Major General Geoffrey T. Keyes's US II Corps (replacement for the US VI Corps transferred out for the Anzio operation) and on 24 January with the French Expeditionary Corps. The French suffered very heavy losses but got the 2nd Moroccan and 3rd Algerian Divisions through the 'Gustav Linie', while the Americans enjoyed the mixed fortune of success with the 34th Infantry Division and failure with the 36th Infantry Division, which was repulsed with very heavy losses. The offensive ground to a halt as the Germans suffered no compulsion to withdraw after the failure of the Anzio operation, and the US II Corps was in turn replaced by Lieutenant General Sir Bernard Freyberg's New Zealand

Corps, which renewed the offensive between 15 and 18 February without appreciable success.

Alexander was well aware that his attempt to storm through the 'Gustav Linie' at Cassino had failed, and called a halt to further operations while the situation was reassessed and Allied forces were reinforced and reshuffled. Thus by the time that the offensive was renewed on 11 May the Allied disposition was (from the coast inland) the US II Corps, the French Expeditionaery Corps, the British XIII Corps under Lieutenant General S. C. Kirkman, the Polish II Corps under General W. Anders, and the British X Corps. On 11 May the Allies went over to the offensive along the 20-mile sector from the sea to a point inland of Cassino, and while the British X Corps and the Polish II Corps managed to get across the Rapido and through the 'Gustav Linie' before being contained, the US II Corps and the French Expeditionary Corps broke through the 'Gustav Linie' in more open country and pressed ahead.

The Americans were checked at San Maria Infante, but the French pushed on and looked set to cut the German lines of communication. Kesselring saw that the German position was lost and ordered a withdrawal on 17 May. On the following day the Poles finally stormed the Cassino position. With the Allied breakthrough of the 'Gustav Linie' and exploitation northwards, the US VI Corps beleaguered at Anzio could finally break out to link up with the rest of the 5th Army. There can be no doubt that the western end of the 'Gustav Linie' gave the Allies the hardest fighting of the whole Italian campaign, and the result was often in doubt because of the enormous strength of the Germans' natural and man-made positions.

Gymnast Original and much disputed Allied plan (spring 1942) for a landing in French North-West Africa as a means of getting US forces into action against Germany and Italy, and of breaking the apparent deadlock in North Africa. The plan exercised Allied planners throughout 1942, and was finally developed into Operation 'Torch'.

H

H2S British radar aid for bomber navigation, also sufficiently discriminating in the image of the ground below it to serve as a bombing aid for night bombers.

H2X US version of H2S.

HA Japanese offensive in the Arakan region of Burma (3/24 February 1944) designed to draw into the area British reserves which could then be destroyed together with the rest of Lieutenant General A. F. P. Christison's British XV Corps, the strategic objective of this limited offensive being a diversion before the implementation of Operation 'U' against Imphal and northeastern India by Lieutenant General Renya Mutaguchi's 15th Army. The spur for operation 'HA' was the December 1943 advance by XV Corps towards the end of the Mayu Peninsula with a view to further operations against the island of Akyab and its tactically important airfield.

The British advance's hesitancy had given Lieutenant General Shojiro Iida, commanding in Burma, time to move in Lieutenant General T. Hanaya's 55th Division as a supplement to the individual infantry regiments holding the area. By the beginning of February 1944 XV Corps had advanced Major General H. R. Briggs's 5th Indian Division from Bawli Bazar to Waybin with brigades disposed forward as far as Maungdaw, which was taken on 9 January, Major General F. W. Messervy's 7th Indian Division from Goppe Bazar and Taung Bazar to Awlanbyin with brigades as far forward as Buthidaung, and Major General C. G. Woolner's 81st West African Division to the east in the Kaladan valley as a flank guard. The 5th and 7th Indian Divisions were linked laterally only by a track running from Waybin to Kwazon over the Ngakyedauk pass and Ngakyedauk valley.

Hanaya's plan was simple, and relied on the particular military virtues of his Japanese soldiers, who were used to operating at a numerical disadvantage and with poor communications in difficult terrain: while the Doi Column pinned the 5th and 7th Indian Divisions with frontal attacks, the Tanahashi and Kubo Forces of the Sakurai Column would depart from an assembly area at Dabrugyaung behind the Japanese right flank to penetrate 'impassable' country between the 7th Indian Division and the outflung 81st West African Division, to reach Taung Bazar behind the left flank of the pinned Indian forces and then fall on their rear. The Sakurai Column departed on 3 February as the Doi Column launched its pinning effort, and reached Taung Bazar on 4 February, thereby cutting the 7th Indian Division's line of communication with Goppe Bazar. At Taung Bazar the Sakurai Column divided, the Tanahashi Force sweeping south-west in a pincer movement against the 'Admin Box' at Sinzweya on the track between the two Indian divisions, and the Kubo Force moving west to cut the 5th Indian Division's line of communication by taking Chota Maughnama on the road to Bawli Bazar.

By 6 February the 'Admin Box' was under siege and Chota Maughnama had been taken. The situation of XV Corps looked precarious, but Lieutenant General W. J. Slim, commanding the British 14th Army, refused to countenance a retreat, and he

73

ordered the encircled forces of the 5th and 7th Indian Divisions to stand and fight with supplies brought in by air. The fighting was bitter in the extreme (as it was so often in the Burma campaign), but the aerial supply system worked well and the two divisions were able to fight their way to contact with each other on 24 February before in turn cutting off part of the Japanese 55th Division. In March XV Corps turned the tables on Operation 'HA' and finally began an effective advance towards Akyab, only to be halted in April by the need to detach forces for the reinforcement of the garrison at Imphal.

Habakkuk British scheme to make vast 'aircraft-carriers' out of an ice/wood shavings 'cement' for stationing in the mid-Atlantic as part of the campaign against German U-boat attacks on convoys in this region that could not be covered by land-based patrol aircraft. The advent of the escort carrier in 1942, and its availability in large numbers from 1943, made the plan superfluous.

Habicht (hawk) Alternative designation of Operation 'Falke', a supplementary envelopment operation planned for Army Group 'South' in the area east of Kharkov, but then absorbed into Operation 'Zitadelle' proper (July 1943).

Haddock British bomber force based in southern France for bombing operations against Italy (June 1940).

Haft Airborne reconnaissance operation by the 1st SAS near Mayenne in France (7 July 1944).

Hagen Linie (Hagen line) German defence line west of Orel, running from Sevsk to Zhidra via Bryansk (summer 1943). This line was schemed by Generalfeldmarschall Günther von Kluge's Army Group 'Centre' as a fall-back position at the base of the German salient round Orel for the 9th Army and the 2nd Panzerarmee in the event that they were driven back by the forces of the Soviet West, Bryansk and Central Fronts. The failure of Operation 'Zitadelle' confirmed the utility of the line as a short-term refuge for the 2nd Panzerarmee and 9th Army (18 July 1943) as they fell back before the Soviet counteroffensive after 'Zitadelle', despite the fact that von Kluge had anticipated a more orderly fallback some two to three months later as a means of shortening his line and so freeing forces for operations in other sectors of the Eastern Front. However, pressured by the Germans' defeat in Operation 'Zitadelle' and by the Allied landings in Sicily (Operation 'Husky') followed by the fall of Mussolini and the defection of Italy from the Axis cause, Hitler ordered a rapid retreat to the 'Hagen Linie' positions even before they were complete, and the Soviet summer offensive of 1943, launched in this sector on 18 August, swept through the 'Hagen Linie' defences and the 9th Army without difficulty.

Haggard Airborne operations by B Squadron, 1st SAS, to cut German rail communications in the area of the Forêt d'Ivoy (10 and 14 August 1944).

Haifisch (shark) Alternative codename for 'Barbarossa'.

Haifisch I (shark I) Simulated preparations for a German invasion of the UK from northern France (1941), designed to conceal the departure of substantial German forces in preparation for Operation 'Barbarossa'.

Haifisch II (shark II) Variation on 'Haifisch I' devised by Generalfeldmarschall Erwin von Witzleben, the German Oberbefelhshaber 'West'.

Hailstone US naval airstrike against Truk Island in the Carolines (17/18 February 1944). The operation was undertaken as a companion to Operation 'Catchpole', the seizure of Eniwetok in the Marshall Islands, as it was expected that the assault on this strategic atoll would prompt an air assault by aircraft based around Rabaul in New Britain and Kavieng in New Ireland, and a combined naval and air assault from the Imperial Japanese Navy's main Central Pacific base at Truk (in fact relegated to a secondary position on 10 February). To counter the latter, Vice Admiral Raymond Spruance and his 5th Fleet moved in for a devastating two-day assault with 5 fleet and 4 small aircraft-carriers, 6 battleships, 10 cruisers and 28 destroyers. Spruance's naval air strength was Task Force 58 commanded by Vice Admiral Marc A. Mitscher, who divided TF58 into three task groups (TG58.1 with the fleet carriers *Enterprise* and *Yorktown*, TG58.2 with the fleet carriers *Essex* and *Intrepid* and the light carrier *Cabot*, and TG58.3 with the fleet carrier *Bunker Hill* and the light carriers *Cowpens* and *Monterey*).

With the decision to adopt Palau at the western end of the Carolines as the Combined Fleet's primary base on 10 February most of Japan's major warships had left Truk, but the huge atoll still contained some 50 merchantmen protected by 3 light cruisers and 8 destroyers, plus some 350 land-based aircraft. In the two days of the onslaught, Mitscher launched some 1,250 sorties by his aircraft, and these scored a quite phenomenal success, destroying on the ground some 220 aircraft and another 30 in the air (for the loss of 35 of their own), and securing a ship tally (in conjunction with the gunfire of Spruance's battleships, which circled the atoll and poured in a devastating fire) of 3 light cruisers, 4 destroyers, 7 fleet auxiliaries, 6 tankers and 17 merchantmen. Apart from the aircraft, the 5th Fleet's only damage was one air-launched torpedo strike on the *Intrepid*, which suffered but little damage. Mitscher's aircraft-carriers paid a return visit to Truk in April and completed the devastation of this huge base. So far as the Imperial Japanese Navy was concerned, a longer-term effect of Operation 'Hailstone' was the politically-motivated sacking of Admiral Osami Nagano, the navy chief-of-staff, in favour of the pliant Admiral Shigetano Shimada.

Halberd British storeship convoy from Gibraltar to Malta (24/28 September 1941). The plan was to emulate Operation 'Substance' in July 1941 and run nine fast merchantmen into Malta with supplies and troops (some of the latter being accommodated on the convoy's close escort) under the cover of Vice Admiral Sir James Somerville's Force H, consisting of the battleships *Nelson*, *Rodney* and *Prince of Wales*, the aircraft-carrier *Ark Royal*, 5 cruisers and 18 destroyers. To facilitate the passage of the convoy, Admiral Sir Andrew Cunningham's Mediterranean Fleet was to make a demonstration at the other end of the Mediterranean, and under cover of these distractions three empty merchantmen were to return from Malta to Gibraltar. All went without hindrance until 27 September, when the first air attacks on the convoy were attempted but driven off by the *Ark Royal*'s aircraft after the *Nelson* had been hit and damaged. Destroyer gunfire also played a great part in deterring the attackers. Reconnaissance aircraft now informed Somerville that the Italian fleet was at sea, and Somerville remained with his damaged *Nelson* and the *Ark Royal* while sending forward Rear Admiral A. T. B. Curteis with the other two capital ships, two cruisers and some destroyers. The Italian fleet then turned for home, and the convoy pushed through a barrage of air attacks (which sank one merchantman) to reach Malta on 28 September.

HALPRO US scheme devised in 1942 for a force of Consolidated B-24 bombers under Colonel Harry A. Halverson to operate against Japanese targets from advanced bases in China. The force was en route to India when it was diverted in Egypt to undertake the first US raid against the Ploesti oil installations in Romania, this first US strategic raid being flown by 13 aircraft on 11/12 June 1942. Other missions against Mediterranean targets then followed, and it was only a depleted force that finally reached India and the 10th Air Force.

Halyard Airborne operation by the Office of Strategic Services to rescue US aircrew held near Prajane in Yugoslavia (2 August 1944).

Hamburg German operation against Soviet partisans operating in the region of Slonim near Baranovichi to the south-west of Minsk (December 1941). The activities of the partisans were as yet relatively small in scale compared with their vigour and impact in the following years, but even at this time the Germans were acutely conscious of the threat thus posed to their extended lines of communication across the western USSR at the time of severe winter conditions and the unfolding of the Germans' desperate effort to reduce Moscow before the arrival from Siberia of fresh troops highly experienced in and equipped for the conduct of winter operations.

Hammer British plan to take Trondheim by frontal assault (16/19 April 1940), the city having fallen to the German 138.Gebirgsjäger Regiment of the German 2nd Mountain Division, which had been delivered to Trondheim (rightly assessed by the Germans as 'the pivot of all [Norwegian] operations') by the ships of Gruppe II (the heavy cruiser *Admiral Hipper* and four destroyers on 9 April. In the surrounding areas the Norwegian 5th Division was managing to check the German advances to the north, east and west, but it was appreciated by the Allied high command that the arrival of men from Generaloberst Nikolaus von Falkenhorst's XXI Gebirgskorps (163rd and 196th Divisions) up the Osterdal and Gudbransdal valleys from Oslo would undo the defence. Thus an Allied grip on central Norway could only be ensured by the delivery of fresh troops for the recapture of Trondheim, which would cut off the 2nd Mountain Division from seaborne reinforcement. Operation 'Hammer' was clearly dependent on the ability of the Royal Navy to escort the necessary troopships, and when this was seen to be too risky against the threat of German bombers of the Luftwaffe's X Fliegerkorps operating from captured bases, Admiral Sir Charles Forbes undertook to examine the possibility that units of his Home Fleet could carry the troops. In the event time to organize the expedition was not available, and it was thus cancelled in favour of the less ambitious Operations 'Maurice' and 'Sickle'.

Handcuff British plan to seize the islands of Rhodes and Scarpanto as part of Operation 'Accolade'. Such schemes had been entertained since as early as May 1943, and on several occasions the men and requisite shipping had begun to assemble. However, by the beginning of August 1943 the tactical scenario for the seizure of Rhodes had altered considerably from the originally-envisaged combined assault with major forces, for the possibility of an armistice with Italy meant that Allied forces might be able to take over this Italian island against negligible resistance.

In overall control of the scheme was General Sir Henry Maitland Wilson's Middle East Land Forces, which would require support (especially in long-range fighters and landing craft) from General Dwight D. Eisenhower's Allied Forces in North Africa. These reinforcements were not forthcoming, and then the 8th Indian Division allocated to the possible landing was transferred to the Italian campaign, so removing the only amphibiously trained formation available to the Middle East Land Forces. Thus Operation 'Handcuff' lapsed, giving the Germans an ideal opportunity to recoup their gains in Rhodes at the time of the Italian armistice. So by 11 September 1943 the 7,000 Germans on Rhodes had seized control of this strategically sited island from the far larger Italian garrison. This was the spur that decided the Allies instead to seize Leros, Kos and several smaller islands off Turkey's Aegean coast between Casteloriso in the south and Samos in the north, an operation that went ahead with the express approval of Prime Minister Winston Churchill between 10 and 17 September 1943.

It was clear, however, that Rhodes was the key to this chain of islands off the south-west coast of Turkey, and that until the German garrison had been overwhelmed and the island brought into the Allied camp, any effective use of their Aegean forces by the Allies was impossible. Plans were thus resumed for a combined operation against the island in October, but the whole scheme was thrown into disarray by the strength and vehemence of the Germans' counterstroke against the Aegean garrisons, which were overwhelmed after a fast build-up of German air strength in Rhodes, Crete and Greece, allowing the German land and airborne forces to retake the islands without undue difficulty. Kos fell to amphibious and airborne landings on 3/4 October, Leros fell to amphibious and airborne landings on 12/16 November, Samos was evacuated on 19/20 November, and Casteloriso also was evacuated on 28 November. It was now decided that as Rhodes was the key to the Aegean situation, its capture in 1944 could be decisive in the conduct of the Balkan campaign and also draw a wavering Turkey into the war on the Allied side. However, the need for all available landing craft at Anzio and later amphibious operations in Italy, northern and southern France, etc. meant that the Middle East Land Forces could not plan effectively and the scheme was finally abandoned.

Hands Up Allied plan for a break-out from the Normandy beach-head after Operation 'Overlord' with the aid of a combined airborne and amphibious assault on the German forces in Quiberon Bay. This area was held only by the refitting 275th Infantry Division of Generaloberst Friedrich Dollmann's German 7th Army, so the chances of effecting a successful lodgement were thought high, with the possibility of an advance to the Loire valley and an eastward advance towards Orléans to encircle the 7th Army unless it shifted forces south from Normandy and Brittany, which would in turn ease the break-out problems of Field Marshal Sir Bernard Montgomery's Allied 21st Army Group.

Hanna German codename to be used to indicate any Allied landing in Denmark.

Hannibal German seizure of the island of Lemnos in the northern Aegean (September 1943) from its Italian garrison after the Allied armistice with Italy.

Hannover I Offensive by Generalfeldmarschall Günther von Kluge's Army Group 'Centre' on the Eastern Front (June/July 1942) to eliminate Soviet positions near Vyazma. Here a relatively small-scale offensive by the 4th Army and the 4th Panzerarmee eliminated the salient that had been pushed into the German line by the southern flank of the Soviet winter offensive of 1941/1942 round Moscow. In the period 18/24 January 1942 Soviet airborne forces had been landed to the rear of the German 4th Army to link up with the partisans holding two large pockets that were seriously affecting the supply position of Army Group 'Centre', and the Soviets sought to link up with the combined airborne and partisan force with an offensive by General Georgi Zhukov's West Front. The forces had not fully joined up by the time the Soviet offensive ended in April 1942, leaving the Germans with the task of tidying up this sector of the Eastern Front. In Operation 'Hannover I', therefore, the 4th Army and the 4th Panzerarmee (the latter due for movement to the south for Operation 'Blau') co-operated in the crushing of the Soviet 33rd Army, the Soviet I Cavalry Corps and the various pockets of Soviet airborne troops, taking some 20,000 prisoners and improving the German line very considerably.

Hannover II Companion offensive by Generalfeldmarschall Günther von Kluge's Army Group 'Centre' to eliminate the Soviet pocket between Byelyi and Sychevka to the west of Moscow. This pocket had been created during the Soviet winter offensive of 1941/1942 as the forces of Lieutenant General I. S. Konev's Kalinin Front swept south-west from Kalinin and the Volga Reservoir (to the north of Moscow) with the object of linking up with the forces of General Georgi Zhukov's West Front near Vyazma in the rear of the German forces seeking to capture Moscow. In the event the link-up was prevented by the determined counterattacks of Generaloberst Erich Hoepner's 4th Panzergruppe (later the 4th Panzerarmee), though the end of the Soviet offensive in April 1942 left the German 9th Army dangerously exposed near Rzhev as the Soviet 4th Shock, 22nd and 39th Armies were disposed to its rear in a large salient stretching towards Vitebsk. By 2 July this salient had been eliminated as a base for the Soviet 39th Army and XXII Cavalry Corps, yielding 50,000 prisoners and shortening the German defence line north of Moscow by a useful 130 miles.

Hansa Overall designation of the German mercantile shipbuilding programme in World War II.

Hardgate Sicilian offensive from the River Dittaino to Aderno (23 July/7 August 1943) by Lieutenant General Sir Oliver Leese's British XXX Corps of General Sir Bernard Montgomery's British 8th Army. This area, to the south-west of Mount Etna, was the key to Messina and the north-eastern tip of Sicily, and was strongly defended by the Gruppe

Schmalz of the 'Hermann Goering' Panzer Division (under the overall command of General Alfredo Guzzoni's Italian 6th Army though tactical command was exercised by Generalleutnant Hans Hube, commander of the German XIV Panzer Corps that was bolstering the Italian defence of the island). The town of Aderno fell on 7 August, opening the way for XXX Corps to advance north-east towards Messina, only after a triple advance by Major General G. G. Simonds's 1st Canadian Division in the west from Agira down the River Salso, by Major General V. Evelegh's 78th Division in the centre from Catenanueva via Centuripe to Aderno, and by Major General D. N. Wimberley's 51st (Highland) Division in the east from the Dittaino downstream of Catenanueva to Biancavilla just to the south-east of Aderno.

Hardihood British plan to aid Turkey should that country enter the war on the side of the Allies (late 1943). This type of scheme had been envisaged as early as 1940, but Turkey had cleverly stayed neutral and received aid from both sides, and by 1943 the Allies were providing aircraft, tanks and anti-tank guns, while the entry of Turkey into the war would have been supported by the arrival in southern Turkey from Syria of 4 infantry divisions and some 18 RAF squadrons. And if the capture of the Dodecanese and other islands in the Aegean could be ensured, further forces could be delivered into Turkey through the port of Izmir. The definitive plan for Operation 'Hardihood' presupposed a Turkish declaration of war on Germany, which would be followed by a four-phase receipt of Allied reinforcements consisting of (first phase) 3 anti-tank regiments and 25 RAF squadrons (mostly fighters) with AA defences, (second phase) 25 more RAF squadrons with AA defences, (third phase) 2 more anti-tank regiments, plus additional AA defences in the form of 2 heavy and 2 light AA regiments, and (fourth phase) 2 armoured divisions.

Hardy Airborne raid by the 2nd SAS to establish a base near Mazignen in France (27 July 1944) for the harrying of those German rail and road communications over which reinforcements could be moved to the Normandy front after the break-out from the 'Overlord' beach-head.

Harlequin A component of the overall 'Cockade' plan designed to provide diversionary action against the German forces in France during 1943. Operation 'Harlequin' was planned as an amphibious training exercise in the English Channel with a feint across the Channel towards the German defences in the Pas-de-Calais. The operation was eventually called off for lack of adequate landing craft.

Harpoon British convoy to ferry in supplies to Malta (5/15 June 1942). The operation was schemed in conjunction with Operation 'Vigorous', the latter being designed to send in 11 ships from the east at the same time that Operation 'Harpoon' delivered 6 ships from the west. The 'Harpoon' convoy sailed from the UK on 5 June with an escort of units from the Home Fleet, and passed through the Straits of Gibraltar on the night of 11/12 June. Though the basic tactical plan was a copy of that which had sent into Malta three successful convoys in 1941 (Operations 'Excess', 'Substance' and 'Halberd'), modifications had to be made for the fact that a large portion of Vice Admiral Sir James Somerville's Force H was absent from Gibraltar for the combined assault on Diego Suarez at the northern tip of Madagascar in the Indian Ocean. Thus Rear Admiral A. T. B. Curteis, in command of the whole operation, had forces from a number of stations, including the battleship *Malaya*, the aircraft-carriers *Eagle* and *Argus*, the cruisers *Kenya*, *Liverpool* and *Charybdis*, and 8 destroyers. The six merchantmen carried some 43,000 tons of cargo, and were to be escorted by Curteis's forces as far east as the Sicilian Narrows, from where they were to dash through to Malta with a close escort under Acting Captain C. C. Hardy and comprising the anti-aircraft cruiser *Cairo*, 9 destroyers and 4 fleet minesweepers. Ahead of the convoy proper, the fast minelayer *Welshman* was to make a run for Malta with ammunition and other special stores.

The convoy was well into the Mediterranean by 14 June, when air attacks began on a force which could not adequately provide its own air defence as the two elderly and thus slow carriers were unable to leave their escorting destroyers and were therefore hampered by a wind from dead astern. One merchantman was sunk, and the *Liverpool* was hit in the engine room and had to detach for Gibraltar, where she arrived on 17 June after being towed most of the way by the destroyer *Antelope*. Heavy but unsuccessful air attacks continued until the convoy reached the Sicilian Narrows in the evening of 14 June and the main escort turned back for Gibraltar. Bereft of proper cruiser escort (unlike the situation in the three 1941 convoys), the 'Halberd' convoy was now to undergo severe tribulations near Pantelleria as a force of 2 Italian light cruisers escorted by 5 destroyers came into the attack. The fleet destroyers of the close escort moved off to intercept the Italian force, but soon suffered the incapacitation of the *Bedouin* and *Partridge*. The *Cairo* and smaller destroyers covered the convoy with smoke and then set off to aid the fleet destroyers, so leaving the convoy entirely unprotected against a severe air attack, which sank one merchantman and crippled a tanker. The Italian surface force then broke off its action with the *Cairo* and her destroyers and moved off to intercept the merchantmen just as another air attack developed. This disabled another merchantman, and the convoy's commodore decided to sink the two crippled ships while the survivors made for Malta at top speed.

Convoy and escort reunited in the afternoon of 15 June and pushed on for Malta, leaving the two crippled destroyers (the *Bedouin* was sunk by the returning Italians while the *Partridge* made it back to Gibraltar). The final approach to Malta was made under heavy air attack, and then the convoy sailed into a minefield, where one merchantman, one minesweeper and three destroyers were damaged, one of the destroyers subsequently sinking. In overall terms the convoy was not a great success, for only 2 of the 6 merchantmen got through, and casualties among the warships amounted to 2 destroyers sunk as well as 1 cruiser, 3 destroyers and 1 minesweeper severely damaged.

Harpune (harpoon) Overall designation of German moves planned for implementation if the Allies should launch an invasion of Norway which, Hitler believed throughout the war, was a primary British target. Prime Minister Winston Churchill would indeed have liked to launch an invasion of this country but, unlike the German leader, was persuaded of the military difficulties of such a project.

Harrod Airborne operations by the French 2ème Regiment des Chasseurs Parachutistes to harass German forces as they retreated near St Gentouse (12 and 27 August 1944).

Hartmut German U-boat operation to screen the surface forces involved in Operation 'Weserübung' from attack by Allied surface units.

Hasenjagd (hare chase) German operation against Soviet partisans operating in the region of Dobruzh near Gomel (6/15 February 1943). This was yet another area in which Soviet partisans based in the impenetrable Pripet Marshes could sally force to strike at important German rear-area installations and communications, producing results out of all proportion to the numbers of men involved.

Hasty (i) US paratroop drop by elements of the 82nd Airborne Division at Trasacco, east of Rome (1 June 1944) to facilitate the approach of Lieutenant General Mark Clark's US 5th Army to the Italian capital, Rome.
(ii) Airborne raid by the 6th Parachute Battalion on Torricelli (1 June 1944).

Hats Operation (30 August/5 September 1940) by the British to reinforce Admiral Sir Andrew Cunningham's Mediterranean Fleet at its base in Alexandria at the eastern end of the Mediterranean, shortly after the entry of Italy into the war on the side of Germany. The ships to be passed through the whole length of the Mediterranean were the battleship *Valiant*, the aircraft-carrier *Illustrious*, the anti-aircraft cruisers *Calcutta* and *Coventry*, and supporting light forces. These forces reached Gibraltar on 29 August and departed on the following day under escort from units of Vice Admiral Sir James Somerville's Force H, which also convoyed vessels taking additional men and armament into the island of Malta. The whole exercise passed without interference by Italian forces.

Haycock Designation of air-mail flights undertaken by de Havilland Mosquitoes from the UK to Yalta and Egypt during the 'Argonaut' Conference (31 January/20 February 1945).

Harry Designation of the Allied air support operation for the crossing of the River Cosina in northern Italy (21/24 November 1944).

Headache British codename for the German 'Knickebein' radio blind-bombing system.

Hedgehog British anti-submarine weapon, a device throwing 24 bombs in an elliptical pattern ahead of the launcher vessel onto a U-boat still held in the ship's sonar.

Heinrich German jamming system against the British 'Gee' navigation aid.

Hela Plan for a maritime evacuation of the German forces in the Kurland beach-head in Latvia (autumn 1944/spring 1945). This plan was expressly vetoed by Hitler, though some units were surreptitiously removed by sea. The Kurland pocket was formed on 10 October 1944 when the forces of General I. Kh. Bagramyan's 1st Baltic Front reached the Baltic Sea just north of Liepaja, cutting off a sizeable portion (24 infantry and 2 Panzer divisions of the 16th and 18th Armies) of Generaloberst Ferdinand Schörner's Army Group 'North' in an area bounded by Tukums on the western shore of the Gulf of Riga and Liepaja on the Baltic. The carrying out of this magnificent movement by the 1st Baltic Front was a classic of logistics and deception, for under the cover of overt preparations for an assault on Riga, the Latvian capital on the right flank of Bagramyan's front. The Soviet commander in a mere six days moved 3 rifle armies, 1 tank army and a number of independent corps (500,000 men and 1,300 armoured vehicles) 100 miles from his right to his left flank. Hitler steadfastly refused to permit an evacuation of the beach-head, which held out until the end of the war, on the grounds that its continued existence would tie down significant Soviet forces, improve Germany's political standing with the Baltic countries with which Germany 'traded', and safeguard the U-boat training area off Danzig. On 25 January 1945 Army Group 'North', now commanded by Generaloberst Dr Lothar Rendulic, was renamed Army Group 'Kurland', but posed no real threat to the Soviets.

Hellhound Allied plan for the total destruction of Hitler's retreat at Berchtesgaden in the Alps by concentrated attacks from heavy bombers (spring 1945).

Henry British operation (13 April 1940) in which some 350 Royal Marines and seamen were landed from two cruisers at Namsos in central Norway in preparation for the delivery of Allied forces for the recapture of Trondheim. This later became Operation 'Maurice'.

Herbstgewitter (autumn storm) German operation against Yugoslav partisans operating in Bosnia (1944) and threatening the already precarious overland communications between the German forces in the Balkans and those in Yugoslavia (both elements comprising the command known as the German Forces in the South-East, headed by Generalfeldmarschall Maximilian von Weichs from his headquarters at Thessaloniki in northern Greece). In August 1944 this command was divided into Generaloberst Alexander Löhr's Army Group 'E' in Greece and Weichs' Army Group 'F' in Yugoslavia.

Herbstlauf (autumn leaf) Operation by Generaloberst Hermann Hoth's 4th Panzerarmee against the Soviet forces around Kransoarmeysk on the junction of the Don-Volga Canal with the River Volga to the south-east of Stalingrad (September 1942). This was a vital point in the Soviets' southern defence perimeter round Stalingrad, where forces that had gathered on the left bank of the Volga could cross to the west bank for the build-up of General A. I. Eremenko's Stalingrad Front that was in November 1942 to launch the southern half of the great pincer movement to trap the 6th Army and part of the 4th Panzerarmee in Stalingrad.

Herbstnebel (autumn mist) **(i)** Germany's last major offensive of the war against the Western Allies, otherwise known as the 'Battle of the Bulge' (15 December 1944/7 February 1945). The strategic situation for this last throw by Hitler was the Allied position at the beginning of December 1944, before the great Belgian port of Antwerp (captured on 4 September but not at first usable as the Germans had mined the estuary of the River Scheldt very heavily and still occupied positions on islands to the north of it until the end of November) could begin to resupply and refuel the Allied armies that were operating over vastly extended lines of communication to English Channel ports in northern France. By mid-December the Allies had halted their breakneck drive from the Normandy break-out, and were embarking on a period of relative inactivity as they prepared for the next major steps, namely the penetration of the 'Siegfried Linie' positions and the crossing of the River Rhine into the heartland of Germany. Hitler therefore planned to smash through the Allied front in the Ardennes (held only by Major General Troy H. Middleton's US VIII Corps of Lieutenant General Courtney H. Hodges' US 1st Army) and then drive north-west to take Antwerp once again, together with its vast stockpiles of Allied supplies, before taking on and destroying piecemeal the Allied forces in the north.

Detailed planning of the offensive was entrusted to Generalfeldmarschall Walter Model's Army Group 'B', and the major forces allocated to the drive were in effect the last of Germany's reserves, namely 10 Panzer and 14 infantry divisions that formed the strength of SS Oberstgruppenführer Sepp Dietrich's 6th SS Panzerarmee in the north, General Hasso von Manteuffel's 5th Panzerarmee in the centre, and General Erich Brandenburger's 7th Army in the south. The 7th Army (LXXX Corps with 2 Volksgrenadier divisions, and LXXXV Corps with 1 Volksgrenadier and 1 infantry division) was the southern flank guard against the attention of Lieutenant General George S. Patton's US 3rd Army, and was intended to hold a line between Luxembourg and Givet while the two Panzerarmees undertook the main drive in the direction of Antwerp. On the left of this offensive the 5th Panzerarmee had the XLVII Panzer Corps (1 Volksgrenadier and 2 Panzer divisions), the LVIII Panzer Corps (1 Panzer and 1 Volksgrenadier division) and the LXVI Panzer Corps (2 Volksgrenadier divisions). On the right of the main offensive the 6th SS Panzerarmee had the II SS Panzer Corps (2 Panzer divisions), the I SS Panzer Corps (2 Panzer, 1 airborne and 2 Volksgrenadier divisions) and the LXVII Corps (2 Volksgrenadier divisions). The task of the 5th Panzerarmee was to break out between Namur and Liège and then head for Antwerp, while that of the 6th SS Panzerarmee was to erupt between Liège and Aachen before making for Antwerp. All Germany's supplies of fuel and advanced weapons were used for the offensive, which was timed for poor weather so that the inability of the Luftwaffe to provide effective cover would not be important as the Allied aircraft would also be grounded.

The German offensive began on 16 December under the cover of low cloud and poor weather, and fell on a totally unprepared US VIII Corps together with two divisions of the US V Corps. Allied intelligence had for the most part discounted any German ability to launch an offensive, especially through the Ardennes region. The only readily available reinforcements for the US 1st Army were the 82nd and 101st Airborne Divisions of Major General Matthew B. Ridgway's US XVIII Airborne Corps, which was resting near Reims. These were rushed up to the front as the US 9th and 3rd Armies (to the south and north of the salient being formed by the German offensive) were ordered to ready their 7th and 10th Armored Divisions to hold the shoulders of the salient as further reinforcements (2nd Armored, 87th Infantry and 17th Airborne Divisions) were brought into the area. In the meantime a mere six US divisions had to check the German thrust, which they did by slowing the progress of the 6th SS Panzerarmee in front of St Vith and by holding Bastogne against the efforts of the 5th Panzerarmee.

81

By 20 December Allied efforts were beginning to take effect, and by 24 December the German offensive had been halted, with the 2nd Panzer Division just short of Dinant which was held by the British XXX Corps. With the forces north of the salient now commanded by Field Marshal Viscount Montgomery's British 21st Army Group and those south of it by Patton's 3rd Army, the Allies then began to squeeze the salient closed with the combined efforts of eight corps, one of the highlights being the relief of the US 101st Airborne Division at Bastogne by the 4th Armored Division. The Luftwaffe gambled all on a massive raid by 800 aircraft against Allied airfields on 1 January 1945, but this German stroke was devastated by the weather, the defences and the sheer inexperience of many aircrew. By 7 February the German ground forces (or what was left of them) were back where they had started, with nothing to show for their efforts except a six-week delay in the Allied advance into Germany.

(ii) German withdrawal from the line of the River Po in northern Italy, a move ordered by Generaloberst Heinrich von Vietinghoff-Scheel for the 10th and 14th Armies of his Army Group 'C', despite the express instructions of Hitler that the army group (with the dubious support of the Army of Liguria provided by Fascist Italy) should fight and if necessary die on the line of the Po. Von Vietinghoff issued his retreat order on 23 April 1943, and this did much to save the army group from complete destruction by the Allied 15th Army Group.

Herbstreise (autumn journey) Planned feint by units of the German navy during the implementation of Operation 'Seelöwe', the object being to draw away from the English Channel British naval forces stationed at Dover and Harwich.

Herbstzeitlose (autumn crocus) Plan for Generaloberst Friedrich Paulus's German 6th Army to extend its left flank northwards towards Saratov between the Rivers Don and Volga (September/October 1942).

Hercules British plan for the capture of Rhodes (March 1944) as proposed to Turkey as an inducement for that country's entry into the war after the breaking of German strength in the Aegean basin. It was planned that two divisions from the forces of Middle East Command should be used for the operation. The plan was cancelled in February 1944, just one month before its implementation, as a result of Turkish reluctance to furnish the Allies with any kind of assistance such as the provision of airfield facilities in Turkey.

Herkules (Hercules) German plan for the capture of the islands of Malta and Gozo with airborne forces operating from Sicily (June 1942). Operation 'Herkules' was schemed by General Kurt Student's XI Fliegerkorps, which planned a major operation using more than 1,100 aircraft to transport and support an assault force consisting of Generalmajor Richard Heidrich's 1st Parachute Division reinforced with the 4th and 5th Parachute Regiments and supported by two Italian formations, the airborne Folgore Division and the airlanding La Spezia Division. The plan was cancelled at the end of July 1942 by Hitler, who had unfortunate memories of the casualties suffered by the Luftwaffe (both aircraft and airborne forces) in the execution of Operation 'Merkur', on the urging of Generalfeldmarschall Erwin Rommel, who insisted that the material and manpower resources for Operation 'Herkules' would be better deployed in support of his offensive towards Egypt and the Suez Canal, which had reached a critical point offering the chances of major strategic success. Hitler was right about the level of casualties that might be expected, but the Axis here lost an excellent opportunity to remove the Mediterranean bastion that had played so important a part in strangling the sea communications from Italy to North Africa upon which the very existence of Rommel's forces depended.

Hermann German operation against Soviet partisans operating in the forest of Naliboka (15 July/15 August 1943).

Herring Allied drop of specially trained Italian partisan forces, numbering some 250 men in all, behind the German lines in the valley of the River Po in northern Italy (March/April 1945). The object of this exercise was to disrupt the lines of communication to Generaloberst Heinrich von Vietinghoff-Scheel's Army Group 'C' as the Allies swept forward in the final stages of the Italian campaign.

Heu Aktion (hay action) German plan to impress large numbers of Ukrainian youths for training as skilled labourers in the German war industries (1942/1943).

H.G. Designation of ocean homeward convoys (together with a numerical suffix) plying from Gibraltar to the UK, and inaugurated in September 1939. These convoys ended in September 1942, homeward bound ships from Gibraltar being included in M.K. convoys.

Highball Designation of a spherical 'bouncing' bomb designed by Dr Barnes Wallis of Vickers along the lines of his 'dambuster' bomb, but in this instance intended for carriage by de Havilland Mosquito light bombers for anti-shipping strikes.

Himmelbett (four-poster bed) Designation of the original German night-fighter network and tactics, in which each target (a British night bomber) needed two radars (one to track the bomber and the other to track the night-fighter, with a ground controller vectoring in the fighter until its own short-range radar picked up the target bomber). A chain of such stations ran round the perimeter of Germany from the North Sea to the Swiss frontier.

Himmler German cover operation to provide a pretext for the invasion of Poland (31 August 1939). The operation was masterminded by Reinhard Heydrich, head of the Sicherheitsdienst, and involved a fake attack on the German radio station at Gleiwitz near the German-Polish frontier. The original plan was for condemned concentration camp inmates to be dressed in Polish uniforms and then left dead (as a result of German 'gun shot wounds' but in fact killed with lethal injections) as proof that the Poles had attacked a target in Germany. The plan was later revised to improve its verisimilitude, the attack being made by SS men in Polish uniform and the dead concentration camp victims being left in German uniform as 'proof' of the Poles' murderous intentions.

Hires Fully developed version of Operation 'Brimstone'.

H.N. Designation of North Sea convoys (together with a numerical suffix) plying between Bergen and Methil, inaugurated on 7 November 1939 and ended on 9 April 1940.

Hobgoblin Allied name for the Italian island of Pantellaria.

Holly Allied codename for Canton Island in the Phoenix group east-southeast of the Gilbert Islands in the Central Pacific. The island was a major staging post in the US maritime lines of communication across the Pacific from the USA to Australia and New Zealand, providing the US, Australian and New Zealand forces of General Douglas MacArthur's South-West Pacific Area and Vice Admiral William F. Halsey's South Pacific Area with most of the *matériel* and supplies they needed for the prosecution of the Allied campaign against the forces allocated to the 17th and 18th Armies of the Japanese 8th Area Army for operations in the Solomons and New Guinea together with their associated but smaller island groups.

Hooker Amphibious landing at Pizzo (on the 'instep' of the Italian 'foot') by British 231st Brigade Group (8/9 September 1943). This landing was designed to speed the advance of Major General Buckhall's British 5th Division by securing beach-heads at Pizzo and Porto San Venere and by cutting the German line of retreat along Highway 18 in northern Calabria. The 231st Brigade Group had to fight a small but bloody engagement with part of the 26th Panzer Division and Gruppe Krüger, being greatly helped by fighter-bomber attacks provided by the Desert Air Force. After linking up with the 5th Division, the 231st Brigade Group led the British advance along the north coast of Calabria, which met no effective resistance after this time.

Horlicks Capture of Biak Island off the north-western coast of New Guinea (27 May/30 August 1944) by Major General H. H. Fuller's US 41st Infantry Division of Lieutenant General Robert L. Eichelberger's US I Corps of General Douglas MacArthur's South-West Pacific Area command. The battle was a particularly vicious one, costing the Americans 524 dead and the Japanese 5,093 dead. Interestingly enough, the loss of Biak was the first dent made in the perimeter fixed in autumn 1943 by General Hideki Tojo, the Japanese prime minister and minister of war, as being Japan's defence line 'with no thought of withdrawal' and running from Timor to the Marianas Islands via north-west New Guinea, Biak Island and the Palau Islands. Thus Admiral Soemu Toyoda detached from Vice Admiral Jisaburo Ozawa's 1st Mobile Fleet an Attack Division (principally the super-battleships *Musashi* and *Yamato* under Vice Admiral Matome Ugaki) to destroy MacArthur's right flank on the sea. The Attack Division was scarcely more than half way to its starting point in the Moluccas Islands when it was recalled for the Battle of the Philippine Sea.

Hornung German operation against Soviet partisans operating in the region of the Pripet Marshes (8/26 February 1943). These partisan forces were provided with leadership and supplies flown in or paradropped by Soviet aircraft based in safe areas, and their bases in the marshes were adequately provided with basic amenities such as hospitals, administration buildings and armouries, enabling these partisans to hold out for long periods between sallies to harass the Germans, either by cutting their lines of communication or by attacking convoys or rear-area installations.

Horse Operation by the 47th Royal Marine Commando at the beginning of Operation 'Elephant'.

Horrified Allied codename for Sicily.

Houndsworth Airborne operation by A Squadron, 1st SAS Regiment, to establish a base in Rouvray (6 June 1944) from which to harass German communications with their forces opposing the Operation 'Overlord' landings in Normandy.

Hubertus German plan for the defence of Moldavia and Bukovina (1944) by substantial portions of Generaloberst Johannes Friessner's Army Group 'South Ukraine', which in August 1944 became Army Group 'South' and was later entrusted to General Otto Wöhler. Commanded by Wöhler, Gruppe Wöhler was tasked with the defence of Moldavia and Bukovina between the Yablonitse Pass and Korneshti and comprised of Wöhler's German 8th Army and General M. Racovitza's Romanian 4th Army. The strategic task of Gruppe Wöhler was to prevent Marshal of the Soviet Union R. Ya. Malinovsky's 2nd Ukrainian Front from breaking through the south-eastern end of the Carpathian Mountains into central Romania before wheeling north-west to push over the Transylvanian Alps into Hungary and Austria. However, the forces available to Army Group 'South' were wholly inadequate for the task of halting the 2nd and 3rd Ukrainian Fronts. In the event Malinovsky did not essay a major offensive into Bukovina, rather pinning the Axis forces in this area with frontal attacks by his 40th Army (in conjunction with the 18th Army of the 4th Ukrainian Front) when the general offensive began on 20 August 1944.

The main weight of Malinovsky's forces fell on Moldavia at the junction of Gruppe Wöhler with Gruppe Dumitrescu (German 6th and Romanian 3rd Armies) holding Bessarabia, the region between Moldavia and the coast of the Black Sea. Here the 6th Tank, 27th, 52nd, 53rd and 7th Guards Armies, supported by the Cavalry Mechanized Group Gorshkov, smashed through the junction of the Romanian 4th and German 6th Armies and made for Galatu on the lower reaches of the River Danube, trapping the German 6th and Romanian 3rd Armies, and securing a bridgehead on 29 August.

The total failure of Army Group 'South' can in part be attributed to the vastly superior Soviet forces opposing it, but also in part to the defection of its Romanian elements on 22 August, when Romania concluded an armistice with the Allies and then declared war on Germany during 25 August after Hitler had

84

ordered Luftwaffe aircraft to bomb those parts of Bucharest containing the palace and the residence of the prime minister. This debacle allowed Malinovsky's armies to reach Bucharest and Ploesti by the end of August before turning west and then north-west towards Hungary. The failure of Operation 'Hubertus' can be seen in the fact that the whole of Romania was in Soviet hands by the early part of October 1944.

Huffduff Allied generic name for H/F D/F (High-Frequency Direction-Finding).

Hunger Food drops by the RAF to the starving population of southern Burma (late summer 1945).

Hurricane I Allied plan for a concentrated bomber offensive against targets in the industrial Ruhr (1944/1945).

Hurricane II Allied plan for a concentrated bomber offensive against industrial targets in all German-controlled areas (1945).

Hurry Operation to reinforce the air defence strength of Malta (31 July/4 August 1940) just after the entry of Italy into the war. The idea was for the semi-expendable training carrier *Argus* to steam from Gibraltar to a point south-west of Sardinia, where 12 Hawker Hurricanes were flown off to Malta.

Husky Allied invasion of Sicily (9 July 1943). This operation was undertaken as a logical strategic successor to the campaign in North Africa, successfully ended in May 1943 with the surrender of the last Axis forces in the theatre. The Allies then wished to launch an invasion of western Europe, but as a landing in northern France was as yet impractical, it was decided that this next major move would have to be undertaken in the Mediterranean theatre. The question that thus presented itself was where such a thrust was to take place, the obvious choices being an advance into southern Italy via Sicily, or an advance through Sardinia and Corsica into northern Italy and southern France. The former, or 'right hook', alternative was chosen as it offered safer maritime communications with North Africa, as it could be covered in its initial stages by fighter aircraft stationed on Malta, and as it would have the effect of drawing German forces farther away from the Eastern Front and the proposed site for the implementation of Operation 'Overlord'. And in grand strategic terms, it was decided early in the planning (and against the wishes of the British, who saw the Italian campaign as a means of avoiding a bloody head-on confrontation with Germany in northern Europe by driving north through Italy and Austria into southern Germany if necessary) that the Italian campaign was not to be a major effort to defeat the Axis powers in Italy, but rather a sustained campaign to draw off as much as possible of Germany's strength from the Eastern Front and from north-west Europe, which were obviously the two decisive theatres.

The first step in the Italian campaign was the reduction of Sicily after a relatively short sea crossing from the Allied base areas around Tunis. To this end the Italian island fortress of Pantelleria and other islands to the west of Malta were neutralized and then seized so that they could offer no threat to the right flank of the Allied invasion, which was preceded by a month-long bombardment of airfields and communications in Sicily, southern Italy and Sardinia by Allied aircraft. The overall command and planning of Operation 'Husky' was entrusted to the 15th Army Group of General the Hon. Sir Harold Alexander, which disposed of two powerful armies for the operation designed to place the Allies on the southern shore of Sicily, defended by General Alfredo Guzzoni's Italian 6th Army with its headquarters at Enna in the centre of the island. The defence itself was entrusted to General Mario Arisio's Italian XII Corps (west of the island) with 3 coastal and 2 infantry divisions, and to General Carlo Rossi's XVI Corps (east of the island) with 2 coastal and 1 infantry divisions plus 2 coastal brigades. In reserve and support were 1 Italian and 2 German divisions, the latter being the 15th Panzergrenadier Division and the 'Hermann Goering' Panzer Division.

Supported by ineffectual airborne landings, the Allied amphibious attack was launched on 10 July after being ferried and escorted from North Africa in the armada of 2,590 ships provided by Admiral of the Fleet Sir

Huskyland

Andrew Cunningham's Mediterranean naval forces command. On the left flank Vice Admiral H. Kent Hewitt's Western Naval Task Force catered for Lieutenant General George S. Patton's US 7th Army, which landed in the Gulf of Gela in two basic groups. On the left Major General Lucian K. Truscott's US 3rd Infantry Division came ashore around Licata with support from the US Rangers and Combat Command 'A' of Major General Hugh J. Gaffey's 2nd Armored Division, and on the right Lieutenant General Omar N. Bradley's US II Corps landed between Gela and Scoglitti with Major General Terry de la M. Allen's US 1st Infantry Division and Major General Troy C. Middleton's US 45th Infantry Division. Air support for the US 7th Army was the responsibility of Major General Edwin J. House's XII Air Support Command. On the Allied right flank Admiral Sir Bertram Ramsay's Eastern Naval Task Force catered for General Sir Bernard Montgomery's British 8th Army which came ashore around Cape Pachino (Lieutenant General Sir Oliver Leese's British XXX Corps with Major General G. G. Simonds's 1st Canadian Division and Major General D. N. Wimberley's 51st Division supported by Commandos and the 231st Brigade Group) and in the Gulf of Syracuse (Lieutenant General M. C. Dempsey's British XIII Corps with Major General H. P. M. Berney-Ficklin's 5th Division and Major General S. C. Kirkman's 50th Division supported by Commandos). Air support for the British 8th Army was the responsibility of Air Vice Marshal Harry Broadhurst's Western Desert Air Force. The US 7th Army had part of the US 1st Infantry Division and the 2nd Armored Division (less Combat Command 'A' already ashore) available as floating reserves, while the British 8th Army had available as reserve (but only in North Africa) Major General V. Evelegh's 78th Division.

The Italians were taken completely by surprise as they had not anticipated any amphibious operations in the poor weather prevailing (largely responsible, together with poor tactical planning, for the overall failure of the airborne operations in the American sector), and the landing rapidly moved into the consolidation phase with powerful gunfire support from Allied warships lying offshore. By 12 July the German XIV Panzer Corps had come into being under Generaloberst Hans Hube to co-ordinate the German (and increasingly to supervise the Italian) defence efforts, and this tendency was evidenced by highly determined German counterattacks on 11 and 12 July. However, the Allies pushed northward with little difficulty until 18 August, when the British 8th Army was stalled in front of Catania, slightly more than half way to the army's final objective, Messina. Though the primary strategic task had been allocated to the 8th Army, the real progress was made by the US 7th Army under the dynamic leadership of Patton. By 23 July his forces had cleared western Sicily and were striking eastward along the north coast towards Messina with the aid of amphibious landings at Sant'Agata (8 August), Cape Orlando (11 August) and Barcellona (15 August) to outflank the resistance now being found mainly by the Germans as they pulled back towards Messina where an evacuation to Calabria in mainland Italy was being started. The 8th Army got under way again on 5 August, but it was the US 3rd Infantry Division that secured the honour of taking Messina in the morning of 17 August as the German rearguards pulled out.

Huskyland Allied codename for Sicily.

H.X. Designation of ocean homeward convoys (together with a numerical suffix) plying from Halifax, Nova Scotia across the North Atlantic to the UK, and inaugurated in September 1939. From September 1942 these convoys started in New York.

Hydra Air raid by some 750 bombers of RAF Bomber Command on the German 'secret weapon' development centre on Peenemünde Island in the Baltic (18 August 1943). This raid did much to delay the development of the V-2 rocket weapon as many of the scientists and technicians involved in the programme were killed or injured, and much of the base's facilities was destroyed or severely damaged.

I

I Japanese offensive to prevent the growth of Allied air power in the south-east Pacific (April 1943) with a sustained offensive launched from the top end of the Solomons and even from the larger airfields around Rabaul in New Britain and Kavieng in New Ireland. The Japanese hoped with this offensive to draw up and defeat the Americans' fighter strength and so delay the impending offensive by Vice Admiral William Halsey's Southern Pacific Area forces up the Solomons towards New Georgia and Bougainville Island. The campaign involved the Japanese operating over very protracted ranges, with the result that mechanical problems and damage became severe difficulties on the long homeward trips, causing the Japanese to lose heavily against US air forces growing almost daily in strength and tactical capability.

Iceberg US invasion of the island of Okinawa (1 April 1945), the main island in the Ryukyu group half way between Formosa and the Japanese home islands, and the ideal base from which to launch the invasions planned against Japan proper. The operation had been considered for some time before its implementation, and it was fully appreciated by the Americans that Operation 'Iceberg' would be both difficult and costly as the island was well defended and possessed a large Japanese civilian population, was comparatively close to Japan (and might thus be reinforced with comparative ease before the actual invasion), and would be defended with more than the normal fanaticism as it was regarded as part of Japan by its defenders. The operation was designed along the lines that had been evolved into thoroughbred amphibious warfare tactics in previous Pacific campaigns, and was entrusted to Lieutenant General Simon B. Buckner's US 10th Army of two corps. The planning staff had to take into account the formidable defence forces of the island, namely the 32nd Army commanded by Lieutenant General Mitsuru Ushijima. This army had comprised the 9th, 24th, 28th and 62nd Divisions together with the 44th Independent Mixed Brigade, but had recently suffered the loss of the 9th Division (moved to Formosa in December 1944) and the 28th Division (located in the Sakishima Gunto). Thus the defence of Okinawa proper was entrusted to the 24th and 62nd Divisions and the 44th Independent Mixed Brigade, supported by the 5th Artillery Command, one divisional field regiment of artillery and the 27th Tank Regiment. The garrison also included seven sea raiding battalions with *Shinyo* suicide boats (three in the Kerama Retto and the other four on Okinawa). When he realized that no reinforcements (or even replacement for the 9th Division) would be forthcoming, Ushijima decided to raise additional forces from his command on the island, and the administrative and support echelons of the ground and air units were thus stripped to find the manpower for two special infantry brigades (one of 6,000 men and the other of 4,500 men) and one special regiment (3,000 men). Ushijima also reduced the sea raiding battalions to one company each, the surplus manpower being used to create three 800-man infantry battalions. Ushijima could deploy some 77,200 regular and 20,000 or more auxiliary (home guard) troops, though US estimates put the total at the unfortunately low figure of 65,000 men located mainly in the area between Naha and Yontan towards the southern end of the island, where there were four important airfields. Ushijima was practical enough to see that he had no chance of defeating the Americans, and instead decided to buy time for Japan by concentrating his forces in strong positions on the southern end of the island (the 62nd Division disposed in the neck of the island between Chatan and Toguchi in the north and between Naha and Yonabaru in the south, with the 24th Division behind the left flank of the Shuri line and the 44th Independent Mixed Brigade behind the line's right flank) and so forcing the Americans to engage in a protracted campaign.

Strategic command of the operation on the US side was the responsibility of Admiral Raymond A. Spruance's 5th Fleet, whose Task Force 51 under Vice Admiral Richmond K. Turner (comprising Rear Admiral M. L. Deyo's Gun-Fire and Covering Force, and Rear Admiral W. H. P. Blandy's Amphibious Support Force of 22 escort carriers) was entrusted with the delivery of the Joint Expeditionary Force in some 1,139 transports, landing craft and auxiliaries. Spruance disposed of more than 300 warships including Task Force 58 (four fast carrier task groups comprising 11 fleet carriers, 6 light carriers, 7 battleships, 15 cruisers and 64 destroyers under Vice Admiral Marc A. Mitscher) and Task Force 57 (one British fast carrier task group comprising 4 fleet carriers, 2 battleships, 5 cruisers and 11 destroyers under Vice Admiral Sir Bernard Rawlings) to soften up and then neutralize as much as possible of the island's defences before the landings were committed, and then to ward off any Japanese naval counteroffensive, however unlikely given the virtually complete destruction of Japan's surface fleet by this time. The 10th Army for the operation was in itself a new formation, but its component parts were for the most part veterans of other Pacific operations. In Major General John B. Hodge's XXIV Corps (the Southern Attack Force) Major General Charles H. Corlett's 7th Infantry Division had seen action on Attu, Kwajalein and Leyte, and the 96th Infantry Division on Leyte, while in Major General Roy S. Geiger's III Amphibious Corps (the Northern Attack Force) Major General William H. Rupertus' 1st Marine Division had seen action on Guadalcanal, New Britain and Peleliu, and the 6th Marine Division on the Marshalls, Guam and Saipan. The 10th Army reserves were Major General Griner's 27th Infantry Division (on the Gilberts, the Marshalls and Saipan), Major General Andrew D. Bruce's 77th Infantry Division (on Guam and Leyte) and Major General Thomas E. Watson's 2nd Marine Division (on Guadalcanal, Tarawa, Saipan and Tinian). Buckner thus had some 182,000 men in seven divisions, of whom 116,000 were to be committed in the initial phase of the operation.

Operation 'Iceberg' called for the four divisions of III Amphibious Corps and XXIV Corps to be landed on an 8-mile stretch of beach on the western side of Okinawa in Hagushi Bay after the Keramo Retto island group to the west of Okinawa had been taken (26/29 March) by the 77th Infantry Division (the Western Islands Attack Group) as a fleet anchorage and base. At the same time that the main landings were being carried out, the 2nd Marine Division was to demonstrate on the eastern side of the island as a diversion, though the 10th Army's contingency plans envisaged that this diversion could be turned into a real landing in Nagagusuka Bay to join up with the main landings should Japanese resistance prove to be stronger than anticipated. In the event the eastern landing was not required, for the main assault went as planned, and by 4 April the US Marines of III Amphibious Corps had advanced north to the Ishikawa Isthmus just south of Onna, while the US Army troops of XXIV Corps had pushed south as far as Kuba, so dividing the Japanese defence into portions in the north and extreme south of the island. The north was reduced by 19 April after some vigorous work by the 6th Marine Division in particular, but the defences in the south were an altogether tougher nut for XXIV Corps to crack as here Ushijima had prepared the immensely strong Shuri Line defences just north of the island's capital, Naha.

Buckner was now faced with the dilemma of undertaking a costly frontal assault or chancing the danger of dividing his forces to launch an amphibious assault in the rear of the Shuri Line. Buckner opted for both, though emphasis in the shorter term was given to a frontal assault after a Japanese suicide attack on 3 May revealed the main features of the Shuri Line. On 7 May Buckner assumed personal command in the Shuri Line battle, and decided that reinforcement was needed to overcome the Japanese two-division front. So III Amphibious Corps was brought south to take over the right-hand sector of the US front facing the Shuri Line, allowing XXIV Corps to concentrate on the left-hand sector. Between 11 and 21 May III Amphibious Corps and XXIV Corps pounded the Shuri Line in the most appalling weather and tactical conditions before Ushijima ordered his surviving forces to fall back to the mountain features of the extreme southern tip of Okinawa as the 6th Marine Division made an amphibious descent south of Naha on 4 June. Attacking on two fronts, the Americans finally overwhelmed the Japanese on 21 June to bring the campaign to an end. Subsidiary to these main efforts had been the capture of Tsugen Shima off the eastern side of the main island by a battalion from the 27th Infantry Division on 10/11 April, and the capture of Ie Shima off the western side of the main island by the 77th Infantry Division between 16 and 21 April. The latter campaign had provided the 10th Army with three Japanese-built airstrips for the use of tactical aircraft supporting operations on the main island.

The whole campaign had been one of appalling severity, costing the Japanese 107,500 known dead and possibly another 20,000 dead in caves sealed by US assault teams armed with flamethrowers and explosives. Large numbers of civilians were killed or committed suicide, but for the first time in the war with Japan an appreciable number of servicemen surrendered to the Americans, in all some 7,400 mostly during the very last few days of the campaign as the 32nd Army was falling to pieces as a cohesive fighting formation. US ground force losses amounted to 7,613 dead (including Buckner, who died as a result of Japanese shelling on 18 June) plus 31,800 wounded in the 10th Army, and 4,900 dead plus 4,800 wounded for the US Navy, which had come under exceptionally heavy *kamikaze* air attack during the campaign, losing 36 ships sunk and 368 damaged. US aircraft losses were 763, a large number by any standards, but those of the Japanese were quite staggering at an overall figure of 7,800 including 1,465 in 1,900 *kamikaze* attacks. Buckner was replaced on 23 June by Lieutenant General Joseph W. Stilwell, and the Ryukyus campaign was declared over on 2 July as the Americans were beginning to realize quite how bloody the whole operation had been. The question now being asked was the cost of the apparently inevitable US invasion of the Japanese home islands given the same type of fanatical resistance. Ushijima's formidable defensive effort had bought Japan three months.

ICHI Japanese offensive in southern and central China (27 May 1944/8 May 1945) to take the bases used by the US air forces in China for the strategic bombing of targets in Japan with Boeing B-29 Superfortress aircraft (XX Bomber Command under Major General Curtis E. LeMay) and for the conduct of local air operations (US 14th Air Force under Lieutenant General Claire Chennault). The offensive was launched by the Japanese 6th Area Army in the triangle bounded in the north by Lake Tung-ting, in the south-east by Canton and in the south-west by the Chinese/Indo-Chinese frontier to the north-east of Hanoi, though the main thrusts were those of the 11th Army's 250,000 men southward from Lake Tung-ting and of the 23rd Army's 50,000 men northwards and north-westwards from Canton. This was the first genuinely large-scale strategic offensive undertaken by the Japanese in China since 1938, and had been accurately predicted by Lieutenant General Joseph W. Stilwell, chief-of-staff to Generalissimo Chiang Kai-shek and commander of the US and Chinese forces in the China-Burma-India Theater. At first Chinese resistance was quite effective, aided as it was by useful tactical air support from the squadrons of the 14th Air force, but on 18 June Changsha fell to the 11th Army, followed by Hengyang on 8 August after an 11-day siege. After this, however, Chinese resistance began to crumble. The 11th Army pressed on to take Lingling on 4 September and Kweilin on 10 November, while the 23rd

Army seized Liuchow on 11 November and the forces from Indo-China captured Nanning on 24 November.

The US Army Air Forces had by this time lost seven of their 12 Chinese bases, forcing the 14th Air Force to fall back towards India and the XX Bomber Command to be shifted to the Marianas early in 1945. The crisis had also persuaded President Franklin D. Roosevelt to urge Chiang that Stilwell should be made commander of all Chinese land forces, but this merely brought to the surface the long-term hostility between Stilwell and Chiang, the latter demanding that Stilwell be replaced. On 18 October Stilwell handed over to Lieutenant General Albert C. Wedemeyer, who became chief-of-staff to Chiang and the commander of the new China Theater which replaced the disbanded CBI Theater.

During late November and early December the Japanese turned west towards Kweiyang and Kunming, but Wedemeyer was able to persuade Chiang that two veteran divisions should be flown in from the Burma front, and these formed the basis of a strengthened Chinese defence that with the aid of the 14th Air Force halted the Japanese in front of Kweiyang. This reverse persuaded the Japanese to call a temporary halt to Operation 'ICHI', and the respite was used profitably by Wedemeyer to revitalize the Chinese forces, with the aid of the extra supplies that were now reaching southern China over the reopened land route from Burma, in preparation for the resumption of 'ICHI' in January 1945.

'ICHI' began again in January 1945 after the Japanese had improved their lines of communication, and considerable gains were made on the coastal regions between Hankow and the Indo-Chinese frontier. At the same time three more US Army Air Force bases fell to the Japanese, the most important being that at Suichuan, which fell in February 1945 at about the time that the 11th and 23rd Armies linked up on the rail line between Canton and Hengyang. Then came a complete surprise for the Allies as the Japanese extended 'ICHI' as Operation 'KO' to an area in central China, where the 12th and 34th Armies went over to the offensive west of Kaifeng between the Hang and Yangtse rivers with the object of taking the air bases at Laohokow and Ankang. The former fell, and the Japanese made substantial advances (netting the spring rice harvest in the process) before they were checked by Chinese reinforcements in April. Again the Japanese shifted emphasis, this time towards the air base at Chihkiang, but their defeat at Changteh on 8 May persuaded the Japanese that 'ICHI' and 'KO' should be terminated, the more so as the Japanese high command insisted that China should become a defensive theatre in order that troops could be moved north to Manchukuo (Manchuria) in the face of an increasingly threatening situation with the USSR. The Chinese went over to the offensive in the south-west during July 1945, and soon cut a corridor through to Indo-China, trapping some 100,000 Japanese troops in various beach-heads along the coast between Hong Kong and Pakhoi, and similar in essence to those already in existence at Swatow, Amoy, Foochow and Wenchow.

Ida German occupation of the Istrian peninsula between Trieste and Fiume (September 1943) after the Allied armistice with Italy, so that communications between Italy and Yugoslavia could be safeguarded.

Ilona German plan for the invasion of Spain (1940/1941) in the event of a British landing in that country.

Impact Operation for British forces to cross Lake Comacchio in northern Italy (1 April 1945). Devised under the control of Field Marshal the Hon. Sir Harold Alexander, the Supreme Allied Commander Mediterranean, by Lieutenant General Mark W. Clark's Allied 15th Army Group as part of the final offensive in Italy, Operation 'Impact' was evolved as a means for Lieutenant General Sir Richard McCreery's British 8th Army to get past the formidable German defences in the region and past the bottleneck of the Argenta gap, in which the natural water obstacles constituted by the River Reno and Lake Comacchio were compounded by a massive minefield in the area of Bastia (to the west of Lake Comacchio en route to the Argenta gap) and by the formidable capabilities of General Richard Heidrich's I Parachute Corps (1st and 4th

Parachute Divisions, 278th and 305th Divisions, and 26th Panzer Division) and LXXVI Panzer Corps (98th and 362nd Divisions, 42nd Jäger Division and 162nd Turkoman Division) of General Traugott Herr's German 10th Army. It was therefore decided that the forces of Lieutenant General Sir Charles Keightley's British V Corps should break through the Argenta gap, aided by an amphibious 'right hook' across Lake Comacchio. To disguise this major undertaking the British designed a deception attack across the spit of land dividing Lake Comacchio from the Adriatic Sea in the hope that the Germans would see this as an attempt to break through to the mouth of the River Po and so switch their forces eastwards away from the main thrust by the British 56th, 8th Indian, British 78th and 2nd New Zealand Divisions.

In its complete complexity Operation 'Impact' called for a frontal attack by the 2nd New Zealand, British 78th and 8th Indian Divisions through the German 98th Division towards Massa Lombarda on 1 April to draw the defence's attention to this sector just as the British 2nd Commando Brigade advanced across the spit to the east of Lake Comacchio and through the German 162nd Division towards Porto Garibaldi with the intention of drawing German attention east again, or alternatively of exploiting any local advantage. Then on 4 April, with German attention split between Massa Lombardo and the spit, the Royal Marine Special Boat Squadron would seize the islands in Lake Comacchio to protect the open flank of the 'right hook' proper on 6 April by the 56th Division (one brigade) supported by the British 2nd Parachute Brigade and Royal Marine Commandos, whose task was to cross Lake Comacchio in amphibious craft to emerge behind the left flank of the 42nd Jäger Division, to take the vital bridge over the Reno at Bastia and to hold the Argenta gap until the arrival of the 8th Indian and 78th Divisions. The whole scheme worked like clockwork, and so successful was the Allied deception scheme for the entire offensive that Generaloberst Heinrich von Vietinghoff-Scheel, commanding the Germany Army Group 'C', fell for the notion that the main Allied effort was to be an amphibious operation against the mouth of the Po, and so sent half of his reserve force, the 29th Panzergrenadier Division, from its position near Bologna, where it posed a distinct threat to the plans of Lieutenant General Lucian K. Truscott's US 5th Army, to the coast near Venice. As the Argenta gap opened to British exploitation, the whole German defence in north-east Italy folded, and the Polish II Corps, and British X and XIII Corps were able to press ahead on the 8th Army's left flank between Bologna and Ferrara. By 23 April the Allied line had advanced to positions just south of the Po as far west as Modena.

Imperator British plan to take and hold Boulogne (or a similar French coastal town) by means of amphibious assault (summer 1942). The plan was devised in response to a request from the USSR for aid at the time of Germany's Operation 'Blau' offensives in the summer of 1942, and was designed to force the Germans to draw from the Eastern Front a sizeable proportion of their air strength to bolster the very limited forces that had been left in Western Europe by the preparations for and execution of Operation 'Barbarossa'.

Independence (i) Plan for the French 1st Army to reduce the German garrisons on the French Atlantic coast (December 1944). These included Lorient (Generalleutnant Wilhelm Russwurn's 265th Division) and St Nazaire, which surrendered only on 8 May 1945, as did the 30,000 men of the 319th Division under Generalmajor Rudolf Graf von Schmettow in the Channel Islands.
(ii) Original designation of Operation 'Venerable'.

Indigo Move of US forces to Iceland (July/September 1941) as replacements for the British forces at that time occupying the country. The first brigade of the US Marine Corps started to arrive in the island on 7 July 1941.

Induction The Luzon invasion part of Admiral Chester W. Nimitz's 'Granite' plan for an eastward Allied thrust across the Pacific to Formosa and China.

Infatuate I Capture of Vlissingen at the southern tip of Walcheren Island (1/6 November 1944) by the British No. 4 Commando and 155th Brigade after crossing from Breskens, recently captured by the Canadian 3rd Division. Walcheren lies on the northern side the estuary of the River Scheldt, and the port of Antwerp could not be used for the movement of supplies to the British 21st Army Group under Field-Marshal Viscount Montgomery until the island had been cleared and the Scheldt swept of mines.

Infatuate II Capture of the rest of Walcheren Island (1/8 November 1944) by Brigadier B. W. Leicester's 4th Special Service Brigade (Nos 41, 47 and 48 Royal Marine Commandos) as part of the Allied scheme to open up the River Scheldt for the movement of shipping to Antwerp for the supply of the British 21st Army Group. The defence was carried out by Generalleutnant Wilhelm Daser's 70th Division of General Gustav von Zangen's German 15th Army, entrusted by Generalfeldmarschall Walter Model's Army Group 'B' with the holding of the Scheldt estuary. By the time of the Allied offensive into Walcheren, the island had been cut off by the advances of the British 52nd Division and the 2nd Canadian Division of the Canadian 1st Army (temporarily under the command of Lieutenant General G. G. Simonds), which had taken South Beveland and North Beveland respectively.

Influx British plan for an invasion of Sicily (1941).

Instep RAF long-range fighter patrols off western France and in the Bay of Biscay to escort aircraft of RAF Coastal Command involved in anti-shipping strike missions.

Insurgent The Mindanao invasion part of Admiral Chester W. Nimitz's 'Granite' plan for an east-west Allied thrust across the Pacific to Formosa and China.

Interlude Invasion of Morotai Island at the northern end of the Moluccas group (15 September 1944) by the US 31st Infantry Division of General Douglas MacArthur's South-West Pacific Area. This step took the US forces half way across to the southern end of the Philippines from the western end of New Guinea. In conjunction with the US Marine landings on Peleliu in the Palau Islands, this brought the combined South-West Pacific Area and Pacific Ocean Areas commands to a converging point for the assault on the Philippines. The reason for MacArthur's assault on Morotai was to obtain a half-finished airfield, but this proved unusable and a new strip was built, this being capable of fighter operations on 4 October and of bomber operations on 15 October, just in time for the invasion of Leyte in the Philippines.

Intransitive British commando liaison mission in Czechoslovakia.

Intruder Allied air operations against specific German activity, the most important of these being night-fighter missions to German night-flying bases for attacks on aircraft either taking off or landing, when they were particularly vulnerable.

Ironclad British operation to capture the port of Diego Suarez at the northern tip of Madagascar (5/7 May 1942). This operation was undertaken at the height of Japan's expansionist programme, the British fearing that the Japanese would be able to secure forward basing rights for their submarines and perhaps maritime reconnaissance aircraft in the Vichy French island of Madagascar, which lay athwart the British convoy routes round the Cape of Good Hope to the Red Sea ports and India. The expedition was mounted by forces from the UK under the escort of parts of Force H from Gibraltar, the rendezvous being made in South Africa where the whole force came under the command of Rear Admiral E. N. Syfret, with Major General R. G. Sturges commanding the land forces, known as Force 121. The naval portion of 'Ironclad' consisted of the battleships *Ramillies* and *Malaya*, the aircraft-carriers *Illustrious* and *Indomitable*, the cruisers *Devonshire* and *Hermione*, 9 destroyers, 6 corvettes and 6 minesweepers. The land forces comprised Brigadier V. C. Russell's 13th Brigade and Brigadier G. W. B. Tarleton's 17th Brigade (of Major General H. P. M.

Berney-Ficklin's British 5th Division, which had been earmarked for service in the Western Desert but which was now split up into brigades for detached service), Brigadier F. W. Festing's 29th Independent Brigade Group and No. 5 Commando.

The object of the whole operation was the naval base of Diego Suarez, located at Antsirane in Diego Suarez Bay to the east of the town proper, but as access to this bay was controlled by French batteries it was thought tactically superior to land in Courrier Bay, to the west of the isthmus connecting Cape Amber with the mainland, before launching an overland advance of some 12 miles to take Antsirane in rear. The landing and initial advance progressed without undue difficulty, but the attack on Antsirane was then checked by strong Vichy French defences in the rear of Antsirane, defences that had not been revealed by photo-reconnaissance flights. The deadlock was broken by the landing of a small party of Royal Marines in Antsirane in a courageous destroyer operation. This demoralized the defence, whose men flocked to surrender. The operation was over by the early morning of 7 May.

The validity of the British reasoning in undertaking the operation seemed to be confirmed on 29 May, when a small Japanese seaplane flew over Diego Suarez. The *Ramillies* immediately got under way as it was thought that the seaplane must have come from a Japanese warship in the offing, though in fact it had been launched from a submarine. While steaming in Diego Suarez Bay the *Ramillies* and a tanker were torpedoed by a pair of midget submarines launched from the parent boat offshore. The battleship was severely damaged and the tanker sunk, indicating that possession of Diego Suarez was not in itself sufficient and that the rest of Madagascar must be brought into the Allied camp. The Vichy French governor of the island steadfastly refused to surrender peaceably, and the British accordingly launched a difficult campaign to reduce the garrison by military strength. In September landings were effected at strategic points round the island (Majunga and Morondava on 10 September, Tamatave on 18 September, and Fort Dauphin and Tulear on 29 September). Combined with an overland advance from Diego Suarez by the 7th South African Brigade, the 29th Independent Brigade Group and the 22nd East African Brigade with South African support moved inland to take the capital, Tananarive, on 23 September and end all Vichy resistance by 6 November at Ambalavao towards the south of the island.

Iron Ring Blockade of Brest by British submarines (March 1941) in an effort to intercept the German warship raiders *Scharnhorst* and *Gneisenau* (battle-cruisers), *Admiral Scheer* (pocket battleship) and *Admiral Hipper* (heavy cruiser) as they returned from forays into the Atlantic.

Isabella Earlier version of 'Ilona', including not only the seizure of mainland Spain, but also the seizure of Portugal, the Canary Islands and the Cape Verde Islands, and a southward extension to seize the French port of Dakar on the West African coast. The implementation of the plan was clearly beyond the capabilities of Germany at the time it was conceived (even allowing for the comparative weakness of the UK in this period), but would have given Germany a commanding strategic position in the Atlantic and West Africa to hinder the movement of British convoys across the Atlantic and also to and from the Middle East and India via the Cape of Good Hope. A strategic corollary of Operation 'Isabella' would have been the seizure of Gibraltar, thus denying the British access to the Mediterranean from the western end.

Iskra (spark) Soviet offensive (11/18 January 1943) to reopen a land corridor to the city of Leningrad, cut off since 15 September 1941 by the arrival of the German 18th Army at Schlüsselburg on the south side of Lake Ladoga. After the failure of a similar offensive at the end of September 1942, the Soviets had planned an altogether more professional operation using larger forces on a smaller front to ensure overwhelming superiority of strength. In the west the 67th Army of General L. A. Govorov's Leningrad Front would advance east across the River Neva between Lake Ladoga and Nevskaya Dubrovka, and in the east the 2nd Shock

Istrien

Army of General K. A. Meretskov's Volkhov Front would push west between Lake Ladoga and Gontovaya Lipka, the two forces planning to meet north of Sinyavino in order to provide a narrow land corridor into Leningrad from the east. The fighting was extremely bitter, as was usual for the Eastern Front at this time, and substantial German forces were nearly cut off on the southern shore of Lake Ladoga, fighting their way out through the so-called 'corridor of death' between Lipka and Sinyavino as the Soviets strove to link up and close the corridor.

Istrien (Istria) Operation by forces of Generalfeldmarschall Maximilian von Weichs' German Army Group 'B' against Soviet partisans operating in the army group's rear areas (January and February 1943).

J

Jagdschloss (hunting castle) German night-fighter control radar.

Jaguar Overall designation of British air reinforcements for Malta (1941).

Jakob German operation against Soviet partisans operating in the area north of Usda (8/12 September 1943).

Jane Landing of the British 29th Independent Brigade Group at Tamatave on the eastern coast of Madagascar (18 September 1942). Undertaken as part of the operations to reduce the Vichy French garrison of the island in the aftermath of Operation 'Ironclad', the landing of Brigadier F. W. Festing's 29th Independent Brigade Group was designed as part of a concentric thrust to the island's capital, Tananarive, with the 22nd East African Brigade that had taken over from the 29th Independent Brigade Group after the initial landing at Majunga on the west coast on 10 September. These forces arrived in Tananarive on 23 September, allowing a joint southward thrust to link up with the South African battalion advancing from Tulear on the south-west corner of the island to trap the Vichy forces in the centre, where the governor surrendered at Ambalavao on 6 November.

Jericho Daring raid by de Havilland Mosquito bombers (18 February 1944) to breach the walls of Amiens gaol and allow the French maquis prisoners inside to escape while the German guards were still stunned.

Jim Crow British fighter patrols in coastal waters to watch for the arrival of any German invasion forces (1940/1941). The concept was later amended to the interception of German fighter-bombers streaking in at low level to make nuisance raids on British coastal towns.

Jockey Designation of the Allied committee planning attacks on German aircraft production capability.

Jockworth Airborne operation by the French 2ème Regiment des Chasseurs Parachutistes to harass German communications near Villefranche (14 August 1944) as the Germans were pulling back in front of the Allied break-out from the Normandy beachhead.

Jolka German plan for the invasion and capture of Switzerland.

Joss Task force of the US 3rd Infantry Division for the landing at Licata in the execution of Operation 'Husky'.

Jostle British electronic countermeasures system similar to 'Airborne Cigar' but operating on different frequencies.

J.T. Designation of South American coastal convoys (together with a numerical suffix) plying from Rio de Janeiro to Trinidad, and inaugurated in July 1943 as the successor to the B.T. convoys inaugurated in November 1942.

Jubilant Allied plan to seize camps in which Allied prisoners of war were being held

(1945) to prevent reprisals by the Germans with imminent defeat facing them.

Jubilee British and Canadian assault on the north French town of Dieppe (19 August 1942). This operation was undertaken for a number of reasons, principally the chance to exercise some of the large numbers of battle-ready troops now awaiting the launch of the 'second front' landings in northern Europe, the testing of the amphibious warfare tactics and weapons developed for the proposed 'second front' operation, the evaluation of the defensive tactics and weapons used by the Germans against an amphibious assault, and the diversion of German forces (especially air forces) from the Eastern Front. Dieppe was chosen as the site for the operation because it was typical of the type of French Channel port that would, it was currently planned, eventually receive the 'second front' operation, because it was within the range of fighters operating from the southern part of England, and because the destruction of the port facilities would have a significant effect on the movement of German coastal convoys along the Channel coast.

The formation selected for the landing was Major General J. H. Roberts' 2nd Canadian Division, which provided 4,921 men for the main assaults, with flanking efforts provided by some 1,057 men of Nos 3 and 4 Commandos (commanded by Lieutenant Colonels Peter Young and the Lord Lovat respectively) plus some US Rangers. The naval forces were commanded by Captain J. Hughes Hallett, and consisted of 9 landing ships infantry and 179 landing craft escorted by 8 destroyers and 39 coastal craft. The air forces allocated to the operation came under the control of Air Vice Marshal T. Leigh-Mallory, and comprised 67 squadrons, no fewer than 60 of them fighter squadrons. Great emphasis was placed on obtaining tactical surprise to get ashore past the defences of the German 302nd Division and the powerful coastal batteries in the area so that a defensive perimeter could be thrown around Dieppe while a special detachment pushed inland to the airfield near St Aubin and destroyed aircraft and facilities before pulling back to the town for the orderly evacuation planned for the evening. The main assault (on the beach just in front of the Casino) was entrusted to the Essex Scottish Regiment and the Royal Hamilton Light Infantry Regiment with support from the 14th Canadian Army Tank Regiment. This force would be flanked to the east by the Royal Regiment of Canada (to take the 'Rommel' battery at Puys) and to the west by the South Saskatchewan Regiment and The Queen's Own Cameron Highlanders (to take the 'Hindenburg' battery behind Dieppe after landing at Pourville). The commando assaults on the outer flanks were designed to take the 'Goebbels' battery (No. 3 Commando to the east), and the 'Hess' and Varengeville batteries (No. 4 Commando to the west).

The whole operation began to go wrong right from the start, for No. 3 Commando was pinned down as it landed and could not reach its objective, though No. 4 Commando was successful and then evacuated as planned. In Dieppe itself the Royal Regiment of Canada on the eastern inner flank was pinned down as it landed, though again the western inner flank fared better and made some (though not the intended) progress. The main landings were a disaster, the forces being pinned down in front of the sea wall after their landing craft had braved a hail of fire to deposit them on the beaches, and the tanks were either unable to cross the sea wall or wiped out as they reached the promenade. The reserve force, the Fusiliers Mont-Royal, were committed at 07.00 but could not improve the situation, and an evacuation was thus ordered at 11.00, being completed by 13.00. The Germans had remained in total control of the situation and lost some 600 men. On the Allied side the Canadians had lost 3,363 men, the Commandos 247, the Royal Navy 550 men plus one destroyer and 33 landing craft, and the RAF 190 men and 106 aircraft.

The lessons were plain, and it was thus decided that the 'second front' landings would have to be made over open beaches rather than in a port area, and that heavy naval gunfire support was essential, together with specialized weapons optimized for beach landing operations. Another important lesson of the Dieppe failure was the need for far better inter-service communications. together with an all-service command structure optimized for flexible control of the whole amphibious operation as an entity rather than as simultaneous operations by the three different services. Also of particular discouragement was the poor showing of the RAF, whose latest Supermarine Spitfire fighters were no match for the German Focke-Wulf Fw 190 fighters.

Judgement Attack by Fairey Swordfish torpedo-bombers of the Fleet Air Arm against units of the Italian fleet at Taranto (11 November 1940). The plan was devised by Admiral Sir Andrew Cunningham, commander-in-chief of the Mediterranean Fleet, and the need to inflict a decisive blow on the Italian battlefleet had been reinforced during 1941 as several convoys to Malta and Alexandria had been threatened in the Sicilian Narrows by these powerful Italian surface forces. Cunningham desired to use the aircraft-carriers *Illustrious* and *Eagle* for the strike, but the latter ship was unavailable at the right time because of the damage caused by the detonation of bombs close alongside during the action off Calabria on 9 July 1940. However, some of her aircraft and aircrews were transferred to the *Illustrious* for Operation 'Judgement', which was to be conducted by two strike forces, the first of 12 and the second of 9 biplane Swordfish aircraft. The plan was implemented when Martin Maryland reconnaissance aircraft had confirmed that the Italian fleet was in Taranto harbour, and the two attack forces lifted off at 20.40 and 21.30 respectively in the evening of 11 November, when the *Illustrious* was some 180 miles to the south-east of Taranto. The first wave attacked at 23.00 on basically a west/east course in two divisions, while the second wave attacked north-west to south-east. The Italians were caught completely by surprise, and considerable damage was inflicted by the British torpedoes, which had been specially modified not to strike the bottom after landing in the water of this comparatively shallow harbour. Only two aircraft failed to return, and the Italians lost the new battleship *Littorio* and the two older but extensively modernized battleships *Caio Duilio* and *Conte di Cavour* sunk, as well as two cruisers and two fleet auxiliaries severely damaged. It was a crippling blow to the Italian fleet, and although some of the ships were eventually returned to service, the air strike had inflicted a mortal blow on Italian naval resolve and morale while boosting that of the British naval forces in the Mediterranean.

Juggler US 8th Air Force attacks on the production centres of Messerschmitt fighters at Regensburg and Wiener Neustadt.

Julius Caesar British plan to repel any combined airborne and seaborne invasion of the UK (1940).

Junior Allied codename for the US 12th Air Force.

Jungle British plan to send forces to Thrace and Anatolia to support Turkey in the event of a German invasion (October 1940). The German high command thought that such an operation could be successfully undertaken by two motorized corps, which could advance into Syria within two months, but the scheme was cancelled by Hitler, who thought that the strategic risks were too high to make the gamble worthwhile. Throughout this period Turkey maintained a steadfast neutrality, being more concerned with the short-term problems posed by Bulgarian designs on Thrace than by any longer-term push by the Germans.

Juno (i) Raid off Norway by the German battle-cruisers *Scharnhorst* and *Gneisenau*, accompanied by the heavy cruiser *Admiral Hipper* (4/13 June 1940). This raid had been planned for 25 May as a means of drawing British naval forces away from the Norwegian coast and so affording a respite to the German land forces in the Vestfjord area (especially Narvik) during the German invasion of Norway. Delays caused Vizeadmiral Wilhelm Marschall to leave Kiel only on 4 June, his three major ships being escorted by four destroyers in the first part of a plan to strike at the Allied forces at Harstad to the northwest of Narvik, where an Allied evacuation was taking place unbeknownst to the Germans. En route Marschall received news of British shipping movements in the North

Jupiter

Sea, and was thus able to intercept on 8 June the tanker *Oil Pioneer* and the empty troopship *Orama*, both of which were sunk. The *Admiral Hipper* and the destroyers were now detached to Trondheim for fuel, while the two battle-cruisers headed north for Narvik, encountering the aircraft-carrier *Glorious* escorted by the destroyers *Acasta* and *Ardent*. All three were sunk. However, the *Ardent* had scored one damaging torpedo hit on the *Scharnhorst*, and Marshall called off further operations, retiring to Trondheim on 9 June. This move in all probability saved from total destruction the lightly escorted British evacuation convoy from the Vestfjord.

(ii) Designation of the beach assigned for the landing of the 3rd Canadian Division and 2nd Canadian Armoured Brigade of Lieutenant General J. T. Crocker's British I Corps of Lieutenant General Sir Miles Dempsey's British 2nd Army in Operation 'Overlord'. The beach ran between the junction point with the British 50th Division at La Rivière ('Gold' beach) in the west and the proposed junction point with the British 3rd Division at Luc ('Sword' beach) in the east.

Jupiter Plan for a British landing in Norway (1942) to capture northern airfields used by the Germans for attacks on the Allied convoys taking supplies round the North Cape to the Soviet port of Murmansk. As early as October 1941 Prime Minister Winston Churchill had proposed an amphibious descent on Trondheim, using mainly Canadian forces. But in the absence of enthusiasm by his military planners, Churchill had postponed the notion for later resurrection as Operation 'Jupiter', given military credibility as a means of safeguarding the Russian convoys but intended as a means of liberating northern Norway. Yet again the planners rejected the notion, but the last use of the concept was as a diversion from the Mediterranean theatre, where Operation 'Torch' was being planned. Continued work on 'Jupiter' thus served to attract the attention of Hitler, who remained firmly convinced between 1940 and 1945 that the Allies intended a descent on his northern flank in this area, and thus kept substantial German forces in Norway throughout the war, even at times when they could have swayed the balance towards the Germans in decisive areas.

J.W. Designation of Arctic convoys (together with a numerical suffix) plying from Loch Ewe to the northern ports of the USSR, and inaugurated in December 1942 as successor to the P.Q. series.

K

K Japanese reconnaissance of Pearl Harbor, the US Pacific Fleet's main base in the Hawaiian Islands, carried out by flying-boats refuelled at French Frigate Shoals from an ocean-going submarine (3 March/30 May 1942). The object of the operation was to provide Admiral Isoroku Yamamoto, commander-in-chief of the Imperial Japanese Navy's Combined Fleet, with accurate and timely intelligence of Pacific Fleet strengths and movements. Admiral Chester W. Nimitz was aware of the Japanese use of French Frigate Shoals, and thus stationed two destroyers of his US Pacific Fleet (plus a supporting oil tanker) over the shoals to deter these Japanese activities. At the crucial time that the US forces were sailing from Pearl Harbor for the Battle of Midway, therefore, Yamamoto was completely in the dark as to movement of US major surface units.

KA Japanese counteroffensive in the Solomon Islands (August 1942) in response to the invasion of Florida and Guadalcanal Islands by Major General Alexander A. Vandegrift's US 1st Marine Division on 7 August under the overall command of Rear Admiral Frank J. Fletcher, with a task force of 3 aircraft-carriers to cover the assault. The Japanese considered Guadalcanal to be essential to the security of Japan's outer defence perimeter, for this island could be developed as a base from which the Allied lines of maritime communication across the Pacific (from the USA to New Zealand and Australia) could be interdicted, so preventing the build-up of forces for a riposte against the 'Greater East Asia Co-Prosperity Sphere'. Heavy Japanese air attacks started later on 7 August as a precursor of Operation 'KA', and Fletcher was forced on 8 August to take the tactical decision to pull his vulnerable carriers and the transports back to Espiritu Santo and New Caledonia, leaving 16,000 marines on Guadalcanal and 6,000 more on Tulagi, together with rations for 37 days and only limited artillery and small arms ammunition. A brief respite was granted to the marines as the Japanese prepared Operation 'KA', and they put this time to good use preparing Henderson Field as a forward strip for fighters and light attack aircraft. Though no land reinforcements for the Japanese on Guadalcanal had arrived by this time, the marines still had to endure daily bomber and naval gunfire attacks.

Then on 18 August one battalion of the Japanese 28th Infantry Regiment, under Colonel Kiyono Ichiki, was landed at Taivu, some 20 miles to the marines' east. After a difficult approach march, Ichiki launched his men in a series of determined assaults against Henderson Field on 20 and 21 August, though they could make no real impression on the marines, who had the benefit of air support as the first tactical aircraft had arrived on Henderson Field on 20 August. Vandegrift then launched his reserve regiment round the Japanese flank, and the Japanese were driven into the sea and totally destroyed, Ichiki committing suicide. More reinforcements for the Japanese were on the way in the form of the 35th Brigade under Major General Kiyotaki Kawaguchi, and this powerful force launched another series of attacks against Henderson Field on 12 September. The Americans were pushed back to within 1,000 yards of the airstrip, but

Kamelie

finally managed to drive the 35th Brigade back on 14 September, leaving 1,200 casualties behind it.

Operation 'KA' was now in full swing as Lieutenant General Harukichi Hyakutake's Japanese 17th Army in the Solomons responded to orders to hold Guadalcanal and to oust the Americans, using the cruisers and destroyers of Rear Admiral Raizo Tanaka's Destroyer Escort Force, nicknamed the 'Tokyo Express' by the Americans, to ferry in troops during the hours of darkness. Soon the 17th Army headquarters together with Lieutenant General Masao Maruyama's 2nd Division and a part of the 38th Division (about 20,000 men in all) were available for the prosecution of Operation 'KA' against the 1st Marine Division, reinforced to a strength of 23,000 by the arrival of the 7th Marine and 164th Infantry Regiments. All was ready for the next Japanese offensive on 23 October, when the 2nd Division attacked Henderson Field from the south. The Americans held firm and on 26 October Maruyama was compelled to fall back after suffering some 3,500 casualties. This exhausted the capability of the Japanese to launch and sustain an offensive, and it was now the turn of the Americans, who were also exhausted.

A lull therefore ensued until December (though the Japanese had been further reinforced in November with a daring daylight run by the 'Tokyo Express'), when on 9 December Major General Alexander M. Patch's Americal Division relieved the totally exhausted 1st Marine Division. Further US expansion into the XIV Corps (formed on 2 January 1943 under Patch) was made possible by the arrival on 17 December of Major General J. Lawton Collins's 25th Infantry Division and Brigadier General Alphonse de Carre's 2nd Marine Division. By January XIV Corps could deploy some 50,000 well trained and well equipped men, while the 17th Army had 25,000 exhausted men who could not be supplied even by the 'Tokyo Express'. The Japanese decided on an evacuation, and by 9 February the last 11,000 survivors of the 17th Army had been taken off by Tanaka's ships, harried all the way to Cape Esperance by XIV Corps.

Kamelie (camellia) German seaborne occupation of Corsica (November 1942) as part of the German seizure of unoccupied France after the Allied landing in North-West Africa, Operation 'Torch'.

KAN Defensive plan devised by the Burma Area Army for the Japanese protection of the Burmese coastline from amphibious attack (1944/1945).

Kaput US 9th Army defeat of a German counterattack by the Panzer Division von Clausewitz of General Walter Wenck's German 12th Army in the sector of Major General Alvan C. Gillem's US XIII Corps (with the object of regaining a portion of the Harz mountains) and the occupation of a length of the River Elbe (15/24 April 1945). The Germans saw their opportunity for a counterattack as the flanking British VIII Corps of the 2nd Army moved north at Uelzen in accordance with the 2nd Army's movement towards Hamburg. The threat of the Panzer Division von Clausewitz was illusory rather than real, but its attack checked the Americans as they used armour, artillery and white phosphorus weapons to halt the Germans and then rout them.

Karlsbad German operation against Soviet partisans operating in the area of the River Beresina (14/26 October 1941). This was at the beginning of the partisan campaign against the invading Germans, and evidence of the importance that the Soviet high command placed in a campaign of continuing disruption in the German rear areas as a standard method of waging war prepared before the beginning of major offensives. Such operations were particularly important in the Beresina sector as this cut the 'Moscow Highway' between Minsk and Smolensk, and along this highway moved much of the equipment and supplies needed by the divisions of Generalfeldmarschall Fedor von Bock's Army Group 'Centre' at this time approaching the gates of Moscow. Quite apart from the slowing of the German offensive, the partisans hoped to ease the pressure on the Soviet pockets in the Germans' rear, notably that at Vyazma which in fact fell on the day that Operation 'Karlsbad' was launched. The conduct of operations against partisans was hampered to a great extent by the fact that the Germans had a double (and sometimes triple) command structure in the occupied territories, with the army responsible for the combat zone and its immediate rear (through a system of town mayors and military commandants), the Ministry for the Occupied Eastern Territories (under Alfred Rosenberg) responsible for 'pacified' areas farther to the rear, and the SS responsible for all police, security and anti-partisan operations.

Kate River crossing exercise by the Canadian II Corps in the UK (spring 1944).

Kater (tomcat) Cover designation of a German night vision device.

KE Sequel to Operation, 'KA', namely the evacuation of the Japanese 17th Army from Guadalcanal (1/9 February 1943). The operation was planned and prepared materially at Rabaul, and began on 14 January 1943 with a run by Rear Admiral Raizo Tanaka's Destroyer Escort Force, nicknamed the 'Tokyo Express' by the Americans, to ferry a special rearguard unit into Guadalcanal. This comprised the 600 men of the Matsuda Unit, which was carried safely in nine destroyers, of which four were damaged on the return trip after being attacked by aircraft from Henderson Field on Guadalcanal. The real evacuation programme consisted of three return trips undertaken between 1 and 9 February. On the first (2/3 February) some 5,935 men were brought out from Cape Esperance and Kamimbo Bay by 1 light cruiser and 20 destroyers, which were attacked unsuccessfully by American PT boats but then lost one destroyer that was mined. On the second trip 1 light cruiser and 20 destroyers were again used, picking up 3,921 men from the same spots on the night of 4/5 February before suffering damage to one destroyer in an air attack on the homeward journey. And on the third trip 1,790 men were lifted from Guadalcanal (18 destroyers) and Russell Island (2 destroyers) on the night of 7/8 February, one destroyer being damaged, again by an air attack. It had been a remarkable operation by any standard, and quite extraordinarily the Americans had failed to respond with determined surface attacks by anything other than coastal craft.

KETSU Japanese plan for the defence of their home islands (1945) against a US invasion. Tokyo was clearly the Allies' primary objective, and to protect the Japanese capital the high command allocated the 1st General Army Headquarters (in Tokyo) to control the three army groups in the central portion of Honshu Island, from south-west to north-east the 13th Area Army (HQ Nagoya) with 6 infantry divisions, the 12th Area Army (HQ Tokyo) with 2 armoured and 18 infantry divisions, and the 11th Area Army (HQ Sendai) with 6 infantry divisions. The reserve for this area was the 36th Army, and the Air General Army controlled such air assets as were left in the theatre. The defence of the rest of the home islands rested with the 2nd General Army Headquarters in Hiroshima, and this controlled the 5th Area Army (HQ Sapporo) defending the island of Hokkaido in the north with 5 infantry divisions, the 15th Area Army (HQ Osaka) defending the eastern tip of Honshu and the island of Shikoku just to its south with 8 infantry divisions, and the 16th Area Army (HQ Fukuoka) defending the eastern island of Kyushu with 2 armoured and 14 infantry divisions. The Japanese had appreciated the likely disposition of the Allied invasions, for the four available armoured divisions were allocated to the real threat areas (Kyushu where operation 'Olympic' was to happen, and the Tokyo area where Operation 'Coronet' was to take place). In all, the forces allocated to the defence of central Honshu and of Kyushu were about half of those available, and amounted to the major formations listed above plus 25 independent mixed brigades, 3 guards brigades and 7 tank brigades. Though Japan would have been much depleted in weapons by the time of the US invasions, there was little doubt in the minds of the American and Japanese planners alike that the determination and numbers of the Japanese defenders would cost the Americans well over 1,000,000 casualties before Japan could be beaten into total defeat.

K.G. Designation of Caribbean convoys

(together with a numerical suffix) plying between Key West and Guantanamo in Cuba, and inaugurated in September 1942.

Kiku Codename for the Japanese 18th Division in Burma.

Kikushi (floating chrysanthemum) Designation of the Imperial Japanese Navy's *kamikaze* aircraft campaign (6 April/11 May 1945) against the US naval forces off Okinawa during the conquest of that island. At the time of the US invasion of Okinawa, the Imperial Japanese Navy had available some 2,000 aircraft that could reach the island (300 with the 1st Air Fleet on Formosa, 800 with the 3rd Air Fleet around Tokyo, 600 with the 5th Air Fleet on Kyushu, and 400 with the 10th Air Fleet on Honshu), despite the preparatory strikes by US carrierborne aircraft which had inflicted great damage on Japanese airfields and aircraft in the area. The Japanese were aware that Operation 'Iceberg' was about to start, and decided on a pre-emptive strike against the US fleet base at Ulithi with 24 explosives-laden Yokosuka P1Y aircraft guided by 4 flying-boats. However, the raid was recalled when erroneous intelligence suggested that there was but 1 US aircraft-carrier at Ulithi, whereas there were in fact 8. On the next day another attempt was made, but only 11 got to Ulithi, one bomber causing damage to the carrier *Randolph*.

Fifty *kamikazes* were launched against the carrier forces decimating Japanese air strength between 18 and 20 March, and scored a crippling hit on the *Franklin* and lesser strikes on the *Essex*, *Wasp* and *Enterprise*. And so the campaign continued, with small- and large-scale *kamikaze* attacks whenever the Japanese could find targets. The first raid using the special Yokosuka MXY7 Ohka suicide aeroplane was made on 21 March, and showed the type's basic vulnerability while being carried by a wholly unmanoeuvrable Mitsubishi G4M bomber. The only successful sortie by the Okha was on 12 April, when 2 out of 12 scored hits, sinking one destroyer and damaging another. These destroyers were on picket duty well clear of the main US naval forces, a ring of such ships being able to provide the radar coverage that gave the defending fighters time to intercept and the major warships time to organize their truly formidable AA defences. In such circumstances mass attacks by *kamikazes* gave the Japanese the chance to swamp the defences, as shown by the first of these on 6 April when 355 *kamikazes* swept in to sink 2 destroyers, 2 ammunition ships and 1 landing ship tank, and to damage some 22 other ships. Attacks were launched on most days that the weather permitted, and the primary targets were the US aircraft-carriers and the shipping packed densely off the beaches of Okinawa, which received no less than 10 major attacks. The campaign ended for the *kamikazes* on 22 June, by which time some 1,900 sorties had been launched and 1,465 aircraft expended, most of them shot down by the fighters or immensely thick barrages of heavy and medium AA fire. The damage to the US Navy was 26 ships sunk and another 164 damaged, plus 4,900 personnel killed and 4,800 wounded, mostly by the *kamikazes*.

Kikusui-1 (floating chrysanthemum 1) Designation of the ultimate Japanese *kamikaze* mission, that of the super-battleship *Yamato* (6/7 April 1945). The concept behind the operation was that the battleship, accompanied by the light cruiser *Yahagi* and eight destroyers, should make a dash from Tokuyama for Okinawa to try to get in amongst the invasion fleet and then beach herself (there being sufficient oil for only a one-way trip to Okinawa) and then cause havoc with her massive main armament (nine 18-inch guns in three triple turrets) while the cruiser and destroyers used their extremely potent 'Long Lance' torpedoes. It was anticipated that the American forces would detect the Japanese force before its arrival and would thus try to intercept it before its arrival off Okinawa, this distraction to the north offering the possibility of great success for the first mass attack by *kamikaze* aircraft, planned for 6 April. The squadron made for Okinawa in close formation with the battleship ringed by the cruiser and seven destroyers, one having dropped out with engine trouble, and was soon spotted by the Americans, who reacted with a large air strike that rapidly obliterated the defences. The *Yamato* was hit by many bombs and torpedoes, and sank with

2,498 men, the *Yahagi* went down with 446 men, and four destroyers (including the one that had suffered engine trouble) were sunk with 721 men. The four surviving destroyers were all badly damaged, but got back to base.

King Designation of General Douglas MacArthur's overall plan for the US reconquest of the southern and central Philippine islands (1944/1945).

King I Proposed opening phase of Operation 'King', namely the conquest of Mindanao by the combined forces of General Douglas MacArthur's South-West Pacific Area and Admiral Chester W. Nimitz's Pacific Ocean Areas. The plan prepared by MacArthur and his chief-of-staff, Major General Richard K. Sutherland, called for US Army forces to invade Mindanao on 15 November 1944 as an initial step into the Philippines, landing at Saragani Bay some 30,000 US troops to crush what was believed to be a small garrison. This would open up the way for a northward push into the rest of the Philippines, or a westward offensive to the Dutch East Indies or China. The whole operation was abandoned in favour of 'King II'.

King II US operation for the reconquest of Leyte Island in the Philippine group (20 October/25 December 1944). This was the first step in the total reconquest of the Philippines that had been the primary objective of General Douglas MacArthur and his South-West Pacific Area command since the expulsion of the Americans in 1942. Since that time there had existed a basic disagreement in strategic aims between Admiral Chester W. Nimitz, the Commander-in-Chief Pacific Ocean Areas, who favoured an east/west thrust across the Central Pacific towards Formosa and China, and MacArthur, who urged a south/north thrust from New Guinea to the Philippines and then if necessary on to Okinawa and the Japanese home islands. President Franklin D. Roosevelt was compelled to adjudicate in this dispute, and came down in favour of MacArthur and an assault on Mindanao, the largest island in the southern Philippines by the combined forces of MacArthur and Nimitz. This decision was endorsed by the 'Octagon' Conference held at Quebec in September 1944, which envisaged first the reconquest of Mindanao in October 1944, then the reconquest of Leyte from 20 December 1944, and then the choice between further progress in the Philippines (to take Luzon and the Filipino capital, the latter by 2 February 1945) or an amphibious assault on Formosa and Amoy off the coast of mainland China (to secure both islands by 1 May 1945).

At this time there was a considerable reshuffle of the US Navy command structure in the Pacific, Admiral William F. Halsey succeeding Admiral Raymond A. Spruance in command of what now became the 3rd rather than the 5th Fleet. This alteration in commanders-in-chief was accompanied by a change in amphibious force commanders, Vice Admiral Theodore K. Wilkinson succeeding Vice Admiral Richmond K. Turner. Spruance and Turner were thus able to set about the planning of future operations while Halsey and Wilkinson concerned themselves with the Philippine operations. One commander who did not change was Vice Admiral Marc A. Mitscher, whose Fast Carrier Task Force (17 fast carriers, 6 new battleships, 13 cruisers and 58 destroyers, with an aircraft strength of 1,100 carrierborne machines) was redesignated Task Force 38 instead of Task Force 58. Mitscher was responsible for a considerable modification in the basic plan for Philippine operations, for on 28 August his TF38 undertook a series of attacks on Japanese positions on Yap, the Palau and Mindanao islands as a precursor for the joint operations to secure Peleliu and Morotai Islands in anticipation of the Mindanao landings. His aircraft flew 2,400 sorties and shot down 200 Japanese aircraft for the loss of only eight of their own number, convincing Mitscher and thus Halsey that the Japanese were far weaker than had been anticipated. On 13 September Halsey thus urged Nimitz to consider the abandonment of the Mindanao operation in favour of an immediate strike into the centre of the Philippines at Leyte. MacArthur thought this an ideal move, and the 'Octagon' Conference endorsed a revised schedule that called for landings on Leyte on 20 October, to be followed by the invasion of Luzon on 20

December while Nimitz's primary offensive forces took a base in the Bonin Islands (20 January 1945) and Ryukyu Islands (March 1945) with a view to major operations from these bases against the Japanese home islands.

American efforts now moved into high gear with a relatively bloodless seizure of Morotai (15 September by MacArthur's forces) and an extremely bloody campaign to take Peleliu (15 September/25 November by Nimitz's forces), while between 10 and 15 October TF38 slashed at all Japanese air and naval bases (in the Ryukyus, Formosa and Luzon) from which counterattacks could be made against the Leyte landings, shooting down more than 500 of 1,000 Japanese aircraft for the loss of 110 US aircraft. Overall control of the Philippines was vested in Field Marshal Count Hisaichi Terauchi's Southern Army, local command being exercised by Lieutenant General Tomoyoki Yamashita's 14th Area Army, which deployed some 265,000 men in nine divisions and three independent mixed brigades in the islands. The defence of the central and southern Philippines was the task of Lieutenant General S. Suzuki's 35th Army with four divisions and one independent mixed brigade. Of this force only Lieutenant General S. Makino's 16th Division was on Leyte, where Lieutenant General Walter Krueger's US 6th Army was to land 174,000 men under the escort and gunfire support of the 700 ships of Vice Admiral Thomas S. Kinkaid's US 7th Fleet. The amphibious force commanders were Vice Admiral Wilkinson (III Amphibious Force, transferred with XXIV Corps from Nimitz's to MacArthur's command for Operation 'King II') and Rear Admiral D. E. Barbey (VII Amphibious Corps). More distant support was provided by Halsey's 3rd Fleet, whose 4 fast carrier task groups were primarily responsible for preventing any Japanese naval counteroffensive against the invasion forces.

The vast invasion fleet arrived off Leyte on 17 October and seized the islands dominating the entrance to Leyte Gulf before launching a sustained two-day bombardment of the invasion area with the support of tactical aircraft from the 18 escort carriers designated to provide the ground forces with support until airfields on Leyte could be captured and brought into use for the 2,500 aircraft of Lieutenant General George C. Kenney's US 5th Air Force. The landings were finally committed on 20 October, with Major General F. C. Sibert's US X Corps (1st Cavalry and 24th Infantry Divisions) on the right and Major General Julian R. Hodge's US XXIV Corps (96th and 7th Infantry Divisions) on the left. By the evening of the first day, 132,400 Americans had come ashore (together with 200,000 tons of supplies), and X Corps had taken the area around Tacloban, together with its airfield, while XXIV Corps had seized the region around Dulag, together with its airfield, putting into American hands two of the island's five airfields (the other three being close to Burauen farther inland from the assault area). Suzuki was ordered to check the Americans on the line between Burauen and Dagami as four battalions and army HQ were rushed onto Leyte, where Yamashita decided the decisive defeat of the Americans would be achieved by a 35th Army reinforced by two divisions and a brigade.

By 24 October the US 6th Army had secured a consolidated beach-head running from Dulag and Burauen in the south to the shores on the Leyte and Samar sides of the San Juanico Strait in the north, while Suzuki mustered his slowly-arriving reinforcements in the Carigara plain, a move that played right into the hands of the US 6th Army, which had now secured all five Japanese airfields. By the end of October the Americans had taken the entire north-eastern corner of Leyte along the line from Carigara to Dulag. As their reinforcements had to come in by sea the Japanese suffered heavy losses at the hands of US aircraft, but between 22 October and 11 December Suzuki had increased Japanese strength on Leyte from 15,000 men to 45,000 men (parts of the 16th, 1st, 26th, 30th and 102nd Divisions eventually) plus 10,000 tons of sorely-needed supplies. By 2 December the strength of the 6th Army on Leyte had reached 183,000 men, and the 32nd Infantry Division had relieved the 24th Infantry Division on 14 November as the Americans continued their methodical but inexorable westward push (using overland and amphibious assaults) from the northern part of their lodgement along the northern side of Leyte towards Pinamopoan.

While Suzuki's attention was engaged by the US X Corps' advance in the north, the US XXIV Corps in the south pushed forward towards Ormoc, the main Japanese base on the island, and to take the southern portion of Leyte. By early December, however, the Americans were stalled by determined if futile Japanese resistance, and Krueger opted for another amphibious assault to unseam the defence. On 7 December the US 77th Infantry Division was thrown ashore just south of Ormoc and captured this key port three days later against minimal resistance. Japanese defences began to crumble from this time, and units of the US X and XXIV Corps met at Cananga on 20 December. Though organized resistance ended on 25 December the Japanese still had many men at loose on the island best on guerrilla warfare, and mopping up lasted until 17 March 1945; even then there was the equivalent of one division in small troublesome pockets, and these remained in action until the end of the war. US ground force losses in the Leyte campaign were 15,584 including 3,508 dead. The Japanese lost at least 80,000, one-third of them during 1945.

King-Pin Allied codename for Général Henri Giraud, French commander-in-chief in North Africa at the time of the Operation 'Torch' landings.

Kipling Airborne raid by C Squadron, 1st SAS, near Mazignen in France to disrupt German communications (29 July 1944).

K.J. Designation of ocean homeward convoys (together with a numerical suffix) plying the route from Kingston, Jamaica to the UK. These convoys were inaugurated on 15 September 1939 and terminated on 8 October 1939.

Klabautermann (bogey man) Operations on Lake Ladoga by German and Italian light naval forces (July/November 1942) directed against the Soviet Ladoga Naval Flotilla with the longer-term objective of cutting the Soviets' supply route to the city of Leningrad across the lake.

Kleine Heidelberg (small Heidelberg) German aircraft-detection equipment using the emissions of British ground-based radars.

Klette (burdock) Designation of two offensives by German ground forces against Soviet partisans operating in the area of Kletnya and Mamayevka (January/February 1943). These partisan forces operated under the direct control of the Soviet high command in Moscow, and in this instance were directed to cut the exposed lines of communication to Generalfeldmarschall Günther von Kluge's Army Group 'Centre' in the area to the southwest of Bryansk. This was part of the Soviet plan for General K. K. Rokossovsky's Central Front, formed from the previous Don Front, to cut off a substantial part of Army Group 'Centre' with a northward punch from the Bryansk-Orel salient. The Soviet offensive began on 25 February 1943 but failed in its strategic objective as the German 2nd Army secured an excellent stop line between Sumy and Rylsk.

K.M.F. Designation of military convoys for Operation 'Torch' (together with a numerical suffix) plying from the UK to North Africa, and later extended to Egypt. These convoys were inaugurated in October 1942.

K.M.S. Designation of ocean outward convoys (together with a numerical suffix) plying the route from the UK to North Africa. Inaugurated in October 1942, these convoys were primarily military in nature, and from April 1943 travelled with O.S. convoys (and with O.G. convoys from July 1943) as far as Gibraltar.

K.N. Designation of US coastal convoys (together with a numerical suffix) plying the route from Key West to New York, and inaugurated in May 1942.

Knickebein (bent leg) German radio blind-bombing system used in the night Blitz against British cities (1940). The system used two intersecting radio beams to mark the bombing point for aircraft fitted with Lorenz equipment.

KO Japanese offensive in central China,

launched (March 1945) as a companion to Operation 'ICHI' farther to the south, and designed by General Y. Okamura (commander-in-chief of the China Expeditionary Army, with its headquarters in Nanking) to eliminate the Chinese salient north of the River Yangtse. This salient had its shoulders at Tungkwan in the north and near Laohokow in the south, with its apex jutting into the Japanese-held portion of China as far east as Kaifeng in the sector held by the 12th and 34th Armies of the 6th Area Army. This Chinese salient was an important Japanese target for the three reasons that it contained a valuable rice harvest, that it sheltered the two major US 14th Air Force bases at Ankang and Laohokow, and that in it lay the strategic rail nexus of Chenghsien. The rice harvest was important to the Japanese as it would bolster their capabilities while reducing those of the Chinese from whom it could hopefully be captured immediately after the harvest; the reduction of the air bases would lessen the threat to significant Japanese targets in China and Manchukuo (Manchuria); and the capture of Chenghsien would allow a useful reduction in Japanese local force strengths by allowing greater strategic mobility and speed as lines radiated from this key city to Peking in the north, to Tungkwan and Sian in the west, to Hankow, Wuchang, Changshah and Canton in the south, and to Suchow and Haichow in the east. Thus Operation 'KO' was more than a mere adjunct to Operation 'ICHI', having decidedly important strategic ramifications of its own, and great efforts were made by the Japanese to secure success.

The operation came as a complete surprise to the Chinese, who were forced back throughout the salient, especially in the south where the air base of Laohokow fell to the chagrin of Lieutenant General Claire Chennault, commanding the US 14th Air Force. However, the Chinese checked the Japanese thrust by mid-April 1945 thanks to the rejuvenating efforts of Lieutenant General Albert C. Wedemeyer, who had succeeded Lieutenant General Joseph W. Stilwell as chief-of-staff to Generalissimo Chiang Kai-shek during the earlier stages of Operation 'ICHI' and was also exercising operational command of the Chinese forces in the field. At about this time Okamura decided that the offensive did not warrant any further expenditure of effort, for the rice harvest had been captured, Chenghsien taken, and one of the two troublesome US air bases seized. Moreover, the threat along the Siberian/Manchukuoan border was looking increasingly dangerous as Soviet troops were moved into the theatre at the time of terminal hostilities in Europe, so Okamura decided to use the strategic mobility provided by possession of Chenghsien to reduce his forces in China as a means of bolstering those in Manchukuo.

Koltso (ring) Soviet operation commanded by General K. K. Rokossovsky to wipe out Generaloberst Friedrich Paulus's German 6th Army trapped in the Stalingrad pocket (9 January/2 February 1943). The operation was undertaken by the Don Front, whose four armies were reinforced by the 57th, 62nd and 64th Armies of General A. I. Eremenko's Stalingrad Front, which was redesignated the South Front on 1 January 1943. The Soviet planning was undertaken at a high level in Moscow when it became fully appreciated that Soviet first impressions, that only a few divisions had been trapped in Stalingrad, were wrong and that one whole army (the 6th Army) and part of another (the 4th Panzerarmee) were in fact encircled. Soviet planning called for the German relief attempt (Operation 'Wintergewitter' controlled by Generalfeldmarschall Erich von Manstein and using Generaloberst Hermann Hoth's Gruppe Hoth of the 4th Panzerarmee) to be defeated comprehensively before the beginning of Operation 'Koltso', and during this time a massive air transport operation was mounted under the personal control of Reichsmarschall Hermann Goering to fly into the beleaguered garrison all necessary fuel, food, ammunition and other supplies, on their return trips the aircraft flying out some 25,000 wounded.

The 6th Army occupied a pocket measuring some 40 miles in length from east to west, and about 20 miles from north to south, and this area contained two major airfields (Gumrak and Pitomnik, the latter having the pocket's only night-flying capability) and five smaller airstrips. At first the aircraft had only some 150 miles to fly, but as Soviet successes against the 4th Panzerarmee and the 6th

Army increased the gap between the two German forces this distance increased eventually to 300 miles, the need for additional fuel reducing the aircraft's freight loads and raising the chance of interception by the increasingly potent fighter force of General S. I. Rudenko's 16th Air Army. Thus the average daily delivery of supplies had fallen from 140 tons in mid-December to 60 tons in mid-January, when Goering was replaced in command of the operation by Generalfeldmarschall Erhard Milch, who managed to boost deliveries to about 80 tons per day before the Soviet ring closing in around the city cost the Germans the remaining airfields and made necessary a recourse to paradrops. In the whole effort the Luftwaffe lost some 490 nearly irreplaceable transport and bomber-transport aircraft.

On 8 January Rokossovsky called on the 6th Army to surrender, and was refused. Operation 'Koltso' thus began at 08.05 on 9 January, the ring round the German pocket comprising (clockwise from the position on the River Volga) the 62nd Army with two pockets on the western bank of the Volga, the 64th Army, the 57th Army, the 21st Army, the 65th Army, the 24th Army and the 66th Army. Pressure was exerted directly on Stalingrad by the two pockets of the 62nd Army in the city, while the southern and northern perimeters were indented by the efforts of the 64th and 66th Armies respectively. The main weight of Operation 'Koltso' lay with the forces to the west, however, and here the 21st, 65th and 24th Armies made important advances, by the night of 13 January advancing as far east as the line of the Rivers Chervlennaya and Rossoshka, in the process taking Karpovka airfield. Conditions were appalling, with driving snow and extremely low temperatures, but the Soviets were far better equipped and fed, for by this time the German garrison was without fuel, desperately short of ammunition, and far below the barest minima of food and clothing. Some 12,000 wounded were without medical support, and later in the campaign these casualties received no food in order to conserve stocks for the fighting men.

By 17 January the Soviets had pushed on farther, having captured the whole western half of the pocket and another five airfields, including the vital Pitomnik on 14 January. Only Gumrak was now in German hands, and this was scarcely usable for snow and runway cratering. On 22 January Rokossovsky launched his men into the final phase of Operation 'Koltso', with the 24th, 65th, 21st and 57th Armies pushing east towards the city. On 26 January elements of the 21st and 62nd Armies made contact, and the German garrison was cut into two pockets in Stalingrad. Paulus controlled that in the south, while that in the north came under the command of General K. Strecker's XI Corps. The end was only days away, but Hitler decided that as no German field marshal had ever surrendered, Paulus should on 31 January be promoted to *Generalfeldmarschall*. On that day Paulus surrendered his pocket, that of Strecker following on 2 February. It was a catastrophic blow for the Germans, losing them vast numbers of men, but more importantly depriving them of the strategic initiative on the Eastern Front, and also dealing a body blow to the morale of the German people, who had come to believe that the German army was all but omnipotent on the Eastern Front. The German dead in Stalingrad are believed to have numbered some 110,000, and about 90,000 Germans were taken prisoner, this latter figure including 24 generals and 2,500 officers. Stalingrad was a defeat from which the German effort in World War II never recovered.

KON Designation of the Japanese plan (spring 1944) to reinforce and hold an inner defence line in the Pacific theatre. It was appreciated by the Japanese that two main US thrusts were being directed against them, namely that of Admiral Chester W. Nimitz's Pacific Ocean Areas from the east across the central Pacific, and that of General Douglas MacArthur's South-West Pacific Area from the south, and that these two thrusts could well meet in the Philippines. The defensive line for 'KON' thus ran from the Marianas via the Palaus and western New Guinea to the Dutch East Indies, and behind this line the Japanese built up troop concentrations, prepared new airfields and gathered the Combined Fleet, the notion being to move men, aircraft and ships rapidly to any sector

107

threatened by the Americans, though the main thrust was expected to be that of MacArthur's forces from New Guinea towards Mindanao in the Philippines. Here the Japanese thought that they could fight a decisive battle against the Americans with a high chance of success. Actual concentrations and contingency plans were frequently altered to meet the shifting perceived threat, but by May 1944 it was clear that the strategic premises upon which Operation 'KON' was based were out of date, and Japanese thinking changed to Operation 'A' as the decisive battle against the advancing US forces.

Konserven (canned goods) German designation for the party of condemned concentration camp inmates used in Operation 'Himmler'.

Konstantin (Constantine) Overall designation of the operation in which German forces occupied those parts of Greece and the Balkans garrisoned by Italian forces up to the time of Italy's armistice with the Allies (September/October 1943). This was the Balkan counterpart to Operation 'Achse' (ii).

Kool US task force in Operation 'Husky'.

Kopenhagen (Copenhagen) German seizure of the pass over Mont Cenis as part of Operation 'Achse' (ii).

Koralle (coral) Telegraphic code address of the headquarters of the Oberkommando der Kriegsmarine at Bernau near Berlin.

Korfu (Corfu) German radar receiver designed to provide the bearing of British and US aircraft using H2S and H2X navigation radar.

Kormoran (cormorant) German operation against Soviet partisans operating in the region of the Novi Borisov-Minsk railway (22 May/20 June 1943). In this key area of Belorussia, substantial partisan forces could operate to good effect from safe havens just to the south in the Pripet Marshes, harrying German rail and road communications with the forces of Generalfeldmarschall Günther von Kluge's Army Group 'Centre' in front of Smolensk. Here the 3rd Panzerarmee and 4th Army were tasked with the defence of Vitebsk and Smolensk, against which the Soviets planned to unleash the forces of General A. I. Eremenko's Kalinin Front (later 1st Baltic Front) and General V. D. Sokolovsky's West Front as part of the late-summer general offensive to free the Dniepr and Smolensk areas from German occupation in the aftermath of Operation 'Zitadelle'. Thus an increasing tempo of partisan operations was ordered in an effort to reduce the volume of supplies reaching German front-line formations, and also to persuade the Germans to pull back combat units for internal-security duties.

Kottbus German operation against Soviet partisans operating in the Polotsk-Borisov-Lepel region (3/23 June 1943). This region lay in the rear of the 3rd Panzerarmee, holding the northern shoulder of Generalfeldmarschall Günther von Kluge's Army Group 'Centre', and was the operational sector allocated to General A. I. Eremenko's Kalinin Front (later 1st Baltic Front) in the Soviet offensive planned for the late summer of 1943. The Soviet partisans were thus tasked with creating havoc on German lines of communication in an effort to divert German front-line units and to hinder defensive preparations.

Kreml (Kremlin) German deception plan of early 1942 designed to instil in the Soviet high command that the German summer offensive of summer 1942 would be directed at Moscow. To this end a series of 'leaks' to foreign pressmen was arranged by Dr Joseph Goebbels's German propaganda ministry, while Generalfeldmarschall Günther von Kluge's Army Group 'Centre' made relatively little concealment of military preparations to this end. The object of this complex plan was to divert the attention of the Soviets from Operation 'Blau' and its successors.

Kreuzotter (viper) German operation against resistance forces in Greece.

Kugelblitz (ball lightning) Massive German operation against partisans operating in eastern Bosnia, western Serbia,

Slovenia and the Adriatic islands (December 1943). The Germans used a total of 19 divisions in this operation, which was planned as a decisive stroke against the communist resistance force in the west and north-west Balkans under the overall leadership of Marshal Tito. The communist partisan movement had come into being almost immediately after the conquest of Yugoslavia by the Germans, but bided its time until after the beginning of Operation 'Barbarossa' before issuing a call to arms. Tito's plans called for dispersed hit-and-run operations against the occupying forces, which would tie down the Germans and Italians, cost the opposition heavily in men and *matériel* and build up the strength and offensive capability of the partisan movement without the need for heavy losses.

The success of Tito's movement is attested by the fact that the Germans had lost control of much of western Serbia by September 1941. There then followed a period of great difficulty as the partisans became more embroiled against the Cetnik royalist resistance under Colonel Draza Mihailovic than against the Germans as each resistance movement sought to bring the other into its fold. The struggle of the Cetniks and the partisans led the former away from their anti-German position, their greater hatred of the partisans persuading them increasingly to co-operate with the Germans against the partisans. In the short term the partisan/Cetnik struggle of 1941 allowed the Germans to recover most of western Serbia by December 1941 during the course of their first offensive against the Yugoslav partisans. This persuaded Tito to fall back into Bosnia and re-establish his forces, which had up to that time consisted mostly of local-defence resistance groups. Tito realized that the war with the Axis would be a long one, and that for his long-term aims of driving out the Axis and establishing a communist state he would need a formal army. The 1st Proletarian Shock Brigade was formed in December 1941, and just 12 months later this People's Liberation Army had grown into a resistance force of some 28 brigades each comprising some 3,000 to 4,000 men and women. Though weapons, ammunition and other requirements were in short supply, the PLA was notable for its high standards of discipline and its excellent care for the wounded.

Tito's forces then started to fight their way northward from Bosnia against the much-strengthened divisions of Generalfeldmarschall Maximilian von Weichs's German Forces in the South-East command. The Allies were highly distrustful of the partisan movement at this time, and no material aid was furnished until mid-1943, by which time the partisans had endured five German offensives against them. From this time onwards a steadily increasing flow of material support began to reach the partisans, who had to endure the Germans' most strenuous offensive against them in Operation 'Kugelblitz', which lasted until February 1944 and drove the partisans back towards Bosnia while capturing Dalmatia and all the offshore Adriatic islands but Vis.

Kurfürst (Elector) Cable address of the headquarters of the Oberkommando der Luftwaffe at Wildpark-Werden near Berlin.

Küste (coast) German air campaign against Warsaw (25 September 1939). Though propaganda during and since the end of the war has put the German aerial assault force for this campaign against the Polish capital at 800 bombers, the true total of aircraft deployed by Generalleutnant Wolfram Freiherr von Richthofen's VIII Fliegerkorps was some 400 bombers, dive-bombers and ground-attack aircraft. The Poles had four times been warned of the dangers inherent in continued defence of the city (by some 100,000 troops), and in the event received some 500 tons of HE bombs from these aircraft. But far greater damage was inflicted by a force of some 30 Junkers Ju 52 tri-motor transports, which unloaded 72 tons of incendiaries over the Polish capital, causing numberless fires that made accurate conventional bombing impossible. The effect of Operation 'Küste' was immediate, for on the next day the capital surrendered without the need for a German ground force assault.

Kutuzov Soviet elimination of the Orel salient (12 July/18 August 1943). Undertaken in the immediate aftermath of the German disaster in Operation 'Zitadelle', this Soviet

K.X.

offensive capitalized on the failing capabilities of the Germans on the Eastern Front to emphasize that the strategic and operational initiatives had passed irrevocably into the hands of Soviet forces that were growing monthly in strength and skill. The offensive was carefully planned, the object being not only to liberate the Soviet territory in the salient, but also to trap as much as possible of the 2nd Panzerarmee (commanded by Generaloberst Walther Model since the dismissal of Generaloberst Rudolf Schmidt on 11 July) and of the 9th Army (commanded by Model), formations of Generalfeldmarschall Günther von Kluge's Army Group 'Centre'. The Soviet offensive was entrusted to the West Front of General V. D. Sokolovsky and the Bryansk Front of General M. M. Popov, which had not been directly involved in the 'Zitadelle' battles that raged just to their south on the right flank of the German salient. The plan was for the 3rd and 63rd Armies of the West Front to drive directly west from the area of Novosil across the River Susha and through the junction of the 2nd Panzerarmee and the 9th Army to take the city of Orel and so pin the Germans in this area while the 3rd Guards Tank Army passed through to exploit farther to the west. At the same time the 11th Guards Army of the West Front was to push straight south from the area of Belev to crush the left shoulder of the German salient and so permit the 4th Tank Army to push through and cut off the 2nd Panzerarmee.

The Germans were well served by their intelligence system, however, and from photoreconnaissance and radio intercepts built up a clear picture of what the Soviets were planning. Though their lack of strength made impossible any counterattack, they were thus able to prepare defences in depth, especially in the sector of General Dr Lothar Rendulic's XXXV Corps which faced the main assault by the 63rd Army. Model exercised operational command of the 9th Army and 2nd Panzerarmee directly, and the 63rd Army was able to make only slow progress towards Orel. The outcome was not in doubt, but the need to force the Germans out of each laid-back defence line threw the scheduling of the Soviet offensive completely out of order. In the north the 11th Guards Army fared better, advancing some 16 miles in two days against bitter resistance. The Soviet advance was slowly checked despite the committal of extra Soviet armies, but then political events elsewhere in Europe took a hand, for on 26 July Hitler heard of the fall of the Italian dictator, Benito Mussolini, and called von Kluge to Germany for orders to evacuate the Orel salient as a means of saving troops for service in an increasingly threatened Western Europe. Von Kluge objected, but Hitler was adamant, especially after the German intelligence services listened in to a radio telephone conversation between President Franklin D. Roosevelt and Prime Minister Winston Churchill about the imminent defection of Italy from the Axis camp.

By early August General K. K. Rokossovsky's Central Front on the southern shoulder of the salient had joined in what was by now a general Soviet offensive, yet the Germans managed to pull back in good order to the half-completed 'Hagen Linie' positions in front of Bryansk on receipt of Hitler's orders for an immediate withdrawal on 1 August. But there was to be no respite for the Germans as Marshal of the Soviet Union Georgi Zhukov was now completing the final plans for the Soviet offensive of 23 August that was to push the Germans back along the whole length of the front from Nevel south to the Black Sea in the operational areas of Army Groups 'Centre', 'South' and 'A'.

K.X. Designation of special Operation 'Torch' convoys (together with a numerical suffix) plying from the UK to North Africa, and inaugurated in October 1942.

L

Lachsfang (salmon trap) Combined German and Finnish operation (1 July/September 1941) to seize the Murmansk railway between Kandalaksha in the north and Belomorsk on the south, a stretch running along the western shore of the White Sea. Success in this venture would have cut off the Soviet forces in the Kola peninsula and Murmansk, making simpler the task of Generaloberst Eduard Dietl's two-division Gebirgskorps in advancing over the River Litsa in the extreme north to take this vital Soviet port. The task was entrusted to the Armeeoberkommando Norwegen of Generaloberst Nikolaus von Falkenhorst, which used General H. Feige's German XXXVI Corps (one Finnish and two German divisions) in the north of the sector and General H. Siilasvuo's Finnish III Corps (one Finnish division) in the south. Little real progress was achieved against the defences of the Soviet 7th and 14th Armies, the latter's Lieutenant General V. A. Frolov being able to use unhindered rail communications to supplement sea lift as a means of rapid reinforcement for Kandalaksha. The whole offensive was bedevilled by rivalry and dissension between the Finnish and German commands, the lack of training in the German troops for forest warfare, determined Soviet resistance, and the foolhardiness of launching three widely-separated thrusts where one concentrated effort might have succeeded.

Ladbrooke Airborne operation by the 1st Air Landing Brigade of Major General G. F. Hopkinson's British 1st Airborne Division to capture the Grande bridge over the River Anapo and then the western suburbs of Syracuse (10 July 1943) during the Sicilian campaign and so speed the advance of Major General H. P. M. Berney-Ficklin's British 5th Division along the eastern coast of the island.

Landbrücke (land bridge) Designation of the German operation to relieve their forces trapped in the Demyansk pocket on the Eastern Front (21 March/21 April 1942). Some 90,000 men of seven divisions of the German II Corps and part of X Corps under General W. Graf von Brockdorff-Ahlefeld had since 8 February been cut off (in what Hitler euphemistically termed an offensive fortress) by the meeting of the Soviet 3rd Shock and 11th Armies. The pocket measured some 40 miles in length and 20 in depth, and hastily-improvised but well-executed airlift operations kept the beleaguered forces adequately supplied until the relief operation could be mounted by the special five-division corps formed for the task under the command of Generalleutnant Walter von Seydlitz-Kurzbach. In one month of intensive operations the relief force drove a narrow corridor through 25 miles of Soviet positions to join up with II and X Corps, allowing substantial reinforcements to be poured into the pocket, which was held as a base for offensive operations during the summer of 1942.

Landgrab US operation to recapture Attu Island in the Aleutians from the Japanese (11/30 May 1943). The island had been taken by the Japanese as part of the Operation 'AL' diversion leading to the Battle of Midway, and was garrisoned by some 3,000 troops, who had to be supplied at great range and in the most hostile climatic and geographical circumstances to no great strategic effect other than the diversion of Japanese resources from important theatres. The garrison on Attu (and that on Kiska) had to endure the tedium and cold of the Aleutians while the Americans kept them under surveillance and bombing attacks to which they could not respond effectively. Towards the end of 1942 the Americans began their countermove, occupying Adak Island on 30 August (rapidly building a tactical airstrip that was operational by 14 September) before moving to Amchitka Island, only 60 miles from Kiska, on 12 January 1943. The US forces then bypassed Kiska, the main Japanese bastion in the Aleutians, and landed on Attu during 11 May 1943. By this time the Japanese garrison on the island was a mere 2,500 men, who came under attack by an invasion force of some 11,000 men of the US 7th Infantry Division. An extremely bloody and bitter campaign was fought over this wholly inhospitable island before the Japanese, out of all but small arms ammunition and reduced to 1,000 men, launched a suicide attack on 28 May. Some 500 men survived the defeat of this effort and tried again on the following night. Early on 30 May the survivors committed suicide, leaving the Americans in possession of the island and 28 prisoners. US losses were 600 killed and 1,200 wounded.

L.E. Designation of local Mediterranean convoys (together with a numerical suffix) plying between Port Said or Alexandria via Famagusta to Haifa or Beirut, and inaugurated in July 1941.

Leader British and US naval air strike against German shipping in Bodo harbour and Norwegian waters (4 October 1943). This operation was made possible by the damage caused to the German battleship *Tirpitz* by British midget submarines in northern Norwegian waters, which allowed major surface units to operate with relative impunity in the North Sea and Norwegian Sea. Under the command of Admiral Sir Bruce Fraser, elements of the Home Fleet escorted the American carrier *Ranger* on the strike, which sank five ships of 20,750 tons and damaged another seven, including a large tanker.

Leatherback Allied codename for Woodlark Island off the southern tip of New Guinea.

Ledo Striptease Advance of the 22nd and 38th Divisions of the Chinese Army in India from Ledo to Shingbwiyang (October 1943). This was a preliminary move for the offensive against Myitkyina long planned by Lieutenant General Joseph W. Stilwell and undertaken at the same time as Major General Orde Wingate's 2nd Chindit Expedition. The rationale of Stilwell's planning was that the location of Lieutenant General N. Tanaka's Japanese 18th Division, in the Hukawng Valley to the north-west of Myitkyina, threatened the vital supply road being built in north-east India from Ledo into southern China, and that this threat could only be removed by the defeat of the 18th Division during an advance by the Chinese 22nd and 38th Divisions to capture Myitkyina, whose loss would deprive the Japanese of their main base in the area. The Chinese divisions reached Shingbwiyang by 30 October 1943 and pushed forward into the Hukawng Valley during November before being checked by the 18th Division. The Chinese advance got under way again in late December but was then halted again in January 1944, resuming only after the arrival of the US 5307th Provision Regiment (otherwise 'Merrill's Marauders'), which allowed the Chinese to pin the Japanese while the Americans launched outflanking movements, until Myitkyina fell with Chindit help on 4 August.

Lehrgang (course) Designation of the evacuation of German forces (General Hans Hube's XIV Panzer Corps) from Sicily to the Italian mainland (11/17 August 1943) in face of Allied victory over the island. The operation was planned and controlled by Oberst Ernst Baade, the German district commandant of the Straits of Messina, with Fregatenkapitän von Liebenstein. With classic efficiency and under circumstances of overwhelming Allied air superiority, these two men managed to effect a superb evacuation with limited resources, using ruthless discipline plus excellent but highly flexible planning to make maximum use of their transports (9 Siebel ferries, 7 ferry barges, 1 naval ferry, 12 landing boats, 41 assault boats and 50 rubber boats). As a preliminary to the evacuation proper, Baade between 1 and 10 August moved some 12,000 men, 4,500 vehicles and 5,000 tons of supplies over to the mainland, and all was ready for the main operation to begin at 18.00 on 11 August under cover of powerful AA defences on both sides of the straits. The strength of the evacuation flotilla varied from time to time, and Allied air strength forced frequent changes in the Germans' operational procedures and actual ferry routes. The evacuation was completed at 06.35 on 17 August, and in the period between 1 and 17 August it is believed that Baade's organization was responsible for the salving of some 60,000 German troops together with a very high proportion of their vehicles, weapons and other equipment and supplies. A comparable Italian evacuation brought some 75,000 men back into Calabria.

Leopard German seizure of the island of Leros in the Aegean Sea (12/16 November 1943). The islands of Leros and Kos, lying to the north of Rhodes and Scarpanto, provided an excellent back-up to the more southerly islands in providing bases from which the Germans could bar Allied access to the Aegean as a means of inducing Turkey to enter the war on the side of the Allies, for while Leros had a good harbour for the basing of light naval forces and seaplanes, Kos could offer a base for landplanes. The islands also formed an admirable offensive base for aircraft and U-boats attacking Allied shipping in the eastern Mediterranean. General Sir Henry Maitland Wilson, the Commander-in-Chief Middle East, had long favoured a descent on the Aegean islands, and had the full support of Prime Minister Winston Churchill in this enthusiasm. However, the Germans had substantial garrison forces on Rhodes, Scarpanto and the other islands, and though British landing forces were available, the Middle East command lacked the landing craft and long-range fighters to make possible a full-scale assault on Rhodes and Scarpanto. Nevertheless, between 10 and 17 September 1943 the islands running between Casteloriso in the south and Samos in the north were all occupied in the aftermath of the armistice with Italy. Some 4,000 men were allocated to Kos (landed by air), Leros (ferried in by destroyers) and Samos (transported from Leros in small craft), with smaller garrisons to bolster the Italian forces on the smaller islands.

In strategic terms the islands were next to useless, however, so long as the German garrison on Rhodes remained intact to block access to the Aegean, and this garrison was never eliminated as a result of the non-implementation of Operation 'Accolade', which vindicated Hitler's refusal to permit the evacuation of the Aegean islands and Crete recommended by Generalfeldmarschall Ferdinand von Weichs, the German commander-in-chief in the Balkans, and Grossadmiral Karl Dönitz, commander-in-chief of the German navy. The Germans now planned a counteroffensive, and by the beginning of November had retaken Kos and most of the smaller islands. On 5 November Leros saw the arrival of Major General H. R. Hall as British commander in the Aegean and of Lieutenant Colonel R. A. G. Tilney as fortress commander for the three British infantry battalions on Leros, which Churchill had decided should be held at all costs despite its isolated position. Kos had fallen to an assault group of Generalleutnant Friedrich-Wilhelm Müller's 22nd Division reinforced by paratroops, and this formation was further augmented to 2,730 men for the proposed descent on Leros, which was to be a combined amphibious and airborne operation. The seaborne landings began on 12 November, and were soon reinforced by the paratroops and further landings on the coast. The British were too widely dispersed and too poorly equipped to check the Germans, who were in full control of the island by 16 November. It was now decided to abandon all the Aegean islands (Samos being evacuated on 19/20 November and Casteloriso on 28 November), the whole Aegean campaign having cost the British army some 4,800 men, the RAF about 115 aircraft and the Royal Navy (including Allied ships under command) 4 cruisers damaged (1 irreparably), 4 destroyers damaged and 6 sunk, 2 submarines sunk, and 10 coastal craft/minesweepers sunk. German casualties were some 4,000 men in all.

Lever British plan for the final destruction of the French battle-cruiser *Dunkerque* in Mers el Kébir (6 July 1940), three days after Force H's gunfire attack on the French North African naval bases.

Lichtenstein German night-fighter radar.

Lichtschlag (thinning) Plan for Generalfeldmarschall Georg von Küchler's Army Group 'North' to improve the position of its extreme southern flank at the junction with Generalfeldmarschall Günther von Kluge's Army Group 'Centre' in the area of Kholm on the River Lovat between Velikuye Luki and Lake Ilmen (October/November 1942). Here the Demyansk salient jutted into the Soviet front very deeply, and von Küchler planned for his 16th Army to straighten the front to the advantage of the Germans by evacuating the Demyansk salient to the line of the Lovat. At the same time von Kluge proposed to evacuate the similar but considerably large Rzhev-Vyazma salient. Hitler absolutely forbade this operationally sensible shortening of the German line on the grounds that it would free forces of Colonel General P. A. Kurochkin's North-West Front and General I. S. Konev's Kalinin Front for employment elsewhere on the Eastern Front. Hitler totally ignored the fact that the straightening of the German line would free German forces for gainful use elsewhere, and also eliminate the dangerous position of the German forces to the immediate north-west of Moscow.

Lifebelt Allied plan to take the Portuguese islands (the Azores, Madeira and Cape Verde groups) in the Atlantic to prevent their use by the Germans as bases for maritime aircraft and U-boats involved in the campaign against Allied shipping in this theatre, and to provide air bases and escort force refuelling points for the Allied units in the Atlantic war.

Lightfoot First phase of the 2nd Battle of El Alamein (23/26 October 1942). This battle was planned by General Sir Bernard Montgomery as the decisive stroke of what had hitherto been a see-saw campaign east and west along the Western Desert as the Axis forces commanded by Generalfeldmarschall Erwin Rommel strove to drive the British back to the Suez Canal and out of Egypt, and as the British and Commonwealth forces under a number of commanders fought to push the German and Italian forces back to Tunisia and then out of North Africa altogether. Supplies and the length of each side's lines of communication had played as decisive a part as tactical and operational expertise in this protracted campaign, and it was this double factor that set the scene for the 2nd Battle of El Alamein, for Rommel's setback in the Battle of Alam Halfa (30 August/4 September 1942) had exhausted his men, cost his vehicle and tank strengths dearly, and used up virtually all the Axis forces' fuel.

Thus Rommel set his Panzerarmee Afrika (renamed the German-Italian Panzerarmee on 25 October) to preparing defensive positions between El Alamein on the coast of the Mediterranean and Qaret el Himeimat on the northern side of the great Qattara Depression. The front was protected by a mass of overlapping minefields covered by artillery, while behind these fields were the Axis infantry and behind them the surviving armour. Rommel was taken off to hospital in Germany during September, leaving General Georg Stumme in command, but by this time all Axis commanders and troops were fully aware that this was the decisive point of the Axis advance, for the position was protected north and south from outflanking movements by the sea and by the depression respectively, and defeat by a frontal assault launched by the 8th Army would result in total catastrophe as the Panzerarmee Afrika lacked the vehicles and fuel for a large-scale retreat.

On the other side of the wire Montgomery also appreciated that the decisive moment had emerged, and that the British were well placed for the battle as the men were available in the right numbers and quality, and that the necessary *matériel* (most notably the US M4 Sherman medium tank that at last gave the British armoured qualitative parity with the German PzKpfw IV) was also to hand. Montgomery realized that the Axis forces' defensive position gave him no room for manoeuvre in the opening phase of the battle, and so planned with exacting method an assault in which the Axis forward minefields, wire and infantry strongpoints would be crushed by a monumental artillery barrage before the infantry moved in to clear the way for a massive armoured punch through the centre of the Axis position. It was this initial break into the Axis position that was Operation 'Lightfoot' which was to be exploited to the west in Operation 'Supercharge'. The forces available to Montgomery were the 3 armoured divisions, 3 armoured brigades (including 1 of infantry tanks), 7 infantry divisions, 2 Fighting French infantry brigade groups and 1 Greek infantry brigade group, while Stumme had 4 armoured divisions (2 German and 2 Italian), 2 motorized divisions (1 German and 1 Italian), part of 1 German motorized division, 4 Italian infantry divisions, 1 Italian parachute division, and 1 German parachute brigade. In all the British had 195,000 men to the Axis forces' 104,000 men (including 50,000 Germans), 1,030 tanks to the Axis forces' 489 tanks (including 211 German), 2,311 pieces of artillery to the Axis forces' 1,219 pieces (including 644 German) and 530 serviceable aircraft to the Axis forces' 350 aircraft (including 150 German).

Montgomery's formations within the 8th Army were Lieutenant General H. Lumsden's X Corps, Lieutenant General B. G. Horrocks' XIII Corps and Lieutenant General Sir Oliver Leese's XXX Corps. An essentially static role was envisaged for XIII Corps (Major General A. F. Harding's 7th Armoured Division, Major General J. S. Nichols's 50th Division and Major General I. T. P. Hughes's 44th Division) on the 8th Army's left flank along the Qattara Depression, where it was to launch a diversionary attack against General Pafundi's Italian X Corps. Here the 1st Fighting French Brigade Group of the 7th Armoured Division was to take Qaret el Himeimat and El Taqa plateau from the Italian Pavia Division to allow the rest of the 7th Armoured Division to pass through as an entity past the Deir el Munassib towards Jebel Kalakh in the event that the opposing Folgore Division did not put up too much of a struggle. The 44th and 50th Divisions of XIII Corps were to undertake pinning attacks against the Brescia Division in the area between the 7th Armoured Division and Ruweisat Ridge, going over to the offensive fully after the break-out by X Corps farther to the north. A more aggressive role was planned for XXX Corps (23rd Armoured Brigade Group, Major General D. N. Wimberley's 51st Division, Major General F. I. S. Tuker's 4th Indian Division, Lieutenant General Sir Leslie Morshead's 9th Australian Division, Lieutenant General Sir Bernard Freyberg's New Zealand Division, and Major General H. D. Pienaar's 1st South African Division) occupying the sector between the Ruweisat Ridge and the sea. Just to the north of the Ruweisat Ridge the 4th Indian Division was to pin the Bologna Division of General Giuseppe de Stefanis's Italian XX Corps while the main effort was made by XXX Corps' other four divisions against General Ennea Navarrini's Italian XXI Corps in the area north of the Miteirya Ridge and south of the Tell el Eisa. On the left flank of this main effort the 1st South African Division was to cross the Miteirya Ridge and engage the Trento Division, while on the right flank the 9th Australian Division was to fulfil a similar function against Generalmajor Kurt Freiherr von Liebenstein's 164th Light Division and any parts of Generalmajor Gustav von Vaerst's 15th Panzer Division in the region. In the centre of XXX Corps' front the 51st (Highland) Division and New Zealand Division were to punch through the Axis forces' forward defences as far as Kidney Ridge, the northern end of XXX Corps' stop line, known by the codename 'Oxalic'. Montgomery expected that the thrust on the right by the 9th Australian and 51st (Highland) Divisions and on the left by the New Zealand and 1st South African Divisions would open two paths through which the tanks of X Corps could flood, Major General R. Briggs's 1st Armoured Division on the right and Major General A. H. Gatehouse's 10th Armoured Division on the left. With X Corps through its positions, the formations of XXX Corps could then start a battle of attrition with the Axis static forces in the area while the two armoured divisions pushed rapidly through to their initial objective ('Pierson') and then their final objective ('Skinflint') with a view to engaging the armoured strength of Generalleutnant Wilhelm Ritter von Thoma's Deutsches Afrika Korps (15th Panzer Division and 21st

Panzer Division) as the first part of Operation 'Supercharge'.

The 8th Army's offensive began with the artillery bombardment that got under way at 21.30 on 23 October. Thirty minutes later both XIII and XXX Corps began their advances under cover of the barrage, and by dawn most of XXX Corps' infantry formations had reached their 'Oxalic' positions. At this time Axis reaction was slow and uncertain, for it was as yet unclear where the main weight of the British effort would fall, and von Thoma was ill (he died of a heart attack during the afternoon, one day before Rommel returned from Germany to assume personal command). The fighting was extremely strenuous in the north, and by the evening the 1st Armoured Division had reached its 'Pierson' positions with most of its units, though the 10th Armoured Division was still held up in its jammed corridor until the New Zealand Division cleared the minefields on 25 October and then moved south-west to ward off the attacks of the 21st Panzer Division so that the 10th Armoured Division could get through to its 'Pierson' position at last. Montgomery at about mid-day on 25 October switched his main effort farther to the north, sending the 9th Australian Division (covered by the 1st Armoured Division) to take the coastal road near Sidi Abd el Rahman. At the same time the New Zealand Division was pulled back while the 1st South African Division and the 4th Indian Division were switched to the north in support of the 9th Australian Division and the 1st Armoured Division. Rommel now felt that he perceived the primary threat, and decided to concentrate his forces in the north, the 21st Panzer Division and General Francesco Arena's Ariete Divisions being called from the south (27 October), and Generalleutnant Theodor Graf von Sponeck's 90th Light Division from the west (28 October). The scene was now set for the 'dogfight' stage of the battle, in which the main strength of the Germans was engaged and subjected to a battle of attrition in the north as Montgomery prepared for the main armoured thrust through the Italian infantry positions just to the south. Severe fighting raged in the coastal region, and the Axis forces used their last reserves of fuel just as the British wished. The Axis position was exacerbated by the fact that two tankers had been sunk in Tobruk harbour before they could disgorge their loads of fuel for the Axis cause. The stage was set for Operation 'Supercharge'.

Lila German occupation of the great French naval base at Toulon in the Mediterranean (27 November 1942) as part of the Axis move into the Vichy-controlled zone in France after the Anglo-American landings in French North-West Africa (Operation 'Torch'). The French moved swiftly to prevent their ships falling into German hands, scuttling 1 battleship, 2 battle-cruisers, 4 heavy cruisers, 3 light cruisers, 30 destroyers, 16 submarines and 19 miscellaneous vessels. Four more submarines escaped from Toulon, 3 reaching the Allies at Algiers while the fourth was interned at Carthage. In this way the French fulfilled the promise made by Admiral Jean Darlan (commander-in-chief of the French navy) to Admiral of the Fleet Sir Dudley Pound (the British First Sea Lord) at the time of France's armistice with Germany in June 1940 that the French navy would under no circumstances fall into German hands.

Lilac US plan to concentrate forces in the Belem-Natal-Recife area of Brazil (1941).

Lilliput Allied supply effort through the small port at Buna after its capture on 14 December 1942. This effort was designed to bolster the offensive capability of the US and Australian forces of General Douglas MacArthur's South-West Pacific Area, operating in the south-eastern end of New Guinea, and consisting primarily of the 7th Australian Division and the US 32nd Infantry Division.

Lilo Proposed breakwater for 'Mulberry', and made up of giant air bags.

Linnet I Plan for Allied airborne forces of Lieutenant General Lewis M. Brereton's Allied 1st Airborne Army to capture Tournai on the River Escaut in western Belgium (September 1944). This strategically important town lay on the junction of General Sir Bernard Montgomery's 21st Army Group and Lieutenant General Omar N. Bradley's

12th Army Group, and the operation was rendered superfluous by the rapid advance of the British XXX Corps of the British 2nd Army, which took the corps past Tournai to Brussels by 3 September. The necessary airborne and air forces were also earmarked for Operation 'Market'.

Linnet II Successor plan to Operation 'Linnet I', designed to seize the 'Maastricht appendix' in the southern part of the Netherlands with forces of Lieutenant General Lewis M. Brereton's Allied 1st Airborne Army (September 1944) as a means of speeding the progress of the US VII Corps and US XIX Corps of Lieutenant General Courtney H. Hodges's US 1st Army through the northern part of the 'Siegfried Linie' defences towards the major concentrations of Generalfeldmarschall Walter Model's Army Group 'B' in the Ruhr and around Köln. Conventional land advances after 15 September 1944 made the scheme unnecessary, especially as the forces were required for Operation 'Market'.

Loincloth Official designation of the 1st Chindit Expedition (8 February/April 1843). The operation was schemed by Brigadier Orde Wingate, an unorthodox British officer with considerable experience of irregular warfare in Palestine and Abyssinia, and whom General Sir Archibald Wavell had been pleased to receive in India during January 1942. This was at the time of Japan's northward thrust from Rangoon, when it was appreciated by the command structure in India that most of Burma would almost inevitably be lost. Wavell appreciated that Wingate's irregular warfare methods might prove singularly useful to the combined British and Indian effort on two scores, namely those of keeping the Japanese off balance by hitting their lines of communication, and of bolstering Allied morale by showing that British, Indian and Gurkha troops could take on and beat the Japanese in jungle warfare, in which the Japanese had acquired an awesome reputation. Wavell was thus persuaded by Wingate that the capabilities of air supply and radio communications made it feasible for a relatively modest force, divided into a number of independent columns, to operate successfully behind the Japanese lines to harass troop movements, cut communications and gather intelligence. Wavell thus sanctioned the formation of the special 77th Indian Brigade, which was to advance into northern Burma and operate in the area east of the River Irrawaddy just to the south of Katha.

The operation was originally to have been supported by an offensive by Lieutenant General G. A. P. Scoones's IV Corps and was planned to coincide with the first British offensive in the Arakan region. However, the lines of communication needed by IV Corps were not ready in time, and Scoones was unwilling to commit his formations east of the Chindwin. Wavell was thus faced with the difficult position of whether or not to commit the 77th Indian Brigade alone. Wavell ordered Operation 'Loincloth' to proceed as planned, the object being to stir up a hornet's nest in the operational areas of the Japanese 18th and 33rd Divisions of Lieutenant General Shojiro Iida's 15th Army, and so encourage greater efforts on the part of British commanders in India once the legend of Japanese invincibility had been destroyed.

On 14 February 1943 the 77th Indian Brigade began its approach marches from Imphal. The brigade was organized as 4 Gurkha and 3 British columns, each consisting of some 400 men, 2 3-inch mortars and 2 medium machine-guns with supplies on some 100 mules, though longer-term supply was reliant on airdrops organized by Major Peter Lord and two RAF squadron leaders. At Tamu the brigade divided into two major parts, the Southern Group (Nos 1 and 2 Columns) crossing the River Chindwin at Auktaung and the Northern Group (Nos 3, 4, 5, 7 and 8 Columns) crossing the same river at Tonhe. The two groups then pressed on to the east, their primary mission being the cutting of the rail line between Mandalay and Mogaung. There were frequent but generally successful brushes with small Japanese parties during this period, but progress was much hampered by the Chindits' erroneous belief that they had to find open ground for air drops to reach them. Once it had been appreciated that the drops could be made in jungle the pace of the advance increased. Diversionary raids were mounted off the line of advance, but the two groups each lost one column dispersed during the early days of March. However, on 3 March No. 1 Column blew the railway just north of Kyaikthin, and three days later Nos 3 and 5 Columns achieved comparable results between Nankan and Bongyaung.

Iida now ordered the concentration of three regiments (one each from the 18th, 33rd and 56th Divisions, and each of three battalions) to eliminate the Chindits, who were now heading for the Irrawaddy, which was crossed with difficulty by five columns between 10 and 18 March. Wingate planned to operate against the Burma Road in the region of Maymyo, with the friendly Kachin Hills and China to his back. However, the area between the Irrawaddy and the River Schweli proved a disaster as it was open and dry country offering little protection to the Chindits, all possible targets were some distance away, and the region was at the very limit of the Chindits' air supply and radio capabilities. Wingate thus decided on 24 March to withdraw, ordering his column commanders to return by the means they thought safest.

One column made for the Kachin Hills, another for China, a third prepared an airstrip and was flown out, and two others opted for the overland retreat back to the Chindwin. But IV Corps had fallen back from the Chindwin, and the Japanese had prepared a cordon defence along the river, catching many Chindits who thought they had reached safety. The Chindits struggled back to India during late March and April 1943, and of the original 3,000 men and 800 mules some 2,180 men and 2 mules returned after covering some 1,000 to 1,500 miles behind the Japanese lines. However, of the survivors a very great proportion was crippled by exhaustion, malnutrition, dysentery and malaria. One of the oddest outcomes of the 1st Chindit Expedition, which was deemed a qualified success by Wavell, was the Japanese Operation 'U', schemed by Lieutenant General Renya Mutaguchi, commander of the 18th Division. He had been much impressed by the Chindits' methods, and proposed a comparable but much larger offensive by the Japanese against Imphal in 1944. This offshoot of the 1st Chindit Expedition matured as the three-division Japanese offensive of 1944.

Look Allied codename for General Dwight D. Eisenhower.

Lost Airborne operation by the SAS to secure intelligence in the Serent area of France (22 June 1944).

Love III Definitive plan for the US assault on the island of Mindoro in the central Philippines (15 December 1944). The South-West Pacific Area command under General Douglas MacArthur had at first proposed that after a swift conquest of Leyte the US forces should make their next effort directly against Luzon, the main Philippine island and the core area of Lieutenant General Tomoyuki Yamashita's 250,000-man 14th Area Army. But the fairly slow pace of the US advance on Leyte meant that the Luzon invasion had to be postponed from December 1944 to January 1945, which meant that tactical air support could not be furnished by Lieutenant General George C. Kenney's 5th Air Force, whose airfields would be waterlogged. Rather than rely on the considerable force of escort carriers to provide the necessary air support, MacArthur decided to improvise a landing on Mindoro so that better-sited airfields could be built on Luzon's doorstep within easy range of Lingayen Gulf and the Manila area. The implementation of Operation 'Love III' was entrusted to the Western Visayan Task Force, comprising two reinforced regiments of the US Army under the command of Brigadier General William C. Dunckel. The assault force sailed from Leyte on 12 December, and on the following day came under attack from some 100 *kamikaze* aircraft, one hitting the flagship *Nashville* and wounding Dunckel. The attack was launched without losses on 15 December, a large beach-head being secured round San Jose on the south-western tip of the island. The building of two airstrips was started, and these were operational by 23 December, allowing the forward stationing of aircraft in preparation for the Luzon landings. The rest of the island was still being mopped up with limited overland advances supported by other amphibious descents round the coast between 21 December and 22 January. From 1 January 1945 the Western Visayan Task Force came under the operational control of

Lieutenant General Walter Krueger's US 6th Army having been relieved for the assault planned against Luzon on 9 January.

Low Ramrod Low-level equivalent to the standard 'Ramrod' operation, designed to penetrate German-controlled airspace below the level of the German radar cover.

Loyton Airborne operation by the 2nd SAS to establish a base near Veney in northern France (12 August 1944).

Lucky Strike Allied scheme to strike south and east towards the River Seine after the break-out from the Normandy beachhead, rather than west towards the ports in Brittany, relying on the development of communications with the 'Mulberry' harbour and with Cherbourg until the port of Le Havre could be captured. It had previously been decided that the Breton ports of Brest and St Nazaire would be essential to the build-up of Allied forces before the decisive eruption into central France could take place. In the event reduced forces were none the less allocated to the move into Brittany, as Major General Troy H. Middleton's US VIII Corps and Major General Walton H. Walker's US XX Corps of Lieutenant General George S. Patton's US 3rd Army were used to secure Brittany, which was garrisoned by General Wilhelm Farhmbacher's German XXV Corps. XX Corps took Nantes with little difficulty, but a harder lot befell VIII Corps, which took Vannes (5 August) and Brest (18 September), but then had to invest Lorient and St Nazaire, which held out against French investment for the rest of the war.

Ludwig German seizure of Livorno after the Italian armistice (September 1943).

Lumberjack Allied offensive between Koblenz and Köln (1/7 March 1945). The offensive was a joint undertaking by Lieutenant General Courtney H. Hodges's US 1st Army and Lieutenant General George S. Patton's US 3rd Army of Lieutenant General Omar N. Bradley's 12th Army Group, and was designed to take the two armies forward through the Eifel region and the defences of Generalfeldmarschall Walter Model's Army Group 'B' to the line of the River Rhine between a point to the north of Köln (in the sector of General Hasso von Manteuffel's 5th Panzerarmee) and Koblenz (in the sector of General Gustav von Zangen's 15th Army). From north to south the US VII Corps was faced by the German LXXXI Corps, the US III Corps by the German LVIII Panzer Corps and part of the German LXXIV Corps, the US V Corps by part of the German LXXIV Corps, the German LXVII Corps and part of the German LXVI Corps, the US VIII Corps by part of the German LXVI Corps and part of the German LIII Corps, and the US XII Corps by part of the German LIII Corps, the German XIII Corps and part of the German LXXX Corps. The US forces made greater progress towards the northern end of the attack, reaching the line of the Rhine in Köln by the evening of 7 March. Far more importantly, however, the armoured Combat Command B of the US 9th Infantry Division, supported by armoured elements of the US 78th Infantry Division, on 7 March secured a bridgehead on the eastern bank of the Rhine at Remagen, where the Ludendorff rail bridge had been incompletely demolished. The way was thus opened for a rapid US exploitation across the natural defence otherwise provided to the Germans by the wide and fast-flowing Rhine, a useful bridgehead having been established by 10 March.

Lustre Operation to ferry British forces into Greece as a reinforcement for that country (5 March 1941). The need for such reinforcements had become apparent early in the year, and urgency was added to the contingency planning by the southward movement of German troops from February and by the accession to the Axis of Bulgaria on 1 March. From 5 March convoys were run from Egypt to Greece every three days. Total losses were 25 ships of 115,000 gross registered tons, though fortunately for the British effort all but seven of these losses occurred in port after the troops had been disembarked. In all some 60,364 men were carried across the eastern Mediterranean under the distinctly hazardous circumstances of Axis air attacks launched from Rhodes and the Dodecanese islands.

Luttich (Liège) Designation of the German counteroffensive (7 August 1944) ordered by Hitler in the area of Mortain. The German leader's reasoning was that the US breakout after Operation 'Cobra' had seen the outpouring of Lieutenant General George S. Patton's US 3rd Army south of Avranches, and that only 25 miles of thinly-held Allied territory separated the German forces at Mortain from the sea at Avranches in Lieutenant General Omar N. Bradley's US 12th Army Group sector. Hitler thus saw a situation in which a strike to the sea would cut off the US 3rd Army for piecemeal destruction as its fuel and ammunition were exhausted, and a right wheel by the German offensive forces to strike into the rear areas of the US forces in the Cotentin peninsula, demoralizing the Allies and wholly reversing the situation in Normandy. Generalfeldmarschall Günther von Kluge, commander-in-chief of Army Group 'B' in northern France, was unable to deter Hitler's enthusiasm, and General Heinrich Eberbach had to give up most of the surviving tanks of his Panzergruppe Eberbach, so renamed from Panzergruppe West after the dismissal of General Leo Freiherr Geyr von Schweppenburg on 4 July. Thus the Germans' last real reserve of armour in northern France, in all some 185 tanks, were committed to a strategic folly. The German XLVII Panzer Corps (2 army and 2 SS Panzer divisions) of SS Obergruppenführer Paul Hausser's German 7th Army attacked westward from Mortain, and made some progress before being checked on 9 August. Allied aircraft, roaming without aerial molestation over the battlefield, ripped the German armour to pieces, rocket-firing Hawker Typhoons playing a decisive part. On 14 August Hitler realized finally that defeat in Normandy was inevitable and called an end to offensive efforts.

Lux Allied codename for convoys sailing towards India with supplies for trans-shipment to China via the Ledo Road.

M

Madison Offensive by Lieutenant General George S. Patton's US 3rd Army against the German-held Metz salient (8 November/13 December 1944). Consisting of the US XI and US XX Corps, the 3rd Army was currently marking time as fuel was short and priority had been given by Lieutenant General Omar N. Bradley's 12th Army Group to Lieutenant General Courtney H. Hodges's US 1st Army on Patton's northern flank. Nevertheless, on the 3rd Army's left XX Corps had reached the River Moselle between Metz and Thionville, while on the army's right flank XII Corps had attained the River Seille above and below Noményafter advancing from Grand Couronné. Further advance was prevented by the inability of the US 5th Infantry Division to reduce the German bastion in the Kronprinz fortress dominating the road between Metz and Nancy at Ars-sur-Moselle. Thus the position rested as Allied forces farther to the north tried to break through the 'Siegfried Linie' defences with little success. The strategic weight was then shifted south again to the 3rd Army's sector, where Patton planned a major drive through Saarlouis for 19 December once the Metz salient had been reduced. The 5th Panzerarmee had been moved north, so the defence of the 125-mile front in Lorraine was left to General Otto von Knobelsdorff's German 1st Army, which had only 9 understrength infantry divisions for the task of halting Patton's three powerful corps of 6 infantry and 3 armoured divisions.

The US offensive was launched under cover of torrential rain; Major General Manton S. Eddy's XII Corps (4th and 6th Armored Divisions plus the 26th, 35th and 80th Infantry Divisions) pushed through the three divisions of General Hoehn's LXXXIX Corps and SS Gruppenführer Hermann Priess's XIII SS Corps to take Moyenvic and Nomény before exploiting towards St Avold and Rohrbach despite counterattacks by the 17th SS Panzergrenadier Division and the 21st Panzer Division. Major General Walton H. Walker's XX Corps (10th Armoured Division plus the 5th, 90th and 95th Infantry Divisions) drove past Metz and General Sinnhuber's LXXXII Corps to reach the Franco-German border on 20 November. Metz was thus isolated, and the task of reducing it fell to Major General J. Millikin's III Corps. The German garrison under Generalleutnant Heinrich Kittel consisted of the 7,000 men of the 462nd Volksgrenadier Division with 30 guns. The city had fallen by 25 November, and the last of the outlying forts capitulated on 13 December, by which time XX Corps had penetrated into the 'Siegfried Linie' defences by taking the bridge over the River Saar between Saarlouis and Fraulautern.

Maggot Fleet Air Arm attack on the German battleship *Tirpitz* lying in the Altenfjord of northern Norway (17 July 1944). The fleet carriers *Formidable*, *Furious* and *Indefatigable* launched 44 Fairey Barracuda strike aircraft escorted by 18 Vought Corsair, 12 Fairey Firefly and 18 Grumman Hellcat fighters, but no hits were scored on the German ship and the British lost two aircraft.

Magic Carpet US programme to

121

Magnesium

repatriate overseas forces and demobilize them after the end of the war.

Magnesium British commando intelligence mission in Czechoslovakia.

Magnet Allied operation to move US ground forces into Northern Ireland (1942) as part of the build-up for subsequent operations on the European mainland.

Mahmoud Special Allied night-fighter operations against German aircraft with rear-facing radar (1944/1945).

Maibaum (May pole) German operation against Yugoslav partisans (1944). The Yugoslav partisan effort under Marshal Tito had by 1944 grown enormously, and comprised the equivalent of 26 divisions, some of them remarkably well equipped, in the bitter struggle with the forces of Generalfeldmarschall Maximilian Freiherr von Weichs's Army Group 'F', which provided the only protection to the four corps of Generaloberst Alexander Löhr's Army Group 'E' in the southern Balkans. Formed on 23 August, Army Group 'E' had 10 divisions (3 of them on Greek islands) and 6 fortress brigades comprising some 300,000 soldiers, 33,000 sailors and 12,000 airmen. At the end of the month the defection of Romania to the Soviet camp unseamed the German position in the eastern Balkans, and Army Group 'E' was ordered to fall back from Greece to a line between Scutari on the Adriatic coast and the Iron Gates pass between southern Romania and Yugoslavia. For lack of adequate transport the garrisons on Crete and Milos were abandoned under the command of General Benthak, and those of Rhodes, Scarpanto, Kos, Tilos and Leros under the command of General Wagner. General Helmuth Felmy's LXVIII Corps pulled out of southern Greece, General Hubert Lanz's XXII Gebirgskorps fell back from Epiros, XIC Corps retreated from Thrace, and XXI Gebirgskorps evacuated Albania, all heading north through southern Yugoslavia towards the plain of the River Sava. The Yugoslav partisans were very active in trying to hamper this retreat so that Marshal of the Soviet Union F. I. Tolbukhin's 3rd Ukrainian Front could cut them off as it swept from Romania and Bulgaria into Yugoslavia, but the Germans were able to fight their way through before the trap closed. The Yugoslav partisans were able to liberate Cattaro (Kotor), Ragusa (Dubrovnik) and Spalato (Split), and to take Zara (Zadar), so that at the end of 1944 they controlled all of southern Yugoslavia as well as 5 large areas (3 around Sarajevo and 2 between Zagreb and Fiume) in German-held northern Yugoslavia.

Maigewitter (May storm) German operation against Soviet partisans operating in the region of Vitebsk (May 1943). This city was an important rail centre for German supplies at the northern end of the Eastern Front, and was one of the major objectives earmarked for General A. I. Eremenko's Kalinin Front in the Soviet offensives planned for the late summer of 1943.

Mailfist British plan for the recapture of Singapore during 1946 using the forces of Lieutenant General O. L. Roberts' XXXIV Corps, namely the 23rd Indian Division, the 81st West African Division and the 3rd Commando Brigade. Port Swettenham in eastern Malaya would have been the base for this operation.

Mainyard Allied codename for Guadalcanal Island in the Solomons chain.

Majestic Revised version of Operation 'Coronet', the second stage of the US invasion of the Japanese home islands scheduled to land on each side of Tokyo on 1 March 1946.

Malicious Allied codename for Palermo in Sicily.

Mallard Airlift of reinforcements for Major General R. Gale's British 6th Airborne Division (6 June 1944) during the implementation of Operation 'Overlord'. Like the US 82nd and 101st Airborne Divisions in the Cotentin peninsula to the west, the 6th Airborne Division had been dropped in slightly the wrong places, but unlike the US formations was at least relatively well concentrated, with much of the 3rd and 5th Parachute Brigades grouped within a triangle some 2 miles wide and 4 miles deep, mostly to the east of the Orne Canal. Brigadier N. Poett's 5th Parachute Brigade (7th, 12th and 13th Battalions) took the bridges over the Orne and Caen Canals and held them until relieved by the British 3rd Division, while Brigadier J. Hill's 3rd Parachute Brigade (8th, 9th and 1st Canadian Battalions) was more scattered but managed to achieve its objectives of blowing the bridges over the River Dives and destroying the Merville battery before being relieved by the 3rd Division. Operation 'Mallard' delivered the 6th Air Landing Brigade in gliders to fields on each side of the River Orne to the south of Ouistreham cleared of German obstacles by the engineers of the 5th Parachute Brigade. The men of the 6th Airborne Division then served as conventional infantry until the end of the Normandy battle, mainly against the German 346th Division of the German LXXXVI Corps within Generaloberst Friedrich Dollmann's 7th Army.

Mallory US contingency plan to bomb the bridges over the River Po in northern Italy.

Mallory Major US campaign against the bridges over the River Po in northern Italy (12/15 July 1944). This was designed to prevent the Germans moving reinforcements south to bolster the formations of Generaloberst Heinrich von Vietinghoff-Scheel's 10th Army and General Joachim Lemelsen's 14th Army falling back towards the 'Gotisch Linie' defences before, respectively, the British 8th Army of Lieutenant General Sir Olver Leese and the US 5th Army of Lieutenant General Mark Clark.

Mammut (mammoth) German early-warning radar.

Mandibles British plan to seize the Italian-held Dodecanese islands (including Rhodes or Leros) in the Aegean Sea (1940/1941). The plan originated with Admiral of the Fleet Sir Roger Keyes's Combined Operations Command in the UK, which saw the Dodecanese islands as ideal targets for commando forces, and in its initial form the plan also embraced the notion of taking Pantelleria Island in the Sicilian Narrows.

Greater importance was attached to the scheme when it was appreciated that British control of the Dodecanese islands might be a useful inducement for the Turks to throw in their lot with the British, and when Axis air power based in the islands began to exact a heavy toll of British shipping (naval and mercantile) in the eastern Mediterranean, but the whole scheme foundered on the objections of Admiral Sir Andrew Cunningham, who appreciated that to secure relatively small strategic advantages his Mediterranean Fleet would have to provide naval cover under very disadvantageous conditions of Axis air superiority. Although the planning for Operation 'Mandibles' never proceeded far past the initial planning stages, one unfortunate consequence was the fact that General Sir Archibald Wavell, commanding in Egypt, had to keep the 7th Australian Division off active service and available in the Nile Delta to provide the main assault force for Rhodes or Leros should the plan be implemented, it being appreciated by all concerned that comparatively small and lightly armed commando forces could not hope to tackle the substantial German and Italian garrisons of the islands.

Mandrel British device for jamming the German ground-based radars used for controlling night-fighters tasked with the interception of British bomber streams.

Manhattan Cover name for the massive but extraordinarily secret project undertaken in the USA by Allied scientists to develop the atomic bomb, first tested with complete success at Alamogordo in the New Mexico desert in July 1945.

Manhole Designation of an Allied mission sent into Yugoslavia (23 February 1944).

Manna (i) Designation of a British combined operation to stabilize the position in Greece as the divisions of Generaloberst Alexander Löhr's Army Group 'E' began to pull out of the country to avoid being cut off as the Soviet forces swept into Yugoslavia and Austria. Under the overall control of Lieutenant General Ronald Scobie's British III Corps, the operation (launched on 4

October 1944) had the dual task of supporting the royalist administration from any attempts by the communist ELAS (Greek People's Liberation Army) to overthrow it, and of preventing the communist regime in Bulgaria from keeping its hold on the Greek provinces of western Thrace and eastern Macedonia, given to King Boris by Hitler in 1941 and still wanted by the new regime despite an agreement that Bulgaria would return to its borders of 6 April 1941. Operation 'Manna' began with the landing of the British 2nd Airborne Brigade to liberate Patras on 4 October, continued with the airdropping of additional airborne units at Eleusis and Megara to move on Athens, and finally witnessed the arrival of Scobie's ground forces at Piraeus in the ships of a combined British and Greek squadron commanded by Rear Admiral Thomas Troubridge. The British did manage to impose a kind of order, but the evacuation of the Germans marked the beginning of the Greek Civil War that continued up to 1948 before the communists were beaten. It is worth noting that the exit of the Germans from Greece was greatly facilitated by a number of agreements with ELAS and its political leadership, EAM (Greek Liberation Committee), whereby German formations were given unimpeded passage on condition they left their heavy weapons for use by the forces of ELAS against the royalists.
(ii) Operation undertaken by British heavy bombers to paradrop food to the starving population of the Netherlands (May 1945).

Maple (i) Allied codename for Port Moresby in New Guinea.
(ii) Airborne raid by the 2nd SAS on Aquilla and Ancena in Italy (7 January 1944).

Marder (marten) German plan for the reinforcement of Italy in the event of a major Allied amphibious assault (December 1942/January 1943). The overall plan ordained that the forces in Italy under the command of Generalfeldmarschall Albert Kesselring should be boosted by 2 infantry divisions from the French command of the *Oberbefehlshaber West*, by 2 infantry or Jäger divisions from the Balkan command of the *Oberbefehlshaber Südost*, and by 5 infantry regiments and 11 infantry battalions from the Replacement Army within Germany.

Margarethe I (Margaret I) Occupation of Hungary by 11 German divisions (9 March 1944). Hitler felt himself forced to make this move by the increasingly ambivalent position of the Kallay administration in Hungary, which was playing both sides of the field in an attempt to mitigate for Hungary the ever worsening position of the Axis. Admiral Miklos Horthy, the regent of Hungary, was closeted with the German leader at Kressheim at the time Operation 'Margarethe I' was launched, and was thus faced with a fait accompli when he swore in a new administration headed by General Dome-Sztojay, the pro-Nazi former ambassador to Berlin, but Horthy refused to step down as regent, and from this time onwards worked increasingly against the interests of Germany.

Margarethe II (Margaret II) German contingency plan to occupy Romania in the event of that country's collapse or defection. In the event, Romania moved into the Soviet camp as a result of a statement by Soviet foreign minister Molotov on 2 April 1944 that the USSR had sent forces into Romania for purely military reasons and desired neither Romanian subservience nor Romanian territory (though no mention was made of the return to Romania of the Bukovina and Bessarabia regions annexed on 26 June 1940). The Germans seem to have been unaware of the conspiracy led by King Michael I to overthrow General Ion Antonescu, the Romanian *Conductor*, and conclude an armistice with the Allies, and it came as a complete surprise when King Michael summoned Antonescu to the palace on 22 August and ordered him to come to an armistice with the Allies. Antonescu refused and was arrested, together with Germany's ambassador and chief military liaison officer. There was little time to implement Operation 'Margarethe II' as the forces of the Soviet 2nd and 3rd Ukrainian Fronts were about to fall on Generaloberst Johannes Friessner's Army Group 'South Ukraine' in northern Romania. Hitler thus contented himself in the short term with ordering the German air units allocated to the defence of the Ploesti oilfields to bomb

Bucharest, with particular emphasis on the palace and the prime minister's residence. This was just what General Sanatescu, the new prime minister, needed as a pretext to declare war on Germany, which he did on 25 August. The full folly of Hitler's reaction was immediately seen on the battlefield, where General P. Dumitrescu's Romanian 3rd Army was paired with the German 6th Army in the Armeegruppe 'Dumitescu' and General Avramescu's Romanian 4th Army with the German 8th Army in Armeegruppe 'Wöhler'. Of the 250 miles of front with the Soviets in Romania, the Romanians held about 100, and they immediately downed arms, seized the crossings over the Rivers Danube, Prut and Siretul for use by the Soviets. The result was total disaster for Army Group 'North Ukraine', which in little more than a fortnight lost virtually all of the 6th Army and part of the 8th Army, in all 16 out of 24 German divisions at a cost of some 105,000 dead and 106,000 taken prisoner.

Marianne German naval raid on shipping off Dover (December 1940).

Marie British and Free French plan to seize French Somaliland with the Free French troops of Général Legentilhomme, Général de Gaulle and Legentilhomme being convinced that the colony and its administration were against the Vichy regime in France (spring 1941). The plan was vigorously opposed by General Sir Archibald Wavell and Général Georges Catroux, the British and French commanders-in-chief in the Middle East, who averred that there could be strong opposition leading to a prolonged campaign in what was currently not a trouble spot. It was then decided to attempt a propaganda campaign in the colony with a view to persuading it to join the Allied cause, and when this in turn proved unsuccessful a blockade of the colony was instituted. This too was abandoned in March 1942 as being counterproductive.

Marita German invasion and conquest of Yugoslavia and Greece (6/28 April 1941). The trigger for the invasion was the 27 March overthrow (in a military coup inspired by King Peter II) of the administration headed by the regent, Prince Paul, who had on 25 March adhered to the Axis cause as a means of staving off Italian, Hungarian and Romanian pressures for annexations of Yugoslav territory. Hitler was so incensed by the overthrow of this agreement, however, that on 27 March he ordered the rapid preparation of the campaign that would bring Yugoslavia firmly under the German heel, and at the same time he decided that the simultaneous conquest of Greece would secure the whole of Germany's southern flank before the launch of Operation 'Barbarossa', and also bail out the Italian forces intractably locked in a hopeless campaign in Albania and north-western Greece. There was little doubt that the German forces could achieve their aims with little difficulty even if the British threw in their lot with the Greeks, but the real disaster of the Balkan campaign, so far as the Germans were concerned, was that it dictated a delay in the start of Operation 'Barbarossa', which was postponed from mid-May to mid-June 1941 with vast ramifications in the fields of operations and grand strategy. Some 33 German divisions, including 6 Panzer divisions, were allocated to the conquest of Yugoslavia, which could call on 28 divisions, 3 of them armoured. It was appreciated that aid would come from Germany's allies in the theatre in return for the meeting of their territorial ambitions, so Italian and Hungarian military contributions were worked into the plan for Operation 'Marita'.

The operational scheme for the invasion of Yugoslavia called for a concerted drive on Belgrade by two major German groupings, Generaloberst Maximilian Freiherr von Weichs's 2nd Army from the area of Austria between Klagenfurt and Graz (XLIX Gebirgskorps and LI Corps), directed southeast down the River Sava through Zagreb to Belgrade after the way had been opened by General Heinrich von Vietinghoff-Scheel's XLVI Panzer Corps (striking south from the region of Barcs in southern Hungary in a double thrust aimed at Zagreb and Sarajevo), and General Günther von Kleist's Panzergruppe von Kleist directed against Belgrade from Romania (General Hans Reinhard's XLI Panzer Corps moving south-west from Timisoara, and General Gustav von Wietersheim's XIV Motorized Corps and the XI

Market

Corps north-west from the region of Sofia in Bulgaria via Nis and down the River Morava to Belgrade). Support for these primary moves was provided by General Vittorio Ambrosio's Italian 2nd Army, whose 14 divisions in 4 corps were to advance from Trieste and Fiume against Ljubljana and south along the Adriatic coast, by 1 Italian division advancing south from the Italian enclave at Zara on the Dalmatian coast, by 4 divisions of the Italian 11th Army moving north from Albania, by the Hungarian 3rd Army striking south from Szeged to take eastern Croatia, and by General Georg Stumme's XL Panzer Corps (of Generalfeldmarschall Wilhelm List's German 12th Army) conquering Yugoslavian Macedonia and taking Skopje.

The whole campaign took just 12 days, and the Axis forces were superbly supported by the tactical aircraft of Generaloberst Alexander Löhr's Luftflotte IV right through the period. The Luftwaffe also played a decisive strategic part with the 'terror bombing' of Belgrade, which thoroughly demoralized the Yugoslavs. Belgrade fell on 12 April and Yugoslavia surrendered on 17 April, yielding 343,700 prisoners to the German casualties of 150 dead and 390 wounded. But 300,000 Yugoslavs escaped the Axis net to form an increasingly powerful resistance movement, initially led by Colonel Draza Mihailovic.

While Yugoslavia was falling to the 2nd Army and the Panzergruppe von Kleist, Greece was fighting back against the offensive of the 24 divisions of the German 12th Army from Bulgaria into Thrace and Macedonia (Generalleutnant Eugen Ott's XXX Corps and General Franz Böhme's XVIII Gebirgskorps against the 8 divisions of the Greek 2nd Army and, in northern Thessaly, the 4 divisions of the British 'W' Force) and from southern Yugoslavia (XL Panzer Corps supported from Albania by the Italian 9th and 11th Armies against the 14 divisions of the Greek 1st Army). The German strategic aim was to use the XL Panzer Corps to strike south between the Pindos mountains and Kozani to cut off the Greek 1st Army, while at the same time isolating the two main groupings in north-western Greece from each other and from the rest of the country. These isolated groups could then be crushed individually with the aid of General Wolfram Freiherr von Richthofen's VIII Fliegerkorps. The collapse of the Yugoslavs in southern Macedonia opened the way for a rapid German advance, Thessaloniki falling on 9 April, Yannina on 20 April, and Athens on 27 April, some three days after Greece's formal surrender had been signed (for the second time as emissaries of the Italian government had not been present at the first!). Any hopes of an orderly Allied withdrawal into the Peloponnese were shattered when a German airborne operation yielded them the bridge over the Corinth Canal on 26 April. German casualties were 1,685 dead and 3,750 wounded, compared with British losses of 12,700 dead plus 9,000 prisoners and Greek losses (in a six-month campaign including the war with Italy in Albania) of 15,700 dead and 218,000 prisoners. During their six-month involvement the Italians lost 13,755 dead, 50,875 wounded, 25,000 missing and 12,370 suffering from frostbite.

Hitler now set about a reorganization of the Balkans to suit his own purposes. Germany took part of Slovenia, Italy received part of Slovenia and much of the Dalmatian coast plus the Bay of Kotor, Bulgaria was awarded Serbian Macedonia, Hungary got Backa, and Montenegro became 'independent'. Italy also established the so-called Kingdom of Croatia incorporating Bosnia and Herzegovina. Germany could also move into the Aegean Sea, German units landing on many islands including Thasos (16 April), Samothrace (19 April), Limnos (19 April), Lesbos (4 May) and Khios (4 May). In terms of men and *matériel* Operation 'Marita' had cost the Germans relatively little, but the real cost of the campaign must be measured by the fact that it deprived Germany of its only genuine (albeit slim) chance of defeating the USSR in Operation 'Barbarossa'.

Market Allied airborne landings in the Netherlands (17 September 1944), designed to take the main crossings over the Zuit Willemsvaart Canal, the River Maas, the River Waal and the River Rhine so that the Lieutenant General Sir Brian Horrocks's XXX Corps of Lieutenant General Sir Miles Dempsey's British 2nd Army could break through the German defences of Generaloberst Kurt Student's 1st Parachute Army to reach the Zuider Zee and so free the estuaries of these major rivers for Allied supply vessels. The detailed planning was undertaken by the Allied 1st Airborne Army commanded by Lieutenant General Lewis H. Brereton, and it was decided that the army's two corps (Lieutenant General F. A. M. Browning's British I Airborne Corps and Major General Matthew B. Ridgway's US XVIII Airborne Corps) would contribute one British and two US airborne divisions plus the 1st Polish Independent Parachute Brigade to the operation, which involved the laying of an 'airborne carpet' to seize and hold the relevant bridges until the formations of the XXX Corps could relieve them. The plan was a logical successor to Operation 'Comet', shelved on 10 September, which placed the primary emphasis on the ground offensive with support from the British 1st Airborne Division and the 1st Polish Independent Parachute Brigade to secure the river crossings by *coup de main* tactics as the ground forces approached them. It was appreciated that this plan had severe tactical and operational limitations, especially as there were some five major and several smaller water crossings to be seized consecutively, and that the Germans would be able to blow at least one of the bridges, negating the whole object of the offensive. The alternative was to seize all the bridges at the same time in Operation 'Market' and to hold them until the ground forces arrived in Operation 'Garden' to 'bounce' over the Rhine and push on to the Zuider Zee. A unified command was essential for Operation 'Market', and to the chagrin of the American commanders it was decided that this should be vested in the British I Airborne Corps commanded by Browning, Brereton's deputy.

The plan finally agreed was that the US IX Troop Carrier command and the British Nos 38 and 46 Groups should transport the airborne forces in 1,300 Douglas C-47 transport/glider tug aircraft, 240 bombers converted into glider tugs, and 2,525 gliders. Once landed, the airborne forces would be supported by No. 83 Group, RAF, for the British 1st Airborne Division, and by elements of the US 8th and 9th Air Forces for the US 82nd and 101st Airborne Divisions.

Nearest the bridgehead over the Meuse-Escaut Canal secured by the XXX Corps (just south of Borkel) would land Major General Maxwell D. Taylor's US 101st Airborne Division, to the north of Eindhoven, to take and hold the bridges over the Wilhelmina Canal at Zon, over the Zuit Willemsvaart Canal at Veghel, and over the River Aa just to the north, together with two subsidiary bridges. Next to the north would land Major General James M. Gavin's US 82nd Airborne Division in the area around Grave to take and hold the only high ground in the region, the Groesbeek, and the bridges over the Maas at Grave, over the Maas-Waal Canal to the west of Grave, and over the Waal on the northern side of Nijmegen, and, farthest to the north, to be relieved by XXX Corps no more than three days after the drop, was to land Major General Roy Urquhart's British 1st Airborne Division in the area between Ede and Oosterbeek to the west of Arnhem to take and hold the bridge over the Rhine at Arnhem and the rail bridge over the same river between Oosterbeek and Arnhem.

The flaws in the plan were several, notably lack of intelligence on German dispositions and strengths in the region, lack of heavy weapons, overestimation of the pace XXX Corps would be able to reach and maintain, inadequate radio ranges, lack of co-ordination between the ground force and air force commands, too great an expectation of the US 82nd Airborne Division in the diversity of tasks it had to achieve, wrong dropping and landing zones for the British 1st Airborne Division (too far from its objectives given the absence of adequate motor transport) and, most importantly, lack of adequate airlift capability. This last meant that the proposed delivery of the XVIII Airborne Corps' airlanding formation, the British 52nd (Lowland) Division, could not be entertained as a practical move until well after the first landings, so losing the element of tactical surprise so essential to airborne forces without heavy weapons, and that even the 1st Airborne Division had to be delivered in two waves, namely Brigadier Gerald Lathbury's 1st Parachute Brigade, Brigadier 'Shan' Hackett's 4th Parachute Brigade and Brigadier 'Pip' Hicks's 1st Air Landing Brigade on the first day in two widely spaced lifts, and

Market

Major General Stanislaw Sosabowski's 1st Polish Independent Parachute Brigade as a reinforcement on the second day.

Although Student's 1st Parachute Army of six or seven divisions was still forming, the makings of an excellent defence were available in the Arnhem area in the form of the headquarters of Generalfeldmarschall Walter Model's Army Group 'B', allowing Model to take personal command of the defence forces available in SS Gruppenführer Willi Bittrich's II SS Panzer Corps (9th and 10th SS Panzer Divisions, refitting after the rigours of the retreat from France) and the three infantry divisions plus miscellaneous units that had been taken under command by Generalleutnant Kurt Chill of the 85th Division. Model could thus call on some 6,000 high-quality German soldiers as an immediate defence force.

At first the Allies thought that success was in their grasp, for most of the initial objectives were attained and XXX Corps made good progress along the single road it was forced to use for its armoured advance. In the south the US 101st Airborne Division was dropped accurately and moved on its objectives, the 506th Parachute Infantry Regiment finding the bridge at Zon blown but none the less being able to cross the canal and press on to the south and the link-up with the advance guard of XXX Corps during the morning of 18 September, allowing the Guards Armoured Division to push on to the St Oedenrode bridge (taken by the 502nd Parachute Infantry Regiment) and the Veghel bridge (taken by the 501st Parachute Infantry Regiment). Thus by 19 September XXX Corps had passed through the US 101st Airborne Division, the only one of the three airborne formations that had undertaken adequate tactical planning for the operation. XXX Corps' next objective was the US 82nd Airborne Division, which had also landed accurately for the 504th Parachute Infantry Regiment to take the Grave bridge and half of the Maas-Waal bridge, for the 505th Parachute Infantry Regiment to take the Groesbeek (an objective not really needed by the airborne forces and needing a full division to hold it against determined counterattack), and for the 508th Parachute Infantry Regiment to try unsuccessfully to take the Nijmegen bridge. XXX Corps arrived in the area in the afternoon of 19 September, and a combined assault by elements of XXX Corps and the 82nd Airborne Division then yielded the Nijmegen bridge on 20 September.

By this time XXX Corps was supposed to be in Arnhem, but opposition was now growing by the hour as the German commanders responded vigorously to the Allied advance, and XXX Corps was checked on the northern bank of the Waal. In Arnhem itself the position of the British 1st Airborne Division was growing acute, for while the 2nd Parachute Battalion under Lieutenant Colonel John Frost had managed to take Arnhem bridge, the rest of the division had been squeezed into a pocket at Oosterbeek. The 1st Polish Independent Parachute Brigade was needlessly dropped on the south bank of the Rhine during 22 September and could neither link up with the rest of the division nor fully withstand the powerful German counterattacks to which it was subjected. Frost and his men on the bridge had run out of ammunition and supplies on 21 September and surrendered, and the position of the survivors of the division was desperate as forward elements of XXX Corps finally managed to cover the last 10 miles from the Waal (despite flank attacks by the 10th SS Panzer Division) to reach the Rhine and establish communication with the Oosterbeek pocket.

By 25 September it was appreciated that XXX Corps could not get across the river to relieve the remnants in the Oosterbeek pocket, and it was decided that as many men as possible (in the event some 2,164) would be ferried across the river to safety before the pocket surrendered. Total British losses were some 7,500 killed, wounded and prisoner. The Poles lost about 1,000 men, and the losses to the Americans were 1,670 dead, wounded and missing in the 82nd Airborne Division, and 2,075 killed, wounded and missing in the 101st Airborne Division. Operation 'Market' had been a failure for a variety of reasons, though none could deny the extraordinary courage of the airborne soldiers, particularly those of the British 1st Airborne Division, which without heavy weapons and many other necessities of modern war had held off a determined and capable enemy for far longer than could have been anticipated when Browning opined before the operation that 'we might be going a bridge too far'.

Maroubra Designation of the 7th Australian Division's forces involved in the Kokoda Trail operations (September 1942/July 1943) against the forces of Major General Tomitara Horii's Japanese 18th Army in New Guinea.

Mars Designation of the US 5332nd Brigade (Provisional) in northern Burma operations.

Mars I Designation of Romanian reinforcements for the Axis summer offensive of 1942 on the Eastern Front.

Mars II Designation of Italian reinforcements for the Axis summer offensive of 1942 on the Eastern Front.

Mars III Designation of the Hungarian reinforcements for the Axis summer offensive of 1942 on the Eastern Front.

Marshall Airborne operation by the 2ème Regiment des Chasseurs Parachutistes to harass the German retreat from Normandy near Corrèze (10 August 1944).

Martin Operational plan for 'Herbstnebel' devised by the Oberbefehlshaber West, Generalfeldmarschall Gerd von Rundstedt.

Masterdom Allied plan for the occupation of Indo-China after the Japanese surrender, planned in association with the comparable Operation 'Bibber' for Thailand. Planned by Admiral Lord Louis Mountbatten's South-East Asia Command, Operation 'Masterdom' called for the movement (by air to Saigon via Bangkok) of the 80th Infantry Brigade of Major General D. D. Gracey's 20th Indian Division, elements of Nos 28 and 684 Squadrons, RAF, and an Allied control commission. This initial step was to be followed by the delivery of the rest of the 20th Division by sea. The total requirement was to move 25,750 men and 2,400 vehicles to Saigon. Here Gracey was to exercise full control of the region until the French could re-establish themselves, issuing orders directly to Field Marshal Count Hisaichi Terauchi, commander-in-chief of the surrendered Japanese Southern Army. The British imagined that there were some 71,000 Japanese under arms in Indo-China, though the reality was something like 2,000 in the headquarters of the Southern Army and of the 38th Army, 8,000 in the 2nd Division, 1,000 in the 55th Division, 7,700 in miscellaneous army units, about 9,000 air personnel at 35 air bases, and about 2,500 naval personnel. About 28,500 men were on the strengths of the forward headquarters of the 38th Army, the 21st and 22nd Divisions, and the 34th Independent Mixed Brigade, all located in northern Indo-China or Thailand and thus the responsibility of the Chinese or occupation forces in Thailand.

Operation 'Masterdom' began on 8 September, but logistic difficulties meant that the 80th Brigade and one squadron of Supermarine Spitfire fighters were not fully assembled until 26 September, by which time Gracey was fully embroiled in the politics of the region, where the Emperor of Annam had abdicated in favour of the Republic of Vietnam and in which large areas were controlled by the Viet Minh communist guerrillas. Gracey's two other brigades, the 32nd and 100th, arrived shortly after this, allowing the British commander to use larger numbers of Japanese troops and thus take a firmer stance with the local dissidents as the troops of Général Paul Leclerc's French administration began to arrive (5th Colonial Regiment and a combat command of the 2nd Armoured Division), with more units (9th Colonial Infantry Division from France and the Far Eastern Brigade from Madagascar) in transit or about to be despatched, and the 3rd Colonial Infantry Division promised for a later date. Small-scale actions kept the Viet Minh under control, and the French began to assume control on 19 December, allowing the British to complete their evacuation of Indo-China by 13 May 1946, when full responsibility was given to Admiral G. T. d'Argenlieu, the French high commissioner.

Mastiff Operation designed to follow Operation 'Birdcage', in which leaflet drops had told Allied prisoners of war that Japan had surrendered. Operation 'Mastiff' was designed to bring physical rather than moral relief to the inmates of the camps. The first 'Mastiff' flights were flown in late August 1945 to known camps in Burma, Thailand and northern Malaya, and by early September the flights had been extended in range to camps in southern Malaya, Singapore, Indo-China, Sumatra and Java. To complement the food and medicine drops of Operation 'Mastiff', special teams were airdropped into the camps to take over administration, medical and food tasks until larger parties could be brought in. By the end of September about 53,700 prisoners and internees had been evacuated to Australia, India and the UK, the total rising to 71,000 by the end of October. By May 1946 some 96,575 prisoners and internees had been evacuated.

Matador Plan devised (August 1941) by Air Chief Marshal Sir Robert Brooke-Popham, the Commander-in-Chief Far East, for an advance by British forces in Malaya to occupy the area of Singora and Patani in southern Thailand should the Japanese move into that country. Brooke-Popham had long considered it strategically wise for the British to occupy portions of the Isthmus of Kra as a natural defence against Japanese movement south into Malaya, and Operation 'Matador' was the outcome of detailed development along this basic train of thought. Singora was the only port with the capacity to supply between three and four Japanese divisions, and its occupation by the British would seriously hamper any Japanese move to the south as the aggressors would be denied the use not only of the port but the airfields in the region as well as the main road and the railway. Brooke-Popham believed that British occupation by three brigade groups, four bomber squadrons and two fighter squadrons would limit any Japanese invasion to a single division supplied with great difficulty overland from Bangkok and threatened by British aircraft operating from Singora and Patani. The plan was approved, but its implementation was delayed and Major General D. M. Murray-Lyon's 11th Indian Division of Lieutenant General Sir Lewis Heath's III Indian Corps was eventually used for conventional defensive operations when it was appreciated that the Japanese had pre-empted Operation 'Matador' with their own landings at Singora and Patani by the 5th and 18th Divisions on 8 December 1941.

Matterhorn Developed version of Operation 'Drake', implemented with the arrival of the US 20th Air Force in China after its activation on 4 April 1944 in response to the directive of the Cairo Conference for the strategic bombing of Japan. Raids began in June 1944 after the completion of the first massive base at Chengtu, built by the efforts of thousands of Chinese labourers, and soon joined by three other Boeing B-29 Superfortress bases. The 20th Air Force's XX Bomber Command was forced to operate with minimal facilities over immensely long ranges, the bombers often staging from rear bases in India laden with fuel and bombs which were used for the smaller number that actually undertook the raids. The first operation, by 98 B-29s against railway workshops at Bangkok in Thailand during 5 June 1944, was not a success. The second raid fared no better, and was this time flown against a steel plant at Yawata on the Japanese island of Kyushu during 15/16 June. Serviceability was low and bombing poor, so the head of the US Army Air Forces, General H. H. Arnold, sent in the redoubtable Major General Curtis E. LeMay to solve XX Bomber Command's problems, which he did with ruthless but practical efficiency. Tactics were revised, units reshuffled and servicing brought up to the mark, so that useful results began to accrue to XX Bomber Command's record. But the real difficulty of the command was the need to operate over very long ranges from indifferent bases, and nothing could alter that. On 15 January 1945 XX Bomber Command flew its last mission from China before transferring to join its sister, XXI Bomber Command, in the Marianas. In 10 months XX Bomber command had flown just 49 missions, averaging about 2 combat sorties per aircraft per month.

Mauerwald Codename for the headquarters of the Oberkommando des Heeres near Angerburg in East Prussia.

Maurice Northern half (16 April/3 May

1940) of the Allied pincer designed to close on the beach-head of the 138th Gebirgsjäger Regiment of the German 2nd Mountain Division at Trondheim in Norway. This German regiment had been delivered at the beginning of Operation 'Weserübung' to Trondheim by the heavy cruiser *Admiral Hipper* and four destroyers, and by mid-April had reached divisional strength and was keeping the 5th Norwegian Division in check as it pushed detachments north to Steinkjer on the rail line to Namsos and south to Dragset on the rail line to Andalsnes and Oslo. It could advance little farther, despite the arrival of the 181st Division as a reinforcement, and awaited the arrival of the 163rd and 196th Divisions of General Nikolaus von Falkenhorst's XXI Gebirgskorps from Oslo up the Gudbrandsdal and Osterdal valleys. The British planned to pinch out this lodgement at Trondheim with a concerted move, Major General A. Carton de Wiart's 146th Brigade being landed at Namsos and Major General B. T. C. Paget's 148th Brigade at Andalsnes on 16 and 18 April respectively. But the two brigades were too late, for the Germans had been reinforced to full mountain-warfare capability whereas the British units were standard infantry brigades, and were checked at Steinkjer and Lillehammer respectively. Reinforcements, consisting of the French 5th Demi-Brigade of Chasseurs Alpins at Andalsnes and the British 15th Brigade at Namsos, did little to improve matters, and on 26 April the leading elements of the 181st and 196th Divisions met at Dragset. It was now clear that the Allied move could not succeed, and on 26 April the Allies decided to abandon central Norway and concentrate their efforts on the German beach-head at Narvik in the north of the country. The 148th Brigade and the 5th Demi-Brigade were evacuated from Andalsnes on 1 May, the Germans taking the town on the following day, while the 146th and 15th Brigades were pulled out of Namsos on 3 May, shortly before the Germans entered the town.

Maus (mouse) Offensive by Generalfeldmarschall Wilhelm List's Army Group 'A' at the extreme south of the German summer offensives of 1942, Operation 'Blau'. The scheme of Operation 'Maus' was for the forces of Army Group 'A' to be divided into two groups, with Generaloberst Ewald von Kleist's 1st Panzerarmee on the line of the River Mius slightly north of Generaloberst Richard Ruoff's Gruppe Ruoff (Ruoff's German 1st Army and General I. Gariboldi's Italian 8th Army) which occupied the length of the lower Mius and the coast of the Sea of Azov to the west of Rostov. Army Group 'A' lacked the strength and bridging equipment for a major thrust across the lower reaches of the River Donets, so instead of advancing from the region of Taganrog to provide the right flank guard for the 6th Army's drive on Stalingrad, Army Group 'A' was directed to move the 1st Panzerarmee forward due east from the area of Artemovsk, some 150 miles to the north, while Gruppe Ruoff pinned the Soviet forces in the region of the Sea of Azov, with an eventual view to the advance of Army Group 'A' over the River Don upstream of Rostov to push into the western Caucasus and the oilfields at Maykop. This plan was subsequently modified into Operation 'Blau III', also known as Operation 'Clausewitz'.

Max Heiliger Designation of the cover under which the spoils of exterminated Jews were banked by the SS.

Maybach Designation of the headquarters of the Oberkommando der Wehrmacht in Berlin (1945).

M.E. Designation of eastbound Mediterranean convoys (together with a numerical suffix) plying from Malta to Alexandria, and inaugurated in July 1940, interrupted during the period in which Malta was besieged, and resumed in November 1942.

Meacon Allied device to mask the emissions of German radio beacons.

Menace British and Free French operation against Dakar in French West Africa (31 August/29 September 1940). After the fall of France in June 1940 the British were alarmed that the Germans could infiltrate forces into Senegal and so gain control of Dakar, allowing German naval and air forces to use the excellent facilities at Dakar as a base for

Mercantile

attacks on British shipping in the eastern Atlantic plying the routes round the Cape of Good Hope and to South America. The British government was thus receptive when Général Charles de Gaulle suggested that his Free French forces should make an attempt to bring Senegal into the Allied fold with British naval and military aid. Planning moved ahead with unusual but commendable speed under the leadership of Vice Admiral J. H. D. Cunningham, previously commander of the 1st Cruiser Squadron in the Home Fleet, and Major General M. N. S. Irwin, the land force commander. Indeed, so speedy was the planning that by the time reliable intelligence arrived that Senegal was firmly committed to the Vichy government and would thus resist strongly any attempt at an Allied occupation, the Allied plans had been finalized and the operation authorized on 27 August.

The invasion force sailed in three groups, that from Scapa Flow consisting of three transports escorted by the cruiser *Fiji* and three destroyers, that from the River Clyde of the cruiser *Devonshire* plus one destroyer and three Free French sloops, and that from Liverpool of three transports escorted by three destroyers. The embarked ground forces comprised 4,200 British and 2,700 Free French troops, whose heavy equipment and other specialized stores sailed with a mercantile convoy to Freetown, Sierra Leone, where the invasion force was to gather for the operation proper. The full naval support group was Force M, consisting of the battleships *Barham* and *Resolution*, the aircraft-carrier *Ark Royal*, the cruisers *Devonshire*, *Fiji* (torpedoed on 1 September and replaced by the *Australia*) and *Cumberland*, 10 destroyers and a number of smaller vessels.

A further note of confusion was added on 11 September when Cunningham received a report that the Vichy French cruisers *Georges Leygues*, *Gloire* and *Montcalm*, escorted by three large destroyers, were believed to be in the area after passing westward through the Straits of Gibraltar. There was considerable confusion in British naval circles (in the UK, at Gibraltar and with Force M) about the likely destination of the Vichy French squadron and how the problem was to be overcome, but the matter resolved itself when the cruisers *Georges Leygues* and *Montcalm* plus the three destroyers put into Dakar, the *Gloire* having been shepherded into Casablanca after suffering mechanical problems. The cruiser *Primauguet*, patrolling from Dakar, was also persuaded to put into Casablanca. The French squadron had in fact been destined for Libreville in Gabon as a bolster against Free French leanings in central Africa (Chad having defected recently to the Allied cause), and its fortuitous presence in Dakar did much to strengthen the pro-Vichy stance of the Senegalese administration, already confident of its ability to resist British naval pressures thanks to the availability of the half-completed battleship *Richelieu*, which had reached Dakar after escaping from France in June 1940.

The British and Free French forces had reached Freetown, just to the south of Dakar, on 14 September and completed their final preparations before heading north in three groups between 19 and 21 September. Two naval bombardments and a naval air strike were undertaken by the British with no success as a result of the excellent use of smoke by the French, and the British ships were hit several times by accurate French gunfire. Cunningham decided that the landing planned for 23 September should not go ahead, though the French attempted such an operation at Rufisque on the eastern side of Hann Bay and were pushed back with a few casualties. The force commanders decided to make a last attempt on 25 September, with the naval forces making an effort to silence the French ships so that a British landing could be made. However, as the ships of Force M moved into position, the *Resolution* was seriously damaged by a submarine-launched torpedo and accurate French gunnery began to make its presence felt. Just before mid-day, therefore, the British commanders decided to abandon Operation 'Menace', and this local decision was rapidly endorsed by the British government.

Mercantile Allied codename for Manus Island in the Admiralty group.

Merchant of Venice Allied code phrase for the capture of Myitkyina in northern Burma (4 August 1944) by the forces of

Lieutenant General Joseph W. Stilwell's Chinese Army in India (30th and 38th Chinese Divisions), supported by Colonel C. N. Hunter's US 5307th Provisional Regiment and Brigadier J. M. Calvert's British 77th Long-Range Penetration Brigade.

Meridian Air attacks by the Fleet Air Arm against the oil refineries at Palembang on Sumatra (24 and 29 January 1945). The two oil refineries at Palembang were the largest in South-East Asia (and between them capable of meeting three-quarters of Japan's total requirement for aviation fuel) and were thus a target of considerable strategic importance. In November 1944 the British Pacific Fleet (intended for service alongside the larger forces of the US Navy in the Pacific) had received a dynamic commander in Admiral Sir Bruce Fraser as it was forming at Trincomalee in Ceylon, with its four fast carriers (*Illustrious*, *Indefatigible*, *Indomitable* and *Victorious*) under the command of Rear Admiral Sir Philip Vian. The British Pacific Fleet was scheduled to move from Ceylon to Australia during January 1945 before joining in Pacific operations, and this gave Vian's carriers an ideal opportunity to raid the Palembang refineries and so confirm the operational capability of their new Grumman Avenger strike aircraft after the limited successes of the two earlier raids, those against the refinery at Belawan Deli in north-eastern Sumatra on 20 December 1944 and 1 January 1945. Vian's 4 aircraft-carriers were escorted by the battleship *King George V*, 3 cruisers and 10 destroyers, and on 24 January launched 43 Avengers escorted by 80 fighters. Very strong AA, fighter and barrage balloon defences were encountered, but the strike cut the output of one refinery by half, while the escort shot down 11 Japanese fighters and destroyed another 30 on the ground at the complex's three defence airfields. A second strike was launched on 29 January, 46 Avengers inflicting sufficient damage on the second refinery to halt its operations totally for two months.

Merkur (Mercury) German airborne and amphibious conquest of Crete (20/31 May 1941). The operation was undertaken in the aftermath of Operation 'Marita' as elements of the German 12th Army mopped up in Greece and the bulk of the German forces used in the Balkan operations was shifted north for the delayed start of Operation 'Barbarossa'. The German fear was now that the British would be able to use Crete as a base for increasingly heavy bomber attacks on the oilfields at Ploesti in Romania, which supplied a decisive and irreplaceable proportion of German oil supplies. German planning was thus unanimous that Crete had to be taken from the Allies, though the question of method was more difficult. A seaborne assault was the logical answer, but the Germans lacked in the Aegean and eastern Mediterranean the naval forces necessary to escort a substantial invasion fleet against the efforts of a determined British Mediterranean Fleet, which had been mauled during the Greek operations but was still a formidable adversary. Here Generalleutnant Kurt Student, commander of the Luftwaffe's XI Fliegerkorps, stepped in with the suggestion that his airborne forces should undertake the task. The idea was immediately attractive to Reichsmarschall Herman Goering, who felt that in this scheme lay the chance for the Luftwaffe to recoup some of the credit it had lost in the Battle of Britain. So Student and Generaloberst Hans Jeschonnek, the Luftwaffe chief-of-staff, were instructed to approach Hitler with the concept. Hitler gave his agreement to the plan, with the sole stipulations that 'Merkur' be undertaken with the forces currently available to XI Fliegerkorps (Generalleutnant Wilhelm Süssmann's 7th Fliegerdivision as the parachute formation and Generalleutnant Hans Graf von Sponeck's 22nd Division as the airlanding formation) by the middle of May so that forces could then be shifted to the Eastern Front.

In overall command of 'Merkur' was Generaloberst Alexander Löhr, commanding Luftflotte II in the Balkans, and with Löhr's support Student was able to secure the services of Generalmajor Julius Ringel's 5th Mountain Division, which was already in Greece, instead of the 22nd Division, which was stuck in Romania without adequate transport. However, Löhr denied Student the full strength of General Wolfram Freiherr von Richthofen's VIII Fliegerkorps as the air support element for the operation as this powerful tactical air formation was required to move north quite soon. Once the decision had been reached, the Germans moved with great speed and vigour, the rest of the 7th Fliegerdivision and the 5th Mountain Division being moved swiftly to the airfields from which the transport force of XI Fliegerkorps would operate. Under the command of Generalmajor Gerhard, this transport force amounted to 500 Junkers Ju 52/3m transport and glider-tug aircraft, and 72 DFS 230 assault gliders. Tactical support would be furnished by some 280 level bombers, 150 dive-bombers and 180 fighters of VIII Fliegerkorps.

The German plan began to develop faults with a total misassessment of the Allied strength on Crete, which the Germans had known to be some 6,000 men in December 1940 but which had now, unbeknownst to the Germans, increased to some 32,000 men under the command of Major General Sir Bernard Freyberg. In addition to the original 6,000-man garrison, Crete was now also held by some 21,000 men of Freyberg's 2nd New Zealand Division and the 6th Australian Division evacuated from Greece, by 5,000 Commonwealth reinforcements from Egypt, and by the 8,000 men of two weak Greek divisions. This amounted to some 40,000 men, against which Student could pit some 8,100 of his 13,000 paratroops and the 14,000 men of the 5th Mountain Division. Where the Germans had advantages, however, were the element of surprise, the quality of their troops, and the virtually total lack in the Allied camp of heavy weapons (Freyberg had only a few captured French and Italian guns and some obsolete British weapons, all without transport, as his artillery, plus 9 elderly tanks and 35 aircraft, all the aircraft being destroyed or evacuated before the beginning of 'Merkur').

The German problem, even without realistic intelligence of Allied strengths and dispositions, was lack of airlift capability, so Student planned to move his airborne forces in two lifts to capture the airfields at Maleme, Rethimnon and Heraklion (together with four other objectives in northern Crete) so that the 5th Mountain Division could then be flown in for the inland development of these three air-heads pending the arrival of seaborne reinforcements (the rest of the 5th Mountain Division from the island of Milos) with heavier weapons and armour. Lohr objected strongly to so dispersed a tactical arrival and asked for a single initial stroke, forcing Student to compromise on three main objectives for the two initial airlifts. In the first lift, to be launched during the morning of 20 May, the Western Group under Generalmajor Eugen Meindl would take Maleme airfield (plus the Tavronitis bridge and Hill 107 commanding the airfield) using most of Major Walter Koch's Airborne Assault Regiment, while the Centre Group under Süssmann seized Canea and Suda slightly to the east with Oberst Richard Heidrich's 3rd Parachute Regiment, the remainder of the Airborne Assault Regiment, one battalion of the 2nd Parachute Regiment and support units. The Centre Group was to be reinforced by the seaborne 100th Mountain Regiment. In the second lift, to be launched during the afternoon of 20 May, the rest of the Centre Group (two battalions of the 2nd Parachute Regiment under Oberst Alfred Sturm) was to take Retimo and its airfield, while the Eastern Group under Oberst Bruno Bräuer was to capture Heraklion with the 1st Parachute Regiment and one battalion of the 2nd Parachute Regiment to open the way for the seaborne arrival of the 5th Mountain Division (less the 100th Mountain Regiment) under Ringel, who would then assume local command.

With hindsight it is possible to see that the German effort was still too dispersed, and allowed for no airborne reserve in Greece for deployment as the tactical situation on the island developed. In this last respect, however, delays in Greece created such a reserve just as it was needed at Maleme. On the Allied side, Freyberg had seen that a landing was imminent (though he envisaged this as being a seaborne operation) and had thus disposed his forces along the northern coast of Crete in well sited positions. The British, Australian and New Zealand battalions were first-class infantry units, but lacked heavy weapons, adequate air defences, useful quantities of motor transport and, perhaps most importantly of all, the communications network that would permit them to operate as a cohesive whole rather than as separate brigades. Heavy air attacks prefaced the arrival of the German airborne assault in the morning of 20 May, when Meindl's Western Group landed accurately but met sterling defence from Brigadier J. Hargest's 5th New Zealand Brigade of five infantry battalions. Unfortunately the New Zealanders had placed too scattered a force on Maleme airfield, which was taken by the Germans, but then the brigade managed to pin down the assault force and inflict heavy casualties on it. The Centre Group also landed with fair accuracy, but was hotly engaged by the Greek 2nd and 8th Regiments and the two other brigades (the 4th and 10th) of the 2nd New Zealand Division, temporarily commanded by Brigadier E. Puttick, as it tried to push down Prison Valley towards Canea, which was held by Major General E. C. Weston's force of Royal Marines, army units and the Royal Naval Base Defence Organization. The Centre Group was sadly mauled by the 4th and 10th New Zealand Brigades.

The Allied defence was now fully aware of what the Germans were doing, and when the first part of the second lift began in the afternoon after delays caused by bottlenecks on Greek airfields, the defence was waiting for it. Thus the second part of the Centre Group failed to take Rethimnon and its airfield against the defence of Lieutenant Colonel I. R. Campbell's 19th Australian Brigade. A similar fate befell the Eastern Group at Heraklion, which was devastated by Brigadier R. H. Chappel's British 14th Infantry Brigade. In Greece Student realized how parlous was the situation, for he knew of the failure at Heraklion, feared a similar result at Rethimnon (though he had heard nothing as a result of radio failure), appreciated that the force at Canea had been halted. Student thus realized that all must now be gambled on the partial success at Maleme, where at least an airfield was in German hands even if dominated by the position of the 22nd New Zealand Battalion on Hill 107. But as Meindl's forces probed towards Hill 107 they found that the New Zealanders had pulled back, and this was the decisive moment, for Student began to pour reinforcements into Maleme from 17.00 on 21 May. The New Zealanders counterattacked but failed, and now realized that the position of the whole of the 5th New Zealand Brigade was no longer tenable. The brigade thus retreated towards Canea, leaving the Germans in control of Maleme and a sizeable air-head.

The Germans were now able to attack Canea with a concerted effort by the Western and Centre Groups, and when Galatas fell on 25 May, Freyberg appreciated that the battle for Crete had been lost as Canea must now fall into German hands, together with the excellent anchorage at Suda Bay, which would allow German seaborne reinforcements to flood into the island despite the total destruction of the first convoy, carrying 4,000 men of the 5th Mountain Division (though only 300 men were lost) by units of the Mediterranean Fleet. With the exception of Greek units and the garrison at Rethimnon (which got the word too late), the Allied forces now fell back towards the south coast at Sfakia, from where some 23,000 were evacuated to Egypt.

By 31 May the campaign was over as the Germans mopped up the last surviving pockets. The cost for the Allies was catastrophic, for the dead amounted to 1,740, the wounded to 3,250 (including 1,740 in German hands), and the prisoners to 11,385. The RAF had lost 46 aircraft, while the Royal Navy had lost 9 warships sunk and another 17 (including 2 battleships) severely damaged. But the cost to the Germans was higher still, for the Luftwaffe lost some 200 aircraft, while the ground forces (Luftwaffe and army) suffered some 10,200 casualties in Crete (1,156 to the 5th Mountain Division, and 1,520 killed, 1,500 wounded and 1,502 missing to the airborne forces). Student's troops had thus suffered something like 55 per cent casualties, leading to a complete reassessment of the airborne forces' role in future German campaigns, and causing Hitler to abandon or query most strongly all serious consideration of further large-scale airborne operations. Operation 'Merkur' may thus be said to have destroyed the German airborne arm as such, its formations thereafter being used mainly as elite infantry divisions. And to the Germans casualty list must be added the men of the 5th Mountain

Division lost when their seaborne convoy was intercepted and destroyed.

M.G. Designation of military convoys (together with a numerical suffix) plying from Malta to Gibraltar, and inaugurated in December 1940.

MI Japanese operation for the capture of Midway Island, and leading to the Battle of Midway (25 May/5 June 1942). This was one of the decisive campaigns of World War II, and resulted in the reversal of Japan's expansion south and east into the Pacific, already checked in the Battle of the Coral Sea, and the removal of the strategic initiative from the Japanese in favour of the Americans. The plan was the brainchild of Admiral Isoroku Yamamoto, commander-in-chief of the Imperial Japanese Navy's Combined Fleet, and was approved reluctantly by the Japanese government on 5 April 1942. Yamamoto had long insisted that protracted war with the USA could only result in defeat for Japan, and that in these circumstances the only way to secure a negotiated peace soon after the beginning of the war was to draw the US Navy's Pacific Fleet into battle under conditions of advantage for the Combined Fleet, to defeat it and then to offer terms to the USA on the basis of the status quo. The Imperial Japanese Army had inclinations along similar lines, but thought that the successful implementation of Operations 'FS' and 'MO' could sever the US lines of communication to Australia long enough for the Japanese to construct an impregnable outer defence perimeter in the Pacific. The army feared that the navy's plans for the occupation of Midway Island as a threat to the Hawaiian Islands would inevitably lead to subsequent naval demands for a combined operation against Oahu Island in the Hawaiian group, but approval of Yamamoto's plan was given when the navy provided assurances that the occupation of Midway (together with the launching of Operation 'AL' against the Aleutians as a strategic diversion) was only a lure to draw out the Pacific Fleet for the decisive battle.

The scheme devised by Yamamoto was essentially simple in concept (though complex in detail) and strategically sound, and used virtually the whole strength of the Imperial Japanese Navy's surface fleet. The plan was predicated on the assumption that of the 4 aircraft-carriers available in May to Admiral Chester W. Nimitz, US Commander-in-Chief Pacific Fleet, at least 1 (*Lexington*) had been sunk in the Battle of the Coral Sea, another (*Yorktown*) had sunk after the battle or was too severely damaged to be operational, and the other 2 (*Enterprise* and *Hornet*) were absent in the South-West Pacific Area. In fact Nimitz had three carriers available for Rear Admiral Frank J. Fletcher (commanding in place of Vice Admiral William F. Halsey, who was ill) as the *Enterprise* and *Hornet* had reached Pearl Harbor to join the *Yorktown*, which had been repaired with extraordinary rapidity (repairs that had been estimated to need 90 days of work were completed between 27 and 30 May by 1,400 men working 24 hours per day).

Yamamoto attached great importance to the distraction of American attention by the activities associated with Operation 'AL', which was to be undertaken just before Operation 'MI' by Vice Admiral Boshiro Hosogawa's 5th Fleet. Escorted by a Main Body (1 heavy cruiser and 2 destroyers), Rear Admiral Sentaro Omori's Attu Occupation Force (1 light cruiser and 4 destroyers escorting 2 transports with 1,000 troops) and Captain Takeji Ono's Kiska Occupation Force (1 light cruiser and 2 destroyers escorting 6 transports with 550 troops) were to land sufficient troops in the Aleutians to establish garrisons while Rear Admiral Kakuji Kakuta's 2nd Strike Force (the light carriers *Ryujo* and *Junyo* escorted by 2 heavy cruisers, 4 destroyers and 1 seaplane tender) struck at Dutch Harbor farther east in the chain of the Aleutians, the whole object being to draw off as much as possible of the Pacific Fleet and/or its reserves to the north.

The main weight of Yamamoto's plan was in the south, where Vice Admiral Chuichi Nagumo's 1st Mobile Force sortied from Hashirajima in Japan on 27 May with the fleet carriers *Akagi*, *Kaga*, and *Hiryu* (with a total of 72 dive-bombers, 90 attack aircraft and 72 fighters) escorted by the battleships *Haruna* and *Kirishima*, the heavy cruisers *Tone* and *Chikuma*, the light cruiser *Nagara*, 12 destroyers and a fleet train of 8 tankers. This was to provide cover and support for Rear Admiral Raizo Tanaka's 2nd Fleet Escort Force, which sailed from Saipan in the Marianas Islands on 28 May with 1 light cruiser and 10 destroyers as escort for the Midway Occupation Force of 5,000 troops in 15 transports, together with a minesweeping group, these being supported by Rear Admiral Takeo Kurita's 2nd Fleet Occupation Support Force (the heavy cruisers *Kumano*, *Mogami*, *Mikuma* and *Suzuya*, 2 seaplane tenders and 3 destroyers) from Guam. The basic plan was for these forces to close in on Midway from the north-west and west in order to attack Midway at dawn on 4 June unless US Navy forces were detected in the area, in which case Nagumo's carrier aircraft would attack these before neutralizing Midway's defences so that the troops could land. To the west lurked a powerful reserve in case US opposition (at sea or on Midway) was stronger than expected. This reserve was Vice Admiral Nobutake Kondo's 2nd Fleet Strike Force (the light carrier *Zuiho* with 24 aircraft, the battleships *Hiei* and *Kongo*, the heavy cruisers *Atago*, *Chokai*, *Myoko* and *Haguro*, the light cruiser *Yura* and 8 destroyers supported by 4 tankers), which was to crush US Navy forces in the region or to shatter the defences of Midway with gunfire. Yamamoto expected that all these operations would finally compel Nimitz to commit all naval forces available at Pearl Harbor, which would then be totally destroyed by the 2nd Fleet in conjunction with his own 1st Fleet Main Body (the light carrier *Hosho* with 19 aircraft, the battleships *Yamato*, *Nagato* and *Mutsu*, the light cruiser *Sendai* and 9 destroyers) from Japan.

Intrinsic to the success of this complex operation, involving as it did some 71 major units of the Imperial Japanese Navy, were security (already breached by the US Navy breaking of the Japanese JN-25 code), good and timely communications (impossible as everything had to be routed through Yamamoto) and accurate reconnaissance to upgrade the current intelligence picture. This last was denied the Japanese by the fact that Operation 'K' had been cancelled, so removing Japan's capability for the aerial reconnaissance of Pearl Harbor, and that the screen of 13 submarines on picket duties between Pearl Harbor and Midway arrived only after the US carrier force had passed to the east. The result was that the Japanese forces did not know of the presence of US naval units near Midway, a situation exacerbated by the fact that neither Nagumo nor Kondo had been informed of the cancellation of Operation 'K', and thus did not think to put up significant aerial reconnaissance patrols.

Thanks to the breaking of JN-25, Nimitz knew what was afoot, and Midway was reinforced to some 3,000 men under the command of the 6th Marine Defense Battalion, extra aircraft were flown in (bringing the island's air strength to 109), and reconnaissance patrols were flown in a great fan from the north-west to the south-west of the island. The naval support for these measures was the dispatch from Pearl Harbor of Fletcher's forces, consisting of Fletcher's Task Force 17 (the fleet carrier *Yorktown* with 13 torpedo bombers, 37 dive-bombers and 25 fighters, the heavy cruisers *Astoria* and *Portland*, and 6 destroyers) and Rear Admiral Raymond A. Spruance's Task Force 16 (the fleet carriers *Enterprise* and *Hornet* with a total of 29 torpedo bombers, 75 dive-bombers and 54 fighters, the heavy cruisers *New Orleans*, *Minneapolis*, *Vincennes*, *Northampton* and *Pensacola*, the light cruiser *Atlanta*, and 11 destroyers). Other forces involved on the US side were Task Group 7.3 (a patrol of four submarines guarding the approaches to Oahu) and Task Group 7.1 (a patrol of 12 submarines in the western approaches to Midway).

As the Japanese forces approached Midway TFs 16 and 17 were ready to the north-north-east of the island, and the Japanese were first sighted at 09.00 on 3 June. Operations began at 04.30 on 4 June, when Nagumo launched a first strike against Midway. The second wave of aircraft on board the Japanese carriers were armed with armour-piercing bombs or torpedoes in anticipation of an American naval counterattack. US aircraft took off from Midway to engage the incoming raid and to attack the carriers, but were generally knocked about by the superior Japanese aircraft and pilots. However, the leader of the Japanese strike called for another raid against the Midway defences, and at 07.00 Nagumo ordered his carrier crews to begin the lengthy task of replacing the second wave's anti-ship weapons with conventional bombs. Work had just begun when Nagumo was informed at 07.28 that a Japanese scout aircraft had spotted 10 US ships some 200 miles to the north-east. The report made no mention of this force's composition, but at 07.58 came another report that the US ships were 5 cruisers and 5 destroyers. Thus work could proceed with the rearming of the second strike, though at this time the carriers' remaining fighters had to be scrambled to intercept an attack by Midway-based aircraft. Then at 08.20 came yet another scout report, this time to the effect that the US naval force included 1 carrier.

Nagumo's position was now impossible, for the scrambled fighters now needed refuelling, the first Midway attack wave was due back, and the second wave was in no position to attempt either sort of attack. While still dithering, Nagumo turned north-east at 09.18 to attack the US forces. Now it was Fletcher's turn, and he launched a first strike at 07.52 from the *Enterprise* and *Hornet*, following with a strike from the *Yorktown* at 09.00 as she was farther to the north. At 09.30 the US torpedo bombers found the Japanese carriers and attacked. But the aircraft were obsolete Douglas Devastators and were destroyed, in the process convincing Nagumo that the Americans' first strike had been beaten, giving the Japanese time to complete the arming of his aircraft for an anti-ship strike. Thus the decks of the Japanese carriers were packed with aircraft as the Douglas Dauntless dive-bombers of Fletcher's first strike arrived overhead and screamed down at 10.25, within five minutes devastating the *Akagi*, *Kaga* and *Soryu*.

Between 19.00 and 19.30 the *Soryu* and *Kaga* sank, and the *Akagi* was finished off with torpedoes on the following day. It was a devastating blow from which only the *Hiryu*, cruising separately, escaped. Thus the sole Japanese carrier launched two strikes, and these found and struck the *Yorktown* between 12.05 and 12.15, and at 14.30. The US carrier was abandoned at 15.00 and later sunk by submarine attack while under tow. Now it was the turn of the *Hiryu*, which was devastated by aircraft from the *Enterprise* at 17.00 and scuttled at 05.10 on the following day, being finished off later by Japanese torpedoes. This was a disaster from which the Japanese could not really recover, though Yamamoto tried desperately during the rest of 4 and 5 June to entice the US forces into combat with his battleship forces. Fletcher made the right tactical and strategic decision, and thus withdrew. The Americans had lost 307 dead and 147 aircraft, as well as one carrier and one destroyer. On the other side the Japanese had lost some 3,500 dead (including highly trained and irreplaceable aircrews) and 332 aircraft, as well as 4 carriers. The Japanese heavy cruisers *Mogami* and *Mikuma* were also damaged in a collision, both ships then being damaged further by air attacks and the *Mikuma* later sinking. The Japanese had suffered a blow of mortal proportions, and Yamamoto had no option but to call off the rest of Operation 'MI', which can justly claim to have cost the Japanese the war. The Battle of Midway was thus one of history's truly decisive battles.

Michaelmas US amphibious operation by the 126th Infantry Regiment of Major General Wiliam H. Gill's US 32nd Infantry Division to capture Saidor on the northern coast of New Guinea (2 January 1944). The operation cost the US forces 55 dead and the Japanese 1,275 dead, and had the effect desired by General Douglas MacArthur's South-West Pacific Area command of cutting the line of retreat for the Japanese 20th and 51st Divisions. Thus instead of falling back relatively easily from the pressure of the forces of Lieutenant General Sir Thomas Blamey's I Australian Corps advancing along the coast of the Huon peninsula (8th and 9th Australian Divisions) and up the Markham valley (7th and 11th Australian Divisions), Lieutenant General Hatazo Adachi's Japanese 18th Army had to retreat through the trackless hinterland to its fall-back positions between Wewak and Mackay to the west.

Micki Maus (Mickey Mouse) German abduction of Admiral Miklos Horthy, the Regent of Hungary (15 October 1944). For some time before this Horthy had maintained clandestine links with the UK and USA, and at the end of September he despatched Lieutenant Marshal Farago on a secret mission to conclude an armistice with the Soviets, who were pressing in on Hungary. A preliminary agreement was signed on 11 October, and the fact of the armistice's existence was broadcast from Budapest on 15 October, leading to an immediate response from the Germans, who knew what was happening. Under the command of SS Obergruppenführer Erich von dem Bach-Zelewski, SS Standartenführer Otto Skorzeny seized Horthy from his palace and took him to Weilheim near Munich. Horthy was later moved to Austria and there released by the Americans at the end of the war. A pro-German puppet regime was formed in Hungary under Major Szalasi and his 'Arrow Cross' party.

Mike I US invasion of Luzon in the Philippine Islands (9 January 1945). This great undertaking was an intrinsic part of the plans of General Douglas MacArthur's South-West Pacific Area, but was not so enthusiastically embraced by the Pacific Ocean Areas command under Admiral Chester W. Nimitz, which was all too aware of the threat to major naval units now posed by Japanese *kamikaze* tactics, especially as Luzon was closer to the main Japanese air bases in Formosa, the Ryukyus and Japan than either Leyte or Mindoro, whose campaigns had been marked by heavy US losses to *kamikaze* aircraft. For this tactical reason, as well as his long-held belief that greater strategic advantage would accrue to the Americans from a blow westward into Formosa and the mainland of China, Nimitz would have preferred that the Luzon invasion not take place. MacArthur had carried President Franklin D. Roosevelt, however, and the plan went ahead, albeit after a delay imposed by the comparatively slow pace of operations on Leyte and the decision first to take Mindoro as a base for the tactical aircraft of Lieutenant General C. Kenney's US 5th Air Force, which had supported MacArthur's ground forces throughout the campaign in New Guinea and the Philippines, and which was now redesignated the Far East Air Forces.

The original date for the start of Operation 'Mike I' had been 20 December 1944, but the Leyte and Mindoro operations, combined with poor weather, resulted in a postponement to 9 January 1945. Under the overall command of MacArthur, the landings were planned with the close support of Vice Admiral Thomas C. Kinkaid's 7th Fleet, whose 850 ships included Rear Admiral Jesse B. Oldendorf's Battle Line, a force of 164 ships including 6 battleships, 6 cruisers and 19 destroyers tasked with the escort of the invasion forces and with the provision of gunfire support for the landings. Oldendorf was supported by an escort carrier group of 17 carriers and 20 destroyers, 10 destroyer transports carrying underwater demolition teams, and 86 other vessels including the essential minesweepers. Oldendorf was to remain in immediate command at the invasion beaches until Kinkaid arrived with the III and VII Amphibious Forces, commanded respectively by Vice Admiral Theodore S. Wilkinson and Vice Admiral D. E. Barbey, when Kinkaid would assume command.

Strategic cover for Operation 'Mike I' was provided by Admiral William F. Halsey's 3rd Fleet. With his fleet centred on the Fast Carrier Task Force of three carrier groups, Halsey left Ulithi on 30 December 1944, and on 3 and 4 January 1945 launched a series of devastating raids against Japanese airfields on Okinawa, Formosa and Luzon. The 3rd Fleet refuelled on 5 January then returned to the offensive with concentrated raids against airfields in northern Luzon (6 and 7 January) and on Formosa (8 and 9 January). During this period Halsey's carriers put up some 3,000 sorties and lost 86 aircraft. However, on the credit side Halsey totally prevented the aerial reinforcement of Luzon, and also caused a considerable degree of damage on his targets, though his efforts were curtailed severely by the weather. After these operations in direct support of Operation 'Mike I', Halsey headed into the South China Sea for strikes against targets in Indo-China, then cruised in the waters to the north in search of the Imperial Japanese Navy's Combined Fleet battleships. Many targets were raided before the 3rd Fleet returned to Ulithi on 25 January to become the 5th Fleet under Vice Admiral Raymond A. Spruance on 26

Mike I

January. In the five months that Halsey had commanded it, the 3rd Fleet had destroyed some 7,000 Japanese aircraft, 90 Japanese warships and about 600 Japanese merchant ships.

The landings on Luzon were the responsibility of the 200,000 men of Lieutenant General Walter Krueger's US 6th Army, and took place in Lingayen Gulf to the north of Manila on the west coast of the island. Krueger planned a two-corps landing in the south of Lingayen Gulf between Damortis in the east and Lingayen in the west. On the left was Major General Innis P. Swift's US I Corps (6th Infantry Division and 43rd Infantry Division, to be reinforced as rapidly as possible by the 32nd Infantry Division), and on the right was Major General Oscar W. Griswold's US XIV Corps (37th Infantry Division and 40th Infantry Division, to be reinforced as rapidly as possible by the 1st Cavalry Division). The task facing the two corps was formidable, for before XIV Corps could undertake its task of driving south to liberate Manila, the capital of the Philippines, the left flank of the US lodgement had to be secured by I Corps from any Japanese counteroffensive from the east or north.

On Luzon the Americans were faced by a formidable adversary in the form of Lieutenant General Tomoyuki Yamashita, commanding the Japanese 14th Area Army under the overall control of Field Marshal Count Hisaichi Terauchi's Southern Army command in Indo-China. The 14th Area Army had some 250,000 men under arms in Luzon, but Yamashita was all too aware of their limitations, for most of his units were understrength and short of supplies as a result of the blockade of the sea lanes between the Philippines and the Japanese home islands by US aircraft, surface ships and submarines. To compound the difficulties of his ground forces, Yamashita had only the most modest air support left after the beginning of January 1945, in the form of 120 aircraft on the strength of the 4th Air Army and 150 aircraft on the strength of the 2nd Air Fleet. It was decided that these should be expended in *kamikaze* attacks on the US invasion fleet, which sailed from Leyte on 2 January. The attacks achieved some successes, including the escort carrier *Ommaney Bay* sunk, another escort carrier damaged, the battleships *California* and *New Mexico* damaged, the cruisers *Australia* and *Louisville* severely damaged, more cruisers damaged to a lesser extent, and several smaller ships (including 5 valuable destroyers) damaged.

By 12 January Yamashita had only 4 liaison aircraft left, so the 4th Air Army's personnel were converted to infantry while the remnants of the 2nd Air fleet were sent back to the 1st Air Fleet on Formosa. After 12 January the Japanese managed to 'make' 27 more aircraft by cannibalization, and these were expended in *kamikaze* attacks on 15, 21 and 25 January. Despite his overall strength of 250,000 at the beginning of the Philippine campaign, Yamashita now had on Luzon a combatant strength of perhaps 90,000 army troops of the 8th, 10th, 19th, 23rd, 103rd and 105th Divisions, the 2nd Armoured Division, the 58th Independent Mixed Brigade and an airborne group. With noncombatants this strength was at least doubled, and Japanese strength was bolstered by some 25,000 naval troops of Vice Admiral D. Okochi's South-West Area Fleet around Manila, which Yamashita had decided to declare an open city. Nevertheless, it was clearly impossible for his forces either to check and defeat the US 6th Army as it landed or to hold the central plain of Luzon against overwhelmingly superior ground and air forces, so Yamashita decided to fight a delaying campaign just inland of the beaches before pulling back into the mountain regions (with his forces in three main groups) to conduct a war of harassment against the Americans. In the north of the island was the Shobo Group, some 152,000 men based on four infantry divisions (the 10th, 19th, 23rd and 103rd), one armoured division (the 2nd) and one independent mixed brigade (the 58th) led by Yamashita from a headquarters at Baguio. In the west (and dominating the important air base at Clark Field from the Cabusilan Mountains) was the Kembu Group, some 30,000 men of an airborne group led by Major General Rikichi Tsukada. And in the south and east was the Shimbu Group, some 80,000 men based on two infantry divisions (the 8th and 105th) led by Lieutenant General Shizuo Yokoyama. From December 1944 onwards well-sited and strongly-defended bases were

140

prepared in these regions, whose defence forces were to operate on a basis of self-sufficiency for as long as they could.

The US invasion fleet entered Lingayen Gulf on 6 January. The warships and naval aircraft then spent three days 'softening up' the beach defences at the base of Lingayen Gulf before the landings started at 09.00 on 9 January. There was no opposition as a result of Yamashita's defence plans, and by nightfall on 9 January the 6th Army had established a beach-head 17 miles wide and 4 miles deep. XIV Corps now began a slow offensive south towards Manila, being much delayed by the fact that the Japanese had pulled up all the rail lines and destroyed all bridges and culverts, while I Corps pushed east towards the line San Jose/Pozorrubio to provide a shield for XIV Corps' left flank. I Corps now began to meet increasing opposition from the Shobo Group as it approached Yamashita's headquarters at Baguio, and on 16 January a Japanese counterattack punched a hole through I Corps nearly to the sea. On 27 January the 32nd Infantry and 1st Cavalry Divisions landed at Lingayen and were moved up to support their respective corps. Spurred on by MacArthur, who wished a rapid advance to Manila so that the US forces would have a good port, secure the all-weather airfields in the area (Clark, Zablan, Nielson and Nichols Fields) for tactical aircraft, and release the prisoners in military and civil camps before the Japanese harmed them further, XIV Corps now headed south at a greater pace but against increasingly determined opposition to reach the outskirts of Clark Field and to take San Fernando on 29 January, forcing the Kembu Group to pull back westward into the Cabusilan Mountains. Further reinforced by the 25th Infantry Division, I Corps had meanwhile advanced east to take San Jose and then pushed on to the eastern coast of Luzon between Baler and Dingalan Bays by 13 February, thereby cutting off Yamashita and his Shobu Group in the north of Luzon.

Mike II Plan for forces of Lieutenant General Walter Krueger's US 6th Army to land in Dingalan Bay, on the east coast of Luzon Island in the Philippines. Eventual success in the eastward drive of Major General Innis P. Swift's US I Corps from Lingayen Gulf made such a landing superfluous.

Mike III Plan for forces of Lieutenant General Walter Krueger's US 6th Army to land at Vigan on the north-west coast of Luzon Island in the Philippines to speed the US advance west of the Cordillera Central massif in the north of Luzon, held by Lieutenant General Tomoyuki Yamashita's Shobo Group of the 14th Area Army. Based on the 10th, 19th, 23rd and 103rd Infantry Divisions, with the 2nd Armoured Division and the 58th Independent Mixed Brigade, the Shobo Group at the end of January 1945 numbered some 110,000 men, and because elements of his army were still heavily involved in the centre and south-east of Luzon, Krueger could deploy only the 25th, 32nd and 33rd Infantry Divisions of Major General Innis P. Swift's US I Corps (supported by part of the 37th Infantry Division) against the Shobo Group. By 26 April the 33rd Infantry Division, with support from the 37th Infantry Division, had taken Yamashita's erstwhile headquarters at Baguio, but the whole of May and June 1945 passed before I Corps could break through the Balete Pass to push on to Bambang and the upper reaches of the Cagayan valley between the Cordillera Central and the Sierra Madre. The 37th Infantry Division pushed down the valley, taking Ilagan (19 June) and Tuguegarao (25 June) before linking up on 26 June with the 511th Parachute Infantry Regiment, which had dropped at Aparri in the extreme north of Luzon on 23 June. Other units had meanwhile advanced up the west coast of northern Luzon, taking San Fernando (26 March) and Vigan (19 April) before advancing along the north coast to Aparri. By the end of June Yamashita had been reduced to some 65,000 men, but these forces now held out for the rest of the war in two major pockets, one in the mountains south of Bontoc (under Yamashita) and the other in the Sierra Madre on the west coast of northern Luzon. There was little point in I Corps attempting to reduce these mountain garrisons, for US casualties would have been enormous for little or no strategic benefit, but the presence of the two Japanese pockets tied

Mike IV

down the 25th, 32nd and 37th Infantry Divisions until the surrender of Japan in September 1945.

Mike IV US amphibious landing at Nasugbu on the western side of south central Luzon in the Philippines (31 January 1945). This landing was undertaken by Major General J. Swing's US 11th Airborne Division (less two battalions) from Lieutenant General Robert L. Eichelberger's US 8th Army in the southern Philippines, and its use to approach Manila from the south-west (in an effort outflank the Japanese defences of the Filipino capital) reflected the burning desire of General Douglas MacArthur to get elements of his South-West Pacific Area forces into Manila as quickly as possible against the forces of Lieutenant General Shizuo Yokoyama's Shimbu Group. There was no opposition as the 11th Airborne Division began to come ashore, and the advance should have been speeded by the dropping of the division's two remaining battalions to take Tagaytay Ridge. The drop took place only on 3 February, however, and overcame only slight Japanese resistance just as the rest of the division arrived. MacArthur's plan had been for a rapid overland advance from south of the city as Major General Oscar W. Griswold's US XIV Corps fought its way from the north, but the 11th Airborne Division was brought to a halt by Japanese naval troops on the south-west approaches to the city.

Manila had been declared an open city by Lieutenant General Tomoyaki Yamashita's 14th Area Army, but its garrison of 17,000 naval troops under Rear Admiral Sanji Iwabuchi none the less decided to hold the city to the last and so prevent the use of its great port by the Americans; rather than try to fight a battle with central control, Iwabuchi divided his forces into independent battle groups allocated to particular sectors of the city. Thus the Americans were committed to the only urban fighting of the Pacific war, though at first the 1st Cavalry Division and the 37th Infantry Division of XIV Corps were reluctant to admit the fact as they advanced from the north with the immediate objective of securing the camp at Santo Tomas in which US civilians were interned. An armoured detachment of the 1st Cavalry Division liberated this camp on 3 February, and elements of the 37th Infantry Division then pushed on to liberate the civilian internees and military POWs held in Old Bilibid Prison. By now the leading units of XIV Corps were in the northern suburbs of Manila, and the battle turned into a grim building-by-building advance as US artillery and house-clearing teams blasted the Japanese back towards the centre of the city. The leading elements of the 1st Cavalry and 11th Airborne Divisions met on 12 February, the day on which the Japanese were left with only Intramuros, the old walled city at the centre of Manila. The Japanese refused to permit the evacuation of civilians, and by the time Manila was finally declared secure by the Americans on 4 March, some 100,000 civilians had become casualties, virtually the entire Japanese naval garrison and some 1,000 Americans had been killed, and the Americans had also suffered about 5,000 wounded.

The task now facing the 6th Army was the elimination of the Shimbu Group in the area of Laguna de Bay and in the Bicol peninsula. Yokoyama's main strength, some 30,000 men, was firmly in command of the southern end of the Sierra Madre as far south as Laguna de Bay along the line Ipo Dam/Wawa Dam/Antipolo. Here the Shimbu Group controlled the water supply to Manila and the direct sea route through the central Philippines, and until they had been winkled out the Americans could neither make full use of Manila harbour nor consider the next step forward towards Japan. In the south of the sector XIV Corps started a major offensive on 8 March with the 1st Cavalry Division in the lead until replaced by the 43rd Infantry Division on 13 March. Supported by the 6th Infantry Division from Major General Innis P. Swift's I Corps, Griswold's formation pushed deep into the centre of Yokoyama's positions until in turn relieved by Major General Charles P. Hall's US XI Corps on 14 March. By the end of March the Americans had reached the eastern side of Laguna de Bay and exposed Yokoyama's left flank. The 6th Infantry Division failed to take the Ipo and Wawa dams during April, but then its successes farther south permitted the 43rd

Infantry Division to be moved to the 6th Infantry Division's support for the offensive which began on 6 May, taking Ipo Dam on 17 May and Wawa Dam on 28 May.

The remnants of the Shimbu Group fell back to an area north of Dinahican on Luzon's coast to the north-east of Luzon, and here survived to the end of the war, finally surrendering with 6,300 men. By this time the maintenance of pressure against the Japanese survivor groups was the task of Lieutenant General Robert L. Eichelberger's US 8th Army, which on 30 June 1945 assumed responsibility from the 6th Army, which was earmarked for the invasion of Japan. The last two groups in southern Luzon were offshoots of the Shimbu Group, namely the 'Fuji' Force of 13,000 men commanded by Colonel Fushijige and a unit of some 3,000 men in Luzon's 'tail' stretching south-east from Laguna de Bay. These were tackled by the 1st Cavalry Division with the aid of Filipino guerrilla forces (which were also heavily involved against the main body of the Shimbu Group). The 'Fuji' Force had been hounded to pieces by the end of April, and the rest of the Bicol peninsula fell by 2 May to a concerted drive from the west by the 1st Cavalry Division and from the east (after a landing at Legaspi on 1 April) by the 158th Regiment Combat Team.

Mike VI Plan by the South-West Pacific Area command for an amphibious landing at Batangas and in Tabayas Bay on the southern side of the main body of Luzon Island. This was rendered superfluous by the success of the 1st Cavalry Division in eliminating the remnants of the Shimbu Group in the area.

Mike VII US amphibious landing at San Antonio in central Luzon (29 January 1945). Undertaken by Major General Charles P. Hall's US XI Corps of Lieutenant General Robert L. Eichelberger's US 8th Army, the landing put the 24th and 38th Infantry Divisions ashore to the north of the Bataan peninsula with the object of taking the naval base at Olongapo and pushing forward to the northern shore of Manila Bay. There were no significant Japanese forces in the Bataan peninsula, but it none the less took XI Corps some two weeks of steady fighting to reach Manila Bay. The corps then undertook the clearing of the Bataan peninsula with an overland advance down the peninsula's eastern side starting on 14 February, and complemented one day later by the landing of one regiment at Mariveles at the tip of the peninsula. Bataan was declared secure on 21 February.

There then remained the four fortresses on islands in Manila Bay. Corregidor was the most powerful of these, and it took 12 days of bitter fighting after the drop of the 503rd Parachute Infantry Regiment on 16 February before the island was declared secure on 28 February. Then Caballo and El Fraile were reduced on 13 April and 18 April respectively by the expedient of pouring diesel oil into the Japanese bunkers for ignition by white phosphorus and HE shells. The Japanese evacuated Canabao just before the Americans landed on 16 April.

To the north of this region the remnants of the Kembu Group were holding out under Major General Rikichi Tsukada. After losing Clark Field, the Kembu Group's surviving 25,000 men had fallen back into the Cambusilan Mountains, where they were kept in check by the 40th Infantry Division of Major General Oscar W. Griswold's US XIV Corps, which was too concerned with the reduction of Manila to undertake anything but containment of this Japanese thorn. Eventually the 40th Infantry Division was supplemented by the 38th and 43rd Infantry Divisions, and the Kembu Force broke up into small guerrilla units on 6 April. These remnants survived to the end of the war, when some 1,500 survivors surrendered. Japanese losses in the Luzon campaign thus amounted to some 190,000, while those of the Americans were 8,000 dead and 30,000 wounded.

Milepost US plan to build up stocks of *matériel*, fuel and other supplies in the Far East to support Soviet forces when they entered the war against Japan on 8 August 1945 with a concentric attack on Manchuria (Japanese Manchukuo) by Marshal of the Soviet Union R. Ya. Malinovsky's Trans-Baikal Front (5 armies), General M. A. Purkaev's 2nd Far Eastern Front (2 armies) and Marshal of the Soviet Union K. A. Meretskov's 1st Far Eastern Front (4 armies). These overran Manchukuo and Korea as far south as the 38th parallel by 22 August, and also took the southern half of Sakhalin Island and the Japanese end of the Kurile Islands.

Millennium British raid by RAF Bomber Command aircraft against Köln (30 May 1942). This was the first '1,000-bomber raid', and caused considerable devastation in the German city.

Mimose (mimosa) Movement of the 17th SS Panzergrenadier Division (June and July 1944) from the area of General Kurt von der Chevallerie's German 1st Army south of the River Loire to the sector of Generaloberst Friedrich Dollmann's 7th Army facing Lieutenant General Omar N. Bradley's US 1st Army at the base of the Cotentin peninsula.

Mincemeat (i) British naval minelaying operation off the Italian port of Livorno (17/30 August 1941). The operation was conceived by Vice Admiral Sir James Somerville of the Gibraltar-based Force H, and used the fast minelayer *Manxman* disguised as a French cruiser between the time she sailed from the UK and returned, except for the period in which she laid her mines on 25 August.
(ii) Allied deception plan (May 1943) to deepen the uncertainty of the Axis powers as to the intended landing site for the Allied invasion of southern Europe. The body of a drowned man was left in the sea off Cadiz with papers identifying him as a courier from the War Office in London to General the Hon. Sir Harold Alexander, General Dwight D. Eisenhower and Admiral Sir Andrew Cunningham with outline plans for the operations that were supposedly being planned against Sardinia and Greece as first steps in the Allied return to Europe. Though the Germans did not remove forces from Italy as a result of this 'plant', it helped considerably in keeping the real plan (for Operation 'Husky') more secure.

Minerva Rescue of Général d'Armée Henri Giraud from southern France by a British submarine (6 November 1942). Captured by the Germans in 1940 and put in a POW camp, Giraud escaped in April 1942 and was later ferried south across the Mediterranean to become commander of the French North African Forces after Operation 'Torch'.

Mistel (mistletoe) German composite attack weapon, comprising a twin-engined bomber with its normal nose replaced by a large shaped-charge warhead and controlled by a single-engined fighter mounted above the fuselage on struts until the final moments of the attack, when the pilot in the fighter released his aircraft for the escape.

Mittelmeer (Mediterranean) Movement of Luftwaffe forces to the Mediterranean theatre (spring 1941) as a reinforcement for the Italian Regia Aeronautica in its operations against Malta and British shipping in the Mediterranean, and as the tactical support element for the Deutsches Afrika Korps being deployed for the assistance of Italian ground forces in the Western Desert. The principal bolster for the Regia Aeronautica was General Hans Geisler's X Fliegerkorps, which began to arrive in Sicily in January 1941, and the North African force began to assemble in the following month.

M.K.F. Designation of Allied military convoys (together with a numerical suffix) plying from the UK to North Africa, and inaugurated in November 1942 in succession to the Operation 'Torch' convoys.

M.K.S. Designation of Allied ocean homeward convoys (together with a numerical suffix) plying from North Africa to the UK, and inaugurated in November 1942 in succession to the Operation 'Torch' convoys. From April 1943 M.K.S. and S.L. convoys sailed in company from the area of Gibraltar.

MO Japanese offensive to take Port Moresby in New Guinea and Tulagi near the eastern end of the Solomons island chain (3/7 May 1942), leading to the Battle of the Coral Sea. The origins of the plan lay with the Imperial Japanese Army, which saw in the primary aspect of the operation a major strategic opportunity for Japan to extend the southern perimeter of her 'Greater South-East Asia Co-Prosperity Sphere' by occupying all of New Guinea and completing its hold on the Solomons as means of severing the lines of maritime communication between the USA and Australia. Admiral Isoroku Yamamoto, commander-in-chief of the Combined Fleet, was at this time preparing Operation 'MI' as a means of bringing the US Pacific Fleet to decisive battle, and argued against the implementation of Operation 'MO' as a diversification of Japanese effort. In the event both 'MI' and 'MO' were implemented at approximately the same time, resulting in a great dilution of effort and forces.

The springboard for Operation 'MO' was provided by the Japanese successes at the end of their first period of conquest, when the Dutch East Indies had been taken, together with western New Guinea. An adjunct to these operations was the capture on 23 January 1942 of New Britain, which fell to Major General Tomitaro Horii's South Seas Detachment of the Japanese army supported by Vice Admiral Shigeyoshi Inouye's 4th Fleet. Rabaul on New Britain was soon under development as the main Japanese naval and air base in the region, whose security was enhanced by the navy's seizure of New Ireland just to the north of New Britain. There had already begun a campaign of bombing to disrupt Australian defences in the area, starting with air attacks on Lae and Salamaua on 21 January as a preface to the Japanese move against Rabaul, whose new bomber base permitted an extension of the Japanese offensive activities as far to the south-east as Bougainville in the Solomons and as far south as Port Moresby (first raid on 3 February) on the south coast of Papua. Port Moresby featured strongly in Japanese planning, for its fine harbour offered just the base needed for Japanese warships to threaten northern and eastern Australia. To ease the task of bombing Port Moresby, some 550 miles from Rabaul, the Japanese decided to seize bases on New Guinea in the form of Lae (forward airfield) and Salamaua (to cover Lae). On 8 March one battalion of the South Seas Detachment's 144th Regiment occupied Salamaua while the 4th Fleet's Maizuru 2nd Special Landing Force occupied Lae and began work on the airfield.

A serious dispute now exacerbated the already strained relations between the Imperial Japanese Army and Imperial Japanese Navy headquarters in Tokyo, for the navy wished to seize Australia as a means of depriving the Allies of their major bastion in the region, while the army demurred on the grounds that the task would need some 12 divisions and too great a tonnage of shipping. By the end of March a compromise had been reached, the navy agreeing to the occupation of all New Guinea at the same time as Samoa, Fiji and New Caledonia were taken in Operation 'FS', which would sever the maritime lines of communications between the USA and Australia, where General Douglas MacArthur had just arrived as commander-in-chief of the Allies' South-West Pacific Area command. These south sea operations were then postponed in favour of the navy-sponsored Operation 'MI', though a more limited local offensive was retained in Operation 'MO', an amphibious attack on Port Moresby, with a secondary operation against Tulagi for the establishment of a seaplane base to reconnoitre far into the Allied lines of communications across the Pacific (once Tulagi was secure, these forces were then to take Mauru and Ocean Islands yet farther to the south-east). Overall control of these operations was vested in the 4th Fleet, and Horii issued his orders on 29 April for landings scheduled to fall on Port Moresby during 10 May.

The naval plan was of typical complexity, involving no fewer than seven elements under separate commanders. For the invasion proper there was Rear Admiral Koso Abe's Port Moresby Transport Force (12 transports), and this was supported by Rear Admiral Sadamichi Kajioka's Port Moresby Attack Force (the light cruiser *Yubari*, 1 minelayer and 6 destroyers) and Rear Admiral Kuninori Marumo's Close Cover Force (the light cruisers *Tenryu* and *Tatsuta*, 1 seaplane carrier and 3 gunboats). More distant cover was provided by Rear Admiral Aritomo Goto's Main Body Support Force, divided into the Close Support Force (the light carrier *Shoho* and 1 destroyer) and the more distant Cover Force (the heavy cruisers *Aoba*, *Kako*,

Kinugasa and *Furutaka*), which was designed also to cover Rear Admiral Kiyohide Shima's Tulagi Invasion Force (1 transport, 2 destroyers and 2 minelayers). It was confidently expected that the US Navy would not let these operations proceed unhindered, so the Japanese included a powerful seventh element in the form of Vice Admiral Takeo Takagi's Carrier Strike Force (the fleet carriers *Zuikaku* and *Shokaku*, the heavy cruisers *Myoko* and *Haguro*, and 6 destroyers), which was to sail from Truk on 1 May with the intention of sailing round the end of the Solomons and then into the Coral Sea, so getting to the east of any US naval forces (believed by Inouye to be no more than one carrier plus supporting ships) that might intervene in Operation 'MO' and thus forcing them into battle.

However, the Japanese naval code had been broken by the Americans, and Admiral Chester W. Nimitz's Pacific Fleet was fully aware of the Japanese plans and could thus prepare a fateful counter, though well aware of the numerical inferiority of the force he could muster under Rear Admiral Frank J. Fletcher. This was Task Force 17 comprising Task Group 17.5 (the fleet carriers *Yorktown* and *Lexington* escorted by 4 destroyers), Task Group 17.2 (the heavy cruisers *Minneapolis*, *New Orleans*, *Astoria*, *Chester* and *Portland* escorted by 5 destroyers) and Task Group 17.3 (the heavy cruisers *Australia*, *Hobart* and *Chicago* escorted by 2 destroyers, and despatched from Australia under the British Rear Admiral J. C. Crace).

The Japanese plan got under way on 30 April, when the Tulagi force sailed from Rabaul under escort of the Close Support Force. Tulagi was occupied without opposition on 31 May and Goto turned back to the west to link up with the cruisers of the Support Force Main Body for the escort of the Port Moresby invasion fleet, which sailed from Rabaul on 4 May. Fletcher was informed of the Tulagi landings at 19.00 on 3 May and headed north with the *Yorktown* (without Rear Admiral Aubrey W. Fitch's *Lexington* and TG17.3, which had not yet arrived at the rendezvous set for 4 May) to bomb the Japanese forces off Tulagi on 4 May before returning to the south and a rendezvous rearranged for 5 May. Throughout 5 and 6 May the US and Japanese forces searched for each other, and at 07.30 on 7 May Crace was detached with his three heavy cruisers to attack the Port Moresby invasion forces. Crace's force survived heavy attacks from land-based aircraft, and the Japanese began to accept that this was the main Allied force in the area. Takagi had now arrived in the Coral Sea, but his aircraft attacked the oiler *Neosho* and a destroyer in the belief that they were a carrier and escort, so allowing Fletcher's carriers to operate with little hindrance. At 11.00 the two US carriers found the Close Support Force to the north of the Louisiade island group off the eastern tip of New Guinea, and attacked the *Shoho* in three waves, the Japanese light carrier sinking at 11.35. It was now clear that there was a very real threat to the transports of the Transport Force, and shortly before the loss of the *Shoho* the Transport Force was ordered back to Rabaul. However, Takagi now realized that there were two US carriers in the region, and he launched a night search by 27 aircraft (of which a mere 6 returned) on 7/8 May.

The decisive day was 8 May, when the US and Japanese carrier forces spotted each other virtually simultaneously and launched strikes. At 10.57 the *Shokaku* was severely damaged, and at 11.18 the *Yorktown* and *Lexington* were badly mauled. The former survived to limp back to Pearl Harbor, but the latter was abandoned, scuttled and then sunk by torpedoes. The Japanese believed that both American carriers had been sunk, but with the *Shokaku* retiring damaged, Inouye ordered the *Zuikaku* back to Truk, and because he was unwilling to risk the invasion without carrier support in the face of increasingly determined attacks from US land-based bombers, postponed Operation 'MO' to 3 July. There followed confusion as Yamamoto countermanded Inouye's orders to Takagi and Goto, but it was too late to find and destroy the surviving Allied forces and on 11 May Yamamoto finally ordered Takagi home.

US losses had been greater than those of the Japanese, but the outcome of the Battle of the Coral Sea must be regarded as an American operational victory as, for the first time in World War II, the Japanese had been checked and compelled to call off an offensive operation, if only temporarily, for the Japanese were determined to press on with the main object of Operation 'MO', the seizure of Port Moresby, and if the navy could not provide the right conditions for an amphibious assault, then an overland effort would be made. The forces for this became available during May after the surrender of Bataan (9 April) and Corregidor (6 May) in the Philippines. Thus the Yazawa and Aoba Detachments from Davao, and the Kawaguchi Detachment from Palau, were added to the South Seas Detachment to form Lieutenant General Harukichi Hyakutake's Japanese 17th Army on 18 May. The plan was now to land at Gona and Buna on the northern side of Papua, and advance over the Owen Stanley Range via Kokoda to take Port Moresby from the northern, landward side. The forces allocated to this effort under Horii were the South Seas Detachment, part of the Yazawa Detachment (Colonel Kiyomi Yazawa's 41st Regiment), part of the Sasebo 5th Special Naval Landing Force, and Colonel Yosuke Yokoyama's 15th Independent Engineer Regiment.

The plan began with the landing on 21 July of 1,800 men of Yokoyama's engineers plus some infantry between Buna and Gona to make a start on turning the trail over the mountains into a road capable of taking at worst mules and at best trucks. Australian opposition was minimal as the Allies thought that the landing presaged yet another advanced airfield, so Yokoyama's men were able to move inland and start work before the arrival of Horii's main force on 21 August. Horii was thus able to ride into Kokoda near the mid-point of the Kokoda Trail on 24 August, his forces now comprising some 8,000 army troops, 3,000 naval construction troops and 450 marines of the Sasebo 5th Special Naval Landing Force. Weather and terrain conditions were appallingly difficult, and the Australians, having at last realized what the Japanese were doing, finally began to work up a substantial defence. The Japanese were still able to push forward as the US and Australian defence under Major General E. F. Herring was still forming and the defence of the trail rested with the militiamen of the Australian 39th Battalion.

The first real check to Horii's advance came between 25 and 28 August at Isurava on the approach to the Templeton's Crossing pass down off the southern side of the Owen Stanley range. Here the Japanese came up against the regulars of the 21st Brigade returned from the Middle East. A determined attack on 29 August forced the Australians back, however, and the Japanese advance moved ahead again, only to be checked at Ioribaiwa (only 30 miles from Port Moresby) on 26 September by the 25th Brigade of the 7th Australian Division. Horii was now ordered to halt offensive operations until he could be supported by an overland advance from Milne Bay in the south-east of the island. Here some 1,500 marines had been landed on 25 August under Commander Shojiro Hayashi (Kure 5th Special Naval Landing Force) under the overall command of Vice Admiral Gunichi Mikawa's 8th Fleet, which was primarily responsible for operations in the Solomons. Hayashi's force pushed westward from Milne Bay, and was reinforced on 29 August by 770 more men of the Kure 3rd and Yokoshuka 5th Special Naval Landing Forces, whereupon Commander Minoro Yana assumed command. On 31 August the Japanese tried to resume the offensive, but were bloodily repulsed by the Australian 25th and 61st Battalions, which then launched a counterattack that drove the Japanese back towards Milne Bay.

The 1,300 Japanese survivors were evacuated on 6 September, realism at last coming to the temporary salvation of the Japanese, who had not appreciated the fact that between 25 June and 20 August the Allies had landed near Milne Bay some 4,500 Australian infantry supported by 3,000 Australian and 1,300 US engineers and artillerymen. Japanese attention was now switched away from the Kokoda Trail operations by the first major reverse to the Japanese forces on Guadalcanal on 15 September, and on 24 September Horii was ordered to fall back along the Kokoda Trail and to establish an impregnable beach-head at Buna. The retreat began on 25 September, the Allies moving in pursuit two days later with the 16th and 25th Brigades of the 7th Australian Division, and the 126th and 128th Infantry Regiments of the US 32nd Infantry Division. The tribulations of the advance were as nothing compared with the disasters of the retreat, and though the Japanese established their beach-head during 12 and 13 November, the garrison was small and pitifully weak from disease and malnutrition. Horii had been drowned, and Operation 'MO' was finally over as the eyes of Imperial General Headquarters in Tokyo were now fixed on Guadalcanal. The Allies too were exhausted and disease-ridden, but the Australians took Gona on 9 December and the Americans overran Buna on 2 January 1943.

Modicum US mission to London (8 April 1942) to present the Marshall memorandum on the eventual Allied invasion of Europe to Prime Minister Winston Churchill, Deputy Prime Minister Clement Attlee, Foreign Secretary Anthony Eden and General Sir Alan Brooke, Chief of the Imperial General Staff. Prepared by General George C. Marshall, the US Army chief-of-staff, the memorandum has three main topics. First, it advised the immediate implementation of Operation 'Bolero' to move 30 US divisions (including 6 armoured) plus appropriate air power to the UK within 12 months. Second, it urged the launch on 1 April 1943 of Operation 'Round-up' to land 30 US and 18 British divisions (including 3 armoured) in France between Boulogne and Le Havre; the first wave was to be 6 divisions and paratroops, and reinforcement at the rate of 100,000 men per week should secure the primary objective of a major lodgement in France from Calais to Deauville via Arras, St Quentin, Soissons and Paris. Third, it called for the start of Operation 'Sledgehammer' on 15 September 1943 to take Cherbourg and the Cotentin peninsula. The British reaction was mixed, and the only portion of the Marshall memorandum to receive full approval was Operation 'Bolero'.

Modified Dracula Extemporized version of Operation 'Dracula', undertaken in May 1945 to take Rangoon once it was realized that Japanese forces in the region were pulling out to the east to hold the area behind the River Sittang.

Monica British tail-warning receiver designed to pick up the radar emissions of German night-fighters closing from the rear.

Monstrous 'Swamp' operation undertaken to destroy the German U-boat *U-616* (13/16 May 1944).

Montclair Definitive version of Operation 'Princeton', the outline plan for the recapture of the Visayas and Mindanao in the Philippines, and of Borneo and the Dutch East Indies. In preparation for operations against Japan, the USA on 5 April 1945 reorganized its command structure in the Pacific, the previous South-West Pacific Area (except the Philippines and Hainan Island) being removed from the command of General Douglas MacArthur as a distraction and reallocated to Admiral Lord Louis Mountbatten's South-East Asia Command (Borneo, Java and Sulawesi) and to Australia (portions of the previous South-West Pacific Area east of Sulawesi), though portions of the latter to the west of the Australian Mandated Territories were during August transferred to SEAC on the request of the Australian administration. Operation 'Montclair' was planned by the original South-West Pacific Area command under MacArthur, and was thus undertaken as a joint US and Australian effort, with the Visayas part falling to Lieutenant General Robert L. Eichelberger's US 8th Army and the Borneo part to Lieutenant General Sir Leslie Morshead's I Australian Corps, available as a formation for mobile operations after the establishment in September 1944 of Lieutenant General V. A. H. Sturdee's Australian 1st Army to replace the miscellany of Australian forces that had been engaged in the blockade of Japanese forces cut off in New Guinea while the 8th Army undertook a comparable task in the island groups to the north of New Guinea.

Although US plans called for the Japanese garrisons in Philippine islands other than Leyte and Luzon to be eliminated by Filipino guerrillas in association with a re-formed Filipino army, MacArthur pre-empted them and on 6 February ordered Eichelberger to mop up Japanese forces in the central and southern Philippines with his 8th Army supported by the amphibious capabilities of Vice Admiral Thomas C. Kinkaid's US 7th

Fleet, and at the same time decided that I Australian Corps should take Borneo to provide the US forces for the invasion of Japan with adequate supplies of oil. Once Borneo had been seized I Australian Corps was, in MacArthur's plan, to go on to the invasion of Java. The US Chief-of-Staff Committee accepted MacArthur's fait accompli on 3 April, just before MacArthur and Admiral Chester W. Nimitz were appointed to command all the land and naval forces respectively in the Pacific Theater.

The operations planned by Eichelberger were in fact a series of overlapping joint undertakings. In the first of these his forces were to take Palawan, the western tip of Mindanao, plus Basilan and Jolo in the Sulu group to secure the entrances to the Sulu Sea and to establish airfields from which operations in Borneo could be provided with tactical air support. In the second the 8th Army was to take the Visayas group (Panay, Cebu, Negros and Bohol). And in the third the US forces were to clear Mindanao. The Japanese forces faced by Eichelberger's command were some 102,000 men of Lieutenant General Sosaku Suzuki's 35th Army, with some 43,000 of these on Mindanao and the other 59,000 scattered over scores of islands large and small. The headquarters of the 35th Army were located on Cebu in the Visayas group, and Eichelberger was under no misapprehension about the difficulty of the task entrusted to his army, which by the middle of April 1945 had launched 38 large and many smaller amphibious landings.

As a preliminary to these far-flung operations, Eichelberger first cleared the maritime route through the Visayan Passages to remove the considerable detour US shipping had been forced to make to avoid these Japanese-held approaches to Manila. At this time the 8th Army held Leyte and a relatively small beach-head on Samar Island over the San Juanico Strait from Leyte, and Eichelberger thus launched his forces in a series of small operations to take the northern shore of Samar and so open the San Bernardino Strait between Samar and Luzon (the Americal Division, landed from Leyte on 19 February), followed by operations to take smaller islands such as Burias (the Americal Division, landed from Leyte on 8 March), Siniara, Romblon and Tablas (part of the 24th Infantry Division, landed from San Jose on Mindoro on 11/12 March), and Masbate (part of the 40th Infantry Division, landed from Leyte on 3 April).

Eichelberger reported the clearing of the Visayan Passages to MacArthur on 5 April, and could now devote his sole attention to the central and southern Philippines, whose liberation had already begun with the landing of the 186th Regiment Combat Team of the 41st Infantry Division, supported by the 6th Amphibious Group, at Puerto Princesa on central Palawan on 28 February. Palawan and its offshore islands were garrisoned by some 2,900 Japanese. By 2 March the surviving Japanese had taken to the mountains, and by 22 April the Palawan group was secure for minimal US casualties, other landings having taken the islands of Dumaran (9 March), Busuanga (9 April), Balabac (16 April) and Pandaman (22 April). The all-weather airfield was in American service by 20 March, allowing tactical strikes against Japanese targets in Borneo and the southern Philippines to start almost immediately, strategic strikes against targets in China following from April.

Next on Eichelberger's list was the western tip of Mindanao, where the rest of the 41st Infantry Division landed around Zamboanga on 10 March, and in two weeks of heavy fighting took the town and its airfield, forcing the local garrison, the 54th Independent Mixed Brigade, to seek refuge in the mountains of the peninsula, where it was harried by Filipino guerrillas for the rest of the war. The 41st Infantry Division now turned southwest to the Sulu archipelago stretching out to Borneo. Basilan was taken against limited opposition on 10 March, and then the 163rd Regimental Combat team was sent to the far south where it took the Tawitawi group on 2 April before falling on Jolo in the centre of the archipelago on 9 April. Again a successful landing was made, but the 4,000 Japanese of the garrison fought stoutly for three weeks until pulling back to the middle of the island, where they held out until the end of June.

The Visayas group was the 8th Army's next objective, and here two formations (the 40th Infantry and Americal Divisions) were used, the former on Panay and Negros Occidental (the portion of Negros to the west of the central mountain chain), and the latter on Negros Oriental, Cebu and Bohol. Part of the 40th Infantry Division, supported by the 9th Amphibious Group, landed to the west of Iloilo on Panay on 18 March, and with Filipino guerrilla aid closed on the 2,750-man garrison holding a position in front of Iloilo. The Japanese fired the town and fell back into the mountains, surviving until the end of the war in limited numbers. The division was then shipped over to Negros Occidental, landing to the south of Bacolod on 29 March. The island was garrisoned by 13,000 Japanese under Lieutenant General Takeshi Kono, and the first of these were encountered as the 40th Infantry Division probed north to Bacolod on 5 April. By 4 June the back of the Japanese defence had been broken and its survivors followed the standard practice of retiring into the mountains where they were hunted by Filipino guerrillas to the end of the war, when a remnant of 6,000 surrendered.

The most severe battle of the campaign was that for Cebu, where Suzuki had some 13,500 Japanese troops to oppose the Americal Division when the Americans landed near Cebu City on 26 March. Fighting its way through well-sited minefields, the division took Cebu City on the following day and pursued the Japanese northwards to prepared positions. Suzuki's forces were winkled out of these on 18 April and then took to the mountains, where parties survived until the end of the war. On 10 April Suzuki and his staff tried to escape to Mindanao in small boats, but were spotted and attacked by aircraft on 19 April. Suzuki was killed, and his successor as commander of the 35th Army was Lieutenant General Gyosaku Moruzumi, the Japanese commander on Mindanao. The last of the Visayas to receive the 8th Army's attention was Bohol, where the reserve regiment of the Americal Division landed on 11 April and overcame limited resistance by 20 April. The regiment was then landed on Negros Oriental during 26 April to supplement the efforts of the 40th Infantry Division in reducing the island by 12 June.

For the loss of 835 dead and 2,300 wounded, the Americans had taken the Visayas against substantial numbers of Japanese, who lost at least 10,000 dead and 500 prisoners to the Americans, and then large numbers to the Filipino guerrillas in the mountains before some 17,500 survivors surrendered at the end of the war. The only Japanese-held island of importance in the Philippines was now Mindanao, held by the 35th Army with the 43,000 men of its 100th Division and 32nd Naval Base Force at Davao towards the south of the island, the 74th Regiment at Malaybay in the centre of the island, and half of the 30th Division at Cagayan on the north coast. However, the Japanese were generally confined to the towns and main roads by Colonel Wendell W. Fertig's 25,000 Filipino guerrillas, who controlled some 90 per cent of the island. The Japanese defence plans were still posited on an American attack from the south, so the 8th Amphibious Group put Major General F. C. Sibert's US X Corps (the 24th Infantry Division from Mindoro and the 31st Infantry Division from Morotai) ashore on 17 April at Parang and Malabang in Illana Bay, on the west of the island. The 24th Infantry Division pushed up the River Mindanao and reached Digos on Davao Gulf during 27 April, then turned north to take Davao on 3 May as the Japanese pulled back along the road to Malaybay. The 24th Infantry Division drove the Japanese back up the Malaybay road only on 10 June. Meanwhile the 31st Infantry Division was pushing along the north-western side of the island towards Cagayan, but was checked short of its objective on 5 May. The way was then opened by a landing in the Japanese rear (in Macajalar Bay to the east of Cagayan) by the 108th Regimental Combat Team during 10 May. The Japanese were now pushed back into the heart of the island. Four more US landings were made between 1 June and 12 July in the south of the island, and the Japanese were firmly contained to sit out the war in two pockets, one of 20,500 men in the centre of the island and another of 2,000 men in the south. The campaign for the Philippines had ended, therefore, where MacArthur first planned to start it, on Mindanao.

During this period I Australian Corps was also reconquering the most important portions of the island of Borneo held by the Japanese 37th Army, with headquarters at

Jesselton, 10 battalions in Brunei and northern Borneo, 1½ battalions in Kuching, 1½ battalions in Bandjermasin, 1 battalion and naval troops at Balikpapan, 1 battalion and naval troops in Tarakan, and 1 battalion at Miri. I Australian Corps began to group on Morotai on 22 February 1945 with Major General E. J. Milford's 7th Australian Division and Major General G. F. Wootten's 9th Australian Division as its principal formations. The first operation was the seizure of Tarakan Island from 1 May by the 26th Australian Brigade Group of the 9th Australian Division, supported by the US 6th Amphibious Group. The Japanese resistance was great, and the island was not declared secure until 24 June, by which time the Australians had lost 225 dead and 669 wounded. Japanese losses were 1,540 dead and 252 prisoners, and 300 men held out until the end of the war. Next came Brunei Bay, the target for the 9th Australian Division (less its 26th Australian Brigade Group) against the Japanese 56th Independent Mixed Brigade. The operation lasted from 10 June to 1 July, by which date the 20th and 24th Australian Brigades had lost 114 dead and 221 wounded, compared with 1,234 Japanese dead and 130 prisoners. The capture of Balikpapan was allotted to the 7th Australian Division supported by the US 8th Amphibious Group. A full strength of 33,500 (including corps troops and attached air units) was brought to bear on excellent fixed defences and a garrison of 4,000 Japanese. The landing began on 1 July after an intense air and naval bombardment, and by the end of the month the surviving Japanese had fled into the interior of Borneo, leaving 1,783 dead and 63 prisoners to the Australians, who had secured their objectives at the cost of 229 dead and 634 wounded. I Australian Corps had taken all three of its objectives in Borneo during these Operations 'Oboe', adding a useful local fuel supply to the Allied effort in the Pacific.

Moonshine (i) British naval operation to pick up vital war supplies from Sweden in converted motor gunboats (13 January/6 February 1945).

(ii) British radar device designed to fool German radar as to the number of aircraft approaching the enemy coast by producing a false picture on the radar screen (1942/1943).

Moorbrand (swamp fire) Operation by Generaloberst Georg Lindemann's German 18th Army of Generalfeldmarschall Georg von Küchler's Army Group 'North' to halt Soviet relief attempts for Leningrad (July/September 1942), principally the offensive of General K. A. Meretskov's Volkhov Front codenamed Operation 'Sinyavino'.

Morgenluft (morning air) Operation by the German forces in southern Tunisia in concert with Operation 'Frühlingswind' (15/22 February 1943) and designed to check the link-up of Lieutenant General K. A. N. Anderson's Allied 1st Army and General Sir Bernard Montgomery's British 8th Army, followed by a drive to the coast at Gafsa, which would divide Generaloberst Jürgen von Arnim's 5th Panzerarmee in the north from Generalfeldmarschall Erwin Rommel's German-Italian Panzerarmee in the south. Rommel proposed a combined offensive by the German-Italian and 5th Panzerarmees under Rommel's sole command, with the 10th and 21st Panzer Divisions of the 5th Panzerarmee undertaking Operation 'Frühlingswind' and a detachment of Generalmajor Kurt Freiherr von Liebenstein's Deutsches Afrika Korps undertaking Operation 'Morgenluft'. General Vittorio Ambrosio, chief-of-staff of the Italian *Comando Supremo*, was unable to impose a single commander on the joint offensives, which was ultimately to lead to operational failure though not tactical defeat.

While von Arnim planned a strike through Faid to Sidi Bou Zid as a means of securing his hold on the Dorsale Orientale, Rommel schemed an offensive from the south through Gafsa and Feriana towards Kasserine, with the object of destroying Lieutenant General Lloyd R. Fredendall's US II Corps (consisting of little more than the US 1st Armored Division of Major General Orlando Ward, reinforced by the 168th Regimental Combat Command of Major General Charles W. Ryder's US 34th Infantry Division) and opening the way between the remnants of the US II Corps and Général de Corps d'Armée L. M. Koeltz's French XIX Corps for an advance through the Dorsale Occidentale on Tebessa in conjunction with a Panzer division from the 5th Panzerarmee.

Commanded by Generalleutnant Hans Ziegler, von Arnim's chief-of-staff, the 10th and 21st Panzer Divisions launched Operation 'Frühlingswind' at 04.00 on 14 February, and immediately made gains and so attracted Allied reinforcements to the northern sector. Rommel attacked on 15 February and soon took Gafsa before pressing on towards Fériana, which fell on 17 February, the day on which von Liebenstein was wounded and handed over command of the Deutsches Afrika Korps detachment to Generalmajor Karl Buelowius.

Dissension now caused Rommel's overall plan to go astray, for while the Deutsches Afrika Korps advanced towards Kasserine and the break through the Dorsale Occidentale, von Arnim was pulling the 10th Panzer Division out of Sbeitla to hold German positions farther to the north, leaving just the 21st Panzer Division to push forward as part of the exploitation towards Le Kef (authorized on 19 February) from Sbeitla via Sbiba, only later being supplemented by the 10th Panzer Division (recalled on 19 February) advancing from Kasserine (which fell on 18 February) via Thala with the support of a diversionary attack towards Tebéssa by the Deutsches Afrika Korps.

Combat Command B of the US 1st Armored Division (supported by Major General Terry de la M. Allen's US 1st Infantry Division) checked the Deutsches Afrika Korps detachment short of Tebéssa on 19 February, while General the Hon. Sir Harold Alexander, the Deputy Allied Commander-in-Chief North African Theatre, sent in from Le Kef units of Major General C. F. Keightley's British 6th Armoured Division to bolster the defences of Major General Manton S. Eddy's US 9th Infantry Division near Thala (British 26th Armoured Brigade) and of the US 34th Infantry Division near Sbiba (1st Guards Brigade). The 10th and 21st Panzer Divisions were thus checked short of these two towns between 19 and 22 February, when Rommel called off the offensive. Though the German operational objectives had not been achieved, the Allies had had their noses severely bloodied and their plans thrown into temporary disarray. German losses were some 2,000 compared with Allied casualties of about 10,000, including 6,500 in the US II Corps.

Morgenrote (dawn) German counteroffensive against the Allied beach-head at Anzio (1/19 February 1944). Thrown ashore in Operation 'Shingle', Major General John P. Lucas's US VI D Corps (initially the US 3rd Infantry Division and part of the British 1st Division, supported by British commandos and US airborne troops) occupied only a relatively small beach-head running from the Mussolini Canal in the south some 12 miles north to the line of the River Moletta, and as far inland as a line just short of Cisterna and Campoleone Station. The opposition was found by the German 14th Army commanded by Generaloberst Eberhard von Mackensen, which was established swiftly in response to the Allied landings. Instead of pressing inland rapidly (as planned) to cut the German 10th Army's lines of communication, Lucas decided to consolidate his beach-head and await the arrival of the corps' armour and heavy artillery. Mackensen was thus able to pin down the Allied forces at Anzio while building up the forces needed for Operation 'Morgenrote', designed to drive VI Corps back into the sea.

The first of these local counterattacks was launched on 1 February by units of General Alfred Schlemm's I Parachute Corps, whose 71st Division, 26th Panzer Division and 'Herman Goering' Panzer Division failed to make any significant inroads in the region of Isola Bella and Carano. The next attack was launched on 3 February, Schlemm's intention being to pinch off the salient towards Campoleone (held by the 3rd Brigade of Major General W. R. C. Penney's British 1st Division) with attacks from the east by the 104th Panzergrenadierregiment of the 3rd Panzergrenadier Division and from the west by the 145th Grenadierregiment of the 65th Division. The Germans managed to take the salient, but failed to crush the 3rd Brigade, although losses to the British were high. The Germans were still attracted by the main road south to Anzio, especially in the area of Carroceto and the Aprilia Factory, now just behind the Allied front since the loss of the Campoleone salient.

Another major counterattack was launched on 7 February by formations of General Traugott Herr's LXXVI Panzer Corps to take these two objectives, which lay just to the British side of the junction between the US 45th Infantry Division and the British 1st Division. Units of the 3rd Panzergrenadier Division, 715th Division and 26th Panzer Division were formed into the Kampfgruppe Gräser commanded by Generalleutnant Fritz-Hubert Gräser of the 3rd Panzergrenadier Division, and on 8 February this group was supplemented by another extemporized grouping under Oberst Schönfeld. The two groups pushed deep into the British 1st Division's positions, and by 11 February had taken Carroceto and the Aprilia Factory, in the process reducing the British division to about half strength.

But all these operations had been little more than spoiling attacks to keep the allies off balance as the main counteroffensive of Operation 'Morgenrote' was prepared for implementation on 16 February as Operation 'Fischfang'. The German plan called for a break to be made (by infantry formations) in the Allied line between Fossa di Spaccasassi in the east and Buonriposo Bridge in the west so that German armoured and motorized formations could pour through the breach either to drive on Nettuno or to crush pockets of Allied resistance with flank attacks. The breakthrough was entrusted to Gräser's 3rd Panzergrenadier Division, Generalmajor Hans-Georg Hildebrandt's 715th Division and Generalmajor Bourquin's 114th Jäger Division, and the exploitation was the task of Generalmajor Fries's 29th Panzergrenadier Division, Generalmajor Hecker's 26th Panzer Division and one battalion of the 4th Panzerregiment. A diversionary attack on Isola Bella was assigned to the 'Hermann Goering' Panzer Division, and I Parachute Corps was tasked with providing a right flank guard for LXXVI Corps.

The Allied defence of this sector was in the hands of the US 45th Infantry Division, with Major General G. W. R. Templer's British 56th Division to its left and the US 3rd Infantry Division to its right. Right from the beginning of the German counteroffensive the fighting was extremely heavy, and by the night of 18/19 February the Germans had driven through the US 45th Infantry Division, only to be checked by the British 2nd Brigade on the corps defence line by Flyover Bridge. It was the end of German attempts to eliminate the Anzio beach-head, and with the arrival from the south-east of the US 1st Armored Division the Allied position was stabilized. Within the beachhead Lucas handed over command to Major General Lucian K. Truscott of the US 3rd Infantry Division on 22 February.

Morgenwind (morning breeze) German occupation of Brac Island in the Adriatic after the Italian armistice (September 1943).

Moses Airborne operation by the French 2ème Regiment Colonial des Parachutistes to aid the maquis near Montmirillon in France (2 August 1944).

Mühle (mill) Headquarters of the Oberkommando der Wehrmacht (1940).

Mulberry Allied artificial harbours sited off the Normandy beaches for the supply of forces in Operation 'Overlord' (June 1944). There were two of these prefabricated harbours, which were built in the UK and towed across the English Channel once the initial lodgement had been achieved, one for the supply of Lieutenant General Sir Miles Dempsey's British 2nd Army and located at Arromanches on 'Gold' Beach, and the other for the supply of Lieutenant General Omar N. Bradley's US 1st Army and located at Colleville on 'Omaha' Beach. The English Channel was swept by severe gales in the period 19/22 June, and the 'Mulberry' at Colleville was destroyed while that at Arromanches was damaged.

München (Munich) German operation against Soviet partisans operating in the region of Radoshkovichi (December 1942).

Musical Newhaven Version of 'Newhaven' using 'Oboe'.

Musical Paramatta British target

marking device with indicators dropped with the aid of 'Oboe'.

Musical Wanganui Air marking equivalent of 'Musical Paramatta'.

Musket Contingency plan for a landing at Taranto in southern Italy by Lieutenant General Mark W. Clark's US 5th Army, using its US VI Corps under Major General Ernest J. Dawley to land the US 1st Armored, 34th and 36th Infantry, and 82nd Airborne Divisions, to be followed ashore by one US or French division yet to be nominated. The plan was prepared at the instigation of General George C. Marshall, the US Army chief-of-staff, who instructed General Dwight D. Eisenhower, the Allied Commander-in-Chief of Allied Forces in North Africa, to use staffs spare at the time of the Sicilian operations to scheme a number of contingency operations. The US 5th Army first prepared Operation 'Brimstone' in association with the French Operation 'Firebrand', but after the initial Allied successes in Sicily it was decided that the US 5th Army might be able to proceed straight to an Italian landing, so after 'Brimstone' had been handed on to the French the US 5th Army set to work on 'Musket' designed to put US forces ashore in the 'heel' of Italy between Taranto and Bari. However, after the fall of the Italian dictator, Benito Mussolini, on 25 July, it was decided that more ambitious operations against Italy could be undertaken, and on 27 July the US 5th Army was instructed to abandon 'Musket' in favour of Operation 'Avalanche' in the Bay of Salerno just to the south of Naples.

Musketeer Cover designation under which the US plans for the reconquest of the Philippine Islands were studied and initially prepared (1943/1944).

Musketry Allied air patrols over the Bay of Biscay (July 1943 onwards) designed to find and destroy German U-boats running on the surface while on transit to or from the hunting areas in the atlantic.

Mustang Allied contingency plan for a rapid overland advance to Naples in the event of an Italian collapse after the Sicilian campaign (summer 1943). The plan envisaged the landing of light forces in the 'toe' of Italy for a fast advance through Calabria and the capture of Naples, through whose port 6 divisions and 43 squadrons of aircraft could be landed for a swift progress to Rome.

Mutton British weapon for use against German bombers (autumn 1940). This Long Aerial Mine consisted of a bomb hanging from a parachute at the end of a long wire, the idea being that swarms of LAMs could be dropped above German bomber fleets to fall and catch in their propellers before being wound up and detonated.

M.W. Designation of Mediterranean westbound convoys (together with a numerical suffix) plying the route from Alexandria to Malta, and inaugurated in July 1940. The M.W. convoys were interrupted at the time of Malta's siege by the Axis powers, and were resumed only in November 1942.

N

N.A. Designation of North Atlantic eastbound military convoys (together with a numerical suffix) plying the route from North America to the UK, and inaugurated in January 1942.

Nabob Allied codename for Northern Ireland.

Nachbarhilfe (neighbourly help) Designation of two German operations against Soviet partisans operating in the region of Kletnya (May/June 1943). This area lay astride the main rail line from Mogilev to Bryansk and Orel, and over this line the Germans were trying to bring up new equipment and reinforcements for the formations of Generaloberst Walter Model's German 9th Army of Generalfeldmarschall Günther von Kluge's Army Group 'Centre' before the launch of Operation 'Zitadelle'. The Soviets were well aware of the Germans' plans for this operation, their last attempt to regain the strategic initiative on the Eastern Front, and at the express command of the *Stavka* (high command) in Moscow, the partisans were very active in harassing German operations aimed at bolstering the 9th Army left wing of the German pincer forces for 'Zitadelle'.

Nachteule (night owl) Ground-attack operations by German night-fighters (November 1944 onwards).

Napfkuchen (large cake) German operation against Yugoslav partisans (December 1943/January 1944).

Nation British plan for the Japanese-inspired Burma National Army of Aung San to defect to the British. The Burma National Army was the military wing of the Burmese nationalist group, the Anti-Fascist Organization, and although the British Force 136 had tried since late 1943 to get into contact with the Anti-Fascist Organization, it was only in late 1944 that this objective was attained, whereupon the Burmese informed the South-East Asia Command of Lord Louis Mountbatten that they planned an armed uprising against the Japanese during 1945. The British were extremely wary of the Burma National Army's longer-term political objectives for an independent left-wing Burma, and thus decided that no weapons would be provided to this organization as such, though smaller groups within the Burma National Army were given weapons. The British also sought to persuade the Burma National Army against an early rising against the Japanese, which could be construed as the Burmese liberating themselves from the occupation forces, but the planned rising went ahead in Rangoon on 27 March 1945. Aung San was cautious about the meeting proposed by General Sir William Slim of the British 14th Army, and delayed for as long as he could before going to Meiktila on 16 May. By this time the Japanese 15th and 33rd Armies had disintegrated, and only the 28th Army was left as an effective fighting formation in south-west Burma, so Slim could see little operational virtue in the Burma National Army, which was however a distinct political menace to the British as it considered itself the provisional government of a liberated country yet refused to undertake such responsibilities as policing.

155

There followed a protracted period of intermittent negotiation before Aung San decided in June that the Burma National Army (now renamed the Patriotic Burmese Forces) could be incorporated into the new British-led Burma Army. The process of enrolling elements of the Patriotic Burmese Forces in the Burma Army began during August 1945, but soon ran foul of Burmese political ambitions, so that the Patriotic Burmese Forces went underground with their weapons, laying up trouble for the future.

Naxos German radar receiver allowing night-fighters to home on the emissions of H2S and H2X navigation radars.

N.E. Designation of Pacific ocean convoys (together with a numerical suffix) plying the route from New Zealand to Panama.

Neptun (Neptune) (i) German offensive by V Corps with the support of I Fliegerkorps (17 April 1943) to wipe out the Soviet beachhead between Novorossiysk and Myskhako. This lodgement, by General I. E. Petrov's Black Sea Group of General I. V. Tyulenev's Trans-Cacuasus Front, posed a threat to the right flank of the German 17th Army of Generalfeldmarschall Ewald von Kleist's Army Group 'A' recently driven back from the Caucasus into the Kuban beach-head on the Taman peninsula.
(ii) Support elements for the 'Nachbarhilfe' operations provided by the forces of Generalfeldmarschall Ewald von Kleist's Army Group 'A'.

Neptune (i) Cover designation for actual 1944 operations within Operation 'Overlord'. This cover was adopted for security reasons during September 1943 on all 'Overlord' planning papers in which the target date and location were indicated.
(ii) Naval operations within Operation 'Overlord'. These plans were extraordinarily complex, reflecting the ambitious assault plan, and were formulated by a special staff under Admiral Sir Bertram Ramsay, the Naval Commander Expeditionary Force. The Allied plan was to land five divisions in the first wave, one division being landed on each of the five beaches, which were allocated in the ratio of three to the British 2nd Army of Lieutenant General Sir Miles Dempsey (on a 30-mile front between the mouth of the River Orne and Port-en-Bessin) and two to the US 1st Army of Lieutenant General Omar N. Bradley (on a 20-mile front between Port-en-Bessin and Les Dunes de Varreville). To carry and escort the assault forces, the Allied naval command provided for two task forces, the Eastern Naval Task Force under Rear Admiral Sir Philip Vian for British forces and the Western Naval Task Force under Rear Admiral A. G. Kirk for US forces. For their tasks the two commanders had very substantial naval assets. The Eastern Naval Task Force had 4 landing ships headquarters, 37 landing ships infantry, 3 landing ships dock, 408 landing craft assault, 11 landing craft headquarters, 155 landing craft infantry (25 of them American), 130 landing ships tank (37 of them American), 487 landing craft tank, 19 landing craft flak, 16 landing craft gun, 83 landing craft support, 22 landing craft tank (rocket), 100 landing craft personnel (smoke and survey) and 952 ferry craft including 396 landing craft vehicle personnel and 240 landing craft mechanized, for a total of 2,426 landing ships and craft. These were supported by 3 battleships, 1 monitor, 13 cruisers (including 1 Polish), 2 gunboats (including 1 Dutch), 30 destroyers (including 2 Norwegian), 14 escort destroyers (including 2 Polish, 1 Norwegian and 1 French), 4 sloops, 42 fleet minesweepers, 87 other minesweepers and danlayers, 19 frigates (including 2 French), 17 corvettes (including 2 Greek), 21 anti-submarine trawlers, 2 minelayers, 90 coastal craft (including 30 American), 1 seaplane carrier and 2 midget submarines. The strength for the Western Naval Task Force was 2 landing ships headquarters, 18 landing ships infantry (including 8 British, 3 landing ships dock (all British), 94 landing craft assault (including 40 British), 189 landing craft vehicle personnel, 15 landing craft headquarters, 93 landing craft infantry, 106 landing ships tank, 350 landing craft tank (including about 120 British), 11 landing craft flak, 9 landing craft gun, 38 landing craft support (including 2 British), 14 landing craft tank (rocket), 54 landing craft personnel (smoke and survey) (including 6 British) and 704 ferry craft

156

including 260 landing craft vehicle personnel and 224 landing craft mechanized, for a total of 1,700 landing ships and craft. These were supported by 3 battleships, 1 monitor (British), 10 cruisers (including 5 British and 2 French), 1 gunboat (Dutch), 30 destroyers, 5 escort destroyers (all British), 59 fleet minesweepers (including 47 British), 62 other minesweepers and danlayers (including 46 British), 12 frigates (including 4 British and 2 French), 4 corvettes (including 2 French), 18 patrol craft, 9 anti-submarine trawlers (all British) and 113 coastal craft (including 32 British). In reserve Ramsay held 1 battleship and 40 minesweepers, while the British home commands contributed 20 destroyers (including 4 American and 2 Polish), 6 escort destroyers, 10 sloops, 32 frigates, 50 corvettes (including 3 Norwegian and 1 French), 30 anti-submarine trawlers, 2 minelayers, 292 coastal craft (including 13 Dutch, 8 French and 3 Norwegian), and 58 anti-submarine vessels. Total strengths were thus 4,126 landing ships and craft, and 1,213 warships. The naval forces included 5 bombardment forces, one for each of the assault beaches, and these were Rear Admiral W. R. Patterson's Force D (2 battleships, 1 monitor, 5 cruisers and 13 destroyers for 'Sword' Beach), Rear Admiral F. H. G. Dalrymple-Hamilton's Force E (2 cruisers and 11 destroyers for 'Juno' Beach), Captain E. W. L. Longley-Cook's Force K (5 cruisers and 13 destroyers for 'Gold' Beach), Rear Admiral C. F. Bryant's Force C (2 battleships, 3 cruisers and 12 destroyers for 'Omaha' Beach) and Rear Admiral M. L. Deyo's Force A (1 battleship, 1 monitor, 6 cruisers and 8 destroyers for 'Utah' Beach).

(iii) Crossing of the River Seine by the British 43rd (Wessex) Division of Major General G. I. Thomas (25/28 August 1944). This spearheaded the advance of the British XXX Corps of Lieutenant General Sir Miles Dempsey's British 2nd Army over the Seine, leading to a rapid advance via Amiens, Arras, Tournai and Brussels, the Belgian capital being reached on 3 September.

Nest Egg British plan to reoccupy the Channel Islands in the event of a German military collapse in the west. The plan was eventually implemented on 8 May 1945 after the surrender of Germany, when the destroyers *Bulldog* and *Beagle* ferried troops to Guernsey and Jersey, and thence to the smaller islands. Generalleutnant Graf von Schmettow on 9 May surrendered the 30,000 German troops (centred on the 319th Division) on the islands, which had been fortified at Hitler's instructions into one of the most powerful fortress areas in the world.

Newhaven British target-marking system used by Bomber Command, aircraft fitted with H2S navigation and bombing radar dropping flares and other indicators to indicate the precise location of the target for the main stream of bombers.

N.G. Designation of US southbound east coast convoys (with a numerical suffix) plying the route from New York to Guantanamo, and inaugurated in August 1942.

Nickel British air raids against Germany (1939/1940), in which no offensive armament was carried but rather loads of leaflets urging the German civil population to abandon the war. Such raids were made by Bomber Command at the express demand of the British government, which feared that the dropping of bombs on German soil would inevitably bring about retribution by German bomber forces, which were wrongly believed to be considerably more powerful than those of Bomber Command. The British aircrews had to endure all the operational disadvantages of offensive warfare, together with the dire winter conditions of the period, yet could achieve little of strategic importance, and learned little about the need for total accuracy of nocturnal air navigation.

Night Light British plan for the invasion of Norway.

Night Ranger Nocturnal version of the 'Ranger'.

Nitelight Designation of sorties by de Havilland Mosquito aircraft to harass German nocturnal troop and vehicle movements in Normandy with the aid of air-dropped flares (June 1944).

157

N.K. Designation of US southbound east coast convoys (together with a numerical suffix) plying the route from New York to Key West, and inaugurated in August 1942.

Noah Airborne raid by the Belgian Independent Parachute company, SAS, to establish a base in the Ardennes (15 August 1944).

Noah's Ark Operation undertaken by Greek guerrilla forces (associated with the democratic cause) to harass the retreat by German forces from Greece (September 1944). Commanded by Generaloberst Alexander Löhr's Army Group 'F', these forces amounted to 300,000 troops of the German army, forming 4 corps with 10 divisions (4 of them on the mainland, and the other 3 on Greek islands together with 6 fortress brigades), 33,000 German sailors (most of them manning coastal artillery batteries) and 12,000 airmen and Flak gunners. Of these four corps, General Helmuth Felmy's LXVIII Corps was in southern Greece, General Hubert Lanz's XXII Gebirgskorps in Epiros, General Paul Bader's XXI Gebirgskorps in Albania, and XIC Corps in Thessaly. Most of XXI Gebirgskorps moved out via Scutari and Cattaro to the north against opposition from the Albanian partisans, while the other three corps had to move through the bottleneck at Skopje in southern Yugoslavia, all the formations being heavily engaged by Greek guerrillas in northern Greece, and XXII Gebirgskorps suffering heavily as it fell back from Yannina. Planned under British supervision, Operation 'Noah's Ark' was schemed as the guerrilla counterpart to the British Operation 'Manna' in southern Greece.

Noball Operations by Allied fighter-bombers and medium bombers against the 'ski site' launching ramps for V-1 flying bombs built by the Germans in northern France and in the Low Countries for the bombardment of the UK (spring 1945). These operations destroyed very large numbers of 'ski sites', but the Germans were still able to launch a moderately intense campaign against southern England. The Allies had also feared for the safety of the land, sea and air forces being grouped in the south for Operation 'Overlord', intelligence reports having credited the V-1s with considerably greater accuracy than in fact they possessed.

Nord (north) Original designation for Operation 'Weserübung'.

Nordlicht (northern light) German plan for the reduction of Leningrad by the beginning of September 1942. The plan was originated by Hitler, who was obsessed by the need to capture the birthplace of the Russian Revolution, and was entrusted to Generalfeldmarschall Georg von Küchler's Army Group 'North' reinforced by four divisions and the super-heavy siege artillery from Generalfeldmarschall Erich von Manstein's 11th Army, which had just battered Sevastopol into submission at the southern end of the Eastern Front. The plan was originated under the designation Operation 'Feuerzauber', but this was changed to 'Nordlicht' on 31 July 1942. The plan was shelved in the aftermath of a Soviet attack near Leningrad, launched to the south of Lake Ladoga on 19 August 1942 by General A. I. Meretskov's Volkhov Front and General L. A. Govorov's Leningrad Front. At this time von Küchler was out of favour with Hitler, and the German leader on 4 September put von Manstein in command of the forces (the German 18th Army) charged with defeating the Soviet drive, a task achieved by the end of September.

Nordmark (Schleswig-Holstein) German naval operation against shipping in the North Sea (18/20 February 1940). Under the command of Vizeadmiral Wilhelm Marschall, the battle-cruisers *Scharnhorst* and *Gneisenau*, escorted by the heavy cruiser *Admiral Hipper* and two destroyers, managed to extricate themselves from the icebound North German estuaries in which they were based with the intention of attacking, in the area between Shetland and Norway, British convoys on the Norway run. Air reconnaissance had warned the British of the German ships' departure, and the only convoy in the area was recalled as a cordon of submarines was disposed to intercept the German ships' likely route and as the main units of Admiral

Sir Charles Forbes's Home fleet were moved into the area from the Clyde. The Germans were hampered by lack of air reconnaissance and lack of targets, and returned empty-handed.

Nordpol (north pole) **(i)** operation planned for Generaloberst Walter Model's German 9th Army of Generalfeldmarschall Fedor con Bock's Army Group 'Centre' (March/May 1942). This operation was schemed in the aftermath of the great Soviet winter offensive round Moscow, launched on 5 December 1941 and finally ended by the complete exhaustion of the Soviet forces at the beginning of April 1942. In the areas of Nelidovo and Belyy, the formations of Lieutenant General I. S. Konev's Kalinin Front had pushed through the German defences into a deep salient that threatened Vitebsk and Smolensk before its forward momentum was checked by General Hermann Hoth's 3rd Panzergruppe at Velizh and Demidov, leaving the Soviet 4th Shock Army in positions just to the north of the Moscow Highway and deep behind the left flank of the 9th Army. The situation stabilized in April, but despite Hitler's reluctant permission for the 9th Army and Generaloberst Georg-Hans Reinhardt's 3rd Panzerarmee to pull back to the Winter Line, the Germans were still in a difficult position with Soviet forces deep past them in each flank, and the portion occupied by the Soviet 39th Army and XXII Cavalry Corps between Belyy in the west and Sychevka in the east was finally extirpated by the 9th Army in a modified Operation 'Feuerzauber' from 2 July. The offensive netted the Germans some 50,000 Soviet prisoners and shortened their defence line before Moscow by about 130 miles. Further operations in this sector were impossible because of the need to support the various Operation 'Blau' offensives in the south.

(ii) German operation against Soviet partisans operating in the region of Smolensk (1 August 1942). In this area, between the leading edges of the two wings of the Soviet winter offensive of 1940/1941, lay the Moscow Highway and the primary rail lines used by the Germans to support their forces before Moscow, so the closure of the neck of the 'cauldron' containing Generaloberst Walter Model's German 9th Army and General Richard Ruoff's 4th Panzerarmee was vitally important to the total success of the Soviet offensive. Thus partisan forces were instructed to move into the area, where they would be supported by elements of the Soviet IV Airborne Corps (notably the 4,000 skilled men of the 8th and 201st Airborne Brigades) dropped in the Germans' rear, in areas to the south-east and south-west of Vyazma, between 18 and 24 January 1942. The combined airborne and partisan forces failed to secure their objectives, however, and were in their turn isolated by the end of the Soviet offensives in April. These surviving Soviet pockets were the objective of the anti-partisan operation, which eliminated one group to the south-east of Smolensk between the Smolensk-Sukhinichi and Smolensk-Bryansk railways, and a second group to the east of Smolensk between the Smolensk-Vyazma and Smolensk-Sukhinichi railways.

Nordsee (North Sea) German operation against Soviet partisans operating in the region of Mogilev (2/5 September 1942). These partisan forces threatened Germany's primary eastward lines of communication to Smolensk, including barge traffic on the River Dniepr.

Nordwind (north wind) German counteroffensive in Alsace (31 December/26 January 1945). Planned by Reichsführer-SS Heinrich Himmler and the SS staff of Army Group 'Oberrhein', the object of this ill-conceived offensive, undertaken by General Friedrich Wiese's German 19th Army at the behest of the SS-dominated and thus semi-independent Army Group 'Oberrhein', was to exploit the salient formed in the German line by the rapid advance (by 15 December 1944) of Lieutenant General George S. Patton's US 3rd Army to Karlsruhe on the River Rhine, just on the junction of General Hermann Balck's Army Group 'C' and Himmler's Army Group 'Oberrhein'. Patton's advance had left the German 19th Army in a re-entrant round Colmar on the 3rd Army's right flank. Here the Germans were faced by the two armies of Lieutenant General Jacob L. Devers's US 6th Army Group, namely

159

Nürnberg

Lieutenant General Alexander M. Patch's US 7th Army and Général d'Armée Jean de Lattre de Tassigny's French 1st Army. Himmler planned a rapid advance to the Saverne Gap by the four divisions of XXXIX Panzer Corps (the 21st and 25th Panzer Divisions, the 10th SS Panzer Division and the 1st Parachute Division) suported to the north by the 36th and 47th Volksgrenadier Divisions and to the south by the 553rd Volksgrenadier Division. This would split the overextended 7th Army into two groups, of which the southern (the US VI Corps comprising the 36th and 79th Infantry Divisions supported by the 12th Armored Division) would be destroyed as the German offensive swept on to retake Strasbourg against the defences of the French 1st Army (3rd Algerian and 1st French Divisions).

Preliminary operations began in the northern sector on 31 January 1944, and the main offensive began against the US VI Corps on 5 January 1945. The Americans pulled back in good order towards the River Moder to the south of the Forêt de Haguenau, and then Himmler launched his secondary attacks, in the centre (around Gambsheim) by the 553rd Volksgrenadier Division and in the south (around Erstein) by the 198th Division supported by the 'Feldhernhalle' Panzer Brigade. It was a promising start for the Germans, but the Allies were determined to hold Strasbourg at all costs, and thus reinforced the French 1st Army. Here the tactical mistakes of SS planning began to show themselves, and the German offensive continued as three generally unrelated local offensives that ended in defeat by 26 January.

Some 11 German divisions, four of them high-grade Waffen-SS formations, had been expended in this senseless operation, which brought disgrace to the hapless Wiese, who was replaced by General Rasp. Himmler was able to persuade Hitler that the plan had been soundly conceived, and was thus promoted to the command of Army Group 'Vistula', being replaced at the head of Army Group 'Oberrhein' by the convalescent SS Oberstgruppenführer Paul Hausser, who now had the unenviable task of holding the Colmar pocket with sadly depleted forces.

Nürnberg (Nuremberg) **(i)** German defence plan for the crossing of the Pyrenees Mountains during any implementation of Operation 'Gisela'.
(ii) German operation against Soviet partisans operating in the region to the east of Lake Bonin (December 1942).
(iii) German development of 'Würzburg' to mitigate the effects of 'Window'.

Nussbaum (nut tree) German meteorological station in the Arctic.

O

O.A. Designation of ocean outbound convoys (together with a numerical suffix) plying from the estuary of the River Thames down the English Channel and into the Atlantic, and inaugurated on 7 September 1939 to end on 24 October 1940. From 3 July 1940 ships of these convoys joined F.N. convoys and moved out through the North-West Approaches.

O.B. Designation of ocean outbound convoys (together with a numerical suffix) plying from Liverpool out into the Atlantic, and inaugurated on 7 September 1939 to end on 21 October 1941 when superseded by the O.N. seies. From 11 July 1940 the O.B. convoys used the North-West Approaches.

Oboe British radar device that permitted bombers to bomb without visual observation of the target.

Oboe I Australian recapture of Tarakan in Borneo (1 May/24 June 1945). This was the first of three operations undertaken by Lieutenant General Sir Leslie Morshead's I Australian Corps in Borneo, whose capture was deemed essential by the Allied high command for the economical prosecution of the war in the Pacific Theater commanded jointly by General Douglas MacArthur (ground forces) and Admiral Chester W. Nimitz (naval forces). Borneo was defended by the Japanese 37th Army with the equivalent of 16 battalions supported by 2 naval units, and contained some of the most important oilfields in the area, whose seizure would not only deprive the Japanese of their output, but also provide the Allies with a ready source of fuel for the offensives planned against the Japanese home islands.

The Australian operations in Borneo were planned in conjunction with the US operations in the southern Philippines, and became feasible with the gathering of I Australian Corps on Morotai from 22 February 1945. Though the US Chiefs-of-Staff Committee (and especially Admiral Ernest J. King) wished the operations of I Australian Corps to be supported by Admiral Sir Bruce Fraser's British Pacific Fleet, Nimitz vetoed the scheme as he needed the British aircraft-carriers for Operation 'Iceberg' (where their armoured flightdecks proved far better able to cope with Japanese *kamikaze* attacks than the unarmoured decks of the more numerous US carriers). Thus the 'Oboe' operations were afforded US Navy support.

Operation 'Oboe I' was designed to wrest Tarakan Island and its oilfield from a Japanese force of some 1,700 servicemen (455th Battalion and 2nd Naval Garrison Unit) and 400 civilians. The island, which lies off the east coast of Borneo, and is about 16 miles long and 11 miles wide, had been virtually isolated by Allied minefields to prevent Japanese tankers from loading at the port, and a four-day clearing operation was undertaken from 27 April 1945 before the 26th Australian Brigade Group of Major General G. F. Wootten's 9th Australian Division was landed on 1 May by the US 6th Amphibious Group under the covering fire of 3 cruisers and 6 destroyers of Vice Admiral Thomas C. Kinkaid's US 7th Fleet. The landing itself was unopposed, but the Japanese fought back with their normal

161

dogged determination in Tarakan town and the hills behind it. The hills had been taken by 4 May, and the town together with its airfield by the following day. Intensive ground-attack operations were flown by the 1st Tactical Air Force (Royal Australian Air Force) and the 13th Air Force (US Army Air Forces), but the island was not declared secure until 24 June, when organized resistance ceased. The Australians lost 225 killed and 669 wounded, while Japanese losses were 1,540 dead and 252 prisoners. The rest of the Japanese garrison took to the hills and held out until the end of the war, when some 300 survivors surrendered.

Oboe II Australian recapture of Balikpapan in Borneo (1/10 July 1945). This point, towards the southern end of Borneo's eastern side, was the terminal (and associated refinery) for the pipeline bringing oil from the two oilfields 25 miles and 50 miles to the north-east. Balikpapan also boasted two airstrips. The Japanese garrison amounted to some 4,000 men of the two-battalion 22nd Special Naval Base Force and the 454th Battalion, and the tactical difficulties posed to Major General E. J. Milford's 7th Australian Division were severe, for the Japanese were well dug-in on the hills overlooking the town, and the approaches from the sea had been liberally mined by the Allies and the Japanese. Minesweeping began on 15 June, and at a cost of 3 sunk and 5 damaged, these craft had completed their task by 1 July, the date scheduled for the Australian landing. Delays in getting the airstrip at Tarakan operational meant that tactical air support had to be furnished at extreme range from Tawitawi, though the activities of Japanese aircraft led Kinkaid to request escort carrier support for his naval forces. Nimitz allocated three such carriers, which arrived on 1 July. Surface forces had meanwhile been preparing for the landing with heavy bombardments of the Japanese positions from the guns of 4 cruisers and 9 destroyers. The 7th Australian Division was landed by the US 8th Amphibious Group on 1 July, and moved inland with commendable speed only to run into stout Japanese defences. Naval gunfire support enabled the division to maintain its progress, however, and the Australians had taken one airfield by 2 July, Balikpapan town by 3 July and the other airfield by 9 July, the Japanese pulling back into the hinterland in their standard fashion for guerrilla warfare. The nearer oilfield was in Australian hands by 18 July, and by the end of the month organized resistance had ended. Australian casualties were 229 dead and 634 wounded, while the Japanese lost 1,783 dead and 63 prisoners, the survivors of the other 2,150 surrendering at the end of the war.

Oboe III Australian recapture of Brunei Bay in Borneo (10 June/1 July 1945). This was the most important oil-producing region of Borneo, as indicated by the strength of the Japanese garrison, the 56th Independent Mixed Brigade with the 371st Battalion on Labuan Island, the 366th and 367th Battalions in Brunei, and the 368th Battalion at Beaufort. The area was again hemmed with substantial minefields, and a US minesweeper group began work on 7 June, losing one vessel in this operation. US tactical aircraft undertook an intense suppression campaign against the Japanese on Labuan Island at Brooketon between 5 and 9 June, and the result of these efforts was that elements of Major General G. F. Wootten's 9th Australian Division (less the 26th Brigade Group) were able to get ashore without difficulty on 10 June. Covered by the gunfire of 4 cruisers and 7 destroyers, the 24th Brigade was landed on Labuan Island and the 20th Brigade at Brooketon. The 24th Brigade was soon able to secure the airstrip on Labuan Island, though the Japanese maintained an organized defence of the western end of the island until 21 June. The 24th Brigade then landed two battalions on the eastern side of Brunei Bay to take Beaufort on 28 June. Meanwhile the 20th Brigade had taken Brunei town on 15 June before advancing south-west along the coast to take Seria on 21 June. Another amphibious landing gave the brigade the towns of Lutong and Miri just over the border in Sarawak. By 1 July the area was secure, the Allies having lost 118 dead (114 Australian and four American) and 221 wounded. Japanese losses were 1,234 dead and 130 prisoners, though again the survivors of the garrison retreated to the jungles inland and held out until the end of the war.

Ochsenkopf (ox head) (i) Offensive by the 5th Panzerarmee towards Beja, Gafour and Teboursouk (26 February/5 March 1943) in conjunction with a similar Operation 'Ausladung'. The plan originated in the erroneous Axis belief that the combined Operations 'Frühlingswind' and 'Morgenluft' had inflicted decisive land and air losses on the Allies, especially Lieutenant General K. A. N. Anderson's Allied 1st Army, allowing the Axis main effort now to be made against General Sir Bernard Montgomery's British 8th Army advancing into southern Tunisia from Libya. General Vittorio Ambrosio, appointed to replace Marshal Ugo Cavallero as chief-of-staff of the Italian armed forces from February 1943, decided that Generaloberst Jürgen von Arnim's 5th Panzerarmee should thus make a number of raids and spoiling attacks before pushing forward its line against the Allied 1st Army in the north of Tunisia.

Though sound in essence, the plan almost immediately foundered on the usual divided command in North Africa, for von Arnim now consulted Generalfeldmarschall Albert Kesselring, the German *Oberbefelhshaber Süd* and commander of Luftflotte II (without even telling Generalfeldmarschall Erwin Rommel, commander since 23 February of Army Group 'Africa') and secured Kesselring's approval for a modification of Ambrosio's basic concept, whereby the raids were abandoned in favour of a revived 'Frühlingswind', in this instance a major thrust by Korpsgruppe Weber towards Béja ('Ochsenkopf') and a subsidiary thrust by Gruppe von Manteuffel towards Djebel Abiod ('Ausladung').

The strategic object of von Arnim's plan was to deprive the Allies of the good tank country between Medjez el Bab and Tunis. 'Ochsenkopf' was the responsibility of Generalmajor Friedrich Weber's Korpsgruppe Weber, a formation based on the commander's 334th Division and strengthened by elements of the 'Hermann Goering' Panzer Division and of the 10th Panzer Division. This was to fall on the formations of Lieutenant General C. W. Allfrey's British V Corps, which was aligned with Major General H. A. Freeman-Attwood's British 46th Division covering Béja, Major General V. Evelegh's British 78th Division covering Teboursouk, and the extemporized 'Y' Division covering Gafour.

The German offensive got under way on 26 February, and made virtually no impression on the British, even where the fighting was at its hardest against the British 46th Division. On 28 February Rommel decreed that the offensive should cease, though only after the Korpsgruppe Weber had attained the objectives set for it by von Arnim. Fighting continued until 5 March, but throughout the Germans and Italians failed to take then hold ground, Weber himself calling off the attacks on 4 March with orders that his men should fall back to defensive positions.

(ii) Overall designation of 'Ochsenkopf' proper and 'Ausladung' as a joint operation, and used in this sense by German higher command echelons.

Octagon Designation of the 2nd Quebec Conference (11/12 September 1944). This was an Allied political and military conference between President Franklin D. Roosevelt and Prime Minister Winston Churchill, each supported by his military advisers. The primary military topics discussed by the leaders were the future conduct of operations against the Japanese in the Pacific and Burma (with special regard to British participation in the Pacific theatre after the defeat of Germany), and the need to maintain Allied pressure in Italy at least until the end of the Gothic Line battles currently in progress. The main political topic was the disposition of Germany after her military defeat.

So far as Burma operations were concerned, the conference directive to Admiral Lord Louis Mountbatten, the Supreme Allied Commander, South-East Command, ordained that the command's primary objective was the recapture of Burma and the reopening of land communications with China, to which end Operation 'Capital' was to be implemented as soon as possible, with Operation 'Dracula' following by 15 March 1945. With regard to Pacific operations, it was decided that a British Pacific

Fleet (with the appropriate fleet train) should be formed and despatched to the region by the beginning of 1945, there coming under the command of Admiral Chester W. Nimitz's Pacific Fleet in operational matters, and that a fleet of between 600 and 800 heavy bombers ('Tiger Force') should be sent to the Pacific as soon as possible after the end of operations against Germany. In Italy, the 'Octagon' conference decided, the Allies should await the outcome of the Gothic Line battles, designed to take the 15th Army Group across the Apennines to the line of the River Adige, just short of the River Piave, before deciding on what should be attempted next, the US desire being to reduce the strength of the 5th Army, while the British plan was still to strengthen the Allied forces with a view to an offensive into Austria and southern Germany. But perhaps the most important result of the 'Octagon' conference was a pair of early Anglo-American plans for defeated Germany.

In the first of these, the country was to be divided into zones of occupation, with the Soviets holding the eastern part of the country, the British the area west of the Rhine and that portion east of the river north of a line from Koblenz along the northern borders of Hesse and Nassau, and the Americans the area east of the Rhine south of the line from Koblenz along the northern borders of Hesse and Nassau; the Americans would also control the ports of Bremen and Bremerhaven. Omissions that were later to become a cause of dissent were lack of any French zone, and lack of any plan for joint occupation of Berlin. The second plan for defeated Germany was the infamous Morgenthau Plan devised by the Secretary of the US Treasury, Henry Morgenthau Jr. This called for the total elimination of German industrial capacity and the expropriation of Germany's raw material resources so that the country would be reduced to a subsistence standard of living with an economy based almost entirely on agriculture. Morgenthau's object was to punish Germany and to prevent her from ever again from developing any warmaking capability. Only extreme pressure from a number of sources prevented this devastating scheme from being presented (in July 1945 at the Potsdam Conference) for adoption as standard Allied policy. Even so, the Germans got wind of the proposal, and the propaganda ministry of Dr Joseph Goebbels was able to make great capital out of the Morgenthau scheme which, Goebbels claimed, was designed to punish all Germany and not just the Nazis. The plan also discouraged those anti-Nazi elements in Germany who wished to surrender the country to the Allies as the price of halting a Soviet invasion with all its attendant barbarities.

O.C. Designation of ocean outward convoys (together with a numerical suffix) plying the route from the UK to Gibraltar, and inaugurated on 1 October 1939. These convoys were halted temporarily in August 1942 and restarted in May 1943, from July 1943 sailing in company with the K.M.S. convoys until the series ended in October 1943.

Oklahoma Designation of the records kept by Lieutenant General Joseph W. Stilwell about his relationship with Generalissimo Chiang Kai-shek and other Allied commanders in the Far East, and about his recall from China on 18 October 1944.

O.L. Designation of ocean outward convoys (together with a numerical suffix) plying the routes from Liverpool between 14 September and 25 October 1940. These were fast convoys, and the series numbered only eight.

Oldenburg Alternative designation for Operation 'Barbarossa' in planning papers.

Olga Designation of the headquarters planned for the Oberkommando der Wehrmacht in Thuringia (1945).

Olive Designation of the operation (25 August/21 September 1944) undertaken by Lieutenant General Sir Oliver Leese's British 8th Army to break through the German defences of the 'Gotisch Linie' in the sector held by General Traugott Herr's LXXVI Panzer Corps (71st and 278th Divisions, 5th Mountain Division, 1st Parachute Division and 162nd Turkoman Division) of Generaloberst Heinrich von Vietinghoff-Scheel's German 10th Army. The British front in this sector was currently held by General W. Anders's II Polish Corps (3rd Carpathian Division and 5th Kresowa Division), with Lieutenant General R. L. McCreery's British X Corps (10th Indian Division supported by the British 9th Armoured Brigade) holding the army's left flank against General Valentin Feuerstein's LI Gebirgskorps (44th, 305th, 334th and 715th Divisions, and 114th Jäger Division).

Leese's plan, approved by General the Hon. Sir Harold Alexander on 4 August, was to form a double strike force to punch through in the Polish sector along the coast, whereas the 8th Army staff had previously planned an inland attack through the mountains. This strike force comprised Lieutenant General E. L. M. Burns's I Canadian Corps (1st Canadian Division and 5th Canadian Armoured Division) on the right and Lieutenant General Sir Charles Keightley's British V Corps (4th, 46th and 56th Divisions, 4th Indian Division and 1st Armoured Division) on the left. This change of plan left the 8th Army with a mere three weeks to prepare the detailed operational orders and organize the movement of the British V Corps and I Canadian Corps from the original forming-up area to the south of Lake Trasimeno to the new start positions behind II Polish Corps. Apart from the men of the assault division, this involved the movement of some 60,000 tanks, vehicles and guns across the Apennines between 15 and 22 August. The 8th Army's tactical plan called for a three-corps advance, with the Poles by the sea for an advance on Pesaro, the Canadians in the centre for an advance on the coast road north of Pesaro before moving on Rimini, and the British inland for an advance through the hills to the east of the Apennines to reach, west of Rimini, the vital Route 9 (key to the Germans' tactical mobility, permitting them to switch mobile formations between General Joachim Lemselsen's 14th Army in the west and the 10th Army in the east). This Allied strength would all fall on the section of front held by the German 1st Parachute, 71st and 278th Divisions.

The 'Olive' plan naturally fell into four phases (the advance to the 'Gotisch Linie' defences, the penetration of these defences, the battle for Coriano Ridge, and the exploitation from this battle. The offensive began on 25 August with total success, advancing to the 'Gotisch Linie' positions by 29 August before the Germans fully appreciated the nature of Leese's plan. German reinforcements were ordered into the sector, but the 'Gotisch Linie' defences behind the line of the River Foglia fell on 30 August before the 26th Panzer and 98th Divisions could get into the line. By 2 September the Germans had formed a cohesive defence, but this was unable to prevent the 8th Army breaking through the 'Gotisch Linie' defences along the whole of its front and pouring through towards Rimini, persuading the command that the armoured forces for the exploitation should be moved up.

But the Germans were still full of fight, and by 4 September the 162nd and 356th Divisions and the 29th Panzergrenadier Division had arrived to bolster the German line, resulting in a distinct slowing of the Allied advance towards the Gemmano and Coriano Ridges. These two features provided some of the worst fighting of the whole Italian campaign. The Gemmano Ridge battle between 9 and 14 September involved the 4th Indian Division and the British 46th and 56th Divisions, while the Coriano Ridge battle between 12 and 19 September needed the British 1st Armoured Division, the Canadian 5th Armoured Division and part of the British 46th Division. By now the Germans had been able to bring in the 90th Panzergrenadier Division and the 20th Luftwaffe Field Division, so they had some 10 divisions to oppose the 8th Army. Finally the German defence broke, and on 21 September the 8th Army took Rimini and was at last in the valley of the River Po. The cost on both sides had been heavy, as indicated by the fact that the British 1st Armoured Division virtually ceased to exist, and that one brigade of the British 56th Division existed only as a cadre. Only after this did the British discover that the Po valley was not the excellent tank country they had supposed, but rather a boggy expanse interweaved by a myriad of water courses admirably suited to the Germans' carefully considered defensive tactics.

Olivenbaum (olive tree) Alternative designation for 'Antimon'.

Olivernte (olive crop) Designation of that portion of Operation 'Ochsenkopf' concerned with the capture of Medjez el Bab (26 February/5 March 1943) by the Korpsgruppe Weber of Generaloberst Jürgen von Arnim's 5th Panzerarmee before the exploitation phase towards Béja, Teboursouk and Gafour. Medjez el Bab was held by Brigadier G. P. Harding's British 138th Brigade of Major General H. A. Freeman-Attwood's British 46th Division, temporarily under command of Major General V. Evelegh's British 78th Division. The fighting was severe, but the Axis forces commanded by Generalmajor Friedrich Weber failed to secure their initial major objective despite local successes during the period at Heidous in the north, on the Tunis road east of Medjez el Bab in the centre and at Sidi Mahmoud in the south.

Olymp (Olympus) German operation against Greek partisans (May/June 1942).

Olympic Designation of the plan for the initial US invasion of the Japanese home islands by Lieutenant General Walter Krueger's US 6th Army, and scheduled for 1 November 1945. The operation was planned without any knowledge of the Allied development of atomic weapons, which ultimately removed the need for the invasion, but all estimates by the US planners were that 'Olympic' would be an exceptionally bloody undertaking, for the Japanese could be expected to resist with more than their usual fanatical courage once the Americans came ashore on the home islands.

The planning of the operation was a monumental undertaking because of the size of the forces involved, and because of the logistical problems of delivering and supporting so many men and machines over so great a distance from their industrial base on the other side of the Pacific Ocean in the continental USA. High command modifications to ease the task of the final assault on Japan were implemented on 5 April 1945, when the Pacific Theater became a joint command under General Douglas MacArthur (ground forces) and Admiral Chester W. Nimitz (naval forces), though the question of command for strategic air support was left open, the matter resting on co-operation between MacArthur and Nimitz on the one hand, and Major General Curtis LeMay, commanding the XXI Bomber Command of the 20th Air Force in the Marianas, on the other. This potential command problem was removed in July 1945, when General Carl A. Spaatz was appointed to head the new Strategic Air Force in the Pacific, whose subordinate command was the 20th Air Force, headquartered in the Marianas, rather than Washington as had previously been the case. Subordinate commands of the 20th Air Force were LeMay's XXI Bomber Command in the Marianas, XX Bomber Command to be based on Okinawa, and VII Fighter Command on Iwo Jima. Tactical air support of the Pacific Theater's ground forces remained the responsibility of Lieutenant General George C. Kenney's Far East Air Force, with headquarters on Okinawa. The US command structure was thus optimized for Operation 'Olympic', the invasion of Kyushu at the south-western end of the Japanese island group, which was authorized on 25 May.

Overall planning was vested in MacArthur's staff, which called for a continuing strategic air campaign against Japan's war industries and internal lines of communication while the US Navy's Fast Carrier Task Force undertook the destruction of Japan's surviving naval and air forces. To this end the five huge bomber bases in the Marianas were to be supplemented by new bases on Okinawa, which by 1 November was to be able to accommodate the 240 squadrons of 60 air groups as well as the logistical bases for the Strategic and Far East Air Forces. For the actual descent on Kyushu MacArthur proposed to use formations already in the Pacific and experienced in war against the Japanese. The overall plan ready by the time of Japan's surrender in August 1945 envisaged that the 6th Army would land at the southern end of Kyushu and occupy the island as far north as the line from Tsuno to Sendai. This would provide the US Navy with an excellent base in the Kagoshima Wan, and also enable forward air bases to be built for the support of Operation 'Coronet', the main step to Honshu Island in 1946. With this primary strategic objective attained, the 6th Army would release four divisions for the Honshu invasion force (1st and 8th Armies).

The detailed plan for 'Olympic' saw the operation progressing in one preliminary and four main phases. In the preliminary phase the US 40th Infantry Division and 158th Regimental Combat Team were to take the islands south and west of Kyushu to provide advanced anchorages, early warning positions and seaplane bases (on D-5 the 158th Regimental Combat Team was to take Tanega Shima, while on D-4 the 40th Infantry Division was to take the Koshiki Retto and neighbouring islands, moving on D-day to seize Uji Gunto, Kusagakijima, Kuro Shima and Kuchino Erabu Shima). After these preliminary moves, the main assault was to be launched simultaneously by three corps, Major General Harry Schmidt's V Amphibious Corps landing its 3rd, 4th and 5th Marine Divisions on the western flank at Kushikino, Major General Charles P. Hall's XI Corps landing its 43rd Infantry, 1st Cavalry and Americal Divisions in the centre in the Ariake Wan between Kanoya and Subishi, and Major General Innis P. Swift's I Corps landing its 25th, 33rd and 41st Infantry Divisions on the eastern flank just south of Miyazaki. During this first phase of the main assault, the US 6th Army's floating reserve (Major General Charles Rider's IX Corps, consisting of the 81st and 98th Infantry Divisions) was to demonstrate off Shikoku, the island between Kyushu and Honshu. The second phase of the assault was to be the consolidation and expansion of the three beach-heads for the building of forward airstrips, and the opening of the Kagashima Wan for US shipppng. To aid the successful completion of the latter task, the two divisions of IX Corps were to be prepared to come ashore if necessary on D+3 at the extreme southern end of Kyushu, on the Satsuma peninsula, for an advance on Kagoshima at the head of the Kagoshima Wan and a link-up with V Amphibious Corps. The third phase was then the joining up of the separate beach-heads to secure a cohesive lodgement as far north as the line from Sendai on the west coast to Tsuno on the east coast, giving the US 6th Army an area some 60 miles wide and on average 50 miles deep. The fourth phase, to be undertaken only if necessary, was an exploitation on Kyushu or in the Inland Sea to secure the US lodgement.

Also available to the US 6th Army were the 11th Airborne and 77th Infantry Divisions on Luzon, and if these 14 divisions could not complete their task Krueger could be reinforced from the forces earmarked for the Honshu landings at the rate of three divisions per month from D+30 onwards. Naval support for these land operations was the responsibility of Nimitz's Pacific Fleet command, for Operation 'Olympic' divided into a 3rd Fleet under Admiral William F. Halsey and a 5th Fleet under Admiral Raymond A. Spruance. The 3rd Fleet was tasked with strategic support of the landings (operating against targets in the Kuriles, Hokkaido and Honshu) with its complement of fast carrier task groups and escorting battleships, cruisers and destroyers, while the 5th Fleet was to convoy and land the US 6th Army, and then to provide it with close support. The 5th Fleet's main strike force was the 1st Fast Carrier Force, and the amphibious operation was entrusted to Vice Admiral Richmond K. Turner's Amphibious Force. The Allies could deploy 14 fleet carriers, 6 light carriers and 36 escort carriers for the operations, together with very powerful battleship and cruiser forces.

The Japanese defence of the area threatened by Operation 'Olympic' was entrusted to the 2nd General Army, with its headquarters at Hiroshima on Honshu. This army group headquarters controlled the 15th Area Army in southern Honshu, and the 16th Area Army in Kyushu, with its headquarters at Fukuoka. The 16th Area Army could call on 14 infantry divisions and 2 armoured brigades in a command structure of 3 armies and 2 other forces. In the north of the island was the 56th Army, while the assault areas of V Amphibious and IX Corps were held by the 40th Army, and those of I and XI Corps by the 57th Army. The strip of Kyushu between the 56th Army in the north and the 40th and 57th Armies in the south was allocated to the Chikugo and Higo Forces. The Japanese air strengths in August 1945 were some 3,800 army aircraft (including 3,000 *kamikazes*) controlled by the Air General Army, and

Omaha

5,145 navy aircraft (including 2,500 trainers to be used as *kamikazes*) controlled by the 3rd, 5th and 10th Air Fleets. Fuel stocks were extremely low, and the 5th Air Fleet had priority in Kyushu, where the 71st, 72nd and 73rd Air Flotillas were tasked with air defence, and the 12th and 13th Air Flotillas with attacks on the US fleet as it approached Kyushu. Another Japanese problem was no overall command.

Omaha Designation of the beach allocated to Major General Leonard T. Gerow's US V Corps of Lieutenant General Omar N. Bradley's US 1st Army in Field Marshal Sir Bernard Montgomery's 21st Army Group for Operation 'Overlord'. The assault formation of the US V Corps was Major General Clarence R. Huebner's 1st Infantry Division, and this was designated to come ashore on 'Omaha' Beach, between Ste Honorine in the east and the Pointe de la Percée in the west, with its 16th Infantry Regiment on the left and the 116th Infantry Regiment (allocated from the 29th Infantry Division) on the right, these two regimental combat teams being followed respectively by the 18th Infantry Regiment and the 26th Infantry Regiment, with the 115th Infantry Regiment to follow on Gerow's command. Farther to the right the US 2nd Ranger Battalion was to land at the Pointe du Hoe and take the German battery on top of the cliffs, and the US 1st Infantry Division was then to push inland to the corps line along the Bayeux-Carentan road, allowing the US 2nd and 29th Infantry Divisions to start coming ashore for an advance westwards to Isigny at the mouth of the Rivers Vire and Aure, and eastwards to Bayeux. The opposition to the US 1st Infantry Division was found by the 916th Regiment of the German 352nd Division of General Erich Marcks's LXXXIV Corps of Generaloberst Friedrich Dollmann's German 7th Army within Generalfeldmarschall Erwin Rommel's Army Group 'B'.

O.N. (i) Designation of North Sea convoys (together with a numerical suffix) plying the route from Methil to Bergen, and inaugurated on 4 November 1939 to end on 5 April 1940. (ii) Designation of ocean outward convoys (together with a numerical suffix) plying the route from UK to Halifax, Nova Scotia, and inaugurated on 27 July 1941 as a replacement for the previous O.B. series.

O.N.S. Designation of ocean outward slow convoys (together with a numerical suffix) plying the route from the UK to Halifax, Nova Scotia, and inaugurated on 26 July 1941 as a replacement for the previous O.B.S. series.

Orange Designation of the US contingency plans prepared before World War II against the eventuality of war with Japan.

Oration Allied mission to the forces of Marshal Tito in Yugoslavia (January 1944).

Orient Long-term German plan for their forces in North Africa and the Caucasus to advance to a link-up in the Middle East (summer 1942). Such plans were never formulated in any great detail, and represented wish fulfilment rather than objective thinking.

Orkan (hurricane) German offensive designed to clear the Crimea of its last Soviet defenders and to take the great fortress of Sevastopol (8 May/9 July 1942). Entrusted to Generalfeldmarschall Fedor von Bock's Army Group 'South', this offensive was designed as a preliminary to the launch of the various Operations 'Blau' in the southern USSR during the summer of 1942, and by clearing the last Soviets out of the Crimea ensured that the right flank of Army Group 'South' was secure and that the German 11th Army of Generaloberst Erich von Manstein could cross the Straits of Kerch to support the 1st Panzerarmee and the 17th Army in their offensive along the eastern coast of the Black Sea after sweeping across the lower reaches of the Rivers Don and Donets.

By mid-December 1941 the Germans had taken all of the Crimea except Sevastopol, but during their great winter offensive of 1941/1942 the Soviets had pushed forces of the 44th and 51st Armies across the Straits of Kerch to retake the Kerch peninsula (from the relatively weak forces of the German XLII Corps under Generalleutnant Hans Graf von Sponeck) as far east as the Kamenskoye isthmus and the city of Feodosiya. Von Manstein had been forced to abandon his operations against Sevastopol and come to the aid of XLII Corps with his XXX Corps just as the German 46th Division evacuated the Kerch peninsula to avoid being cut off by Soviet forces landed at Feodosiya. The arrival of von Manstein and reinforcements remedied the situation, though the forces of Lieutenant General D. T. Kozlov's Crimean Front (thus renamed from Caucasus Front on 28 January) launched renewed offensives 27 February, 13 March, 26 March and 9 April before halting their efforts only through complete exhaustion. In this Soviet beachhead during the spring of 1942 were the 17 infantry divisions and 3 infantry brigades (supported by 2 cavalry divisions and 4 tank brigades) of Lieutenant General S. I. Chernyak's Soviet 44th Army and Lieutenant General K. S. Kolganov's Soviet 47th Army of the Crimean Front, and von Manstein decided to expel these Soviet forces before returning to the task of crushing Sevastopol without any distraction. This city was left under investment by the German LIV Corps, which had given up most of its German divisions for von Manstein's Kerch operations, undertaken by 6 German divisions (including the new 22nd Panzer Division) and 3 Romanian divisions. The Germans' numerical inferiority was offset by the availability of Generloberst Wolfram Freiherr von Richthofen's VIII Fliegerkorps, a superb tactical support formation provided by Generaloberst Alexander Löhr's Luftflotte IV.

The German offensive opened on 8 May, and by the evening XXX Corps had punched a hole through the Soviet 44th Army's front, allowing the 50th, 28th Gebirgsjäger and 22nd Panzer Divisions to wheel north on the following day and drive 11 Soviet divisions into the Sea of Azov by 11 May. Von Manstein had meanwhile been driving east with the rest of the 11th Army, and reached Kerch on 16 May. The Soviets could not maintain a beach-head on the peninsula, and on 20 May the last elements of the 44th Army were evacuated by sea to the Kuban across the Straits of Kerch, leaving 170,000 prisoners, 1,140 guns and 260 tanks.

Von Manstein was now free to turn his attention to the reduction of Sevastopol. Commanded by Lieutenant General I. E. Petrov, the garrison of Sevastopol was found by the Independent Coastal Army, comprising about 100,000 men of 7 infantry and 1 unmounted cavalry divisions supported by 3 marine infantry brigades led by Vice Admiral F. S. Oktabrsky. Two more infantry brigades were landed during the battle, giving the Soviets a total strength of some 70 battalions. The defences themselves were formidable, and consisted of some 3,600 fortifications (both permanent and extemporized) over a depth of some 15 miles round the city, with 600 guns (including 4 305-mm weapons in 2 twin turrets) and 40 tanks. The extreme difficulty of the terrain was also another significant factor in the defence's favour. On the other side of the wire, the 11th Army mustered some 11 divisions including the 2 of the Romanian Mountain Corps which occupied the western side of the investment on the Yaila Heights. The Germans had no tanks, but had been provided with three battalions of assault guns, and also had 700 pieces of artillery (including two 60-cm Karl mortars and one 80-cm Gustav rail gun), 24 rocket-launcher batteries and some 600 aircraft of VIII Fliegerkorps' 7 bomber, 3 Stuka and 4 fighter groups, supported by 17 Flak batteries.

Von Manstein was in no doubt of the difficulty facing his army, and opted for simultaneous attacks from the north (General Erich Hansen's German LIV Corps) and from the south (Generalleutnant Maximilian Fretter-Pico's German XXX Corps). The perimeter of Sevastopol had been reduced in the first attack (December 1941) to about two-thirds of its original extent, but still measured some 16 miles in width, the front running from the mouth of the River Belbek in the north, down across the River Chernaya to the east of the Fedyukhin Heights, to a point just east of Balaclava in the south. The German attack started on 7 June, the main task being entrusted to LIV Corps in the north though XXX Corps to the south had the greater strength. The fighting was enormously costly in men and *matériel*, but LIV Corps moved steadily down the valley of the Belbek to take Fort Stalin, while XXX Corps pushed through to the forward edge of the

Soviet defences on the Sapun Gora. It was now clear that the greater effort should have been made in the XXX Corps sector, but von Manstein decided to stick to his original plan as any change would have resulted in a delay, and the German command had warned the 11th Army that delay would cost it the support of VIII Fliegerkorps, which was needed to support the 'Blau' offensives. The 50th Division of LIV Corps finally crossed the Chernaya to take the Inkerman defences on XXX Corps' right flank, and on 28 June the 22nd and 24th Divisions of XXX Corps crossed North Bay in assault boats to take the Soviet defences on the far side and so open the way into the Soviets' rear. This spelled the end of any meaningful Soviet resistance, but rather than risk his men in urban fighting, von Manstein ordered that what was left of Sevastopol be shelled and bombed into submission.

Between 30 June and 2 July the Soviet command was evacuated from Sevastopol by submarine as the remnants of the garrison fell back to the Kersonese Peninsula to the west, where on 4 July the Soviets' main strength, some 30,000 men, finally surrendered. The last pockets on the peninsula capitulated on 9 July. German casualties in the campaign had been 24,111 killed and wounded, but the 11th Army took some 95,000 prisoners and 460 guns. Only in the extreme south of the Crimea was there still Soviet resistance, in the form of partisans operating out of the mountains, thus the 11th Army was available for further operations. But Hitler, so impressed with the 11th Army's triumph that he promoted von Manstein to *Generalfeldmarschall* on 4 July, decided that this proven army should not now be transferred to the Kuban but rather to the other end of the Eastern Front, where it would reduce Leningrad. LXII Corps was left as garrison of the Crimea while XXX and LIV Corps moved north with all the heavy artillery and four infantry divisions. The 11th Army's other formations were dispersed as reinforcements to points as diverse as Smolensk and Crete.

Orphan   Developed version of 'Aphrodite'.

O.S.   Designation of ocean outward convoys (together with a numerical suffix) plying the route from the UK to Freetown, Sierra Leone, and inaugurated on 24 July 1941. The series was stopped temporarily in September 1942 and restarted in February 1943. From April 1943 the O.S. convoys sailed with K.M.S. convoys as far as Gibraltar.

Oskar (Oscar)   Attack by German S-boats on shipping off Dover (December 1940).

Ostgoten (East Goths)   German organization of home defence units in eastern Germany (1944/1945).

Ostmarkflug (Austria flight)   Alternative designation for 'Weiss'.

O.T.   Designation of US coastal and central Atlantic convoys (together with a numerical suffix) plying the route from New York to the Caribbean and North Africa, and inaugurated in February 1943 as a means of sending fast tankers to North Africa for the support of the armies involved in Operation 'Torch' and its exploitation.

Otto   (i) German operational study for the restoration of the monarchy in Austria (1937).
(ii) German occupation of Austria (12/13 March 1938). Hitler had long wished to unify Austria with Germany, and had aided the Austrian Nazis agitating for just such an event. But when Chancellor Kurt von Schuschnigg announced on 9 March 1938 that there would be a plebiscite (on terms unfavourable to the Austrian Nazis), Hitler saw that he must use military might to force the issue and called in General Ludwig Beck, the army chief-of-staff, and Generalmajor Erich von Manstein, deputy chief-of-staff, to urge rapid preparations for a push from southern Germany to Vienna by 12 March. Both Beck and von Manstein argued that the only available formations, VII and XIII Corps together with the 2nd Panzer Division, were not ready for such an operation, but then improvized the undertaking in just five hours so that the operation orders could go out during the afternoon of 10 March. Hitler then forced the replacement of Schuschnigg by Dr Arthur Seyss-Inquart, the Austrian

Nazi leader, on 11 March with the threat of an invasion if the plebiscite was not called off, and then went ahead with the extemporized invasion on 12 March despite the protests of Generaloberst Walther von Brauchitsch, the commander-in-chief of the German army, and of Generalleutnant Max von Viebahn, the Oberkommando der Wehrmacht director of operations. Both were unhappy with the nature of German policy, and also feared Allied intervention should Austria be invaded. The actual invasion was undertaken without opposition, and the Allies refused to do anything but protest, so Seyss-Inquart was able to declare the *Anschluss* (annexation) on 13 March, whereupon Austria became the Ostmark of the Greater German Reich.

(iii) Original codename under which the invasion of the USSR was planned for eventual implementation as Operation 'Barbarossa'.

Outdistance British commando liaison mission in Czechoslovakia.

Outmatch Designation of patrols by de Havilland Mosquito aircraft in the Bay of Biscay and over the Western Approaches to tackle German bombers, especially those carrying anti-ship missiles (June/September 1944).

Outstep British long-range fighter patrols off Norway to escort anti-ship strike missions by Coastal Command aircraft (1944/1945).

Overlord Allied invasion of northern France (6 June 1944). Such an operation had been long wished by the Allies, and the final 'Overlord' plan was accepted in outline at the 'Trident' conference in Washington during 1943 after the Allied planners had appreciated that any premature effort (such as Operation 'Sledgehammer' in 1942 and Operation 'Round-up' in 1943) stood little real chance of success against an enemy who maintained strong forces in France under an able leadership. The Allies therefore decided to bide their time (despite Soviet insistence that a 'second front' be opened against the Germans in the west as a means of easing pressure on the Eastern Front) until they had the right strength of adequately trained and equipped forces, supported by the necessary naval and air forces, for a decisive stroke. This decisive stroke was not to be merely the occupation of a substantial lodgement in German-occupied France, but the beginning of a major strategic drive through France and into Germany with the object of Germany's total defeat.

Planning for Operation 'Overlord' was undertaken by a number of teams under the control of SHAEF (Supreme Headquarters Allied Expeditionary Forces) but closely supervised by the Combined Chiefs-of-Staff Committee. Heading SHAEF was General Dwight D. Eisenhower, with Air Chief Marshal Sir Arthur Tedder as his deputy and Lieutenant General Walter Bedell Smith as his chief-of-staff. Command of the invasion forces was vested in Field Marshal Sir Bernard Montgomery. There had been considerable pressure for a joint command of the Allied forces for 'Overlord', with Montgomery heading the Anglo-Canadian forces and Lieutenant General Omar N. Bradley the US forces, but Eisenhower insisted on a single commander for the one army group that would launch the landing and undertake the breakout from the beachhead, though the arrival of more troops in France in the exploitation after the break-out would make necessary the formation of two army groups, one Anglo-Canadian under Montgomery and one US under Bradley, whereupon Eisenhower would assume command in France over both army group chiefs.

Initial Allied thoughts had centred upon a landing in the Pas-de-Calais region, which offered good terrain across a relatively narrow water crossing, but it was soon clear that this was just what the Germans were expecting, the *Oberbefehlshaber West* (Generalfeldmarschall Gerd von Rundstedt) and the commander-in-chief of Army Group 'B' (Generalfeldmarschall Erwin Rommel) having disposed Generaloberst Hans von Salmuth's powerful German 15th Army in this area with 14 first-line infantry divisions (plus another 3 refitting or forming) and 5 first-line Panzer divisions (plus another 2 refitting or forming). So Allied thoughts were switched farther to the west, where the beaches of Normandy (between Le Havre to the east and Cherbourg to the west) offered adequate sites for the

Overlord

landing against the German 7th Army of Generaloberst Friedrich Dollmann (14 first-line infantry divisions, including 2 parachute divisions, and another infantry division forming). Normandy was also attractive from the operational viewpoint as the crossing was the next shortest after that to the Pas-de-Calais, and from the tactical viewpoint because it lay within fighter range of southern England and because the country was suitable for the tactics in which the Allied formations had been trained. It is worth noting that the Allied formations to be used in 'Overlord' were well trained and well equipped but, for the most part, untried in battle.

The first real plan for the Normandy landings was known as the COSSAC plan, named for the Chief-of-Staff Supreme Allied Commander staff under Lieutenant General Sir Frederick Morgan. This plan was devised in late 1943, and immediately fell foul of Eisenhower and Montgomery. The American commander objected to the plan because it called for a narrow-front landing by 3 divisions only, with a mere 2 more divisions as floating reserve, because it failed to allow for a rapid build-up in the beach-head area, and because it made no provision for the capture of Cherbourg at the head of the Cotentin peninsula. Eisenhower was adamant that the early seizure of a major port was essential for the assured delivery of the follow-on forces and the supplies that were essential for the beach-head to be maintained against the powerful German counteroffensive that must inevitably be launched once the Germans had established the real nature of the Allied effort. Montgomery objected to the COSSAC plan on the grounds that it provided too narrow a landing, especially as by D+12 some 12 divisions were scheduled to come ashore over the same beaches, this figure increasing to 24 divisions by D+24. In these circumstances Montgomery anticipated that the beach areas would become huge traffic jams, throwing Allied operations completely out of gear and constituting ideal targets for German air (and missile) activity. Montgomery went one step further than criticizing the COSSAC plan and also suggested his ideal concept, in which a broad-front landing would be made only after the successful completion of an Allied air offensive to eliminate German air units in the area. Montgomery thus advocated that the British and US armies should each have their own group of landing beaches, each beach being used for a single corps (both assault divisions and follow-up divisions) and sufficiently separated from other beaches so that each corps could have freedom of tactical action in developing its beach-head before the entire army group moved rapidly to secure at least two major ports or groups of smaller ports, ideally one to each army. Though his objections to the COSSAC plan were different from those of Montgomery, Eisenhower also saw his subordinate's point of view, and modifications were worked into the basic COSSAC scheme.

Thus the 'Overlord' plan added two more beaches ('Sword' Beach at Lion-sur-Mer on the left and 'Utah' Beach at Les Dunes de Vareville on the right) so that 5 divisions could be landed in the first assault wave, joining the 3 airborne divisions already landed, against the 4 German divisions of General Erick Marcks's LXXIV Corps (of which only Generalleutnant Wilhelm Richter's 716th and Generalleutnant Krauss's 352nd Divisions would be fully engaged, for just parts of Generalmajor Bernhard Klosterkemper's 91st and Generalleutnant Karl-Wilhelm von Schlieben's 709th Divisions would come under attack after the 'Utah' Beach landings. This meant that effectively 8 Allied divisions would be attacking 3 German divisions, offering better chances of success than the COSSAC scheme, which had 3 Allied divisions assaulting 2 German divisions. Other advantages of the revised plan were the availability of 7 Allied divisions to follow the assault wave, and the fact that the westward extension of the assault area to include 'Utah' Beach on the eastern side of the Cotentin peninsula allowed for a rapid development north through the peninsula to Cherbourg even if the Germans managed to hold the line of the River Vire to prevent the other Allied forces sweeping west into the Cotentin peninsula.

There can be little doubt that the revised plan was considerably superior to its predecessor, but its development meant that 'Overlord' had to be postponed from early May to early June 1944, the precise date of the invasion being determined by the need for a full or almost full moon for the nocturnal delivery of the 3 airborne divisions, coinciding with low water shortly after dawn so that the Allied air forces could provide tactical air support for the airborne forces and deal with any last German gun emplacements before the assault proper began at low water. This last was necessary as Rommel had developed the number and capability of the German obstacles and mines on the beaches, and these would only be exposed at low water. These considerations indicated an invasion between 5 and 7 June 1944, weather permitting, so detailed plans were worked out by Montgomery's 21st Army Group staff and troops began to move up towards their loading areas for Operation 'Neptune', the naval operation that would take them across the English Channel to Normandy.

As these preparations were instituted, the Allies had two other tasks to undertake before the invasion. The first was the use of strategic air power in concert with the tactical air forces to reduce the Germans' defence capability in north-west Europe (without any concentration on targets that would indicate Normandy as the designated invasion site). The second was the implementation of a series of complex dissimulation moves designed to make the Germans think that the landings would take place in the Pas-de-Calais region, and thus maintain their forces in this region to the detriment of the garrison in Normandy.

The Allied strategic air forces in Europe had been put at Eisenhower's disposal for the run up to 'Overlord'. Under the command of Lieutenant General Carl A. Spaatz, these strategic formations were Air Chief Marshal Sir Arthur Harris's RAF Bomber Command in the UK, Lieutenant General James H. Doolittle's US 8th Air Force in the UK, and Lieutenant General Nathan F. Twining's US 15th Air Force in Italy, which were to be used at Eisenhower's behest to supplement the efforts of his own tactical air arms in England (under the command of the 'Overlord' air commander, Air Chief Marshal Sir Trafford Leigh-Mallory), namely Major General Hoyt S. Vandenberg's US 9th Air Force and Air Marshal Sir Arthur Coningham's 2nd Tactical Air Force. From January 1944 onwards these air armadas concentrated on targets in occupied Europe with emphasis (in order of priority) on aircraft production, railways, V-1 sites and airfields (January), V-1 sites, airfields and railways (February), railways, aircraft production, V-1 sites, coastal fortifications and airfields (March), railways, airfields, V-1 sites, coastal fortifications and shipping (April), and railways, rolling stock, road bridges, coastal radar installations, V-1 sites and coastal fortifications (May). The object of this campaign was to halt the movement of German reserves, to cut German lines of communication, to destroy the V-1 sites which could (the Allies believed) jeopardize the landings, to eliminate German aircraft and air facilities in France and the Low Countries, and to destroy the coastal radars and fortifications that might warn of the invasion and then severely damage the assault forces at sea.

Less obvious, but still as important, was the dissimulation programme, and in this field the Allies achieved a masterstroke, convincing the Germans of the existence of two major formations that did not in fact exist. The first of these was the US 1st Army Group under Lieutenant General George S. Patton, which the Germans believed was grouped in Kent and Sussex for a descent on the Pas-de-Calais with 25 infantry and armoured divisions plus 5 airborne divisions. The second phantom formation was the British 4th Army, which the Germans believed was assembling in Scotland under Lieutenant General Sir A. F. A. N. Thorne for an invasion of Norway, where Generaloberst Nikolaus von Falkenhorst had 11 divisions. Hitler's intuition told him that the Allies would indeed land in either of these two places, and this certainty on the part of the German leader coincided with German staff appreciations about the threat to the Pas-de-Calais to prevent reinforcement of Normandy. It was just as important for the deception to be maintained after the implementation of 'Overlord', so that the German 15th Army was not used as a source of reinforcement for the 7th Army. To this purpose two aircraft sorties were flown and two tons of bombs dropped east of Le Havre for every one sortie and one ton of bombs west of that port in the period immediately

Overlord

after D-Day, and so convincing were these Allied deceptions that for seven weeks after D-Day the Germans thought that another (and larger) landing would be made in the Pas-de-Calais. Other elements of the Allied deception plan were designed to mislead German intelligence as to the real strength of the Allies in the UK, and whereas on 31 May the Allies had some 52 divisions in the UK (only 37 of them fit for continental operations), the Germans believed that the total was 87 combat divisions including 8 airborne divisions.

So successful had the Allied air offensive been that Luftflotte III under Generalfeldmarschall Hugo Sperrle had a mere 420 aircraft in northern France to pit against an Allied aerial armada of some 10,521 combat aircraft (3,467 four-engined bombers, 1,645 twin-engined bombers and 5,409 single-engined fighters and fighter-bombers), 2,355 transport aircraft and 867 gliders, the last two categories being used to transport some 27,000 men of the three Allied airborne divisions committed during the night of 5/6 June as the vanguard of the Allied assault.

The Allied assault forces were gathered in the south of the UK for their embarkation. On the left of the Allied assault Lieutenant General Sir Miles Dempsey's British 2nd Army was to land Lieutenant G. T. Bucknall's British I Corps ('Sword' and 'Juno' Beaches) and Lieutenant General J. T. Crocker's British XXX Corps ('Gold' Beach), while on the right Bradley's US 1st Army was to put ashore Major General Leonard T. Gerow's US V Corps ('Omaha' Beach) and Major General Joseph L. Collins's US VII Corps ('Utah' Beach). The objective of the four landings of the three eastern corps was by the end of the first day to secure a consolidated beach-head some 5 to 6 miles deep between the mouth of the River Dives at Cabourg and the mouth of the River Vire at Isigny (and including the cities of Bayeux and Caen), while the US VII Corps was to take an area on the eastern side of the Cotentin peninsula stretching from the mouth of the Vire in the south to Quinneville in the north, and as far inland as Pont l'Abbé on the River Douves. The flanks of the beachhead were to be secured first by airborne operations, in the east (in the British I Corps' sector) by Major General Richard Gale's British 6th Airborne Division, and in the west (in the US VII Corps' sector) by Major General Matthew B. Ridgway's US 82nd Airborne Division and Major General Maxwell B. Taylor's US 101st Airborne Division.

Once these flanking operations had been launched, the seaborne assault forces were to arrive in three echelons. In the assault wave the British I Corps was to land on 'Sword' Beach Major General G. T. Rennie's British 3rd Division (gathered in southern Sussex and embarked at Shoreham) supported by the British 27th Armoured Brigade and commandos, and on 'Juno' Beach Major General R. F. L. Keller's 3rd Canadian Division (again gathered in southern Sussex and embarked at Shoreham) supported by the Canadian 2nd Armoured Brigade and commandos. The British XXX Corps was to land on 'Gold' Beach Major General D. A. H. Graham's British 50th Division (gathered in Hampshire and embarked at Portsmouth) supported by the British 8th Armoured Brigade and commandos. Specialised armour was provided for these British formations by the 'funnies' of Major General Sir Percy Hobart's British 79th Armoured Division. The US V Corps was to land on 'Omaha' Beach Major General Clarence R. Huebner's US 1st Infantry Division (gathered in Dorset and embarked at Weymouth) supported by US Rangers; and the US VII Corps was to land on 'Utah' Beach Major General Raymond O. Barton's US 4th Infantry Division (gathered in Devon and embarked at Torquay and Dartmouth). In the follow-up wave these corps were to be reinforced with their organic divisions, the British I Corps with Major General D. C. Bullen-Smith's 51st (Highland) Division (gathered in Essex and embarked at Southend), the British XXX Corps with Major General G. W. E. J. Erskine's 7th Armoured Division and Major General E. H. Barker's 49th Division (gathered in northern Essex and Suffolk, and embarked at Felixstowe), the US V Corps with Major General Charles H. Gerhardt's 29th Infantry Division (gathered in Cornwall and embarked at Fowey) and Major General Walter M. Robertson's 2nd Infantry Division (gathered in south Wales and embarked at Swansea), and the US VII Corps with Major General Manton S. Eddy's 9th Infantry Division (gathered in Somerset and embarked at Bristol) and Brigadier General Jay W. MacKelvie's 90th Infantry Division (gathered in south Wales and embarked in Cardiff). In the follow-up corps wave the assault corps of the initial wave were to be reinforced by the British VIII and XII Corps and by the US XIX Corps.

First of the Allies to land were the airborne divisions, which began to arrive during the night of 5/6 June. The British 6th Airborne Division was not too badly scattered and managed to secure its primary objectives, but the US 82nd and 101st Airborne Divisions were woefully dispersed and were generally unable to secure their primary objectives behind 'Utah' Beach. Of the assault formations, the US 4th Infantry Division arrived slightly to the south of its intended landing area at La Madeleine on 'Utah' Beach, but got ashore without undue difficulty and pushed inland towards Ste Mère Eglise and the main road from Carentan to Cherbourg, meeting increased resistance from the German 919th Regiment as it moved forward. By midnight the division had landed 21,328 men, 1,742 vehicles and 1,950 tons of stores, and had lost 197 men killed, wounded and missing. The US 1st Division on 'Omaha' Beach had a far harder time of it, and was totally unable to break through the defences of the 916th Regiment to reach the Isigny-Bayeux road 3 miles from the beach. During the night the 29th Infantry Division was landed in support of the 1st Infantry Division, but in the short term little could be achieved, and the US V Corps suffered some 2,000 casualties during the day before its men were able to push inland through German defences shattered by the gunfire of Rear Admiral A. G. Kirk's Western Naval Task Force destroyers.

The Anglo-Canadian landings were opposed (west to east) by the German 726th, 915th and 736th Regiments, and fared somewhat better than those of the Americans. The British 50th Division got off 'Gold' Beach and advanced some 6 miles towards Bayeux by the end of the day. The 3rd Canadian Division had greater difficulty in landing, but then pushed forward from 'Juno' Beach some 8 miles towards its objective, Carpiquet airfield. The British 3rd Division also came ashore without undue difficulty on 'Sword' Beach, and then pushed inland to relieve the British 6th Airborne Division and to advance towards Caen and Troarn. The casualties of the British 2nd Army were some 3,000 men during 6 June.

The German riposte to the landings was patchy, not being helped by the fact that Marcks was away in St Lô for his 53rd birthday and Rommel was in Germany for a conference, with Generalleutnant Dr Hans Speidel, the Army Group 'B' chief-of-staff, deputizing for him in France. Nevertheless word of the invasion passed rapidly from LXXIV Corps to the 7th Army to Army Group 'B' and to the *Oberbefelhshaber West*, who ordered the 12th SS Panzer Division and Panzer-Lehr Division to ready themselves for a rapid counterattack while he cleared the matter with the Oberkommando der Wehrmacht and Hitler. But Hitler refused to let von Rundstedt commit this powerful armoured force at what could have been the decisive moment. Instead the Führer ordered that no overt moves were to be made until there had been time for the situation to clarify itself. So the local armoured formation, the 21st Panzer Division, was kept immobile until 14.30, and SS Oberstgruppenführer Sepp Dietrich's I SS Panzer Corps (SS Gruppenführer Fritz Witt's 12th SS Panzer Division and Generalleutnant Fritz Bayerlein's Panzer-Lehr Division) until 17.00. Speidel warned Dollmann that the daylight movement of I SS Panzer Corps would result in heavy losses from Allied tactical aircraft, and this proved to be the case, establishing an ominous precedent for the Germans in the months to come. The two divisions found it difficult to concentrate, and then suffered heavy losses to the activities of Allied fighter-bombers (many fitted with devastating rocket armament) as they moved forward towards the fighting, arriving only on 8 and 9 June respectively. Generalleutnant Edgar Feuchtinger's 21st Panzer Division was in army group reserve closer to the sea, and was able to intervene more rapidly, initially with its infantry units and then with its armour in support of the 716th Division. During the afternoon of 6 June the 21st Panzer Division pushed forward between

Oxalic

'Juno' and 'Sword' Beaches, advancing almost as far as Douvres before it was pushed back again almost out of petrol and having lost 40 of its 197 tanks and assault guns. Delays imposed by Hitler had thus cost the Germans their only real chance of driving the Allies back into the sea.

Both sides were now beginning to move in substantial reinforcements. The German 7th Army was assigned to dealing with the US 1st Army. General Leo Freiherr von Geyr von Schweppenburg's Panzergruppe 'West' staff (eventually commanding XLVII Panzer Corps, I SS Panzer Corps and II SS Panzer Corps, but currently limited to three Panzer divisions), and under the personal supervision of Rommel, tried to handle the British by retaking Bayeux and pushing on to the sea before destroying the two groups into which the British would have thus been divided. It was a vain hope, for by the morning of 10 June the Allies had consolidated their beachhead into a cohesive whole soon to be supported by two 'Mulberry' artificial harbours. The Allied front ran from Crisbecq some half way up the eastern side of the Cotentin peninsula to Ouistreham at the mouth of the River Orne, and contained 10 infantry divisions, 3 airborne divisions and 3 armoured divisions.

Operation 'Overlord' had worked magnificently, and the Allies were in France to stay, with the planners now working on the optimum way for the British to draw in the German reserves (especially the armoured formations) so that the Americans could break out in the west as a consequence of Operation 'Cobra'. Thus there was still some dire fighting to be undertaken around Caen and south of Bayeux, while the US 1st Army got the ball rolling once more with the seizure of the Cotentin peninsula. By 17 June the US 90th Infantry Division, flanked by the 90th Infantry and 82nd Airborne Divisions, had driven west from Ste Mère Eglise through the German 243rd and 91st Divisions to reach the west coast of the Cotentin peninsula between Cartaret and Portbail. From this line the 9th, 79th and 4th Infantry Divisions then advanced north to take Cherbourg on 27 June. German resistance on the Cotentin peninsula ended on 30 June in the Cap de la Hague, and the Allies could then be reinforced and supplied through a major port.

Oxalic Designation of the final objective for the British XXX Corps of General Sir Bernard Montgomery's British 8th Army in the 2nd Battle of El Alamein (24 October 1942). This objective was a line running along the western side of the Miteirya Ridge northwest to a point just north of Kidney Ridge.

Oxtail British plan to form an anti-shipping unit for operations in the Pacific with 'Highball' weapons (July 1944).

Oyster Attack by RAF Bomber Command aircraft on the Philips radio factory at Eindhoven in the Netherlands (6 December 1942).

P

Pampa Designation of Allied meteorological flights over Germany and eastern Europe.

Pancake US bombing offensive against German supply dumps in the region of Bologna in northern Italy (October 1944). Bologna was the focal point of the road and rail communication in the area, allowing the Germans to bring up men and *matériel* for the reinforcement of their defences facing Lieutenant General Mark W. Clark's US 5th Army on the western side of Italy and Lieutenant General Sir Richard McCreery's British 8th Army on the eastern side, and also permitting German forces to be switched relatively easily from one sector of the defensive front to another. Bologna thus became a primary target after the Allied breakthrough of the 'Gotisch Linie' defences in August and September 1944, resulting in this air campaign against German supply dumps.

Pantaloon Allied codename for Naples in southern Italy.

Panther **(i)** Move of No. 1 Group, RAF Bomber command, to France (2 September 1939). In France this group became part of the Advanced Air Striking Force.
(ii) Plan for German forces to make an enveloping movement east of Kharkov (July 1943). It had been proposed that this be an offensive of limited scope to be undertaken in conjunction with Operation 'Habicht' by Generaloberst Hermann Hoth's 4th Panzerarmee and General Wilhelm Kempf's Armeegruppe 'Kempf' of Generalfeldmarschall Erich von Manstein's Army Group 'South', but Hitler and General Kurt Zeitzler, the chief-of-staff of the Oberkommando des Heeres, then decided that Operation 'Zitadelle' would benefit from lack of German distraction, and Operation 'Panther' was cancelled.
(iii) German operation against Soviet partisans operating in the region of Generalfeldmarschall Erich von Manstein's Army Group 'South' (April 1943).

Panther Linie (Panther line) German defence line in the USSR, running from Narva on the Gulf of Finland (north) to the Sea of Azov near Melitopol (south) via Lake Peipus, the River Sozh, Gomel, the River Dniepr and Zaporozhye. Otherwise known as the Ostwall (the counterpart to the Westwall in France), this major strategic defence line was proposed by General Kurt Zeitzler (the chief-of-staff of the Oberkommando des Heeres) after Operation 'Zitadelle', whose failure clearly signalled that the German had lost the strategic initiative on the Eastern Front. Hitler was at first opposed to the construction of such a line (he argued that the materials and construction manpower were needed for the Westwall, and that the availability of defence works in their rear would induce German commanders in the East to fall back) but on 12 August he agreed to the start of work. Before this time, however, the German forces in the East had already begun work using slave labourers to throw up earthworks (there being wholly inadequate stocks of concrete, barbed wire and mines in the East for anything but this), and these were expanded as a result of Hitler's order. In the north the work fell to Generalfeldmarschall

Panzerfaust

Georg von Küchler's Army Group 'North', in the centre to Generalfeldmarschall Günther von Kluge's Army Group 'Centre', and in the south to Generalfeldmarschall Erich von Manstein's Army Group 'South' and Generalfeldmarschall Ewald von Kleist's Army Group 'A', all using vast quantities of slave labour as a supplement to the German armies' engineers and rear-echelon troops.

The need for effective fixed fortifications is indicated by the abysmally low strength of German formations on the Eastern Front. For example, Army Group 'South' held a sector 450 miles in length with 37 infantry divisions whose real strength was each on average that of a regiment. Thus each division had between 1,000 and 2,000 rifles to cover 12 miles of front, allowing for no defence in depth. Army Group 'South' also had 17 Panzer and Panzergrenadier divisions, but again real strengths were as low as 40 tanks to each Panzer division and on 7 September Army Group 'South' had just 257 tanks and 220 assault guns. Hitler expressly ordered that no withdrawal should be made to the 'Panther Linie' defences, which were often sited poorly and inadequately constructed for the task of halting what were now highly trained and well equipped Soviet armies, but by the end of September the eight German armies of Army Groups 'Centre', 'South' and 'A' had been pushed back to the rudimentary 'Panther Linie' defences by the Soviet summer offensive of 1943, launched from north to south by General A. I. Eremenko's Kalinin Front, General V. D. Sokolovsky's West Front, General M. M. Popov's Bryansk Front, General K. K. Rokossovsky's Central Front, General N. F. Vatutin's Voronezh Front, General I. S. Konev's Steppe Front, General R. Ya. Malinovsky's South-West Front and General F. I. Tolbukhin's South Front, all co-ordinated by Marshal of the Soviet Union Georgi Zhukov.

By the end of 1943 the Soviets had driven right through the 'Panther Linie' defences in three vast areas. In the north Eremenko's 1st Baltic Front sundered through the 3rd Panzerarmee between Nevel and Vitebsk. In the centre the Bryansk Front and Rokossovsky's Belorussian Front smashed the German 9th and 2nd Armies between Mogilev and Kiev, the latter falling to the jubilant Soviets on 6 November. And in the south the 1st Ukrainian, 2nd Ukrainian, 3rd Ukrainian and 4th Ukrainian Fronts (commanded respectively by Vatutin, Konev, Malinovsky and Tolbukhin) tore through the German 8th Army, 1st Panzerarmee and 6th Army between Cherkassy and the Sea of Azov, pushing on in the south as far west as Kherson at the mouth of the Dniepr on the Black Sea, so cutting off the German 17th Army in the Crimea, to which it retreated from its Kuban beach-head under pressure from General I. E. Petrov's North Caucasus Front. The turn of the very northern end of the 'Panther Linie' defences came later, for it was between January and March 1944 that the powerful forces of General L. A. Govorov's Leningrad Front, General K. A. Meretskov's Volkhov Front and General M. M. Popov's 2nd Baltic Front pushed the German 18th and 16th Armies of Army Group 'North' (commanded by von Küchler and, from 29 January, by Generalfeldmarschall Walter Model) back to the 'Panther Linie' defences, breaking through them in a massive offensive launched on 4 July.

Panzerfaust (tank fist) German seizure of Burberg Castle in Budapest (16 October 1944) at the time that Admiral Miklos Horthy broadcast to the Hungarian people that he had secured an armistice with the Soviets. At this time Horthy was kidnapped by the Germans, who were prepared for Hungary's defection and had thus undertaken extensive contingency plans for implementation at the time of Horthy's removal. A puppet government was installed in Budapest, but the Germans' reaction had totally alienated an already unenthusiastic nation, and the result was that General B. Dalnoki Miklos, commander of the 1st Hungarian Army, defected to the Soviets after telling the Hungarians to treat the Germans as foes, and Colonel General L. Verres, commander of the 2nd Hungarian Army, was arrested at the orders of Generaloberst Johannes Friessner, commander of the German Army Group 'South', before he could emulate this act.

Paravane Sinking of the German battleship *Tirpitz* by British bombers (12 November 1944). The very existence of this massive and extremely powerful capital ship in Norwegian waters was an impediment to the activities of the British Home Fleet, and a constant threat to the Allied convoys taking war supplies to the Soviet port of Murmansk via the Arctic convoy route round the North Cape. While in northern Norwegian waters the *Tirpitz* had been attacked on 16 occasions (6 times by RAF bombers and the other 10 times by Fleet Air Arm strike aircraft) between 28 January 1942 and 29 October 1944. By October 1944 the German battleship had moved some 200 miles south from Altenfjord, and now lay in Tromsofjord, some 3 miles to the west of Tromso town. On 29 October a force of 38 RAF Avro Lancaster four-engined bombers, operating from a Soviet base and each carrying one 12,000-lb 'Tallboy' penetration bomb, set off to attack the *Tirpitz*, which was damaged at the stern by a near miss, the best the RAF bombers could manage in adverse bombing conditions of patchy cloud. Air Chief Marshal Sir Arthur Harris decided that another raid was in order, and Operation 'Paravane' was launched as soon as the weather permitted, on 12 November, by 32 Lancasters each armed with a single 'Tallboy'. Poor liaison meant that German fighter cover from Bardufoss did not appear, and the Lancasters were able to enjoy perfect bombing practice. The *Tirpitz* was hit by at least two bombs (another three close alongside causing additional damage) and capsized. The ship came to rest with her superstructure on the bottom of Tromsofjord, and of the 1,000 or so men trapped inside her, some 85 were rescued when a hole was cut in the ship's exposed bottom. The *Tirpitz* had previously survived some 19 bomb hits (including one 12,000-lb and five 1,600-lb weapons) in raids which had cost the British 32 aircraft (13 RAF and 19 Fleet Air Arm).

Paukenschlag (drum roll) German U-boat offensive off the eastern coat of the USA (January/June 1942). The operation was planned by Admiral Karl Dönitz, commander of Germany's U-boat arm, to capitalize on the USA's unpreparedness for war, as evidenced along her eastern seaboard by lack of escorted convoys, continued illumination of navigation aids and lack of coastal black-out. Dönitz decided on the operation during 9 December 1941, just two days after the USA's entry into World War II, but had to contend with the fact that while he wished to despatch a first strike wave of 12 Type IXC boats, he could in fact send only 5 because Hitler insisted that the 6 boats on watch round the Straits of Gibraltar should not be removed. The initial 5 boats arrived off the USA on 13 January, two days before 4 more Type IXC boats left Brest and Lorient to supplement their effort. Later even the relatively small Type VIIC boats crossed the Atlantic to this fruitful hunting ground, and from February Dönitz was able to extend his boats' area of operation to the Caribbean as far as Venezuela. This effort was greatly aided by the availability of a few Type XIV 'milch cow' boats, which were able to ferry over the Atlantic fuel and other supplies sufficient for about a dozen attack boats, allowing Dönitz to keep some 27 U-boats operational between Nova Scotia and British Guiana. This was the second 'happy time' for the U-boats, which sank some 455 ships (including many tankers) while operating up to 300 miles off the US eastern seaboard. These sinkings totalled some 196,243 tons in January, 286,613 tons in February, 354,489 tons in March, 276,131 tons in April, 451,991 tons in May and 416,843 tons in June. Losses of U-boats in the Atlantic and Caribbean during the same months were 1, 2, 3, 2, 1 and 2.

However, in April the USA initiated a limited convoy system, extended in May to nonstop convoys between Halifax and Key West, and together with increasing anti-submarine capability and skill, this began to whittle away Germany's advantages. These were already under threat at home by Hitler, who was unwilling that boats be despatched to the other side of the Atlantic at a time he felt the Mediterranean and Norway were 'zones of destiny'. Thus Grossadmiral Erich Raeder, commander-in-chief of the German navy, did not demur when Hitler insisted that of the 41 new U-boats delivered in the first half of 1942, 26 should be used off Norway and another 2 in the Mediterranean, leaving only 13 to replace the total of 13 boats Donitz had lost in the Atlantic. From June, therefore, Dönitz called his singleton boats out of US coastal waters to re-form the 'wolf packs' of the central Atlantic, and Operation 'Paukenschlag' was over, defeated as much by Hitler and Raeder as by the Americans.

Paula (i) German air operation designed to crush the remnants of the French air force (3 June 1940). The operation was planned by Generalfeldmarschall Hermann Goering, and used II, IV and V Fliegerkorps (1,200 bombers) escorted by 350 fighters of Fliegerführer Nr 3 to attack air stations and depots in the region of Paris. Moderate casualties were suffered by both sides, but the German offensive failed to secure its primary objective of eliminating French air strength before the opening of Operation 'Rot' on 5 June.
(ii) German operation against Yugoslav partisans operating in Serbia (1943).

Paula Linie (Paula line) Designation of the German defence line on the River Sillaro in northern Italy. Like most of the secondary defence lines prepared by the Germans along rivers in northern Italy, the 'Paula Linie' had only moderately effective defences, and was breached by General W. Anders II Polish Corps (3rd Carpathian and 5th Kresowa Divisions) and Lieutenant General S. C. Kirkman's British XIII Corps (10th Indian Division) of Lieutenant General Sir Richard McCreery's British 8th Army on 15 April 1945. The defence lay in the hands of General Eugen Meindl's I Parachute Corps (26th Panzer Division, 1st and 4th Parachute Divisions, and 278th and 305th Divisions) of General Traugott Herr's German 10th Army. The British corps attacked north-west with the strategic object of punching through the German lines of communication to the north-east and Austria, causing them to fall back from Bologna, to the west of which the US 5th Army of Lieutenant General Lucian K. Truscott was very temporarily stalled. Anders's forces entered Bologna on 21 April, by which time the Americans were pushing through to the valley of the River Po in hot pursuit of General Joachim Lemelsen's German 14th Army. It was at this stage that Generaloberst Hans von Vietinghoff-Scheel realized that the end for his Army Group 'C' must come sooner rather than later, and that despite Hitler's orders to the contrary he must seek a rapid surrender to avoid needless casualties.

Peanut American codename (semi-official) for Generalissimo Chiang Kai-shek.

Pedestal British supply convoy to Malta (11/13 August 1942). The operation was undertaken as efforts to resupply Malta during June from the British bases at each end of the Mediterranean had failed, but the island's fighter strength had been bolstered most usefully by aircraft ferried in from the west and flown to the island. This meant that Malta was in a strong position to beat off the efforts of the Italian Regia Aeronautica and the German X Fliegerkorps, and also to aid incoming convoys during the last and most fraught stage of their voyages. The failure of the June efforts had provided useful tactical lessons, however, and 'Pedestal' was planned with a diversionary convoy from Alexandria, and considerably greater air power for the convoy escort.

The whole operation was led by Vice Admiral E. N. Syfret, commanding Force H, and his escort force included Rear Admiral A. L. St G. Lyster's carrier squadron (the *Victorious*, *Indomitable* and *Eagle* with 72 fighters) later supplemented by the *Furious*, which was to fly off 38 Supermarine Spitfire fighters to increase Malta's air strength. Other units of Syfret's command were the battleships *Nelson* and *Rodney*, 7 cruisers (one of them the AA ship *Cairo*) and 24 destroyers. Of this overall strength, Rear Admiral H. M. Burrough was to take the cruisers *Nigeria*, *Kenya*, *Manchester* and *Cairo* together with 12 destroyers through to Malta as close escort for the 13 merchantman and tanker. Syfret planned to operate to the west of the Sicilian Narrows with the rest of his force, strengthened by the 8 destroyers previously used to escort the *Furious*, until Burrough returned with the close escort. Underway refuelling capability would be available from two oilers escorted by four corvettes. The last component of this large plan was a force of 8 British submarines, of which some were to patrol off Italian bases and the others to the north of the convoy's route in a position to intercept any Italian warships heading south to attack the convoy. Syfret met the convoy off the River Clyde on 3 August, and convoy plus escort passed through the Straits of Gibraltar on 10 August, the day on which the diversionary convoy provided by the British Commander-in-Chief, Mediterranean (Admiral Sir Henry Harwood) left Port Said under escort of Rear Admiral Sir Philip Vian's 15th Cruiser Squadron. The diversionary convoy turned back on 11 August, but Vian led his forces in a gunfire attack against Axis positions on Rhodes during 13 August before returning to Egypt.

However, the Axis powers were well aware of what was under way, and agents on Algeciras (opposite Gibraltar on the Spanish mainland) relayed news of the convoy as it passed through the Straits of Gibraltar, allowing the Germans and Italians to set in motion a considerable offensive plan despite the unavailability of Italy's 4 battleships for lack of fuel. Involved in the Axis planning were Admiral Arturo Riccardi (head of the Italian navy), General Rino Corso Rougier (head of the Italian air force), Generalfeldmarschall Albert Kesselring (*Oberbefehlshaber Süd*) and Admiral Weichold (Germany navy liaison officer to the Italian navy), who had at their disposal 16 Italian and 5 German submarines (tasked with attacking the convoy between the Straits of Algiers and the Sicilian Narrows), 784 aircraft (447 bombers, 90 torpedo-bombers and 247 fighters tasked with attacks on the convoy from as far to the west as they could operate), 18 torpedo craft (tasked with attacks on the convoy between Cape Bon and the island of Pantelleria) and a major surface force of 6 cruisers and 11 destroyers (tasked with finishing off the convoy in conjunction with air attacks). The Axis powers had thus grouped powerful forces to prevent the arrival of a convoy on which the continued defiance of Malta depended, especially as the tanker *Ohio* was bringing in the fuel on which the defence effort rested.

Axis aircraft started to shadow convoy W.S.21S and its escort from the morning of 11 August, and from this time it was clear that determined resistance would be encountered by the Allied operation. The Germans drew first blood, the *U-73* torpedoing and sinking the aircraft-carrier *Eagle* at 13.15 on 11 August half way between Algiers and the southern tip of Majorca. This valuable if elderly campaigner had played a decisive part in Mediterranean operations, in the course of nine ferry trips flying off 183 Spitfires to Malta during 1942. The escorting destroyers salved some 900 of her crew of 1,160. Shortly after this the *Furious* completed her flying-off operation and turned back to Gibraltar, the destroyer *Wolverine* of her escort ramming and sinking the Italian submarine *Dagabur*. At 20.00 some 36 German bombers evaded the British fighter screen and attacked the convoy without success, though the AA guns of the warships claimed several victims among the attackers. Worse was in store for 12 August, when the Hawker Sea Hurricane fighters took a heavy toll of two Axis air raids launched during the morning from the bases at Decimomannu and Elmas in Sardinia. Some 100 aircraft were despatched, and the attackers lost 28 of their number for little real gain other than slight damage to one freighter (which straggled and was finished off during the night by an Italian torpedo boat) and a near miss for the carrier *Victorious* (on whose armoured flightdeck a bomb broke up). The most damaging raid of the day arrived at 18.35, and these 100 aircraft launched a well co-ordinated attack that resulted in considerable damage to the carrier *Indomitable*, causing her airborne aircraft to be shifted to the *Victorious*, now the only workable British carrier left. The destroyer *Foresight* was also hit, being abandoned and sunk later by a British torpedo. Some recompense was gained by the destroyer *Ithuriel*, which sank the Italian submarine *Cobalto*.

Then at 19,00, just to the north of Bizerta, Syfret turned back with the main strength of Force H, leaving the convoy under the close escort of Burrough's force. This was the turning point of 'Pedestal' for just one hour later the Italian submarines *Axum* and *Dessie* launched 8 torpedoes at the British force. Five of these struck home, sinking the AA cruiser *Cairo* and badly damaging the flagship *Nigeria*, which turned back for Gibraltar, and the tanker *Ohio*. Another air attack followed, the fighter cover from Malta having just turned for home as the convoy lacked its only two fighter direction ships, the *Nigeria* and *Cairo*. This attack by 20 aircraft damaged 2 more merchantmen that were picked off in the night by Italian torpedo boats, and to cap this tale of early evening disaster, the Italian submarine *Alagi* sank another merchantman and damaged the cruiser *Kenya* at 22.00. It was now the turn of the torpedo boats, which in two attacks early on 13 August (by 1 boat at 01.30 and by 2 boats between 03.15 and 04.30) sank 4 more merchantmen and the cruiser *Manchester*, and damaged another merchantman as the convoy hugged Cape Bon.

The German and Italian forces were now poised to finish off convoy W.S.21S, but then fell out with each other over the question of fighter support, which was sufficient to escort the bombers or the 2 squadrons of Italian cruisers (2 ships from Cagliari and 4 ships from La Spezia) but not both. Kesselring and Fougier wanted bomber escort, and Weichold and Riccardi demanded cruiser escort, a dilemma arbitrated by Benito Mussolini in favour of the air commanders. It was the wrong decision, for the two attacks (the first by 12 German aircraft and the second by 5 Italian aircraft) launched during the morning of 13 August succeeded in sinking only 1 more merchantman, whereas the abandoned surface vessel attack (by 6 cruisers and 11 destroyers) would almost certainly have destroyed the remnants of the convoy, even if heavy losses to the Italians had been caused by the six British submarines covering the last leg of the route to Malta. To add injury to insult, the Italian cruiser force was intercepted by the British submarine *Unbroken* to the north of Sicily as the Italians were returning to port. The *Unbroken* scored torpedo hits on the heavy cruiser *Bolzano* and the light cruiser *Muzio Attendolo*, causing each of them damage that took more than a year to repair. The last Axis success was the sinking of a straggling merchantman by German aircraft at 19.00 on 13 August.

Supported by 1 destroyer and 2 minesweepers, the desperately important *Ohio* limped into Malta on 15 August after fighting off more air attacks, finding in Grand Harbour 4 other merchantmen. Burrough had turned back as planned at 16.00 on 13 August, and 'Pedestal' had got to Malta some 32,000 tons of supplies from the 85,000 tons loaded in the Clyde. This delivery allowed Malta to hold out, while the 10,000 tons of fuel delivered by the *Ohio* allowed the Malta-based strike aircraft and submarines to return to the offensive at just the right time to cripple the Axis cross-Mediterranean supply effort designed to allow Generalfeldmarschall Erwin Rommel's forces to inflict the decisive defeat on the British forces in Egypt. 'Pedestal' was the last of the major supply operations to Malta, and while it was a tactical defeat for the British, it secured longer-term strategic success in the Mediterranean and North Africa.

Penitent Plan by Field Marshal the Hon. Sir Harold Alexander's 15th Army Group to take the ports of Split, Sibenik and Zara on the coast of Yugoslavia (spring 1945) as a means of shipping the British 8th Army across the Adriatic Sea to capitalise on the success of Marshal Tito's Yugoslav forces by driving north into Austria. Alexander had long been obsessed with the need to outflank the German defences in northern Italy, where the Allies and the Germans were nicely balanced, and at the time when it was assumed that the 15th Army Group would reach the River Adige by the winter of 1944 he had ordered that three British divisions be prepared for withdrawal from the line for training in amphibious operations; this initial plan supposed a major amphibious operation across the Adriatic, but Tito's successes along the coast led Alexander to revise his scheme, which was now that light forces and commandos should be landed at the three ports in question to aid Tito and to develop the ports and their inland communications so that the 8th Army could be moved across the Adriatic for a rapid development into southern Austria.

However, it was too late by the time Alexander had formulated his scheme, for the Allied armies had not pushed far enough north by the advent of winter, the US chiefs-of-staff were opposed to the development of another operational front in the Mediterranean theatre, the growing civil war in Greece was absorbing three divisions (the 4th Indian Division and the British 4th and 46th Divisions of the British X Corps), and Tito was becoming totally disillusioned with the half-hearted support he was receiving from the Western Allies, especially as politically-sympathetic Soviet forces were already operating in northern and eastern Yugoslavia. Winston Churchill also pointed out that Yugoslav operations by the British in February 1945 were far too late to have any material effect on the outcome of the war.

Perch Deep outflanking movement by Major General G. W. E. J. Erskine's British 7th Armoured Division within Lieutenant General G. T. Bucknall's British XXX Corps (12/14 June 1944). The object of this operation was to break past the sterling defence of Generalleutnant Fritz Bayerlein's Panzer-Lehr Division of XLVII Panzer Corps at Tilly-sur-Seules by a south-west advance towards Caumont before the division wheeled south-east to take Villers Bocage, and so deepen the British position to the west of Caen. Support for this bold move was provided by the British 50th Division, with the British 1st Airborne Division available for paradropping should the situation warrant it. In a wider context, Lieutenant General Sir Miles Dempsey hoped that this operation would allow his British 2nd Army to break south-east across the River Orne into the better tank country around the upper reaches of the River Aure. The offensive made some progress, but was stalled by the excellent defence of the Panzer-Lehr Division and by the inability of the 50th Division to move up in close support of the overextended 7th Armoured Division.

Perpetual Allied Eastern Task Force landing at Bougie in Algeria during Operation 'Torch' (11 November 1942).

Performance Partially successful breakout of Norwegian merchantmen, supported by British warships, from Sweden to the UK (1/4 April 1942). This operation was a logical successor to a similar effort in January 1941, when some 5 Norwegian merchantmen had broken out through the Skagerrak from Gothenberg and reached the UK under escort of two cruiser and destroyer forces despatched to their aid by Admiral Sir John Tovey, commanding the Home Fleet, and a second effort was ordered on 11 March 1942. Weather and operational problems caused the operation to be postponed to 1 April, when 10 merchantmen left Gothenberg. No aircraft or warship cover could be provided during the first day, but on 2 April a force of 6 destroyers and units of RAF Fighter and Coastal Commands were despatched. But 5 of the merchantmen were lost in the Skagerrak to determined efforts by German surface forces, 1 was so severely damaged that the British destroyers sank her, 2 returned to Gothenberg, and only 2 reached the UK.

Persecution Landing by Major General H. H. Fuller's US 41st Infantry Division at Aitape on the northern coast of New Guinea, undertaken with the same division's landing at Hollandia and complemented by the landing of Major General F. A. Irving's US 24th Infantry Division at Tanahmerah Bay slightly farther to the west of Hollandia (22 April 1944). This was part of the scheme devized by General Douglas MacArthur's South-West Pacific Area for Lieutenant General Robert L. Eichelberger's US I Corps of Lieutenant General Walter Krueger's US 6th Army in a rapid 'coastal-hopping' campaign designed to move the US forces as rapidly as possible westwards along the north coast of New Guinea in preparation for a return to the Philippines. 'Persecution' was the first of this series, and was undertaken after a careful programme of misinformation which persuaded Lieutenant General Hatazo Adachi that his Japanese 18th Army was to be threatened by a frontal assault in the area of Wewak, the next logical target for the combined Australian and US forces that were just completing the reconquest of the Huon peninsula area of New Guinea, where US forces were operating along the coastal region north of the Finisterre and Saruwaged ranges, and the Australians in the Markham and Ramu valleys farther inland. The Hollandia and Aitape operations were thus highly successful masterstrokes, undertaken with the support of Rear Admiral D. E. Barbey's 7th Amphibious Force of the US 7th Fleet (Vice Admiral Thomas Kinkaid) and Lieutenant General George C. Kenney's US 5th Air Force together with elements of the Royal Australian Air Force. Close air support of the landings was entrusted to a force of eight escort carriers provided by the US 5th Fleet. The invasion forces sailed from Finschhafen and Goodenough Island on 16/18 April, and

Petersburg

rendezvoused with the carrier force on 20 April.

US estimates had put the Japanese strength at some 14,000 in Hollandia (where the real strength was in fact about 11,000, most of them administrative troops) and about 3,500 in Aitape (where the real strength was about 1,000), and the Japanese command was in total disarray at the time, the 18th Army having just come under control of the 2nd Area Army, which had ordered Adachi to pull his 3 divisions back from the area of Madang and Wewak to Hollandia, the commander of the 6th Air Division having just been relieved for the loss of most of his aircraft to the series of devastating raids launched against the Hollandia region and its airfields by the USA Fast Carrier Task Force between 30 March and 3 April, and Rear Admiral Endo having arrived from Wewak at the end of March to take over command of the region's naval forces. This meant that local command had devolved on Major General Kitazono, previously a transport force commander near Wewak, who had arrived only 10 days before the American invasion.

In the landings the 24th Infantry Division came ashore unopposed at Tanahmerah Bay and moved east to link up with the 41st Infantry Division's beach-head at Hollandia, where two regimental combat teams had come ashore against light opposition. At Aitape the 163rd Regimental Combat Team of the 41st Infantry Division also landed without serious problems from the Japanese, who had moved inland as the Americans landed. The 24th and 41st Infantry Divisions linked up on 26 April, and the region's three airfields were soon in service for Allied aircraft.

The Imperial General Headquarters saw that this American move required a complete reassessment of the Japanese position in New Guinea, and Adachi was on 2 May ordered to forget the 1943 defence line (running through Wakde and Sarmi) in favour of a new line running though Biak Island and Manokwari, though on 9 May this revised defence line was altered to one running from Sorong to Halmahera, with Biak and Manokwari to be held only as outposts since Allied air attacks from Hollandia had already begun against targets in Western New Guinea, in the process causing severe damage to the convoy bringing in the Japanese 32nd and 35th Divisions to reinforce the Japanese 2nd Area Army in that area. The 32nd Division had lost one regiment and all its artillery, while the 35th Division was now little more than four battalions strong with only very limited artillery support. Adachi was now ordered to fall back some 400 miles to join the 2nd Area Army, but realized that an inland retreat round the US positions in his rear was impossible, so he decided on a do-or-die counterattack on Aitape and Hollandia, where the US I Corps had set about preparing a defence against the inevitable counterattack, which Adachi launched on 10 July after the US I Corps had been reinforced by Major General William H. Gill's US 32nd Infantry Division of Major General Charles P. Hall's US XI Corps. The Japanese were held with little difficulty, Adachi calling off his offensive on 3 August, and their dead at Aitape and Hollandia were 8,370 and 4,441 respectively to US figures of 440 and 87 respectively. Even while Adachi was making these last desperate attempts to effect a breakthrough to the rest of the Japanese forces on New Guinea, MacArthur had pre-empted him with a series of devastating moves (to Wakde Island on 17 May, Biak Island on 27 May, Numfoor on 2 July and Sansapor on 30 July), that completely isolated the Japanese in New Guinea. Operation 'Persecution' was thus a strategic stroke of the first magnitude.

Petersburg Allied contingency plan for the evacuation of New Guinea in the event that the Japanese managed to take Guadalcanal in the Solomons chain.

Petworth Allied codename for the Italian island of Lampedusa to the south-west of Malta.

Phoenix Designation of the breakwaters for 'Mulberry' artificial harbours, made from concrete caissons sunk to constitute an outer breakwater.

Picador Version of 'Barrister', intermediate between this initial plan and the fully developed 'Menace'.

Piccadilly Fly-in strip and stronghold for Operation 'Thursday', otherwise the 2nd Chindit Expedition (March 1944) of Major General O. C. Wingate's 3rd Indian Division. 'Piccadilly' was located to the north-west of Bhamo in the great eastern loop of the River Irrawaddy by that town. This was to be one of the two landing strips for Brigadier J. M. Calvert's 77th Indian Infantry Brigade, and once this brigade had moved out to its operational area, the 'stronghold' battalion of Brigadier W. D. A. Lentaigne's 111th Indian Infantry Brigade was to land and set up its fortress position. Just before the launch of Operation 'Thursday' on 5 March, it was discovered by air reconnaissance that there were signs of activity on 'Piccadilly', and this strip was dropped from Wingate's plans, the whole of the 77th Indian Infantry Brigade being landed instead at 'Broadway'.

Picket I British operation to deliver nine Supermarine Spitfire fighters to Malta (21 March 1942). The aircraft were flown off the carrier *Eagle*.

Picket II British operation to deliver seven Supermarine Spitfire fighters to Malta (29 March 1942). The aircraft were flown off the carrier *Eagle*.

Pierson Designation of the first objective for the British X Corps in General Sir Bernard Montgomery's 8th Army during the 2nd Battle of El Alamein (24 October 1942). Running north and south just to the west of Kidney Ridge, 'Pierson' was to be reached by the British 1st and 10th Armoured Divisions by dawn on 24 October after advancing through the corridors cleared by the infantry formations of the British XXX Corps.

Pigstick British plan for the landing of one division at the southern end of the Mayu peninsula in the Arakan region of Burma (spring 1944) to help in the destruction of the Japanese forces pinning the 5th and 7th Indian Divisions of Lieutenant General A. F. P. Christison's XV Corps on the 'Tunnels' road between Wabyin and Kwazon. The operation was a response to Lieutenant General T. Hanaya's Operation 'HA', in which his 55th Division had spoiled XV Corps' offensive of December 1943 and then launched a counteroffensive. The effective use of Lieutenant General Sir William Slim's 14th Army air transport strength allowed the 5th and 7th Indian Divisions to hold out despite the Japanese investment, and 'Pigstick' was designed by Admiral Lord Louis Mountbatten's South-East Asia Command to regain the initiative. The plan meant that Operation 'Tarzan' would have to be abandoned, but was deemed feasible if the Chinese forces in Yunnan would go over to the offensive to distract Japanese attentions in northern Burma. Severe logistical and political difficulties intervened (centring respectively on lack of amphibious capability and on Generalissimo Chiang Kai-shek's refusal to permit a Chinese offensive until an amphibious operation had retaken the Andaman Islands, Moulmein or Rangoon, or until the British and Indians had taken Lashio or Manadalay), and on 9 January the plan was cancelled. By this time Slim had prepared only initial plans, which called for an advance by the 5th and 7th Indian Divisions towards the tip of the Mayu peninsula, covered by detached brigades inland in the Kaladan and Lemro valleys, while one division (probably the British 2nd Division) landed at the tip of the Mayu peninsula and crossed the River Mayu estuary to cut the Japanese lines of communication before the combined Allied force advanced overland to take Akyab.

Pig Trough Projector used by the Royal Navy. This device was fitted with an anti-roll system, and was designed to fire the Short Aerial Mine anti-aircraft weapon.

Pilgrim Definitive British plan to take the Portuguese island groups in the Atlantic (July 1941). This plan combined the previous Operations 'Thruster' (the Azores), 'Springboard' (Madeira) and 'Puma' (the Canaries and the Cape Verdes) into a single operation to be undertaken by one infantry division plus detachments of the special forces (about 24,000 men in all), escorted by 1 battleship, 4 aircraft-carriers, 3 cruisers and 27 destroyers, and supported once ashore by 2 squadrons of RAF fighters. The men and landing craft for this operation were kept under orders for the last six months of 1941, though the task was simplified after the receipt of news that in the event of any German invasion of the Iberian peninsula the Portuguese government would evacuate itself to the Azores, whereupon it would accept British or American forces into the islands. The plan was eventually cancelled in February 1942 when more useful commitments for the landing craft and naval forces were fixed.

Pillar Box Multi-barrel projector used by the royal Navy for the launching of Short Aerial Mine anti-aircraft weapons.

Pinetree Allied codename for the headquarters of the US 8th Air Force.

Piperack British electronic countermeasures system to jam the airborne interception radar of German night-fighters (1944/1945).

Pirate Amphibious training exercise undertaken by the British I Corps in preparation for Operation 'Overlord' (1943).

Pistol Airborne raid by the 2nd SAS on German targets in the Saverne gap in France (15 September 1944).

Plan 21 Plan prepared by Lieutenant General Shojiro Iida's Japanese 15th Army for an invasion of Assam at the end of 1942. The object of this offensive was to capitalize on the Japanese successes in Burma (before the end of the campaign with the 1942 spring monsoon) by advancing into Assam against British and Indian forces still trying to reorganize themselves after their losses in the Burma campaign. Plan 21 called for the 33rd Division to advance from Kalewa to take Dimapur and Silchar, for the 18th Division (reorganized as a mechanized formation) to pass through the 33rd Division to deal with any counterattack and take Golaghat, and for a detachment of the 18th Division to advance up the Hukawng valley to take Ledo. The plan was cancelled on 23 December 1942.

Plan Dog US Navy contingency plan to aid the UK in a war with Germany and Italy whilst the USA was still at peace with Japan (spring 1941).

Plan X Allied plan for the reconquest of Burma as far south as the line between Lashio and Kalewa (1943). This could not be undertaken fully in 1943 because of Japanese moves and an Allied lack of strength, but began in October 1943 with the advance of Lieutenant General Joseph W. Stilwell's Chinese Army in India forces (the Chinese 22nd, 30th and 38th Divisions). Stilwell was unhappy that no major British offensive was planned for north and central Burma in 1943, and feared that the Japanese would use this lack of opposition to undertake their own operation, namely an advance into northeastern India, where the vital supply road to China was being built from the railhead at Ledo. Stilwell therefore decided on a spoiling offensive towards Myitkyina through the Hukawng valley and Lieutenant General N. Tanaka's 18th Division of Lieutenant General Renya Mutaguchi's Japanese 15th Army.

Progress through the Hukawng valley was slow as a result of Tanaka's careful and effective delaying tactics, and it was only with the arrival of Brigadier General Frank Merrill's US 5307th Provisional Regiment in late February 1944 that greater progress was made, the Chinese pinning the Japanese while the Americans undertook hooking movements to bring them into the rear of the Japanese blocks. The Chinese and American forces closed in on Myitkyina during May 1944, but failed to take this vital city against determined Japanese resistance, and it was only with the arrival of the 77th Indian Brigade at the end of the 2nd Chindit Expedition (Operation 'Thursday') that the Allies were able to take Myitkyina as the Japanese evacuated it on 3/4 August. However, the essentials of Plan X then matured towards the end of 1944 as Stilwell's last offensive as chief-of-staff to Generalissimo Chiang Kai-shek and US commander in the China-Burma-Indian Theater.

Apart from expelling the Japanese from northern Burma, the primary object of this renewed offensive was to reopen land communications with China via the Burma Road from Mandalay once this had fallen to the British, though Stilwell planned a link road between the transport heads at Ledo on the Ledo Road and Mongyu on the Burma Road. The Japanese defence in this region was in the hands of the 53rd Division of Lieutenant General S. Katamura's Japanese 15th Army, through farther to the south lay the 18th and 56th Divisions of Lieutenant General Masaki Honda's Japanese 33rd Army, respectively covering the northern and north-eastern approaches to Mandalay. Now available to Stilwell's Northern Combat Area Command were Brigadier General J. P. Willey's Mars Force, General Sun Li-jen's New Chinese 1st Army (Chinese 30th and 38th Divisions), and General Liao Yueh-shang's New Chinese 6th Army (Chinese, 14, 22nd and 50th Divisions), while operating in close touch in southern Yunnan were the 11th and 20th Army Groups of General Wei Li-huang's Chinese 'Y' Force. Stilwell could also call on the British 36th Division provided by Admiral Lord Louis Mountbatten's South-East Asia Command by General Sir George Giffard's 11th Army Group, which became Lieutenant General Sir Oliver Leese's Allied Land Forces South-East Asia on 12 November 1944.

The Allied advance began on 15 October 1944. In the west the British 36th Division moved south from Mogaung towards Indaw (captured on 10 December 1944), Myitson (21 February 1945), Mogok (19 March) and Kyaukme (31 March). In the centre the New Chinese 6th Army moved on Shwegu (7 November 1944) and across the upper reaches of the River Shweli to Hsipaw (16 March 1945). And in the east the New Chinese 1st Army with aid from the Chinese 'Y' Force advanced from Myitkyina to Bhamo (15 December 1944) and Lashio (7 March 1945). All these forces were aided by the implementation of Operation 'Extended Capital' to their west during the same period, and linked up with each other between 24 and 30 March in the area of Hsipaw, the Chinese 'Y' Force having met the New Chinese 1st Army at Mongyu on 27 January.

The usual problems had been encountered in the course of this large-scale operation, though added difficulties were the strained relations of Stilwell and Chiang Kai-shek, and the inroads of the Japanese Operation 'ICHI' in China proper. The first resulted in Chiang's insistence that Stilwell be removed, which occurred on 18 October 1944 after the American commander's promotion to full general. Stilwell was replaced by three US officers, namely Lieutenant General R. A. Wheeler as Deputy Supreme Commander, South East Asia Command, Lieutenant General Albert C. Wedemeyer as chief-of-staff to Chiang Kai-shek (as commander-in-chief of the Chinese forces) and Lieutenant General D. I. Sultan as commander of the Northern Combat Area Command. The second problem resulted in Chiang Kai-shek's removal of two divisions for deployment against 'ICHI' during the second half of December 1944. Stilwell was replaced just as his offensive was starting, and this led to certain modifications in the original concept of trapping the Japanese 33rd Army after the 53rd Division had held Bhamo for a month up to 15 December before fighting its way out to link up with the 56th Division just as Chiang Kai-shek called away the best two Chinese divisions in the theatre. In these circumstances Sultan could not hope to fulfil Stilwell's original intentions and instead concentrated on the opening of the road between Ledo and Mongyu by taking the Japanese-held portion between Bhamo and Lashio.

Plan Y Allied plan for the reconquest of central Burma (1943). This could not be undertaken during 1943 because of Japanese moves and an Allied lack of strength, but was then developed into Operation 'Capital' and then Operation 'Extended Capital' envisaging a three-pronged advance on Mandalay and Meiktila (the British and Indians from the west, the Americans and Chinese from the north, and the Chinese from the east).

Plan Z (i) Allied plan for the reconquest of southern Burma (1943). This could not be undertaken during 1943 for a variety of reasons, but was then developed into Operation 'Dracula' for the seizure of Rangoon and southern Burma. The collapse of the Japanese defensive effort in the region then led to the recasting of this plan as Operation 'Modified Dracula'.

(ii) Japanese scheme promulgated by Imperial General Headquarters in Tokyo during May 1943 for a major offensive/defensive strategy in the Pacific. The plan took no heed of the lessons of the Battle of

Plenaps

Midway and the implications of the Guadalcanal campaign, and ordained that a Japanese defensive perimeter should be established along a line from the Aleutians to Wake Island, to the Marshall Islands, to the Gilbert Islands, to Nauru Island, to the Bismarck Islands, to New Guinea and to the Malay barrier, with defensive garrison bastions in strategic areas and the Combined Fleet based at Truk for easy movement to any threatened sector. In the event of an Allied attack, the Japanese were to draw the attack towards the nearest main force, which would destroy the attacker with land- and carrier-based aircraft, Allied aircraft-carriers and then troop transports being specifically identified as the primary and secondary targets for Japanese aircraft. If the attackers managed to secure a beach-head, then the Japanese defence forces were under no circumstances to allow the inland development of the beach-head into an effective lodgement but were to counterattack until the beach-head had been totally eliminated.

The effect of Plan Z was thus to disperse Japanese forces in a large number of operationally defensive bastions over so large an area that supply and reinforcement were next to impossible as US submarine strength and carrierborne air strength grew. In addition, while it made sense to call on the defenders to fight a protracted battle until counter-offensive forces could be rushed in from the nearest main bastion, the Japanese plan made no allowances for the Americans' overwhelming *matériel* superiority, which permitted them to deal separately with the island garrison and the counteroffensive force moving into the area. Finally, the Americans merely ignored any bastions not on their direct axes of strategic advance, leaving them to be contained by secondary forces (and thus 'to wither on the vine') as the Americans pushed on to the next major objective. This meant that by the end of World War II the Pacific was dotted with isolated Japanese garrisons that had contributed nothing to Japan's war effort, and in the process starved and suffered dreadfully from the many endemic diseases of the region.

Plenaps Plan for the British, Dutch and American naval forces in the Far East to operate jointly in the event of war with Japan (December 1941). In the event the British and Dutch co-operated closely (as laid down in the A.B.C.2 scheme and the Anglo-Dutch proposals of 27 April 1941), while the Americans operated separately for the purpose of ensuring the defence of the Philippines, though maintaining touch with the British and Dutch in accordance with the A.B.C.1 agreement.

Plough Allied plan for the training of US and Canadian troops in the art of snow warfare (1943), the object being an Allied descent on German-held north Norway.

Ploughman Overall designation of the 'Siren Tour' campaign to upset the nocturnal rhythm of German life with long-range sorties by de Havilland Mosquito bombers which attacked a string of successive targets (1944/1945).

Plum Allied codename for the Philippine Islands.

Plunder Offensive by Field Marshal Lord Montgomery's British 21st Army Group across the River Rhine north of the Ruhr (23 March 1945). Other than 'Overlord', this was the largest operation undertaken by the British in World War II, the 21st Army Group being able to call on 1,284,715 men of Lieutenant General Sir Henry Crerar's Canadian 1st Army (8 divisions), Lieutenant General Sir Miles Dempsey's British 2nd Army (11 divisions including 3 armoured and 2 airborne, plus 4 armoured brigades, 1 infantry brigade and 1 commando brigade) and Lieutenant General William H. Simpson's US 9th Army (11 divisions including 3 armoured). The army group could call on 5,481 pieces of artillery (field, anti-tank and anti-aircraft).

The German opposition was found by Generaloberst Johannes Blaskowitz's Army Group 'H', which disposed of two armies in the form of General Günther Blumentritt's 25th Army and General Alfred Schlemm's 1st Parachute Army. The Germans expected that Montgomery's Rhine-crossing assault would take place downstream of Emmerich, and here the 25th Army, the stronger of Blaskowitz's two weak armies, was disposed. This left the 1st Parachute Army to cover the 45-mile sector between Emmerich and Duisburg with a mere 8 poor divisions in 3 corps (2 each with 3 divisions and 1 with 2 divisional formations). The strongest of these corps was II Parachute Corps, located at Rees, which had a mere 12,000 men. The 1st Parachute Army's sole mobile reserve was XLVII Panzer Corps with the 116th Panzer Division and the 15th Panzergrenadier Division, the designations covering a woeful weakness in armour, 35 tanks between them. Both the Oberkommando der Wehrmacht and Generalfeldmarschall Albert Kesselring, now the *Oberbefelhshaber West*, expected that the Allies would preface the obviously forthcoming operation with an airborne asault, probably against the high ground covering Wesel, the primary strategic target in the sector, and so allocated to Army Group 'H' a complete Flak corps to supplement the army group's already powerful artillery forces which included a *Volks* artillery corps and a *Volks* rocket-launcher brigade.

So far as Montgomery's plans were concerned, he had decided that the main effort should in fact be made upstream of Emmerich, in the sector where the British 2nd Army faced the German 1st Parachute Army. Montgomery's original plan had called for II Canadian Corps (Canadian 2nd Army) and the US XVI Corps (US 9th Army) to be allocated to Dempsey's 2nd Army for 'Plunder', but vociferous objections by the Americans led to a modification whereby the 9th Army undertook its parallel Operation 'Flashpoint' just to the right of the British 2nd Army. The Allied plan was thus for the British 2nd Army to cross the Rhine (between 900 and 1,500 ft wide in this area) at Rees against the right wing of the German II Parachute Corps (6th and 8th Parachute Divisions), at Xanten against the left wing of the German II Parachute Corps (7th Parachute Division) and the right wing of the German LXXXVI Corps (part of the 84th Division), and at Wesel against the centre of the German LXXXVI Corps (part of the 84th Division), and for the US XVI Corps of the 9th Army to cross at Walsum against the left wing of the German LXXXVI Corps (180th Division supported by the 'Hamburg' Division). Montgomery planned to reallocate Wesel to the Americans once the bridgehead on the eastern bank of the Rhine had been secured so that Simpson would have the use of two bridgeheads for the launch of his two-corps exploitation.

The whole operation was a monumental exercise in logistics, for the Allied planners had decided on a huge artillery preparation (the British 2nd Army had 60,000 tons of additional ammunition), and the establishment of bridges would also be a vast undertaking, requiring the services of 37,000 British and 22,000 American engineers. The 2nd Army had 30,000 tons of engineer equipment as part of its allocation of 118,000 tons of additional stores, and the US 9th Army had 138,000 tons of additional stores. But before the bridges could be thrown across the Rhine, the Allied assault formations had first to cross this mighty river and establish bridgeheads on the far bank. This task was undertaken by large numbers of assault craft and amphibious vehicles, while the movement of heavier weapons and bridging equipment was entrusted to a special Royal Navy detachment under Vice Admiral Sir Harold Burrough and equipped with 45 landing craft medium and a similar number of landing craft vehicle personnel. These were shipped to Ostend from the UK in a landing ship dock and then moved under their own power to Antwerp for collection and delivery to the Rhine by a fleet of army tank transporters.

Elaborate deception and camouflage schemes were adopted in an effort to conceal this mass of Allied preparation from the Germans, and it was also decided that while the artillery deluged the German forward positions on the Rhine, the Allied air forces would operate slightly farther to the rear in the period before the assault to seal off the battlefield. In this campaign RAF Bomber Command and the US 8th and 9th Air Forces flew some 16,000 sorties between mid-February and 21 March, and dropped 49,500 tons of bombs on the German rear areas, effectively destroying all lines of communication. Between 11 and 21 March this effort was supplemented by the tactical operations of the British 2nd Tactical Air Force and the US XXIX Tactical Air Command, which between them flew 7,300 sorties.

Plunder

Montgomery's huge artillery bombardment was launched at 17.00 on 23 March, and continued with breaks until 09.45 on the following morning. During the night the first assault crossings were successfully made. In the north Lieutenant General Sir Brian Horrocks's British XXX Corps put across just north of Rees 4 battalions of Major General T. Rennie's 51st (Highland) Division. Slightly farther to the south Lieutenant General Sir Neil Ritchie's British XII Corps put across opposite Xanten Major General C. M. Barber's 15th (Scottish) Division. Farther south still the 1st Commando Brigade crossed to Wesel and engaged the 180th Division in the wasteland that had been the city, and in the extreme south of the operation Major General John B. Anderson's US XVI Corps sent over Major General Leland S. Hobbs's 30th Infantry Division and Major General Ira T. Wyche's 79th Infantry Division between Wesel and Walsum.

The Germans, shattered by artillery fire on top of the weeks-long aerial bombardment and total defeatism at this last stage of the war, offered only minimal resistance and the Allies thus secured extensive bridgeheads all along their front. But dawn saw a reversal of this trend, especially in the north, where the German airborne formations began to fight back with extreme tenacity. Blaskowitz thought that he had perceived the nature of the Allied offensive, and so ordered XLVII Panzer Corps south from the 25th Army's sector with its 116th Panzer and 15th Panzergrenadier Divisions. The Germans had been deceived by their belief that the Allied strategy was plain, for they had anticipated an airborne operation at the same time as the crossing, probably deep in the German rear to create an air-head that would be held until relief/exploitation forces arrived to complete the vertical envelopment of the 1st Parachute Army with conventional ground operations.

However, Montgomery was tactically as astute as ever, and instead opted for an airborne drop (Operation 'Varsity') shortly after the crossing and barely 5 miles into the German rear at Hammilkeln to open the German centre. Under the command of Lieutenant General Matthew B. Ridgway's US XVII Airborne Corps, Major General E. Bols's British 6th Airborne Division and Major General William E. Miley's US 17th Airborne Division landed with minimal casualties, took or silenced most of the German heavy artillery batteries, and then drove west through the Diersfordter Forst to link up with the British XII Corps. XVII Airborne Corps also took key points on the River Issel, which runs parallel to the Rhine between Wesel and Emmerich, and which could have been used by the Germans as an effective fall-back line. Caught between two forces, the German 84th Division was virtually destroyed, and by nightfall on 24 March the Allies had secured a bridgehead some 30 miles wide and up to 5 miles deep.

It was now time for the consolidation and development phase so that Montgomery could commit his other 4 corps to the exploitation. By 26 March the development was well under way, with seven 40-ton bridges open to Allied traffic across the Rhine, allowing Montgomery to move into the bridgehead two important armoured formations, namely Major General L. O. Lyne's British 7th Armoured Division of the British XII Corps and Brigadier General John M. Devine's US 8th Armored Division of the US XVI Corps. By midnight on 28 March these two formations had permitted a considerable increase in the size of the Allied bridgehead, the 7th Armoured Division having pushed forward some 20 miles (as far as Borken) and the 8th Armored Division about 25 miles (as far as Haltern), with other elements of the British 2nd and Canadian 1st Armies driving into northern Germany and towards southern Holland, and the US 9th Army pushing south into the northern part of the Ruhr industrial complex between Duisburg and Essen. Still farther to the south Lieutenant General Courtney H. Hodges's US 1st Army of Lieutenant General Omar N. Bradley's US 12th Army Group had broken out of its Remagen bridgehead and swept both east and north. Leading elements of the US 9th and 1st Armies (the 8th Armored Division and Major General Maurice Rose's US 3rd Armored Division) met at Lippstadt east of the Ruhr during 2 April, trapping the remnants of Generalfeldmarschall Walter Model's Army Group 'B' (5th Panzerarmee and 15th Army) in the Ruhr pocket together with LXIII Corps of the crushed 1st Parachute Army. This pocket contained 19 divisions in 5 corps, which Hitler designated the 'Ruhr fortress'. The Allies pushed on to the east and their link-up with the Soviets on the River Elbe, leaving the Ruhr pocket to be crushed by the specially formed US 15th Army which was commanded by Lieutenant General Leonard T. Gerow with 18 divisions of the US 1st and 9th Armies in 5 corps. Model committed suicide on 21 April, and on the same day Generaloberst Josef Harpe of the 5th Panzerarmee surrendered the pocket, which yielded 325,000 prisoners including 29 generals.

Pluto Common designation of the Pipe Line Under The Ocean, a group of four 3-in. pipes laid some 170 miles across the English Channel from Sandown on the Isle of Wight to Cherbourg at the north of the Cotentin peninsula. The line was completed in July 1944, and allowed some 250,000 gallons of petrol to be pumped from the UK to France every day for the nourishment of the Allies' offensive effort.

Pointblank Overall designation of the combined bomber offensive undertaken by the British and US strategic bomber forces in Europe, and fixed at the Casablanca conference (January 1943) in the 'Pointblank Directive'. The primary object of the plan was to organize British and US strategic bombing efforts to ensure 'the progressive destruction and dislocation of the German military, industrial and economic system, and the undermining of the morale of the German people to a point where their capacity for armed resistance is fatally weakened'. Overall control of the offensive was entrusted to the British Chief of the Air Staff, Marshal of the Royal Air Force Sir Charles Portal, though the real implementation of the scheme was left to Air Chief Marshal Sir Arthur Harris (head of RAF Bomber Command) and Lieutenant General Ira C. Eaker (head of the US 8th Air Force).

Though the two air forces should have been able to dovetail their activities nicely, the British operating at night and the Americans by day, there remained fundamental differences of strategic aim which bedevilled the whole 'Pointblank' campaign, for whereas the Americans believed in selective attack on key industries and transport centres using precision daylight attacks, Harris remained firmly wedded to the concept of general area attack in the belief that there were no vital industries whose destruction could not be compensated by the use of alternatives, dispersed production and stockpiles. Harris thus opted for general attack which, he believed, would ultimately result in the total dislocation of the German war-making capability and thus the attainment of the objective of 'Pointblank'.

Within the original 'Pointblank' directive the primary objectives for Allied bombing were listed as U-boat construction yards, the German aircraft industry, transportation, oil plants and other targets in Germany's war industry. Other targets were mentioned, these including U-boat bases in western France, Berlin, industry in northern Italy, German warships in harbour, and (when the Allies invaded the continent) any targets tactically advantageous for continental operations. The directive was reviewed at the Washington conference in May 1943, and though the basic objects remained relatively unaltered, it was decided that the Allied bomber forces should also concentrate on the destruction more specifically of German fighter aircraft in the air, and on the production centres for such aircraft, the rationale being that the destruction of Germany's air strength was 'essential to our progression to the attack of other sources of the enemy war potential'. In other words, only the destruction of the Luftwaffe would permit the bomber forces to concentrate effectively on those targets whose destruction was sought in the original directive.

The plan was adopted in definitive form during June 1943, but was never implemented fully as a result of the tactical latitude given to the bomber force commanders in the UK, and in Italy when the US 15th Air Force started to operate from bases in that country. The Americans therefore continued with precision attacks, and the British with general attacks, and only rarely were the efforts co-ordinated so that the two different attack techniques were applied to the same targets.

Pöhn German operation against Soviet partisans operating in the area of the rail line between Brest-Litovsk and Pinsk (March 1943). This rail line was one of the primary lines of German communication in the central sector of the Eastern Front, a fact well appreciated by the Soviet high command in Moscow, which instructed its partisan forces based in the Pripet Marshes (on whose edges lies Pinsk) and other areas to strike at it whenever possible, and in particular when the Germans were preparing an offensive in the sector. The partisan operations that spurred 'Pöhn' were designed to reduce the flow of supplies and equipment towards Generalfeldmarschall Gunther von Kluge's Army Group 'Centre', by which Operation 'Zitadelle' was being prepared in the aftermath of the German disaster at Stalingrad.

Polaire Airborne operation by the French Force 136 to aid Laotian resistance groups operating against the Japanese near Xiengkhouang (1/27 December 1944).

Polarbär (polar bear) Airborne drop of a battalion of the Lehr-Regiment Brandenburg zbV 800 on Antimachia airfield on Kos (3 October 1943). The island had been occupied by the British on 14 September as a preliminary to Operation 'Accolade' for the capture of Rhodes, and by 17 September had established a garrison of some 1,600 men of the 1st Durham Light Infantry and No. 2909 Squadron of the RAF Regiment, supported by the Supermarine Spitfire fighters of No. 7 Squadron, South African Air Force; there were also some 4,600 Italians on the island. The overall British command was exercised at great range by Lieutenant General Sir Desmond Anderson, commander of the British III Corps in Persia and Iraq. The German counter to this occupation was planned by Generalfeldmarschall Maximilian Freiherr von Weichs, the *Oberbefehlshaber Südost*, who used one battalion of the 440th Grenadierregiment (stationed in Mytilene and Khios) and part of Generalleutnant Friedrich-Wilhelm Müller's 22nd Division (stationed in Crete) for the task of retaking the Aegean islands taken by the British during September. The German task force was shipped in four transports plus a few ferries and landing craft, and assaulted the island's north and south coasts at 06.00 on 3 October, just 30 minutes before the Brandenburg unit dropped on the airfield. The British could do no more than fight a delaying action with their ill-equipped troops, and by nightfall the Germans were in command of Kos, the survivors of the British garrison having fallen back into the mountains on the south coast by the early hours of 4 October. Only about 100 men were brought off by the Royal Navy, leaving 1,500 dead and prisoner in German hands. The Germans lost some 85 men, and had returned to their bases by 5 October, leaving a small garrison on the island.

Poppy Allied codename for New Caledonia Island.

Popular Designation of RAF photo-reconnaissance sorties by single-engined aircraft to gain overall coverage of the French coast. Undertaken mainly at low level, these operations helped Allied planners to develop a clear picture of the French coastline with a view to selection of landing sites for the Operation 'Overlord' landings.

Porcelain Allied codename for Kwajalein atoll in the Marshall Islands.

Port T Allied codename for Addu Atoll at the southern end of the Maldive Islands in the Indian Ocean.

Portcullis Designation of the last westward operation from Egypt to take supplies into Malta (1/9 December 1942). This convoy operation was undertaken after the success of Operation 'Stoneage' in November, and in it 4 merchantmen left Port Said on 1 December, being joined off Benghazi by one tanker ferrying furnace fuel for the naval surface forces based in Malta. The escort was provided by 4 cruisers of Rear Admiral A. J. Power's 15th Cruiser Squadron plus 10 destroyers. The merchantmen reached Malta on 5 December without any interference from the Germans and Italians, and all had been unloaded by 9 December.

Poseidon German occupation of Samos

Island (November 1943). At the time of the Italian armistice with the Allies in September 1943, the British had decided that Rhodes would be taken (probably by the 10th Indian Division and the 9th Armoured Brigade provided by General Sir Henry Maitland Wilson's Middle East Land Forces command) in Operation 'Accolade', but that operation required fighter cover which could only be provided from the three airfields on Kos. It was therefore planned that Kos should be taken as a preliminary to 'Accolade', and that at the same time Leros and Samos farther to the north should be occupied, the former as it possesses a good anchorage, and the latter as it covers the approaches to the Turkish port of Smyrna, where Allied troops and equipment would be landed in the event of Turkey entering the war on the Allied side after the successful implementation of 'Accolade'. It was also decided that these and smaller islands would be ideal bases from which Long-Range Desert Group and other raiding organizations could operate against German garrisons in the Aegean.

By the end of September 2,700 troops of Brigadier F. G. R. Brittorous's 234th Infantry Brigade had been delivered to these three main islands, and Brittorous had been appointed to command both the Leros garrison and the British forces in the Aegean. However, it soon became clear that Brittorous could not deal adequately with both tasks, and Major General H. R. Hall was appointed on 1 November to command in the Aegean, with his headquarters on Samos, where he arrived on 11 November. On the following day the Germans began their operation to take Leros, succeeding by 16 November. It was now clear that 'Accolade' could not be launched (especially as Kos had fallen to the Germans on 3/4 October), and that there was little point in maintaining any real presence in the Aegean, and it was decided that the surviving British garrisons should be evacuated, the British departure from Samos taking place without German interference on 19/20 November. The Germans were thus able to implement Operation 'Poseidon' without interruption.

Postern Combined US and Australian operation to clear Lieutenant General Hatazo Adachi's Japanese 18th Army from the Huon peninsula region of New Guinea (4 September 1943/26 April 1944). Under the overall command of General Douglas MacArthur, the South-West Pacific Area command had succeeded in defeating the Japanese Operation 'MO' aimed at Port Moresby, and by January 1943 had taken the Japanese beach-heads at Gona and Buna from which 'MO' had been launched. This provided the Allies with an ideal starting point for an advance along the northern coast of New Guinea as the first step in MacArthur's proposed 'Reno' counteroffensive towards the Philippines. Such an advance would form the left arm of a pincer (whose right arm would be the US Navy forces advancing up the chain of the Solomon Islands) designed to destroy the Japanese forces in New Guinea and also to cut off Lieutenant General Imamura's 8th Area Army in the Bismarck Archipelago.

At the beginning of 1943 the 18th Army had a mere one division in east New Guinea, but Imamura soon despatched to Wewak the 20th and 41st Divisions to bolster this formation, which was disposed farther to the southeast covering the Allied approaches to the Huon peninsula. During January Kangaforce of Lieutenant General E. F. Herring's I Australian Corps fought off several Japanese attempts to take Wau and its airfield, which would provide the Allies with a suitable base for operations in the Huon peninsula. Late in the month the 17th Australian Brigade was flown in to reinforce Kangaforce, and together these two Australian units drove the Japanese back to the coast. This persuaded Imamura that Lae was threatened, and he therefore forwarded the headquarters of the 18th Army and 7,000 men of the 51st Division from Rabaul. The men sailed in 8 transports escorted by 8 destroyers, but the convoy was spotted in the Bismarck Sea by Allied aircraft and heavily attacked on 1/2 March. All 8 transports were sunk, together with 4 of the destroyers, though the surviving 4 were able to rescue some 3,000 soldiers from the sea before returning to Rabaul.

There matters rested as both sides built up their forces. MacArthur had hoped to resume offensive operations in May, but delays to the

Postern

build-up of the 7th Amphibious Force meant that it was the end of June before Operation 'Postern' could be undertaken by MacArthur's revived forces (the US Alamo Force commanded by Lieutenant General Walter Krueger with the US 32nd and 41st Infantry Divisions, and the Australian New Guinea Force commanded by Herring with, at various times, the 3rd, 5th, 7th, 9th and 11th Australian Divisions). For air support MacArthur's ground elements had squadrons of the Royal Australian Air Force and of Major General George C. Kenney's US 5th Air Force. To protect his right flank as the main operations in the Huon peninsula got under way, MacArthur sent part of Alamo Force to take Woodlark and Trobriand Islands in Operation 'Chronicle' on 30 June, the same day that a battalion of the US 32nd Infantry Division's 162nd Infantry Regiment was landed at Nassau Bay to the south-east of Salamaua, the main Japanese bastion in the lower end of the Huon gulf, to link up with Major General S. G. Savige's 3rd Australian Division, whose 15th and 17th Australian Brigades were now the primary Australian units in the region. The 162nd Infantry Regiment was brought up to full strength and Savige's command (now the equivalent of three brigades) moved concentrically on Salamaua.

The fighting was as severe as the terrain, and slow progress was the order of the day, which fell in with MacArthur's plan to use Salamaua as a decoy to draw Japanese reserves from Lae, which was the first real objective of the offensive. At this stage the Japanese 18th Army had the 41st Division in Wewak, the 20th Division at Madang, and the remnants of the 51st Division at Salamaua and Lae. MacArthur's plan was to use mainly Australian forces at this stage of the offensive, and he had available (apart from the 3rd Australian Division) Major General G. A. Vasey's 7th Australian Division in Port Moresby and Major General G. F. Wootten's 9th Australian Division in Milne Bay. While the 3rd Australian Division pinned the Salamaua garrison, MacArthur completed planning for Lae, which was to be taken in a pincer movement by the 9th Australian Division (landed by sea on 4 September near Hopoi to the east of Lae) and the US 503rd Parachute Infantry Regiment (dropped on 5 September at Nazdab in the Markham valley to the north-west of Lae) supported by the 7th Australian Division (airlifted into Nazdab from 7 September after the Americans had cleared up local resistance). The whole operation worked just as planned, and resulted in the capture of Salamaua on 12 September (by Major General E. J. Melford's 5th Australian Division, which had replaced the exhausted 3rd Australian Division) and of Lae on 16 September.

MacArthur now controlled the Huon gulf and wasted no time in consolidation before harrying the off-balance Japanese. So on 21 September the US 7th Amphibious Force loaded the 9th Australian Division's 20th Brigade at Lae for an attack on Finschhafen. Major General Yamada was expecting an attack from Lae, and had thus disposed three-quarters of his force (reinforced by one regiment of the 20th Division) covering the southern and western approaches to Finschhafen. Thus there was only slight opposition to the 20th Australian Brigade's landing at Katika some 6 miles north of the town, though the Japanese later managed to check the brigade on the River Bumi as the Australians moved on Finschhafen. By 26 September the brigade had crossed the river and resumed its advance on the town, and after a heavy bombardment on 1 October the Australians stormed into Finschhafen as the Japanese pulled out.

MacArthur's plan now called for continued amphibious advance round the coast of the Huon peninsula, but it was first necessary to secure the left flank of the combined Australian and US forces by clearing the Japanese out of the valleys of the Markham and Ramu rivers on the inland side of the Saruwaged and Finisterre mountain ranges. So when Allied forces began to arrive in Nazdab, an independent company was sent probing up the Markham valley, this company taking the village of Kiaipit on 19 September after an advance on 30 miles. At Kiaipit the Japanese had built a landing strip, and this was rapidly developed so that from 21 September the 21st and 25th Australian Brigades could be flown in from Nazdab. By 4 October these two brigades had pushed forward to Dumpu in the Ramu valley, and here the headquarters of the 7th Australian Division were established. However, the Japanese controlled the passes over the Finisterre range leading down to Bogadjim on the coast just south of Madang, and Vasey appreciated that his division needed reinforcement before it could break through to the coast.

Back at Finschhafen, meanwhile, the rest of the Japanese 20th Division under Lieutenant General S. Katagiri had arrived from Madang to reinforce Yamada's remnant, which was holding the high ground round Satelberg, some 6 miles inland from Finschhafen. Katagiri launched a series of counterattacks from 16 September, but the 20th Australian Brigade fought these off and, after reinforcement by the 26th Brigade, the full 9th Australian Division went over to the offensive on 25 September, whereupon the Japanese fell back along the coast towards Sio, which the 20th Australian Brigade took on 15 January 1944 just before it was replaced by the 8th Australian Brigade of the 5th Australian Division, which took over from the 9th Australian Division.

The Japanese 20th and 51st Divisions were now in full retreat (the latter from Lae over the trackless Saruwaged range where it lost 2,100 of its 8,600 men), but both were cut off when the US 32nd Infantry Division landed its 126th Infantry Regiment at Saidor on 2 January 1944. Adachi ordered the survivors of the two divisions to make their way back to Madang as best they could to join up with the 41st Division brought forward from Wewak. The tribulations of the Japanese were enormous as they made their way northwest through the jungle, bypassing the US positions at Saidor wherever they could, and though Adachi tried to ferry in supplies by barge, these were generally intercepted and sunk. The survivors began to reach Madang in mid-February.

The 8th Australian Brigade reached Saidor on 10 February, allowing the US regiment to push forward towards Bogadjim aided by the seaborne delivery of two fresh battalions to Yalau Plantation on 5 March. Moves were also taking place inland, where the 15th and 18th Australian Brigades of the 11th Australian Division had relieved the 15th and 21st Australian Brigades of the 7th Australian Division at Dumpu from the beginning of January. On 20 January the two fresh brigades sallied forth, and by 22 January the 18th Australian Brigade had cleared the Kankiryo Saddle pass over the Finisterre range, while two days later the 15th Australian Brigade passed round the end of the range to threaten Bogadjim from the west. There followed a pause as the Allies consolidated, and it was only in March that the advance was resumed. On 21 March elements of the 18th Australian Brigade linked up with the US 126th Regiment from Saidor, and on 13 April the brigade took Bogadjim.

Operation 'Postern' was completed by the seizure of Madang (on 24 April by the 8th and 15th Australian Brigades) and Alexishafen (on 26 April by a battalion of the 8th Australian Division). At this time Major General A. J. Boase's 11th Australian Division replaced the 7th Australian Division in command of all Australian forces in the area. MacArthur's forces had already made the next jump along the coast of New Guinea, landing at Aitape and Hollandia on 22 April, so 'Postern' ended with a period of consolidation in the Huon peninsula as the Australians harried isolated Japanese pockets with active patrolling. Forces were also pushed forward to Hansa Bay (16 June), and patrols reached as far west as the River Sepik.

Postklystron German jammer against H2S and H2X radar.

Pot of Gold US plan to send forces into northern Brazil (1940).

P.Q. Designation of arctic convoys (together with a numerical suffix) plying the route from Iceland to ports in the northern USSR, and inaugurated in September 1941. This series was replaced by the J.W. series in December 1942.

Pounce Operation in Java by the British 5th Parachute Brigade Group (winter 1945). Under the command of Brigadier J. H. N. Poett, the brigade had been in India for Operation 'Zipper', and was moved to Malaya on 17 September 1945 before switching to Singapore and allocation to the British XV Corps. This corps was moved to Java in October, and the 5th Parachute Brigade left

195

for the island on 18 October as part of the British force intended to intern all Japanese troops and civilians on the island, and to keep peace (threatened by the extremist Indonesian nationalist faction) until the Dutch could send forces back to the East Indies to assume control of their colony. The 5th Parachute Brigade arrived in Batavia in December, and was judged ready for action on 20 December, and it was sent east to assume control of the Semarang region of north central Java, where lawlessness was rife. The brigade was grouped in Semarang by 14 January 1946, allowing the 49th Indian Brigade to return to the rest of the 23rd Indian Division around Batavia in western Java. Unlike the other British forces in Java, the 5th Parachute Brigade had a relatively uneventful sojourn on the island, and was relieved by the Dutch 'T' Brigade Group by 26 April before moving back to Singapore.

Priceless Overall designation of the Allied invasion of the Italian mainland after the fall of Sicily in Operation 'Husky'. The term was used in high command planning for the strategic objectives of General Dwight D. Eisenhower, the Allied Commander-in-Chief, Allied Forces in North Africa, working through General the Hon. Sir Harold Alexander's Allied 15th Army Group. The raw concept was developed in Operation 'Avalanche' and Operation 'Baytown', undertaken respectively by Lieutenant General Mark W. Clark's US 5th Army and General Sir Bernard Montgomery's British 8th Army.

Primrose British operation (16 April 1940) in which small Royal Marine and Royal Navy landings were made at Andalsnes, Aalesund and Molde in central Norway in preparation for larger landings planned for the recapture of Trondheim. The plan was developed into Operation 'Sickle'.

Princeton US outline plan for the recapture of the Visayas and Mindanao in the Philippines, and of Borneo and the Dutch East Indies (1943/1944).

Privet British aerial minelaying operations off Danzig.

Projekt 25 (project 25) Portion of Operation 'Marita' concerned with the conquest of Greece separate from that of Yugoslavia.

Providence Allied recapture of the area of Buna and Gona on the northern coast of Papua (20 November 1942/22 January 1943). Buna and Gona were the beach-heads from which the Japanese South Seas Detachment under Major General Tomitara Horii had launched the overland assault on Port Moresby in Operation 'MO', and the defeat of this Japanese offensive opened the logical necessity of depriving them of their beach-heads before the Allied forces of General Douglas MacArthur's South-West Pacific Area went properly over to the offensive against the Japanese bastions in the Huon gulf region. Under MacArthur's impatient overall command, operations were undertaken by Lieutenant General Sir Thomas Blamey's forces, consisting primarily of the 6th and 7th Australian Divisions and part of the US 32nd Infantry Division, supported by elements of the Royal Australian Air Force and US Army Air Forces under the control of Major General George C. Kenney's Allied Air Forces, South-West Pacific.

The task of driving the South Seas Detachment back over the Kokoda Trail fell mainly to the 16th and 25th Australian Brigades of the 7th Australian Division, and by 28 October 1942 the Australians had expelled the Japanese from the last of their prepared defensive positions on the Kokoda Trail, and began to come down off the northern slopes of the Owen Stanley range towards the northern plain of Papua, where the Japanese had established strong defensive perimeters around their beach-heads. Between 4 and 12 November effective air support enabled the 7th Australian Division to break through the Japanese positions in front of the River Kumusi and start the final drive towards the coast, where the Japanese had constructed a series of well sited and carefully built positions from Cape Endaiadere to Gona as the main defence for Buna and Sanananda. By 19 November the 16th Australian Brigade had been halted in front of Sanananda, and the 25th Australian Brigade in front of Gona.

MacArthur realized that there would have to be further reinforcement and resupply before Operation 'Providence' could start, and airfields were built at Popondetta and Dobodura for transport aircraft. Here the Allied forces came under the command of Lieutenant General E. F. Herring's I Australian Corps, the American forces being supervised by Lieutenant General Robert L. Eichelberger. Apart from the two Australian brigades that had moved up along the Kokoda Trail, other units were a battalion of the US 126th Infantry Regiment (across the Owen Stanleys by the Kapa Kapa Trail to reach Bofu on 16 November), the 2nd and 10th Australian Battalions (by air from Milne Bay on 5 October to secure the airstrip at Wanigela down the coast from Buna), the US 128th Infantry Regiment (by air from Port Moresby to Wanigela on 14 October) and the rest of the US 126th Infantry Regiment (by air from Port Moresby to Pongani by mid-November after the US 128th Infantry Regiment had sailed in native craft from Wanigela to prepare an airstrip). This allowed the main strength of the US 32nd Infantry Division to assemble at Pongani, some 30 miles south of the Japanese beach-head, and to start an advance up the coast to supplement the efforts of the 7th Australian. Division.

The US 32nd Infantry Division had been halted in front of Japanese outposts by 20 November. It was at this time that the Allied command was reorganized, the US 127th Infantry Regiment flown into Pongani to bring the US 32nd Infantry Division up to full strength, and the 21st and 30th Australian Brigades of the 6th Australian Division flown in to take over from the two exhausted brigades of the 7th Australian Division. There was also a command modification on the Japanese side, where Lieutenant General Hatazo Adachi assumed command of the newly formed Japanese 18th Army in New Guinea on 25 November. Adachi tried to run reinforcements and supplies into the Papuan beach-head, but Allied air power dealt very severely with these destroyer operations, and only a small number of men and a few supplies were delivered.

The Allies were now, it seemed, well placed to crush the Japanese, and after a determined 10-day assault the 21st Australian Brigade captured Gona on 9 December and so breached the northern side of the Japanese perimeter. But elsewhere the Allies failed to make significant progress against superb Japanese defence from excellent positions. With MacArthur's urging, Herring grouped his forces (strengthened by some tanks and the 18th Australian Brigade from Milne Bay) for the capture of Cape Endiaidere and Buna, leaving Sanananda to be mopped up after the southern breach had been made. The weather was appalling and the fighting desperately severe as the Allies pushed forward throughout December, picking off each Japanese position before they could advance to tackle the next. The task was completed only on 3 January 1943, leaving Sanananda to be tackled by the 18th Australian Brigade, the 127th Infantry Regiment (US 32nd Infantry Division) and the 163rd Infantry Regiment (US 41st Infantry Division). Sanananda was crushed between 12 and 16 January, and between then and 22 January the Australians and Americans mopped up along the coast to bring 'Providence' to a close. The whole Papua undertaking had cost the Japanese some 12,000 casualties, while those of the Americans were 2,800 and of the Australians 5,700. Fought at about the same time as the Guadalcanal battle, the campaign in 'Providence' provided striking evidence of the Japanese capability in defensive fighting, and provided little comfort for the operations ahead.

Publican Rocket-launched version of 'Foxer'.

Puddle Airborne reconnaissance operation by the 153rd Gurkha Parachute Battalion in the Myitkyina region of Burma (3 July 1943).

Pugilist-Gallop Breakthrough of the Mareth Line by the British 8th Army (20/27 March 1943). The comparative success of Operation 'Frühlingswind' and Operation 'Morgenluft' in February 1943 had persuaded Generalfeldmarschall Erwin Rommel and his Army Group 'Africa' that the threat of Lieutenant General K. A. N. Anderson's Allied 1st Army from the west had been contained, even if temporarily, and that the primary threat to the Axis powers' narrow beach-head in Tunisia came from the British

Pugilist-Gallop

8th Army of General Sir Bernard Montgomery in the south. Thus he removed the 15th and 21st Panzer Divisions from Generaloberst Jürgen von Arnim's 5th Panzerarmee for General Giovanni Messe's Axis 1st Army, which was to halt the advance of the 8th Army at Medenine in Operation 'Capri', launched and defeated on 6 March 1943.

There now followed an alteration of the Axis command in Tunisia when Rommel was recalled on 9 March. Von Arnim succeeded to the command of Army Group 'Africa', the 5th Panzerarmee was taken over by General Gustav von Vaerst, and Messe received an extremely able chief-of-staff in Generalmajor Fritz Bayerlein. The importance of the Tunisian beach-head to the Axis cause even at this late stage is attested by the fact that with the approval of Hitler and Mussolini Generalfeldmarschall Albert Kesselring, the German *Oberbefelhshaber Süd*, flew to Tunisia to confer with the senior Axis commanders and passed on the order that there was to be no further retreat, the beach-head being maintained between Cape Serrat in the north and Mareth in the south. To this end von Arnim's command was strengthened to 16 divisions by the delivery of the 'Hermann Goering' Panzer Division, the Division 'von Manteuffel' and the 999th Division, the last a formation of military prisoners being given a last chance to rehabilitate themselves. However, though the formation strength of the Axis was impressive, its manpower and weapon strengths were not, and many of the units were exhausted. Moreover, the German and Italian staffs were frequently at loggerheads with each other, and the Italians could not maintain anything like a significant supply of equipment, supplies and fuel to Army Group 'Africa' because of the depredations of the British air and naval forces based in Malta, now supplemented by Allied units from North-West Africa and the Western Desert. At the beginning of 1943 the Italians had available some 300,000 tons of shipping for the North Africa route, and of these some 87,000 tons had been sunk in January and 69,500 tons in February.

Meanwhile the Axis forces were faced with the threat of two very powerful Allied armies whose efforts were co-ordinated, under the overall command of General Dwight D. Eisenhower, by General the Hon. Sir Harold Alexander's 18th Army Group. On 14 March Alexander issued instructions to his command, to the effect that the Allied 1st Army was to maintain pressure against the 5th Panzerarmee in the north with its French XIX Corps, while Alexander took the US II Corps under army group command to harass the Axis lines of communication (in the centre of the sector, just north of Gabes) by advancing on Maknassy and Gabes, while the British 8th Army smashed through the Mareth Line defences in the south and drove on Gabes. With the Axis forces then compressed into a beach-head in central and northern Tunisia, the Allies would launch a concentric offensive to crush them by 15 May at the latest so that the schedule laid down at the Casablanca conference for Operation 'Husky' could be ensured.

Thus the scene was set for Operation 'Pugilist-Gallop', the British 8th Army assault on the Mareth Line, which was sited on a natural bottleneck between the Wadi Zeuss and the Wadi Zigzaou at the point at which the 8th Army hoped to wheel north into southern Tunisia round the Gulf of Gabes. Here the coastal strip is only some 22 miles wide, bounded at its north-eastern end by the Sebkra Oum ez Zessar marshes on the sea and at its south-western end by the Matmata hills, an ideal spot for an Axis mine-protected defence line just in front of Mareth town. Axis pioneers had been hard at work to improve the original French frontier defences, and the Mareth Line thus consisted of some 100,000 anti-tank and 70,000 anti-personnel mines laid in two main belts, one just behind the Wadi Zeuss and the other just forward of the Wadi Zigzaou. The belts were joined by subsidiary minefields, and the whole position was liberally strewn with barbed wire and mutually-covering 'nests' of pillboxes. The main features of the line were known to the British from French officers in the Allied forces, and from extensive photo-reconnaissance of the Axis developments.

The Axis static defences were entrusted to two Italian corps. Nearer the coast was General Orlando's XX Corps (the Young Fascist Division with 5 battalions, the Trieste Division with 6 battalions, the German 90th

Light Division with 6 battalions and the Spezia Division with 7 battalions). Nearer the Matmata hills was General Berardi's XXI Corps (the Pistoia Division with 5 battalions and the German 164th Light Division with 4 battalions). These essentially static formations were covered to the rear by the 15th Panzer Division (5 miles north-west of Mareth with 32 serviceable tanks), the 10th Panzer Division (south-west of Sousse) and the 15th Panzer Division (south-west of Gabes). The 10th and 15th Panzer Divisions had a total of 110 serviceable tanks, and protection for the vulnerable Tebaga gap into the Axis rear areas was provided by the Raggrupamento Sahariano (the equivalent of 7 battalions).

Montgomery planned for the Axis static formations to be crushed in the coastal sector of the Italian XX Corps by Lieutenant General Sir Oliver Leese's British XXX Corps (Major General J. S. Nichols's British 50th Division, Major General D. N. Wimberley's 51st (Highland) Division and Major General F. I. S. Tuker's 4th Indian Division) so that a breach could be made for the armour of Lieutenant General B. G. Horrocks's British X Corps (Major General R. Briggs's British 1st Armoured Division and Major General G. W. E. J. Erskine's British 7th Armoured Division) to erupt into the enemy's rear with the object of driving straight through to Gafsa and Sfax in preparation for a nonstop drive to Sousse and Tunis. To cut the Axis forces' line of retreat, Lieutenant General Sir Bernard Freyberg's New Zealand Corps (Freyberg's own 2nd New Zealand Division, Brigadier C. B. C. Harvey's British 8th Armoured Brigade and Général de Division Henri Leclerc's 'L' Force) was to sweep deep round the southern flank through Wilder's Gap in the Matmata hills to assault the Tebaga gap defences and so break through to the coast near Gabes well to the Axis rear. The Axis forces suffered from an enormous quantitive disadvantage compared with the Allied forces, for whereas the former had only some 142 tanks the latter had 743, and this disadvantage was carried over to field artillery (447 to 692), anti-tank artillery (728 including dual-purpose 88-mm Flak guns to 1,033) and aircraft (123 to 755, the latter excluding the aircraft of the North African Strategic Air Force made tactically available on 20 and 21 March).

Montgomery's main frontal assault was to start on 20 March, but as his corps had a 120-mile approach march to the Tebaga gap Freyberg departed on 18 March. Two days before this the British had started preliminary operations against the Mareth Line defences, the 201st Guards Brigade of the 7th Armoured Division probing into the defences of the 90th Light Division south-east of Mareth, and the 69th and 153rd Brigades (of the 50th and 51st Divisions respectively) establishing a bridgehead through the Wadi Zeuss defences of the Young Fascist and Trieste Divisions just inland of the coastal marshes. The offensive proper got under way at 22.30 on 20 March with a large artillery barrage, under cover of which the 50th Division secured a bridgehead over the Wadi Zigzaou. General Sozzani's Young Fascists did not break, however, and soon the 50th Division was on the defensive, much hampered by the onset of torrential rain, which turned the ground into a quagmire and the Wadi Zigzaou into a torrent. By 22 March the division had only one small foothold left on the northern side of the Wadi Zigzaou after counterattacks by Generalmajor Willibald Borowietz's 15th Panzer Division. By this time the New Zealand Corps was hotly engaged in the Tebaga gap and unable to break through rapidly as Messe had sent in the 21st Panzer Division supported by Generalmajor Kurt Freiherr von Liebenstein's 164th Light Division pulled out of the Mareth Line.

Montgomery's basic plan had thus failed, but the British commander now decided on a swift evolution of his basic plan to take advantage of X Corps' armoured superiority. The weight of the infantry attack was now switched inland, the 4th Indian Division being directed to outflank the end of the Mareth Line in the Matmata hills and fall on Beni Zelten (28 March) with its 5th Indian Brigade (via Ksar el Hallouf) and 7th Indian Brigade (by means of a wider sweep through the Matmata hills). To maintain frontal pressure on the Mareth Line the 7th Armoured Division was thrown into the fray in this sector, but the key to Montgomery's revised scheme was the despatch on 23 March

199

of the XXX Corps' headquarters and the 1st Armoured Division to reinforce the New Zealand Corps at the Tebaga gap. The 1st Armoured Division grouped to the south-east of the gap during the night of 25 March, and from 16.00 on 26 March supplemented the New Zealand Corps' efforts in Operation 'Supercharge'. This sector was beyond the reach of any Allied heavy artillery, but this was more than balanced by the availability of some 22 fighter-bomber squadrons, which decimated all Axis transport and armour in the Tebaga gap area. Under Horrocks' command the Allies smashed through the Tebaga gap, but rather than press on straight to the coast Horrocks decided to mop up, and this gave Messe just enough time to fall back relatively intact from the Mareth Line to another excellent defensive position, this time just 8 miles long on the Wadi Akarit to the north of Gabes. Messe had lost some 16 battalions, 31 guns and 60 tanks, but had spoiled Montgomery's chance of a pellmell advance to Tunis.

Puma British plan to take the Canary island group from Portugal (April/May 1941). The plan began to take shape (together with those for the similar Operations 'Springboard' and 'Thruster') in July 1940 when the British feared that the success of the Germans in mainland Europe might persuade them to move against Portugal (possibly with the support of Spain) and its strategically placed island possessions in the Atlantic. These would provide the Germans with ideal forward bases for aircraft and submarines operating against the convoys on which the UK's continued survival depended, so contingency plans were considered for the seizure of these islands should Germany move against Spain and/or Portugal. The plans for three separate operations in the Atlantic were eventually combined into Operation 'Pilgrim', and the threat to these islands meant that the necessary forces (land, sea and air) were earmarked for this operation over a considerable period.

Pumpkin Operations by Major General D. T. Cowan's 17th Indian Light Division south of Tiddim in central Burma (December 1943). The object of these activities was to open the road to Fort White and thence to Kalewa on the River Chindwin for the general advance of Lieutenant General Sir Geoffrey Scoones' IV Corps, itself designed as a spoiling operation against the Japanese offensive expected in the spring of 1944. The 17th Indian Light Division was unable to make significant progress against Lieutenant General G. Yanagida's Japanese 33rd Division, which was building up its strength and positions for its part in the advance of Lieutenant General Renya Mutaguchi's Japanese 15th Army in Operation 'U' against Imphal and Kohima.

Pussta (puszta) Limited offensive by Generaloberst Ernst Busch's German 16th Army to restore the position of Generalfeldmarschall Georg von Küchler's Army Group 'North' just south of Demyansk between Dedno and Pustynya (October/November 1942). Here the Soviet 3rd and 4th Shock Armies of General P. A. Kurochkin's North-West Front had formed a deep salient during the Soviet late-winter offensive between January and March 1942.

Python Repatriation scheme for time-expired British troops in the Far East (1945).

Q

Q British plan to destroy the naval base at Singapore to prevent its use by the Japanese (February 1942). This denial scheme had its origins in the Royal Navy, which planned that the dockyard staff should undertake the demolition work under the command of Rear Admiral E. J. Spooner before their evacuation in the closing stages of an unsuccessful British defence of Singapore Island. However, the naval personnel were evacuated relatively early in the final campaign, and the implementation of 'Q' was left somewhat imprecisely to Major General D. M. Murray-Lyon's 11th Indian Division within Lieutenant General Sir Lewis Heath's III Indian Corps. The army troops were little experienced in the demolition of naval facilities, and coupled with the decision to leave the demolitions to the last minute, this meant that much of the naval facility on the Johore Strait fell intact into the hands of the Japanese, though the floating dock was scuttled, the King George V graving dock was incapacitated, cranes were destroyed and fuel tanks either fired or holed by 9 February 1942, when the Japanese Guards, 5th and 18th Divisions crossed the Johore Strait to secure a lodgement in the north-west of the island.

Q.P. Designation of Arctic convoys (together with a numerical suffix) plying the route from ports in the northern USSR to Iceland and the UK, and inaugurated in September 1941. In December this Q.P. series was replaced by the R.A. series.

Quadrangle Designation of the operation organised by Admiral Sir Henry Harwood, the Commander-in-Chief Mediterranean, to run a series of four convoys into Malta from Egypt (December, 1942/January 1943). Given the success of the previous Operations 'Stoneage' and 'Portcullis', Harwood decided that these final relief convoys for Malta should each consist of 2 merchantmen with minimal escort, sailing as far as Benghazi with normal Western Desert convoys before breaking off to Malta under final escort of Rear Admiral A. J. Powers's Malta-based Force K, which averaged 1 cruiser and 5 destroyers, in case the Italians sortied from Taranto. The 4 convoy operations were designated 'Quadrangle A', 'Quadrangle B', 'Quadrangle C' and 'Quadrangle D', and on each occasion empty ships were passed east from Malta, this number including the 4 survivors of the 'Pedestal' convoy.

Quadrant Designation of the 1st Quebec Conference (14/24 August 1943). Attended by President Franklin D. Roosevelt and Prime Minister Winston Churchill, together with their political and military staffs, the 'Quadrant' conference was called to decide matters of immediate and long-term importance to the two western Allies, matters which would involve the USSR and China being specifically excluded. The primary result of the conference was a joint commitment by the USA and UK to Operation 'Overlord', to be launched on or about 1 May 1944 with the object of securing a lodgement including one or more Channel ports so that the Allies could then secure additional area in France for the ground and air exploitation of the initial success with 'operations designed to strike at the heart of Germany and to destroy her mili-

Quarterback

tary forces'. The basis of the invasion of Europe should be the COSSAC plan, it was decided, and to facilitate the successful implementation of 'Overlord' the conference also decided that General the Hon. Sir Harold Alexander's Allied 15th Army Group in Italy should exploit its offensive towards Milan and Turin, so pinning as many German divisions as possible, and that the allocation of resources to the Mediterranean should be limited to those required for the success of the Milan/Turin operations, with no thought for the British desire for development into Austria and southern Germany.

It was also decided that an American officer should be appointed to command 'Overlord' (in fact General Dwight D. Eisenhower) though Churchill had previously promised the command to General Sir Alan Brooke, Chief of the Imperial General Staff and the chairman of the Chiefs-of-Staff Committee. For his acquiescence in the matter of Eisenhower, Churchill was permitted to insist on the appointment of Admiral Lord Louis Mountbatten to the post of commander-in-chief, South-East Asia Command. Churchill also wished to secure Allied approval for Operation 'Culverin' against northern Sumatra, but this was not forthcoming. The real point at issue between the Allies was not so much where their ground forces should be deployed, but the relative allocation of amphibious capability. This was effectively decided by the Americans, who had by far the larger production capacity and need for such craft, and on 6 June 1944 the allocation was 3,696 in the UK for 'Overlord', 3,866 in the Pacific for the twin offensive thrusts of General Douglas MacArthur and Admiral Chester W. Nimitz (both moves jealously preserved by Admiral Ernest J. King, the US Navy commander-in-chief, against the scaling-down efforts of Brooke), and 1,037 in the Mediterranean where, against the wishes of the British, the Americans insisted that the US and rearmed French forces should land between Toulon and Marseilles at about the same time as 'Overlord' was implemented. Thus was born Operation 'Anvil', on which the Germans would supposedly be crushed by the hammer of 'Overlord'.

Quarterback Allied codename for Lieutenant General Joseph W. Stilwell.

Queen Offensive by Lieutenant General Omar N. Bradley's US 12th Army Group on the Roer plain (16 November/15 December 1944). The offensive arose from an inter-Allied command conference on 18 October, which decided that despite the continued nonavailability of Antwerp as a major supply port for the Allied forces in North-West Europe there should be a major effort to get a substantial bridgehead over the River Rhine before the arrival of winter. Field Marshal Sir Bernard Montgomery, commanding the 21st Army Group, argued that operations south of the Ardennes (especially those by Lieutenant General George S. Patton's US 3rd Army directed at the Saar) should be halted unless they could be supplied from Marseilles, so that all available supplies and fuel could be used for a northern strike at the Rhine. General Dwight D. Eisenhower refused to entertain any such notion, but decided that the 12th Army Group, with British support, would make a major effort towards the Rhine; there thus appeared Operation 'Queen', in which Bradley would supervise a major offensive by Lieutenant General Courtney H. Hodges's US 1st Army and Lieutenant General William H. Simpson's US 9th Army (brought into the line north of the US 1st Army after arriving from Brittany in September).

Planned for the beginning of November, 'Queen' called for a rapid advance to and over the River Roer, after which the US 9th Army would wheel north to Krefeld and the US 1st Army would strike east to Köln and Bonn. At much the same time Lieutenant General Sir Miles Dempsey's British 2nd Army would advance from the Nijmegen area to clear the Reichswald area before moving south between the Rivers Maas and Rhine. The Germans would thus be expelled from the lower Rhineland, it was expected, leaving the Allies with a 100-mile front along the Rhine between Bonn and Arnhem. When the weather permitted, the US 1st and 9th Armies would cross the Rhine south of Köln and north of Düsseldorf to encircle the Ruhr.

Patton was not to be deterred, however, and launched his Saar offensive on 3

November. The one positive hope for Bradley in these circumstances was that Generalfeldmarschall Gerd von Rundstedt, the *Oberbefelhshaber West*, would send his mobile reserves south to oppose Patton. This did not occur, for von Rundstedt appreciated that the Americans were planning an offensive east from the Aachen area. Bradley's forces had themselves been weakened, moreover, by the need to lend Montgomery two divisions which had not yet been returned, and the result was a postponement of the offensive to 11 November, when it was planned to unleash 4 divisions of the 1st Army and 4 divisions of the 9th army on a 25-mile front between the Hurtgen Forest and Geilenkirchen against General Ernst Brandenburger's German 7th Army and General Hasso von Manteuffel's 5th Panzerarmee of Generalfeldmarschall Walter Model's Army Group 'B', in all some 14 divisions (reinforced to 17 divisions during the campaign) including 5 infantry, 2 Panzer and 2 Panzergrenadier in the 5th Panzerarmee.

The Germans knew that the Americans were coming, and also enjoyed the benefits of exceptional fixed and field fortifications. The Allies hoped to break through this front with a massive carpet bombing effort by Allied bombers, but the need to wait for adequate weather led to further delay, pushing the start of 'Queen' back to 16 November when 2,500 Allied bombers dropped 9,400 tons of bombs on the Germans' front-line positions. These were little damaged thanks to their great strength, and the Germans were thus able to emerge unscathed to decimate the American advance. There followed nearly one month of desperate fighting more reminiscent of the Western Front in World War I than of the mobile operations of World War II, and when the US offensive petered out on 15 December with the launch of the Germans' great 'bulge' offensive in the Ardennes, the average advance had been a mere 8 miles. The US 9th Army had reached the line of the flooded Roer between Jülich and Linnich at the end of November, but it took the US 1st Army another two weeks to reach the Roer opposite Düren.

The lesson was clear, for the Germans still controlled the series of seven dams farther up the Roer, which could be used to flood the lower reaches and so make conventional warfare next to impossible. The Americans had tried and failed to secure these dams (the US V Corps suffering dreadfully in its efforts to take the Roer and Erft dams, whose destruction by the Germans would release a flood 25 feet deep and 1.5 miles wide near Düren) and the RAF had tried to burst them with bombs. Moreover, the Germans had moved SS Oberstgruppenführer Sepp Dietrich's 6th SS Panzerarmee west of the Rhine for 'Herbstnebel', and this could have been used to deal with any breakthrough towards Köln and Düsseldorf. The Allies were stalemated.

Quick Anger Offensive against Arnhem by I Canadian Corps (12 April 1945). Under Lieutenant General C. Foulkes, this corps had been despatched from Italy in February 1944 to bring Lieutenant General Sir Henry Crerar's Canadian 1st Army up to strength. On 1 April the army got back from the British 2nd Army Lieutenant General G. G. Simonds's II Canadian Corps, and was instructed by Field Marshal Lord Montgomery's 21st Army Group to undertake a double task, namely the clearance of those parts of the Netherlands still in the hands of General Günther Blumentritt's German 25th Army of Generaloberst Johannes Blaskowitz's Army Group 'H', and the winning of a corridor between the River Weser and the Zuider Zee for an advance north-west to Wilhelmshaven and Emden, with the British XXX Corps as the left flank guard for Lieutenant General Sir Miles Dempsey's British 2nd Army as it pushed into northern Germany towards Hamburg. The clearance of the Netherlands was entrusted to I Canadian Corps (1st Canadian Division and 5th Canadian Armoured Division), which reached and took Arnhem with a fine pincer movement on the third day of the offensive and then swept on to the Zuider Zee at Harderwijk. Blumentritt then ordered the sea dikes to be opened, but Crerar achieved a local armistice with Blumentritt so that this move would not devastate much of the lowest-lying parts of the Netherlands, the armistice also stipulating that the Germans would make no effort to shoot down RAF bombers

Quick Anger

dropping food to the Dutch population in Operation 'Manna'.

The second task allocated to the Canadian 1st Army was more difficult, and fell to II Canadian Corps. This went over to the offensive for the rapid liberation of Zutphen and Almelo (6 April) followed by that of Groningen and Leeuwarden (10 April) and an advance into Germany aided by the capture of crossings over the Orange Canal by the 2ème and 3ème Regiments Coloniaux des Parachutistes at Assem and Meppel. However, once II Canadian Corps was in Germany it met fierce resistance from General Straube's II Parachute Corps, requiring assistance from army group in the form of the 5th Canadian Armoured Division, the Polish 1st Armoured Division and the British 3rd Division. By 5 May the corps was on the outskirts of Wilhelmshaven and Emden. The double offensive cost the Canadians 5,514 casualties.

R

R Japanese operation to capture Rabaul in New Britain and Kavieng in New Ireland (23 January 1942). Rabaul was the primary target, for it offered an excellent land-locked harbour as a base for Vice Admiral Shigeyoshi Inouye's 4th Fleet tasked with the defence of the central sector of Japan's southern defence perimeter. New Britain had also been identified since September 1941 as the long-term headquarters of Lieutenant General Imamura's 8th Area Army to control army forces in New Guinea and in the Solomons. The envisaged defence perimeter was to run south through the central Pacific and then turn west in the Ellice Islands, the southern sector taking in the western end of the Solomon Islands, the southern portion of Papua and all of New Guinea, Timor Island and Java Island before turning north-west towards the Malay Barrier. Together with the nearby Admiralty Islands, New Britain and New Ireland were ideal base areas for the completion of the southern sector as the main harbour at Rabaul was backed by a lesser harbour at Kavieng, and the two islands could rapidly be developed with airfields for the long-range bombers on which the Imperial Japanese Army and the Imperial Japanese Navy depended for far-flung operations in the Pacific. The defences of the two islands were softened up by land-based aircraft operating from Truk, the main base of Admiral Isoroku Yamamoto's Combined Fleet, before the assault force arrived and landed with little opposition. Rabaul was soon in full operation as a naval and air base for softening-up operations in New Guinea and Papua, the targets for Operations 'RE' and 'RI', while longer-term plans were implemented for the defence of the islands, which the Japanese saw as the ideal bastion against any Allied offensive towards the Philippines from the south, and as the perfect outer defence for Truk.

R4 British contingency plan for the seizure of the ports of Stavanger, Bergen, Trondheim and Narvik in Norway should the Germans react strongly to the implementation of Operation 'Wilfred' (April 1940). Operation 'R4' called for immediate response as soon as German forces violated Norway's territorial waters, and to ensure speed of response the cruisers *Devonshire*, *Berwick*, *York* and *Glasgow* embarked troops at Rosyth on 7 April, while the men and transports for the Trondheim and Narvik landings were assembled in the Clyde together with the cruiser *Aurora* and 6 destroyers, all under the command of Admiral Sir E. R. G. R. Evans. 'Wilfred' was never initiated, however, as the Germans struck first with Operation 'Weserübung', and since 'R4' could not hope to wrest the desired ports from the Germans who had taken them the plan was abandoned on 9 April.

R.A. Designation of Arctic convoys (together with a numerical suffix) plying the route from ports in the northern USSR to Loch Ewe, and inaugurated in December 1942 as a replacement for the previous Q.P. series.

Rainbow (i) Generic designation of US contingency plans for war with the Axis powers (1940/1941).
(ii) Offensive by the Chinese 'Y' Force down the River Salween in southern China (10

May/August 1944). Undertaken at the sensible instigation of Lieutenant General Joseph W. Stilwell with the full approval of Generalissimo Chiang Kai-shek, 'Rainbow' was designed to put into Chinese hands the region containing Myitkyina, Bhamo and Lashio, so easing the overland supply route to China. The offensive was entrusted to General Wei Li-huang's 'Y' Force, which comprised the 11th and 20th Army Groups with some 72,000 men in 12 divisions for the short-term objective of taking Tengchung, Lungling and Mangshih so that the Chinese would have the stretch of the Burma Road to the west of the Salween and the complete supply route could be brought into service as soon as Stilwell's northern Combat Area Command had taken the Burmese portion.

Planned by Wei Li-huang, the offensive lacked any real co-ordination, for while the 20th Army Group was to cross the Salween and advance over the Mamien and Tatangtzu passes in the Kaoli Kung mountain range to reach the River Shweli for a drive on Tengchung, the 11th Army Group was to move as three separate entities with the 39th Division of the 2nd Army crossing the Salween north of Hueijan to take the Hungmushu pass in the southern Kaoli Kungs and attack the remains of the Hueijan bridge from the rear, with the rest of the 2nd Army crossing the Salween south of Pingka for the capture of this town and then Mangshih, and with the 71st Army following the 2nd Army to branch off for the capture of Lungling. The Japanese defence was entrusted to Lieutenant General S. Matsuyama's 56th Division of Lieutenant General M. Honda's 33rd Army, and this division had a strength of only some 11,000 men to face a numerically superior Chinese force which was, however, very short of supplies and ammunition for a protracted campaign.

The 53rd and 54th Divisions of the 20th Army Group got under way smartly on 10 May, but were soon stalled in front of the Mamien and Tatangtzu passes, which the Japanese had covered with permanent fortifications. The 2nd Army, with the 88th Division of the 71st Army under command, also made good initial progress and invested Pingka on 17 May before sending its main strength to establish a block on the Burma Road south-west of Mangshih (so cutting the Japanese 56th Division's lines of communication) and to invest Lungling. The 71st Army now followed the 2nd Army across the Salween and joined the 88th Division for an assault in Lungling. This effort was bloodily repulsed between 9 and 13 June, and the Japanese commander now switched his main defence south to resecure his severed communications, leaving only small forces to hold the Mamien and Tatangtzu passes. Matsuyama moved with considerable speed, and by 14 June was in a position to counterattack at Lungling, driving the 10,000 men of the two Chinese divisions back into the hills by 17 June.

To compound the problems of the Chinese, the 2nd Army at this juncture decided to abandon its block on the Burma Road (on the grounds that it had not received its fair share of available army supplies) and fell back to Pingka. The 56th Division thus secured its lines of communication, though the Chinese 20th Army Group at this time broke through the Mamien and Tatangtzu passes and headed for the valley of the Shweli and its important centre of communications at Tengchung. The 39th Division had also made progress to secure the eastern side of the Hungmushu pass, but instead of being advanced to attack Hueijan as planned, it was diverted south to attack Lameng. By the end of June the Chinese were thus outside Tengchung, Lameng and Pingka, but were unable to press their offensive with any real vigour. Matsuyama now had single battalions invested in Tengchung, Lameng and Pingka, but had the rest of his force (minus 3,000 casualties) to the west of the stalled Chinese. All Wei Li-huang could do at this time was to press ahead with the sieges of Tengchung, Lameng and Pingka.

By the third week in July the 20th Army Group had five divisions outside Tengchung, and with the aid of bomber support from the US 14th Air Force the army group fought its way into the walled town on 4 August. Even so, Japanese resistance continued for another month. The same type of battle was waged at Lameng, where the Chinese 11th Army Group was still outside the walls during August. Operation 'Rainbow' had failed to secure the swift advantage demanded of it in southern China, and the campaign in northern Burma was further delayed as a consequence. It was only when the Northern Combat Area Command began its own offensive on 15 October that the 'Y' Force was able to get under way once more.

Rainbow-1 US pre-war plan for the defence of the western hemisphere (as far south as 10 degrees South) between Greenland in the east and Hawaii, US Samoa and Wake to the west. The plan was cancelled in May 1942.

Rainbow-2 US pre-war plan for the extension of 'Rainbow-1' to the western Pacific, including Guam and the Philippines. The plan was cancelled in August 1941.

Rainbow-3 US pre-war plan for the extension of 'Rainbow-1' to South America. The plan was cancelled in August 1941.

Rainbow-4 US pre-war plan for the modifications of 'Rainbow-1, 2 and 3' in the event of British and French hostilities with Germany, Italy and (possibly) Japan. The plan was cancelled in May 1942.

Rainbow-5 US implementation of A.B.C.1 (spring/summer 1942).

Raincoat Breakthrough of the German 'Bernhardt Linie' positions in the Monte Camino region of Italy by the US II Corps and British X Corps (2/10 December 1943). Planned by Lieutenant General Mark W. Clark's US 5th Army under the overall supervision of General the Hon. Sir Harold Alexander's 15th Army Group, 'Raincoat' was designed to punch a hole through the southern defences of the 'Bernhardt Linie' (held from west to east by the 94th Division, the 15th Panzergrenadier Division, the 29th Panzergrenadier Division, the 44th Division, the 5th Mountain Division and 305th Division of General Hans Hube's XIV Panzer Corps within Generaloberst Heinrich von Vietinghoff-Scheel's 10th Army) and thus allow the Allies to close up on the main defences of the 'Gustav Linie' in front of Cassino.

The US 5th Army envisaged a three-phase assault. In the first phase (Operation 'Raincoat' proper) Lieutenant General R. L. McCreery's British X Corps (Major General J. L. I. Hawkesworth's 46th Division and Major General G. W. R. Templer's 56th Division) and Lieutenant General Omar N. Bradley's US II Corps (Major General Fred K. Walker's US 36th Infantry Division and the 1st Special Service Force, with the US 3rd Infantry Division available from army reserve if required) would take Monte Camino, the southernmost bastion of the German defence. In the second phase the US II Corps would move ahead of the British X Corps to take Monte Lungo and Monte Sammucro, the centre and northernmost bastions of the German defence, while Major General John P. Lucas's US VI Corps (34th and 45th Divisions) held the Germans along the Colli-Atina road in the hills above Venafro. And in the third phase the Allies would exploit into the valley of the River Liri with a view to pushing up the valley of the River Rapido to Cassino.

The beginning of 'Raincoat' was marked by a heavy artillery bombardment of the defences of Generalmajor Eberhardt Rodt's 15th Panzergrenadier Division, complemented by a massive air offensive. Neither achieved significant results as a result of the Germans' deeply buried positions. Thus the Allied infantry, spearheaded by the British 56th Division, were faced with a succession of uphill assaults as the German positions were slowly taken in individual assaults. The position at the peak of Mone Camino fell only on 6 December, and the clearance of the rest of the Monte Camino took another four days, with casualties to the British X Corps of some 1,000. The second phase of the operation began on 7 December, as the British X Corps was still embroiled on Monte Camino. The US II Corps initially made good progress, but was then seriously checked by Generalmajor Fries's 29th Panzergrenadier Division.

The offensive was resumed on 15 December, and by 17 December the Americans had taken Monte Sammucro and Monte Lungo. Major General Fred K. Walker's US 36th Division was totally exhausted by its considerable efforts, and the casualties in the US II Corps had been heavy. The US VI Corps fared no better against Generalleutnant Dr Franz Beyer's 44th Division and Generalleutnant Julius Ringel's 5th Mountain Division, the tide turning in the Allies' favour only with the arrival of the mountain-trained 2nd Moroccan Division, under General de Division André Dody as the precursor of General de Corps d'Armée Alphonse Juin's French Expeditionary Corps. In this sector the Germans were finally pushed back to the main 'Gustav Linie' defences by 29 December.

However, the offensive had failed in its main purpose, which was to put the Allies in a strong position no more than 30 miles from the Anzio beach-head area of Operation 'Shingle' (which had been fixed for no later than 15 January 1944 so that its amphibious craft could be redeployed to northern Europe for Operation 'Overlord') by the time winter ended the 1943 campaigning season. 'Shingle' was implemented despite Clark's urging that it be abandoned, and in January the Allies were thus faced with a difficult task, especially as seven divisions had been withdrawn from Italy for 'Overlord' at the time of the 'Bernhardt Linie' battles, when the Allies had 13 divisions (4 British, 3 Commonwealth, 5 US and 1 French, all of them in the operational zone) in Italy to the Germans' 18 (only 11 of them in the operational zone, and 5 of the 7 German mobile divisions in the process of replacement by 4 infantry divisions). The Allied divisions shipped north between the Volturno and 'Bernhardt Linie' battles were replaced in December 1943 and January 1944 to bring Allied strength to 5 British, 5 Commonwealth, 1 Polish, 5 US and 2 French divisions (18 divisions in all), while the Germans had been bolstered to 23 divisions, but though the Allied operational-zone advantage at this time was 3 divisions compared with 2 at the time of the 'Bernhardt Linie' battle, the new divisions were inexperienced in the conditions of Italian warfare.

Ramrod British light bomber raid against a specific target in occupied Europe (1941 onwards) with the intention that German fighters should be scrambled to intercept the bombers and then be tackled by the escorting British fighters on terms disadvantageous to the Germans. The double object of this type of operation was that targets should be bombed to useful effect, and that German fighter strength in North-West Europe should be whittled away.

Ranger British low-level fighter-bomber sweeps over occupied Europe against German targets of opportunity.

Rankin A Plan for Allied forces to move into northern Europe before the date set for Operation 'Overlord' in the event that Germany's military or economic position deteriorated suddenly (1943/1944). In this event the Allies would undertake an 'Overlord' type operation against the Cotentin peninsula (January 1944) or the Normandy coast (April 1944) with the object of defeating Germany as rapidly as possible. 'Rankin A' also envisaged supplementary or diversionary landings in the Pas-de-Calais region and/or in the south of France.

Rankin B Plan for Allied forces to move into France should the Germans evacuate their forces from major parts of occupied Europe (1943/1944). In this eventuality the Allies would undertake an invasion of France in the Cotentin peninsula with the object of securing the rapid defeat of Germany; it was also envisaged that forces would be landed in the south of France.

Rankin C Plan for Allied forces to move into Europe in the event of a German surrender (1943/1944). In this eventuality the Allies would land in France with the object of ensuring German adherence to the surrender terms, with US forces in France, Belgium and southern Germany, and British forces in northern Germany and the rest of liberated Europe.

Rashness Revised version of 'Carbonado'.

Rattle Allied Combined Operations HQ conference to discuss amphibious tactics and techniques with a particular emphasis on the use of such tactics in Operation 'Overlord' (1943).

Ratweek Bombing offensive by the Allies' Balkan Air Force, undertaken in conjunction with Yugoslav partisan harassment operations against the German forces of Generaloberst Alexander Löhr's Army Group 'E', and designed to hinder the latter's evacuation of Greece to join up with the main forces of Generalfeldmarschall Maximilian Freiherr von Weichs's Army Group 'F' in Yugoslavia (1/7 September 1944). The withdrawal of Löhr's army group (LXVIII Corps in southern Greece, XIC Corps in north-eastern Greece, XXII Gebirgskorps in north-western Greece and XXI Gebirgskorps in Albania) was necessitated by the development of the Soviet autumn offensive of 1944 into the Balkans, followed by the defections of Rominia and Bulgaria from the Axis cause. In the autumn there was thus a great chance that Lohr's 345,000 German soldiers, sailors and airmen would be cut off in the southern Balkans.

Army Group 'E' was formed on 23 August 1944, and one day later it was ordered to fall back into southern Yugoslavia along the line from Scutari to the Iron Gate pass via Skopje. However, by this time the Bulgarian 5th Army, now fighting alongside the Soviets, had captured Nis behind the left flank of the proposed line for Army Group 'E', and Löhr was forced to adopt a line farther to the north, and established his headquarters at Sarajevo by 15 November. In the course of this retreat the Greek guerrilla forces had harried the 315,000 retreating Germans (some 30,000 men having been abandoned in the Greek islands), and this effect was greatly supplemented by the activities of 'Ratweek', which failed however to slow the German retreat sufficiently for Marshal of the Soviet Union F. I. Tolbukhin's 3rd Ukrainian Front to cut the Germans' line of retreat by an advance farther to the west. As it was the Soviets with Yugoslav support captured Belgrade on 20 October, vindicating Löhr's choice of a more westerly line of retreat through Skopje, Mitrovica, Novi Pazar and Visegrad rather than the more obvious line from Skopje to Nis, Kraljevo and Belgrade.

Raubtier (beast of prey) Offensive of the German 18th Army (March 1942) to check a Soviet offensive to the north of Novgorod on the northern shore of Lake Ilmen. Though Stalin was not displeased that Leningrad be invested by the Germans, he did not wish this key city to fall, and its relief was thus one of the primary objectives of the offensive in the north undertaken as part of the Soviet general winter offensive of 1941/1942. The main offensive weight of the strike was borne by General K. A. Meretskov's Volkhov Front, which was formed in 17 December 1941 with the 4th, 52nd, 59th and 2nd Shock Armies. Meretskov's offensive began on 7 January 1942 with a probing attack westwards across the frozen River Volkhov (immediately to the north of Novgorod) by the 6 divisions and 6 brigades of Lieutenant General G. G. Sokolov's 2nd Shock Army with the intention (from 13 January) of smashing through General F. W. von Chappuis's German XXXVIII Corps to the rear areas of Generaloberst Georg von Küchler's German 18th Army and then wheeling north towards Leningrad with the aid of flanking support by Lieutenant General N. K. Klykov's 52nd Army and Major General I. V. Galanin's 59th Army.

The fighting took place on a frozen swamp under the direst conditions, and in the following month the Soviets advanced some 40 miles, about half the distance to Leningrad. In the second week of March Major General I. I. Fedyuninsky's 54th Army launched a subsidiary offensive south-west from Kirishi to link up with the 2nd Shock Army (now commanded by Major General A. A. Vlasov) for the final push to Leningrad. The two armies finally got within 15 miles of each other, in the process nearly isolating Generaloberst Johannes Blaskowitz's German I Corps.

Up to this time the defensive effort of the 18th Army had been extemporized, with ad hoc units thrown in to plug gaps and to try to stem the Soviet advance. Since 17 January the army had been commanded by General Georg Lindemann after the elevation of von Küchler to replace Generalfeldmarschall Wilhelm Ritter von Leeb as head of Army Group 'North', and Lindemann was now in a position to undertake a more permanent reversal of the Soviets' fortunes with attacks on the shoulders of the salient to the north of Novgorod. From the north the SS Police Division of I Corps struck south, and from the south the German 56th and 126th Divisions of XXXVIII Corps (supported by the Spanish 250th Division) struck north, the Germans meeting on 19 March and thus cutting off some 130,000 Soviets in the Volkhov pocket. Meretskov managed to open up a small relief corridor for a short while, but this had no material effect on the position of the pocket, which finally capitulated in June 1942 yielding Vlasov, 33,000 prisoners, 600 guns and 170 tanks.

Ravenous Plan for the advance of Lieutenant General G. A. P. Scoones's IV Corps across the River Chindwin into northern Burma, to be undertaken in concert with an amphibious attack on Akyab (Operation 'Cannibal') and a seaborne descent on Rangoon and southern Burma (Operation 'Anakim') as the major components of the British plan for the reconquest of Burma in 1943. Within this overall scheme Brigadier O. C. Wingate planned to launch his Operation 'Loincloth', the 1st Chindit Expedition, in which the 77th Indian Brigade would harass Japanese communications in front of the IV Corps' advance and then fall back onto the corps as it pushed across the Chindwin. 'Ravenous' was postponed time and again for logistical and manpower reasons, and was then redesigned as a limited offensive from Assam to gain footholds in northern Burma, to improve the air supply route to China and, if the Chinese would co-operate, to push farther into northern Burma with a view to developing additional airfields and a radar chain for the protection of Assamese air bases. Further delays prevented the implementation of the overall scheme during 1943, and with the eventual abandonment of Operation 'Cannibal' and then of Operation 'Anakim', 'Ravenous' was eventually translated into Operation 'Capital' itself developed into Operation 'Extended Capital' after the Japanese had launched their own Operation 'U' as a counter to the British build-up in the area of Imphal and Kohima.

Razzle British pyrotechnic device, designed for air-dropping on German forests.

RE Japanese operation against Milne Bay at the eastern tip of Papua in concert with Operation 'MO' (25 August/6 September 1942). The operation was undertaken by the Imperial Japanese Navy's 8th Fleet (based at Rabaul on New Britain under Vice Admiral Gunichi Mikawa, and the successor of the 4th Fleet for South-West Pacific operations since 14 July) at the behest of the Imperial Japanese Army, which needed support in its operations along the Kokoda Trail to take Port Moresby. Since 18 May 1942 Papua had been the responsibility of Lieutenant General Harukichi Hyakutake's Japanese 17th Army, whose primary interest was in the Solomons operations. Although the 8th Fleet was already overextended with operations in the Solomons, Mikawa responded to Hyakutake's request that he aid Major General Tomitaro Horii's South Seas Detachment on the Trail with a diversionary landing on Rabi and Samarai Islands in the Louisiade group in Milne Bay by elements of the 8th Fleet, so that a seaplane base could be built for the flank protection of the Kokoda Trail operations.

In the second week of August Japanese photo-reconnaissance revealed that the Australians were building a new airstrip near Gili Gili at the head of Milne Bay, and at this time it was decided to change the Japanese objective to this more important area, whose capture would provide the Japanese with a complex of three airfields for the bombing of Port Moresby and northern Australia. The army was to have contributed the Kawaguchi Detachment of the 17th Army for the operation, but this was diverted to Guadalcanal and not replaced, leaving the operation in the hands of the navy. The men of the marine landing force were transported for 'RE' in the light cruisers *Tenryu* and *Tatsuta* plus 5 destroyers, but the squadron was spotted and attacked by aircraft as it approached Rabi Island at the north of Milne Bay.

The invasion went ahead at 23.30 on 25 August, the original 1,500-men assault force of the Kure 5th Special Naval Landing Force and the Sasebo 5th Special Naval Landing Force, under Commander Shojiro Hayashi, being reinforced on 29 August to 2,400 men by the Kure 3rd Special Naval Landing Force and Yokosuka 5th Special Naval Landing Force under Commander Minoro Yana, who assumed local command from Hayashi. What the Japanese did not know, however, was that the Australian garrison had been reinforced at the insistence of General Douglas MacArthur, commanding the South-West Pacific Area, by 4,500 infantry of the 18th Australian Brigade between 25 June and 20 August. These combat troops were supplemented by about 3,000 Australian and 1,300 US engineers and artillerymen. Under the command of Lieutenant General F. F. Rowell's I Australian Corps based in Port Moresby, the garrison was fully alert, and there developed a small but exceptionally bloody battle for the area.

The Japanese advanced westward from their landings at Waga Waga and Ahioma, taking K. B. Mission and Rabi on 27 August, but were then halted on the edge of Airstrip No. 3 during 28 August. Yana's reinforcements provided short-term help, but on 31 August the 61st Australian Battalion spearheaded the Allied counterattack that repulsed the final Japanese effort. Mikawa ordered an evacuation on 6 September, and 3 more destroyers were sent to the area to assist, but the Japanese evacuated only 1,320 men including 320 seriously wounded. Of the 2,400 troops landed, therefore, some 1,080 had been killed or posted missing. It was a serious reverse for the Japanese, spelling the end of any chance to provide the South Seas Detachment with any effective air support as it began the descent from the Owen Stanley range towards Port Moresby.

Rebecca H British blind-navigation radio device (1944/1945).

Reckless US assault on the Japanese base area of Hollandia in New Guinea (22 April 1944). This operation was part of a daring three-pronged amphibious assault planned by General Douglas MacArthur's South-West Pacific Area command to outflank the forces of Lieutenant General Hatuzo Adachi's Japanese 18th Army still engaged to the east with the forces of Lieutenant General E. F. Herring's I Australian Corps in the exits from the Huon peninsula. This would provide the US forces with the excellent anchorage in Humboldt Bay off Hollandia and also the airfield complex around Lake Sentani just inland of Hollandia, so speeding the advance of MacArthur's forces to the west in preparation for the US return to the Philippines.

The task was entrusted to Lieutenant General Robert L. Eichelberger's US I Corps of Lieutenant General Walter Krueger's US 6th Army, which was to land two regimental combat teams of Major General F. A. Irving's US 24th Infantry Division in Tanahmerah Bay near Wakde in the west of the operation, two regimental combat teams of Major General H. H. Fuller's US 41st Infantry Division in Humboldt Bay in the centre of the operation, and one regimental combat team of the 41st Infantry Division (to be reinforced by one regimental combat team of Major General William H. Gill's US 32nd Infantry Division) at Aitape in the east of the operation.

US intelligence suggested that there might be 14,000 Japanese at Hollandia, and probably 3,500 (but possibly 6,500) at Aitape. However, the Japanese in New Guinea were in the throes of a reorganization after the disaster of the operations in the Huon peninsula, and the 18th Army had recently come under command of the 2nd Area Army, which had ordered a withdrawal of Adachi's three forward divisions from the area of Wewak to Hollandia, which was to become the main Japanese base in central New Guinea. But at the time of the American assault there were only 11,000 Japanese in Hollandia and 1,000 in Aitape, most of them administrative troops. Moreover, local commanders had also been reshuffled, and none of them had been in the area for more than a few weeks, Rear Admiral Endo and Major General Kitazono having arrived only 3 weeks and 10 days earlier respectively.

Supported by Lieutenant General George C. Kenney's US 5th Air Force and Rear Admiral D. E. Barbey's US 7th Amphibious Force of the US 7th Fleet, the landings were universally successful. At Hollandia the US 41st Division landed unopposed after the Japanese defenders fled inland from the rigours of the cruiser bombardment of the beaches, abandoning their fixed defensive positions in the process. The Americans advanced inland against negligible opposition, capturing two of the three airfields around Lake Sentani by 26 April and linking up with the US 24th Infantry Division, which had taken the third airfield after advancing from Tanahmerah Bay. This American success was achieved with few casualties, but completely destroyed the integrity of the Japanese defence line fixed at the end of 1943. With Wakde and Sarmi now no longer feasible as main bastions, Imperial General Headquarters in Tokyo ordered the establishment of a new line running through Biak Island and Manokwari, later modified to Sorong and Halmahera with Biak and Manokwari as forward outposts.

Adachi was now faced with the problem of retreating some 400 miles to join the 2nd Area Army in western New Guinea. Though his orders instructed him to bypass the new US positions, Adachi was all too aware of the problems of such a retreat and decided to attempt a breakthrough at Aitape and Hollandia. The Japanese attacked on 10 July, and suffered some 50 per cent casualties before conceding defeat on 3 August. The battle for Hollandia was less severe than that for Aitape, and cost the Americans 87 dead to a Japanese equivalent of 4,441 before Adachi moved inland to face the dire prospect of a long westward infiltration without supplies and medicine.

Red US contingency plans before World War II for war with the UK.

Red Admiral Allied contingency plan for an airborne operation to seize the Kiel Canal linking the North Sea and the Baltic through Schleswig-Holstein (May 1945).

Red Ball Designation of the complex system of one-way express lorry routes through France from the Channel ports to keep the Allied armies supplied with all necessities before the opening of Antwerp as a forward supply port (July/December 1944).

Red Line Designation of the Allied radio link with the headquarters of General Dwight D. Eisenhower after the Allied landings in France during 'Overlord'.

Red Vault US II Corps operation in Tunisia (March 1943).

Regate (regatta) German operation against Soviet partisans operating in the region south of Gorki in Belorussia, to the south-west of Smolensk (3/8 October 1942). This area was fundamental to the rear-area security of Generalfeldmarschall Gunther von Kluge's Army Group 'Centre', and thus a natural target for the activities of Soviet partisans.

Regenbogen (rainbow) German naval operation against convoys J.W.55B (19 ships to the USSR) and R.A.55A (22 ships from the USSR), leading to the sinking of the German battle-cruiser *Scharnhorst* (30/31 December 1943). This double movement was a likely target for the Germans' heavy warships in Norway, and was thus covered by Vice Admiral R. L. Burnett's cruiser force (*Belfast*, *Sheffield* and *Norfolk*), longer-range protection being afforded by the battleship *Duke of York*, the cruiser *Jamaica* and 4 destroyers of Admiral Sir Bruce Fraser's Home Fleet operating from Iceland. The Germans were ready to respond to so tempting a target, and when aerial reconnaissance reported J.W.55B as '40 troop transports', the Germans assumed that a major raid on Norway was about to materialize. This estimate was later revised, the Germans appreciating that the sighting was more probably of a normal Arctic convoy with a strong escort (in fact 14 destroyers).

The die was cast on 25 December, when the German naval high command ordered Konteradmiral Erich Bey to sea from Altenfjord with the *Scharnhorst* and 5 destroyers. A patrol line of 8 U-boats was stretched out to the south from a point to the west of Bear Island, and the Luftwaffe was scouring the area with aircraft. Fraser and Burnett were informed by the Admiralty that the *Scharnhorst* was out. The convoy J.W.55B was moving east-north-east just to the south of Bear Island at 04.00 on 26 December, with Fraser's squadron moving north-east some 210 miles to the south-west and Burnett's squadron moving south-west some 150 miles to the east of the convoy, whose safety was Fraser's primary concern. The German squadron was heading north into a point right between the converging courses of the two British squadrons, and the destroyers were finding it difficult to keep up with the *Scharnhorst* in the deteriorating weather. At 07.30 Bey ordered his destroyers to fan out on a search to the south-west, and thereafter the *Scharnhorst* was on her own, being picked up on the *Belfast*'s radar at 08.40. The *Scharnhorst* was illuminated by starshell at 09.24, and five minutes later taken under fire by the squadron of 3 cruisers as she turned south. She hauled round to the north-east once she had distanced herself from the cruisers. The cruisers could at first follow this move on radar, but could not keep pace with the *Scharnhorst*, so Burnett decided to keep his force between the *Scharnhorst* and the convoy.

The sense of Burnett's move became clear just after 12.00, when the *Scharnhorst* was again picked up on radar. Both sides opened fire, the British cruisers coming off worse but persuading Bey to turn south, where Fraser's squadron was waiting for him. At 16.17 the *Scharnhorst* was picked up on the *Duke of York*'s radar, and at 16.50 the German battle-cruiser was illuminated by starshell from the shadowing *Belfast*, whereupon the *Duke of York* and *Jamaica* opened fire. Caught between the fires of Fraser's and Burnett's squadrons, there was no escape for the *Scharnhorst*, especially when the British battleship's 14-in. shells plunged into her at long range. The *Scharnhorst* was turned into a blazing wreck and sank at 19.45, taking with her all but 39 of her crew, which had numbered more than 2,000 at the beginning of the sortie. Like other German major surface vessels, the *Scharnhorst* had shown herself to be magnificently designed and constructed, for it had taken at least 13 14-in. shell hits, about 12 hits from the cruisers and 11 hits from the 55 torpedoes fired to sink her.

Regenfass (water butt) German operation against Soviet partisans operating in the region of Ushachi in Belorussia to the south of Polotsk (April 1944). This area was held by Generaloberst Georg-Hans Reinhardt's 3rd Panzerarmee of Generalfeldmarschall Walter Model's Army Group 'Centre'. The region was earmarked for the main offensive by General I. Kh. Bagramyan's 1st Baltic Front in July 1944, and was thus a primary target for Soviet partisan operations.

Regenschauer (rain shower) German operation against Soviet partisans operating in the region of Ushachi in Belorussia to the south of Polotsk (April 1944), and undertaken as a companion offensive to 'Regenfass'.

Reinhardt Linie (Reinhardt line) German defence line in Italy, running north-east from its link with the 'Gustav Linie' at Sant'Ambrogio (on the junction of the Rivers Liri and Rapido to form the River Garigliano) via Monte Cesima to Castel di Sangro back on the 'Gustav Linie' in the Apennines. Otherwise known as the 'Bernhardt Linie', the 'Reinhardt Linie' formed the outer defence of the 'Gustav Linie', and was itself protected by the 'Barbara Linie' between the lower reaches of the River Volturno and the Garigliano. Constructed in the autumn of 1943 at the instigation of General Hans Hube, commanding XIV Panzer Corps in Generaloberst Heinrich von Vietinghoff-Scheel's German 10th Army, the 'Reinhardt Linie' was based on the natural defence provided by the Mignano defile, and though intended (like the 'Barbara Linie') as a tactical delaying position in front of the main 'Gustav Linie', it was in many ways superior as a strategic block to the entrance of the Liri valley and the approaches to Rome. Hube appreciated that the 'Reinhardt Linie' was too far forward from the 'Gustav Linie' for an ideally co-ordinated defence, but with his corps engineers he constructed well-sited positions that made full use of the terrain's features to provide deep rather than linear defences. The Allies broke through this line in Operation 'Raincoat'.

Reise Würzburg (giant Wurzburg) German night-fighter control radar.

Renate (Renata) German E-boat attack on British shipping off Dover (January 1941).

Reno Series of five plans for the advance of US forces of General Douglas MacArthur's South-West Pacific Area through the Bismarck archipelago, New Guinea and the eastern part of the Dutch East Indies to invade the Philippine Islands (1942/1944). This was the basic strategic scheme to which MacArthur worked between mid-1942 and mid-1944 with the object of recapturing the Philippines as the major stepping stone in his northward advance to the Japanese home

Rentier

islands, a scheme MacArthur and his chief-of-staff, Lieutenant General Richard K. Sutherland, advocated as being decisively superior to the alternatives advocated by Admiral Chester W. Nimitz's Pacific Ocean Areas (an advance to the Marianas Islands via the Gilbert and Marshall Islands, followed by an offensive to Iwo Jima in the Bonin Islands and then to Okinawa in the Ryukyu Islands) and by Admiral Ernest J. King's US Navy Operations Staff (an advance to the Marianas Islands via the Gilbert and Marshall Islands, followed by an offensive to Formosa off the coast of mainland China).

The basic 'Reno I' plan outlined the concept of the South-West Pacific Area. The concept was then fleshed in slightly by 'Reno II', which was delivered to Washington in August 1943 and postulated an orderly progress (under cover of US land-based air power) via New Britain (so that the Japanese 8th Area Army and 8th Fleet headquarters and base areas could be destroyed), the northern coast of New Guinea, Halmahera, Morotai and Manado into Mindanao. The plan was refined into 'Reno III' by September 1943, and now featured the concept of bypassing New Britain (which was to be reduced later, together with New Ireland) in February 1944, followed by the occupation of the northern coast of New Guinea in two phases by October 1944, followed by the capture of Halmahera and Manado in December 1945, and ending with the invasion of Mindanao in February 1945. 'Reno IV' appeared in March 1944, and suggested that the US forces should bypass Truk to the south with the object of landing on Mindanao during November 1944 and on Leyte during January 1945. In July 1944 there appeared 'Reno V', which advocated that US forces should strike from the western end of New Guinea and Morotai against southern Mindanao (25 October 1944) and Leyte (15 November 1944), followed by large-scale landings in Lingayen Gulf on 1 April 1945 to start the reconquest of Luzon.

US Army and Army Air Force planners found much to criticize, but the scheme formed the basis on which the final invasion of the Philippines was based, though the schedule was advanced as a result of US Navy revelations about Japanese air strength in the region.

Rentier (reindeer) Offensive from northern Norway by the German Gebirgskorps to retake Petsamo in northern Finland from the Soviets and to drive on Murmansk (June/July 1941). This area had been taken by the 104th Division of the Soviet 14th Army during the 'Winter War' between the USSR and Finland in 1939 and 1940. The area contained nickel mines vital to Germany's war economy, and was thus a major target during the opening stages of the German campaign against the USSR. The Soviet defence of this sector was entrusted to the two divisions of Lieutenant General V. A. Frolov's 14th Army of Lieutenant General M. M. Popov's North Front (the Leningrad Military District until the outbreak of war). The offensive was undertaken by the Gebirgskorps of General Eduard Dietl within Generaloberst Nikolaus von Falkenhorst's 'Norway' Army, and made very little progress before being halted on the River Litsa by Frolov's army, which had been bolstered by an extemporised division made up of sailors and conscripted civilians. However, Petsamo had been retaken in the 15-mile advance.

Reservist Allied seizure of vital points in Oran during the opening stages of Operation 'Torch'.

Retribution Overall designation of Allied naval measures against Axis shipping involved in the withdrawal from Tunisia (May 1943). The operation was controlled by Admiral Sir Andrew Cunningham, who used a force of 18 British destroyers and a number of Malta-based coastal flotillas for the purpose of intercepting any Italian surface forces that tried to undertake an evacuation of the Axis powers' crumbling beach-head in Tunisia. Three of the destroyers were damaged by Allied air attacks before Cunningham ordered that their upperworks should be painted red as an identifying mark. In the event only the smallest of evacuations was attempted, resulting in the sinking of a number of coastal craft as well as 2 Italian merchantmen of the Skerki Bank on 9 May.

Only a few hundred men succeeded in reaching Sicily after the fall of Tunisia.

Reunion Operation to recover US air force personnel incarcerated in Romania (1945).

Rhein (Rhine)   Early version of 'Danzig'.

Rheinübung (Rhine exercise)   Foray into the North Atlantic by the German battleship *Bismarck* escorted by the heavy cruiser *Prinz Eugen* (18/27 May 1941), leading to the loss of the *Bismarck*. Both ships had recently been completed and Grossadmiral Erich Raeder, commander-in-chief of the German navy, thought that a commerce-raiding cruise into the Atlantic would be the best way for the two vessels to cut their operational teeth. The British Admiralty was aware that the two ships had been completed, and that they might sortie with the pocket battleship *Lützow* and the light cruisers *Emden* and *Köln*. The British thus put substantial forces on full alert, and intensified patrol operations (air and sea) between Iceland and Norway, the area through which any German squadron would have to sail to reach the Denmark Strait (between Greenland and Iceland) or Faroes-Iceland gap to break out into the North Atlantic and its convoy routes. In fact only the *Bismarck* and *Prinz Eugen* were finally earmarked for the sortie ordered by Raeder on 2 April 1941 with the object of large-scale devastation of convoys. The original plan was for the battle-cruisers *Scharnhorst* and *Gneisenau* to sortie from Brest at the same time on a diversionary raid, but both ships were damaged and thus unable to participate even though the raid was postponed after the *Prinz Eugen* suffered mine damage in the Baltic on 23 April. Vizeadmiral Günther Lütjens, commanding the Atlantic sortie, suggested that 'Rheinübung' should be postponed until the *Scharnhorst* and *Gneisenau* had been repaired or, indeed, until the new battleship *Tirpitz* had been commissioned, but this would have led to unacceptable delays and the operation was ordered to proceed with the *Bismarck* and *Prinz Eugen* alone. Unlike the orders given to the *Scharnhorst* and *Gneisenau*, now lying at Brest after a similar operation in the Atlantic, Lutjens was given permission for Kapitän Lindemann's *Bismarck* to attack convoys with battleship escort if this would allow Kapitän Brinkmann's *Prinz Eugen* to get in amongst the merchant shipping. However, Lütjens was under strict instructions not to jeopardize his squadron in any way against superior naval forces or if there was no worthwhile convoy in the offing.

The two German ships sailed from Gdynia in the Baltic on 18 May, and on 20 May emerged from the Kattegat into the North Sea. But by 21 May the British were aware of the two ships' movement, and Admiral Sir John Tovey was informed that his Home Fleet would be reinforced by the aircraft-carrier *Victorious* and the battle-cruiser *Repulse*. By 22 May the British had aerial photographs of the 2 German ships lying in the Korsfjord to the south of Bergen. There were suggestions that the 2 German ships might be covering a German assault on Iceland, but Tovey remained convinced that the Germans were about to launch another major offensive by surface ships into the North Atlantic. Thus Tovey strengthened British patrols between the Orkneys and Greenland (via the Shetlands, the Faroes and Iceland), and sent Vice Admiral L. E. Holland's Battle-Cruiser Squadron (the battle-cruiser *Hood*, the new battleship *Prince of Wales* and 6 destroyers) to Hvalfjord in western Iceland as cover for the Denmark Strait. Further aerial reconnaissance on 22 May showed that the *Bismarck* and *Prinz Eugen* had sailed from the Korsfjord, and Tovey departed Scapa Flow at 22.45 with the new battleship *King George V*, and *Victorious*, 4 cruisers and 7 destroyers, this force being joined later by the battle-cruiser *Repulse* from the Clyde.

Against advice from his officers, Lütjens had decided to break through the ice-narrowed 60-mile Denmark Strait rather than the 300-mile gap between the Faroes and Iceland, which would have given him quicker access to the Atlantic against a mere three cruisers before the Battle-Cruiser Squadron and the Home Fleet could close in on him. As it was the German squadron was picked up on the radar of the British cruiser *Suffolk* at 19.22 on 23 May, and thereafter the Germans were shadowed by the *Suffolk* and *Norfolk* under the command of Rear Admiral W. F.

Rheinübung

Wake-Walker, whose radio reports started the two British main forces closing in on the anticipated position of the German squadron. At 05.35 on 24 May the *Hood* and *Prince of Wales* sighted the German ships and immediately altered course to close the range (possibly so that the *Bismarck* would be unable to use long-range plunging fire to strike a mortal blow through the thin horizontal armour of the elderly *Hood*). At 05.52 Holland ordered his two ships to open fire on the leading German ship, which was now the *Prinz Eugen* as the two had changed places during the night. However, the *Prince of Wales* correctly identified the *Bismarck* and opened up on her.

The crisis came at 06.00 just as Holland ordered a turn to port to bring his after guns to bear. A 15-in. salvo from the *Bismarck* smashed down on the *Hood*, which blew up and disappeared in three or four minutes, leaving just three survivors out of a complement of 95 officers and 1,324 men. The Germans then turned their attentions to the *Prince of Wales*, which was already having trouble with her main guns, and soon landed four 15-in. and three 8-in. shells on the British battleship, one hit landing on the compass platform and killing or wounding everyone on it but the ship's captain and a signaller. Captain J. C. Leach broke off the action at 06.13 as he was heavily outgunned, but he had nevertheless managed to hit the *Bismarck* twice, one of the 14-in. shells gashing open an oil bunker and so hampering the German flagship through loss of fuel (which also left a telltale slick in the sea) and contamination of the surviving fuel with sea water. Lütjens therefore decided to abandon 'Rheinübung' and at 08.01 he radioed his intention of making for St Nazaire.

Meanwhile the British were reassessing their position after the wholly unexpected loss of the *Hood*. While the Wake-Walker took the *Prince of Wales* and the Battle-Cruiser Squadron destroyers under command and continued to shadow the German ships, the Admiralty set about increasing the strength of the forces opposing the *Bismarck* and *Prinz Eugen* by calling in Force H from Gibraltar (the battle-cruiser *Renown*, the aircraft-carrier *Ark Royal* and the cruiser *Sheffield*) plus the battleship *Rodney* and her 4 destroyers, which were escorting the troopship *Britannic* from the River Clyde to New York. Tovey by now appreciated that Lütjens might make for a French port or return to Germany rather than continue with the original raiding scheme, and disposed his forces accordingly. However, the speed of the German squadron was still too great for Tovey's liking, and during the night of 24/25 May a strike by Fairey Swordfish torpedo-bombers of the untried *Victorious* was sent in. Lieutenant Commander E. Esmonde led his aircraft with great skill, and managed to score one torpedo hit on the *Bismarck*. The torpedo failed to detonate, but all the aircraft managed to return to their carrier.

Matters now took a more ominous turn for the British, for Lütjens ordered the *Prinz Eugen* to break off on an independent raiding mission, and then the *Suffolk* lost radar contact with the German battleship at 03.06 as the *Bismarck* turned south-east towards the French coast. Moreover, the British ships were running short of fuel and having to break away for replenishment (leaving in the Atlantic only the *King George V* of the 22 ships that had sailed on 22 May), and a radio message from the *Bismarck* was incorrectly triangulated, leading Tovey to believe that the German battleship was trying to return to Germany and persuading him to turn north-west at 10.47 on 25 May. But the crucial moment came at about 10.30 on 26 May, when a Consolidated Catalina of RAF Coastal Command spotted the *Bismarck* steaming south-east towards Brest, now only 690 miles distant. A signal was flashed out, and it was immediately apparent that the Home Fleet could not intercept in the immediate future.

Success for the British now rested with Admiral Sir James Somerville's Force H, which at 14.50 launched a strike by Swordfish torpedo-bombers from the *Ark Royal*, the pilots fully appreciating that they must slow the *Bismarck* for the *Rodney* and *King George V* to intercept before they too had to break off for fuel. The strike was a disaster, for the pilots attacked the cruiser *Sheffield*, which had been sent ahead by Somerville to shadow the *Bismarck*. Luckily for the British, the torpedoes failed to work, exploding as soon as they hit the water. A second strike was flown off at 19.10, the torpedoes being fitted with contact rather than magnetic-proximity detonators. A German U-boat watched the take-off but could not interfere as it was out of torpedoes. Greater success attended the second strike, for between 20.47 and 21.25 on 26 May the Swordfish scored two hits, the first hitting the armour belt and causing no damage but the second striking the stern to damage the propellers and jam the rudders. The fate of the *Bismarck* was now sealed, for the great ship was seriously slowed and could not steer.

The *Bismarck* circled twice and then settled on a north-north-westerly course towards the two British battleships. First the *Bismarck* ran into a flotilla of five British destroyers commanded by Captain Sir Philip Vian, but so accurate was the battleship's gunfire that of the 16 torpedoes launched at long range by the destroyers in a very heavy sea, only two struck the battleship, causing no significant damage. Meanwhile the *Norfolk* was vectoring in the *King George V and Rodney*, and at 08.47 on 27 June the two British battleships opened fire at 25,000 yards, soon closing to 16,000 yards. At 10.15 Tovey had to break off for fuel, but by this time the *Bismarck* was a blazing wreck without effective armament. At 10.36 the *Bismarck* sank, according to the British finished off by two torpedoes from the cruiser *Dorsetshire*, and according to the Germans scuttled by her crew. Only 110 survivors were picked out of the water, some 2,190 others having been killed or otherwise going down with their ship.

The *Prinz Eugen*, meanwhile, had refuelled at sea on 24 May, but then started to develop engine problems on 26 May and so turned back towards France, reaching Brest unhindered on 1 June. And so ended 'Rheinübung', which had been a disaster for the Germans but also a great blow to the British. Apart from the loss of the *Hood* and damage to the *Prince of Wales*, the operation to sink the *Bismarck* revealed the severe tactical limitations imposed on Atlantic operations in the absence of underway replenishment tankers, and also how dangerous the German fleet would have been had its Plan 'Z' construction programme been completed before the outbreak of war, for the chase of 1 battleship and 1 heavy cruiser had required the British to use 8 capital ships (2 aircraft-carriers and 6 battleships/battle-cruisers), 11 cruisers, 22 destroyers and 6 submarines with great dislocation of convoy escort and the like.

Rhombus Allied meteorological flights over the North Sea.

Rhubarb British fighter-bomber sweep over occupied Europe and Germany (1941–5), the objects being to harass German communications by destroying transport in target-of-opportunity attacks, to keep the German defences on a state of constant alert, and to destroy any German fighters sent up to intercept the raiders.

Rhumba Plan for the transfer of US forces and logistics from British bases to France after the implementation of Operation 'Overlord'.

RI Japanese operation to secure Buna and Gona as beach-heads for the implementation of the overland offensive against Port Moresby in Papua (21/29 July 1942). The plan was the responsibility of Lieutenant General Harukichi Hyakutake's Japanese 17th Army, which had been formed on 18 May 1942 (after the end of Japanese operations in the Dutch East Indies and on Bataan) to run Japanese land operations in New Guinea and the Solomon Islands with the primary objects of capturing New Caledonia, Fiji, Samoa and Port Moresby. In this way Allied communications between the USA and Australasia would be severed, and the Allies deprived of the southern base area for any northward advance towards the Philippines. The 17th Army succeeded (and absorbed) Major General Tomitaro Horii's South Seas Detachment, and during June began to form at Truk and Rabaul (and in the Palaus) with the Aoba, Kawaguchi and Yazawa Detachments freed by the end of earlier operations.

Operations 'MI' and 'MO' were at this time just starting, and all looked promising for the joint offensive into the South Pacific by the Imperial Japanese Army and Imperial Japanese Navy. Then the Battles of the Coral Sea and Midway stopped both in their tracks, and Operation 'MO' had to be rethought as an overland advance on Port Moresby while

Ringbolt

the plans for seaborne assaults on New Caledonia, Fiji and Samoa were temporarily cancelled. The operation in New Guinea was recast as an advance across the Owen Stanley mountain range from a consolidated beachhead at Buna and Gona on the north-eastern side of Papua.

For this operation Hyakutake assigned the South Seas Detachment reinforced with the 15th Independent Engineer Regiment, for though intelligence reports indicated that the Kokoda Trail was passable, the Japanese hoped to be able to develop it into a road capable of taking trucks, or at worst pack horses. Lae and Salamaua were already in Japanese hands as advanced air bases for the bombing of Port Moresby, but could be nothing more than intermediate steps on the route to Buna and Gona. Hyakutake could achieve little without the navy, and such support was initially supplied by Vice Admiral Shigeyoshi Inouye's 4th Fleet at Rabaul. This formation was replaced on 18 July by Vice Admiral Gunichi Mikawa's 8th Fleet, which initially possessed 5 heavy cruisers, 3 light cruisers, 5 submarines, several destroyers and the 25th Air Flotilla. With Mikawa's assistance, Hyakutake planned to secure his beach-head with the 1,800 men of the Yokoyama Force, commanded by Colonel Yosuke Yokoyama and comprising 1 battalion of the 144th Regiment, 1 company of marines of the Sasebo 5th Special Naval Landing Force, Yokoyama's own 15th Independent Engineer Regiment and a number of artillery, anti-aircraft and service units.

The Yokoyama Force embarked during 18 July on 3 high-speed transports, and was escorted on the trip from Rabaul by the light cruiser *Tatsuta*, the minelayer *Tsugaru*, and the destroyers *Asanagi*, *Ukuzi* and *Yuzuki*. As the forces boarded, Mikawa was completing the plans for the complementary Operation 'RE' to establish a seaplane base in the Louisiade Islands off Milne Bay, later changed to a landing in this bay to take the three airstrips built there by the Australians. The convoy sailed to Gona without opposition and the troops began to land on 21 July against no ground opposition. A few Allied aircraft appeared later in the day and damaged 2 of the transports, but all the soldiers bar 40 got ashore safely. Yokoyama grouped his force between Buna and Gona, and on 22 July the marines reached Buna and began to prepare an airstrip as the battalion of the 144th Regiment, with engineer support, pushed inland as rapidly as it could to take Kokoda in the northern foothills of the Owen Stanleys. Lieutenant Colonel Hatsuo Tsukamoto's force met only limited oposition (from Australian militiamen) on its advance to Kokoda, which was occupied on 29 July. Between 18 and 21 August the rest of Horii's forces (numbering some 8,000 army troops supported by about 3,000 naval construction troops and 450 marines of the Sasebo 5th Special Naval Landing Force) landed at Gona. Horii himself landed on 21 August and reached Kokoda on 24 August, so the full-scale drive on Port Moresby began shortly afterwards from the advance position secured by Tsukamoto at Deniki.

Ringbolt Allied codename for Tulagi Island in the Solomons group.

Richard (i) Designation of German plans for a naval war with communist Spain (1937). (ii) German codeword to signal an Allied landing at Anzio south of Rome (in fact Operation 'Shingle').

River British codename for the German 'X-Gerät' blind-bombing system.

RO Japanese operation to reinforce the air strength of Rabaul with aircraft delivered by aircraft-carriers (1 November 1943) in anticipation of the US offensive against Bougainville in the central Solomons. At this time Vice Admiral Ryunosuke Kusaka's 11th Air Fleet in New Britain had only some 200 aircraft, and in Operation 'RO' another 172 aircraft were delivered from the stocks of Admiral Mineichi Koga's Combined Fleet. 'RO' was scheduled for 28 October, but at this time the Combined Fleet's plans were in disarray in the aftermath of an abortive sortie from Truk on 5 October to try to intercept the US Fast Carrier Task Force, which had sortied from Pearl Harbor for an attack on Wake Island. The carriers thus unloaded their charges on 1 November. The operation was undertaken successfully, and had been inspired by a similar undertaking organized by Admiral Isoroku Yamamoto at the end of March 1943 in preparation for Operation 'I', when more than 100 aircraft and their crews were unloaded from the 4 fleet aircraft-carriers of Vice Admiral Chuichi Nagumo to bolster the 11th Air Fleet in desperate efforts to strike at the growing US base areas in New Guinea and Solomons.

Roadstead British offensive air sweeps against German coastal shipping (1941 onwards).

Rob Roy Designation of the air operation to ferry supplies to Major General R. Gale's British 6th Airborne Division in the 'Overlord' landings (6 June 1944).

Robinson (i) Designation of the headquarters of the Oberkommando der Luftwaffe in East Prussia.
(ii) British bomber attack on the Le Creusot works of the Schneider armament group (17 October 1942).

Rockbottom Designation of special airlift operations over the 'Hump' air route from India to China (autumn 1943).

Rodeo Designation of sweeps over northern Europe by fighters of RAF Fighter Command (1941/1945) with the object of attacking targets of opportunity and of tackling German fighter forces based in the northern part of occupied Europe.

Roger British plan to take Phuket Island off the western coast of Malaya (spring 1945). The plan was formulated within the overall scheme by Admiral Lord Louis Mountbatten's South-East Asia Command for the recapture of Malaya. The command felt that the correct strategic approach was that adopted by the Japanese, namely a landing in the Kra isthmus of Thailand followed by a southward advance to Singapore. To this end the command proposed that Phuket Island should be taken as an initial move to provide the British assault forces with an advanced air and naval base. Detailed planning fell to Lieutenant General Sir Oliver Leese's Allied Land Forces, South-East Asia, which decided that 'Roger' could be undertaken on 1 June 1945 by two divisions supported by a single commando brigade, this making possible the implementation of Operation 'Zipper' in the area of Port Swettenham and Port Dickson in October 1945 for an advance to Singapore by the period December 1945/March 1946.

The operation was to be supervised by the new XXXIV Indian Corps (commanded initially by Lieutenant General H. L. Davies and from 12 March by Lieutenant General O. L. Roberts) with the 23rd Indian Division, the 81st West African Division and the 3rd Commando Brigade. The forces allocated for 'Roger' were also earmarked for Operation 'Dracula', and the plan was delayed by lack of shipping, but 'Roger' was finally rendered obsolete by the collapse of the Japanese in August 1945.

Romulus British operation for the clearance of the Arakan coast of Burma as far south as Akyab (December 1944) in preparation for Operation 'Talon' to capture Akyab. The operation was ordered by Admiral Lord Louis Mountbatten's South-East Asia Command in November 1944, and marked a radical change from the previous policy of containment on this front as Mountbatten needed formations from this front for operations elsewhere. Thus the successful conclusion of 'Romulus' and 'Talon' was to be followed by the immediate release to other duties of the 3rd Commando Brigade, followed in February and March by two divisions to be nominated.

'Romulus' was entrusted to Lieutenant General A. F. P. Christison's XV Indian Corps. In October 1944 this corps had comprised 4 infantry divisions, 1 tank brigade, 1 commando brigade and 1 infantry brigade with which to oppose the Japanese 55th Division of Lieutenant General S. Sakurai's 28th Army. From July onwards, however, Sakurai ordered the bulk of the 55th Division to fall back towards the Kaladan estuary, leaving only the Sakura Detachment to oppose the British formations. General Sir Henry Giffard, commanding the 11th Army Group, then ordered Lieutenant General Sir William Slim's 14th Army to thin XV Indian Corps by going over to the offensive and

219

achieving decisive local results. From this demand came 'Romulus', in which XV Indian Corps would advance to the capture of northern Arakan in a triple thrust with Major General G. N. Wood's 25th Indian Division on the right by the sea, Major General H. C. Stockwell's 82nd West African Division in the centre in the valley of the River Mayu, and Major General F. J. Loftus-Tottenham's 81st West African Division on the left in the valley of the Kaladan. Christison anticipated that Japanese resistance would stiffen along the line from Donbaik to Myohaung via Rathedaung, and therefore proposed that while his 3 forward divisions pinned the Japanese along this line with determined attacks, Brigadier G. R. Hardy's 3rd Commando Brigade would land in the Japanese rear on the Myebon peninsula, followed by Major General C. E. Lomax's 26th Indian Division, after the Arakan Coastal Forces had severed Japanese maritime communications. The assigned forces would then invade Akyab Island in 'Talon' and so free the formations required by higher command.

In preparation for the offensive proper, Christison launched his divisions on a number of preparatory attacks designed to provide XV Indian Corps with adequate start lines after the monsoon, the 25th Indian Division clearing the coast around Godusara and moving east of the Mayu range to a position astride the Maungdaw-Buthidaung road to cover the assembly area of the 82nd West African Division in the valley of the River Kalapanzin, and the 81st West African Division starting a sweep down the valley of the Kaladan as early as October 1944 to reach its concentration area around Tinma by the end of November. With the Sakura Detachment of the 55th Division fully engaged in the Mayu region, Sakurai during November ordered Lieutenant General S. Miyazaki's 54th Division to form Major General T. Koba's Matsu Detachment to hold the Kaladan valley.

Christison's final plan was formalized on 23 November, and called for a general advance starting on 13 December. In this advance the 74th Indian Brigade of the 25th Indian Division was to advance south along the coast with naval support and naval supply, and the rest of the 25th Indian Division was to push down the Mayu range and the western bank of the River Mayu before crossing the Mayu to take Rathedaung, the division then concentrating for a drive to Foul Point at the tip of the Mayu peninsula. The 82nd West African Division was to move south along the eastern side of the Mayu to take Htizwe before advancing via Kanzauk to relieve the 81st West African Division in the Kaladan valley, and then to move south along the river in boats to take Myohaung and Minbya. At this stage 'Talon' was to be unleashed by the 3rd Commando Brigade followed by the 26th Indian Division and a regiment of the 50th Indian Tank Brigade. Thereafter there was to be a general exploitation against the Japanese 28th Army in the Kaladan valley area. The offensive began on time and, after some brisk fighting, began to secure its objectives in advance of the schedule envisaged. The 74th Indian Brigade reached Foul Point on 27 December, and by the end of the year the 81st West African Division held an ideal base area in the Teinnyo-Myohaung area against the Matsu Detachment, and was awaiting the arrival of the 82nd West African Division for the major drive down the Kaladan.

Rooftree   Joint plan by the US Army and US Navy for Operation 'Torch'.

Rooster   Designation of the airlift operation undertaken (January 1944) to move the Chinese 22nd Division into the build-up area for Lieutenant General Joseph W. Stilwell's Chinese Army in India offensive through the Hukawng valley towards Myitkyina in northern Burma.

Roses   Allied codename for Efate Island in the New Hebrides group.

Rösselsprung   (knight's move) German air and sea offensive against Allied convoys for ports in the northern USSR (1/10 July 1942). This was a crucial period for the USSR, which was in the throes of checking the German army's various Operations 'Blau', and the Allies were thus making determined efforts to get through as many weapons and supplies as possible. The Germans were well placed to intercept these convoys with Norway-based sea and air power. In Narvik were the pocket battleships *Admiral Scheer* and *Lützow* together with 6 destroyers, and at Trondheim were the battleship *Tirpitz* and the heavy cruiser *Admiral Hipper* together with 4 destroyers. In addition, Generaloberst Hans-Jürgen Stumpff's Luftflotte V disposed of powerful and experienced anti-shipping air formations at many Norwegian bases, 7 of them ideally located for the interception of British convoys rounding the North Cape as far out as a point half way between Bear Island and Spitzbergen Island. The British were not aware of the political and strategic restrictions that hemmed in the tactical and operational flexibility needed by Admiral Schniewind, the German commander-in-chief afloat, for a successful foray, and therefore decided that USSR-bound convoys would receive escort by substantial surface forces only as far east as Bear Island, convoys thereafter having to rely on submarine escort for protection against the German heavy surface units

Thus was set the scene for the most disastrous of the Arctic convoys, P.Q.17, which sailed from Reykjavik in Iceland on 27 June. The convoy comprised 35 merchantmen (22 American, 8 British, 2 Soviet, 2 Panamanian and 1 Dutch) escorted by Commander J. E. Broome's force of 6 destroyers, 4 corvettes, 4 armed trawlers, 3 minesweepers, 2 submarines and 2 auxiliary anti-aircraft vessels. More distant cover was provided by Rear Admiral L. H. K. Hamilton's cruiser squadron (the British *London* and *Norfolk* and the US *Tuscaloosa* and *Wichita*, plus 3 destroyers), and in reserve against major German reaction was Admiral Sir John Tovey's Home Fleet force (the British battleship *Duke of York*, the US battleship *Washington*, the aircraft-carrier *Victorious*, the cruisers *Nigeria* and *Cumberland*, and 14 destroyers).

The convoy was spotted by German U-boats and aircraft on 1 July as it headed well north to pass between Bear and Spitzbergen Islands to keep as far from the German bases as possible. During the evening of 1 July P.Q.17 passed the homeward-bound Q.P.13, and shortly after this the Germans launched their first significant attack, Heinkel He 111 torpedo-bombers being beaten off without loss to the Allied convoy. Hamilton and his cruisers had now overtaken the convoy and were lurking to the north, and for the next two days no attacks materialized as the convoy was shielded by heavy fog. Meanwhile the Germans had been moving their heavy forces up toward Altenfjord, the *Tirpitz* and the *Admiral Hipper* reaching the Lofoten Islands on 3 July, by which time the *Scheer* had arrived in Altenfjord. The British Admiralty was aware that the *Tirpitz* and *Admiral Hipper* had sailed from Trondheim, but did not know of the German squadron's present location, and was also unaware of the movement of the Narvik force, which had been depleted when the *Lützow* and 3 destroyers ran aground near Narvik.

By 4 July the German ships were gathered in Altenfjord, and the convoy suffered its first losses, in this inital instance to He 111 torpedo-bombers. At 08.30 a single merchantman was torpedoed, and at 20.30 3 more merchantmen became victims of a determined attack by about 24 He 111s. Two of these ships were sunk by the British escort, but the third ship, a Soviet tanker, managed to keep up with the convoy despite her damage. The Germans were now caught in the mess of restrictions imposed by Hitler on the use of heavy surface forces in the Barents Sea, so the *Tirpitz*, *Admiral Hipper* and *Scheer* remained in Altenfjord while reconnaissance of various types was used to establish the position of the Home Fleet, Hitler's standing orders dictating that German major surface assets should not sail until the position of British aircraft-carriers had been determined. The 3 German surface vessels thus remained in Altenfjord until the late afternoon of 5 July, while Admiralty uncertainty as to their position led to disaster for P.Q.17. There had been a gap in the British aerial reconnaissance pattern, and Admiral Sir Dudley Pound felt at the Admiralty that while it was known at 20.30 on 4 July that the *Tirpitz* and *Scheer* were in Altenfjord, it was likely that all 4 German heavy warships (the accident to the *Lützow* was unknown) would put to sea to fall on the convoy any time after 02.00 on 5 July.

The Admiralty had to balance the threat offered by the surface forces against that of the air forces, and decided that the former was greater, especially as the cruiser escort had been ordered to stand on past its normal turn-back point after the Home Fleet units had retired as planned shortly after 12.00 on 4 July. There followed a sequence of three catastrophic but understandable signals. At 21.11 on 4 July the Admiralty signalled 'Most Immediate. Cruiser force withdraw to westward at high speed', followed at 21.23 by 'Immediate. Owing to the threat of surface ships convoy is to disperse and proceed to Russian ports' and finally at 21.36 by 'Most Immediate. My 9.23 of the 4th. Convoy is to scatter'. The convoy was thus on its own against the efforts of the Luftwaffe and the German U-boat arm in latitudes where the protection of the summer nights is short. Broome wished to stay with the convoy, but Hamilton was confident that the orders of 21.11 and 21.23 meant that the two escort forces were to fall back on the Home Fleet for a concentrated descent on the German forces sortying from Altenfjord.

The convoy scattered at 22.15, and of the 30 ships at this time only 11 finally reached Archangel between 11 and 25 July. The other 19 were sunk, 9 of them by aircraft and the rest by 82 torpedoes fired by U-boats. German losses were 2 bombers, 3 torpedo-bombers and 2 reconnaissance aircraft, and for this the Germans destroyed 99,316 of the 156,492 tons of cargo loaded, together with 430 of 594 tanks, 210 of 297 aircraft and 3,350 of 4,246 vehicles. Late on 4 July Hitler gave his permission for the surface vessels to sortie, and this they did at 11.00 on 5 July. During the day the success of aircraft and U-boats became clear, and the ships were ordered back at 22.00. In the Allied camp there were great repercussions, and Winston Churchill was so shocked by the catastrophe that he refused permission for the next P.Q. sailing until September 1942. In this time the British had improved their methods, so that while 13 of the 40 merchantmen were lost, the Germans also paid a heavy price in the form of 4 U-boats and 41 aircraft.

Rot (red)   **(i)** German plan for the invasion of France as part of a two-front war with Czechoslovakia and France (1935/1937).

(ii) Second phase of the German conquest of France (5/22 June 1940). This phase had been prepared while the Allies were evacuating the British Expeditionary Force and elements of the French 1st Army from Dunkirk, the German Panzer forces pinning the beachhead while the infantry formations of Generaloberst Fedor von Bock's Army Group 'B' and Generaloberst Gerd von Rundstedt's Army Group 'A' held the line of the River Somme which the Germans had reached during the first phase of 'Gelb', with useful bridgeheads at Abbeville, Amiens, Péronne and Rethel for the implementation of 'Rot'. By 4 June Général Maxime Weygand, the French commander-in-chief, could muster 71 divisions for the defence of central and southern France, whereas the Germans now totalled 143 divisions, 7 more (3 from Poland, 3 from the training army and 1 from Denmark) than they deployed for the start of 'Gelb' on 10 May.

The German plan was in essence a twofold one, with the armoured and motorized force of Army Groups 'B' and 'A' driving forward from the Somme into central and western France, and the more static formations of Generaloberst Wilhelm Ritter von Leeb's Army Group 'C' moving forward in the region from Luxembourg and the Swiss frontier to pass between the fortresses of the Maginot Line before turning to crush the French forces against the line. In the north, the French 10th and 7th Armies (commanded respectively by Général Altmayer and Général Frère) were faced by Army Group 'B' comprising the German 2nd and 9th Armies, but spearheaded by General Ewald von Kleist's Panzergruppe von Kleist (XIV Motorized Corps and XVI Panzer Corps) and General Hermann Hoth's Panzergruppe Hoth (XV Panzer Corps). In the centre the French 6th and 4th Armies (commanded respectively by General Touchon and General Réquin) were faced by Army Group 'A' spearheaded by General Heinz Guderian's Panzergruppe Guderian (XXIX Panzer Corps and XLI Panzer Corps). In the south, in the sector covered by the Maginot Line, the French 2nd, 3rd, 5th and 8th Armies (commanded respectively by Général Freydenberg, Général Condé, Général Bourret and Général Laure) were faced by the German 1st and 7th Armies. Paris, the French capital, was covered by the Army of Paris.

The Germans knew exactly what they were about to do, but the French were in a more difficult state. Although discouraged by their failures in Operation 'Gelb', they had not lost spirit completely, but were apprehensive at facing a triumphant German army without the support of the British and Belgians. The whole of their strategic defence planning had been defeated, and new plans were nowhere near complete, while the whole command structure had been disorganized by the replacement of Général Maurice Gamelin as commander-in-chief by Weygand, and by the reorganization of the command structure after the loss of northern France. It was here that the first blow of the renewed German offensive was to fall, on the 10th and 7th Armies of Général Besson's French 3rd Army Group (10th, 7th and 6th Armies). The 10th and 7th Armies could offer no defence in depth, being stretched along the lower Somme in a series of strongpoints at the rate of 1 division to every 8 miles of a front on which the Germans had 7 bridgeheads.

The German offensive was launched on 5 June by XV Panzer Corps and the Panzergruppe von Kleist, the former debouching from its bridgehead at Longpré on the lower Somme and the latter using its XIV Motorized Corps to push forward from Amiens and Péronne slightly farther up the river. The French resisted stoutly for two days, and von Bock was giving serious thought to the reinforcement of the XIV Motorized Corps with XVI Panzer Corps when he heard that the 4th and 9th Armies had broken through on the Chemin-des-Dames to reach the River Aisne at Soissons. Then came the news that the XV Panzer Corps had also broken through to reach Forges-les-Eaux. Besson ordered an immediate retreat, but this left behind the French and one British division that had been holding the forward line. These formations fell back towards the sea, when some 46,000 men surrendered at St Valéry-en-Caux during 12 June.

Fanning out as they moved forward, the units of the XV Panzer Corps drove west and south, key points and dates during its advance being Rouen, Cherbourg (18 June), Alençon, Rennes (18 June), Brest (19 June), Nantes (19 June), Saumur (19 June), Royan (25 June) and St Jean-de-Luz on the Spanish frontier (27 June). But two days after the start of the Army Group 'B' offensive, Army Group 'A' had joined in, adding to the agony of France. Here the attack was launched against the French 4th Army by the German 2nd and 12th Armies, and though the French again put up a determined resistance for the day, there was no way in which they could long check the Germans, and later on 9 June the two corps of Panzergruppe Guderian moved into the van and struck out to the south, XXXIX Panzer Corps towards Pontarlier on the Swiss border, and XLI Panzer Corps towards Belfort slightly farther to the north (22 June).

Meanwhile the Panzergruppe von Kleist had been switched from its bridgeheads at Amiens and Péronne before piercing the French front just to the west of Reims at the junction of the French 6th and 4th Armies. Paris had been declared an open city on 12 June, the date on which the Germans had generally reached the line of the Rivers Seine, Oise and Marne, and the victorious Germans entered the French capital on 14 June as their armoured forces were still pouring out of the west and south. The main weight of the southern exploitation fell to the Panzergruppe von Kleist, which sent its XIV Motorized Corps forward in two columns, one up the line of the River Yonne towards Creusot, St Etienne and Vichy (20 June) and the other on a more south-westerly route via Briare (18 June) to Angoulême, and forwarded its XVI Panzer Corps along the upper Seine toward the Rivers Saône and Rhône to reach Dijon (16 June) and Lyons (20 June).

Two days later the German Operation 'Tiger' had trapped the French 2nd Army Group in the Vosges region, and the battle for France was over. The organised resistance of the French had ended on 18 June, two days after the installation of Marshal Henri Pétain as the French leader in place of Paul Reynaud. Pétain immediately sought an armistice with Germany, this being signed on 22 June to come into effect on 25 June. The battle of France had cost the French 92,000 dead, 250,000 wounded and 1,450,000 prisoners, whereas the losses of the Germans were 27,074 dead, 111,034 wounded and 18,384 missing. The armistice divided France into two portions, the occupied zone in the north and along the west coast (giving Germany air and naval bases for the prosecution of the war against the UK), and the unoccupied zone in the south, where the Germans pulled back slightly from the extreme limits of their advances.

Rot-Grün (red-green)   German plan for a two-front war with France and Czechoslovakia (1935/1937).

Roundhammer Allied plan for an invasion of Europe intermediate in scope between Operation 'Round-up' and Operation 'Sledgehammer' (1943), the concept being adopted at the 'Trident' Conference in May 1943 as a result of the urging of General George C. Marshall, the US Army Chief-of-Staff, that the Allies should concentrate their European effort on a selected area to ensure 'a decisive invasion of the Axis citadel'. The result was Operation 'Roundhammer', basically an improved version of 'Round-up' with a proposed implementation date of 1 May 1944, by which time the USA proposed to have available in the UK some 29 divisions. The object of the operation was the capture of a large European lodgement which could then be used as the basis for decisive operations against Germany as the assault forces were built up a rate of 3 to 5 divisions per month. From this basic concept via Operation 'Skyscraper' grew that for Operation 'Overlord', the definitive plan for a cross-Channel landing that matured in July and August 1943 before it was finalized by the Allied leaders at the 'Quadrant' Conference.

Round-up Designation of a US-originated plan (1942) for a major Allied landing in northern France. The plan was developed at the instigation of General George C. Marshall (Chief-of-Staff of the US Army) by Major General Dwight D. Eisenhower (head of the US Army's strategic planning department), and was presented to President Frankling D. Roosevelt on 1 April 1942. 'Round-up' was conceived as the middle stage of a three-phase offensive against Germany. The first phase was Operation 'Bolero', which envisaged the build-up of American forces in the UK so that by April 1943 there were 30 US divisions (including 6 armoured divisions) across the Atlantic together with the appropriate strategic and tactical air formations (delivered in Operation 'Sickle'). The successful implementation of 'Bolero' would be followed on 1 April 1943 by 'Round-up', in which 45 infantry and 3 armoured divisions (30 American and 18 British) would begin to land (6 divisions supported by airborne forces in the first wave) between Le Havre and Boulogne with the object of taking a sizeable beach-head that could be reinforced at the rate of 100,000 men per week to secure a lodgement running from Deauville to Calais via Paris, Soissons, St Quentin and Arras, but extended later to include Angers. The third phase of this American plan would be operation 'Sledgehammer', to be launched on 15 September 1943 to take Cherbourg and the Cotentin peninsula.

The British were not impressed with 'Round-up' which, they felt, had no strategic objective other than the obtaining of a lodgement, faced severe terrain problems in the landing phase, and would be opposed by the powerful German 15th Army of Generaloberst Hans von Salmuth, whose formation had received favoured treatment in the supply of men, weapons and other *matériel* because of the very contingency the Americans were now advocating. By August 1942 'Sledgehammer' had been abandoned and 'Round-up' modified to include 27 US and 21 British divisions. By November 1942, at the time of the Casablanca Conference, 'Round-up' was planned round 30 divisions (including 6 armoured), but was cancelled at this conference in favour of a British-sponsored plan for the opening of hostilities against Italy with a landing in Sicily (Operation 'Husky') followed by landings on mainland Italy.

Rover Designation of British air reconnaissance sweeps over Norway (1941/1945).

Royal Flush Designation of Allied air support operations for 'Overlord' (6 June 1944).

Royal Marine British offensive against German riverine and canal traffic (10/31 May 1940), air-laid mines being dropped in the River Rhine and other German waterways.

The plan had been proposed by the British early in 1940 in the form of mines laid in the Rhine at Strasbourg to float down the river, but the French had objected to the notion until an inter-Allied meeting on 28 March, when they gave their permission for the operation to begin on 4/5 April (mines put into the Rhine at Strasbourg) and 15 April (air-laid mines in many German rivers and waterways).

R.S. Designation of West African ocean convoys (together with a numerical suffix) plying the route from Gibraltar to Freetown, Sierra Leone, and inaugurated in February 1943.

Rubble Breakout by Norwegian merchant ships from Sweden to the UK (23/25 January 1941). The 5 merchantmen were lying in Gothenburg and, with the support of the British Admiralty, decided to make a run for the UK via the Skaggerak. The ships sailed in the afternoon of 23 January and passed through the Skaggerak without interception, thereafter meeting with two cruiser and destroyer forces despatched by Admiral Sir John Tovey, Commander-in-Chief of the Home Fleet. All the ships got to Scapa Flow safely, though the Germans launched heavy air attacks on the escapers, and the combined force narrowly missed an accidental interception by the German battle-cruisers *Scharnhorst* and *Gneisenau* as the German warships headed north in preparation for a foray into the North Atlantic.

Rübezahl (turnip number) German operation against Yugoslav partisans.

Ruffian Alternative British codename to 'River' for the German 'X-Gerät' blind-bombing system.

Rugby Airborne operation by the US 1st Provisional Airborne Division as part of Operation 'Dragoon' (15 August 1944). Commanded by Major General Robert T. Frederick, the US 1st Provisional Airborne Division comprised the US 517th Parachute Infantry Regiments, the US 509th and 551st Parachute Infantry Battalions and the British 2nd Parachute Brigade, and the division's task was to land at 07.00 some distance behind the assault beaches to open the way into the Argens and Nartuby valleys near Le Muy for Major General Lucian K. Truscott's US VI Corps of Lieutenant General Alexander M. Patch's US 7th Army. It was expected that the landings would move inland without undue resistance from Generalleutnant Otto Fretter-Pico's 148th Division and Generalleutnant Johannes Bässler's 242nd Division of General Friedrich Wiese's German 19th Army. Most of the drops took place on target and the paratroops had little difficulty in securing their objectives against limited German resistance, but the US 509th Parachute Infantry Battalion was dropped too close to the coast near St Tropez, storming the German defences from the rear and entering the coastal resort long before the Allied schedule. The rest of the 1st Provisional Airborne Division received its heavy weapons during the afternoon (the transport gliders had been forced to turn back during the morning because of poor visibility) as it forged its way south to link up with the US 36th Infantry Division advancing from its landings at Agay and St Raphaël.

Rumpelkammer (junk room) German campaign against the UK with V-1 missiles launched from Heinkel He 111 bombers (5 September 1944/14 January 1945). In the course of this campaign the He 111 aircraft of Kampfgeschwader 3 and Kampfgeschwader 53 launched 1,200 V-1s against England, of which 66 hit London, 1 hit Manchester and 168 landed elsewhere in England. The campaign cost the Germans 41 bombers, some 20 shot down by the RAF fighter defences, and the others crashing into the North Sea as they flew at low altitude (to avoid radar detection) towards their missile-launch positions.

Rupert (i) Combined British and French attempt to take the port of Narvik in northern Norway from the German forces commanded by Generalleutnant Eduard Dietl. The town had been taken on 9 April at the beginning of Operation 'Weserübung' by the 139th Gebirgsjägerregiment of the 3rd Mountain Division, ferried to the port in the 10 destroyers of Kommodore Paul Bonte's

Gruppe I naval force. The town was surrendered by a Quisling, and Dietl was able to secure the area (and its arsenal) against the efforts of the 6th Norwegian Division. It had been planned that the Gruppe I destroyers withdraw after landing Dietl's force, but the tanker with their fuel was sunk and the destroyers thus had to remain in Ofotfjord.

The German position was precarious in the extreme, and had the Allies moved with speed it is likely that they would have retaken Narvik without difficulty. Plans had been laid as early as December 1939 for an operation against Narvik, the main exit for Swedish iron ore during the winter when the Baltic is frozen, but the plan had been postponed for fear that it would prompt a German counter-landing, and was revived only on 10 April, with Major General P. J. Mackesy in command of the land forces and Admiral of the Fleet Lord Cork and Orrery in command of the associated naval forces, which were already in action (the 1st Battle of Narvik, resulting in the loss of two British and two German destroyers, and the killing of Bonte). The rest of the German destroyer force was eliminated in the 2nd Battle of Narvik on 13 April, but Dietl made good use of this reverse to reinforce his 2,000 soldiers by forming the 2,600 surviving German sailors into five 'mountain marine' battalions equipped with captured Norwegian weapons.

It was anticipated that the Germans could now be dislodged without difficulty as they were cut off from seaborne resupply and reinforcement, and wholly at the mercy of the British naval forces free to operate in the Ofotfjord. However, there were serious differences between Mackesy and Cork and Orrery, Mackesy insisting that an assault landing could not be made on Narvik. The British advance guard was therefore landed at Harstad on the island of Hinnoy, leaving the 24th Guards Brigade with the prospect of a 60-mile advance across two fjords before it could close on Dietl's force. Mackesy was constantly at odds with Cork and Orrery, whose insistence on a revision of the army command led to the replacement of Mackesy by Lieutenant General C. J. E. Auchinleck.

With the rest of Norway now mostly in German hands, it was decided that the Narvik operation had gained in strategic importance as the only realistic way left to the Allies of blocking a large portion of Germany's iron imports. Auchinleck's force was thus reinforced by Général de Division Marie-Emile Béthouart's French 1st Light Division. This comprised the 27th Chasseur Demi-Brigade, the 13th Foreign Legion Demi-Brigade and the 1st Carpathian Chasseur Demi-Brigade (the last comprising Poles), and this division landed at Ankenes, Bjerkvik, Elvenes and Foldvik between 28 April and 7 May. It took the Allies some time to ready themselves, and this gave the Germans time to reinforce Dietl, who received an airdropped parachute battalion on 15 May, and later the hurriedly-retrained 137th Gebirgsjägerregiment was also airdropped. Moreover, the 2nd Gebirgsjäger Division was moving north from Trondheim to the relief of the German forces in Narvik, though this development was halted by part of the 24th Guards Brigade, which landed at Bodo on 15 May and blocked the Germans.

All was set for the battle of Narvik, with the Allies deploying 13 battalions to the Germans' 10. The Allied offensive began on 13 May, when Béthouart moved his 27th Demi-Brigade from Elvenes to join the 13th Demi-Brigade at Bjerkvik while General Bohusz-Szyszko's 1st Demi-Brigade occupied a commanding position at Ankenes. The Allies now had a change of heart and ordered the abandonment of the effort. Béthouart protested that it would be simpler to take Narvik and re-embark in the port, and it was then decided that Narvik would be taken. On May 28 the 13th Demi-Brigade, reinforced by the Norwegians, took the town and forced Dietl and his surviving forces up the iron-ore railway towards the Swedish frontier and internment, but before this happened the Allies pulled out on 7/8 June after demolishing Narvik's port. The 25,000 Allied troops were landed in Scotland, and despite the demolitions the Germans shipped out from Narvik their first load of iron ore during January 1941.

(ii) Airborne operations by the 2nd SAS to cut rail lines in the region of Bailly-le-France (4 August 1944).

Rutter Initial version of Operation 'Jubilee', planned in April 1942 for implementation at the end of June, but then postponed for weather reasons and then abandoned. The belief expressed in the basic concept by Winston Churchill led to the resurrection of the notion as 'Jubilee'.

S

S-1 Allied codename for the atomic bomb.

Safari British concept for an Allied combined air and sea landing in Denmark no earlier than 1 May 1943. The concept originated with Winston Churchill, who remained constantly sceptical of the Americans' desire for a single massive landing on the coast of occupied Europe. Churchill thought that greater results might accrue to the Allied cause from a series of six simultaneous landings in occupied Europe between Norway and southern France, for whereas some of these might find themselves embroiled against superior forces, others might have relative 'walk-overs' against inferior German forces and thus secure valuable lodgements with minimal casualties. Churchill's primary objective was northern Norway (Operation 'Jupiter'), where he thought the initial landing should be made, but this would be greatly aided by landings or feints at Denmark, the Netherlands, Belgium, the Pas-de-Calais (where Churchill proposed a major air battle), the Cotentin peninsula, Brittany, St Nazaire and the mouth of the River Gironde. Churchill anticipated that some four of these landings might be successful in securing a major port, and this would allow some 700,000 Allied troops to be landed in the first 15 days of the whole operation. Churchill's plans were eventually abandoned at American and British military insistence as militarily unsound as they were too diffuse and thus offered no real concentration of effort or aim against Germany proper.

Salesman Airborne raid by the French 3ème Regiment Colonial des Parachutistes near Sussac in central France (10 August 1944).

Sampson Designation of a British blind-bombing attack using the 'Gee' bombing aid.

Samwest Airborne operation by the French 3ème Regiment des Chasseurs Parachutistes to establish a base in the Forêt de Duault (6 June 1944).

San Antonio I Initial raid by Brigadier General H. S. Hansell's US XXI Bomber Command from bases in the Marianas (24 November 1944). The raid was sent against the Nakajima aero-engine factory at Musashi near Tokyo, and was undertaken by 111 Boeing B-29 Superfortress heavy bombers (led by Brigadier General Emmett O'Donnell) on the instructions of the 20th Air Force headquarters in Washington, where General Henry H. Arnold and the Joint Chiefs-of-Staff Committee exercised total control. Only 24 aircraft found and bombed the target with great inaccuracy, and the raid was not a success because of inadequate tactics (mainly a reliance on bombing from very high altitude).

San Antonio II Follow-up raid by XXI Bomber Command B-29s against Musashi (27 November 1944).

Sardine Allied landing in the northern reaches of the Adriatic Sea.

Satin US plan for Lieutenant General Lloyd R. Fredendall's US II Corps of Lieutenant General K. A. N. Anderson's

Allied 1st Army to drive on Sfax (December 1942) before the Axis powers could develop a strong defence on the area.

Saturn (i) Soviet plan for the recapture of Rostov-na-Donu at the same time as the elimination of the German pocket in Stalingrad (December 1942). The operation was planned as the successor to the Soviet offensive by the South-West and Stalingrad Fronts that had trapped Generaloberst Friedrich Paulus's German 6th Army in Stalingrad, to capitalize on the disarray of the Axis forces (in particular the Romanians) on the southern sector of the Eastern Front and so succeed in a major strategic blow down the River Don to the Sea of Azov. Operation 'Saturn' was confirmed by the *Stavka* (Soviet high command) in Moscow during 3 December, and envisaged a thrust by General N. F. Vatutin's South-West Front (the 1st Guards Army, the 5th Tank Army and the 21st Army) down the Don from Nizhne Chirskaya while the Don Front (General K. K. Rokossovsky with the 65th Army, the 24th Army and 66th Army) and the Stalingrad Front (General A. I. Eremenko with the 62nd Army, the 64th Army, 57th Army and 51st Army) closed in to crush the German 6th Army in Stalingrad.

It was soon realized by the Soviets, however, that their forces in the south were insufficient for two strategic blows at the same time, and it was thus decided to postpone 'Saturn' until Stalingrad had been reduced. This thinking was confirmed by the presence of two powerful German groupings (Generaloberst Karl Hollidt's Armeegruppe Hollidt near Tormosin and Generaloberst Hermann Hoth's Armeegruppe Hoth near Kotelnikovo), which could have taken any Soviet advance in flank as it struck down the Don. As it was, the Soviet high command decided that while the Don Front (together with the 62nd and 64th Armies of the Stalingrad Front) contained the Germans in Stalingrad until the Soviets were ready to crush them, the South-West Front and the Stalingrad Front should remain poised on the defensive to deal with the inevitable German counteroffensive to relieve Stalingrad (Operation 'Wintergewitter'). With the later development of 'Saturn' (ii), the original 'Saturn' (i) was retrospectively renamed 'Great Saturn'.

(ii) Soviet offensive designed to eliminate the advantages accruing to the Germans as a result of Operation 'Wintergewitter' (16/31 December 1942). Originated by the *Stavka* (Soviet high command) in Moscow, this revised plan called for a joint offensive by General N. F. Vatutin's South-West Front and the left wing of General F. I. Golikov's Voronezh Front to cut the lines of communication of Generalfeldmarschall Erich von Manstein's Army Group 'Don', and to take the airfields at Tatsinskaya and Morozovsk, from which was operating the German airlift to Generaloberst Friedrich Paulus's 6th Army trapped in Stalingrad. To this end the South-West Front and attached portion of the Voronezh Front were to strike south-east towards Nizhni-Astakhov and Morozovsk.

By now known as 'Little Saturn' to distinguish it from the original 'Saturn' (now 'Great Saturn'), the Soviet offensive got under way with a concentrated bombardment of General Italo Gariboldi's Italian 8th Army, which was holding the south bank of the River Don between the Hungarian 2nd Army and Generaloberst Karl Hollidt's Armeegruppe Hollidt. The bombardment totally discouraged the Italians, and the Soviet forces of Lieutenant General V. I. Kuznetsov's 1st Guards Army (South-West Front) and Lieutenant General F. M. Kharitonov's 6th Army (Voronezh Front) smashed through the Italian front to penetrate some 40 miles into the Axis rear by 19 December, when they captured one of the main supply dumps of Army Group 'Don' at Kantemirovka. The destruction of the Italian 8th Army was completed by Lieutenant General D. D. Lelyushenko's 3rd Guards Army (South-West Front), which crushed the Italians' right wing and helped to trap its remnants at Verchnyakovski, where some 15,000 survivors eventually surrendered.

The overextended Germans had no rear-area formations to check the Soviets, and the mobile forces of the 1st Guards Army, 3rd Guards Army and 6th Army (4 tank corps and 1 mechanized corps) exploited deep into the German rear, the Soviet XXIV Tank Corps advancing 150 miles into the rear of Armeegruppe Hollidt to launch a surprise onslaught against Tatsinskaya airfield on 24 December, and the Soviet XXV Tank Corps and I Guards Mechanized Corps falling on Morozovsk airfield. Both airfields were lost to the Germans, together with large numbers of irreplaceable aircraft (Junkers Ju 52 transports at Tatsinskaya, and Heinkel He 111 bomber-transports at Morozovsk). The depth of the Soviet push had completely uncovered the left flank of Armeegruppe Hollidt, which was still striving to push through to Stalingrad in Operation 'Wintergewitter', and the Romanian divisions Hollidt used in a desperate effort to remedy the situation were most severely handled. The German command in the USSR felt that there was a good chance that Army Group 'Don' and Army Group 'A' might now be cut off by a Soviet offensive towards Rostov-na-Donu, but as everything had to be referred to Hitler in Germany (and thus suffered undue delay as the Führer was in conference with the Italians), local decisions became the order of the day, especially as Armeegruppe Hollidt was now just 30 miles from the 6th Army in Stalingrad. It was vital for the Germans to stem the unhindered rampage of the 1st Guards Army, the 3rd Guards Army and the 6th Army. Thus General Otto von Knobelsdorff's XLVIII Panzer Corps (reinforced by an extra Panzer division) was sent south-west towards Morozovsk to prevent the Romanian 3rd Army from being cut off on the upper reaches of the River Chir on the left flank of Generaloberst Hermann Hoth's Armeegruppe Hoth. Hoth was himself forced to give up his 6th Panzer Division (LVII Panzer Corps) as additional support for the Romanian 3rd Army.

So far the Soviets had confined their effort to the German forces to the west of Operation 'Wintergewitter', but on 24 December they extended their effort to the east of the faltering German thrust, which had been halted on 23 December by the 5th Shock Army, 51st Army and 2nd Guards Army of General A. I. Eremenko' Stalingrad Front. The Stalingrad Front had now concentrated its hold on the lower Chir and the River Myshkova, and Eremenko was ready to launch his counteroffensive, initially against the Romanian 4th Army on the right flank of Armeegruppe Hoth. Here the 51st Army unleashed its VI Mechanized Corps on the right and its III Guards Mechanized and XIII Mechanized Corps on the left to punch through the Romanians towards Kotelnikovo. These forces struck deep into the Romanian rear, and Hoth was forced to pull back his LVII Panzer Corps (17th and 23rd Panzer Divisions) which was already under intense pressure from II Guards Mechanized Corps and VII Tank Corps of the 2nd Guards Army attacking south-west from the Myshkova. Kotelnikovo, from which 'Wintergewitter' had started on 12 December, fell to VI Tank Corps on 29 December.

Farther to the north-west the 5th Shock Army and 5th Tank Army had also gone over to the offensive across the lower Chir, and the plight of the Germans was acute, with a renewed possibility that Army Group 'Don' and Army Group 'A' would be cut off. Even Hitler was persuaded of the need for retreat, and on 28 December he sanctioned a withdrawal to a line from Konstantinovsk to Armavir via Salsk. By the end of the year the Soviets had completed 'Saturn', and now turned their attentions towards yet another offensive before the Germans could gather breath.

(iii) Allied plan to base air forces in Turkey for the provision of air support in Operation 'Hercules' (spring 1944). The plan was based on the capture of Rome in January 1944, which would free three groups of medium bombers for transfer to Cyrenaica. From here the bombers could start the process of wearing down German air and naval strengths in the Aegean pending the delivery to Turkey of 17 fighter squadrons (assuming Turkish permission). Then the Allies could mount an intensive air campaign against the Germans in the Aegean while 2 divisions were prepared in the Middle East for the amphibious assault on Rhodes during March 1944 if shipping permitted, with Kos and Leros as alternatives requiring reduced transport. During this preparatory phase, Allied supplies would be shipped to Smyrna and, if possible, into the Black Sea where a flotilla of 6 to 8 British submarines (supported by a depot ship) would operate after the implementation of 'Hercules' and a Turkish entry into the war on the side of the Allies. The plan was abandoned at the end of

January 1944 because the Turks steadfastly refused to allow the entry of Allied Air units onto their soil, and because amphibious transport was not available for 'Hercules'.

Saucy Developed but scaled-down version of Operation 'Anakim' adopted by the Allies at the 'Trident' Conference of May 1943 for implementation in the autumn of 1943. The plan called for a three-pronged Allied offensive southward through northern Burma, with the British advancing from Imphal, Lieutenant General Joseph W. Stilwell's Chinese Army in India from Ledo, and the Chinese 'Y' Force from Yunnan. An advance in the Arakan region was to complement the British effort from Imphal. The plan was greatly delayed and hampered by Generalissimo Chiang Kai-shek, who wished to use Chinese forces more in China, and also to see a greater Allied (and particularly British) interest in the war against the Japanese in Asia.

S.C. Designation of ocean homeward convoys (together with a numerical suffix) plying the route from Halifax, Nova Scotia to the UK, and inaugurated in August 1940. Between September 1942 and March 1943 the S.C. series originated in New York.

Schamil (Shamil) German plan for an airborne operation by the Lehr-Regiment Brandenburg zbV 800, a special operations unit, to seize Maikop and Grozny (July/August 1942). These two towns were the centres of oil production and refining in the northern half of the Caucasus, and as such were prime objectives (with Baku on the Caspian coast) for the 1942 summer offensive of Generalfeldmarschall Wilhelm List's Army Group 'A'. The plan was for the Lehr-Regiment Brandenburg to drop in advance of the 1st Panzerarmee to take the towns by *coups-de-main* so that the Soviets would not be able to destroy the oil facilities, but Maikop fell with little difficulty on 9 August, and the Germans failed to penetrate deeply beyond the River Terek in the region of Grozny, so obviating the need for the airborne operation against this centre.

Schildkröte (tortoise) Defence line of Generaloberst Karl Hollidt's German 6th Army in the southern USSR (1943). This new 6th Army was formed from the previous Armeegruppe Hollidt in February 1943, and held the line of the River Mius against General R. Ya. Malinovsky's South Front as part of the defence found by Generalfeldmarschall Erich von Manstein's Army Group 'South' (later Generalfeldmarschall Ewald von Kleist's Army Group 'A'). The line suffered the same problems as other German defences on the Eastern Front, namely lack of construction time, lack of men, lack of equipment, lack of materials and lack of weapons, and was thus punctured with little difficulty by General F. I. Tolbukhin's South Front during the opening stages of the Soviets' general offensive of August 1943.

Schlingpflanze (liana) German plan to widen the corridor between Staraya Russa and Demyansk at its narrowest point between Ramushevo (on the River Lovat) and Saluchi (July/August 1942). The pocket was held by General W. Graf von Brockdorff-Ahlefeldt's II Corps of the 18th Army of Generalfeldmarschall Georg von Küchler's Army Group 'North' against the 11th Army, 34th Army and 3rd Shock Army of the North-West Front commanded by Lieutenant General P. A. Kurochkin. Hitler saw the Demyansk salient as a threat poised over the Soviet rear areas in the north, and thus insisted that the salient be maintained and even enlarged. The position was finally abandoned on 1 February 1943 in the face of massive Soviet offensives on the northern half of the Eastern Front.

Schnee (snow) Transfer of German reinforcements to Norway (December 1942).

Schneehase (alpine hare) German operation against Soviet partisans operating in the region of Polotsk (February 1943). On this upper section of the River Dvina were vulnerable points in the supply system to Generalfeldmarschall Georg von Küchler's Army Group 'North', which was under steady pressure from the Soviet Volkhov, North-West and Kalinin Fronts, and whose supplies were therefore a valuable target for Moscow-commanded partisans.

Schneesturm (snow storm) German operation against Yugoslav partisans operating in Bosnia (1943).

Schnepfe/Wildente (snipe/wild duck) German double operation against Soviet partisans operating from the marshes to the north of Vitebsk (1/7 November 1943) and so posing a threat to the supply lines of Generalfeldmarschall Günther von Kluge's Army Group 'Centre' and Generalfeldmarschall Georg von Küchler's Army Group 'North'.

Schulung (lesson) German operational study for an invasion of Czechoslovakia as part of a two-front war (1935).

Schwarz (black) German overall plan for the seizure of control in Italy should that country fail militarily or defect to the Allies. The plan had its origins in a gloomy forecast (by the Oberkommando der Wehrmacht in May 1943) of Italy's continued role as partner to Germany. Hitler thus ordered that Operation 'Alarich' be prepared for the seizure of northern Italy by an army group headquarters established in Munich under Generalfeldmarschall Erwin Rommel. This initial plan called for the occupation of northern Italy by some 6 or 7 divisions drawn from the Eastern Front and supplemented to a total of 13 or 14 divisions, as the situation demanded, by divisions drawn from France and other areas from which formations could be spared. These forces would secure a firm German base into which Generalfeldmarschall Albert Kesselring could withdraw his forces from southern Italy. The plan was put tentatively into operation during the Sicilian campaign, when Rommel was called from Greece to assume command of Army Group 'B' in Munich, Generalfeldmarschall Gerd von Rundstedt was instructed to despatch 2 divisions from France (and to earmark another 4 for later despatch), II SS Panzer Corps (with 2 SS Panzer divisions) was pulled out of the Eastern Front, and General Kurt Student, the commander of XI Fliegerkorps (the 1st and 2nd Parachute Divisions) was flown to Rome to take command of the 3rd Panzergrenadier Division and prepare for the airlift of the 2nd Parachute Division from southern France. If 'Alarich' were implemented fully, it would be Student's task to take Rome and the Italian government, and to find and liberate Benito Mussolini, the Italian dictator who had been deposed on 25 July.

At this stage (28 July) 'Alarich' was abandoned in favour of 'Achse', a plan for German control of a hostile Italy. Included in this revised scheme were control of the Italian frontiers, the seizure of the ports of northern Italy (Genoa, La Spezia, Livorno, Trieste, Fiume and Pola), the disarmament of Italian forces except those prepared to fight alongside the Germans under German command, the evacuation of German forces from Sardinia and Corsica, the occupation of Elba, the withdrawal of Generloberst Heinrich von Vietinghoff-Scheel's German 10th Army to the region around Rome, the establishment of German forces of Army Group 'B' on a line across Italy from Elba to Civitanova via Perugia, the seizure of Italian warships and merchantmen by the German navy, the seizure of Italian air assets (especially anti-aircraft guns) by the German air force, and the occupation of Italian-held portions of southern France by von Rundstedt's troops.

Schwarz I and **II** (black I and II) German double operation against Yugoslav partisans operating in Bosnia (early May/15 June 1953).

Scipio (i) Original Allied plan for the seizure of Dakar in French West Africa (summer 1940). The plan had its origins in the desire of Prime Minister Winston Churchill and Free French leader Général Charles de Gaulle to bring Vichy France's overseas territories into the Allied fold. Clearly the most important of these were French North Africa, French West Africa and French Indo-China, where it was hoped a blend of Allied propaganda followed by the arrival of French ground forces would sway the political balance without the need for conflict. Of the three main targets, French West Africa offered the best chance of success, and the British and French leadership thus considered the landing of a small French force (about one brigade in strength) at Dakar in Senegal, or at Conakry in French Guinea, or at Douala in the French Cameroons.

However, the political sponsors of the plan failed to take into account the facts that the leadership of the colonies might adhere strongly to the Vichy cause and that naval support for these administrations might be provided from France, and when these considerations were finally taken into account during August 1940 it was decided that a greater British involvement would be necessary to provide the strength necessary for a *coup-de-main* against Dakar, now fixed as the target for the initial effort of what had now become a military rather than political operation. This resulted in a change of codename to 'Menace'.

(ii) British 8th Army breakthrough of the Wadi Akarit Line in southern Tunisia (5/6 April 1943). General Giovanni Messe's Axis 1st Army had fallen back to this line after the 8th Army's success on the Mareth Line, and prepared to hold strong defences on what was the last natural barrier to the 8th Army's advance into the southern end of the coastal plain of Tunisia. Messe had been able to start preparing defences on this formidable barrier only on 27 March, for up to that time the Italian Comando Supremo in Rome had ordained that the 8th Army would be unable to breach the defences of Mareth Line without a protracted battle. The Italian XX Corps under General Giuseppe de Stefanis was given responsibility for developing the defences, but was seriously hampered by lack of mines and barbed wire, so that the line consisted primarily of the man-improved Wadi Akarit (running inland some 4 miles from the coast of the Gulf of Gabes), the precipitous Djebel Roumana and the Djebel Tebaga Fatnassa complex, covered by some anti-tank ditches, small minefields, gun positions and a few extemporized machine-gun nests.

While General Enea Navarrini's Italian XXI Corps held the inland sector (west of the Djebel Haidoudi) with the Pistoia Division, a detachment of the 15th Panzer Division, the survivors of the German 164th Light Division and the remnants of the Raggrupamento Sahariano, the Wadi Akarit was the responsibility of XX Corps, which located (east to west) the Young Fascist Division (in the coastal sector), two battalions of Generalleutnant Theodor Graf von Sponeck's German 90th Light Division, the Trieste Division, and the Spezia Division (linking XX Corps with the Pistoia Division on the eastern flank of XXI Corps. In reserve Messe held the 361st Panzergrenadierregiment and 190th Anti-Tank Regiment (90th Light Division) in the Fatnassa area, and Generalmajor Willibald Borowietz's 15th Panzer Division (less the detachment with XXI Corps) and the first-class 200th Panzergrenadierregiment (90th Light Division) in the Roumana area.

Commanding the British 8th Army, General Sir Bernard Montgomery was faced with an Axis defence position held by a single depleted corps with only modest artillery and armour support, but the nature of the Wadi Akarit position meant that the British could not fruitfully use their very considerable quantitative advantages in men, artillery and armour. Montgomery's plan was therefore to breach the Axis position with Major General D. N. Wimberley's 51st (Highland) Division of Lieutenant General Sir Oliver Leese's British XXX Corps so that the various formations of Lieutenant General M. C. Dempsey's British X Corps could pour through and develop their exploitation to the north, thus resuming the pellmell advance to Sfax, Sousse and Tunis envisaged at the time of the Mareth Line battle in March. Montgomery's exploitation was based on Lieutenant General Sir Bernard Freyberg's 2nd New Zealand Division leading the advance to the airfields around Mezzouna, where Major General R. Briggs's British 1st Armoured Division would take over.

However, once detailed planning was begun and the relevant reconnaissances undertaken, it became clear that the Axis strength was greater than had been anticipated, and Leese decided that the initial assault should be undertaken by two divisions, Major General F. I. S. Tuker's 4th Indian Division supplementing the coastal effort of the 51st (Highland) Division (against the Young Fascist, 90th Light and Trieste Divisions) with an inland drive against the Spezia Division between the Djebel Roumana and the Djebel Tebaga Fatnassa. Neither Wimberley nor Tuker liked the tasks allocated to their divisions, the latter complaining that his division would be enfiladed by the

233

Scorcher

Axis fire from the Djebel Roumana and Djebel Tebaga Fatnassa. Leese was persuaded, with Montgomery's agreement, to change the plan to an assault on the Djebel Roumana (held by the Trieste and Spezia Divisions) on 6 April by the 51st (Highland) Division, while the main effort was made by the 4th Indian Division against the monumentally complex Djebel Tebaga Fatnassa posiition (held by the 361st Panzergrenadierregiment and part of the Pistoia Division), which the division was to take on the night of 5/6 April before bridging the anti-tank ditch below it for the exploitation.

The third component of the revised plan was a central assault by the 69th Brigade of Major General J. S. Nichols's British 50th Division against the anti-tank ditch between the Djebel Roumana and El Hachana at the eastern end of the Djebel Tebaga Fatnassa complex. Somewhat counterproductive diversions were also laid on, by the British 1st Armoured Division against the Djebbbel Haidoudi pass in the Italian XXI Corps' sector, and by the 201st Guards Motor Brigade of the 51st (Highland) Division in the coastal sector against the Young Fascist and 90th Light Divisions. The whole width of the British assault was a mere 8 miles between the Gulf of Gabes and the Chott el Djerid, a marshy lake which the British believed to be impenetrable but which was in the process of drying out.

The strength of the Axis position was great, and Messe believed that Montgomery would attack only at the time of the next full moon on 19/20 April. Montgomery also thought that a night assault was essential, but opted for the darkness of the new moon on 5/6 April, when the 4th Indian Division moved off with the 7th Indian Brigade in the lead to take Rass Zouai, where the 5th Indian Brigade would pass through it to take the Fatnassa ridge, the object being to capture or neutralize the Axis positions on the Djebel Tebaga Fatnassa by 08.30 on 6 April. The 4th Indian Division was generally successful, the 7th Indian Brigade taking Ras Zouai by 24.00 and pushing on to the Djebel Tebaga Fatnassa by 04.00 while the 5th Indian Brigade wheeled slightly right towards the gap between Point 152 (at the eastern end of the Djebel Tebaga Fatnassa) and El Hachana. The British 69th Brigade made little impression in its sector, but the 152nd and 154th Brigades of the 51st (Highland) Division fared better, the former taking the Djebel Roumana and pushing on towards Point 112, while the latter broke through the left flank of the Trieste Division and headed for the coastal road running north from Gabes to Sffax.

By 12.00 on 6 April the 5th Indian Brigade was being counterattacked by the 200th Panzergrenadierregiment and the 154th Brigade was receiving the attentions of the 15th Panzer Division. Leese had ordered the movement of the 2nd New Zealand Division (X Corps) at 11.10, the division being instructed to use the junction of the 50th and 51st Divisions as its route into the Axis rear. Plans were also laid for the continuance of the battle on 7 April with the support of the army's artillery (which would barrage the Axis rear areas) and the armour of X Corps, but the situation was now swaying against the Axis forces, though Messe was not yet convinced that the battle was lost. Generaloberst Jürgen von Arnim, commanding Army Group 'Africa' and presently at Messe's headquarters, thought differently and ordered a retreat to start at nightfall.

Messe jumped the gun and got away the best of his Italian troops in the limited motor transport available to the 1st Army, leaving the Germans and some of the Italians to escape on foot if they could. Von Arnim's reasoning was that as defeat was probable, it was better to pull back a short way in good order, especially as the Axis forces' right flank in southern Tunisia was seriously threatened by the advance of Lieutenant General George S. Patton's US II Corps, which linked up with Montgomery's left flank on 8 April between Gabes and El Guettar. But Messe would have no truck with intermediate stop lines and pulled well back, the Spezia and Trieste Divisions to Enfidaville and the Young Fascist Division to El Djem. The Axis position in southern Tunisia was thus lost. Operation 'Scipio' had cost the 8th Army 1,289 casualties, while the Axis losses included some 7,000 prisoners as well as a substantial number of dead and wounded.

Scorcher British plans for the defence of

Crete (May 1941). At the time of the Greek campaign in April 1941, the garrison of Crete consisted of 3 British battalions (the 14th Brigade of the new British 6th Division), and a number of half-trained and poorly-equipped Greek units, reinforced during early May by the Royal Marine Naval Base Defence Organization under Major General E. C. Weston. The importance of Crete in strategic terms was well understood by the Allies, and though it was appreciated that the Italians would in the short term be unable to undertake the conquest of the island, the Germans were believed to be an altogether more formidable proposition, as they might undertake the venture to prevent the British establishing bases from which naval and air forces could raid into the Aegean and as far north as the vital Romanian oilfields.

On 30 April it was decided to entrust overall command of the island to Major General B. C. Freyberg, commander of the 2nd New Zealand Division recently evacuated from southern Greece. Freyberg assumed command at the beginning of May, and quickly assessed the defence needs of the island, which could only be invaded with any practicality along its northern shore, where there is a coastal plain for the development of the landings. There was little thought given to the possibility of a large-scale airborne invasion, but the plan devised by Freyberg none the less retained its basic validity against this contingency. From the Allied point of view the island's main assets were the harbour at Suda and the three airfields, and these areas were each entrusted to a brigade-sized formation. From west to east these areas were Maleme airfield (Brigadier E. Puttick with the 5th and 10th New Zealand Brigades of the 2nd New Zealand Division, which Puttick now commanded), the Suda-Canea region (Weston with his Royal Marines and other units), the Heraklion area (Brigadier B. H. Chappel with the 14th Brigade) and the Rethimnon-Georgeopolis area (Brigadier G. A. Vasey with the 19th Australian Brigade). The Greek units were divided among the Allied formations. Freyberg's plan was to hold these vital points and defeat any invasion on the beaches and/or airfields. Heavy weapons were in very limited supply, and communications all but nonexistent, so great emphasis was placed on local initiative and rapid response to any German approach. Air defence was also scarce, the garrison having just 32 heavy and 36 light AA guns, and no aircraft. Group Captain G. R. Beamish had commanded four squadrons (Nos 33, 80 and 112 Squadrons of the RAF and No. 805 Squadron of the Fleet Air Arm), but the hectic pace of operations against an overwhelming German air superiority meant that when the squadrons were withdrawn to Egypt on 19 May they had a mere four Hawker Hurricane and three Gloster Gladiator fighters between them. The Allied forces on Crete numbered some 30,000 men.

Sealion Allied contingency plan for the evacuation of Lieutenant General R. L. McCreery's British X Corps from the northern sector of the beach-head at Salerno for rapid movement to reinforce Major General Ernest J. Dawley's US VI Corps in the southern sector of the beach-head (13 September 1943). This plan was evolved in outline only, and resulted from the anxiety felt by Lieutenant General Mark W. Clark's US 5th Army staff about the continued viability of the overall Allied beach-head after the launch of Operation 'Avalanche', where the German 10th Army of Generaloberst Heinrich von Vietinghoff-Scheel was launching determined counterattacks with the aid of useful Luftwaffe raids against the beach-head and the ships supporting it. The operation was planned with great reluctance by Commodore G. N. Oliver under the supervision of Vice Admiral J. Kent Hewitt, both naval commanders appreciating that any evacuation would be costly in the extreme. The Allied 15th Army Group commander, General the Hon. Sir Harold Alexander, arrived in the beach-head during 15 September and ordered an end to the preparations.

Seaslug Allied US patrols over the Bay of Biscay (July 1943) to intercept German U-boats transiting between French bases and their operational areas at the height of the Battle of the Atlantic. During the month 13 U-boats were lost to Allied air attack in the Bay of Biscay.

235

Seatrain Reverse counterpart of Operation 'Sealion', namely an Allied contingency plan for the evacuation of Major General Ernest J. Dawley's US VI Corps from the southern sector of the beach-head at Salerno for rapid movement to reinforce Lieutenant General R. L. McCreery's British X Corps in the northern sector of the beach-head (13 September 1943). The reasoning of the US 5th Army staff was the same as that for 'Sealion', despite the objections of the naval planners that any such move would mean the loss of all the supplies landed with the corps that was to be moved, but the plan was scotched by General the Hon. Sir Harold Alexander, who arrived to take personal note of the situation on 15 September.

Seelöwe (sealion) German plan for the invasion of the UK (summer 1940). As early as the winter of 1939/1940 Grossadmiral Erich Raeder, commander-in-chief of the German navy, had foreseen the need for an invasion of the UK if that country refused to capitulate after the defeat of France, and set his staff to the preparation of preliminary plans. Raeder appreciated that the German army would regard any such invasion as little more than the assault crossing of a larger-than-average river, whereas he knew that such a crossing could face highly adverse weather and sea conditions, and would also encounter the full strength of the formidable Royal Navy even after the necessary operational pre-condition (Luftwaffe elimination of the RAF) had been achieved. Raeder presented his initial ideas to Adolf Hitler on 21 May, but the German leader was at that time preoccupied with the course of operations in France and paid scant heed to Raeder's ideas. It was only after the capitulation of France on 25 June that Hitler began to devote his full energies to the question of the UK, and on 2 July (three days after receiving an initial assessment prepared by General Alfred Jodl, chief-of-staff of the Oberkommando der Wehrmacht) Hitler ordered preliminary planning, this being extended on 16 July by the Führerbefehl Nr 16, which laid out the objectives of what had now become Operation 'Seelöwe'.

According to the directive, 'The aim of this operation is the elimination of the British homeland as a base for the further prosecution of the war against Germany, and, if necessary, to occupy it completely,' yet Hitler was still convinced that he could reach an accommodation with the British, and so delayed the start of full-scale preparations until he had made a 'last appeal to reason' in a speech on 19 July. On 22 July the British refused even to consider the German offer, so Hitler ordered that 'Seelöwe' be prepared for commitment in mid-September, while the Luftwaffe of Reichsmarschall Hermann Goering set about the destruction of the RAF as the necessary precondition of the invasion. The German army had little experience with an operation of the scale envisaged, but set about its task with the usual methodical professionalism (even if lack of understanding of the realities of amphibious warfare was evident), under the direct supervision of Generalfeldmarschall Walther von Brauchitsch (commander-in-chief of the German army) and Generaloberst Franz Halder (chief-of-staff of the German army).

The initial German scheme was delivered to Hitler on 13 July (three days before Führerbefehl Nr 16) and was built around the use of combat-experienced divisions (with supporting elements) drawn from Generalfeldmarschall Gerd von Rundstedt's Army Group 'A' (based in northern France) and Generalfeldmarschall Fedor von Bock's Army Group 'B' (based in western France). The army plan called for the initial assault wave (11 infantry and 2 mountain divisions) to be transported across the Channel to secure (over a period of three days) a number of relatively small and unconnected beach-heads between Ramsgate and Lyme Bay. In this tactically and operationally unsound scheme 6 divisions from Army Group 'A' (the 3 corps of Generaloberst Ernst Busch's 16th Army) were to be shipped from Rotterdam, Vlissingen, Ostend, Nieuport, Dunkirk, Calais and Boulogne to be landed between Ramsgate and Bexhill, 4 divisions of Army Group 'A' (the 2 corps of Generaloberst Adolf Strauss' 9th Army) were to be shipped from Le Havre to be landed between Brighton and the Isle of Wight, and 3 divisions of Army Group 'B' (1 corps of Generalfeldmarschall Walther von Reichenau's 6th Army) were to be shipped from Cherbourg to be landed in

Lyme Bay. These 13 assault divisions would be delivered in two waves (the first delivering 90,000 men, 650 tanks and 4,500 horses, and the second 160,000 men, 60,000 horses, between 30,000 and 40,000 vehicles and 500 field howitzers), and would then be supplemented by 28 more divisions for the exploitation. This reinforcement would be delivered in three waves, the first consisting of 6 Panzer and 3 motorized divisions in three army corps plus the 7th Fliegerdivision and the 22nd Division in one Luftwaffe corps, the second of 9 infantry divisions, and the third of 8 infantry divisions.

The object of the assault by the divisions of Army Group 'A' was to secure a consolidated beach-head (up to 20 miles deep) between Ramsgate and Bognor Regis, after which the Germans would advance, to their first objective, a line stretching from Gravesend to Southampton and giving the Germans a secure lodgement in most of south-east England. With the arrival of reinforcements (the 28 divisions mentioned above), the Army Group 'A' divisions would sweep forward to their second objective, a line running from Maldon on the east coast of Gloucester on the River Severn, via St Albans and Oxford. The conurbation of London would not be assaulted in this phase, but cut off for subsequent reduction if the British failed to capitulate. At the same time the Army Group 'B' divisions in Lyme Bay would break out of their beach-head to secure the west country before supplementing Army Group 'A' for a northern advance that was expected to reduce the rest of the UK in about one month.

The paradox of the German situation in July 1940 was that the German navy, which had been the original sponsor of the 'Seelöwe' concept when the army was wholly unenthusiastic, was becoming increasingly disenchanted with the notion as the army's enthusiasm grew. Raeder's objections centred on the difficulty of undertaking the operation because of damage to the invasion ports caused by the implementation of Operations 'Gelb' and 'Rot', the unpredictability of weather and sea conditions in the English Channel, Germany's lack of adequate landing resources (requiring the collection and modification of coastal craft and barges from all parts of occupied Europe) and, perhaps most significantly, the inability of the German navy to secure the crossing lanes for the reinforcement divisions against opposition from the Royal Navy. The naval arguments were compelling, and their meaning was not lost on the army, which was forced to scale down its plans to fit more closely the convoy and escort capacity offered by Raeder. Even so, there remained a fundamental difference between the maximum that Raeder could offer and what the army saw as its minimum for a successful assault, so Hitler had to force a compromise on the two services at the end of August.

The 6th Army landing in Lyme Bay was abandoned as an element of the assault phase, and the efforts of the 16th and 9th Armies were scaled down. The 16th Army was now to use 1 mountain and 3 infantry divisions in two landings (between Folkestone and New Romney, and between Camber and Hastings), and the 9th Army was now to use 2 infantry and part of 1 mountain division in two landings (between Hastings and Eastbourne, and between Beachy Head and Brighton) for the rapid delivery of 2 more infantry divisions and the rest of the mountain division. The 7th Fliegerdivision was to make parachute landings for the capture of the high ground north-west of Dover. The initial beach-head was defined as a line from the middle of East Kent to Brighton, giving the Germans a lodgement some 15 miles deep into which the second wave could be delivered for an exploitation to secure a line from the estuary of the River Thames via the North Downs to Portsmouth. Thus a first wave of 7 infantry, 2 mountain and 1 parachute divisions would receive a second wave of 4 Panzer, 2 motorized and 2 infantry divisions reinforced by 2 motorized regiments, a third wave of 6 infantry divisions (plus an airlanding division if required), and an unspecified fourth wave. If circumstances demanded (and shipping permitted), the 6th Army would be moved into the west country at the time the third and fourth 16th Army and 9th Army waves were delivered. On 6 September the 6th Army came under the command of Generalfeldmarschall Wilhelm Ritter von Leeb's Army Group 'C', which replaced Army Group 'B' on that date. The army was still unhappy with this revised plan, which promised landings on a front that the army planners believed to be too narrow, but Raeder was adamant that this was the best that his resources would permit.

At this time the British defence was adequately organized on paper but still suffering from the catastrophes of France and the Dunkirk evacuation, and hopelessly short of trained men and weapons (especially artillery and armour). Under the overall control of the War Office in London, the defence of the most threatened sector in the south-east was entrusted to XII Corps (Kent, Sussex and Surrey), which controlled the 1st, 45th and New Zealand Divisions, the 29th Brigade Group and the 1st Motor Machine-Gun Brigade. To the west of XII Corps was V Corps (Hampshire, Wiltshire, Somerset and Dorset), which controlled the 3rd, 4th and 50th Divisions, the Australian Infantry Force, the 21st Army Tank Brigade and 1 brigade of the 2nd Armoured Division. Farther west still was VIII Corps (Devon and Cornwall), which controlled the 48th Division and the 70th Brigade Group. East Anglia was the responsibility of II and XI Corps, which between them ordered the 15th, 18th, 52nd and 55th Divisions, and the 37th Brigade Group. In reserve for these most threatened sectors were the two corps of the GHQ Reserve, namely VII Corps in Surrey and Berkshire with the 1st Armoured Division, the 1st Canadian Division and the 1st Army Tank Brigade, and IV Corps north of London with the 2nd Armoured Division (less the brigade in the west country), the 42nd and 43rd Divisions, and the 21st Brigade Group. London was defended by three infantry brigades, the East Midlands and the north-east of England by I and X Corps (5 infantry divisions and 1 army tank brigade), the West Midlands, Wales and the north-east of England by III Corps (2 infantry divisions, 1 infantry brigade, 1 motor machine-gun brigade and 1 army tank brigade), Scotland by 3 infantry divisions and 1 motor machine-gun brigade, and Northern Ireland by 2 infantry divisions and 1 infantry brigade.

Frantic German preparations continued throughout late July and August, but were much hampered by the activities of British bombers, which had as their primary target the ports in which the invasion transport was being gathered and modified, but on 11 September Hitler announced that the countdown for 'Seelöwe' would begin on 14 September for a landing at dawn on 24 September. On 14 September Hitler postponed his decision for three more days, and on 17 September he postponed 'Seelowe' indefinitely because the Luftwaffe had manifestly failed to subdue the RAF in the Battle of Britain. Hitler ordered that the invasion fleet be returned to normal service, but only in such a way that it could be rapidly reassembled for a revival of 'Seelöwe' in the spring or summer of 1941. In March 1942, with his forces deeply committed in the USSR, Hitler ordered that 'Seelöwe' be put on one-year notice, and the scheme was effectively forgotten.

Selenium Royal Navy offensive against German shipping off Norway (January/February 1945). The offensive was of particular importance to the Allies, as Hitler's insistence that Norway was a 'zone of destiny' meant that at the time of the Russo-Finnish armistice of 4 September 1944 there were in northern Norway and Finland some 170,000 men of 7 German divisions whom the German authorities wished to evacuate from Narvik, which was also the main shipment port for the Swedish iron ore on which Germany placed so great an industrial reliance. By the beginning of 1945 the evacuation was in progress using some 200 ships (380,000 tons) reserved in northern Norway against just such an eventuality. The British realized that the evacuation was wholly dependent on the delivery of motor transport and bunker fuel to Narvik by German tankers, and thus decided on a major effort (by major surface forces, submarines, coastal craft and the strike aircraft of No. 18 Group of RAF Coastal Command) to prevent the arrival of this fuel. Overall command was vested in Admiral Sir Henry Moore, commander-in-chief of the Home Fleet, who had to contend with imprecise intelligence, the difficulty of Norwegian coastal waters and the vagaries of the winter weather.

Nevertheless some significant successes were gained. On 6/8 January the Norwegian-manned motor torpedo boats of the 54th Flotilla sank 3 laden iron-ore transports. On

11/12 January the cruisers *Norfolk* and *Bellona* under Rear Admiral R. R. McGrigor sank 2 merchantmen and 1 of 6 escorts. Aircraft also laid mines during the month, in which the Allied tally was 12 ships of 20,043 tons sunk (almost the same as that achieved by the aircraft of No. 18 Group). A sweep was also undertaken against 3 German destroyers that left Narvik on 26 January to move into the Baltic, and though 1 German ship was heavily damaged and another less badly afflicted, 2 of the destroyers reached Kiel on 1 February. The fourth large German destroyer in northern Norway sailed on 5 February for the Baltic, joining up with the repaired destroyer of the earlier movement. Both were again hit, this time by bombs, but made it to Kiel during March.

Semmering Linie (Semmering line) German defence line in Norway.

Senger Linie (Senger line) Designation of a German defence line in south central Italy (spring 1944), otherwise known as the 'Führer Linie'. This line was held by Generalleutnant Fridolin von Senger und Etterlin's German XIV Panzer Corps (th 15th Panzergrenadier Division, and the 71st and 94th Divisions) within Generaloberst Heinrich von Vietinghoff-Scheel's 10th Army. The line was designed as a fall-back position covering the entrance to the valley of the River Liri to the north of the main German defence line in the sector, the 'Gustav Linie', and ran roughly parallel to (but between 10 and 15 miles north of) this latter defence. The 'Senger Linie' defences were based on the Tyrrhenian Sea at Terracina, and then ran inland between the Monti Ausoni and Monti Aurunci into the valley of the River Liri (from Pico to Piedimonte San Germano via Pontecorvo on the Liri). The line then ran just to the north of Cassino before ending at Terelle on the western slopes of the Apennine mountains. The line was designed as the last German barrier to an Allied advance up the valley of the Liri towards Rome.

The breaking of this line was the second phase of General the Hon. Sir Harold Alexander's Operation 'Diadem', whose first phase was the defeat of the Germans at Cassino and the breaching of the 'Gustav Linie', and third phase a rapid exploitation of success in the second phase to reach Valmontone (in conjunction with a breakout from the Anzio beach-head by the US VI Corps) and so cut off the German 10th Army (rather than take Rome, which had political but certainly no military value). With Lieutenant General Sir Oliver Leese's British 8th Army (British XIII, Polish II and British X Corps) co-operating in the northern sector of the offensive to effect the final reduction of the German strongpoint at Cassino (held by Generalmajor Richard Heidrich's superb 1st Parachute Division), Lieutenant General Mark W. Clark's US 5th Army was to play the major role in the offensive, deploying Major General Geoffrey T. Keyes's, US II Corps (US 85th and 88th Divisions) on the coastal sector, and Général de Corps d'Armée Alphonse Juin's French Expeditionary Corps (French 1st Motorized Division, 2nd Moroccan Division, 3rd Algerian Division and 4th Moroccan Mountain Division) on the right.

The plan schemed by Clark was a coastal advance by the US II Corps while the French Expeditionary Force advanced to take Monte Maio just over the 'Gustav Linie' and then wheeled right via Ausonia and Castelnuovo into the Liri valley at Pontecorvo. Juin objected to this simplistic tactical scheme on the grounds that his formations would be caught in the valley of the Liri by German fire from the mountains on each flank, and that it would be better to press on from Monte Maio into the Montio Aurunci using the mountain-warfare capabilities of his French colonial troops, thus avoiding the main strength of the German defence in the Liri valley) to break through a flank of the 'Senger Linie' defences. Clark readily agreed to this modification.

The offensive began on 11 May 1944 and, despite the Allies' overall superiority of 12 divisions to 6, only the French made real progress through Generalleutnant W. Raapke's 71st Division. By 17 May Général de Division Brisset's French 1st Motorized Division had reached Monte d'Oro and Général de Division Sevez's 2nd Moroccan Division had taken Esperia, and Generalfeldmarschall Albert Kesselring saw that the 'Gustav Linie' had been breached in the south-west. He thus ordered an immediate withdrawal, and Cassino finally fell to the Poles on 18 May. Meanwhile Général de Brigade A. Guillaume's 4th Moroccan Mountain Division was pressing through the defences of Generalleutnant G. Pfeiffer's 94th Division and advancing into the Monte Aurunci to take its dominating peaks of Monte Petrella, Monte Revole and Monte Faggeta. In the Liri valley Lieutenant General E. L. M. Burns's I Canadian Corps had replaced the British XIII Corps and took Pontecorvo in the centre of the 'Senger Linie' on 19 May, and on the same day the French 1st Motorized Division took Pico slightly farther to the west.

The 'Senger Linie' was breached, and by 23 May the Germans were in severe difficulties as Major General Lucian K. Truscott's US VI Corps erupted from Anzio to meet the US II Corps on 25 May on the shores of Lake Fogliano to the south-east of the beach-head. The French Expeditionary Corps and I Canadian Corps were pushing forward at the same time, and the first two phases of 'Diadem' had been completed successfully. Then on 25 May Clark altered Alexander's overall plan (as had been presaged by Clark's orders to Major General John P. Lucas before the launch of Operation 'Shingle'), ordering the US VI Corps to make not for Valmontone to the north-east but for the Alban hills to the north as a preliminary move towards Rome, and so was lost a perfect opportunity to cut off all of XIV Panzer Corps, and also elements of LXXVI Panzer Corps which had been containing the Anzio beach-head.

Serail (harem) Designation of the headquarters of the Oberkommando der Wehrmacht at Berchtesgaden in southern Germany.

Serrate Radar device allowing British night-fighters to close on the emissions of German night-fighters.

Sesame Allied air attacks on German positions in the Futa and Il Giogo passes to the north of Florence (9/11 September 1944). These two passes were the main avenues of advance for Lieutenant General Mark W. Clark's US 5th Army against the German 'Gotisch Linie' defences in northern Italy, both passes being held by the 4th Parachute Division of General Alfred Schlemm's I Parachute Corps (4th Parachute, 334th and 362nd Divisions) of General Joachim Lemselsen's German 14th Army, with General Valentin Feuerstein's LI Gebirgskorps of Generaloberst Heinrich Vietinghoff-Scheel's German 10th Army on its left flank. Under the command of General the Hon. Sir Harold Alexander, commanding the Allied 15th Army Group in Italy, Clark now planned to break through the 'Gotisch Linie' defences in the Apennine mountains and reach the key communications nexus at Bologna before the arrival of winter brought the 1944 campaigning season to an effective end.

The British 8th Army had already punched its way through the 'Gotisch Linie' defences on the Adriatic Sea sector at the eastern end of the German line, and the German 10th Army had lost three of its divisions in the vain attempt by Generalfeldmarschall Albert Kesselring's Army Group 'C' to stem the British offensive. Now it was Clark's turn to assault these formidable defences in the hills and mountains of the Apennines. The main task was allocated to the US II Corps under Major General Geoffrey T. Keyes (US 34th, 85th, 88th and 91st Infantry Divisions), with Lieutenant General S. C. Kirkman's British XIII Corps (British 6th Armoured, British 1st and 8th Indian Divisions) on its right. Clark's plan was for the US II Corps to seek to deceive the Germans as to its real intentions by advancing astride Route 65 leading to the Futa pass, with the US 34th Infantry Division on the western and the US 91st Infantry Division on the eastern side. As these two divisions closed on the Futa pass, the US 85th Infantry Division would drive forward in the main effort through the Il Giogo pass (believed to be less strongly held) with the US 91st Infantry Division coming to its support from the west. The US 88th Infantry Division would be held back to exploit the sector in which the greater success was achieved. Operational cover for the whole enterprise was to be provided by the British XIII Corps, which was to attack farther to the east on the Faenza and Forli roads against the German 715th Division of LI Gebirgskorps. The British 1st Division was tasked with advancing up the Faenza road, and the 8th Indian Division up the Forli road. In the event, Kesselring was taken in by the Allies' operational deception, and until too late believed that the main effort was being made by the British XIII Corps against Faenza and Forli with the intention then of taking Imola and advancing on Bologna from the southeast.

Operation 'Sesame' was launched by the Desert Air Force on 9 September with the object of softening the German defences in the two passes. More than 2,000 sorties were flown by medium bombers and fighter-bombers during the five days of the air offensive, and though some damage was caused, the German defence was too well entrenched and too battle-experienced to suffer decisive casualties. The US 5th Army offensive got under way on 10 September. By 12 September the US 34th and 91st Infantry Divisions had forced the 4th Parachute Division (which had all three of its regiments in the line and thus had no reserve) back into the main defences of the Futa pass. One day later the US 85th Infantry Division closed on the Il Giogo pass and the offensive proper was launched as the efforts of 'Sesame' tailed off. In four days the US divisions made no real impression on the doughty 4th Parachute Division, and suffered very heavy casualties into the bargain. However, to the east the British XIII Corps was faring better against the German 715th Division, and on 17 September a combined effort by the US 85th Infantry and British 1st Divisions caused the loss of the 4th Parachute Division's left-flank defences on the east of the Il Giogo pass. By 18 September the US II Corps held a 7-mile section of the 'Gotisch Linie' defences.

Kesselring realized only at this stage that the road to Imola through the Il Giogo pass was open, and pulled the German 44th and 362nd Divisions (from LI Gebirgskorps and XIV Panzer Corps) from the 10th Army sector to try to hold Firenzuola. The divisions began to arrive on 20 September, and were too late to check the development of the US II Corps salient through the 'Gotisch Linie' defences as the 4th Parachute Division, exhausted by its magnificent efforts, was forced to pull back from the Futa pass and Firenzuola on 21 September. The Allied plan had called for the fresh US 88th Infantry Division to move up for an exploitation towards Bologna, but as the 8th Army was currently stalled after the San Gemmano and Coriano ridge battles, Alexander ordered Clark to send the US 88th Infantry Division towards Imola and thus towards the rear areas of the 10th Army checking the British. However by 27 September the Americans were held at Monte Battaglia in front of Imola as Kesselring threw in any units he could. The fighting lasted some 10 days and halted the US 88th Infantry Division. The winter weather had now arrived, and given the determination and skill of the German defence, Clark decided to call a halt and consolidate.

Setting Sun Designation of the overall US strategic air campaign against Japan (1944) using the US 20th Air Force's growing Boeing B-29 Superfortress strength. The air force was divided into two commands, XXI Bomber Command operating from Chinese bases, and XX Bomber Command from bases in the Marianas. The offensive was planned in concert with the activities of the US Navy's great fleet of submarines in the Pacific, which was strangling the maritime lines of communication over which Japan had to import the raw materials and fuel needed for her war effort. The major objective of the air offensive was thus to strike with great precision at war-making industries and communications in Japan, so that even those limited imports that got through the submarine net could not be turned into aircraft, ships, tanks etc.

Sextant Designation of the inter-Allied conference at Cairo (22/26 November and 3/7 December 1943). The main political leaders in attendance were President Franklin D. Roosevelt, Prime Minister Winston Churchill and Generalissimo Chiang Kai-shek, each accompanied by high-ranking government and military aides. The primary objectives of the conference were to plan the implementation of the agreements reached at the Quebec Conference, to agree the course of American, British and Chinese action against Japan, and (Roosevelt and Churchill) to

241

formulate a post-war settlement of Europe. Premier Joseph Stalin refused to travel as far as Cairo at the time the Soviet army was involved in a major offensive, and the break during the 'Sextant' Conference allowed Churchill and Roosevelt to travel with their aides to meet Stalin at Tehran for the 'Eureka' Conference. Little was decided at the 'Sextant' Conference, for most major military problems required Stalin's input, and the British and Americans could not agree on any genuine strategy for the prosecution of the war in South-East Asia given the intractability of Chiang and diverging US and British opinions of the theatre's importance before the outcome of the European and Pacific campaigns had been decided. Moreover, the British tried to use the conference to urge the importance of the Mediterranean theatre while the Americans were adamant that Operation 'Overlord' must remain the Allies' main effort in the European theatre, leading to a direct assault on Germany, its armies and its war-making potential.

Another problem to rear its head was the Allies' general shortage of amphibious capability, which meant that of the three amphibious operations envisaged before 'Overlord' only one could be undertaken. The three were Operation 'Shingle' against Anzio in Italy, Operation 'Hercules' against Rhodes in the Aegean, and Operation 'Buccaneer' against the Andaman Islands in the Indian Ocean as a stepping stone to Malaya and the Dutch East Indies.

The main decisions reached during the 'Sextant' conference were a dedicated affirmation for the simultaneous (or nearly simultaneous) launch of Operations 'Overlord' and 'Anvil' as a priority over all other European operations (a decision conveyed at the 'Eureka' Conference to Stalin), the use of 2 US divisions for 'Anvil' followed by 10 more US divisions from the USA, the prosecution of the Italian campaign for the capture of Rome and an advance to the line of Pisa and Rimini, and the retention of 68 landing ships tank in the Mediterranean until 15 January (six weeks later than originally planned). This last meant the cancellation of 'Buccaneer' (to the chagrin of Roosevelt, who had promised Chiang that the operation would proceed), the implementation of 'Shingle' and the possible undertaking of 'Hercules' if other considerations could be achieved.

Seydlitz (i) Offensive by the German 9th Army near Belyy (July 1942). This operation was undertaken as part of the general improvement of the German line to the west of Moscow, turned into a massive series of salients and re-entrants by the Soviet winter offensive of 1941/1942. The Soviet Belyy salient, just to the west of Sychevka, had been created between January and April 1942 by the offensive of Lieutenant General I. S. Konev's Kalinin Front against Generalfeldmarschall Günther von Kluge's Army Group 'Centre'. A great salient had been driven by the Soviets towards Smolensk, but this had been divided into two halves by the counteroffensive towards Belyy launched by the 3rd Panzergruppe. The eastern half was now held by the Soviet 39th Army supported by XXII Cavalry Corps, and von Kluge decided that Generaloberst Walter Model's 9th Army should destroy the salient, so shortening the German defence line by 130 miles. As well as improving the German line, the elimination of the salient netted the Germans some 50,000 Soviet prisoners and considerable quantities of *matériel*.

(ii) German operation against Soviet partisans operating in the region of Dorogobuzh (25 June/27 July 1943). Lying on the upper reaches of the River Dniepr between Smolensk and Vyazma, this region was vital to the defences and communications of Generalfeldmarschall Günther von Kluge's Army Group 'Centre' at the point where the 3rd Panzerarmee and 4th Army would receive the brunt of the Soviet late-summer offensive from 23 August. Aimed at liberating Smolensk and opening the way for an offensive to retake Belorussia, the Soviet offensive in the sector would be entrusted to General A. I. Eremenko's Kalinin Front (later renamed the 1st Baltic Front) and General V. D. Sokolovsky's West Front.

Shadow 82 Plan for US air forces to relieve RAF squadrons in Northern Ireland (1942).

Shaker Illumination and marking of

nocturnal targets for RAF Bomber Command aircraft by pathfinders using 'Gee'.

Shakespeare Airborne operation by the Belgian Independent Parachute Company, SAS, to attack German rear-area installations near Tornade in France (31 July 1944).

Sharpener Allied designation of the headquarters of General Dwight D. Eisenhower near Portsmouth for the final preparation of Operation 'Overlord' (May 1944).

Shellburst Allied designation of the headquarters of General Dwight D. Eisenhower near Bayeux in northern France after the launch of Operation 'Overlord' (August 1944).

Shingle Allied landing at Anzio in central Italy (22 January 1944). The operation was planned in November 1944 by General the Hon. Sir Harold Alexander's Allied 15th Army Group, at the urging of Prime Minister Winston Churchill, as a means of speeding the advance of Lieutenant General Mark W. Clark's US 5th Army along the western side of Italy towards (but not into) Rome. The operation was initially to have used a single US division landed no later than 15 January 1944 (when the required amphibious shipping was to be removed from the Mediterranean in preparation for Operation 'Overlord'), the exact date of the landing being determined by the arrival of the US 5th Army at a point some 30 miles to the south of the proposed beach-head after breaking through the 'Bernhardt Linie' and 'Gustav Linie' positions. At the same time the Germans were finally coming to a conclusion in their dispute as how best to defend Italy, Hitler deciding in favour of holding southern Italy in the scheme proposed by the *Oberbefehlshaber Süd*, Generalfeldmarschall Albert Kesselring, rather than securing northern Italy in the plan proposed by the commander-in-chief of Army Group 'B', Generalfeldmarschall Erwin Rommel. As a result Kesselring was appointed to the command of a new Army Group 'C' controlling all German forces in southern and northern Italy. Kesselring immediately set about preparing a new army headquarters (the 14th Army under Generaloberst Eberhard von Mackensen) for the control of operations in Italy west of the Apennine mountains, leaving Generaloberst Heinrich von Vietinghoff-Scheel's 10th Army to concentrate on the defence of eastern Italy. So just as the Allies were preparing a bold outflanking movement at Anzio, the Germans were establishing an effective theatre command with a capable but as yet uncommitted army headquarters under its direct control.

Meanwhile various delays had postponed the removal of Allied amphibious transport capability to the UK, and it was now possible to shift Operation 'Shingle' towards the end of January 1944 as Clark's forces had as yet failed to make the necessary inroads through the 'Bernhardt Linie' and 'Gustav Linie' defences. At the end of December it was decided to make 'Shingle' a two-division landing by Major General John P. Lucas's US VI Corps, but there now entered a dangerous diversion of aims, for whereas Alexander instructed Clark that the aim of the operation was 'to carry out an assault landing on the beaches in the vicinity of Rome with the object of cutting the enemy lines of communication and threatening the rear of the German XIV Corps', Clark told Lucas that he was merely 'to seize and secure a beachhead in the vicinity of Anzio' and later 'to advance on the Alban Hills'. So while the British wanted a landing followed by a swift and fully-committed advance, the Americans envisaged a landing which would be consolidated before any advance was undertaken, Clark being determined that the problem of German counterattacks that beset Operation 'Avalanche' at Salerno should not be repeated at Anzio with Operation 'Shingle'.

The Allied plan was finalized on 12 January (three days after the US VI Corps had been replaced in the line south of Cassino and moved to its embarkation points at Salerno) as part of a five-phase Allied winter offensive against a German army believed to be exhausted and virtually without reinforcements of reserves. Operation 'Shingle' was designed as the third of these phases (the first two being the Allied offensives against the 'Gustav Linie' and 'Senger Linie' positions, and the last two the link-up with the US VI Corps and the destruction of XIV Panzer

Corps). On 16 January Clark renewed his offensive against Cassino on the 'Gustav Linie' in an effort to draw German reserves south, for it was appreciated by the Allies that the Germans could move forces against the beach-head more rapidly than the Allies could pour troops into it. It was therefore vital to Allied plans that the German lines of communication south of Rome be seriously interdicted by air power to slow the development of the inevitable German counteroffensive. Kesselring was fully aware that an amphibious landing might happen (German contingency plans envisaged such an outflanking operation in places as diverse as Istria, Ravenna, Civitavecchia, Livorno and Viareggio) and had organised a number of extemporised local commands to deal with any such operation. In the Anzio sector were General Alfred Schlemm and the headquarters of I Parachute Corps.

The final plan for 'Shingle' was completed in some three weeks, and called for the US VI Corps to be moved from Salerno by a mainly American task group commanded by Rear Admiral Frank J. Lowry with Rear Admiral Thomas H. Troubridge commanding the British element. For the landing Lucas could use Major General Lucian K. Truscott's US 3rd Infantry Division (controlling the 7th, 15th and 30th Infantry Regiments, the 504th Parachute Infantry Regiment, the 509th Parachute Infantry Battalion, the 1st, 3rd and 4th Ranger Battalions, and the 751st Tank Battalion), Major General W. R. C. Penney's British 1st Division (commanding the 2nd and 3rd Infantry Brigades, the 24th Guards Brigade and the 46th Royal Tank Regiment) and Brigadier T. D. L. Churchill's 2nd Special Service Brigade (commanding the 9th and 43rd Royal Marine Commandos). In reserve (to be committed at Clark's discretion) Lucas had Major General Ernest N. Harmon's US 1st Armored Division (less Combat Command B and thus comprising the 1st Armored Regiment and the 6th Armored Infantry Regiment) and Major General William W. Eagles's US 45th Infantry Division (comprising the 157th, 179th and 180th Infantry Regiments, and the 645th Tank Destroyer Battalion).

The plan put into effect by Lucas was for the US 3rd Division to land its three infantry regiments in the south (between Nettuno and the Mussolini Canal) with the 504th Parachute Infantry Regiment following them ashore, for the three Ranger battalions to land in the centre (between Anzio and Nettuno) with the 509th Parachute Infantry Regiment following them ashore, and for the British 2nd Infantry Brigade to land in the north (between Anzio and the River Moletta) with the 2nd Special Service Brigade following it ashore. The rest of the British 1st Division was to be maintained as floating reserve as the assault forces consolidated a beach-head between the Mussolini Canal and the Moletta via Padiglione. The British would hold the left of the beach-head and then exploit towards Campoleone up the Albano road, and the Americans would hold the right of the beach-head before exploiting towards Cisterna. Only after this enlarged beach-head had been secured would Lucas envisage the landing of the US 1st Armored and 4th Infantry Divisions for the assault towards the Alban Hills.

In themselves, the 'Shingle' landings were the most successful of World War II in any theatre, for there was opposition only from two German battalions and some shore batteries, which were silenced by the guns of 4 light cruisers and 24 destroyers. So by 24.00 on 22 January the US VI Corps had got ashore 36,034 men, 3,069 vehicles and 90 per cent of the corps' assault equipment at the cost of 13 men dead, 97 wounded and 44 missing. The news of the Allied landing was flashed to Kesselring as rapidly as possible, but there was nothing that the Germans could do within the next two days as forces were brought in to contain the beach-head. This gave the US VI Corps 48 clear hours in which to smash north-west some 12 miles to sever XIV Panzer Corps' lines of communication at Velletri and Valmontone. Instead Lucas consolidated the beach-head and worked to build up his corps' supplies, and only on 24 January did the commander begin a cautious advance just as the first German forces arrived in the area.

As soon as word of the landing reached Kesselring's headquarters, the relevant contingency plan was set in motion to move to Anzio forces for Schlemm's I Parachute

Corps (the 'Hermann Goering' Panzer Division from Frosinone and the 4th Parachute Division from Terni), General Traugott Herr's LXXVI Panzer Corps from the River Sangro (the 26th Panzer Division, and the 3rd and 29th Panzergrenadier Divisions) and von Mackensen's 14th Army headquarters from northern Italy together with the 65th and 362nd Divisions. But so severe was the threat to the integrity of the German defences in southern Italy that the Oberkommando der Wehrmacht ordered the *Oberbefehlshaber West* (Generalfeldmarschall Gerd von Rundstedt) to send in the 715th Division from Marseilles, and the *Oberbefehlshaber Süd-Ost* (Generaloberst Alexander Löhr) to hand over the 114th Jäger Division from the Balkans.

By 23 January the first elements of the 'Hermann Goering' Panzer Division (supported by a miscellany of Flak guns and field artillery) had arrived, but von Mackensen and Kesselring could start to think of a counterattack only on 28 January, by which time the US 1st Armored and 45th Infantry Divisions were assembling in the area of Padiglione Wood, and the north-eastern perimeter of the beach-head had been pushed out some 2 miles by the advances of the British 1st and US 3rd Divisions towards Campoleone and Cisterna respectively. The divisions were checked short of their major obejctives by the 3rd Panzergrenadier Division and the 'Hermann Goering' Panzer Division respectively, and von Mackensen now had 3 divisions and the equivalent of another in miscellaneous units, the total rising to 8 divisions by the end of the month; it was now too late for the US VI Corps to attempt a major move against the 10th Army's lines of communication, and the corps was effectively trapped in the beach-head by aggressive and skilful counterattacks. The corps survived these counterattacks (the last failed on 19 February) and was eventuually taken over by Truscott, reinforced with the British 5th, US 34th and US 36th Infantry Divisions plus the 1st Special Service Force, and broke out of its beach-head on 23 May, linking up with the US II Corps two days later.

Shipmate Allied designation of the headquarters of General Dwight D. Eisenhower near Portsmouth for the beginning of Operation 'Overlord' (June/July 1944).

SHO Designation of the plan promulgated (24 July 1944) by the Imperial General Headquarters in Tokyo for the strategic conduct of all Japanese operations from that time onwards in a great arc running from Manchukuo (the Japanese puppet state in Manchuria) through the Pacific Ocean to the Southern Region. The plan was prepared in the aftermath of the Japanese defeats in the Battle of the Philippine Sea and on the island of Saipan (soon to be joined by Tinian and Guam) in the Marianas, and the beginning of US air raids on the Japanese home islands. These events had led to the fall on 18 July of the administration headed by General Hideki Tojo, to be replaced on 22 July by a government led by General K. Koiso and Admiral M. Yonai. The evident fact that the Japanese planners had to face was that the enemy (in this instance the Americans) were overwhelmingly stronger than the Japanese in the air, on land and at sea, and that the US offensive against Japan would have to be met and defeated in the area of the Philippines, Formosa and Japan; here the defence would enjoy the benefits of interior (and hence shorter) lines of communication, and of lengthy preparation.

Operation 'SHO' thus ordered a defensive concentration on the line running from the south in the Philippines via Formosa, the Ryukyu Islands and the Japanese home islands to the Kurile Islands in the north. Within this basic framework the Japanese undertook plans for defensive campaigns in key geographical regions (Operations 'SHO-1' to 'SHO-4') for implementation as and when required. Parallel to this Pacific planning, Operation 'ICHI' was to be pursued in China with the objects of denying the US Army Air Forces the bases from which they could bomb Japan, of securing the Chinese harvest and of inflicting on the Chinese a decisive defeat so that Japanese ground and air forces could be redeployed to theatres that were becoming a greater threat to Japan. In Field Marshal Count Hisaichi Terauchi's Southern Region the Japanese defence was a joint army and navy responsibility by area, but in September the two services agreed on

245

a combined defence for Sulawesi (2nd Area Army with 6 infantry and 1 air divisions), Borneo (37th Army with a miscellany of garrison units), the Andaman Islands and the Nicobar Islands, and in October the army assumed sole responsibility for the defence of these islands.

SHO-1 Japanese overall defence plan for the Philippines Islands within the framework of the 'SHO' scheme. The plan was ready for implementation at the end of August 1944. Of the defence sectors envisaged in the 'SHO' scheme, this was the one that the Japanese thought most likely to receive a direct US assault during 1944, and it was essential that the assault be defeated (causing the Americans casualties as heavy as those the Japanese were prepared to accept) to check the momentum of the US advance and maintain uninterrupted maritime communications between Japan and the Dutch East Indies, from where the Japanese war effort derived almost all its fuel. In these circumstances, the Japanese realized, their navy might be isolated in the north without fuel, or in the south without ammunition and necessary replacements. There were thus compelling strategic reasons for the retention of the Philipines, and in this area the Japanese thought that they had an operational 'ace' in the fact that for the first time in the Pacific war the US forces would be operating with only carrier-based air power in a region where the Japanese could deploy massively superior land-based air power at short range.

In simple terms, therefore, the object of 'SHO-1' was to use land-based air power to neutralize the carrier-based air power of any US invasion force as it closed the Philippines, and so permit Admiral Soemu Toyoda's Combined Fleet (tactically and operationally weakened by its losses in the Battle of the Philippine Sea) to destroy the invasion force without hindrance from US aircraft. The task of neutralizing US carrier air power was entrusted to the Imperial Japanese Navy's 1st and 2nd Air Fleets (the former based in the Philippines under Vice Admiral Takujiro Onishi, and the latter training in the Japanese home islands, under the command of Vice Admiral Shigeru Fukodome, until moved to the Philippines at the implementation of 'SHO-1' to link up with the 1st Air Fleet as Fukodome's 1st Combined Base Air Force) supported by the Imperial Japanese Army's 4th Air Army with its 2nd and 4th Air Divisions. The Japanese appreciated that the Combined Fleet might be unable to prevent the US landings, and so based Lieutenant General Tomayuki Yamashita's 14th Area Army in the islands. The Japanese were generally short of shipping, and Field Marshal Count Hisaichi Terauchi, commanding the Southern Region from Saigon, ordered Yamashita to concentrate on the defence of the main Philippine island, Luzon.

Yamashita assumed his command on 6 October, and decided to use three infantry divisions (8th, 193rd and 105th) and two independent mixed brigades (55th and 58th) for Luzon's defence. For the central and southern islands, which were of secondary importance, he allocated Lieutenant General Sasuku Suzuki's 35th Army with its 16th Division on Leyte, its 30th Division defending Davao in southern Mindanao, its 100th Division in central and northern Mindanao, and its 102nd Division and an independent mixed brigade in Panay, Negros and Cebu. As a central reserve Yamashita had the 2nd Armoured Division (still in Manchukuo), and the 1st Division (still in Shanghai) and the 26th Division. Later in the year Yamashita was reinforced by the 10th Division (from Formosa) and the 23rd Division (from Manchukuo). The 2nd and 4th Air Divisions had 8 air regiments between them, and the 4th Air Army had also been allocated the 30th Fighter Group from Japan with 10 air regiments. The army also controlled the 4 air regiments of the 7th Air Division in Sulawesi, and it was planned to fly in another 13 air regiments (from Malaya, Indo-China, Formosa, China and Japan) to produce a total of 34 air regiments. Thus was set the scene for the climactic campaign for the Philippines, which resulted in the Japanese loss of the islands and also in the largest naval battle the world has ever seen, the four-part Battle of Leyte Gulf (24/25 October 1944).

'SHO-1' began tentatively on 15 September, when the US assault on Morotai and the Palau Islands confirmed Terauchi in his belief that the US invasion of the Philippines was imminent and that he should forward to the islands all designated reinforcements. The trigger for the implementation of 'SHO-1', however, was the strike undertaken against Japanese air strength in the Ryukyus, Formosa and Luzon by the 15 fast carriers of Admiral William F. Halsey's US 3rd Fleet. In the course of this operation (10/17 October 1944) the Americans lost 26 aircraft and suffered damage to 2 cruisers, whereas the Japanese admitted to the loss of 320 aircraft while claiming that they had sunk 2 battleships and 11 aircraft-carriers. This monstrous overclaim by Japanese land-based air units persuaded the Imperial General Headquarters to alter the parameters of 'SHO-1'. All Japanese land-based aircraft were ordered to implement their part of the operation immediately, and the 350 aircraft of the 2nd Air Fleet (together with the 150 carrier aircraft of the 3rd and 4th Carrier Squadrons withdrawn from the Mobile Force of Vice Admiral Jisaburo Ozawa) were sent to Formosa rather than Luzon, being forwarded to Luzon only on 18 October, the date by which the 1st Air Fleet had been reduced to some 100 aircraft. Furthermore, on Luzon a reluctant Yamashita was ordered to fight the decisive land battle on Leyte rather than on Luzon; in fact only two days after the start of the US invasion of Leyte on 20 October did Yamashita start to obey this order to change his operational planning completely, ordering Suzuki to concentrate his army on Leyte. It was too late to affect the outcome of the land battle.

Meanwhile Toyoda launched the naval side of Operation 'SHO-1' in all its complexity on 17 October, with the constituent forces coming under the control of Vice Admiral Gunichi Mikawa's South-West Area Fleet as they approached the Philippines. The naval portion of 'SHO-1' called for a four-sided descent on the US invasion fleet off Leyte. Vice Admiral Takeo Kurita's 1st Strike Force, 5th Fleet was ordered to sail from Singapore and refuel in Brunei Bay before dividing into two parts before approaching the US forces via the Sibuyan Sea and San Bernardino Strait (Kurita's Force 'A', otherwise the Centre Force) or the Surigao Strait (Vice Admiral Shoji Nishimura's Force 'C', otherwise the Southern Force). Vice Admiral Kiyohide Shima's 2nd Strike Force, 5th Fleet was ordered to sail from the Ryukyus via the Pescadores Islands to link up as the Northern Force with Nishimura's Southern Force in the attack through the Surigao Strait, and Vice Admiral Ozawa's Mobile Force, Strike Force was ordered to sail from the Inland Sea in the Japanese home islands as a decoy for the 10 fleet carriers of Halsey's Task Force 38. Toyoda planned that with Halsey lured away to the north by Ozawa, the other three Japanese forces could fall on Vice Admiral Thomas C. Kinkaid's 7th Fleet off Leyte and, unhindered by US carrier-based aircraft, destroy its amphibious vessels with gunfire and torpedoes.

The forces involved on each side were prodigious, fully vindicating the description of the Battle of Leyte Gulf as the world's greatest sea battle in numerical as well as strategic terms. On the Japanese side Kurita's Centre Force comprised the super-battleships *Yamato* and *Musashi*, the battleships *Nagato*, *Kongo* and *Haruna*, the heavy cruisers *Atago*, *Takao*, *Chokai*, *Maya*, *Myoko*, *Haguro*, *Kumano*, *Suzuya*, *Chikuma* and *Tone*, the light cruisers *Noshiro* and *Yahagi*, and 15 destroyers. Nishimura's Southern Force was also a powerful outfit, comprising the battleships *Yamashiro* and *Fuso*, the heavy cruiser *Magami* and 4 destroyers, supplemented by Shima's Northern Force of the heavy cruisers *Nachi* and *Ashigara*, the light cruiser *Abukuma* and 7 destroyers. To complete the Japanese offensive disposition there was Ozawa's Mobile Force comprising the fleet carrier *Zuikaku*, the light carriers *Zuiho*, *Chitose* and *Chiyoda*, the hybrid battleship/carriers *Ise* and *Hyuga*, the light cruisers *Oyoda*, *Tama* and *Isuzu*, and 8 destroyers. The air strength of the Mobile Force was some 116 aircraft (including 80 fighters) on the 4 carriers, while the hybrid battleship/carriers had no aircraft.

If the Japanese 68-ship line-up was impressive, that of the Americans was doubly so, their 275 ships and 1,500 aircraft being divided into two fleets. Around Leyte for the escort and protection of the invasion forces was Kinkaid's US 7th Fleet which, apart from 600 or more vessels in the III and VII Amphibious Forces (Task Force 79 and 78 respectively), had Rear Admiral Thomas L.

247

SHO-1

Sprague's Escort Carrier Group (Task Group 77.4) comprising Task Unit 77.4.1 (6 escort carriers, 3 destroyers and 5 escort destroyers), Task Unit 77.4.2 (6 escort carriers, 3 destroyers and 5 escort destroyers) and Task Unit 77.4.3 (6 escort carriers, 3 destroyers and 4 escort destroyers) with a total of 503 aircraft (304 fighters and 199 attack aircraft). Also part of the 7th Fleet was Rear Admiral Jesse B. Oldendorf's Battle Line (Task Group 77.2) comprising 6 battleships, 3 heavy cruisers, 5 light cruisers, 29 destroyers and 45 PT boats for the gunfire support of the invasion and defence of the amphibious fleet and attached escort carriers. The primary offensive capability of the US Navy in the area was Halsey's 3rd Fleet, with its Fast Carrier Task Force commanded by Vice Admiral Marc A. Mitscher. The operation part of the 3rd Fleet in the Battle of Leyte Gulf was Task Force 38, which was at three-quarter strength as Vice Admiral J. S. McCain's Task Group 38.1 was on its way to Ulithi to refuel and resupply its 2 fleet carriers, 2 light carriers, 3 heavy cruisers and 14 destroyers. For the battle Halsey and Mitscher thus deployed Rear Admiral G. F. Bogan's Task Group 38.2 (3 fleet carriers, 2 light carriers, 2 battleships, 4 light cruisers and 18 destroyers) off San Bernardino Strait, Rear Admiral F. C. Sherman's Task Group 38.3 (2 fleet carriers, 2 light carriers, 4 battleships, 4 light cruisers and 14 destroyers) off Luzon, and Rear Admiral R. E. Davison's Task Group 38.4 (2 fleet carriers, 2 light carriers, 1 heavy cruiser, 1 light cruiser and 11 destroyers) off Leyte. Mitscher's carriers fielded a total of 835 aircraft.

Operation 'SHO-1' got off to a bad start for the Japanese, Kurita's 1st Strike Force being spotted by US submarines as it headed north-east after refuelling in Brunei Bay. Off Palawan Island the submarines reported the position, strength and course of the Centre Force, and then the *Dace* and *Darter* moved into the attack, the former sinking the heavy cruiser *Maya*, and the latter damaging the heavy cruiser *Takao* (which had to turn back to Brunei Bay) and sinking the heavy cruiser *Atago*. Kurita pressed on regardless of the loss of his flagship (the *Atago*) together with most of his signals staff. In the morning of 24 October Kurita moved round the south of Mindoro Island, and the scene was set for the Battle of the Sibuyan Sea, the first of the Battle of Leyte Gulf's four component actions.

Halsey appreciated that he could leave Nishimura and Shima to Kinkaid, and so concentrated the air efforts of TG 38.2 against the Centre Force, with particularly emphasis on the super-battleship *Musashi*. Between 10.26 and 13.50 TG 38.2 flew 259 sorties to the Sibuyan Sea. Hit by 19 torpedoes and 17 bombs, the huge *Musashi* sank with about half her crew at 18.00, and other casualties in the Centre Force were the heavy cruiser *Myoko*, which had to be sent back to Brunei Bay in seriously damaged condition, and three other cruisers damaged. Kurita broke away to the west, persuading Halsey that he was retreating, but then reversed course to the east again. This caused delay to Kurita's force, making it impossible for the Centre Force to co-ordinate its northern attack on the US 7th Fleet with the southern attack to be launched by Nishimura and Shima. Even so Kurita pressed on, passing through the San Bernardino Strait at 23.30 on 24 October on its way to the third component action of the Battle of Leyte Gulf, the Battle off Samar.

But meanwhile the second component, the Battle of Suriagao Strait, was about to unfold as Nishimura's and Shima's forces closed on Leyte from the south after rounding Negros and Bohay Islands. With the Southern Force some 90 minutes ahead of the Northern Force, the Japanese began to penetrate into Surigao Strait early in the morning of 25 October. The Americans knew just what was coming and had laid careful plans for the destruction of the Southern Force, which would first be assaulted by torpedo-firing PT boats, then by torpedo-firing destroyers, and finally by the Gun Line, especially the six battleships of Rear Admiral G. L. Weyler which, with Oldendorf's cruisers, formed a horizontal line across the Japanese axis of advance so that all heavy guns could be brought to bear on the Japanese van. The PT boats attacked between 23.00 on 24 October and 03.00 on 25 October, but failed to score. Greater success attended the efforts of the destroyers, which sank three of the four Japanese van destroyers (*Michishio*, *Asagumo* and *Yamagumo*) and crippled the battleship *Fuso*, which broke in two and sank at 04.30.

248

It was now the turn of the Battle Line, which opened fire at 03.53 and lobbed 285 14-in. and 16-in. shells at the Japanese using radar ranging and laying. The *Yamashiro* was hit repeatedly and sank at 04.19, but the badly damaged *Mogami* managed to retire only to collide with Shima's flagship *Nachi* at 04.30 as the second Japanese force pressed north into the Surigao Strait even though it had lost the cruiser *Abukuma* torpedoed by a PT boat at 03.25. At 04.25 Shima decided on a prudent withdrawal, later losing the crippled *Mogami*.

But as Kinkaid and his staff were celebrating their victory in Surigao Strait, they received the astounding news that Task Group 77.4's escort carriers had come under attack in the Battle off Samar. Kinkaid had not been informed by Halsey that the latter was pulling back from San Bernardino Strait Vice Admiral Willis A. Lee's Task Force 34 (an extemporized force of 6 battleships, 4 cruisers and 8 destroyers drawn from Task Force 38) for support of his carriers against the Mobile Force, and through this gap in the US defences Kurita had sailed to engage the dreadfully vulnerable escort carriers of Task Group 77.4 Closest to the Japanese attack was Rear Admiral Clifton A. F. Sprague's TG 77.4.3 with the escort carriers *Fanshaw Bay*, *St Lo*, *White Plains*, *Kalinin Bay*, *Kitkun Bay* and *Gambier Bay* escorted by the destroyers *Hoel*, *Heermann*, *Johnston*, *Dennis*, *Butler*, *Raymond* and *Roberts*. C. A. F. Sprague was faced by a Japanese force of 4 battleships, 6 heavy cruisers and 10 destroyers. With his aircraft armed for ground-support operations over Leyte, C. A. Sprague could only run, and this he did most effectively despite the considerably slower speed of his force in comparison with that of the Japanese. The US commander used a rain squall and smoke to break away from the Japanese, and then sent in his destroyers to slow the attackers. It was a confused battle characterized by extreme courage and determination on the part of the Americans but lack of concerted effort by the Japanese ships, and while the Americans lost the *Gambier Bay*, *Hoel*, *Johnston* and *Roberts*, the Japanese lost the heavy cruisers *Suzuya*, *Chokai* and *Chikuma*. At 09.23 Kurita decided to withdraw, wrongly believing that he was up against Task Force 38. The trial of TG 77.4.3 was not over, however, for later in the morning the *St Lo* was hit by a *kamikaze* aircraft and later sank.

While these events had been unfolding, away to the north Halsey had been pulled in by the deception threat posed by Ozawa and steamed off in pursuit at 23.45 on 24 October. By this time Halsey had ordered TG 38.1 back from Ulithi (the group then being diverted to the support of the 7th Fleet's escort carriers) and gathered TG 38.2, TG 38.3 (less the *Princeton* sunk by land-based Japanese aircraft earlier in the day) and TG 38.4. TF 38 was without its battleships and cruisers, which had been formed into TF 34 under Lee to guard San Bernardino Strait, but Lee followed some three hours behind Halsey (so letting Kurita through the San Bernardino Strait) before again turning at 11.15 on 25 October for a belated attempt to engage Kurita and so protect TG 77.4.3. Halsey's reconnaissance aircraft spotted the Mobile Force at 02.20 on 25 October, and at 08.45 the first of four US strikes was launched to start the last of the four components of the Battle of Leyte Gulf, namely the Battle of Cape Engano.

Ozawa had turned north late on 24 October to draw TF 38 away from Leyte, but was now faced by the overwhelming air strength of TF 38, which flew 527 sorties to sink the carriers *Chitose*, *Zuikaku* and *Zuiho*, and the destroyers *Akitsuki*. The air strikes also damaged the carrier *Chiyoda*, which was finished off (together with the destroyer *Hatsusuki*) by a force of 4 cruisers and 10 destroyers under Rear Admiral Du Bose, detached by Halsey at 14.15. The battle came to a close at 24.00 on 25 October when TF 34 caught the destroyer *Nowaki* in San Bernardino Strait and sank her with gunfire.

The battle had eventually involved 244 ships, of which 32 were sunk. The Japanese had lost 3 battleships, 4 carriers, 10 cruisers and 9 destroyers totalling 306,000 tons, whereas the American losses had been 1 carrier, 2 escort carriers and 3 destroyers totalling 37,000 tons. The defeat of the Japanese was almost inevitable, and had the monumental effect of stranding Yamashita in the Philippines and so allowing the conquest of these islands, which split the Japanese strategic defence wide open, and also isolated the remnants of the Japanese navy in two groups, that in the south without ammunition and spare parts, and that in the north without fuel. The pitiful remnants of Japan's once-mighty naval air arm had been destroyed at sea and over Luzon to no real effect.

SHO-2 Japanese overall defence plan for Formosa and the Ryukyus within the framework of the 'SHO' scheme. The plan was ready for implementation at the end of August 1944. Formosa was defended by the Formosa Army (10th, 50th and 66th Divisions) and the 8th Air Division, while the Ryukyus were entrusted to the 32nd Army (9th, 24th, 28th and 62nd Divisions). In Formosa the 10th Division was posted to the 14th Area Army in November and replaced by the 12th Division from Manchukuo. Formosa was not assaulted by the Allies, and the Ryukyus became the target of Operation 'Iceberg'.

SHO-3 Japanese overall defence plan for Kyushu and Honshu Islands in the Japanese home islands within the framework of the 'SHO' scheme. The plan was ready at the end of October 1944, with its details embodied in Operation 'KETSU' of December 1944. Kyushu and southern Honshu were the responsibility of Field Marshal S. Hata's 2nd General Army, using the 16th Area Army (14 divisions, 7 independent mixed brigades and 3 tank brigades) for Kyushu and the 15th Area Army (9 divisions and 4 independent mixed brigades) for southern Honshu. Central and northern Honshu fell to Field Marshal G. Sugiyama's 1st General Army, which deployed from south to north the 13th Area Army (6 divisions, 3 independent mixed brigades and 1 tank brigade), the 12th Area Army (18 divisions, 7 independent mixed brigades, 2 armoured divisions, 3 tank brigades and 3 Imperial Guards brigades for Tokyo) and the 11th Area Army (6 divisions and 2 independent mixed brigades). Under the control of Imperial General Headquarters reserves could be drawn from the 17th Area Army's seven divisions in Korea, and air support was provided by General M. Kawabe's Air General Army with the 1st and 6th Air Armies in Japan and the 2nd Air Army in Korea.

SHO-4 Japanese overall defence plan for Hokkaido Island and the Kurile Islands within the framework of the 'SHO' scheme. The plan was ready for implementation at the end of October 1944, with its final development embodied in Operation 'KETSU' of December 1944, which added the defence of the southern half of Sakhalin Island to the original scheme. The defence was allocated to the 5th Area Army (5 divisions and 2 independent mixed brigades) answering directly to Imperial General Headquarters in Tokyo.

Shrapnel British plan for the seizure of the Cape Verde Islands (spring 1941). This preliminary plan was later absorbed into Operation 'Pilgrim'.

Shred British naval minelaying operation off Norway (March 1945). Germany was still making extensive use of Norwegian coastal waters for the movement of iron ore convoys from Narvik, but these waters were inaccessible to British warships because of the presence of German minefields. The alternative was to force German shipping into the hands of MTB flotillas lurking outside the Leads by the laying of British minefields, a task difficult because of the depth of the water. However, during March one such operation was carried out to produce off Stadtlandet a minefield that sank a large ship on 22 March.

Siberien (Siberia) German ocean rendezvous in the Indian Ocean between Mauritius and Australia (1939/1943). At this rendezvous surface raiders could meet their supply vessels and replenish their stocks of ammunition, comestibles and fuel as a means of extending the operational endurance of their sorties. The 'Siberien' rendezvous was used successfully by the raiders *Pinguin*, *Orion*, *Atlantis* and *Komet*. The *Pinguin* (known to the Germans as Ship 33 and to the British as Raider F) sailed on 22 June 1940 and sank 28 ships (136,551 tons) before being sunk by the British cruiser *Cornwall* on 8 May 1941. The *Orion* (Ship 36, Raider A) sailed on 6 April 1940 and sank 9 ships (57,774 tons) before returning to base on 21 August 1941. The *Atlantis* (Ship 16, Raider C) sailed on 31 March 1940 and sank or captured 22 ships (145,697 tons) before being sunk by the

British cruiser *Devonshire* on 22 November 1941. And the *Komet* (Ship 45, Raider B) sailed on 9 July 1940 and, with the aid of Soviet icebreakers, completed a voyage through the North-East Passage to the north of the USSR to debouch through the Bering Strait into the Pacific. She sank 6 ships (42,959 tons) before returning to Germany. The rendezvous was later used for German ships and U-boats transiting between Germany and Japan.

Sickle (i) British landing at Andalsnes to the south of Trondheim in Norway (18 April 1940). This was the southern component of a plan (whose northern half was Operation 'Maurice') to land sufficient forces on each side of Trondheim to launch a pincer attack for the recapture of the city, taken on 9 April by the German 138th Gebirgsjägerregiment transported in the heavy cruiser *Admiral Hipper* and four destroyers of the German naval Gruppe II. XXI Corps under Generaloberst Nikolaus von Falkenhorst began to reinforce the garrison on Trondheim into the full 2nd Gebirgsdivision and 181st Division with a view to advances through the defences of the Norwegian 5th Division down the Osterdal and Gudbrandsdal towards Oslo and the 196th and 163rd Division. Under the command of Brigadier H. de R. Morgan, the leading elements British 148th Brigade were landed at Andalsnes from the cruisers *Galatea* and *Arethusa*, the AA cruisers *Carlisle* and *Curacao*, and 2 destroyers commanded by Vice Admiral Sir G. F. B. Edward-Collins. The rest of the brigade was landed later in two waves (2,200 men in the cruisers *Galatea*, *Sheffield* and *Glasgow* plus 6 destroyers, and 1,600 men in the cruisers *Manchester*, *Birmingham* and *York* plus 3 destroyers). Thus 4,800 British troops moved south-east to Dombas as the preliminary to an advance north up the rail line to Trondheim. Command was assumed by Major General B. C. T. Paget on 26 April, and under the overall control of Lieutenant General H. R. S. Massy (heading all British forces in Norway other than those in Narvik) the brigade was instructed to forget Trondheim temporarily and move to the support of the Norwegian 2nd Division in the Gudbrandsdal against the German 163rd Division. The brigade had got as for as Lillehammer by 21 April, but could achieve little against the Germans without heavy weapons and motor transport. On 24 April the British decided to abandon central Norway, and the 148th Brigade was ordered to pull out, which it did on 1 May in the same force of cruisers and destroyers that had delivered it in the middle of April.

(ii) Overall designation of the build-up of US air power in the UK for the air offensive against Germany (1942/1943), in short the aerial counterpart of Operation 'Bolero'. The programme was slow to get under way as its priority was relatively low and diversions were often made, for example two groups of Boeing B-17 Fortresses to the US 12th Air Force in North Africa during 1943, and one group of Consolidated B-24 Liberators to the US 5th Air Force in the South-West Pacific Area during the late summer of 1943.

Siegfried (i) Original designation of the German summer offensives of 1942 on the Eastern Front, later retitled 'Blau'. As originally schemed by the Oberkommando des Heeres under the direct stimulus of Adolf Hitler, who had lost interest in Moscow, Operation 'Siegfried' was to clear the Soviets from the area west of the River Don, establish powerful strategic defences along the Don between Voronezh and Stalingrad, and take the north-western Caucasus as far east as the River Manych (including the oilfields at Maikop)' together with the passes over the Caucasus mountains which would make possible a subsequent advance to the southern oilfields at Grozny and Baku.

(ii) Baseline German plan for the occupation of Italian-held portions of southern France as part of Operation 'Achse' (ii). The scheme was later developed into 'Attila' (implemented in November 1942), though the Italian sectors in France were taken over by the troops of Generalfeldmarschall Gerd von Rundstedt's *Oberbefehlshaber West* command in France only after the Italian armistice of September 1943, the whole undertaking being completed within 12 hours of the executive order.

Siegfried Linie (Siegfried line) Designation of the major defence line in the west of Germany, essentially a counterpart to the

Silberfuchs

French Maginot Line, but constructed to more modern concepts with better anti-tank defences and less reliance on fixed fortifications mounting heavy-calibre guns. The line ran from Kleve on the Dutch/German border to the east of Nijmegen (where the River Rhine crosses into the Netherlands) along the German frontier south to the Swiss frontier to the north-east of Basle. The 'Siegfried Linie' was also known to the Germans as the 'Westwall', especially after the line had been modified and developed from July 1944, after a period of neglect, as the major check to the Allies' eastward offensive towards Germany.

Silberfuchs (silver fox) German offensive, with Finnish support, to take the port of Kandalaksha on the White Sea (July 1941), and thus isolate the Soviet forces in the Kola peninsula for subsequent destruction (so that the Germans could secure the major port of Murmansk and secure their grasp on the nickel-mining area of Petsamo) as well as launching a southward advance towards Lakes Onega and Ladoga (as a preliminary to a German assault on Leningrad from the north). German planning began in December 1940 and envisaged that Generaloberst Nikolaus von Falkenhorst's AOK Norwegen would reinforce the Finns, two German divisions being moved in June 1941 from northern Norway into central Finland where, with one Finnish division, they formed General H. Feige's German XXXVI Corps. Von Falkenhorst's plan was for XXXVI Corps to advance east from the railhead at Kemijarvi to retake Salla (taken from the Finns by the Soviets in the Winter War of 1939/1940) and then advance on Kandalaksha, while 200 miles to the north Generalleutnant Eduard Dietl's Gebirgskorps retook Petsamo and advanced on Murmansk, and 100 miles to the south Major General H. Siilasvuo's one-division Finnish III Corps advanced to take Kestenga and Ukhta before driving forward to Loukhi to the south of Kandalaksha on the rail line from Leningrad to Murmansk. In overall strategic terms the plan was poor, providing three widely separated efforts rather than a single decisive thrust, and took little note of the fact that the German divisions were ill trained and poorly equipped for forest warfare. Operation 'Silberfuchs' began on 1 July, and the two German divisions fared notably worse than the single Finnish division committed against the two-division XLII Corps of Lieutenant General V. A. Frolov's Soviet 14th Army. Lieutenant General M. M. Popov's North Front made good use of its lateral rail communications to reinforce its 14th Army, and the combined German and Finnish offensive was checked by December after making relatively small gains in the centre and north.

Silberstreif (silver lining) Overall designation of German propaganda operations.

Silver A Designation of a British commando intelligence operation to establish liaison with the Czech resistance (1942).

Silver B Designation of the communications mission connected with Operation 'Silver A'.

Sinyavino Designation of a Soviet offensive designed to lift the siege of Leningrad and to link Leningrad with the Coastal Command beleaguered in the Oranienbaum beach-head to the west of the city on the southern side of the Gulf of Finland (7 January/end of March 1942). At this time Leningrad was invested on its Karelian (northern) side by the Finnish IV Corps of the Karelian Army of Marshal Baron C. G. E. Mannerheim's Finnish Army Group, and on its southern side by the German 18th Army, commanded by Generaloberst Georg von Küchler (from 18 January General Georg Lindemann) in Generalfeldmarschall Wilhelm Ritter von Leeb's (from 18 January Generaloberst Georg von Küchler's) Army Group 'North', which had drive its L Corps through to Schlüsselburg on the southern shore of Lake Ladoga to the east of Leningrad, and its XXVI Corps through to Peterhof on the southern shore of the Gulf of Finland to the west of Leningrad. In Leningrad were trapped a vast civil population and Lieutenant General L. A. Govorov's Leningrad Front (in the north-west the 23rd Army facing the Finns, and in the south the 42nd Army checking the German XXVIII Corps, and the 55th Army plus the Neva Group checking the German L Corps). The Leningrad Front also controlled one formation outside the Leningrad pocket, namely the 54th Army holding the area from the southern shore of Lake Ladoga at Lipka to Kirishi on the River Volkhov against the German L Corps and I Corps. In the Oranienbaum beach-head was the Coastal Command, which also came under the control of Govorov, and this was contained by the German XXVI Corps. To the south-east of the beleaguered city, between the 54th Army at Kirishi and Novgorod on the northern shore of Lake Ilmen, was General K. A. Meretskov's Volkhov Front (2nd Shock, 4th, 52nd and 59th Armies) opposite the German XXXVIII Corps and the right wing of the German I Corps.

The overall Soviet plan called for a deep westward thrust between Gruzino and Novgorod by the Volkhov Front's 2nd Shock Army (under Lieutenant General G. G. Sokolov, later Major General A. A. Vlasov) before it wheeled north to link up with Lieutenant General I. I. Fedyuninsky's 54th Army advancing during the second week in March from a point just north of Kirishi, so trapping the German I Corps. The two armies were then to drive north to link up with the 55th Army advancing south from Leningrad. As the two forces met the German L Corps would be trapped in the Schlüsselburg corridor. The operation began on 7 January, and was defeated by the 18th Army's Operation 'Raubtier'. At the same time the Soviet 42nd Army attempted to drive across the Peterhof corridor to relieve the Coastal Command, but was halted in its tracks by the German XXVIII Corps with support from XXVI Corps. Fighting continued to the end of March without much movement.

Siren Tour Air raids undertaken by small numbers of British bombers against German targets (1940/1941) with the major objects of causing air raid alarms, so disturbing the sleep of German industrial workers, and of keeping the anti-aircraft defences on the full-time alert as a means of reducing their efficiency.

Skinflint Designation of the final objective of the British X Corps of General Sir Bernard Montgomery's 8th Army in the 2nd Battle of El Alamein (24 October 1942). This was an oval area on the Rahman Track, to the south of Tell el Aqqaqir and west of Kidney Ridge, behind the main defensive positions of the 15th Panzer Division and the Littorio Division. The 1st and 10th Armoured Divisions of X Corps finally broke through 'Skinflint' on 4 November after the 'dogfight' of Operation 'Supercharge'.

Ski Site Allied designation of the ramp sites in northern France and the Low Countries from which Oberst Wachtel's Flakregiment 155(W) launched its V-1 cruise missiles from 12/13 June 1944. Intelligence reports had informed the Allies of the existence and nature of the 'Ski Sites', and photo-reconnaissance first recorded the type in October 1943, allowing the preparation of the 'Noball' offensive that started on 5 December 1943 and ended on 12 June 1944 after 23,196 tons of bombs had been dropped on 96 'Ski Sites'.

Skyscraper Allied plan for a cross-Channel attack (spring 1943). This was the last such plan prepared by the Combined Commanders' staff before the formation of the COSSAC organization headed by Lieutenant General Sir Frederick Morgan, and as such Operation 'Skyscraper' provided one of the starting points for the planning of Operation 'Overlord'. The concept of this plan was to allow Allied planners to break away from the overly complex developments of Operation 'Round-up', and also to permit a more realistic assessment of the amphibious capability required for major cross-Channel operations. 'Skyscraper' proposed two simultaneous Allied landings in northern France (one in the Cotentin peninsula for the capture of Cherbourg, and the other north of Caen) by 4 assault divisions, in preparation for a follow-up force of 6 divisions. Support for 'Skyscraper' was to be provided by 4 airborne divisions (dropped and landed south of the landings to interfere with the forward movement of German reserves) and 18 Commandos (for special assault missions). The 'Skyscraper' plan went little further than this outline for the landings, but was based on the premise that the Allied forces would then advance basically north-east towards the line of the River Seine (though it was also appreciated that extra port facilities might be gained by the capture of Le Havre) as the first step towards the capture of Antwerp so that major Allied forces could be built up in the region between the Pas-de-Calais and Antwerp for a narrow-front thrust into northern Germany.

S.L. Designation of ocean homeward convoys (together with a numerical suffix) plying the route from Freetown, Sierra Leone to the UK, and inaugurated in September 1939. The series was suspended temporarily between October 1942 and March 1943, and from May 1943 travelled home from the region of Gibraltar with M.K.S. convoys.

Slapstick Capture of Taranto by the British 1st Airborne Division (9 September 1943). The origins of the plan lay in the early days of September 1943, at just the time the Allies were putting together the final details for the US 5th Army's Operation 'Avalanche' and the British 8th Army's Operation 'Baytown' was being implemented. The Allied planners at this time realized that though all major formations and amphibious transport were earmarked for these two major undertakings, there were also two other tempting targets for large-scale *coup-de-main* assault. The first of these comprised the islands of Sardinia and Corsica (the first held by the 90th Panzergrenadier Division and the second by the Brigade Reichsführer-SS), and the second was the clutch of ports in the 'heel' of Italy (Taranto, Brindisi, Otranto and Bari).

The renascent French forces commanded by Général d'Armée Henri Giraud in North Africa were allocated to the Sardinian and Corsican operation using any shipping available in North African ports, and Major General G. F. Hopkinson's British 1st Airborne Division was designated for the 'heel' landings, which were hastily improvised under the designation Operation 'Slapstick' for the capture of Taranto, which would allow the British V Corps (British 1st, 4th and 78th Divisions) to come ashore in Italy without difficulty despite the cancellation of the corps' proposed Operation 'Goblet'

against Crotone. There was no airlift capacity available (else the British 1st Airborne Division would have been used in 'Avalanche') and virtually no amphibious shipping, so it was decided that given the poverty of the Axis defence (Taranto being held by the Italian navy, and German presence in the 'heel' being confined to a single parachute regiment), the cruisers and destroyers of Commodore W. G. Agnew's 12th Cruiser Squadron could be used for the transport and landing of the division.

The strategic rationale of the operation was that the capture of the 'heel' would provide the British with a clutch of ports for the supply of the 8th Army during its advance up the eastern coast of Italy, leaving the ports on the western side of the country for the US 5th Army. The only proviso demanded by Admiral of the Fleet Sir Andrew Cunningham's Mediterranean Fleet was that it have absolute assurance that the Italian fleet was sailing to surrender (as a result of the Allied armistice with Italy) before the 12th Cruiser Squadron (reinforced by the US cruiser *Boise* and the British minelayer *Abdiel*) was released for 'Slapstick'.

The British 1st Airborne Division was loaded at Bizerta in two echelons (the first consisting of the divisional headquarters, the 1st and 4th Parachute Brigade Groups and the 9th Field Company RE, and the second of the 2nd Parachute Brigade Group, the 1st Airlanding Brigade Group and the Glider Pilot Regiment), and was escorted to Taranto by a Malta-based force comprising the battleships *Howe* and *King George V* (plus escorting destroyers) commanded by Vice Admiral A. J. Power. The first echelon was landed without incident on 9 September, and the 12th Cruiser Squadron returned to Bizerta to load the second echelon as the leading elements of the British 1st Airborne Division fanned out from the port lest the Germans of the 4th Parachute Regiment attempt to intervene. The only disaster of 'Slapstick' was the loss of the *Abdiel*, which swung at her mooring on 10 September and detonated a German magnetic mine, which broke the ship in two and sank her with 48 sailors and 120 paratroops.

The British entered Bari and Brindisi on 11 September, the day on which Hopkinson was mortally wounded and replaced by Major General E. E. Down. The success of 'Slapstick' persuaded the Combined Chiefs-of-Staff that substantial reinforcement would be profitable, and Major General D. Russell's 8th Indian Division was forwarded from Egypt, arriving from 23 September (and so putting paid to British plus for operations against Rhodes), six days after the headquarters of Lieutenant General C. W. Allfrey's British V Corps had been established at Taranto. Major General V. Evelegh's British 78th Division had begun to disembark at Bari on 22 September, and the Special Service Brigade began to arrive on 28 September. With his corps assembled, Allfrey was instructed to hold a watching brief over the 'heel' area until he could link up on the right flank of the British XIII Corps for the capture of Foggia (and its strategically important airfields) at the end of September.

Sledgehammer US plan for an Allied landing of limited aims to take the Cotentin peninsula of northern France together with its major port at Cherbourg (autumn 1942, later amended to 1943) as an emergency operation to be undertaken in the event that either the USSR or Germany seemed in danger of imminent military collapse. In this way the Allies hoped to be able to capitalize on their 'Bolero' build-up (for Operation 'Round-up', proposed for the spring of 1943) either to help the USSR or to seal the fate of Germany. The plan was proposed in the spring of 1942 by the US Army strategic planning department under Major General Dwight D. Eisenhower, and subsequently underwent considerable development to keep abreast of current war situations, but always fell foul of the British, who felt that the move was fraught with military dangers and offered little real strategic advantage because of its inbuilt limitations. These fears were generally well founded, and the British reservations about the plan gradually infected the Americans. As a result it was decided in August 1942 to abandon the concept in favour of Operation 'Torch' using the same scale of forces but in a theatre of less possible resistance and thus able to exert a direct influence on the outcome of the war, in this instance North Africa where large numbers of French troops were based and might thus come over to the Allied cause.

Snelgrove Airborne operation by the French No. 4 Squadron, 2ème Regiment des Chasseurs Parachutistes to harass German lines of retreat near Creuse in France (12 August 1944).

Soapsuds Intermediate designation of Operation 'Tidal Wave' (1 August 1943) after the initial 'Statesman'.

Sodium Designation of a British commando intelligence mission in Czechoslovakia.

Sonnenblume (sunflower) Designation of the movement of German troops to North Africa (January/February 1941). The operation arose from the inability of Marshal Rodolfo Graziani's Italian 10th Army to deal with Major General R. O'Connor's British Western Desert Force in Libya. Hitler was unwilling to commit German forces to offensive action in North Africa, but on 11 January 1941 announced that he was prepared to allocate forces (including armoured units) as a 'blocking group' for the defence of Tripolitania. Under the overall command of Generalleutnant Erwin Rommel, Generalmajor Johannes Streich's 5th Light Division and Generalmajor Heinrich von Prittwitz und Gaffron's 15th Panzer Division were to form the Deutsches Afrika Korps.

Rommel reached Tripoli on 12 February, and his first combat units started to land two days later, at much the same time as the first elements of X Fliegerkorps detached from Sicily under Generalmajor Stefan Fröhlich, the Fliegerführer Afrika. At the insistence of Hitler (whose allocation of the 15th Panzer Division was dependent on their compliance), the Italians had agreed to pull back no farther than Sirte in the Gulf of Sirte, so maintaining a presence in Cyrenaica, and here a new commander, General Italo Gariboldi, was trying to restore the cohesion and morale of the 10th Army. Rommel appears to have been little concerned with the letter of his orders, and thus decided by 1 March that the best way to defend Tripolitania was an offensive from Sirte to take the marshy region 20 miles west of El Agheila, which could be held by small armoured forces behind mine and wire defences. By 13 March the 5th Light Division had moved up to this point, found no British opposition and, with the Italian Ariete Division, set about improvizing defences.

With Tripolitania thus secure, Rommel's fertile mind began to envisage greater things when Axis intelligence confirmed that most of the Western Desert Force had been pulled back to Egypt, leaving the defence of Cyrenaica to the precarious corps command of Lieutenant General Philip Neame's Cyrenaica Command with Major General M. D. Gambier-Perry's British 2nd Armoured Division (two understrength brigades in the region of Mersa Brega), Major General L. J. Morshead's 9th Australian Division (one full-strength and two understrength brigades in the region of the Jebel Akhdar between Benghazi and Derna) and the 3rd Indian Motorised Brigade (in El Adem). The British thought that there would be no Axis offensive, and Neame was ordered to maintain a static defence, though in the event of an Axis drive he was given authority to fall back as slowly as possible, with the object of buying time for reinforcements to arrive after a period of some two months.

Rommel now suggested to Gariboldi, his immediate superior, that their combined forces should launch a surprise attack before the onset of summer weather in May. Gariboldi agreed, and the two commanders secured permission for an offensive to retake Cyrenaica and then (with enormous optimism given the state of Axis reserves and lines of communication) advance into Egypt with the longer-term possibility of an offensive to the Suez Canal. The attack started on 24 March, when the Germans seized El Agheila as a prelude to an advance by the 5th Light Division, the Brescia Division and the Ariete Division (later supplemented by parts of the 15th Panzer Division and the Trento Division). By 25 April the exhausted Axis forces had pushed through the Halfaya Pass on Egypt's western frontier and come to a halt after a devastating campaign that had returned Cyrenaica to Axis control, and on 11 April cut off in Tobruk the 9th Australian Division reinforced by one brigade of Major General J. D. Laverack's 7th Australian Division. The defensive nature of 'Sonnenblume' had been completely forgotten.

Source Attack on the German battleship *Tirpitz* by British midget submarines (22 September 1943). Under the command of Captain W. E. Banks, the 12th Submarine Flotilla was formed on 17 April 1943 to train midget submarine crews and develop the appropriate tactics for the attack planned by Rear Admiral C. B. Barry and his staff. The midget submarines were to be towed to within a short distance of the target area by parent boats, and between 30 August and 1 September these larger boats arrived at Loch Cairnbawm in Scotland for final trials and training. On 11/12 September the force set out, with the *Truculent, Syrtis, Sea Nymph, Stubborn, Thrasher* and *Sceptre* towing the $X 6$, $X 9$, $X 8$, $X 7$, $X 5$ and $X 10$ respectively towards northern Norway. The exact location of the *Tirpitz* and other targets was as yet uncertain, but photo-reconnaissance would reveal this in time for final instructions to be radioed to the attack force. The attack information was sent on 14 September, this establishing that the $X 5$, $X 6$ and $X 7$ would attack the *Tirpitz* in Kaafjord, that the $X 9$ and $X 10$ would attack the battle-cruiser *Scharnhorst* in Kaafjord, and that the $X 8$ would attack the pocket battleship *Lützow* in Langefjord, another subsidiary of Altenfjord.

The trip northward was full of incident, for on 16 September the $X 9$ dived and was never seen again, the $X 8$ had to be scuttled on 17 September after becoming unserviceable, and several of the tows parted. The attack was finally committed on 20 September, when the four surviving X boats slipped their tows and headed for Altenfjord. The $X 10$ was unable to attack because of problems with her compass and periscopes, and withdrew on 22 September to meet the *Stubborn* off Norway on 28 September. As it was, the $X 10$'s target had moved on 21 September, so even if the boat had been fully serviceable there would have been little for her to do. The attack was now reduced to that on the *Tirpitz* by $X 5$, $X 6$ and $X 7$. $X 5$ failed to attack, and is believed to have been sunk by the Germans on 22 September. Thus the effort against the huge German battleship was eventually made by

256

the *X 6* and *X 7*, whose four-man crews behaved with exemplary courage and extreme skill to lay their four great side charges close under the *Tirpitz*'s hull, those of the *X 6* just off her starboard quarter, and those of the *X 7* under the hull just fore and aft of midships. After dropping their charges the crew of the *X 6* scuttled their craft and were picked up by the Germans, who then warped the *Tirpitz* away from the position where the *X 6* had gone down (and thus away from the *X 6*'s charges). The *X 7* placed both her charges and then tried to escape, only to find the gate in the anti-torpedo booms closed. She was then damaged and her commander decided to abandon the boat after the crew had scrambled onto a nearby gunnery target. The commander got onto the target but the boat then sank, only one of the three men on board managing to get out with the aid of his escape gear. The explosion that caused the damage to the *X 7* was the simultaneous detonation of all four charges at 08.12. Though the *Tirpitz* was not irretrievably crippled, she was severely damaged as the concussion lifted the ship several feet into the air to come down with so great a shock that all three sets of main-propulsion turbines were badly disabled. The Germans estimated that it would be April 1944 before this and other damage could be repaired. The commanders of the *X 6* and *X 7* were each awarded the Victoria Cross for this incredibly gallant action.

Spätlese (late vintage) German operation against Soviet partisans operating in the region north of Smolensk (18 September 1942). The operation was undertaken in an effort to eliminate the Moscow-controlled partisan forces who were seriously affecting the flow of supplies (and also the rear-area security) of elements of Generalfeldmarschall Günther von Kluge's Army Group 'Centre', most notably the German 9th Army in the Rzhev salient.

Spelter British commando intelligence mission in Czechoslovakia.

Sphere British air patrol of the Straits of Dover (1941 onwards).

Sphinx US programme to develop weapons and tactics specifically suited to operations against Japanese fortifications on Pacific islands.

Spinach British air mining area in the Baltic Sea off Gdynia.

Splice British operation to reinforce the air defences of Malta with Hawker Hurricane fighters (21 May 1941). This operation was presaged by a preliminary undertaking of 27 April, which involved ferrying the aircraft and pilots of No. 249 Squadron from the UK in the elderly carrier *Argus*, transferring them to the *Ark Royal* at Gibraltar, and then flying them off to Malta from a point to the west of the Sicilian Narrows at the same time that naval reinforcements (the cruiser *Dido*, the fast minelayer *Abdiel* and 6 destroyers) sailed through to Malta. Operation 'Splice' was similar in concept, the Hurricane fighters arriving from the UK in the carrier *Furious*, which then transferred some of the aircraft to the *Ark Royal* before the two carriers sailed from Gibraltar to fly off the 48 fighters on 27 May. Another such operation was undertaken on 15 June, the *Furious* having ferried 47 Hurricanes to Gibraltar for onward movement towards Malta by the newer *Ark Royal* and *Victorious* escorted by Vice Admiral Sir James Somerville's Force H. The operation was repeated on 27 and 30 June to fly off the latest batch of 64 fighters delivered to Gibraltar by the *Furious*. Two more operations in September 1941 delivered another 49 Hurricanes from the *Ark Royal* and *Furious*. Finally during that year, a force of 37 Hurricanes and 7 Bristol Blenheim light bombers was embarked on the *Ark Royal* and *Argus* and flown off to Malta on 13 November. The unfortunate result was the loss of the *Ark Royal* to the German *U-81* as the British carrier was returning to Gibraltar.

Spoof Designation of diversionary raids undertaken by British light bombers (1944/1945) with light bombs to draw the attention of the German defences (especially night-fighters) away from the area of major raids.

Spooner Allied codename for New Zealand.

Spotter British operation to deliver 15 Supermarine Spitfire fighters to Malta (7 March 1942). The aircraft were flown off the aircraft-carriers *Eagle* and *Furious*, and all reached the island without incident.

Spring Offensive by II Canadian Corps (2nd and 3rd Canadian Divisions) near Falaise in conjunction with Operation 'Cobra' (25 July 1944). The operation was undertaken from the line reached by the corps in Operation 'Goodwood', which had ended five days earlier, and was designed to exert pressure on the German forces containing the Allies at the eastern end of the Normandy lodgement so that Generalfeldmarschall Günther von Kluge (the *Oberbefehlshaber West* and also commanding Army Group 'B') could not divert troops to the west to help check the breakout of Lieutenant General Omar N. Bradley's US 1st Army at St Lô in 'Cobra'. The tactical objective of Lieutenant General G. G. Simonds's II Canadian Corps in 'Spring' was to secure the Bourguebus ridge and the northern end of the road to Falaise so that after the success of 'Cobra' Field Marshal Sir Bernard Montgomery's 21st Army Group could exploit to the south and then to the east. The operation succeeded admirably in its primary role, for while the Canadian attacks on the Bourguebus ridge were repulsed bloodily, they succeeded effectively in slowing the redeployment of SS Oberstgruppenführer Sepp Dietrich's I SS Panzer Corps and SS Gruppenführer Willi Bittrich's II SS Panzer Corps of General Heinrich Eberbach's 5th Panzerarmee, so that it was 29 July before the 2nd and 116th Panzer Divisions were able to reach the breakout area at Avranches, south of St Lô.

Springboard British plan for the seizure of the Atlantic island of Madeira (spring 1941). This plan was the partner to Operations 'Puma' and 'Thruster' for the capture of all the Atlantic islands, but there were great difficulties in the fact that the total British amphibious capability of the period was sufficient for about one brigade group. The plan was designed as a means of projecting British anti-submarine capability towards the central Atlantic (and of denying the Germans the ability to base U-boats and maritime reconnaissance aircraft in the island) at a time when it was expected that Operation 'Felix-Heinrich' against Spain and Gibraltar would be launched as soon as Germany had dealt with the USSR (Operation 'Barbarossa') in the late autumn of 1941. As it was, 'Barbarossa' was delayed by Operation 'Marita' and the determination of the Soviet resistance, and Hitler never really had the opportunity for 'Felix-Heinrich'. On the British side 'Springboard' was eventually built into the overall 'Pilgrim' plan.

Sprotie (sprat) German codeword to signal an Allied landing on the coasts of the southern Adriatic Sea.

Squid British anti-submarine weapon, consisting of three or six gyro-stabilized mortars designed to fire a triangular pattern of 385-lb bombs to land 300 yards ahead of the launch vessel on a U-boat still held in the ship's sonar detection range.

SR Japanese operation to seize Lae and Salamaua in south-eastern New Guinea (8/10 March 1942). These two places were required as advanced air bases for the bombing campaign planned by the Japanese against Port Moresby. The main Japanese bases in the theatre were located around Rabaul in New Britain, some 550 miles to the north, and though both bombers and escorting fighters could operate over this considerable radius, it forced a reduction in the bombers' load and in the fighters' time over the target. The region around Lae offered good sites for advanced air bases, with Salamaua offering defensive positions against any Allied counterattack from the south and west, the more so as most of the civilians in the area had fled in the bombing that preceded the Japanese capture of Rabaul and Kavieng. The task was allocated by Imperial General Headquarters in Tokyo to Major General Tomitaro Horii's South Seas Detachment, the army formation that had been responsible for the capture of New Britain and New Ireland as the headquarters and base area for Vice Admiral Shigeyoshi Inouye's 4th Fleet.

Given the absence of Allied ground forces in the area, Horii decided that a single battalion with marine support was adequate for the task, and decided on part of the 144th Regiment, which was ferried from Rabaul in transports escorted by the light cruiser *Yubari*, the destroyers *Mutsuki, Yayoi, Mochizuki, Oite, Asanagi* and *Yunagi*, and the minelayer *Tsugaru* (flagship). The landing at Salamaua was made at 01.00 in 8 March by the battalion of the 144th Regiment, and at 02.00 the Maizuru 2nd Special Naval Landing Force occupied Lae. Finschhafen was taken two days later, by which time the army troops had been re-embarked, leaving the naval engineers and marines to establish the necessary air bases and communications facilities.

The only opposition to Operation 'SR' came from the US Navy, which had the carriers *Enterprise* and *Yorktown* south of New Guinea at the time. On 10 March the two carriers launched a strike force of 90 aircraft against the invasion flotillas off Lae and Salamaua, and the aircraft caused very considerable destruction: 4 Japanese transports were sunk, and 13 other vessels were damaged to greater or lesser degree. But the strike did nothing to affect developments ashore, and the Japanese were soon in full control of the Huon peninsula. This was just part of the Japanese extension to the south-east, where Imperial General Headquarters wished to establish a powerful strategic barrier against any Allied counteroffensive into the Bismarck Sea. Further advances during March witnessed the Japanese occupation (followed by airfield construction) of Buka, Bougainville and the Shortland Islands at the northwestern end of the Solomons chain, of Manus Island in the Admiralties group, and of Halmahera between the western tip of New Guinea and Mindanao in the south of the Philippines. Thus Rabaul, the key to Japan's defence of her south-eastern perimeter, was hedged about defensively by Japanese-held islands all containing useful naval and air bases.

S.R. Designation of West African ocean convoys (together with a numerical suffix) plying the route from Freetown, Sierra Leone to Gibraltar, and inaugurated in February 1943.

S.T. Designation of West African coastal convoys (together with a numerical suffix) plying the route from Freetown, Sierra Leone to Takoradi, Gold Coast, and inaugurated in December 1941.

Stalemate US seizure of the Palau Islands as part of Operation 'Granite' (15 September/25 November 1944). These islands formed the main southern anchorage of the Japanese Combined Fleet from February 1944, and were desired by the Pacific Ocean Areas command under Admiral Chester W. Nimitz as an advanced base for operations against the Philippine islands. The main long-range defence of the islands lay with the new 14th Air Fleet, which was being built up from the remnants of the 11th Air Fleet largely destroyed over the 2nd Area Army's operational area. Under the overall command of the 31st Army, the Palau Islands were garrisoned from March 1944 by one regiment detached from the 35th Division pending the arrival of the 14th Division from China during April.

The US forces were indeed interested in the Palaus, but not just as a stepping stone to the Philippines. The islands also formed a vital link in the chain of support for the Japanese forces in New Guinea, and for this reason Vice Admiral Marc A. Mitscher's Fast Carrier Task Force (3 carrier task groups supported by 6 fast battleships, 13 cruisers and 26 destroyers) of Admiral Raymond A. Spruance's US 5th Fleet struck at the islands on 30/31 March in preparation for the US Army's Hollandia operation in New Guinea. The destroyer *Wakatake* and 28 merchant ships totalling 129,807 tons were sunk, some 30 aircraft were destroyed, and the approaches to the main anchorage were mined. Koga was immediately impressed with the new vulnerability of the Combined Fleet's main anchorage, and ordered a withdrawal to Tawitawi (between Borneo and the Philippines).

The pace of US operations in the central and south-western Pacific was now increasing, and the Philippines were targeted for assault by combined US Navy and US Army forces during October 1944. To this end, therefore, it was decided to secure advanced bases (that for the US Navy in the Palaus and that for the US Army on Morotai) which were to be assaulted simultaneously on 15 September. The Morotai operation by the US 31st Infantry Division met no opposition and succeeded without difficulty. The same could not be said of Operation 'Stalemate' undertaken against the Palaus by Admiral William F. Halsey's US 3rd Fleet.

The defence was centred on the 14th Division, which Lieutenant General Sadal Inouye deployed mainly on Babelthuap, the largest of the Palau Islands. The US plan, however, was to take only the two southern islands (Peleliu and Angaur) so that the Kossoi Passage could be cleared of mines and the anchorage used for the Philippine operations. The target area was softened up by gun bombardment and air strikes from the escort carriers of Vice Admiral Theodore S. Wilkinson's III Amphibious Force, and on 15 September some 23,400 men of the US 1st Marine Division (Major General Roy S. Geiger's II Amphibious Corps) began to land on Peleliu against a Japanese defence of 10,500 men. The initial beach-head was taken by the US Marines against the usual fanatical resistance by the Japanese, but by the end of 16 September the island's airfield had been occupied (though not consolidated) by the Americans as the Japanese pulled back to their main defence position at the north-western tip of the island. This position enabled the Japanese to command the airfield, and it was only on 1 October that the US Marines had advanced far enough to allow the airfield to be used. By 7 October the strip had been developed sufficiently for bombers to use it.

However, the battle for Peleliu was far from over, and it required anotherr six weeks of bitter fighting before the island was declared secure on 25 November. On 17 September, meanwhile, the US 81st Infantry Division was landed by III Amphibious Force on Angaur at the extreme south of the group against moderate opposition, and by 20 September the island was secure apart from one small pocket at the north-west tip of the island. On 21 September the airfield on Angaur came into use by Consolidated B-24 Liberator heavy bombers. The last stage of the campaign was the seizure of Ulithi atoll (between the Palaus and the Marianas) by a regimental combat team of the US 81st Infantry Division. The Americans landed on 23 September only to find that the Japanese had pulled out earlier in the month. The excellent anchorage at Ulithi was soon developed at the US Navy's main forward base in the Pacific, taking over from Eniwetok.

Stalin Line Soviet defence line in the western USSR (1941). This covered the full depth of the vast Soviet frontier with the Western nations, running from its northern extremity at Narva on the Gulf of Finland to a southern terminus just west of Odessa on the Black Sea. From Narva the line ran south along the length of the River Velikaya (via the eastern side of Lake Peipus), and then cut across from Idritsa to Polotsk on the upper River Dvina before leaving this river at Vitebsk to move south-east to Orsha on the River Dniepr. The line then followed the southward run of the Dniepr via Moghilev and Rechitsa to a point south of the Pripet Marshes where the Dniepr meets the River Pripet, swung south-west across the grainlands of the Ukraine to reach the River Dniestr just to the east of Kamenets-Podolsk, and completed its run to the Black Sea down the Dniestr. The line had been constructed between 1929 and 1935 (and thus well before the westward extension of the USSR's frontiers at the expense of the Baltic states and Poland) to protect the USSR's current boundaries. It was by no means continuous, but rather a belt of defensive fire points (some 2 km in depth) together with artillery emplacements strengthened to resist heavy shellfire. After the USSR's westward expansion this system was run down, and stripped of its weapons and garrisons. Immediately before the German invasion of June 1941 Stalin ordered the reactivation of the line and of the special defensive sectors in Karelia and at Polotsk, Koroshten and Kiev.

By 9 July the Germans had closed up to the 'Stalin Line' along most of its length, the most notable exceptions being the sector behind the Pripet Marshes, where the Soviet 21st and 5th Armies (of General D. G. Pavlov's West and Colonel General M. P. Kirponos' South-West Fronts respectively) were checking the German 6th Army and 2nd Panzergruppe (of Generalfeldmarschall Gerd von Rundstedt's Army Group 'South' and Generalfeldmarschall Fedor von Bock's Army Group 'Centre' respectively), and the sector on the lower Dniestr, where the Soviet 18th and 19th Armies of the South-West Front were holding back the German 11th and Romanian 4th Armies of Army Group 'South'. To balance these failures, the Germans had by this same date secured two significant breakthroughs, one in the north around Vitebsk (in the sector of Army Group 'Centre') by Generaloberst Hermann Hoth's 3rd Panzergruppe, and one in the south around Zhitomir (in the sector of Army Group 'South') by Generaloberst Ewald von Kleist's 1st Panzergruppe. Very soon after this the German forces punched through the ineffective 'Stalin Line' along its whole length.

Stamina Allied air support operation for Lieutenant General Sir Geoffrey Scoones' IV Indian Corps at Imphal (18 April/30 June 1944). The operation was started as Lieutenant General Renya Mutaguchi's Japanese 15th Army was launching Operation 'U' against Imphal and Kohima as the planned prelude to an invasion of north-east India, the British object being to stockpile all necessary supplies for a 30-day siege (2,800 tons of supplies, 300 tons of ammunition and 80 tons of engineer stores by the end of April) in IV Indian Corps' base area around Imphal. This required a daily lift of 245 tons, but weather and other circumstances reduced this to 148 tons per day for a month-end total of 1,926 tons. During May the daily rate improved to 194.8 tons (for the delivery of 6,040 tons) and during June to 362 tons (for the delivery of 10,858 tons). The monthly delivery of men by airlift was 1,479 in April, 5,011 in May and 6,071 in June; in overall terms 'Stamina' delivered 18,824 tons and 12,561 men, shortfalls of 8,669 tons and 5,939 men on the target figures. The return flights from Imphal evacuated about 13,000 casualties and 43,000 non-combatants.

Stanza British plan to build up a forward base at Rangoon for further advances into South-East Asia (1945). The plan proposed that the port be opened as soon as possible after the liberation of Rangoon with the object of handling some 7,500 tons (including some 1,500 tons of oil products) per day. This would allow the establishment of a dump holding sufficient supplies and fuel for 45 days of operations by two full corps (just under seven divisions) and one group of RAF aircraft. 'Stanza' also provided for the development of four airfields within four months, rising to seven airfields by the end of 1945. The implementation of 'Stanza' was made possible by Operation 'Modified Dracula', and the port began to receive ships on 8 May 1945.

Star Soviet offensive for the recapture of Kharkov (1 February/26 March 1943). This was one of the most important objectives of the Soviet winter/spring offensive of 1943, designed to push the German Army Group 'A' (Generalfeldmarschall Maximilian Freiherr von Weichs) and Army Group 'Don' (Generalfeldmarschall Erich von Manstein) back from the line of the River Don into the Ukraine. This general offensive began on 12 January 1943 between Orel in the north and Rostov-na-Donu in the south, using Lieutenant General M. A. Reiter's Bryansk Front, Colonel General F. I. Golikov's Voronezh Front, General N. F. Vatutin's South-West Front and General A. I. Eremenko's South Front, and by the end of the month had pushed the Soviet front forward to the line of the Rivers Oskol, Donets and Don against the efforts (from north to south) of the German 2nd Army, the Hungarian 2nd Army, the Italian 8th Army, the Romanian 3rd Army and the German 4th Panzerarmee. Major elements of the German 2nd and Hungarian 2nd Armies were cut off by the flood of Soviet armour, and the Axis position deteriorated sharply. However, the dispersion of the Soviet effort allowed many of the isolated Axis units to make their way back to their parent formations, even though 86,000 prisoners (most of them Hungarians) were taken by the Soviets.

The *Stavka* (Soviet high command) now decided on a move that had distinct operational dangers, for instead of a direct thrust by the Voronezh Front towards Kharkov, it opted for a divergent operation (one half of the front striking west towards Kursk and the other moving south-west towards Kharkov) to exploit the 200-mile gap ripped in what had been Army Group 'B' between Generalfeldmarschall Günther von Kluge's Army Group 'Centre' and Army Group 'Don' (the latter renamed Army Group 'South' on 6 February). On 1 February this gap witnessed the movement of substantial Soviet forces. For while the 13th and 38th Armies of the Voronezh Front moved off west towards Kursk, and the 60th, 40th and 3rd Tank Armies of the same front struck out west in the direction of Kharkov, the 6th Army and 1st Guards Army of the South-West Front diverged to the south-west with the object of taking Mariupol on the Sea of Azov and so cutting the lines of communication to Army Group 'Don' and to Generalfeldmarschall Ewald von Kleist's Army Group 'A' in the Caucasus.

The spearhead of Operation 'Star' was the thrust of Lieutenant General P. S. Rybalko's 3rd Tank Army on the southern flank of the Voronezh Front. This drove forward from Kupyansk on the Oskol towards Kharkov on 1 February, and on 5 February (three days after the fall of the last German pocket in Stalingrad) it reached the Donets to the east of Kharkov. Though the Soviet army was checked by SS Gruppenführer Paul Hausser's II SS Panzer Corps, it was already clear that the great area between Kursk and Kharkov via Belgorod was threatened by the Soviet advance, as were the lines of communication to Army Group 'Don' and the remnants of Army Group 'A'.

By the end of January Army Group 'A' had fallen back into a beach-head in the Kuban, and on 2 February the South Front was revitalized by the replacement of Eremenko by General R. Ya. Malinovsky. Two days later the South Front had advanced the Soviet line in the south over the lower Don to Shakhty and Novocherkassk, and four days later Rostov-na-Donu was liberated, so isolating the 17th Army in the Kuban. Farther to the north the Voronezh Front was in full spate, retaking Volchansk, Belgorod, Oboyan and Kursk, and on 11 February reached the suburbs of Kharkov with the 69th Army and VI Guards Cavalry Corps, which again were checked but not halted by II SS Panzer Corps. Between these southern and northern flanks of the Soviet offensive the South-West Front had also been making important gains as the 6th and 1st Guards Armies supported by Group Popov crossed the Donets and struck out towards the Dniepr crossing at Dnepropetrovsk and Zaporozhye, deep in the rear of Army Group 'Don'.

Hitler at this time adamantly refused to permit any German withdrawal behind the line of the River Mius, and there was thus good reason for the Soviets to hope for the trapping of the 1st Panzerarmee, the 4th Panzerarmee and the Armeegruppe Hollidt against the Sea of Azov. Von Kluge and von Manstein flew to confer with Hitler on 6 February, and the German leader reluctantly agreed to a withdrawal to the line of the Mius in the south. At this time Army Group 'B' was put into reserve, its surviving combat formations being allocated to Army Groups 'Centre' and 'South'. The Soviets were now beginning to lose momentum, and when General K. K. Rokossovsky's new Don Front (ex-Stalingrad Front) tried to drive through to von Kluge's rear behind the Orel salient with a left hook from the Soviet salient around Kursk, it was checked by a German 2nd Army counterattack at Sevsk. The situation was still threatening for the Germans as on 16 February General H. Lanz's Armeegruppe Lanz (III SS Panzer Corps and Korpsgruppe Raus) had abandoned Kharkov against all orders. One day later Hitler arrived in Zaporozhye to sack von Manstein, who survived as a result of a piece of the most extraordinary tactical genius that not only halted but threw back the Soviets despite a German numerical inferiority of one to seven.

The main threat to the Germans was now the Soviet salient developed towards Dnepropetrovsk by the 1st Guards and 6th Armies with Group Popov, and von Manstein quickly improvised a pincer movement to eliminate this salient. While the Korpsgruppe Raus of the Armeegruppe Kempf (General Werner Kempf) held the Soviets to the west of Kharkov, on 19 February II SS Panzer Corps of the same grouping struck south from Krasnograd towards Pavlograd, and scattered IV Guards Rifle Corps. Three days later the southern half of the pincer swung into action as, under von Manstein's personal control, Generaloberst Hermann Hoth launched his 4th Panzerarmee (General Otto von

Knobelsdorff's XLV Panzer Corps and General Friedrich Kirchner's LVII Panzer Corps) to link up with II SS Panzer Corps near Pavlograd.

Farther to the east on the southern side of the salient General Eberhard von Mackensen's 1st Panzerarmee also had its part to play, the army's XL Panzer Corps under General Sigfrid Henrici smashing Group Popov near Krasnoarmeysk. The Soviet high command believed that this extraordinary effort was merely a means for the Germans to ensure that the 1st Panzerarmee and Armeegruppe Hollidt could pull back from the Mius to the Dniepr, and so ordered the South-West Front to pin the Germans along the Mius. But by this time the 4th Panzerarmee had linked up with II SS Panzer Corps and Korpsgruppe Raus and, after regrouping between 4 and 6 March, had advanced some 150 miles to threaten Kharkov once more. This move punched through the junction between the Voronezh Front and the South-West Front. The Germans re-entered Kharkov on 12 March, and retook Belgorod six days later. It was only at this stage that the Soviet high command appreciated the brilliance of von Manstein's moves, which now threatened to cut off the Voronezh and Central Fronts. Stalin thus ordered a withdrawal of some 40 miles to the Donets, the 3rd Tank Army fighting its way out from the region of Kharkov. General Georgi Zhukov was ordered in to halt what Stalin saw as the Soviet rot, and with the aid of three specially allocated armies (the 1st Tank, 21st and 64th Armies) managed to stabilize the position by the time the spring thaw arrived on 26 March. Von Manstein's blow had cost the Soviets some 40,000 casualties, 600 tanks and 500 guns. Operation 'Star' had been defeated, and the Germans were back on the line of the Mius and Donets. The Soviet army was by no means defeated in any long-term way, but von Manstein had saved Army Group 'South' and also proved that the German army still retained very great operational expertise and strength, especially when it could deploy small numbers of high-grade formations such as II SS Panzer Corps.

Starfish British decoy flares, designed to resemble German markers and so lure German bombers away from their designated targets (autumn 1940).

Starkey Combined RAF and US Army Air Force offensive against German air strength in the West by means of a feint against Boulogne (25 August/9 September 1943).

Starvation Mining campaign undertaken by the US XX Bomber Command from the Marianas to mine Japanese harbours and the waters around the Japanese home islands with a view to preventing the arrival of raw materials convoys from overseas, and to halting the use of coastal shipping as a replacement for overland routes destroyed by conventional bombing (1945).

Statesman Initial plan for a US bomber campaign against the Romanian oilfields at Ploesti, eventually developed in 'Soapsuds' and 'Tidal Wave'.

Steiermark (Styria) German codename for the headquarters of Reichsführer-SS Heinrich Himmler.

Steinbock (ibex) Series of German air raids (the 'baby Blitz') against London and other major British targets (21 January/29 May 1944). Under the command of the Angriffsführer England (Generalmajor Dietrich Peltz), the German forces available for this small offensive against the UK amounted during the third week of January 1944 to 524 bombers and fighter-bombers, of which 462 were serviceable. Most of the aircraft were Junkers Ju 88 and Dornier Do 217 twin-engined bombers, though other types were the Heinkel He 177 four-engined bomber, the Junkers Ju 188 twin-engined bomber, the Messerschmitt Me 410 twin-engined fighter-bomber and the Focke-Wulf Fw 190 single-engined fighter-bomber. Hitler was adamant that the war should once again be taken to the British, but Peltz was in little doubt that the aircraft and men available to him were woefully inadequate for the task, especially against a British defence honed to a peak by years of war and deploying good AA guns, excellent radar, an advanced control system and the formidable de Havilland Mosquito night-fighter. The best for which Peltz could hope was that most of his crews could find and attack targets marked by his best crews.

The tenor of the whole campaign was set by the inaugural raid, launched against London by every serviceable aircraft (447 machines) on 21 January 1944. Some 500 tons of bombs were carried, but of this total only 32 tons were dropped in London and another 236 tons on land. The next raid was launched on 29 January, this time by 285 aircraft, and the tonnage delivered to London was 36.5 compared with 158 dropped on land. The German losses in these two raids were 57 aircraft, an unacceptably high 7.8 per cent of sorties flown. London was the target right through February, when seven raids delivered low tonnages and suffered losses of 75 aircraft (5.2 per cent). March, April and May 1944 saw the diversification of the offensive to targets as far separated as Hull and Falmouth, but results were still poor, and in March losses amounted to 75 aircraft (8.3 per cent), in April in 75 aircraft (8.7 per cent) and in May to some 50 aircraft (about 10 per cent).

The campaign ended with the raid of 29 May against Falmouth and Portsmouth. By this time the Germans were suffering from the loss of aircraft at a time when it was clear that the Allied invasion of Europe was imminent, and though the object of the offensive had been altered from pure retaliation to dislocation of the Allied invasion preparations (hence the later concentration on ports such as Falmouth, Weymouth, Portsmouth, etc.), it was clear by May at the latest that German offensive air assets should be husbanded against the unleashing of the Allied invasion.

Sternenlauf (star track) German operation against Soviet partisans operating west of Dubrovno on the main rail and road link towards Moscow (23 January/12 February 1943). This double link was the main supply and reinforcement artery for Generalfeldmarschall Günther von Kluge's Army Group 'Centre', against which the Soviets were making a great effort between November 1942 and July 1943 in preparation for the offensive to liberate Belorussia in the late summer of 1943.

Stettin German occupation of Memel (23 March 1939). Part of East Prussia up to the time of the Treaty of Versailles in 1919, Memel and its largely German population had since been a part of Lithuania but subject to German ambitions of annexation into the 'Greater German Reich'. After an ultimatum to Lithuania, Memel was reoccupied by the Germans in a short and bloodless operation watched by Hitler from the pocket battleship *Deutschland*.

Stichling (stickleback) German codeword to signify the launch of any Allied invasion in the Aegean region.

Stoneage British supply convoy operation to Malta (17/20 November 1942). Undertaken as the Allied 1st Army delivered into North-West Africa during Operation 'Torch' was beginning its eastward approach to Tunisia, and as the British 8th army in the Western Desert was sweeping west (liberating Tobruk on 13 November and Benghazi on 20 November) towards Tunisia, Operation 'Stoneage' was designed to ensure the relief of Malta. The convoy of 2 US, 1 Dutch and 1 British merchantmen was assembled at Alexandria after passing north through the Suez Canal, and left for Malta on 17 November under escort of the four cruisers of Rear Admiral A. J. Power's 15th Cruiser Squadron, together with 17 destroyers. Axis air attacks started on 18 November, and initially the only casualty was the cruiser *Arethusa*, which was torpedoed but managed to get back to Alexandria, albeit with 155 dead. The convoy was buffeted by adverse weather and renewed Axis air attacks, but with most of the relevant African shoreline in Allied hands, British fighters were able to provide excellent cover, allowing the unharmed convoy to steam into Malta early on 20 November with an escort reduced to the cruiser *Euryalus* and 10 'Hunt' class escort destroyers. By 25 November the convoy had been unloaded, its most important supply being aviation fuel, which at last permitted the small-scale delivery by submarine to be ended.

Stopper British air patrols off Brest (1941/

1942) to watch for signs of German warship activity and to attack U-boats on passage.

Störfang (sturgeon trap) Alternative name for the capture of Sevastopol in the Crimea (2 June/2 July 1942) by the German 11th Army of Generaloberst Erich von Manstein.

Stosser (falcon) German airborne operation to disrupt the Allied rear area near Belle Croix in Belgium as part of Operation 'Herbstnebel' (15/16 December 1944). Commanded by Oberstleutnant Friedrich-August von der Heydte, this parachute force numbered some 1,200 men in all, but only some 300 men actually dropped behind the Allied lines because the low performance of the Junker Ju 52 transport aircraft crews ensured that three-quarters of the German force dropped inside the German lines. The task entrusted to von der Heydte was to cut the roads over which Lieutenant General Courtney H. Hodges's US 1st Army could rush reinforcements to check the advance of SS Oberstgruppenführer Sepp Dietrich's 6th SS Panzerarmee. The landings were a total disaster as they occurred at night and in unsuitable terrain, and generally failed in their objectives. Most of the errant paratroops had been rounded up by 18 December after hiding and watching impotently as three US divisions moved over the roads the German airborne force had tried to cut.

Strangle Allied air offensive designed to cut the maritime, road and rail lines of communication to the German armies south of Rome (19 March/11 May 1944). The object of this major undertaking was to destroy Germany's capability to move supplies, fuel, *matériel* and reinforcements south of a line between Pisa and Rimini, and thus break the deadlock between the opposing land forces by allowing the Allies to build up a decisive numerical advantage before the resumption of the 'Gustav Linie' battle in the spring/summer of 1944. Under the overall command of Lieutenant General Ira C. Eaker, the commander-in-chief of the Mediterranean Allied Air Forces, the two main Allied air formations involved in the campaign co-ordinated by Major General John K. Cannon's Mediterranean Allied Tactical Air Force were Brigadier General Gordon P. Saville's XII Air Support Command (US 12th Air Force) and Air Vice Marshal H. Broadhurst's Desert Air Force (Mediterranean Allied Tactical Air Force), supported by Major General Nathan F. Twining's Mediterranean Allied Strategic Air Force. During the campaign some 20,000 tons of bombs were delivered on targets such as railway defiles, marshalling yards, bridges and tunnels, and though some useful results were achieved (some 10 major supply arteries being cut), these were insufficient to prevent the Germans moving adequate forces and resources to check the Allies' May 1944 offensives. During March, for example, the German forces under Generalfeldmarschall Albert Kesselring received a daily ration of 1,357 tons of supplies (compared with a requirement of 2,261 tons). However, the expedients adopted by the Germans to ensure continued supplies seriously eroded their reserves of motor fuel.

Stratford British plan for a landing in southern Norway by five battalions of Major General P. J. Mackesy's 49th Division (spring 1940). This was part of a proposed development of Allied operations into the Scandinavian theatre in an effort to forestall German moves in the same direction. The whole plan was approved at the beginning of February 1940. One demi-brigade of French Chasseurs Alpins and one brigade of British regular troops were to be shipped into Narvik before advancing up the main rail line to occupy the important Swedish iron ore fields at Gallivare. A mixed force of two or three brigades was to be sent to the support of the Finns against the USSR, but was to operate to farther south than the head of the Gulf of Bothnia for logistic reasons. The 49th Division was to occupy the southern Norwegian ports of Stavanger, Bergen and Trondheim (Operation 'Stratford'), and a formation of one regular and two territorial British divisions was to be withdrawn from the British commitment to France for operations in Sweden against any German countermove. The plan thus envisaged the delivery of 100,000 men and 11,000 vehicles to Scandinavia in an operation taking 11 weeks. The key to the whole concept was Trondheim, where Allied troops were to be

265

landed as fast as the Norwegian roads and railways could shift them to their operational areas. Operation 'Stratford' was scheduled to begin on 28 February, but Norway was determined to maintain her neutrality as long as possible (especially after the 'Altmark incident' of 16 February, in which the British destroyer *Cossack* had boarded the German freighter *Altmark* in Norwegian waters and freed British prisoners taken by the pocket battleship *Admiral Graf Spee*), and this exceptionally difficult strategic undertaking was cancelled on 29 February.

Stream British landing at Majunga in Madagascar (10/11 September 1942). It had become clear in the aftermath of Operation 'Ironclad' against Diego Suarez that the Vichy French administration of Madagascar would not capitulate willingly to the British, and there thus remained the possibility of an intensification of the Japanese submarine offensive in the Mozambique Channel. Through this strategically important passage moved most of the convoys carrying British reinforcements and *matériel* to North Africa, the Middle East and India, and during June and July 1942 Japanese submarines had indeed operated in these waters, sinking 20 ships of 94,000 tons before withdrawing during July. It was therefore essential that Madagascar (and especially its west coast ports of Majunga, Morondava and Tulear) be brought into the Allied fold. To this end Operation 'Stream' secured Majunga when Brigadier F. W. Festing's British 29th Infantry Brigade Group was landed there on 10 September. The brigade was later re-embarked for the landing at Tamatave on the island's east coast (18 September), its place being taken by the 22nd East African Brigade, which advanced inland towards the capital, Tananarive, which fell on 23 September.

Strike Final offensive in Tunisia by Lieutenant General K. A. N. Anderson's Allied 1st Army to defeat Generaloberst Jürgen von Arnim's Army Group 'Africa' (General Giovanni Messe's 1st Army and General Gustav von Vaerst's 5th Panzerarmee) in its final beach-head around Bizerta and Tunis (6/12 May 1943). The operation was planned by General the Hon. Sir Harold Alexander's 18th Army Group as successor to Operation 'Vulcan'. The main task was entrusted to Lieutenant General B. G. Horrocks's British IX Corps (British 6th and 7th Armoured Divisions, British 4th Division, Indian 4th Division, 25th Tank Brigade and 201st Guards Motor Brigade), which was to use its two infantry divisions to break through the Axis defences in front of Massicault (some 25 miles south-west of Tunis) so that the British 6th and 7th Armoured Divisions could exploit into the Axis rear. As a preliminary to this move, Lieutenant General C. W. Allfrey's British V Corps (British 1st, 46th and 78th Divisions) was to take the Djebel Bou Aoukaz and so provide a left-flank guard for IX Corps, holding back one division for exploitation. At the same time, in the north of the 1st Army's sector, Lieutenant General Omar N. Bradley's US II Corps (US 1st Armored and 1st, 9th and 34th Infantry Divisions) was to take the high ground to the east and west of Chouigui, the crossings over the River Medjerda at Tebourba and Djedeida, and then Bizerta, while in the south of the 1st Army's sector Général de Corps d'Armée L. M. Koeltz's French XIX Corps (Division d'Oran, Division d'Alger and Division du Maroc) was to take the Djebel Zaghouan.

Alexander emphasized that the main objects of the operation were to take Tunis and to trap in northern Tunisia (well away from the Axis embarkation points in the Cap Bon peninsula) as great a part as possible of the Axis forces, and this could only be achieved by passing the British 6th and 7th Armoured Divisions through the British 4th and 4th Indian Divisions on 6 May so that they could take the high ground some 6 miles west of Tunis and so prevent the Axis forces from developing the anti-tank defence that would provide a narrow escape corridor to the south-east.

The offensive began as planned on 6 May, and though progress was made, this failed to achieve the speed desired by Alexander. Worn out by months of fighting without rest or even adequate reinforcement (of men and equipment), the Axis forces disintegrated as an army group but continued to offer determined resistance on an individual formation basis. Von Arnim could no longer exercise control, therefore, but in the north the 5th Panzerarmee fell slowly back under pressure of the US II and British IX Corps towards Bizerta and Tunis (along the line Tebourba-la Mohammedia-Djebel Oust), while in the south General Hans Cramer's Deutsches Afrika Korps (with the 10th Panzer Division and the 'Hermann Goering' Panzer Division under command) fell back before the British V and French XIX Corps towards the Cap Bon peninsula (along the line Djebel Oust-Zaghouan. At the eastern end of the Axis line, along the Gulf of Tunis coast, the Axis 1st Army held its positions against a comparatively inactive British 8th Army and ensured that the Cap Bon peninsula was in Axis hands for the planned evacuation.

Though Messe was not told of the decision, von Arnim and von Vaerst had no intention of seeking to hold either Bizerta or Tunis, where the port installations and other facilities were destroyed on 6 May, just one day before these cities fell to Major General Manton S. Eddy's US 9th Infantry Division and Major General G. W. E. J. Erskine's British 7th Armoured Division respectively. The Axis defence was now split into pockets, but still continued to fight doggedly against the rampant Allied forces even though they could not hope to halt the Allied progress. On 9 May von Vaerst and the remnants of the 5th Panzerarmee surrendered to the US II Corps, and the area of Tunisia north of the capital was in Allied hands, leaving two Axis groupings (named Armeegruppe von Arnim and Armeegruppe Messe on 11 May) holding out against the Allied 1st and British 8th Armies respectively. On 12 May von Arnim and Messe surrendered separately, and the North African campaign of World War II was over. Some 250,000 Axis prisoners were taken, and amongst the Allied 1st Army's booty were some 600 undamaged Axis aircraft abandoned for lack of fuel, a commodity whose unavailability (together with that of ammunition) had bedevilled the final resistance of Army Group 'Africa'.

Strongpoint Major reorganization of Lieutenant General Claire L. Chennault's US 14th Air Force in China (1945).

Stud Allied air operations in direct support of Field Marshal Sir Bernard Montgomery's Allied 21st Army Group in Operation 'Overlord' (6 June 1944). These operations were entrusted to Air Marshal Sir Arthur Coningham's British 2nd Tactical Air Force and Lieutenant General Lewis H. Brereton's US 9th Air Force under the overall command of Air Chief Marshal Sir Trafford Leigh-Mallory, the Allied air commander-in-chief.

Student Joint German and Italian plan to reintroduce Fascism to Italy after the overthrow of Mussolini (July 1943) and the Italian armistice with the Allies (September 1943). This vain hope rested with the Fascist puppet government under Mussolini, established in northern Italy by the Germans after the rescue of the Italian dictator in Operation 'Eiche'.

Sturmflut (tidal wave) Final stage of Operation 'Morgenluft' by the Deutsches Afrika Korps (19/22 February 1943). This last effort was directed against the US positions in the Kasserine Pass by the assault group of the Deutsches Afrika Korps commanded by Generalmajor Karl Bülowius under the overall leadership of Generalmajor Kurt Freiherr von Liebenstein but in fact controlled by Generalfeldmarschall Erwin Rommel, commander-in-chief of the German-Italian Panzerarmee. By 17 February Operations 'Morgenluft' and 'Frühlingswind' had both achieved their primary objectives but, ever the opportunist, Rommel was avid to exploit the Allied evacuation of the Dorsale Occidentale by advancing through the Kasserine Pass to take Tebessa and so disrupt the rear areas of the US II Corps and French XIX Corps of Lieutenant General K. A. N. Anderson's Allied 1st Army, and then striking out towards Bone and Constantine to defeat the 1st Army in its entirety. Rommel asked for the co-operation of Generaloberst Jürgen von Arnim's 5th Panzerarmee in this undertaking, but von Arnim responded that, while the 10th and 21st Panzer Divisions were under Rommel's control for the operation, he believed that the optimum move was now an advance farther to the north-west against Le Kef with a view to an exploitation from the River Medjerda towards Beja. A third view in the matter was that of the Italian Comando Supremo, which on 19 February ordered that Rommel's combined force should strike north with the object of cutting off the British V Corps or at least of driving it back to the Algerian frontier.

While the German *Oberbefelhshaber Süd* (Generalfeldmarschall Albert Kesselring) was adjudicating between the three parties, Rommel decided to pre-empt the decision, and thus launched Operation 'Sturmflut' at 04.50 on 19 February, moving out from the town of Kasserine which had been taken on 18 February as the culmination of 'Morgenluft'. Rommel planned to use his well-proved tactics of speed and movement with comparatively small forces to ensure success against an opponent in considerable command and tactical disarray as a result of 'Morgenluft' and 'Frühlingswind'. Such a move was well within the capabilities of the Deutsches Afrika Corps' assault group, which was to be reinforced after it had taken the Kasserine Pass by Generalleutnant Wolfgang Fischer's 10th Panzer Division diverted from the Fondouk region on 19 February. The Kasserine sector was the responsibility of Lieutenant General Lloyd R. Fredendall's US II Corps, whose 1st Armored Division (Major General Orlando Ward) was reorganizing itself at Tebessa. Kasserine Pass was itself held by Colonel Alexander N. Stark's Stark Force, with the British 26th Armoured Brigade available as reserve (near Thala) with the approval of the 1st Army.

Rommel's expectations of a rapid breakthrough and exploitation at Kasserine were not fulfilled, however, and the Deutsches Afrika Korps' assault group was able to break through only on 20 February as Stark Force disintegrated. Thereafter the Deutsches Afrika Corps' assault group swept forward to the Djebel el Hamra, where it was finally checked by Combat Command B of the US 1st Armored Division and by elements of the US 1st Infantry Division, while the 10th Panzer Division advanced towards Thala against strengthening opposition from the British 26th Armoured Brigade supported by Nick Force.

The Axis commanders were now seriously worried by Rommel's lack of progress and the approach of General Sir Bernard Montgomery's 8th Army to the Mareth Line, and on 21 February the Comando Supremo ordered Rommel to break off the offensive and return to his start line. The Allied air forces were beginning to dominate the battlefield, and the Germans suffered heavy losses as they pulled back towards Kasserine Pass with the Allies in pursuit. By 24 February the pass was once more in Allied hands, and 'Sturmflut' was over, the day for such extemporized forays with limited *matériel* and fuel resources being long past.

Style British troop convoy to Malta (31 July/4 August 1941). This improvised operation was undertaken to deliver to the island those troops left at Gibraltar by the grounding of the troopship *Leinster* at the beginning of Operation 'Substance'. The operation was undertaken by ships of Vice Admiral Sir James Somerville's Force H, and the 1,800 troops and airmen (the latter made up mostly of vital maintenance crews) destined for the Malta garrison were carried on the cruisers *Hermione* and *Arethusa*, and on the fast minelayer *Manxman*, escorted by two destroyers. This force left Gibraltar on 31 July and made a fast passage to Malta, delivering the men and some supplies before departing the island on 2 August to regain Gibraltar on 4 August. The most eventful part of the operation was the ramming and sinking of the Italian submarine *Tembien* by the *Hermione* off Tunis on 2 August.

Substance British convoy to Malta (21/27 July 1941). At this time Malta's garrison was in sore need of reinforcements and supplies, but as no convoy could be passed westward through the Mediterranean from Alexandria, it was decided to try an eastward convoy from Gibraltar. The British plan was that the troopship *Leinster* and six storeships should be passed to Malta while the auxiliary *Breconshire* and six empty merchantman escaped from the island to Gibraltar. The significance of the operation is attested by the fact that Vice Admiral Sir James Somerville's Force H was temporarily reinforced by a detachment of the Home Fleet in the form of the battleship *Nelson* and the cruisers *Edinburgh*, *Manchester* and *Arethusa*. The convoy departed the River Clyde on 11 July and reached Gibraltar on

19 July, allowing the operation proper to begin on 21 July. An immediate problem was the grounding of the troopship *Leinster*, and though some 3,200 of the 5,000 troops and airmen on board were transferred to other ships, the balance of 1,800 was left for Operation 'Style', undertaken a few days later.

The British plan was for Admiral Sir Andrew Cunningham's Mediterranean Fleet to sortie from Alexandria in order to deal with the Italian fleet if it sailed from Taranto, Palermo and Messina, for a patrol group of 8 submarines to lurk on the likely approach routes of any Italian surface forces, and for the convoy to head east under escort of the reinforced Force H (2 battleships, 1 aircraft-carrier, 5 cruisers and 18 destroyers), which would turn back in the Sicilian Narrows, leaving the convoy to proceed to Malta under the close escort of Rear Admiral E. N. Syfret's force (comprising the cruisers *Edinburgh*, *Manchester* and *Arethusa*, the fast minelayer *Manxman* and 10 destroyers) as the ships from Malta escaped westward.

The operation proceeded without undue incident until 23 July, when the convoy was south of Sardinia and came under heavy air attack. Despite the efforts of the fighters flown off the carrier *Ark Royal*, the first casualties were the *Manchester*, which was so heavily damaged by a torpedo that she had to return to Gibraltar, and the destroyer *Fearless*, which had eventually to be sunk by the British. The vital storeships were undamaged, however, and reached the Skerki Channel at 17.00 for the final dash to Malta after the main strength of Force H had turned back. Air attacks on the convoy continued, but the only casualty was again a warship, this time the destroyer *Firedrake*, which was detached to Gibraltar. Syfret turned north after nightfall, deciding that the longer passage would be more than balanced by freedom from Axis minefields and the possibility of losing shadowing aircraft in the dark, and the commander was proved right. Early on 24 July one of the storeships was torpedoed and damaged by a Pantelleria-based torpedo craft, but managed to get through to Malta. At daybreak the cruisers headed independently for Malta as there was now no chance of Italian interception by Italian heavy warships, unloaded their troops and stores, and made off to Gibraltar late on 24 July. Later on the same day the storeships and their destroyer escort arrived safely as the empty ships that had broken out from the island headed for Gibraltar, all arriving despite the attentions of the Axis air forces. Finally, Somerville again headed for Malta to provide air cover over Syfret's returning force, and by 27 July Force H was safely back at Gibraltar.

Südsee (South Pacific) German plan to restore mercantile shipping links with Japan by means of the North-East Passage round the north of the USSR (1942) once that country had been defeated.

Sulphur British commando intelligence mission in Czechoslovakia.

Sumac Allied codename for Australia.

Sumpf (swamp) German plan to widen the salient west of Staraya Russa (November 1942) with an advance to the north by Generalfeldmarschall Ernst Busch's German 16th Army in Generalfeldmarschall Georg von Küchler's Army Group 'North'. The Soviet opposition was found by Lieutenant General P. A. Kurochkin's North-West Front in this sector, whose massive series of salients and re-entrants had been created by the northern flank portions of the Soviet army's great winter offensive of 1941/1942 and maintained since that time by Hitler's steadfast refusal to give up even the most dangerously exposed salients, which he regarded as launch points for offensives into the Soviet rear areas.

Sumpfblüte (swamp flower) German operation against Soviet partisans operating in the region of Dorogobuzh (6/18 July 1942). This was one of the main areas into which the Soviet high command had ordered that the 8th and 201st Airborne Brigades of the Soviet VIII Airborne Corps be dropped between 8 and 24 January 1942 in an effort to co-ordinate and bolster the partisan forces which were attempting to seal the gap between the southern side of the salient formed by Lieutenant General I. S. Konev's Kalinin Front and the northern side of the salient created by General Georgi Zhukov's

Sumpffieber

West Front to the west of Moscow during the great Soviet winter offensive of 1941/1942. Had the Soviets been able to close the gap between Vyazma and Smolensk, they would have trapped the German 4th and 9th Armies, and the 3rd and 4th Panzerarmee of Generalfeldmarschall Fedor von Bock's Army Group 'Centre'. As it was, the Germans were able to stabilize the position by the end of April, when the onset of the spring thaw combined with total exhaustion to halt the Soviet efforts. During the rest of the year the German command tried to re-order its front to the west of Moscow by eliminating surviving pockets of airborne troops and partisans (supported by parts of the Soviet 33rd Army, which had broken through the German 4th Army's front to link up with the partisans and then been cut off by German counterattacks between Vyazma and Spas Demensk) in its rear, Hitler having forbidden the abandonment of any salients created by the Soviet advances.

Sumpffieber (malaria) German operation against Soviet partisans operating in the region of Ossipovichi (9 February/9 March 1942).

Sundance Allied codename for Majuro atoll in the Marshall Islands.

Sunrise (i) British Bomber Command daylight attack on the German battle-cruisers *Scharnhorst* and *Gneisenau*, and on the heavy cruiser *Prinz Eugen*, lying in Brest and La Pallice (24 July 1941). The raid was undertaken by Handley Page Hampdens and Halifaxes, Boeing Fortresses and Vickers Wellingtons, and resulted in substantial British losses (17 aircraft) for negligible damage to the German ships.
(ii) Designation of the talks between the Allies and the SS about the possibility of a German surrender in Italy (April/May 1945). The talks were initiated by SS Obergruppenführer Karl Wolff (the German armed forces' plenipotentiary to the Fascist government of North Italy, and the officer responsible for the internal security of German-occupied northern Italy) by means of intermediaries in Switzerland with Field Marshal the Hon. Sir Harold Alexander and a few other high-ranking Allied commanders of the 15th Army Group. Wolff's object was to secure terms for Army Group 'C'. Wolff's plans were hampered by the removal of Generalfeldmarschall Albert Kesselring to the position of *Oberbefehlshaber West*, and the new German commander in Italy, Generaloberst Heinrich von Vietinghoff-Scheel, refused to have anything to do with Wolff's scheme until he had informed Hitler of the withdrawal of Army Group 'C' to the line of the River Po, and then permitted Wolff to travel to Alexander's headquarters at Caserta on 28 April, a surrender being negotiated with effect from 18.00 on 2 May.

Supercharge (i) Designation of the 'dogfight' stage of the 2nd Battle of El Alamein (2/5 November 1942). The plan evolved from the development of Operation 'Lightfoot' between 24 and 28 October, when General Sir Bernard Montgomery's British 8th Army had failed to secure the rapid breakthrough anticipated against Generalfeldmarschall Erwin Rommel's German-Italian Panzerarmee to release the British 1st and 10th Armoured Divisions of Lieutenant General H. Lumsden's British X Corps into the rear areas of the combined German and Italian forces under Rommel's command. In its original form on 29 November, Operation 'Supercharge' envisaged a final breakthrough in the north, but when he appreciated that Rommel had moved Generalleutnant Theodor Graf von Sponeck's German 90th Light Division forward into the coast road sector nearly reached by Lieutenant General Sir Leslie Morshead's 9th Australian Division, Montgomery rapidly switched his point of attack farther to the south, into the sector covered by General Wilhelm Ritter von Thoma's Deutsches Afrika Korps and the left wing of General Giuseppe de Stefanis's Italian XX Corps.

The British plan was thus for Lieutenant General Sir Oliver Leese's British XXX Corps to continue to exert infantry pressure on the Axis Front, forcing Rommel to commit his last reserves (General Francesco Arena's Ariete Division and General Francesco La Ferla's Trieste Division, the first an armoured formation and the second a motorized formation), while the equivalent of one brigade was

Supercharge

withdrawn from each of three divisions (Major General I. T. P. Hughes's British 44th Division and Major General J. S. Nichols's British 50th Division of Lieutenant General B. G. Horrocks's British XIII Corps, and Major General D. N. Wimberley's British 51st Division of the British XXX Corps) to reinforce Lieutenant General Sir Bernard Freyberg's 2nd New Zealand Division, which was to make the decisive effort around Kidney Ridge against the Italian infantry holding the forward positions in front of Generalleutnant Gustav von Vaerst's 15th Panzer Division and Generalmajor von Randow's 21st Panzer Division. Though depleted in numbers (of both men and tanks) and short of fuel, these formations were still formidable adversaries, and were flanked to the north by the German 90th Light Division and to the south by Generalmajor Kurt Freiherr von Liebenstein's 164th Light Division. Once Freyberg's division (with support on its left flank from the 51st Division) had made the initial breakthrough on a 4,000-yard front using the British 151st and 152nd Brigades (each aided by one regiment of Valentine tanks and with the three-regiment 9th Armoured Brigade in close support with its 40 Grant, 39 Sherman and 53 Crusader tanks), Major General R. Briggs's British 1st Armoured Division would debouch through the gap with its two armoured brigades (39 Grant, 113 Sherman and 119 Crusader tanks) and engage the 15th and 21st Panzer Divisions to the west of the Rahman Track. The 15th Panzer Division at this time had 51 tanks, and the 21st Panzer Division mustered 44 tanks, with 7 more available from Deutsches Afrika Korps headquarters and between 15 and 25 from the 90th Light Division.

Montgomery planned to unleash 'Supercharge' behind a concentrated but comparatively short barrage on the night of 31 October/1 November, but was persuaded by Freyberg to postpone the start until the night of 1/2 November to give the troops some rest and allow the completion of the 2nd New Zealand Division's reinforcement. The artillery bombardment began at 01.05 on 2 November with the two infantry brigades following it closely and reaching all their objectives by 06.15 to permit the 9th Armoured Brigade to begin the exploitation proper, followed somewhat slowly (to Freyberg's consternation) by the 1st Armoured Division. Having undertaken a diversion to the south, Major General A. F. Harding's British 7th Armoured Division was now pulled out of the British XIII Corps with its 54 Grant and 26 Crusader tanks (British 22nd Armoured Brigade) and allocated to the British X Corps for the exploitation.

Despite the attentions of Air Vice Marshal Sir Arthur Coningham's Western Desert Air Force, however, Rommel was able by nightfall on 2 November to organize a new defence position in front of the British armour. The German commander was then informed by von Thoma that the activities of British attack aircraft, the German tanks' shortage of fuel and the total absence of Axis reserves meant that the continued maintenance of this position was at best problematical, and Rommel made the only decision available to him, namely a withdrawal to positions reconnoitred at Fuka. Moreover, by this time Axis tank strength had fallen to 187 tanks, including 155 Italian vehicles wholly incapable of halting the Shermans used by the British.

First to move were the infantry-based Italian X and XXI Corps, leaving Rommel's mobile formations (Italian XX Corps, Deutsches Afrika Korps, 90th Light Division and 19th Flak Division) to conduct a fighting withdrawal in the face of the British advance. The Axis withdrawal started at 13.30 on 3 November, but was then halted at the express order of Hitler. The German leader later reversed his instructions, giving Rommel the freedom of action he so desperately needed, but by then it was too late for an orderly withdrawal, and on 4 November the 8th Army ripped a 15-mile gap in the German and Italian front near Tell el Aqqaqir, allowing the armour of X Corps to smash through the Ariete Division and capture von Thoma. Only fragments of the four German divisions escaped, as did most of the Trieste and Littorio Divisions, but the Italian infantry (the Bologna Division, and General Masina's Trento, General Brunetti's Brescia and General Scattaglia's Pavia Divisions) plus the airborne Folgore Division of General

Supercharge

Frattini, were lost, together with the headquarters of the Italian X Corps.

Operation 'Supercharge' had thus succeeded in its primary objective, and of the 108,000 Axis troops involved at El Alamein, some 25,000 were killed or wounded, and another 30,000 (including 10,725 Germans) were taken prisoner, and the British also captured 1,000 guns and 320 tanks. The 8th Army's losses were 13,560, including 4,610 killed or missing, and some 150 tanks were lost. The strategic impact of 'Supercharge' was enormous, for combined with Hitler's halt order it destroyed the German-Italian Panzerarmee as an effective offensive force. The 8th Army moved off to the west in pursuit of the German-Italian Panzerarmee, its X and XXX Corps reaching Mersah Matruh on 7 November, Tobruk on 12 November, Benghazi on 19 November and El Agheila on 17 December. Here X Corps took over lines of communication duties from Tobruk, leaving X Corps to continue the advance with its 7th Armoured, 51st and 2nd New Zealand Divisions. Tripoli was reached on 23 January 1943, and here the Free French Force 'L' commanded by Général de Division Henri Leclerc arrived from Chad to join the advance to the Mareth Line, which the 8th Army reached on 16 February.

(ii) Breakthrough of the Tebaga Gap by the New Zealand Corps to complete the Allied outflanking movement round the Mareth Line in Operation 'Pugilist' (26/27 March 1943). The original plan devised for the Mareth Line battle by General Sir Bernard Montgomery's British 8th Army had been for Lieutenant General Sir Oliver Leese's British XXX Corps to make a frontal breakthrough of the Mareth Line defences (General Berardi's Italian XXI Corps and General Orlando's Italian XX Corps), by which time Lieutenant General Sir Bernard Freyberg's New Zealand Corps (the 2nd New Zealand division, the British 8th Armoured Brigade and the Fighting French Force 'L') would have completed a 120-mile flank march to reach and break through the Tebaga Gap (held by General Mannerini's Raggrupamento Sahariano) to debouch into the coastal plain of southern Tunisia and so take Gabes, thus cutting the lines of communication to (and also line of retreat for) General Giovanni Messe's Axis 1st Army as it pulled back from the Mareth Line.

'Pugilist' failed as such on 22 March when the British XXX Corps could not drive through the Mareth Line and when the New Zealand Corps could not break through the Tebaga Gap in the face of determined counterattacks by Generalmajor Hans Georg Hildebrandt's 21st Panzer Division and Generalmajor Kurt Freiherr von Liebenstein's 164th Light Division. Little deterred by this setback, Montgomery swiftly developed 'Pugilist' into a new 'Supercharge', in whch the Axis forces on the Mareth Line would be pinned by the British XXX Corps while Lieutenant General B. G. Horrocks's British X Corps (including Major General R. Briggs's British 1st Armoured Division) moved as rapidly as possible through Wilder's Gap in the southern end of the Matmata Hills to reinforce the New Zealand Corps at the Tebaga Gap. This wide outflanking movement was covered by an inner flank move by Major General F. I. S. Tuker's 4th Indian Division, which advanced its 5th and 7th Indian Brigades from Medenine through the northern end of the Matmata Hills in an apparent effort to move past the end of the Mareth Line to take Matmata and Toujane.

While the British XXX Corps (Major General A. F. Harding's British 7th Armoured Division, Major General J. S. Nichols's British 50th Division and Major General D. N. Wimberley's British 51st Division) continued to pressure the Axis forces in the Mareth Line, on 23 March the 4th Indian Division and the British X Corps moved off to the south on their separate tasks, which Montgomery planned to unleash simultaneously with an attack on the Mareth Line by the 7th Armoured Division so that the Germans and Italians (already in dire straits of mobility thanks to the efforts of Air Vice Marshal H. Broadhurst's Western Desert Air Force) would be faced with three widely separated attacks and thus unable to reinforce any of the potential breakthrough sectors. However, it was at the Tebaga Gap that 'Supercharge' was expected to yield the greatest results, especially as some 22 squadrons of fighter-bombers were allocated to

272

provide close air support for the attack, scheduled for 16.00 on 26 March.

The plan was for the 5th New Zealand Brigade (2 infantry battalions and 2 armoured regiments) and 6th New Zealand Brigade (1 infantry battalion and 1 armoured regiment) to attack astride the road to El Hamma against some two German battalions (of the 164th Light Division) on a 2,000-yard front with the 8th Armoured Brigade in immediate support. After an advance of some 2,500 yards the New Zealanders would allow the 1st Armoured Division to pass through to its staging area on the road to El Hamma, some 5,000 yards from the operation's start line. When the moonlight was adequate, the 1st Armoured Division (with its 2nd Armoured Brigade in the lead) would strike towards El Hamma and Gabes. 'Supercharge' proceeded much as planned, but as a result of the sterling German defence at the Tebaga Gap after the 1st Armoured Division had got through, the New Zealand Corps was unable to get through to reinforce the 1st Armoured Division at El Hamma fast enough for a concerted effort against Gabes. Thus Messe was able to extricate most of his German and Italian forces (except some 16 infantry battalions, 31 guns and 60 tanks) to the Wadi Akarit positions farther to the north.

Super Gymnast Final development of Operation 'Gymnast', soon superseded by Operation 'Torch' as an alternative to Operation 'Sledgehammer' against a target in northern Europe. The concept had originated as the British Operation 'Acrobat', and was then developed as the British 'Gymnast', which proposed the landing of 55,000 British troops in French Algeria should the British 8th Army make sufficient progress in Cyrenaica to draw off major Axis reserves and make possible a westward drive to the Tunisian frontier. The British were opposed to the American-sponsored 'Sledgehammer', which they claimed would put ashore in a dangerous position Allied forces insufficient to defeat the 40 to 44 German divisions in northern France, and thus without strategic purpose. Nevertheless the Americans wished to get their ground forces into action against the Germans during 1942 if possible, and the desirability of such an operation against French North Africa (where large numbers of French troops were stationed and might be expected to join the Allied cause) was agreed at the 'Arcadia' Conference in Washington during December 1941.

The original 'Gymnast' scheme was reworked during January 1942 (after the resolution of Anglo-American difficulties in which the British proposed that 100,000 men should be landed, whereas the Americans wished to use 200,000 men in the initial lodgement, rising to 300,000 men as the Allied forces moved east) to produce the Anglo-American Operation 'Super Gymnast', which proposed that 3 British and 3 US divisions should be landed in French Morocco and French Algeria on 15 April 1942, while 3 US divisions were shipped across the North Atlantic to Northern Ireland, so freeing 3 British divisions for operational service. The target date proved wholly optimistic (especially as the Axis forces forced the British back from Cyrenaica to the Gazala Line, and as Allied amphibious capability was required during this period for other purposes, such as Operation 'Ironclad') and as a result 'Super Gymnast' was postponed, being revived in July 1942 as a means of easing German pressure on the USSR and getting US forces in contact with the Germans during 1942, and 'Super Gymnast' was finally developed into the definitive Operation 'Torch' for November 1942.

Super Round-up Final development of Operation 'Round-up'. This plan was adopted as Allied policy in July 1942, when it was agreed between the Americans and British that an Allied landing would be made as soon as possible after Operation 'Torch' (in the summer of 1943) in considerable strength (30 US and 18 British divisions) in the area of northern France between Calais and Dieppe. The proposed launch date for this operation was 1 April 1943, and under the command of General Dwight D. Eisenhower the Allies would try to use some 7,000 landing craft to land on a six-division front that could then be reinforced at the rate of some 100,000 men per week under an Allied air umbrella of 5,800 aircraft (3,250 American and 2,550 British). However, faced with very serious British reservations about the operation (especially after the fiasco of Operation 'Jubilee'), the 'Super Round-up' plan was postponed at the Casablanca Conference of January 1943 in favour of the British-sponsored Operation 'Husky' against Sicily.

S.W. Designation of military convoys (together with a numerical suffix) plying the route from Suez to Durban or the Cape of Good Hope, and inaugurated in June 1940 to end in August 1943 after the termination of the North African campaign.

Swallow Airborne drop of part of the Company Linge near Vermork in Norway to prepare for the arrival of a gliderborne force (18 October 1942).

Swamp Designation of any all-out search by Allied air and naval units for a spotted U-boat.

Switchback Reduction of the Breskens pocket behind the Leopold Canal by the 3rd Canadian Division (6 October/2 November 1944). This pocket was held by Generalmajor Kurt Eberding's 64th Division of General Gustav von Zangen's 15th Army within Generalfeldmarschall Walter Model's Army Group 'B', and lay on the southern side of the estuary of the River Scheldt, effectively denying the Allies ship access to the port of Antwerp (captured on 4 September 1944), especially as the Germans also held the islands of Walcheren, North Beveland and South Beveland on the northern side of the estuary. This sector was the responsibility of General Sir Henry Crerar's Canadian 1st Army, and more specifically of Lieutenant General G. G. Simonds's II Canadian Corps, which lacked the resources for the reduction of the Breskens pocket during September as its 3rd Canadian Division was engaged farther west along the coast in the reduction of Boulogne and Calais. Later during September the task devolved completely on Simonds, who assumed command of the Canadian 1st Army when Crerar was taken ill, Major General Foulkes taking over II Canadian Corps.

Major General Spry's 3rd Canadian Division became available at the beginning of October, and Simonds started the detailed planning of extensive operations to clear the whole of the Scheldt estuary and the area of Antwerp. Operation 'Switchback' began at 05.30 on 6 October when the 7th Canadian Brigade crossed the Leopold Canal at Eede and secured two small bridgeheads, which were consolidated against fierce resistance into a single bridgehead on 9 October, the day on which the German defence was outflanked by the landing of the 9th Canadian Brigade across the mouth of the Braakman at the eastern end of the pocket. The division's last brigade, the 8th Canadian Brigade, was now sent into this beach-head and the German defence began to falter as the Canadians pushed forward along two axes. The Germans abandoned Eede on 14 September, and four days later the British 157th Brigade of Major General Hakewill-Smith's British 52nd Division took over from the 7th Canadian Brigade. Breskens itself fell on 21 October, and the final resistance in the pocket ceased at Zeebrugge on 2 November, just six days before the last German defenders on Walcheren surrendered, and the Allies were able to start using Antwerp from 29 November.

Sword Designation of the beach landing area allocated to the British 3rd Division in Operation 'Overlord' (6 June 1944). This beach was the easternmost of the Allied assault areas, and stretched between the mouth of the River Orne in the east to its junction with 'Juno' Beach at a point between Luc and Langrune in the west. The area was held by part of the German 736th Regiment of Generalleutnant W. Richter's 716th Division within General Erich Marcks' LXXXIV Corps of Generaloberst Friedrich Dollmann's German 7th Army. The area behind 'Sword' Beach was the assault area of Major General R. Gale's British 6th Airborne Division, whereas the beach itself was the target for Major General T. G. Rennie's British 3rd Division of Lieutenant General J. T. Crocker's British I Corps within Lieutenant General Sir Miles Dempsey's British 2nd Army. The divisional landing was made by the British 8th Brigade, followed by the British 185th and 9th Brigades, and supported by the British 27th Armoured

Brigade. Flank protection was provided to the east by the 1st Special Service Brigade and No. 4 Commando, and to the west by No. 41 Royal Marine Commando of the 4th Special Service Brigade. By the end of 6 June the 'Sword' Beach area in British hands had a width and depth each of some 4 miles after the division had checked a counterattack during the afternoon by the 21st Panzer Division of XLVII Panzer Corps.

Swordhilt Allied plan to seize a beachhead south of Brest to aid the break-out from Normandy (summer 1944). The plan was developed in parallel with Operations 'Lucky Strike', 'Beneficiary' and 'Hands Up' by Lieutenant General Omar N. Bradley's US 1st Army Group, and envisaged the use of amphibious and airborne forces to secure viable port facilities on the Atlantic coast of the Breton peninsula.

Symbol Designation of the Allied heads-of-government conference at Casablanca (14/23 January 1943). The conference was deemed necessary after the successful launch of Operation 'Torch' in November 1942 to assess the needs and objectives of the Western Allies' strategy (without the intrusion of diplomatic matters) for 1943 and later, and more specifically whether or not Operation 'Round-up' should follow as had been arranged in July 1942. On the American side the chief persons at the 'Symbol' Conference were President Franklin D. Roosevelt, Harry Hopkins (the president's personal adviser), Admiral William D. Leahy (the president's chief-of-staff and chairman of the Joint Chiefs-of-Staff Committee, much incapacitated by illness during the 'Symbol' Conference), Admiral Ernest J. King (commander-in-chief of the US Fleet), General George C. Marshall (US Army chief-of-staff) and Lieutenant General H. H. Arnold (commander of the US Army Air Forces). On the British side the main protagonists were Prime Minister Winston Churchill, General Sir Alan Brooke (Chief of the Imperial General Staff and chairman of the British Chiefs-of-Staff Committee), Admiral Sir Dudley Pound (the First Sea Lord and Chief of the Naval Staff), Air Chief Marshal Sir Charles Portal (Chief of the Air Staff), Vice Admiral Lord Louis Mountbatten (head of Combined Operations) and Field Marshal Sir John Dill (Head of the British Joint Staff Mission in Washington). Later arrivals for the 'Symbol' Conference were General Dwight D. Eisenhower (Allied Commander-in-Chief, North African Theatre), General the Hon. Sir Harold Alexander (Commander-in-Chief, Middle East) and Air Chief Marshal Sir Arthur Tedder (Air Commander-in-Chief, Mediterranean), and also the two main contenders for leadership of the Free French, namely Général de Division Charles de Gaulle and Général d'Armée Henri Giraud.

As had been the case with comparable conferences in the preceding 14 months, the 'Symbol' Conference ended with a series of compromises that fully satisfied neither party, though in this conference it was generally the British who got their way. The outcomes of the conference in more tangible form were the 'Pointblank' directive for the prosecution of the Allied bomber offensive against Germany, the development of US operations in the Pacific (further advances along New Guinea's northern coast and the capture of the Caroline and Marshall island groups) to capitalise on the success of US Army and US Navy forces in New Guinea and the Solomons respectively, the postponement of any cross-Channel attack on France until 1944, the development of further Allied offensives in the Mediterranean with the launch of Operation 'Husky', the allocation of the highest priority to the building of anti-submarine capability (corvettes, sloops, frigates, escort destroyers and escort carriers) as the German U-boat threat in the Atlantic was reaching a peak unsupportable by the Allies, and the adoption of an 'unconditional surrender' policy for the prosecution of the war with Germany and Japan.

TA (i) Japanese offensive effort to retake the US beach-head around Cape Torokina on Bougainville Island in the Solomons group (8 March 1944). This extensive beach-head had been secured in the Empress Augusta Bay area by Major General Allen H. Turnage's US 3rd Marine Division of Lieutenant General Alexander A. Vandegrift's I Amphibious Corps in the highly successful and little opposed Operation 'Toenails' during November 1943 to complete the eastern portion of the 'Elkton' plan. As soon as the initial beach-head had been secured, Major General Robert S. Beightler's US 37th Infantry Division moved into it from 8 November, and the two US divisions then expanded the beach-head into a lodgement containing a fighter airstrip, a bomber base and a good forward anchorage, the strategic reasoning of Admiral William F. Halsey being that this US lodgement would contain the Japanese forces on the island (40,000 men of the 6th and 17th Divisions, commanded by Lieutenant General Harukichi Hyakutake's Japanese 17th Army, plus some 20,000 naval troops) as well as provide a base area from which Rabaul could be neutralized and the Japanese lines of communication from Rabaul to New Guinea and the Solomons interdicted by the use of US air and naval power. The first Japanese counterattacks failed, and by the beginning of 1944 the lodgement contained three airfields, a naval base and a vast supply dump defended by the Americal and 37th Infantry Divisions.

Lieutenant General Imamura, commanding the Japanese 8th Area Army in Rabaul, was convinced that the US forces intended to seize the whole of Bougainville and, after a flying visit to Hyakutake's headquarters on 21 January, ordered that the Empress Augusta Bay lodgement should be destroyed as soon as possible by the Japanese 6th Division (reinforced by two battalions of the 17th Division) with the air support of the 4th Air Army. In the event the Americans forestalled the Japanese, for US aircraft from the Empress Augusta enclave made life so difficult for the 4th Air Army over New Britain that after a massive battle on 19 February the remnants of the air army were called back to Truk, leaving New Britain and the Solomons without Japanese air cover. Hyakutake pressed on with his plans, however, and Operation 'TA' was launched by some 15,000 troops on 8 March under the cover of a heavy artillery bombardment.

The fighting followed the standard course of such Pacific war battles, with the Japanese notable for the ferocity and courage of their offensive against overwhelmingly superior US firepower. The first attack lasted for one week, and the Japanese made useful progress before being hurled back. Three more attacks were made in the next 10 days before the 8th Area Army ordered Hyakutake to call off the offensive on 25 March. The Japanese had lost some 6,000 men, and the fighting capability of the 17th Army had been broken despite the availability of another 32,000 men. The Americans were later pulled out off the island, being replaced by Australians, and though fighting flared up shortly at the end of the year, the isolated 17th Army was generally left to rot without adequate food, medicine, clothing and other supplies.

(ii) Japanese plan to reinforce the Philippines (late 1944). This reinforcement came mainly from the Kwantung Army in Manchukuo, the Japanese puppet state in Manchuria, and consisted of the 2nd Armoured Division, the 8th Division and the 23rd Division.

T.A. Designation of military convoys (together with a numerical suffix) plying the route from the UK to the USA, and inaugurated in March 1942 using large liners.

Table Tennis Seizure of Numfoor Island at the western end of New Guinea by US forces of General Douglas MacArthur's South-West Pacific Area command (2/7 July 1944). This was the penultimate 'hop' of MacArthur's magnificent amphibious campaign along the northern coast of New Guinea, and was planned while the US 41st Infantry Division was still hotly engaged on Biak Island just to the east of Numfoor in Geelvink Bay. Biak had been invaded because (among other reasons) the South-West Pacific Area command needed advanced airfields from which Lieutenant General George C. Kenney's US 5th Air Force could support further land operations, and Biak contained one of the only two airfield complexes left to the Japanese 2nd Area Army. However, the determination of the Japanese resistance meant that the 5th Air Force could not use Biak during June and July, and MacArthur decided on another landing in the same area to secure the three airfields on Numfoor, which Allied intelligence estimated to have a garrison of some 3,000 men.

The island's defences were softened by an intensive bombardment by the cruisers of Vice Admiral Thomas C. Kinkaid's US 7th Fleet, supported by 14 destroyers, and then the US 158th Regimental Combat Team was landed on 2 July, meeting little resistance from the shattered Japanese and thus capturing the north-western airfield without difficulty. A prisoner of war claimed to the Americans that there were in fact 5,000 Japanese on the island, and during the next two days the 158th Regimental Combat Team was thus reinforced by the 1,500 men of the US 503rd Parachute Infantry Regiment, which was dropped on the airfield in US hands. In fact the defence was totally disorganized, and by 6 July all three airfields were in American hands, the operation being completed on the following day for the total loss of 63 Americans and 2,328 Japanese. The loss of Numfoor made the Japanese 2nd Army's position in the eastern part of the Vogelkop wholly untenable, and this fact was recognized by the army, which pulled its 35th Division at Manokwari back to Sorong at the extreme west of New Guinea. In combination, the attack on Biak Island (followed by that of Numfoor Island) threatened to make a major dent in the strategic defence line ordained by Imperial General Headquarters as the 'KON' plan at the end of 1943 and running from the Marianas Islands south-west to the Palau Islands then south to Biak Island and west to the tip of New Guinea and finally south-west to Timor Island. Accordingly Admiral Soemu Toyoda, commander-in-chief of the Combined Fleet since the loss of Admiral Mineichi Koga in an air crash on 31 March, detached Vice Admiral Matome Ugaki's Mobile Force Vanguard (consisting of the super-battleships *Yamato* and *Musashi*, supported by older battleships, light aircraft-carriers, cruisers and destroyers) from Vice Admiral Jisaburo Ozawa's 1st Mobile Fleet for the support of reinforcement operations for the garrisons of the 2nd Army. But Ugaki's force had only just reached Halmahera when it was recalled on 11 June to join the rest of the 1st Mobile Fleet for the Battle of the Philippine Sea in Operation 'A'. This powerful naval force could have made a considerable difference to the progress of MacArthur's offensive in New Guinea, and its recall is striking evidence of Japan's inability to cope with simultaneous offensives by the powerful formations of the US Army and US Navy.

T.A.G. Designation of Caribbean convoys (together with a numerical suffix) plying the route from Trinidad to Guantanamo, Cuba, and inaugurated in August 1942 as a replacement for the T.A.M. series started in July 1942.

Taifun (typhoon) Designation of the German offensive against Moscow (2 November/5 December 1941) as the culmination of Operation 'Barbarossa'. The operation was ordered specifically by Adolf Hitler on 6 September 1941 in his Führerbefehl Nr

35, which established that the army group commanded by Marshal of the Soviet Union Semyon Timoshenko was to be destroyed east of Smolensk by pincer attacks directed on Vyazma (starting by the end of September) so that Generalfeldmarschall Fedor von Bock's Army Group 'Centre' could then drive on Moscow with its left flank on the upper reaches of the River Volga and its right flank on the River Okha. The detailed planning of the operation was entrusted to the Oberkommando des Heeres, which co-ordinated its efforts closely with those of Army Group 'Centre', both staffs appreciating that as much as they faced the Soviet armies they also faced a race against time since the weather was likely to break by the beginning of October, the autumn mud then presaging the arrival of frozen winter early in December.

At this time the delay imposed upon Germany's plans against the USSR by Operation 'Marita' became apparent as a strategic folly of the first order. The German problem was compounded by an erroneous intelligence assessment of the strength facing Army Group 'Centre' in front of Moscow, this being reckoned as the seven armies of Lieutenant General I. S. Konev's West Front and two armies of Lieutenant General A. I. Eremenko's Bryansk Front to Timoshenko's south. The Germans rightly reckoned the Soviet front-line strength at between 70 and 100 divisions, but failed to appreciate the presence of Marshal of the Soviet Union S. E. Budenny's Reserve Front behind the Vyazma Defence Line.

The operational scheme devised by Army Group 'Centre' and OKH was simple in concept (the well-established double pincer movement, in this instance designed to close at Vyazma on the Moscow Highway some 80 miles from the Germans' start line, trapping the bulk of the Soviet forces), though difficult to execute because of the strengthening Soviet resistance against German forces approaching the point of exhaustion and now sorely in need of reinforcement and refitting. The northern arm of the pincer consisted of Generaloberst Adolf Strauss's 9th Army with Generaloberst Hermann Hoth's 3rd Panzergruppe inside it, and the southern arm was similarly constituted of Generalfeldmarschall Günther von Kluge's 4th Army with Generaloberst Erich Hoepner's 4th Panzergruppe outside it. The northern arm (under Strauss's command) could deploy 18 infantry, 2 motorized and 3 Panzer divisions, while the southern arm (under von Kluge's command) could deploy 15 infantry, 2 motorized and 5 Panzer divisions. Once the pincer had closed on Vyazma, the 3rd Panzergruppe was to spearhead the northern advance against Moscow (along the axis from Belyy to Rzhev and Kalinin, and thus forming the left-flank guard for the main offensive against any attempt at intervention by the Soviet Kalinin and North-West Fronts) and the 4th Panzergruppe the southern advance (along the axis from Yukhnov to Moscow) to encircle the Soviet capital.

It had been hoped that Generaloberst Heinz Guderian's 2nd Panzergruppe (to be redesignated the 2nd Panzerarmee on 6 October, and consisting of 6 infantry, 4 motorized and 5 Panzer divisions in 2 infantry and 3 Panzer corps) would be able to move sufficiently far up from the south (together with Generaloberst Maximilian Freiherr von Weichs's 2nd Army of 8 infantry divisions) to take part in the main offensive, but as this proved impossible the 2nd Panzergruppe and 2nd Army were allocated the important secondary task of driving north-east from Novgorod Severski towards Orel and Tula with the object of piercing through the Bryansk Front and forming a right-flank guard for the main offensive against any Soviet attempts at intervention from the south. The whole operation involved a considerable reshuffling of formations, and though the operational capability of Army Group 'North' and Army Group 'South' was impaired by their loss of 7 (2 motorized and 5 Panzer) and 9 (5 infantry, 2 motorized and 2 Panzer) divisions respectively, Army Group 'Centre' was not bolstered as much as it might have been, for its formations had been reorganized on virtually a wholesale basis, with a consequent loss of operational cohesion. Guderian was to move off on 30 September, with the main offensive following on 2 October. Von Bock thus controlled 48 infantry, 8 motorized and 14 Panzer divisions, and air support for the whole undertaking was entrusted to 1,000 aircraft provided by

II and VIII Fliegerkorps of Generalfeldmarschall Albert Kesselring's Luftflotte II. Von Bock had only two divisions in reserve, and the OKH had no more to give him.

German intelligence now put the opposition at 80 infantry, 11 tank divisions or brigades, and 9 cavalry divisions, whereas in fact Timoshenko's West Theatre had Konev's West Front (6 armies) and Eremenko's Bryansk Front (4 armies) in the front line, with Budenny's Reserve Front (6 armies) echeloned behind them to provide defence in depth. The Soviets mustered some 800,000 men in 83 infantry divisions, 9 cavalry divisions and 13 tank brigades (770 tanks). Air support was provided by some 360 aircraft.

Operation 'Taifun' started as planned on 30 September, when the 2nd Panzergruppe surged forward through the Ermakov Group, on the left flank of the Bryansk Front, towards Sevsk and Orel. The latter fell on 3 October after the 2nd Panzergruppe had advanced some 130 miles, and at the same time General Joachim Lemelsen's XLVII Panzer Corps (one of Guderian's three Panzer corps) had peeled off to the north in an attempt to cut off the Bryansk Front.

The Soviet resistance in this sector now began to stiffen, and Major General D. D. Lelyushenko was sent forward from Moscow to organize the defence of Mtsensk with extemporized forces. Heavy fighting followed in this sector, to the north-east of Orel. Bryansk fell on 6 October to the 17th Panzer Division on the extreme left of Guderian's advance, and two large pockets of Soviet troops were formed with the co-operation of the 2nd Army, which linked the 2nd Panzerarmee with the 4th Panzergruppe. To the north of Bryansk was the 50th Army, and to the city's south the 3rd and 13th Armies.

Things were going well for the fast-moving Germans, but they were worried by the growing resistance of the Soviets, and by the fact that the first snow of winter fell on 6 October. Eremenko and his Bryansk Front headquarters were out of touch with Moscow, and on 8 October Eremenko ordered his encircled forces to break out to the east, a move possible because the Germans had so far thrown only a cordon round the pockets. The remnants surrendered on 17 (northern pocket) and 25 October (southern pocket), yielding 50,000 prisoners. Farther to the east Guderian was making only slow progress, for the only practical road north-east from Orel had broken up under the weight of traffic it was carrying (and the Soviets were proving adept at the whole spectrum of demolitions and booby traps), cross-country movement being impossible as the continued snow melted as it reached the ground, forming the impenetrable autumn *rasputitsa* (mud). Guderian was also suffering from a surfeit of Hitler-inspired orders, requiring him to undertake (all at the same time) the capture of Tula to the north-east, the capture of Kursk to the south, and the elimination of the two Soviet pockets to the west. Progress was made, however, and by 30 October Guderian had pushed forward to the outskirts of Tula and had taken Kursk.

Away to the north the two arms of von Bock's primary pincer movement had been under way since 2 October with the object of trapping as much as possible of the West Front before it could fall back to the defences of the Vyazma Defence Line, which stretched north/south just to the west of Vyazama as far north as a point to the east of Lake Seliger, and as far south as a point just north of Bryansk. As with Guderian's southern offensive, the northern pincer at first moved with great speed and considerable success in the last of the autumn's fine weather. The 9th Army and the 4th Panzergruppe (the northern arm) broke through the Soviets' main defences at the junction of the 30th and 19th Armies just north of Dukhovshchina, allowing Hoth to launch General Ferdinand Schaal's LVI Panzer Corps towards Kholm and Vyazma, and General Georg-Hans Reinhardt's XLVI Panzer Corps towards Rzhev on the upper Volga. By 10 October the northern arm of the pincer had pierced the Vyazma Defence Line between Vyazma and Sychevka, and pushed forward as far as Gzhatsk on the rail line from Smolensk to Moscow.

Similar success attended the efforts of the 4th Army and 4th Panzergruppe (the southern arm) which fell on the Soviet 24th and 43rd Armies and routed them before driving through the Vyazma Defence Line. On 4 October the southern arm took Spas

Taifun

Demensk and Kirov, and one day later seized Yukhnov and Mosalsk before being slowed in the approaches to the Mozhaisk Defence Line by 10 October. The Soviet position was critical, and on 5 October Stalin authorized the West and Reserve Fronts to pull back east of the Vyazma Defence Line in an effort to avoid total encirclement and destruction by Army Group 'Centre'. The 31st and 32nd Armies of the Reserve Front were ordered to check the Germans while this wholesale withdrawal was effected, but to complicate the issue, the Soviet high command now decided to reorganize its forces in the sector, and in the process of this reshuffle the high command in Moscow lost complete control of the situation. The result was inevitable, and by 7 October the 3rd and 4th Panzergruppen had created a great pocket to the west of Vyazma. In this pocket were trapped most of the 19th, 20th, 24th and 32nd Armies, together with the Boldin Group. The Soviets continued to fight, but were demoralized and poorly led.

On 13 October the great Vyazma pocket collapsed, yielding the Germans some 650,000 prisoners and vast quantities of *matériel* (including more than 1,000 tanks and 4,000 guns). The Soviets had lost more than 45 divisions, nearly half of the forces at their disposal at the beginning of 'Taifun'. The civil population of Moscow clearly thought that the end was at hand, and from 16 October the roads east from the Soviet capital were jammed with refugees, seriously hampering the arrival of reinforcements drawn in from the east. Stalin ordered that Moscow be ordered into a state of siege on 19 October, and the situation began to stabilize. More importantly, however, Stalin summoned from the Leningrad front General Georgi Zhukov to co-ordinate the Soviet resistance on the Mozhaisk Defence Line, now the main barrier between Army Group 'Centre' and Moscow. Zhukov ordered that all stragglers and lost detachments be rushed to the Mozhaisk Defence Line, where the defences were being prepared by Major General S. I. Bogdanov. From 14 October Major General K. K. Rokossovsky's 16th Army, Major General K. D. Golubev's 43rd Army, Lieutenant General I. G. Zakharkin's 49th Army and Major General D. D. Lelyushenko's 5th Army were allocated to hold the line with 14 infantry divisions, 16 tank brigades and 40 rifle regiments (a total of 90,000 men).

It was at this time that the Soviet high command began to commit forces from the Far East, and other reinforcements were being made available from Lieutenant General P. A. Kurochkin's North-West Front and Timoshenko's South-West Front. Zhukov assumed control of the whole sector on 10 October, the previous West and Reserve Fronts being amalgamated as Zhukov's West Front, with Konev as his deputy. Seven days later Konev was despatched to form a new Kalinin Front (22nd, 29th and 30th Armies and the Vatutin Group) in an effort to check the 3rd Panzergruppe, which had taken Kalinin on 14 October and thus threatened to envelop Moscow from the north if it could get round the Volga Reservoir and advance down the eastern bank of the Volga Canal to the Soviet capital. Konev's task was thus to hold the east/west sector of front running west from Kalinin to Ostashkov at the southern end of Lake Seliger. Zhukov was faced with an impossible task on the Mozhaisk Defence Line, and by 18 October the line had been pierced by General G. Stumme's XL Panzer Corps at Mozhaisk, by General Adolf Kuntzen's LVII Panzer Corps between Borovsk and Maloyaroslavets, and by General Hans Felber's XIII Corps at Kaluga. By 30 October the Germans had driven through the Mozhaisk Defence Line along its full length, and were only some 40 miles from Moscow, whose three defence lines were being strengthened continuously by civilian labour, three-quarters of which were women.

But at this time the weather broke completely, a fact not appreciated in the OKH orders of 14 October, which directed that the 2nd Panzerarmee was to take Tula and then envelop Moscow from the south, that the 2nd Army was to advance from Kursk to Voronezh, that the 4th Army was to pin the Soviet forces west of Moscow, that the 3rd and 4th Panzergruppen were to envelop Moscow from the north-west, and that the 9th Army was to move north-east towards Vishni Volochek to support Generalfeldmarschall Wilhelm Ritter von Leeb's

Army Group 'North'. The orders were issued by Generalfeldmarschall Walther von Brauchitsch, commander-in-chief of the German army, and brought protests from von Bock, whose army group frontage was thus extended to 600 miles from the original 400 miles of 2 October despite the losses of the first stage of 'Taifun'. Von Bock wanted to attack Moscow along the shortest route and with his forces concentrated, but von Brauchitsch was adamant despite warnings from Army Group 'Centre' about the worsening weather, the German formations' lack of fuel, supplies and winter clothing, and the impossibility of the ground, over which only tracked vehicles and captured Soviet carts could move.

Consolidation of current positions and preparations for the final German drive towards Moscow occupied the period from 30 October to 15 November, and the German situation can be regarded only as parlous. In a report tendered on 6 November, the Oberkommando der Wehrmacht reckoned that as a result of *matériel* and manpower deficiencies the 101 infantry divisions on the Eastern Front (excluding Finland) should be reckoned as no better than 65 divisions, that the 17 Panzer divisions had the combat capability of a mere 6 Panzer divisions, and that the real strength of all 136 German divisions on the Eastern Front was that of just 83 divisions, or just over 60 per cent of its establishment capability; with the weather worsening and the Soviets beginning to receive reinforcements from the east, this position could only worsen.

Despite this gloomy situation, the OKH at Hitler's insistence on 7 November issued orders for a resumption of the 'Taifun' offensive on the supposed grounds that the Soviet defence was incapable of holding its current positions with a continuous defence. Yet during the first 14 days of November the West Front was reinforced with 100,000 men, 300 tanks and 2,000 guns. Thus when 'Taifun' was resumed on 15 November Army Group 'Centre' could muster 58 divisions (38 infantry, 7 motorized and 13 Panzer) against the Soviet Kalinin, West and South-West Fronts, which between them deployed 91 formations (60 infantry divisions, 14 cavalry divisions and 17 tank brigades). Of the last, several were equipped with the new and extremely formidable T-34, against which German tanks and anti-tank guns were relatively impotent. The Soviets were also better acclimatized to and equipped for the weather, and despite their losses of *matériel* during the previous five months of mobile fighting were still well provided with artillery (especially of the heavier types which had not been deployed against the German 'Barbarossa' offensive).

The story of Germany's last effort against Moscow is simple, for while the Panzer formations managed to advance to within a few miles of the city, the Germans were unable to make the decisive breakthroughs either north or south of the capital and were eventually checked on 5 December. In the north the 3rd Panzergruppe managed to reach the Volga Canal against the West Front, and in the south the 2nd Panzerarmee drove past Stalinogorsk towards Ryazan but could get no farther than Mikhaylov and Gorlovo before being halted by the South-West Front. By 3 December von Bock was ordered to sanction some local withdrawals in the face of Soviet counterattacks, and 'Taifun' had failed. On 5 December the offensive was formally abandoned, and von Brauchitsch decided to retire. Even Hitler was forced to reconsider his desire that Moscow be taken, and on 8 December the German leader signalled his acceptance of the army's decision. The repercussions in Germany were severe, and at a meeting on 19 December von Brauchitsch was formally replaced as commander-in-chief of the army by Hitler, and von Bock was replaced as commander-in-chief of army Group 'Centre' by von Kluge. From this time onwards Hitler interfered more in the conduct of operations, and the failure of 'Taifun' thus had a decided (and malign) effect on the operational conduct of the war by the Germans.

Talisman Early version of Operation 'Eclipse' (ii).

Talon Final British and Indian offensive in the Arakan coastal region of Burma (4 January/9 February 1945) in succession to Operation 'Romulus'. In this area Lieutenant General Sir Philip Christison's XV Indian

Corps of Lieutenant General Sir William Slim's 14th Army was faced by Lieutenant General S. Miyazaki's Japanese 54th Division of Lieutenant General S. Sakurai's 28th Army, and the division's role was to hold the coastal plain as long as it could to prevent XV Indian Corps from crossing the Arakan Yomas into the plain of the River Irrawaddy and so cutting the lines of communication ot Lieutenant General S. Katamura's 15th Army (in the valley of the River Sittang) and Lieutenant General M. Honda's 33rd Army (in the valley of the River Salween), the main formations of Lieutenant General H. Kimura's Burma Area Army. The 28th Army had previously included the 2nd Division, but this had been posted to the 33rd Army and then on to Indo-China, leaving Sakurai with the 54th and 55th Divisions, the latter holding the Irrawaddy delta and southern Burma, previously the 2nd Division's sector.

'Romulus' had taken the 81st and 82nd West African Divisions of XV Indian Corps south down the valley of the River Kaladan, and the 25th Indian Division to Foul Point at the tip of the Mayu peninsula, so Sakurai thus had little option but to base his defence on the two main passes over the Arakan Yomas, that between An and Ngape in the north leading to the Irrawaddy at Minbu, and that at Taungup in the south leading to the Irrawaddy at Prome. Miyazaki thus concentrated his overextended force at Kangaw (the 154th Regimental Group covering An) and at Taungup (the 121st Regimental Group), though important roles were allocated to the comparatively small forces holding Akyab Island (the Matsu Detachment of the 111th Regimental Group) and the Myebon peninsula (at the mouth of the Kaladan) and Ramree and Cheduba Islands farther to the south. Miyazaki appreciated correctly that Christison needed these islands to secure his flank before any inland move, to serve as bases for British tactical support aircraft, and to form the base area for the 14th Army's vital southern ports. This last was indeed one of the two primary Allied requirements of Operations 'Romulus' and 'Talon', namely the elimination of the 28th Army so that some of XV Indian Corps could be reallocated, and so that the ports of Akyab and Kyaukpyu (the latter on Ramree Island) could be used to supply XV Indian Corps and also the 14th Army as it advanced south after Operation 'Extended Capital'. It was planned that 46,000 men should be supplied through Akyab, requiring the unloading of 850 tons per day during February and March 1945, dropping to 600 tons per day from May onwards, when the surplus divisions of XV Indian Corps were to be reallocated. Kyaukpyu would supply 36,000 men, requiring the unloading of 450 tons per day in February rising to 650 tons per day from March in order to develop a stockpile for the 14th Army.

Operation 'Talon' was the responsibility of XV Indian Corps, whose formations were Major General G. N. Wood's 25th Indian Division, Major General C. E. N. Lomax's 26th Indian Division, Major General F. J. Loftus-Tottenham's 81st West African Division, Major General G. McI. I. S. Bruce's 82nd West African Division, and Brigadier G. R. Hardy's 3rd Commando Brigade. Naval support was provided by Rear Admiral B. C. S. Martin's Force W, and air support was entrusted to Air Vice Marshal the Earl of Bandon's No. 224 Group, RAF. 'Talon' was due to begin on 3 January 1945, when the 25th Indian Division and the 3rd Commando Brigade were to land from 12.30. However, on 2 January an artillery observation officer saw no sign of a Japanese garrison (which had been withdrawn on 31 December 1944 as it was wholly outflanked by the advance of the 81st West African Division on the mainland) and the operation went ahead without opposition or bombardment.

Even before this, however, Christison had planned his next move, in this instance against the Myebon peninsula, where there was still a Japanese garrison. The joint force commanders now worked quickly to prepare a double operation against the Myebon peninsula and against Ramree Island, the former to allow an overland advance against An and the latter to complete the Allied hold on the Arakan coast's two best ports. The Myebon peninsula landing was to take place on 12 January, with the 3rd Commando Brigade securing a beach-head through which the 74th Indian Brigade of the 25th Indian Division was to pass on its way to attack

Kangaw. The operation went as planned, and by 17 January the whole of the Myebon peninsula was in British hands, and the 74th Indian Brigade had begun its exploitation towards Kangaw on the far side of the estuary of the River Myebon.

Farther to the north the 82nd West African Division, now commanded by Major General H. C. Stockwell, had relieved the 81st West African Division in the Kaladan valley and pushed south to take Mychaung on 25 January as it tried to cut the 54th Division's lines of communication at Kangaw. The landings on Ramree Island were launched on 21 January, when the 71st Indian Brigade of the 26th Indian Division came ashore just to the west of Kyaukpyu and secured a beach-head. On the following day the 4th Indian Brigade of the same division passed through and developed the attack to the south in the direction of Mayin on the island's west coast. The defence (by one battalion of the 121st Regimental Group) now stiffened, and Lomax had to commit his whole division to a methodical elimination of the Japanese defenders. Ramree itself fell on 9 February, and recognizing that further resistance was counterproductive, Miyazaki ordered the survivors to be evacuated on this same day. An air attack by the 5th Air Division allowed one Japanese destroyer and a squadron of motor launches to pick up 500 Japanese troops, and fighting finally ended on 17 February. Cheduba Island had been evacuated by the Japanese, and the landing by Royal Marine Commandos on 26 January met no resistance. After the clearance of Ramree Island the 26th Indian Division was relieved (by the 22nd East African Brigade from corps reserve) so that it could ready itself for the assault on Taungup.

Meanwhile the 25th Indian Division was involved in one of the bloodiest battles of the entire Burma campaign as it moved against Miyazaki's main position at Kangaw, held by the 154th Regimental Group. Wood planned his attack with the 3rd Commando Brigade in the lead to secure a beach-head over the Daingbon Chaung, allowing the 51st Indian Brigade to pass through and link up with the 74th Indian Brigade advancing from its crossing of the Min Chaung to the north. The two Indian brigades would then move against Kangaw from the south, the 154th Regimental Group thus being trapped between the Indians and Commandos and the 82nd West African Division moving south. The landings were launched on 21 January, and Miyazaki immediately ordered the Matsu Detachment (Major General T. Koba) to fall back in front of the West Africans and keep open the road to the An pass. Vicious fighting continued until 18 February, although Miyazaki had ordered a general withdrawal towards the An pass early in February when he realized that the success of the 26th Indian Division on Ramree Island raised the possibility of a landing in his rear. Yet by determined fighting and excellent tactical thinking Miyazaki had kept most of his division intact, delayed the Allied advance and maintained Japan's hold on the An pass (111th and 154th Regimental Groups, both somewhat depleted) and on the Taungup pass (virtually full-strength 121st Regimental Group).

Christison was still prepared to continue, but a halt was now forced on XV Indian Corps by developments elsewhere. The Chinese desperately needed additional airlift capacity, and Lieutenant General Sir Oliver Leese (Commander-in-Chief, Allied Land Forces South-East Asia) decided that XV Indian Corps' air supply should be terminated and the 25th and 26th Indian Divisions withdrawn, the former to India and the latter to prepare for Operation 'Dracula'. Christison was nevertheless instructed to press ahead with the forces left to him, and sporadic fighting continued up to 1 May. An was taken on 23 April and Taungup fell on 29 April. Further operations would have permitted XV Indian Corps to open the way across the Arakan Yomas, but the implementation of Operation 'Modified Dracula' on 2 May gave Rangoon to the British, and with it the best supply facilities in the region.

TAN Japanese *kamikaze* raid on the US naval base and anchorage in Ulithi atoll (11 March 1945). The raid was undertaken by 24 converted twin-engined naval bombers from Kyushu. Only 15 aircraft reached Ulithi at dusk, and one of them dived into a small island, believing it to be an aircraft-carrier. The only significant damage was caused to the carrier *Randolph* by another aircraft.

Tanne (fir) German attempt to seize of Suusaari Island (15 September 1944). The operation as originally planned had envisaged that both Suusaari (in the Gulf of Finland) and the Aaland Islands (in the Gulf of Bothnia) should be taken simultaneously (to prevent the Finns handing them over to the Soviets) and thus to bottle Soviet naval units in the Gulf of Finland, but in the event shipping was available for only one component, and Hitler chose the area nearer the main Soviet naval base at Kronshtadt. Finland was currently negotiating with the USSR for an armistice, and the Soviets had agreed to negotiate if all foreign troops had left Finland by 15 September. Hitler was incensed at this defection, and ordered the operation on 13 September believing that the Finns would not oppose the German landing. This was not the case, however, and the Germans were driven off with very heavy casualties by the Finns with support from Soviet aircraft. The effect was to strengthen Finnish determination for peace with the USSR, a preliminary peace treaty being signed on 19 September.

Tannenbaum (Christmas tree) German plan for the seizure of Switzerland (1940).

Tannenburg Designation of Hitler's headquarters in the Black Forest (25 June/6 July 1940) for the final stages of Operation 'Rot'.

Tarzan British plan for operations in northern Burma (dry season 1943/1944). Prepared by the staff of General Sir Claude Auchinleck, the Commander-in-Chief India, Operation 'Tarzan' was submitted to the Combined Chiefs-of-Staff Committee on 27 September 1943, and proposed a triple thrust each supported and preceded by long-range penetration groups. In overall terms the 'Tarzan' plan called for the Chinese 'Y' Force in Yunnan to take the area of Lashio and Bhamo, for Lieutenant General Joseph W. Stilwell's Northern Combat Area Command to move from Ledo against Myitkyina before advancing on Bhamo and Katha, and for British airborne forces to take Indaw and then hold it through the monsoon season with the aid of air support. Subsidiary to these main operations, but nevertheless important as a means of pinning the Japanese defence, would be advances by IV Indian Corps from Fort White and Tamu to the River Chindwin, and by XV Indian Corps in the Arakan to the line Kyauktaw-Indin. Only the British part of the operation was planned in any detail, and this envisaged that three long-range penetration groups would move into Burma on about 15 February 1944, one moving towards Gangaw and Pakkoku, one towards Katha and one towards Bhamo and the Gokteik Gorge. Diverted by these and other operations (such as those of IV and XV Indian Corps beginning in January), the Japanese would then be unable to contest a landing by two airborne battalions at Indaw on about 15 March. With the airfield thus secured, two brigades of a division previously withdrawn from the Arakan front would be flown into Indaw during the following week, the third brigade moving overland from Imphal.

The staff assessment was that some 20 transport squadrons (500 aircraft) would be needed for the operation, which though schemed with Chinese and US participation in mind, was not wholly dependent on the co-operation of 'Y' Force and the Northern Combat Area Command. Auchinleck fully appreciated that lack of such support would severely curtail the offensive impact of the Indaw operation, even though it was unlikely that the Japanese could defeat the division in the area given the nature and strength of Allied air power over Burma. The initial reaction to the plan was one of guarded approval with the proviso that it needed to be recast with significantly reduced airlift requirements, and Auchinleck by October had revised his scheme to the level of 11 or 12 squadrons (275 to 300 aircraft). The Chinese were unhappy with the plan, though, especially as it placed great responsibility on the Chinese without a concomitant burden on the British. For this reason Generalissimo Chiang Kai-shek asked for the plan to be revised as a scheme for the complete reconquest of Burma.

This was clearly impossible for a variety of logistic reasons, and 'Tarzan' was cancelled in January 1944 at the suggestion of Admiral Lord Louis Mountbatten, Commander-in-Chief South-East Asia Command, in the hope that Operations 'Gripfast' and 'Pigstick' could be substituted so that the Allies could undertake at least some offensive action in Burma during the early part of 1944.

Taubenschlag (dovecote) German plan for Generalfeldmarschall Erich von Manstein's 11th Army to launch an offensive towards Toropets (October/November 1942). The object of the operation was the reduction of the pressure on Generalfeldmarschall Georg von Küchler's Army Group 'North' by the Soviet Volkhov and North-West Fronts by a threat to the Soviets' rear on their left flank, on the junction with the Kalinin Front, but though the bulk of the 11th Army had been diverted north after the fall of Sevastopol, army headquarters had only reached Vitebsk when it was ordered south once more, being transformed into Army Group 'Don' at Novocherkassk on 27 November to help deal with the steadily worsening position to the west of the German 6th Army beleaguered in Stalingrad.

Tauern Linie (Tauern line) Designation of a German defence line in Norway.

T.A.W. Designation of Caribbean convoys (together with a numerical suffix) plying the route from Trinidad to Guantanamo, Cuba, and inaugurated in July 1942 only to be replaced from August 1942 by the T.A.G. series.

Taxable British radar decoy operation to make the Germans think that an invasion of the Pas-de-Calais was imminent (6 June 1944). This was part of the deception scheme to protect Operation 'Overlord', and involved RAF aircraft dropping large quantities of 'Window' over a small southbound 'invasion' convoy in the English Channel so that German radar operators would assess its size as much greater than reality.

T.B. Designation of military convoys (together with a numerical suffix) plying the route from the USA across the Pacific to Sydney, Australia, and inaugurated in January 1942 as part of the build-up of supplies and forces in this vital back for what was to become General Douglas MacArthur's South-West Pacific Area.

T.E. Designation of Mediterranean coastal convoys (together with a numerical suffix) plying the route from Gibraltar to North African ports, and inaugurated in November 1942 after the successful launch of Operation 'Torch' in order to keep the American, British and (later) French troops adequately supplied as they moved east towards Tunisia.

Teacup Allied codename for Manus Island in the Admiralty group of the Bismarck archipelago.

Teardrop US Navy sweep against German U-boats (April/May 1945). During these two months US Navy forces sank 10 U-boats in the Atlantic.

Telegraph Allied codename for Lieutenant General Walter Bedell Smith, chief-of-staff to General Dwight D. Eisenhower.

TEN Japanese plan for the air defence of the Japanese home islands (January 1945). In its initial form 'TEN' was devised by the Imperial General Headquarters in Tokyo as a means of co-ordinating more closely the air defence assets of the Imperial Japanese Army and Imperial Japanese Navy under the army's 1st Air Army. This controlled the 10th, 11th and 12th Air Divisions (400 fighters and 45 reconnaissance aircraft) allocated respectively to the 12th, 15th and 16th Area Armies, and also supervised various naval fighter units totalling 160 aircraft. It was appreciated, however, that these forces could hope to deal only with the US strategic bomber offensive from the Marianas, and that further air assets would have to be deployed for attacks on the invasion of Japan that would inevitably come. By March 1945, therefore, Imperial General Headquarters had developed 'TEN' into an offensive/defensive scheme for air attacks designed to destroy US invasion forces before they could land on Japanese soil. The formations tasked with this responsibility were the 3rd, 5th and 10th Air Fleets and the 6th Air Army in Japan, the 1st Air Fleet and 8th Air Division in Formosa, and units of the 5th Air Army in China. Naval air units were entrusted with attacks on US naval forces while army air units dealt with the amphibious forces. The Japanese also appreciated that *kamikaze* attacks offered them the best chances for success, and all air formations involved in the 'TEN' programme were instructed to inculcate such a spirit amongst their pilots. In keeping with this tactical decision the 10th Air Fleet was fully equipped with *kamikaze* aircraft (700 aircraft by the end of March rising to 2,000 aircraft by the end of April), and the 6th Air Army numbered about 350 such aircraft in its total of 700 machines.

It was also decided by Imperial General Headquarters that as the situation in the Southern Region was essentially hopeless, the theatre's air assets should be returned to Japan for more profitable employment. Thus Imperial General Headquarters ordered the Southern Army to return 6 air regiments from the 2nd Air Division in the Philippines, the 30th Fighter Group from the Philippines, the transport element of the 1st Airborne Group in the Philippines, 2 air regiments and 1 heavy bomber squadron from the 7th Air Division in Sulawesi, and 1 heavy bomber squadron from the 9th Air Division in Sumatra. The much-reduced 2nd and 7th Air Divisions were allocated to the 3rd Air Army, and the personnel of the 4th Air Division and 1st Airborne Group were transferred as infantry to the 14th Area Army as their original formations were now bereft of aircraft. By the end of March 1945, therefore, Operation 'TEN' could call on some 2,100 army and 3,100 navy aircraft for the defence of Japan against US attack. What 'TEN' could not provide, however, was adequate fuel for sustained operations or for the continued training of the mass of aircrews, whose standards can best be described as poor.

Tentacle   British plan for floating concrete airfields.

Terminal   **(i)** Royal Navy operation to prevent the Vichy French from scuttling their warships and destroying waterfront installations in Algiers harbour at the time that Operation 'Torch' was launched (8 November 1942). The operation was undertaken by the destroyers *Broke* and *Malcolm*, and was severely handicapped by the fact that the ships could not find the harbour entrance in the dark and also came under heavy fire from the shore batteries. The *Malcolm* had to pull out with heavy damage, and it was only on her fourth attempt that the *Broke* found the harbour entrance and managed to break through the boom to land her American troops. The *Broke* was then forced by severe damage from Vichy French guns to pull out of Algiers, and the destroyer sank on 9 November.

(ii) Designation of the inter-Allied conference held at Potsdam (15/28 July 1945). This was the last of the 'big three' conferences in World War II, and was designed to settle Allied differences about the post-war disposition of Europe and to decide on how best to end the war with Japan. Winston Churchill wished the conference to be held as soon as possible after the end of hostilities with Germany, and though president Harry S Truman (who had succeeded to the presidency only one month earlier on the death of President Roosevelt) agreed that it was necessary to thrash out matters with Premier Joseph Stalin, he was adamant that he had to remain in the USA until the Congress had passed his budget proposals in July. Truman suggested a venue in Alaska or Vienna, but then agreed to Stalin's suggestion that the 'Terminal' Conference should be held in the Berlin suburb of Potsdam.

Initial meetings began on 15 July, but plenary sessions had to wait until 17 July, when Stalin arrived. The Soviet leader immediately proposed that Truman should be chairman, and the conference soon got under way with the decision that a Council of Foreign Ministers should be established to draft peace treaties and the like. This initial decision was not matched by further agreement, for while Churchill and Truman wished the USSR to abide by the terms agreed at the Yalta Conference for the disposition of eastern Europe, Stalin was clearly set on bringing these countries into the Soviet orbit as satellites rather than on enticing them into association with the USSR as free states after the election of truly democratic governments. Stalin also wished to claim war reparations from Italy, which the UK and USA wished to treat leniently as she had joined the Allied cause in 1943, and the situation was reversed in the cases of Romania, Bulgaria and Hungary, which had all joined the Soviets late in the war. No decisions were reached at the 'Terminal' Conference on these matters, which were referred to the Council of Foreign Ministers. The whole question of war booty was also referred to the Council of Foreign Ministers.

The 'Terminal' Conference was interrupted on 25 July when Churchill and his deputy, Clement Attlee, returned to the UK for the outcome of the British general election. The result was declared on 26 July, the coalition government of Churchill being replaced by a Labour administration under Attlee, and on 28 Attlee returned to Potsdam as head of the new British government for the final four meetings, which decided on the disposition and denazification of Germany, the establishment of new frontiers for Poland, and the prosecution of the war against Japan.

So far as Germany was concerned, the 'Terminal' Conference decided that 'all German land, sea and air forces, the SS, SA, SD and Gestapo, with all their organisations, staffs and institutions, including the General Staff, Officers' Corps, Reserve Corps military schools, war veterans' organizations, and all other military and quasi-military organizations, together with all clubs and associations which serve to keep alive the military tradition in Germany, are to be completely and finally abolished.' War criminals were to be arrested for trial, and all high-ranking Nazi officials and service personnel were to be interned. Nazi party members were to be banned from public office, and from positions of responsibility in public or private undertakings. War reparations were to be extracted by the victors from each nation's zone of occupation.

So far as Poland was concerned, the Allies started from the premise that while the USSR would receive that part of Poland to the east of the Curzon Line, Poland would be compensated by territory taken from defeated Germany. In the event the USSR annexed those parts of Poland it wanted, and at the same time allocated its puppet regime in Poland the portions of Germany as far west as the Rivers Oder and Neisse. This gave Poland some of Germany's richest agricultural and industrial territories, and uprooted many millions of ethnic Germans who flocked to the west.

At the end of the 'Terminal' Conference Attlee and Truman were joined by Generalissimo Chiang Kai-shek in issuing the Potsdam Declaration (the USSR not then being at war with Japan), which stated, 'We call upon the government of Japan to proclaim now the unconditional surrender of all the Japanese armed forces.... The alternative for Japan is prompt and utter destruction.' Japan refused even to answer, and the result was the dropping of two bombs (on Hiroshima on 6 August and on Nagasaki on 9 August) to bring World War II to an end.

T.F. Designation of central Atlantic convoys (together with a numerical suffix) plying the route from Trinidad to Freetown, Sierra Leone, and inaugurated in November 1942.

Theseus German plan for the seizure of French North Africa and French West Africa, but including the Portuguese Cape Verde Islands (summer 1942). This scheme was the logical successor to Operation 'Felix-Heinrich', and was designed to deny the British any western access to the Mediterranean as well as providing the German navy and air force with bases ideally situated for the prosecution of the war against British maritime communications across the South Atlantic and round the Cape of Good Hope. The rationale of this plan was first expressed in Hitler's Führerbefehl Nr 32, issued on 11 June 1941 and looking to the period after the successful implementation of Operation 'Barbarossa'.

Thesis British air offensive against German targets in Crete (July 1943). This was part of the Allied effort to pin German and Italian forces in the eastern Mediterranean, and served also to help persuade the Axis command in the period just before the launch of Operation 'Husky' against Sicily that Allied forces might be preparing an invasion in the eastern Mediterranean, on Crete or some of the Aegean islands, or even in Greece. The effect of these and other diversionary measures was that extra German forces were moved into Greece, Crete, Rhodes and other Greek islands.

Thruster British plan for the seizure of the Azores Islands in the event that Germany moved against Spain and Portugal (June 1941). Operation 'Thruster' was schemed in concert with Operation 'Springboard' against Madeira and Operation 'Puma' against the Canary Islands, and for much of 1941 forces were kept on the alert for any or all of these operations in the UK, Gibraltar or Sierra Leone. In July 1941 the three separate operations were combined into the single Operation 'Pilgrim', to use some 24,000 men and all available amphibious capability.

Thunderclap Allied plan to end the war against Germany by the total destruction of Berlin, Leipzig, Dresden and Chemnitz from the air (1945). Some preliminary raids were undertaken (including the total destruction of Dresden), but the speed of the final Soviet advance made unnecessary the full implementation of the scheme, which was not liked by air planners as it was designed not just to end the war but to convince the Germans that any organized resistance after the formal end of hostilities would be futile, and merely bring about massive retribution. It was also intended as a warning to the Soviets of Allied strategic air power.

Thursday Designation of the 2nd Chindit Expedition (5 March/12 August 1944). This operation was undertaken in conjunction with an advance towards Myitkyina by Lieutenant General Joseph W. Stilwell's Northern Combat Area Command, and may thus be regarded as the successor to the abandoned Operation 'Tarzan' as one of the objectives for the Chindits, otherwise Major General Orde Wingate's 3rd Indian Division. The area in which the Chindits were designed to operate lay in the great eastward bend of the River Irrawaddy between Myitkyina in the north and Katha in the south, and was part of the sector allocated to Lieutenant General Renya Mutaguchi's Japanese 15th Army. However, at the very time Operation 'Thursday' was launched Mutaguchi was about to start his own Operation 'U' against Imphal and Kohima, so his three main formations (the 15th, 31st and 33rd Divisions) were fully employed on the Chindwin sector against Lieutenant General G. A. P. Scoones's IV Indian Corps of Lieutenant General Sir William Slim's 14th Army.

There were thus only a few scattered units in the area into which the 3rd Indian Division was inserted, the object of Wingate's operation (as defined in the 'Quadrant' and 'Sextant' Conferences) being to harass the Japanese rear areas and to establish blocks on the roads and rail lines up which Lieutenant General M. Kawabe's Burma Area Army could funnel reinforcements to Lieutenant General M. Honda's 33rd Army facing Stilwell's forces, so facilitating the Northern Combat Area Command's task of taking Mogaung and Myitkyina plus a buffer belt some 50 miles deep to the south of these two towns. Kawabe's only in-theatre reserve was the 24th Independent Mixed Brigade, but this was deployed in battalion packets as protection against Allied airborne assaults on the vital rail line from Tenasserim to Mandalay, so the arrival from Formosa of Lieutenant General K. Takeda's 53rd Division was a great boon. Mutaguchi was relying on this division as his army reserve for 'U', but Kawabe allocated it instead to the operations necessary to defeat 'Thursday'.

Since Operation 'Loincloth' Wingate had made great improvements in his long-range penetration concept, and the 3rd Indian Division was far better trained and prepared for operations behind the Japanese lines than the 77th Indian Brigade had been. The core of the 3rd Indian Division was provided by three British brigades from the British 70th Division, which had been disbanded for this purpose in October 1943. The division also had three Indian brigades, Wingate's concept being that only three brigades should be engaged operationally at any one time, leaving the other three available as reinforcements or replacements as the situation demanded. Each brigade comprised four battalions and support elements, and each battalion was designed to move as two columns, each numbering some 400 men. 'Thursday' was supported by Colonel P. Cochran's 1st Air Commando, and the plan was that Brigadier B. E. Fergusson's British 16th Brigade should march to its operational area from Ledo, while Brigadier J. M. Calvert's 77th Indian Brigade and Brigadier W. D. A. Lentaigne's 111th Indian Brigade would be airlifted (the advance parties by glider to prepare airstrips on which the balance of the brigades could be landed by transport aircraft).

The 16th Brigade began its 350-mile overland advance on 5 February 1944, and Wingate hoped that the three brigades could co-operate in the capture of the communications nexus at Indaw, together with its airfield, so that a division could be flown in to hold the area as a base for the Chindit columns roving the Japanese rear areas and wreaking havoc. Wingate was told by Admiral Lord Louis Mountbatten's South-East Asia Command that he could have only the 3rd West African Brigade (of his own 3rd Indian Division) for the defence of Indaw, but felt that his brigades would still be able to operate effectively for periods of up to three months, after which they would be replaced by the other three brigades of the 3rd Indian Division.

'Thursday' proper began on 5/6 March with the air delivery of the 77th and 111th Indian Brigades, at just the time that the Japanese 15th Army was moving forward against IV Indian Corps. The task allocated to the 77th Indian Brigade (of five rather than the standard four battalions) was to land at 'Broadway' and 'Piccadilly', and then to move south-west to cut the road and rail line north from Indaw at Mawlu, so severing the lines of communications of Lieutenant General S. Tanaka's 18th Division opposing the Northern Combat Area Command. Calvert hoped to achieve this end by using three battalions for blocks, one to protect his airstrip and one to sever the road between Bhamo and Myitkyina on the eastern side of the Irrawaddy. At the last minute it was believed that the strip at 'Piccadilly' was compromised, and Calvert decided to accept the delay of landing his complete brigade at 'Broadway'. The fly-in was beset by several problems, but in the four-day operation some 12,000 men and 3,000 mules of the 77th and 111th Indian Brigades were landed, together with supplies and two troops of artillery (one of field guns and the other of light AA guns).

On 6/7 March the 111th Indian Brigade began to arrive at 'Chowringee' south-east of Indaw, but Lentaigne soon discovered that this strip was potentially vulnerable to air and ground attack, and the rest of the 111th Indian Brigade was landed at 'Broadway' (see above) before setting off south across the Irrawaddy. Only part of the 111th Brigade managed to cross before Japanese interference decided Wingate that Lentaigne should operate with a depleted brigade while Calvert took over those units still north of the Irrawaddy. By this time Calvert had placed an extremely strong block, complete with extensive defences, across the rail line just north of Mawlu at 'White City'.

Lentaigne was now operating south of Indaw with a view to preventing the arrival of Japanese reinforcements before the British 16th Brigade arrived for the assault on Indaw. However, Lentaigne was too late to prevent Major General Hyashi's 24th Independent Mixed Brigade delivering three battalions to Indaw by 21 March, supplementing the 4th Regiment, and the attack by Fergusson's brigade on 26 March was repulsed. Fergusson fell back towards his airstrip at 'Aberdeen', and though Lentaigne finally managed to cut rail communications to Indaw from the south, Hyashi had managed to reinforce Indaw to a total of nine battalions with the aid of units from the 18th and 56th Divisions.

The situation for the Japanese was nonetheless serious, and Kawabe seriously considered instructing Mutaguchi to call off 'U' because of the danger to the 15th Army's communications, though the local Japanese commander persuaded his superior that this was unnecessary. The Japanese effort was not directed at 'Broadway' and 'White City', the Chindits' main airstrips and bases behind Japanese lines, but Wingate had realized that such an event was all too likely, and had dictated that the defence of such bases was best ensured by the use of powerful static forces supported by 'floater' units. The latter patrolled round the base, warned of Japanese attacks and then counterattacked the flanks or rear of the Japanese as they assaulted the base. Ground attacks on 'Broadway' and

Thursday

'White City' were beaten off, as were air attacks by the Japanese 5th Air Division, but the Japanese were now using 11 battalions against the Chindits, including one diverted from Mutaguchi's 33rd Division.

Even so, the threat at Imphal and Kohima was developing against the British, and Slim was faced with the need for air-transportable and jungle-trained reinforcements for Imphal. The theatre's only such units were the three uncommitted brigades of the 3rd Indian Division, and Slim finally decided that while his 14th Army would take the British 23rd Brigade (as the left-flank guard for XXXIII Indian Corps as it advanced from the Brahmaputra valley towards Imphal and Kohima), Wingate would be able to keep the British 14th Brigade and the 3rd West African Brigade for operations in central Burma, which Wingate believed were progressing satisfactorily, especially as Brigadier T. Brodie's British 14th Brigade and Brigadier A. H. Gillmore's 3rd West African Brigade started their fly-in to 'Aberdeen' on 23/24 March, and as the 77th Indian Brigade had under Calvert's energetic leadership taken Mawlu and a mass of useful intelligence information.

Then disaster overtook the Chindits, for on 24 March Wingate was killed in an unexplained air crash, and with him died much of the 3rd Indian Division's forward planning and forceful leadership (especially in promoting the Chindit concept to sceptical higher commanders). Lentaigne was promoted to fill Wingate's shoes, and command of the 111th Indian Brigade went to Brigadier J. R. Morris though, in the absence of Morris on detached operations with Morrisforce, actual command devolved on Major J. H. Masters. At the beginning of April, therefore, Lentaigne had five somewhat depleted and scattered brigades under command, while Hyashi had the equivalent of one full division with heavier weapons than the Chindits, but without the level of air support available to them.

Hyashi now decided to eliminate 'White City' in an attack launched on 5 April. Exceptionally heavy fighting followed until 17 April, and though Hyashi's 24th Independent Mixed Brigade suffered very heavy casualties it failed to wrest 'White City' from the 77th Indian Brigade reinforced by the 3rd West African Brigade, despite the fact that the Japanese had deployed the equivalent of a division against 4 British, 1 Gurkha and 2 Nigerian battalions. The exhausted Japanese were forced to pull back to Indaw on 18 April. While Hyashi's main effort had been devoted to 'White City' the other brigades of the 3rd Indian Division had been running fairly rampant throughout the Chindits' operational area, the 111th Indian Brigade destroying Japanese supply dumps near Banmauk, the British 14th Brigade blowing the main railway bridge in the Bonchaung Gorge as well as destroying 21 dumps and cutting the railway south of Indaw in 16 places, and the British 16th Brigade taking the airfield to the west of Indaw. The overall effect on 'U' was considerable, for the Japanese lines of communication to the 31st Division in front of Kohima and to the 15th Division in front of Imphal were totally destroyed. Further success was enjoyed east of the Irrawaddy by the Gurkhas of Morrisforce, who completely disrupted Japanese communications between Bhamo and Myitkyina.

By the end of April the Chindits were clearly dominant in their operations, and were playing a useful part in aiding the Northern Combat Area Command while hindering the activities of the Japanese 15th Army. At this point South-East Asia Command imposed a change of operational plan on the 3rd Indian Division, which had thus to abandon its efforts against the Japanese lines of communication and to assist the Northern Combat Area Command more directly in the capture of Mogaung and Myitkyina. It was planned that these two objectives be attained before the advent of the monsoon, so 'Aberdeen', 'Broadway' and 'White City' were abandoned as the 3rd Indian Division shifted its focus north, where the 111th Indian Brigade was to block the rail line to Mogaung and Myitkyina at 'Blackpool' (between Hopin and Taungni) with the 77th Indian Brigade providing an eastern flank guard while the British 14th Brigade and 3rd West African Brigade covered the western flank. The British 16th Brigade, now in very poor condition after its long approach march from Ledo and then its period of sustained operations, was flown out.

The plan did not work, for 'Blackpool' was an inadequate site for the block, which the 111th Indian Brigade was in any event neither trained nor equipped to construct. 'Blackpool' was created on 7 May, and soon faced determined opposition from the Japanese 53rd Division, which made its major effort from 20 May. By 25 May 'Blackpool' had been overrun, the 77th Indian Brigade and 3rd West African Brigade being unable to assist as the former was separated from 'Blackpool' by the flooded River Namyin and the latter was tied down at Lake Indawgyi, where the Chindits' increasing number of sick and wounded were being evacuated by flying-boat. The fall of 'Blackpool' was a severe blow to the Allies, for on 17 May the leading elements of the US 5307th Provisional Regiment and a regiment of the Chinese 30th Division had seized Myitkyina airfield as the first part of their attack on this strategically sited town. Now Japanese reinforcements, in the form of the fresh 53rd Division, could flood north unimpeded from Indaw to bolster the Myitkyina garrison and the 18th Division at Kamaing, where Tanaka's division was hard pressed by the Chinese 22nd and 38th Divisions. The British 14th Brigade and 3rd West African Brigades were effectively out of action in the malarial hotbed around Lake Indawgyi, and the 111th Indian Brigade was in poor state after the 'Blackpool' fighting, so the only available Chindit formation was the 77th Indian Brigade.

Calvert was thus ordered to take Mogaung at any cost while some 30,000 Chinese reinforcements were flown intoo Myitkyina airfield so that Stilwell's forces could take the town (and its road, rail and river communications), which the 33rd Army reinforced with soome 3,000 men of the 56th Division commanded by Major General Mizukami. Outnumbered some 15 to 1, Mizukami faced an extraordinarily difficult task, but his defence of Myitkyina must be noted as one of the best such actions of World War II, for the defence lasted 76 days. The 33rd Army was allocated the newly-arrived 53rd Division which, with little opposition at Indaw and 'White City', was ordered north to relieve Myitkyina. However, the division was still not within striking distance of Myitkyina when Calvert launched the 77th Indian Brigade's assault on Mogaung with some preliminary operations at the beginning of June, and Honda immediately ordered Takeda to hold Mogaung, initially with the 128th Regiment.

Unaware of the relative weakness of the Japanese defence, Calvert had decided on a systematic approach through the outlying villages in an effort to mitigate casualties to his decimated brigade, and to give time for the Chinese 22nd and 38th Divisions to arrive after defeating the 3,000-strong 18th Division at Kamaing (16 June). By 12 June the 77th Indian Brigade numbered a mere 550 combat-ready men and, with only small numbers of Chinese reinforcements arriving at a time when his exhausted men were falling rapidly to a number of illnesses, Calvert decided on an all-out effort from 23 June, and Mogaung finally fell on 26 June as the last Japanese pulled out to the south-west.

Calvert was now down to 300 fit men, having suffered some 950 casualties and 150 sick since 17 May. It was clear that the shattered Brigade had to be withdrawn, and the 111th Indian Brigade was also evacuated after a final successful action at Padiga. There remained the British 14th Brigade and 3rd West African Brigade, and these were in action at Taungni and Sahmaw until 12 August, when they too were flown out. Stilwell was reinforced with elements of Major General F. W. Festing's British 36th Division from 15 July, and Myitkyina finally fell on 4 August, the day after Mizukami ordered Colonel Maruyama to abandon the town with all surviving Japanese troops; Mizukami then committed suicide. Operation 'Thursday' had cost the 3rd Indian Division some 5,000 casualties, but it had achieved great things, even if many of the later operations fell outside the brief Wingate had fixed for his men, and were thus undertaken with the wrong training and equipment.

Tidal Wave Attack on the Ploesti oilfields in Romania by US bombers (1 August 1943). The oilfields and eight associated refineries produced about 10 million tons of fuel annually, and this tonnage was of signal importance in maintaining the German war effort. For this reason, therefore, Ploesti was designated a vital strategic target for Allied bombing as early as January 1942, and the first attack was launched on 11 June 1942 by the 12 Consolidated B-24D Liberator heavy bombers of the HALPRO detachment in Egypt. The damage caused was minimal, but the raid served to confirm the importance and the vulnerability of the target area in German minds. Thus steps were taken to improve Ploesti's defences (fighters, AA guns and smoke generators) so that other raids would face a more difficult task.

The major US Army Air Force effort was planned as Operations 'Statesman' and 'Soapsuds', but finally came to fruition as Operation 'Tidal Wave' under the control of Major General Carl A. Spaatz's North-West African Air Force. Five groups of B-24 bombers were allocated to the mission, namely the North-West African Air Force's own 98th and 376th Bombardment Groups (Heavy), the US 8th Air Force's 44th and 93rd Bombardment Groups (Heavy) from the UK, and the 389th Bombardment Group (Heavy) initially allocated to the 8th Air Force but diverted while still in the USA. US planning called for the mission to be despatched from Benghazi on a low-level strike in the hope of taking the Germans and Romanians by tactical surprise. A total of 177 Liberators took off on 'Tidal Wave', and over the Mediterranean separated into five streams for the approach flight, which was already being monitored by the alert Germans. The 376th BG(H) and the following 93rd BG(H) made navigational errors and headed for Bucharest before realizing the fact and turning back, only 6 aircraft of the 376th BG(H) then bombing Ploesti while the other aircraft attacked targets of opportunity. The 44th and 98th BG(H)s made accurate approaches, but were faced by fully alerted defences, including a Flak train moving at maximum speed along the track used by the two groups as their lead-in to the target. The 389th BG(H) also bombed with good accuracy. Over the target area and on their exit the bombers were engaged by fighters, and total losses were 41 over the target and another 13 approaching or departing the target area.

Some 40 per cent of the Ploesti refinery capacity was destroyed, but as the Germans needed only 60 per cent of total refinery capacity to process the available oil, the results of the raid were minimal as the Germans within a few days restored production to its previous levels. Ploesti exercised a fascination for the Americans, and over the following year another 20 raids were launched against the refineries and the complex's transportation system before the refineries shut down on 24 August 1944, just six days before the Soviets reached Ploesti. In the course of some 7,500 bomber sorties the Americans dropped about 13,500 tons of bombs on Ploesti and lost 350 heavy bombers.

Tigar 1C Allied construction project for the road between Ledo and Kunming so that supplies could be carried by truck to the Chinese forces of Generalissimo Chiang Kai-shek, thus obviating the need for the airlift operation 'over the hump' of the eastern Himalayas. Up to May 1943 the Allies had worked on the principle of reopening the Burma Road so that China-bound supplies could be delivered to Rangoon by ship and then moved by rail to Lashio, the Burmese end of the Burma Road to Kunming. From the 'Trident' conference onwards, however, the Allies began to reveal considerably more realistic opinions about the liberation of southern and central Burma, and all mention of the Burma Road was tacitly dropped in favour of positive opinion for a new supply road running basically south-east some 483 miles from the railhead at Ledo in north-east Assam, across the mountains, jungles and swamps of northern Burma to Wanting in Yunnan, where it would link with the original Burma Road.

Pending the completion of this new road, the 'Trident' Conference decided that the monthly airlift 'over the hump' should be increased to 10,000 tons by the autumn of 1943 after an increase to 7,000 tons in July. In the event the July tonnage was a mere 4,500 tons, and continued difficulties were encountered in building up the tonnages for delivery to the Chinese forces and to Lieutenant General Claire L. Chennault's US 14th Air Force, which had an ever-increasing demand as the war, progressed. Both the British and the Americans proposed plans for the Ledo Road, but the plan of Brigadier General Raymond Wheeler was chosen and responsibility was thus given to the Americans under Colonel Arrowsmith and later on General Pick.

Work started on 25 December 1942 from Ledo with the object of building the 103-mile stretch to Shinbwiyang in the Hukawng valley by the end of 1943. From here the gravel-covered three-lane road would advance to Myitkyina and then cross the River Irrawaddy to Bhamo, where it would link with the pre-war British road to Namkham, and then push forward to meet the Burma Road at Mong Yaw. Progress over the later stages was much dependent on the progress of operations in north Burma, but the Ledo Road was officially opened on 31 January 1945, and soon after this the combined Burma and Ledo Roads complex was renamed the Stilwell Road by Chiang.

Tigar 26A US plan to move the supply base for Lieutenant General Claire L. Chennault's 14th Air Force from Kunming to Kweilin to ease the supply situation for the Boeing B-29 Superfortress bombers starting operations from China (1944).

Tiger (i) Designation of half of the final phase of Germany's military defeat of France, namely the offensive by Generaloberst Erwin von Witzleben's German 1st Army of Generaloberst Wilhelm Ritter von Leeb's Army Group 'C' through the Maginot Line (13/22 June 1940). This was the northern half of a pincer designed to meet General Friedrich Dollmann's German 7th Army (Operation 'Bär') in the region of Epinal and Nancy, so trapping the 17 divisions of Général d'Armée Gaston Pretelat's French 2nd Army Group (Général d'Armée Condé's 3rd Army, and the 5th and 8th Armies). Operation 'Tiger' was launched as the German armoured formations of General Heinz Guderian's Panzergruppe Guderian (within Generaloberst Gerd von Rundstedt's Army Group 'A') were pushing south from Châlons and Verdun between the upper reaches of the Rivers Marne and Meuse, so threatening the rear of the French 2nd Army Group. 'Tiger' began two days before 'Bär', and von Witzleben pushed forward 7 divisions against Général de Corps d'Armée Hubert's Saar Detachment (1 French and 1 Polish division).

The Germans at first made negligible progress against determined resistance, but during the night of 14/15 June Hubert was ordered to fall back as part of a movement to align the 2nd Army Group between Geneva and Dôle, which eased the task of the German 7th Army in 'Bär'. Greater weight was added to these twin operations by the subordination of Panzergruppe Guderian (and the German 16th Army on its left) to Army Group 'C' by an Oberkommando des Heeres order of 17 June. Guderian immediately ordered his formations to wheel 90 degrees left, XXXIX Panzer Corps being directed towards Belfort in support of the 7th Army, and XLI Panzer Corps being directed towards Epinal in support of the 1st Army. The French 2nd Army Group was thus trapped between three infantry armies pushing forward from the Maginot Line, and two Panzer corps in their rear. Pretelat had been separated from his command by now, with Condé assuming overall control in his stead, but the 400,000 men of the 2nd Army Group (together with the 2nd Army) were cut off when the 1st Panzer Division met the leading elements of the 7th Army at Montreux-les-Vieux on 18 June. The French were short of ammunition and surrendered on 22 June.

(ii) British fast merchant convoy from Gibraltar to Egypt carrying tanks and aircraft (5/12 May 1941). The Royal Navy had grave doubts about the wisdom of running a vital convoy through the full length of the Mediterranean, especially as the Italian air force had recently been reinforced by a specialist Luftwaffe anti-shipping formation (Generalleutnant Hans Geissler's X Fliegerkorps), but the British political and military leadership insisted that reinforcement of British forces in Egypt was vital if General Erwin Rommel's forces (recently reinforced by the 115th Panzer Division to raise German tank strength in North Africa to 488, including 122 heavy tanks) were to be halted and repulsed in Operation 'Battleaxe'. General Sir Archibald Wavell had under his command in Egypt sufficient personnel to man another 6 armoured regiments, and the plan was thus to send through 5 fast merchantmen loaded with 295 tanks and 50 Hawker Hurricane fighter aircraft, escorted by Vice Admiral Sir James Somerville's Force H reinforced with ships destined for Admiral Sir Andrew Cunningham's Mediterranean Fleet at Alexandria. These ships were the battleship *Queen Elizabeth* and the cruisers *Naiad* and *Phoebe* from the Home Fleet. At the time the convoy was sailed X Fliegerkorps was being transferred from Sicily to North Africa, so German air opposition was negligible after the 'Tiger' convoy passed through the Straits of Gibraltar on 6 May. Force H escorted the merchantmen as far east as Cap Bon, with six of its destroyers continuing to the handover point south of Malta, where the Mediterranean Fleet assumed responsibility. Two ships were mined on the night of 7/8 May and one later sank, but this was the only loss during the operation, in the course of which Cunningham took the opportunity to shell Axis positions at Benghazi and to pass into Malta 3 tankers and 4 supply ships. The 4 surviving merchantmen unloaded at Alexandria some 238 tanks and 43 fighters.

(iii) Final exercise for the 'Utah' Beach landing of Major General J. Lawton Collins's US VII Corps of Lieutenant General Omar N. Bradley's US 1st Army in preparation for Operation 'Overlord'.

T.J. Designation of South Atlantic convoys (together with a numerical suffix) plying the route from Trinidad to Rio de Janeiro, Brazil, and inaugurated in July 1943 replacing the T.B. series inaugurated in October 1942.

T.M. Designation of Central Atlantic convoys (together with a numerical suffix) plying the route from Trinidad to Gibraltar, and inaugurated in January 1943 as special tanker convoys bringing fuel across the Atlantic for the Allied 1st Army fighting its way east towards Tunisia after the Operation 'Torch' landings.

T.O. Designation of Central Atlantic convoys (together with a numerical suffix) plying the route from North-West Africa via the Caribbean to New York, and inaugurated in November 1942 as the series returning to the Caribbean and the USA the fast tankers associated with Operation 'Torch' and its exploitation.

TO Designation of that part of the Japanese Operation 'ICHI' designed specifically to take the US air bases at Hengyang, Lingling, Kweilin and Liuchow in southern China (June/September 1944). The task was entrusted to the 11th and 23rd Armies of the Lieutenant General Okamura's 6th Area Army under the overall control of the China Expeditionary Army.

Toenails US seizure of the New Georgia island group in the central Solomons (21 June/6 October 1943). This was the second stage in the Solomons campaign undertaken as part of the overall 'Elkton' plan by Vice Admiral William F. Halsey's South Pacific Area forces, and was designed to coincide with the operations against Salamaua and Lae in New Guinea by the South-West Pacific Area forces of General Douglas MacArthur as the two-pronged US offensive closed in on the Japanese 8th Area Army (Lieutenant General Hitoshi Imamura) on New Britain and New Ireland. Although he was part of Admiral Chester W. Nimitz's Pacific Ocean Areas command, Halsey was operationally controlled by MacArthur, and Operation 'Toenails' was planned as a stepping stone towards Bougainville at the north-western end of the Solomons so that the important airfield at Munda could be used for the land-based air support of further operations. The trouble lay in the fact that the New Georgia islands are a complex of close-lying islands surrounded by shallow water and reefs, so Halsey's staff came immediately to the conclusion that the assault would need first to take the outlying islands and then, using these as advanced bases, close on Munda indirectly as no heavy ships could get within gunfire range.

The Japanese defence numbered some 11,000 men scattered to defend all likely landing spots, and the 8th Area Army and 4th Fleet were ready to despatch reinforcements. The naval forces commanded by Rear Admiral Minoru Ota (Kure 6th and Yokosuka 7th Special Naval Landing Forces) were responsible mainly for Munda and for Vila on Kolombangara Island, while army units of the 38th and 51st Divisions were tasked with the defence of other areas under the overall command of Lieutenant General Noburu Sasaki's South-East Detachment, a joint army/navy command controlled by

Lieutenant General Harukichi Hyakutake's Japanese 17th Army responsible for the defence of the Solomons.

Detailed planning of the US operation was entrusted to Rear Admiral Richmond K. Turner's III Amphibious Force, and while the operation was prepared US aircraft raided the Japanese positions (especially airfields) and ships laid minefields which caused moderately heavy losses to the Japanese destroyer operations ferrying in men and supplies. The landings were planned in two phases for 30 June 1943. At dawn the Eastern Landing Force under Rear Admiral George H. Fort was to land the 4th Marine Raider Battalion (to be followed by the 1st Battalion, 103rd Infantry Regiment during the following day) at the extreme south-eastern point of New Georgia Island, while elements of the 2nd Battalion, 103rd Infantry Regiment landed at Oleana Bay on the southern side of Vangunu Island to the east of New Georgia Island. After these initial objectives had been secured, the rest of Major General John H. Hester's US 43rd Infantry Division (plus additional units of Turner's Western Landing Force) would land its 172nd Infantry Regiment on the northern shore of Rendova Island just to the south of Munda at the western end of New Georgia Island. From Rendova Island the 43rd Infantry Division would then cross to New Georgia Island east of Munda and close in on the airfield with air support from a strip improvised at Segi.

The plan was altered at the last minute when Australian coastwatchers reported that the Japanese were moving larger numbers of troops towards the Segi area. Thus Lieutenant Colonel Michael S. Currin's 4th Marine Raider Battalion was landed on 21 June and secured the Segi area against limited opposition. The Americans immediately began to develop an airstrip while Currin undertook an attack on Viru, whose capture on 1 July secured the US position at Segi. On the previous day the landing of the 172nd Infantry Regiment on Rendova Island had proceeded with hitches but without significant casualties as the Japanese had not expected a landing on the island, whose 250 naval defenders took to the hills after some skirmishes. On 2/3 July the US 169th and 172nd Infantry Regiments of the US 43rd Infantry Division crossed to New Georgia Island and, after landing at Zanana, began to advance west on the River Bariki and Munda. By 5 July both regiments were ashore, and extra pressure on the Japanese began to develop as a Northern Landing Force under Rear Admiral W. L. Ainsworth on 4/5 July landed part of the 1st Marine Raider Regiment and the 145th and 148th Infantry Regiments (of the US 37th Infantry Division), under Colonel Harry Liversedge, at Rice Anchorage on the northern side of New Georgia Island with the object of advancing south against Enogai Inlet and Bairoko Harbour, and so threaten Munda from the north.

So far the US operations had proceeded much as planned, but on the night of 6/7 July the Japanese launched a major counterattack against the inexperienced 169th Infantry Regiment and came close to destroying it before Hester's personal intervention rallied the Americans. The 169th and 172nd Infantry Regiments then advanced again, although the rate was too slow to please senior US commanders, especially after another Japanese counterattack on 16/17 July. It was clear that reinforcement and reorganization were required, and on 16 July the US XIV Corps was activated under Major General Oscar W. Griswold to supervise the US forces on New Georgia, now comprising the 37th and 43rd Infantry Divisions after the 103rd and 161st Infantry Regiments had been landed on 18 July. On 1 August the US forces finally emerged from the jungle onto the outskirts of Munda airfield, but it was 5 August before the last elements of the Japanese defence had been quelled in the Munda area. By 15 August the airfield was in full US service as the 43rd Infantry Division (commanded since 29 July by Major General John H. Hodge) moved north to assist the 37th Infantry Division against the 6th Kure Special Naval Landing Force at Bairoku Harbour, the last Japanese outpost on New Georgia Island, which fell on 22 August after the surviving defenders had been evacuated to Vila by barge. The last Japanese resistance on the island ended on 24 August after the arrival of yet more reinforcements, in the form of elements of the 25th Infantry Divisions.

Yet the New Georgia Island operations had dealt with only half of the Japanese garrison in the group. During the course of the New Georgia fighting, the other garrisons had been reinforced to some 10,000 men despite losses during the naval battles (on 5/6 July and 12/13 July) of Kula Gulf and Kolombangara, which were Japanese tactical victories. Most of the Japanese were disposed for the protection of the airfield at Vila on Kolombangara Island to the north-west of New Georgia Island, but there were also Japanese forces on Arundel and Vella Lavella Islands, and these three bastions had to be eliminated before the US position in the group could be considered secure. Turner planned to attack Kolombangara as soon as the New Georgia operation was complete, but then a more attractive alternative was perceived, namely the bypassing of the island by landings on Arundel and Vella Lavella, which would isolate the Japanese defenders on Kolombangara and condemn them 'to wither on the vine' as the US forces pushed up the chain of the Solomons with the aid of air support from Munda and an airstrip built on Vella Lavella. Thus was born the concept of isolating rather than destroying Japanese bastions wherever possible, with a consequent saving in US lives and a speeding of the rate of advance.

The Vella Lavella operation began on 15 August as the fighting on New Georgia continued, a reinforced regiment of the 25th Infantry Division landing on the south-eastern tip of the island and securing a beachhead large enough for the construction of an airfield at Barakoma. By the end of September New Zealand forces had relieved the Americans on Vella Lavella, and on 6 October the last Japanese were evacuated from the island. Arundel Island was taken against serious resistance between 27 August and 20 September, and this allowed Vila airfield to be neutralized by USA artillery located on Arundel's northern shore. As early as 13 August Imperial General Headquarters had realized that the Japanese grip on the central Solomons could not be maintained, but it was not until the end of September that Hyakutake could evacuate the surviving Japanese (some 9,000 in all) from the New Georgia group to Bougainville, clearly the next objective for Halsey's forces. 'Toenails' had cost the Americans some 1,000 dead, while the Japanese losses were probably 3,000 dead and 7,000 wounded, yet the defence of the central Solomons had lasted four months, and given the Japanese that much more time to bolster their defences on New Britain and New Ireland, which they confidently expected the Americans to attack.

Tolstoy Designation of the inter-Allied conference held at Moscow (9/16 October 1944). The conference was organized at the suggestion of Prime Minister Winston Churchill, who was concerned about the progress of events in eastern Europe and thus wished to consult Premier Joseph Stalin about the post-war disposition of Greece and Poland. President Franklin D. Roosevelt declined to accompany Churchill as he was too involved in the US presidential election campaign. Churchill was accompanied to Moscow by Anthony Eden (the British Foreign Secretary), General Sir Hastings Ismay (Churchill's chief-of-staff) and Field Marshal Sir Alan Brooke (Chief of the Imperial General Staff and chairman of the Chiefs-of-Staff Committee). The USA was represented by Averell Harriman, the American ambassador to the USSR. The main Soviet protagonists were Stalin and his foreign minister, Molotov.

Stalin and Churchill settled to business without delay, and an initial agreement was made about spheres of influence in eastern Europe (Romania: USSR 90 per cent and the others 10 per cent; Greece: UK 90 per cent and the USSR 10 per cent; Yugoslavia: 50 per cent to each side; Hungary: 50 per cent to each side; and Bulgaria: USSR 75 per cent and the others 25 per cent).

Eden and Molotov later argued about the percentages, but these problems were minimal compared with those of Poland, which was represented by two governments in exile, namely that in London (Prime Minister Stanislas Mikolajczyk and Foreign Minister Tadeusz Romer) and that in the USSR (the 'Lublin National Committee'). The 'Tolstoy' Conference sought to reach agreement on the eastern frontiers of post-war Poland, and on the formation of a government representing the aspirations of both governments in exile. Much to the dismay of the Mikolajczyk faction, Churchill forced a compliance with the previously secret agreement of the Tehran Conference (that Poland east of the Curzon Line, in all some 48 per cent of the pre-war country, should be allocated to the USSR) in the hope of persuading the USSR to agree to a bipartite post-war state in which both eastern and western factions would anticipate. It was an abject defeat for the west on Poland, the country on whose behalf the UK had gone to war in 1939.

Other suggestions of the 'Tolstoy' Conference were for a British and American offensive through Switzerland to outflank the southern end of the 'Siegfried Linie' defences (flatly refused by Churchill), for the movement of 60 Soviet divisions and their support elements east for the initiation of hostilities against Japan (fraught with logistic difficulties pointed out by Stalin), recognition of General de Gaulle's Fighting French as the government of France (agreed by all parties), and the division of Germany into two parts, Wurttemberg and Bavaria being allocated to Austria to form a Danubian Confederacy (discussed but not finalized).

Tombola (i) Allied underwater pipeline to enable tankers to discharge their loads while lying off Ste Honorine des Pertes (September 1944). The object of this device was to shorten the overland supply route to the Allied forces advancing towards Germany.
(ii) Airborne operations by the 2nd SAS to aid Italian partisans near Reggio (4/7/9 March 1945).

Tonga Overall designation of the British 6th Airborne Division's activities in Operation 'Overlord' (6 June 1944). The British I Airborne Corps was commanded by Lieutenant General F. A. M. Browning, but of the corps' two divisions and several independent brigades, only Major General Richard Gale's British 6th Airborne Division was to be used in the airborne role, though the 1st Special Service Brigade was to come under divisional command after landing conventionally over 'Sword' Beach. In order of importance, the tasks allocated to the 6th Airborne Division were the capture and retention of the bridges over the River Orne and adjacent Caen Canal, the silencing of the Merville battery so that the British 3rd Division could land on 'Sword' Beach, and the guarding of the 3rd Division's left flank by the destruction of the four bridges over the River Dives which might otherwise be used for counterattacks by formations of Generaloberst Hans von Salmuth's German 15th Army. With these primary objectives attained, the division was to be reinforced by its third brigade (the 6th Air Landing Brigade) and the 1st Special Service Brigade to deal with any German incursions into the area east of the 3rd Division (between the Orne and the Dives as far south as Caen). The two brigades that were to be landed in the assault phase of the operation were Brigadier Nigel Poett's 5th Parachute Brigade and Brigadier James Hill's 3rd Parachute Brigade, the former tasked with the Orme and Caen Canal operations, and the latter with the Merville battery and Dives operations.

The 5th Parachute Brigade's task was undertaken successfully after the brigade landed to find its bridge objectives already taken by the glider-landed *coup-de-main* party delivered in advance of the main landings. The brigade's 7th Parachute Battalion held the bridges against the 192nd Panzergrenadierregiment until relieved by the 1st Special Service Brigade at 13.45 on 6 June, and the 12th and 13th Parachute Battalions took and held Le Basse de Ranville and Ranville until relieved by the 3rd Division. The drop of the 3rd Parachute Brigade was altogether more scattered, and though the 8th Parachute Battalion landed near the Bois de Bavent before moving off to destroy the Dives bridges and then retire once more to the Bois de Bavent, the 1st Canadian Parachute Battalion and the 9th Parachute Battalion were dropped in entirely the wrong places (north-west of Vareville) and had lengthy moves before the Canadians destroyed their allocated Dives bridges and the British silenced Merville. During the evening Brigadier the Hon. H. K. M. Kindersley's 6th Air Landing Brigade arrived as reinforcement for the division, landing in gliders on each side of the Orne south of Ouistreham.

Topflight Allied signal to release information about Operation 'Overlord'.

Tora Japanese map exercise to test and assess Allied capabilities and intentions in the Pacific and Chinese theatres (winter 1943).

Torch Allied landing in French North Africa (8 November 1942). Evolved from Operations 'Acrobat', 'Gymnast' and 'Super Gymnast', Operation 'Torch' had a sound military rationale, but was also planned (largely by the Americans) as a means of getting US ground forces into the war against Germany and, assuming the success which the operation indeed enjoyed, of raising the morale of the American people with an operation of major strategic importance and under American leadership. Although US strategic doctrine called for a direct rather than an indirect approach to Germany, designated the primary enemy by the Allied leaders, it was appreciated in Washington that British reservations about the direct assaults (Operations 'Round-up' and 'Sledgehammer') meant that no such cross-Channel operations would be undertaken until mid-1943 at the very earliest, so principles were sacrificed for an indirect but more rapidly implemented assault. Though it would have been possible for the USA to provide forces and *matériel* for the British-led effort in the Western Desert, it was decided instead to open a new theatre which could be commanded by an American, in this instance Lieutenant General (soon General) Dwight D. Eisenhower, the commanding general European Theater of Operations, US Army.

Another reason for the choice of an American commander was the attitude of the French in North Africa, amongst whom distrust of the British was strong (especially after the operation against the French fleet at Mers el Kebir in July 1940). It was nevertheless hoped that an agreement could be reached with the French before the landings were committed or, failing that, during the initial phases of 'Torch', so that a bloodless or comparatively bloodless invasion would be followed by the wholesale adherence to the Allied cause of the substantial French forces in North Africa. These forces amounted to 120,000 men (55,000 in Morocco, 50,000 in Algeria and 15,000 in Tunisia), and while the Allies appreciated that the French equipment was obsolete, training standards were high and the delivery of Allied weaponry would turn the French formations into first-class fighting assets. The French air force in North Africa amounted to some 500 obsolete aircraft, but the units of the French navy in North and West African ports were formidable, consisting as they did of the battleships *Jean Bart* and *Richelieu*, 4 cruisers, 7 or more destroyers, 8 or more submarines and many smaller craft.

The Allied leaders met in London during July 1942 to thrash out the final problems associated with the commital of US ground forces into action with the Germans, and late in the month President Franklin D. Roosevelt authorized 'Super Gymnast', henceforth designated 'Torch'. Command was entrusted to Eisenhower as the Commander-in-Chief Allied Expeditionary Forces, and with Eisenhower the two most important figures in the Allied Force Headquarters were the deputy commander-in-chief, Major General (soon Lieutenant General) Mark W. Clark, and the chief-of-staff, Brigadier General (soon Major General) Walter Bedell Smith, all working closely with the Combined Chiefs-of-Staff Committee. The original concept for 'Torch' was based on two landings, one by the Americans and the other by the British. The American commander was Major General (soon Lieutenant General) George S. Patton, while the British commander was at first Lieutenant General the Hon. Sir Harold Alexander (soon appointed Commander-in-Chief Middle East), then Lieutenant General Bernard L. Montgomery (soon appointed to command the 8th Army), then Lieutenant General W. H. E. Gott (killed in an air crash), and finally Lieutenant General K. A. N. Anderson.

The plan for 'Torch' was that Allied forces should seize the French territories of Morocco, Algeria and Tunisia in North Africa, though it was appreciated that while landings were practical in Morocco and Algeria, an eastward land advance to Tunisia might well have to be undertaken against Axis forces, for though the terms of France's 1940 armistice with Germany and Italy prohibited the presence of Axis forces in

French North Africa, there was every reason to believe that the landing of Allied forces in Morocco and Algeria would signal an Axis descent on Tunisia from forward bases in Sicily. Despite the length of coastline open to invasion, the choices facing the Allied planners were complicated by the presence of German U-boats in the Atlantic and Mediterranean, the large numbers of Axis attack aircraft located in Sicily and Sardinia, the possibility of determined French resistance, and also the chance that Spain might intervene on the side of the Axis.

By September 1942 it had been decided by the planners that there would be three rather than two landings. Under the command of Patton, with Vice Admiral H. Kent Hewitt as naval commander, the Western Task Force would sail from Virginia in the USA and land on the Atlantic coast of French Morocco around Casablanca. Under the command of Major General (soon Lieutenant General) Lloyd R. Fredendall, with Commodore T. H. Troubridge as naval commander, the Centre Task Force would consist of US forces from the UK shipped and escorted by the British to land in French Algeria around Oran. And under the command of Major General Charles W. Ryder, with Vice Admiral Sir Harold Burrough as naval commander, the Eastern Task Force would consist of a small US landing force (to be followed by substantial British forces) from the UK shipped and escorted by the British to land in French Algeria around Algiers. Overall naval command was vested in Admiral Sir Andrew Cunningham, with Vice Admiral Sir Bertram Ramsay as his deputy, and the two air commanders were Brigadier General (later Major General) James H. Doolittle for the Western and Centre Task Forces, and Air Marshal Sir William Welsh for the Eastern Task Force.

Once the Allied forces had landed (with the Americans in the van in an effort to placate the French), they would form the Allied 1st Army (with, it was hoped, an increasing number of French troops) under Anderson and dash east to Tunisia in the hope of forestalling the development of an Axis beach-head in that territory. In a successful effort to maintain security the Allied forces sailed in small groups from a number of ports on both sides of the Atlantic, the plans still being flexible as a result of a decision to leave it until the last minute for Admiral Jean Darlan (head of the Vichy French armed forces and the senior representative of the Vichy regime in North Africa) and Général d'Armée Henri Giraud (the highest-ranking pre-war French officer to have escaped from the Germans and come over to the Allies) to influence events on the French side. Giraud had been rescued from southern France in a British submarine and taken to the 'Torch' headquarters in Gibraltar, but the French commander adamantly refused to travel to North Africa to try to swing the Vichy forces towards the Allied cause unless he was appointed to command the whole of 'Torch'.

The Allied landings were thus made on 8 November over a wide and extremely divided front with no real information about the likely French reaction, the US plans having been made largely on the estimates (both accurate and inaccurate) provided by Robert Murphy, the senior US diplomat in North Africa. In the sector of the Western Task Force the main objective was Casablanca, a major political prize as well as the port through which much of the Allied force could be fed and supplied; but this was too tough a nut for the transatlantic force to crack, and Patton descided on three smaller landings. In the south Major General Ernest J. Harmon put ashore at Safi some 6,500 men of the US 2nd Armored and 9th Infantry Divisions, and secured a disorganized beach-head against stiff local resistance before moving out against Casablanca on 9 November. Harmon's force was hotly engaged by Vichy forces at Bou Guedra before news of the ceasefire reached both sides. In the centre of the Western Task Force's sector Major General Jonathan Anderson put ashore at Fedala some 16,000 men of his US 3rd Infantry Division; again there was French resistance as the Americans built up their beach-head and then struck south towards Casablanca, and news of the ceasefire reached the Americans as they were about to open their artillery bombardment of the city. In the north of the Western Task Force's sector Major General Lucian K. Truscott landed at Fehdia some 9,000 men of the US 2nd Armored and 9th Infantry

Torch

Divisions; again French resistance was encountered, and Truscott's force had moved only a short way before news of the ceasefire reached it on 11 November. In the middle of the Allied assault area Fredendall's Centre Task Force also made three landings (two west of Oran and one east of the city) with some 22,000 men of Major General Orlando Ward's US 1st Armored Division and Major General Terry de la M. Allen's US 1st Infantry Division; again the French resisted as the 1st Armored Division moved inland to tackle Oran from the south and as the 1st Infantry Division attacked from east and west. The French at Oran capitulated at 12.00 on 10 November.

In the east lay the most important preliminary objective of 'Torch', namely the great city of Algiers with its port, two airfields and extensive communications, all the objectives of Ryder's Eastern Task Force. The landings were again effected in three main areas, with 7,200 British of the 11th Brigade Group responsible for the Blida sector, 4,350 Americans of the US 34th Infantry Division's 168th Regimental Combat Team (with some 1,000 British commandos) for the Sidi Ferrouch area just to the west of Algiers, and 5,700 Americans of the US 34th Infantry Division's 39th Regimental Combat Team (plus some 200 British commandos) allocated the Cap Matifou sector just to the east of Algiers. The British landed without opposition, but the Americans met some resistance.

As part of the Eastern Task Force's activities, Operation 'Terminal' was launched on 8 November in an effort to secure for the Allies the key points of the Algiers waterfront. Although the objectives (a fuel depot, a power station, the seaplane base, the port with its jetties and moles, and the post offices) were taken, the assault force had eventually to surrender. The senior French officer in Algiers was Darlan, and during the afternoon of 8 November he was authorized by the Vichy government to negotiate a local armistice through the agency of Général de Corps d'Armée Alphonse Juin. On 9 November Clark arrived in Algiers and on 10 November arranged a ceasefire for the rest of North Africa. Meanwhile Anderson had arrived in Algiers on 9 November and started the organissation of his 1st Army for the 380-mile drive on Tunis and Bizerta, the Allies' two main targets in Tunisia.

The planners were worried, however, by the fact that under the able and energetic leadership of Generalfeldmarschall Albert Kesselring, the German *Oberbefehlshaber Süd*, the Axis powers had started to pour German and Italian troops into Tunisia from 9 November. First to arrive were a number of fighters and dive-bombers to protect the Axis beach-head area from the disruptive efforts of Allied forces, and these were followed by Luftwaffe ground personnel to open up the Tunisian end of the air bridge to ferry Axis ground forces, which began to arrive from 11 November (under Oberst Lederer) in the form of the 5th Parachute Regiment and 104th Panzergrenadierregiment, the Italians following on 12 November with the leading elements of the Superga Division. The forces were readily available in the form of the reinforcements standing by in Sicily and southern Italy for Generalfeldmarschall Erwin Rommel's German-Italian Panzerarmee in the Western Desert. By the end of November some 15,000 troops had been airlifted into Tunisia and another 1,900 (plus heavy weapons and supplies) moved by sea. The headquarters of the initial controlling formation, General Walther Nehring's XC Corps, was established on 16 November, and the Axis powers were in business.

The French were in two minds about the approach they should adopt to the Axis powers in Tunisia, where the ports and airfields of Tunis and Bizerta had soon been occupied, for they had received no directive from Darlan or from France. Thus it was only in mid-November that a weak cordon was thrown around the area in which the Germans and Italians were establishing their beach-head. The Allied 1st Army was pouring east all this time, and came into contact with Axis forces on 20 November. On 4 December Hitler appointed Generaloberst Jürgen von Arnim to command the new 5th Panzerarmee, specially formed in North Africa to control three Panzer and three Panzergrenadier divisions under the overall control of the Italian Comando Supremo, though von Arnim was answerable directly to Kesselring. Thus the first phase of Operation 'Torch' came to an end with the Allied forces poised to secure what they thought would be a comparatively painless victory in Tunisia. The 1st Army attacked on 25 November, but was checked without undue difficulty by XC Corps. Thereafter the fighting intensified, though Anderson was unable to bring his full strength to bear as a result of logistic inadequacies in his rear and the inability of the divided Allied air command to furnish the right type of air support. On 24 December Eisenhower visited Anderson and was forced to agree that a rapid capture of northern Tunisia was out of the question.

Toreador British plan for a two-division airborne operation in central Burma to open the way for the 14th Army (1944).

Tornado US assault on Wakde Island off northern New Guinea and on Sarmi (17 May/2 September 1944). This was the logical successor to the Hollandia operation in the fast-moving westward advance of the South-West Pacific Area forces of General Douglas MacArthur, and was undertaken while the Hollandia operation was still under way with the double object of providing Lieutenant General George C. Kenney's US 5th Air Force with an area suitable for heavy bomber bases, and of denying Lieutenant General Hatazo Adachi's Japanese 18th Army fallback position (with the 2nd Army) after its pending defeat at Hollandia and Aitape. Wakde had recently seen the construction of a Japanese airstrip, and lying some 120 miles west of Hollandia but just 2 miles offshore near Toem and Sarmi, the island was admirably suited to MacArthur's 'coast-hopping' progress, especially as a mainland airstrip had been built at Toem and a third was under construction.

The unit entrusted with the landing was the 163rd Regimental Combat Team of Major General H. H. Fuller's US 41st Infantry Division, the unit which had spearheaded the Aitape landing. The operation began on 17 May with an unopposed landing at Toem, and on the following day US artillery was lined up on the New Guinea shore to support naval gunfire in covering the landings on Wakde. These landings were achieved without incident, but as it attempted to push inland the 163rd Regimental Combat Team was met by determined Japanese opposition, numbering some 800 men. It took the Americans two days to overrun the island, which measures 2 miles in length and 1 mile in width, and at the end there were only four survivors of the Japanese garrison. The island's airstrip came into use by tactical aircraft on 21 May, in time to support the coastal drive launched by the 41st Infantry Division at the insistence of Lieutenant General Walter Krueger's US 6th Army. Krueger rightly reasoned that with most of the Japanese 36th Division holding the area between Toem and Sarmi the US hold on Wakde would be threatened. There followed more than one month of heavy fighting before the region was reasonably secure, and the final Japanese resistance was not overcome until the beginning of September.

The fighting in 'Tornado' had been particularly severe, the Americans losing 646 dead and the Japanese some 3,899 dead, a ratio in favour of the Americans of 1:6, the lowest of the 'coast-hopping' campaign. It had by then been discovered that the area was unsuitable for heavy bombers (as was the Sentani airfield complex at Hollandia), so MacArthur moved boldly forward to Biak with the 41st Infantry Division even as part of that formation was still fighting its way forward to Sarmi.

Tortue (tortoise) Plan by the French resistance, with support from the Special Operations Executive and Office of Strategic Services, to hinder the road movement of German reinforcements to Normandy after the launch of Operation 'Overlord' (6 June 1944). The plan was formulated in conjunction with the French railways' Operation 'Vert', and achieved considerable success with guerrilla action.

Totalize Canadian offensive to take Falaise (7/11 August 1944). The object of the operation was for Lieutenant General Sir Henry Crerar's Canadian 1st Army to crush the German forces to the south of Caen as the US 1st Army of Lieutenant General Courtney H. Hodges was breaking out of the Normandy lodgement area at Avranches to the west, and the primary objective of the operation was Falaise. Crerar allocated

Tractable

Lieutenant G. G. Simonds's II Canadian Corps to the task with its two infantry (Canadian 2nd and British 51st) and two armoured (Canadian 4th and Polish 1st) divisions. The opposition was found by Generalfeldmarschall Günther von Kluge's Army Group 'B', and more specifically by SS Oberstgruppenführer Sepp Dietrich's I SS Panzer Corps (the 85th, 89th and 272nd Divisions and the 12th SS Panzer Division) of General Heinrich Hans Eberbach's 5th Panzerarmee, which had organized a defence based on two strong lines.

The offensive began at 23.30 on 7 August after some 1,000 heavy bombers had dropped 5,000 tons of bombs on the German positions, supported in this effort by the massed fire of 720 pieces of artillery. Four mechanized columns from the two infantry divisions (two tank brigades on the flanks and two infantry brigades carried in armoured personnel carriers in the centre) punched through the German front line and headed south for the headquarters of I SS Panzer Corps. By dawn the Canadians had advanced 3 miles, but then became bogged down in strengthening resistance, for despite the collapse of the 89th Division and the near collapse of the 272nd Division (on the German flanks), the 85th Division was holding with the able support of SS Oberführer Kurt Meyer's 12th SS Panzer Division. Simonds then decided to commit Major General G. Kitching's Canadian 4th Armoured Division (on the right flank, just to the north of Bretteville) and Major General S. Maczek's Polish 1st Armoured Division (on the left flank, just to the east of Hautmesnil). Both armoured divisions were new to combat, and here matters began to go seriously wrong with the Canadian II Corps' offensive. During the next two days the corps pushed on another 5 miles, but the last two days of 'Totalize' were marked by stagnation as the Canadian advance was halted by strenuous German counterattacks. However, by this time the American breakout from Avranches was well under way, and the notion entered the mind of Lieutenant General Omar N. Bradley, commander of the US 12th Army Group, that the rapid eastward progress of the US 1st and 3rd Armies opened the way for the German 5th Panzerarmee and 7th Army, together with the Panzergruppe Eberbach, to be trapped in a large pocket south of Falaise. 'Totalize' was thus developed into Operation 'Tractable'.

Tractable Development of II Canadian Corps' offensive in Operation 'Totalize', designed to close the neck of the Falaise salient against the US 1st Army of Lieutenant General Courtney H. Hodges and so trap considerable German forces, notably SS Oberstgruppenführer Sepp Dietrich's 5th Panzerarmee, SS Oberstgruppenführer Paul Hausser's 7th Army and General Heinrich Hans Eberbach's Panzergruppe Eberbach (14/16 August 1944). The neck of the salient, created largely by the Germans' westward advance from Mortain against the US breakthrough at Avranches on the western side of the Cotentin peninsula, was about 25 miles wide, and the Allies hastened to improvize Operation 'Tractable' before the Germans could pull back. Bradley hoped that Major General Wade H. Haislip's US XV Corps would be allowed to attack north to meet II Canadian Corps, but Field Marshal Sir Bernard Montgomery was jealous of his 21st Army Group's operational area and decided that 'Tractable' would use only Lieutenant General Sir Henry Crerar's Canadian 1st Army, which would also leave Haislip's corps free for a larger enveloping movement near the Seine if Allied plans progressed according to intention. Thus a golden opportunity was lost, for at the time Haislip was preparing a northward advance to Argentan in the direction that would allow him to link with Lieutenant General G. G. Simonds' II Canadian Corps advancing south to Falaise.

The Canadians attacked on 14 August, and soon managed to break through the 5th Panzerarmee's forward positions and reach a point some 3 miles north of Falaise, but there was still a neck of 15 miles in the German salient's eastern end, and Bradley ordered Haislip to make for Dreux and the River Seine as Montgomery still believed that the Canadians could close the gap. By 15 August the Allies were pounding the shrinking pocket with artillery and aerial weapons, and the German position was worsened by the disappearance within the pocket of Generalfeldmarschall Günther von Kluge, commander of the German Army Group 'B'. Hitler appointed Hausser to temporary command with the instruction to destroy the Allied forces threatening the 5th Panzerarmee, the 7th Army and Panzergruppe Eberbach. Von Kluge reappeared on 16 August and persuaded Generaloberst Alfred Jodl (chief-of-staff of the Oberkommando der Wehrmacht) that evacuation of the Falaise position was essential if the seven corps within the pocket were not to be eliminated.

The evacuation started after nightfall on 16 August, the day on which the Canadians finally took Falaise. In fact von Kluge did not wait for permission from OKW or from Hitler, but on his own initiative started the withdrawal, his intention being to save as many as possible of the 23 threatened divisions. Dietrich's first desire was to save his beloved II SS Panzer Corps, and this had been extricated by 17 August, the day on which Dietrich formally succeeded Eberbach as commander of the 5th Panzerarmee. Thereafter the 5th Panzerarmee and Panzergruppe Eberbach tried to hold the shoulders of the pocket so that the 7th Army could pull back the 40 miles from the western end of the German salient. During the night of 16/17 the 7th Army fell back to the eastern side of the River Orne after a stealthy retreat of 15 miles.

On 18 August Hitler appointed Generaloberst Walter Model to take over from von Kluge, who committed suicide shortly afterwards; but Model fully realized that von Kluge had done the right thing, and so ordered the evacuation to continue. The Allies were pressuring the pocket with six corps (II Canadian Corps of the Canadian 1st Army, British XII, XXX and VIII Corps of the British 2nd Army, and US VII and V Corps of the US 1st Army), and on 20 August the net was finally closed on the German armies, trapping 2 army headquarters, 4 corps headquarters and 10 divisions. Yet the net was not complete, and German forces in the small pocket just west of Chambois and St Lambert continued to filter out even as scenes of the most terrible carnage were witnessed in the pocket as massive air and ground attacks were launched on the trapped formations. Between 20,000 and 40,000 Germans escaped, but they had to leave all their heavy weapons, and the Allies took some 50,000 prisoners. On the battlefield were enormous quantities of destroyed *matériel* and some 10,000 German bodies. Even so, if Haislip's corps had been permitted to move north on 13/14 August (or if II Canadian Corps had been able to move as fast as Montgomery wished), there is every likelihood that three complete armies would have been bagged.

Trajan Linie (Trajan line) German and Romanian defence line in northern Romania, designed as the main defence line for Generaloberst Johannes Friessner's Army Group 'South Ukraine' (August 1944). This line covered the western approaches to the Romanian coastal plain along the Black Sea, but Hitler forbade any withdrawal to the line until it was too late, for the main offensive by Marshal R. Ya. Malinovsky's 2nd Ukrainian Front coincided with Romania's surrender (23 August) and then declaration of war on Germany (25 August).

Transfigure Allied plan to use Lieutenant General Lewis H. Brereton's Allied 1st Airborne Army in a major operation against the road network in the region of Orléans and Paris (16/17 August 1944). This was one of 16 such operations considered but not implemented by the 1st Airborne Army, which was established on 20 June 1944 to control Major General Matthew B. Ridgway's US XVIII Airborne Corps (Major General James M. Gavin's 82nd Airborne Division and Major General Maxwell D. Taylor's 101st Airborne Division), Lieutenant General F. A. M. Browning's British I Airborne Corps (Major General Roy Urquhart's 1st Airborne Division, Major General Richard Gale's 6th Airborne Division, the 1st Polish Independent Parachute Brigade, and the 1st Special Service Brigade), and the British 52nd Division.

Trappenfang (bustard trap) German operation to take the Kerch peninsula at the eastern end of the Crimea (November 1941). The operation was part of the double offensive undertaken in the Crimea by General Erich von Manstein's German 11th Army of Generalfeldmarschall Gerd von Rundstedt's Army Group 'South'. The army had forced its way through the isthmus of Perekop on 28 October 1941 with the object

303

of taking Sevastopol and destroying all Soviet forces in the area, namely Colonel General F. I. Kuznetsov's 51st Independent Army of Vice Admiral G. I. Levchenko's Crimea Command. As the 11th Army pushed into the Crimea it found itself faced with operations on two diverging axes, one south towards Sevastopol and the other east against the remnants of the 51st Independent Army retiring towards the Kerch peninsula. Von Manstein rightly allocated priority to the Sevastopol operations, but detached Generalleutnant H. Graf von Sponeck's newly arrived XLII Corps to push the 51st Independent Army off the Kerch peninsula. Von Sponeck achieved his task by 16 November, when the last units of the 51st Independent Army were evacuated for the Kuban after abandoning all their heavy equipment and weapons. In the Kuban the 51st Army received a new commander, Lieutenant General V. N. Lvov and, under control of Lieutenant General D. T. Kozlov's Transcaucasus Front, was rebuilt and paired with Lieutenant General S. I. Chernyak's 44th Army for a return to the Crimea. The landings began on 26 December 1941 when the 51st Army landed 13,000 men at Kerch and the 44th Army landed 3,000 men near Feodosiya in the rear of the German opposition, which amounted to only the 46th Division. From 29 December the Soviets landed another 23,000 men at Feodosiya. Von Sponeck abandoned the Kerch area and fell back to Feodosiya to avoid being cut off, and was later relieved of his command by Hitler, court martialled and sentenced to death, though the sentence was transmuted to life imprisonment. Von Manstein was forced to break off his operations against Sevastopol to reinforce XLII Corps with the 132nd and 170th Divisions of XXX Corps, delaying the capture of this great city to the middle of 1942.

Trappenjagd (bustard hunt) German operation to eliminate the Soviets from the Kerch peninsula (8/15 May 1942) before concentrating on the reduction of Sevastopol. Generaloberst Erich von Manstein's German 11th Army had been forced to break off its operations against Sevastopol in December 1941 to assist Generalleutnant H. Graf von Sponeck's understrength XLII Corps against the invasion of the eastern Crimea at Kerch and Feodosiya by Lieutenant General V. N. Lvov's 51st Army and Lieutenant General S. I. Chernyak's 44th Army of Lieutenant General D. T. Kozlov's Transcaucasus Front (later the Caucasus Front and, from 28 January 1942 after its move into the Kerch area, the Crimean Front). Von Manstein assumed personal command of the dangerous situation near Feodosiya and, on 15 January 1942, launched an attack on a force believed to number some eight divisions with a mere three reinforced German divisions. Feodosiya was retaken by the Germans, yielding 10,000 prisoners and 170 guns, but despite the loss of this port the Soviets were able to build up their forces with movements across the ice from the Kuban. Stalin and the Soviet high command urged Kozlov to great efforts in his attempts to break out of the Kerch peninsula and advance to the relief of Sevastopol, but the 44th and 51st Armies were unable to make significant headway in offensives launched on 27 February, 13 March, 26 March and 9 April.

By April the Soviets were totally exhausted, and von Manstein felt that it was time for a major effort to expel the Crimean Front so that the 11th Army could complete its operations against Sevastopol. Von Manstein thus removed as many German formations as possible from the siege of Sevastopol, which was left to LIV Corps and the Romanians, and concentrated XXX and XLII Corps against the Crimean Front, which now fielded Major General K. S. Kolganov's 47th Army in addition to the 44th and 51st Armies. Von Manstein had 6 German divisions (including the new 22nd Panzer Division) and 3 Romanian divisions for Operation 'Trappenjagd', and was supported by Generaloberst Wolfram Freiherr von Richthofen's VIII Fliegerkorps of Generaloberst Alexander Löhr's Luftflotte IV, but was still outnumbered heavily by the Soviets' 17 infantry divisions, 3 infantry brigades, 2 cavalry divisions and 4 tank brigades. The German commander thus opted for a risky plan in which his motorized forces would drive straight for Kerch through Soviet defences lacking in depth, relying on VIII Fliegerkorps for support and a number of assault boat landings on his flanks to disrupt any Soviet attempts to take his main thrust in flank.

On 8 May the Germans broke through on a 3-mile front and dashed towards Kerch, which they reached on 15 May just as the 50th Division, the 28th Gebirgsjäger Division and the 22nd Panzer Division completed the destruction of eight soviet divisions they had pinned against the Sea of Azov. XXX and XLII Corps had suffered some 7,500 casualties, but the Soviets had been driven out of the Kerch peninsula by 20 May, and had also suffered immensely heavy losses including 170,000 prisoners, 1,100 guns, 250 tanks, 3,800 vehicles and 300 aircraft. Indeed, so comprehensive was the defeat that few Soviets managed to reach the safety of the Kaman peninsula in the Kuban. Von Manstein could now devote his energies solely to the reduction of Sevastopol.

Treibjagd (driving hunt) German operation against partisans in Yugoslavia.

Trident Designation of the second inter-Allied conference held in Washington (15/25 May 1943). This was a conference of President Franklin D. Roosevelt and Prime Minister Winston Churchill, the Western Allied leaders, and their staffs to confirm earlier decisions and to clarify matters left nebulous at the Casablanca Conference. The most important problem facing the conference was the nature of Allied operations in Europe, where the USA wished to pursue as rapidly as possible the development of a direct assault on Germany by means of a cross-Channel operation, and where the UK adhered to the potentially less costly indirect approach through Europe's 'soft underbelly' with an advance through Italy to Austria and southern Germany. Thus the most important single decision of the 'Trident' Conference was an Allied commitment to launch a major offensive (Operation 'Roundhammer', soon to become Operation 'Overlord') across the English Channel against the German forces in France. The target date was 1 May 1944, and the Allies agreed to have ready some 29 divisions by that date, with facilities for reinforcements to be shipped to France at the rate of 3 to 5 divisions per month after the initial lodgement had been secured.

Agreements ancillary to this main undertaking were continued development of Operation 'Sledgehammer' for an emergency return to the continent in the event of a German collapse, and agreement on the so-called Eaker plan of Major General Ira C. Eaker for a four-phase air assault on the Germans in northern Europe (the disruption of the German military, industrial and economic system, the undermining of German morale, the whittling down of German fighter strength, and the ever-deepening penetration of German airspace by Allied aircraft engaged on these tasks). In return for their agreement on the cross-Channel operation, the British won approval from the Americans for continued operations against Italy (using forces drawn from a maximum of 27 allocated to the Mediterranean theatre for offensive and garrison duties). Other agreements were the need to bomb Ploesti from North African bases, the urgent requirement to continue the war against the German U-boat fleet with all possible strength, and British responsibility for an Allied seizure of the Azores. There was also a unanimous reaffirmation of the Casablanca decisions on the desirability of aiding the USSR, of bringing Turkey into the war and of re-equipping the French forces.

The 'Trident' Conference was concerned mainly with European matters, but the course of the war against Japan was also discussed, and here the Allies agreed an overall strategy based on a six-phase war considered without time limits and presupposing full co-operation between the Americans, British and Chinese. In the first phase the Chinese would improve their overall position in China, the Americans would open communications into the Celebes Sea, and the British (with US support) would recapture Burma. In the second phase the Americans would recapture the Philippines while the British conducted operations around the Strait of Malacca and the Chinese prepared an offensive towards Hong Kong. In the third phase the Chinese would retake Hong Kong while the British continued with their activities round the Strait of Malacca and the Americans operated in the northern half of the South China Sea. In the fourth phase the three Allied countries would prepare a massive strategic air campaign against Japan from Chinese bases. In the fifth phase this air offensive would be implemented; and in the sixth phase US forces (with British and Chinese assistance) would invade the Japanese home islands.

Within the context of this overall concept, the 'Trident' Conference adopted US proposals that air operations in and from China should be stepped up, that the USA should build up its supply effort to China from India with the aid of operations in northern Burma, that the Japanese should be expelled from the Aleutian Islands, that the Marshall and Caroline island groups should be taken in a major offensive by the forces of Admiral Chester W. Nimitz's Pacific Ocean Areas command, that the rest of the Solomons and Bismarck archipelagos should be taken, that the rest of New Guinea to be wrested from the Japanese, and that operations against Japanese lines of communication should be stepped up. At British insistence it was decided that no major land operations should be undertaken in central and southern Burma, and Operation 'Anakim' was thus postponed.

In the short term, therefore, the 'Trident' Conference' called for the continuation of Mediterranean and South-West Pacific Area operations, and the development of major operations in the central Pacific. But most important of all was the longer-term US and British commitment to Operation 'Overlord' and an all-out offensive across north-western Europe.

Trigger Allied plan to establish in the USA a model air-defence sector based on the RAF pattern that had proved so successful in 1940 and 1941.

Trinity Successful operational test of the world's first atomic device at Alamogordo, New Mexico (16 July 1945).

Trojanisches Pferd (Trojan horse) German cover plan for Operation 'Margarethe'.

Troopers Allied cable address of the British War Office.

Trueform Airborne raid by the Belgian Independent Parachute Company, SAS, against German petrol dumps at Pacy in France (17 August 1944).

Truncheon British plan for a landing at Livorno in north-west Italy (1941).

T.S. Designation of West African coastal convoys (together with a numerical suffix) plying the route from Takoradi, Gold Coast to Freetown, Sierra Leone, and inaugurated in August 1942 as successor to the short-lived L.S. series started in April 1942.

T.U. Designation of US military convoys (together with a numerical suffix) plying the route from the UK to the USA, and inaugurated in September 1943.

Tual French Force 136 airborne mission to aid Laotian resistance groups near Vientiane (February 1945).

Tube Alloys Allied codename for the atomic bomb.

Tulsa Early plan by General Douglas MacArthur's South-West Pacific Area for the capture of Rabaul (1942/3). The most important town on New Britain, Rabaul had been captured on 23 January 1942 by Major General Tomitara Horii's South Seas Detachment as the main base area for Vice Admiral Shigeyoshi Inouye's 4th Fleet (and perhaps more importantly the 24th Air Flotilla) tasked with the consolidation of Japan's defensive perimeter in the south-east Pacific, and later as the offensive/defensive core for Vice Admiral Gunichi Mikawa's 4th Fleet (plus the 25th Air Flotilla) and Lieutenant General Hitoshi Imamura's 8th Area Army. Rabaul was the key to what the Americans called the Bismarck Barrier, and blocked the Allies' primary approach routes to the Philippines and to Truk, main southern bastions of the Imperial Japanese Army and Imperial Japanese Navy respectively. US planning was thus centred initially on a twin drive towards Rabaul by MacArthur's forces in New Guinea and by Vice Admiral William F. Halsey's South Pacific Ocean Area in the Solomons, and recognizing this fact the Japanese from 24 December 1942 vested overall control of the area in Vice Admiral Ryunosuke Kusaka's South-Eastern Area Fleet (8th Fleet and 11th Air Fleet) with the support of Imamura's army forces. However, during 1943 Allied planning began to shift away from Rabaul, for operational experience had showed that the best way to deal with major Japanese bastions was to neutralize rather than destroy them, with consequent savings in Allied lives and time. Rabaul would clearly be a tough nut to crack, so the 'Quadrant' Conference of August 1943 agreed that Rabaul should be bypassed by the Allied advance, relatively small forces being left to contain the area after it had been rendered impotent by the destruction of its aircraft and the severing of Japanese lines of communication to the area.

Tungsten Attack on the German battleship *Tirpitz* by aircraft of the Fleet Air Arm (3 April 1944). This great German warship was available in Norwegian waters for attacks on Allied convoys routed round the North Cape on their way to the ports of the northern USSR, and the threat of her very presence severely curtailed the operational flexibility of Admiral Sir Bruce Fraser's Home Fleet, which had to maintain powerful forces at Scapa Flow lest the Germans attempt a foray into the Barents Sea or even into the North Atlantic. The immediate spur for Operation 'Tungsten' was the sailing of the important J.W.58 convoy just as Allied intelligence revealed that repairs to the *Tirpitz* (crippled in Operation 'Source', the midget submarine attack of September 1943) were complete. Detailed planning of 'Tungsten' was entrusted to Vice Admiral Sir Henry Moore, who had available the fleet carriers *Victorious* and *Furious* (each to carry 21 Fairey Barracuda strike aircraft and some fighters) and the escort carriers *Emperor*, *Fencer*, *Pursuer* and *Searcher* (carrying Grumman Wildcat, Grumman Hellcat and Vought Corsair fighters). Each of the strike forces was to be escorted by 40 fighters, and the *Furious* and *Fencer* maintained a reserve of fighters to protect the British ships. Of the 42 strike aircraft (of which only 40 undertook the raid), 10 each carried 1,600-lb armour-piercing bombs, 22 each carried three 500-lb semi-armour-piercing bombs and the final 10 each carried high explosive and anti-submarine bombs. The first wave of the British attack reached the target area in Kaafjord just as the *Tirpitz* was weighing anchor for steaming trials, and only minimal opposition was encountered by the strike aircraft as the escorting fighters managed to cripple most of the *Tirpitz*'s fire-control systems with gun fire. The results of the strike were the loss of 2 British aircraft (1 fighter and 1 Barracuda) in exchange for 9 bomb hits, which caused extensive but not crippling damage to the battleship. The second strike arrived once the *Tirpitz* had anchored again, and another 5 hits were scored for the loss of 2 aircraft. However, the armour-piercing bombs had been dropped from too low an altitude and failed to inflict decisive damage, so the battleship was out of action for only three months. Of the *Tirpitz*'s 438 casualties in the operation 122 had been killed. Moore had planned to repeat the raid on the following morning, but after receiving the aircrews' reports Moore decided that the *Tirpitz* was badly enough damaged not to warrant a risky second effort against alerted defences.

Turbinlite (i) Designation of US twin-engined Douglas Havoc aircraft fitted with nose-mounted searchlights and radar to illuminate German nocturnal aircraft, which would then be shot down by Hawker Hurricane fighters accompanying the 'Turbinlite' aircraft (1940/1941).

(ii) Allied scheme to provide US night-fighter units with RAF training and equipment (1942).

Twilight Version of the 'Setting Sun' concept proposed by Lieutenant General Joseph W. Stilwell, chief-of-staff to Generalissimo Chiang Kai-shek, and actually adopted by the Combined Chiefs-of-Staff planners as more practical than 'Setting Sun'. Proposed by the US Army Air Forces, 'Setting Sun' proposed to establish on Chinese bases near Changshah a force of between 10 and 20 Boeing B-29 Superfortress groups (rising eventually to 30 groups) supported initially by 2,000 and later 4,000 Consolidated B-24 bombers converted into transport aircraft to ferry supplies from India. The air force planners estimated that if five missions per month were carried out by 28 B-29 groups, Japan could be brought to her knees in six months or, more realistically, that a campaign started in October 1944 with smaller numbers (but increasing as B-29 production permitted) could permit an Allied occupation of Japan from September 1945. Evolved by Stilwell with Major General George E. Stratemeyer (commanding the Eastern Air Command, South-East Asia Air Command), Operation 'Twilight' suggested that the transport aircraft component be scaled down and that the B-29s be based near Calcutta to shuttle forward for operations to bases near Kweilin. At these advanced bases the bombers would offload excess fuel and take on bombs. The 'Twilight' plan ensured greater security for the bombers, as well as a larger measure of self-sufficiency, and would have made it possible for ten groups to begin operations by April 1945. The disadvantage of 'Twilight' compared with 'Setting Sun' was that Kweilin is 200 miles farther than Changshah from Japan. In the event 'Twilight' was superseded by Operation 'Matterhorn' based on Chengtu, some 400 miles farther still from Japan, the US reasoning being that the necessary bases could be readied in 1944 rather than 1945.

T.X. Designation of Mediterranean local convoys (together with a numerical suffix) plying the route from Tripoli, Libya to Alexandria, Egypt, and inaugurated in February 1943.

Typhoon US seizure of Sansapor at the western tip of New Guinea (30 July 1944). This virtually unopposed landing by the US 6th Infantry Division of Lieutenant General Walter Krueger's US 6th Army cost 2 American and 374 Japanese dead, and brought to a close the strategic portion of General Douglas MacArthur's South-West Pacific Area offensive along the northern coast of New Guinea, in the process opening the way for the Allied return to the Philippines after the capture of Morotai as an advanced port and forward air base area. With Sansapor in US hands some 120,000 Japanese, the remnants of seven formations (the 5th, 32nd, 35th, 36th, 46th and 48th Divisions and the 7th Air Division) of Lieutenant General Hatazo Adachi's 18th Army and of the 2nd Army within Lieutenant General K. Anami's 2nd Area Army, were isolated in New Guinea and Timor without chance of reinforcement or resupply, and were thus condemned to wait out the war in conditions of increasing malnutrition and disease.

U

U Offensive against Imphal and Kohima by Lieutenant General Renya Mutaguchi's Japanese 15th Army from central Burma (7 March/22 June 1944). Planned by Mutaguchi under the supervision of Lieutenant General Shozo Kawabe's Burma Area Army, Operation 'U' was an extremely bold effort to spoil the Allied offensive that was clearly imminent as an advance over the River Chindwin towards Mandalay, and involved the 15th Army in an all-out drive to seize the Manipur plain in which are situated Imphal and Kohima (the only logical jumping-off points for the Allied offensive) and to cut the Allied lines of communication to northern Assam, supply base for Lieutenant General Sir William Slim's 14th Army and for the Chinese and American forces commanded in northern Burma and south-western China by Lieutenant General Joseph W. Stilwell. Mutaguchi had planned such an operation for some time, and 'U' was timed to coincide with the full development of Operation 'HA' in the Arakan region, where Lieutenant General T. Sakurai had succeeded in attracting the 5th Indian, 7th Indian, 25th Indian, 26th Indian, 81st West African and 82nd West African Divisions plus a parachute brigade and a commando brigade.

The Japanese plan had been conceived on the basis of a 15th Army strength of four divisions, but Kawabe never in fact planned that Mutaguchi should have Lieutenant General K. Takeda's 53rd Division when it arrived from Formosa, and Mutaguchi's plans were further disrupted when the 15th Division (commanded by Lieutenant General M. Yamauchi until he died of malaria during the Imphal battle, and replaced by Lieutenant General U. Shibata) was delayed in Thailand, arriving tired and ill-equipped to reinforce the 15th Army only on 11 February after the personal intervention of Field Marshal Count Hisaichi Terauchi, commander-in-chief of the Southern Region. Apart from the 15th Division, Mutaguchi's other two formations were the 31st Division (commanded by Lieutenant General K. Sato) and the 33rd Division (commanded by Lieutenant General G. Yanagida until superseded for timidity early in the campaign by Lieutenant General N. Tanaka).

The Japanese commander planned a triple advance from the line of the Chindwin. In the south the 33rd Division would advance from Kalewa on 7/8 March and divide into three columns, that on the left being directed against Tiddim with the 215th Regiment, that in the centre moving against Tongzang with the 214th Regiment, and that on the right comprising Major General T. Yamamoto's 33rd Infantry Group (reinforced 213rd Regiment, plus most of the division's wheeled vehicles) to take Tamu and link with the 15th Division. With their first objectives taken the left and centre columns were to join at Tongzang and move north towards Imphal, where they would cut the track west to Silchar and rejoin the 33rd Infantry Group. In the centre of the Japanese front the 15th Division would move off from Thaungdut on 15/16 March and divide into two columns, that on the left deploying one battalion of the 60th Regiment to link up with the 33rd Division's right-hand column on the Shenam Saddle, and that on the right having the 51st Regiment plus parts of the 60th and 67th Regiments for its advance on Sangshak and then a southward advance on Imphal to cut it off from the north before destroying the 14th Army's formations in the Imphal plain. In the north the 31st Division was to depart on its 100-mile approach march from the area just to the north of Homalin on 15/16 March and divide into three columns, that on the left having Major General M. Miyazaki's 31st Infantry Group (58th and 128th Regiments) for its advance via Ukhrul to invest Kohima from the south, that in the centre having the 138th Regiment for its move to Jessami and an investment of Kohima from the east, and that on the right having one battalion of the 138th Regiment to invest Kohima from the north and prevent the arrival of Allied reinforcements from Dimapur. Thus the 33rd and 15th Divisions would tackle Imphal (the 33rd Division having most of the army's armour and heavy artillery), while the 31st Division was tasked with the elimination of Kohima (and its 4,000-ft pass on the road from Dimapur to Imphal) in the north so that Allied reinforcements could not intervene in the major battle around Imphal.

Mutaguchi expected that his 15th Army could complete Operation 'U' in some three weeks, after which the army could be supplied from captured British stocks until a road had been driven through from Kalewa to Imphal via Palel just north of the Shenam Saddle. The Japanese thus carried supplies for just the three weeks allocated by Mutaguchi to the operation. But already Kawabe was beginning to have doubts about the practicality of the undertaking, and the same sentiments were expressed by Lieutenant General Tazoe, commanding the much depleted 5th Air Division that was intended to provide air support for the 15th Army.

Facing the 15th Army Lieutenant General Sir William Slim's 14th Army (under the control of Admiral Lord Louis Mountbatten's South East Asia Command and General Sir Henry Giffard's 11th Army Group) deployed Lieutenant General G. A. P. Scoones's IV Indian Corps in the Manipur plain region, with Lieutenant General M. G. N. Stopford's XXXIII Indian Corps farther back to hold the valley of the River Brahmaputra and its communications vital to the continued Allied effort in Burma and China. IV Corps was tasked with preparing and then launching the 14th Army's eastward move across the Chindwin (Operation 'Capital'), and had three divisions, namely Major General D. T. Cowan's 17th Indian Light Division, Major General D. D. Gracey's 20th Indian Division, and Major General O. L. Roberts's 23rd Indian Division, as well as the 254th Indian Tank Brigade. At the time the Japanese were getting under way the two-brigade 17th Indian Light Division was in position round Tiddim (as far north as Tongzang and as far south as Fort White), the three-brigade 20th Indian Division was located in the Kabaw valley between Sittaung and Tamu, and the three-brigade 23rd Indian Division was in reserve at Imphal (less the 49th Indian Brigade at Ukhrul and Sangshak) with the 254th Indian Tank Brigade. The 14th Army appreciated that the tactical situation in central Burma made it possible for the Japanese to attempt a long-range infiltration campaign, but Slim wrongly estimated that the Japanese could deploy only two regiments in such an effort, and therefore raised no objection when Operation 'Thursday' was committed on 5/6 March to deliver the 3rd Indian Division for the 2nd Chindit Expedition. However, contingency plans for a Japanese offensive were in existence, Scoones intending to pull the 17th Indian Light and 20th Indian Divisions back to the Imphal plain where they could be reinforced with Major General H. R. Briggs's 5th Indian Division and Brigadier M. R. J. Hope-Thompson's 50th Indian Parachute Brigade flown in from the Arakan front. Scoones could then use these four divisions as a concentrated force with armour and overwhelming air support to crush any Japanese offensive. As the Imphal plain was being prepared as the base area for 'Capital' there were large numbers of noncombatants in the area, and Slim planned to fly out these 40,000 men in the aircraft bringing in the 5th Indian Division and 50th Indian Parachute Brigade (Operation 'Stamina').

The stage was thus set for the climactic battles of 'U', which pitted some 120,000 Allied soldiers (9 British, 16 Gurkha and 24 Indian battalions, plus 120 tanks) against just under 90,000 Japanese (26 battalions) supported by about 7,000 Indian collaborators of the Indian National Army's 1st

Division allocated to the Japanese 15th and 31st Divisions. But while the Japanese could call on no reinforcements (excluding some 4,000 men included in the Japanese total above), Scoones could call on XXXIII Indian Corps, which was much reinforced during the campaign and eventually comprised Major General J. M. L. Grover's British 2nd Division, Major General F. W. Messervy's 7th Indian Division, Brigadier L. E. C. M. Perowne's 23rd Indian Brigade (from the 3rd Indian Division), Brigadier W. I. Nonweiler's 3rd Special Service Brigade and Brigadier P. C. Marindin's Lushai Brigade, in all some 75,000 men (3 Gurkha, 11 Indian and 20 British battalions) plus the armour of the 149th Regiment, Royal Armoured Corps.

The key to the defence of Imphal and Kohima by IV Indian Corps was timely withdrawal and concentration when the Japanese attacked, especially as the 17th Indian Light Division had to fall back about 100 miles. Scoones and Slim were surprised by the strength and speed of the Japanese advance, but managed to pull back the 17th Indian Light and 20th Indian Divisions in good order, though two brigades of the 23rd Indian Division were sensibly detached south to aid the 17th Indian Light Division. The Japanese 31st Division cut off Kohima on 4 April, and Imphal was invested by the Japanese 15th and 33rd Divisions on 5 April. Already the schedule fixed by Mutaguchi was slipping, and this was to bedevil the Japanese as they ran out of food, ammunition and medicine. By this time the movement of the 5th Indian Division from the Arakan front was well under way, the division coming under command of IV Indian Corps on 19 March less its 161st Indian Brigade under Brigadier D. F. W. Warren at Kohima under command of XXXIII Indian Corps.

The Japanese 31st Division completed its investment of Kohima on 7 April and there followed a tiny but exceptionally bitter 12-day battle in this small but very precipitous region as the Japanese 58th Regiment tried to take Kohima and as the Japanese 138th Regiment attempted to overrun the west of the 161st Indian Brigade at Jotsoma on the road to Dimapur. Help was on its way as Stopford pushed forward his British 2nd Division with its British 5th Brigade in the lead. On 14 April the British 5th Brigade overwhelmed the Japanese roadblock at Zubza and pushed on to relieve the 161st Indian Brigade at Jotsoma. By 18 April the brigade had pushed past two more roadblocks and relieved Kohima. Once the garrison had been reinforced and resupplied, the 5th Brigade pulled back as part of the British 2nd Division's effort to take the Japanese 31st Division in a pincer movement beginning on 26 April with the 5th Brigade on the left and the 6th Brigade on the right. The move was only partially successful, the 5th Brigade again linking up with the Kohima garrison on 27 April but the 4th Brigade being held on Mount Pulebadze and taking GPT Ridge at the south of Kohima only on 4 May.

By now the Japanese 58th Regiment had been reinforced by the 124th Regiment. Between 4 and 7 May the battle in Kohima was taken over by the 6th Brigade (British 2nd Division) and 33rd Indian Brigade (7th Indian Division), but these two brigades failed to take the Japanese line between the District Commissioner's Bungalow and Jail Hill. The attack was renewed on 11 May and the position fell on 13 May. Between 15 and 31 May the 33rd Indian Brigade was heavily repulsed on Gun Spur and Hunters Hill in the Naga Village to the north-east of Kohima, and between 25 and 28 May a similar fate befell the British 2nd Division on the Aradura Spur to the south of Kohima. Finally the 7th Indian Division broke through the Japanese line near the Naga Village on 1 June, allowing the 5th Brigade to outflank the Aradura Spur on 5 June and so render the Japanese position untenable. But already (31 May) the Japanese had begun to pull back, and the British 2nd Division pushed south towards Imphal.

All this while IV Indian Corps had been involved in desperate fighting against the Japanese 15th and 33rd Divisions. Scoones's tactical plan was based upon the Allied retention of fortified boxes round each supply dump and the six airfields, using his 4 divisions, 1 parachute brigade and 1 armoured brigade supported by the formidable tactical air support afforded by the 27 fighter and fighter-bomber squadrons of Air Marshal Sir John Baldwin's 3rd Tactical Air

Force at the disposal of the corps. Even so, the original IV Indian Corps' defence perimeter had to be contracted to an inner perimeter with the 5th Indian and 23rd Indian Divisions holding the north-east sector against the Japanese 15th Division and the 20th Indian and 17th Indian Light Divisions holding the south-east and south sectors against the Japanese 33rd Division. Despite this the Japanese were able to penetrate the defence with attacks towards Sengmai, Nunshigum, Palel and Ningthoukhong. Imphal was besieged for 88 days, and it was only on 22 June that the 5th Indian Division was able to break out and link up with the British 2nd Division at Milestone 107 just north of the Imphal perimeter.

The Japanese were now exhausted, and what was left of the 15th Army started to pull back to the Chindwin. Yet the Allies were unable to break the Japanese, and despite the loss of some 53,500 men (including 30,500 dead) Mutaguchi was able to return to his start line against an indifferent pursuit. Allied casualties had been 16,700, about one-quarter of them at Kohima. After the battle IV Indian Corps was pulled back to India with its 17th Indian Light and 20th Indian Divisions, and XXXIII Indian Corps (British 2nd, 5th Indian, 23rd Indian and 11th East African Divisions) took over the pursuit to the Chindwin, which the Allies reached only during the early part of December 1944.

U.C. Designation of ocean outbound convoys (together with a numerical suffix) plying the route from the UK to the Caribbean, and inaugurated in February 1943 as special tanker convoys.

U.G. Designation of military convoys (together with a numerical suffix) plying the route from the USA to North Africa, and inaugurated in October 1942 for the delivery of troops allocated to Operation 'Torch'.

Undergo Reduction of the Calais pocket by Major General Spry's 3rd Canadian Division (25 September/1 October 1944). The clearance of the coast between Dieppe and Antwerp was allocated to Lieutenant General G. G. Simonds's II Canadian Corps of Lieutenant General Sir Henry Crerar's Canadian 1st Army after Hitler had instructed Generaloberst Hans von Salmuth's 15th Army to hold the Channel ports indefinitely. The defence was entrusted to a mixed bag of 7,500 German troops commanded by Oberstleutnant Schröder. A Canadian assault on 24 September failed after 600 of 900 heavy bombers failed to lay the required carpet of bombs through the defences, but on 30 September/1 October a second assault proved successful.

Undertone Offensive by the US 3rd and 7th Armies south of the River Mosel to clear the 'Saar-Palatinate triangle' as the third stage of the Allies' advance to the River Rhine (12/21 March 1945). The operation was originally schemed as a limited advance through the hitherto untouched 'Siegfried Linie' defences in the sector held by Lieutenant General Alexander M. Patch's US 7th Army within Lieutenant General Jacob L. Devers US 6th Army Group, the object being to pierce the 'Siegfried Linie' between Saarbrücken and Haguenau and then advance as far north-east as Kaiserslautern using the army's 12 divisions allocated (from north to south) to Major General Frank W. Milburn's US XXI Corps, Major General Wade H. Haislip's US XV Corps and Major General Edward H. Brooks's US VI Corps at the US 7th Army's junction with General d'Armée Jean de Lattre de Tassigny's French 1st Army. Complicated political and military considerations then intervened, and a limited supporting role originally entrusted on the US 7th Army's northern flank to Lieutenant General George S. Patton's US 3rd Army of Lieutenant General Omar N. Bradley's 12th Army Group was developed into the major portion of the offensive, now designed to witness the US 7th Army's offensive in the south to breach the 'Siegfried Linie' and so pin the German forces in the sector while Patton's forces flooded forward over the northern half of the 'Saar-Palatinate triangle' to secure the line of the Rhine between Koblenz and Ludwigshafen after the energetic US commander had (in the space of a mere five days) shifted the weight of his army south from Brohl and Koblenz on the Rhine to Cochem and Nette on the Mosel.

Undertone

The 'Saar-Palatinate triangle' was a major German salient jutting into the Allied line south of the Mosel, and was held by SS Oberstgruppenführer Paul Hausser's Army Group 'G' at the express instructions of Adolf Hitler, who refused to take the advice of his advisers that the army group should be pulled back from the 'Siegfried Linie' to the better defensive line offered by the Rhine. Germany had invested enormous energies and resources to the construction of the 'Siegfried Linie', and Hitler would hear of no withdrawal from its supposedly impregnable defences. Hausser had originally controlled three armies, but the 19th Army had been placed under direct control of the Oberkommando der Wehrmacht after its evacuation of the Colmar pocket. Hausser thus controlled in the south General Hans Felber's 7th Army (LXXXIX, XIII and LXXX Corps, and commanded temporarily by General Hans von Obstfelder) and in the south General Hermann Foertsch's 1st Army (LXXXII, LXXXV, XIII SS and XC Corps). Though formidable on paper, these formations were drastically understrength and poorly trained, and the German forces in the sector (from south to north the 19th, 1st and 7th Armies) had only 13 divisions with which to face 1 French and 21 American divisions. The best of the German divisions were Generalleutnant Hans Degen's 2nd Gebirgsdivision and SS Gruppenführer Karl-Heinrich Brenner's 6th SS Gebirgsdivision.

The main weight of Operation 'Undertone' was allocated to the US 3rd Army, which deployed Major General Troy H. Middleton's two-division US VIII Corps to keep watch on Koblenz, Major General Manton S. Eddy's US XII Corps (5th, 76th, 89th and 9th Infantry Divisions, and 4th and 11th Armored Divisions) in the centre (against the left wing of the German 7th Army) with Bingen and Bad-Kreuznach as its objectives, and Major General Walton H. Walker's US XX Corps (26th, 80th and 94th Infantry Divisions, and 10th Armored Division) on the right (against the right wing of the German 1st Army) with Kaiserslautern as its objective behind the sector of the 'Siegfried Linie' held by the rest of the German 1st Army against the US 7th Army, which was to pin these German forces as the US XX Corps swept into their rear.

The 'Undertone' offensive was launched on 12 March, and by 14 March the US XII Corps had secured a bridgehead over the Mosel at Treis with its 5th and 90th Infantry Divisions, permitting Eddy to loose the 4th and 11th Armored Divisions towards Worms (via Bad Kreuznach and Kirn respectively) through the sketchy defences of General Gustav Hoehne's LXXXIX Corps and Generalleutnant Ralph Graf von Oriola's XIII Corps. The only serious problem encountered was Generalmajor M. von Lauchert's 2nd Panzer Division, which troubled the 4th Armored Division near Bad Kreuznach. The US XX Corps had also broken through General Walter Hahm's German LXXXII Corps in its sector south of Trier with the 26th, 80th and 94th Infantry Divisions, allowing Walker to send forward his 10th Armored Division (supplemented from 17 March by the 12th Armored Division from the US 7th Army) in the direction of Kaiserslautern and Ludwigshafen. By 19 March the 4th Armored Division was just 12 miles south-west of Mainz and the 10th and 12th Armored Divisions were 15 miles from Kaiserslautern. Two days later the 90th Infantry Division was taking Mainz, the 4th Armored Division was in Worms, the 11th Armored Division was advancing south of Worms, the 12th Armored Division was in Ludwigshafen and the 10th Armored Division was approaching Landau. The US 3rd Army, with the able and timely support of Major General Otto P. Weyland's XIX Tactical Air Command, had driven through the 'bad tank country' of the Hunsdruck area with commendable speed and very light losses.

The US 7th Army got under way on 15 March, and even with the support of Brigadier General Glenn O. Barcus's XII Tactical Air Command faced an altogether more difficult task. On the right of the army's operational area the US VI Corps had to retake the ground lost in the Germans' Operation 'Nordwind', and General Erich Petersen's German XC Corps delayed VI Corps for four days before the Americans could close up to the 'Siegfried Linie' defences behind the River Lauter. It then took another three days for VI Corps to break through between Wissem-

313

bourg and Pirmasens, even with the support of the US 14th Armored Division from 18 March.

Greater success attended the efforts of the six-division XV Corps against SS Gruppenführer Max Simon's XIII SS Corps and of the XXI Corps against General Baptist Kniess's German LXXXV Corps. The US 45th Infantry Division secured a breakthrough at Uttweiler, and the US 6th Armored Division was thus able to exploit in the direction of Kaiserlautern from 20 March after the fall of Zweibrücken. Operation 'Undertone' was capped on the night of 22/23 March when units of the US 5th Infantry Division secured a bridgehead across the Rhine opposite Oppenheim. Two days later the US XII and XX Corps had passed five divisions over the Rhine and were developing their advance towards Aschaffenburg and Hanau.

Unity Allied cable address for the headquarters of General Dwight D. Eisenhower.

Unternehmen 25 (operation 25) Alternative designation for the German seizure of Yugoslavia (6/17 April 1941), otherwise known as Operation 'Marita'.

Uranus Soviet offensive to cut off and encircle the German forces attacking Stalingrad (19/30 November 1942). While General A. I. Eremenko's Stalingrad Front was supporting the efforts of Lieutenant General V. I. Chuikov's Soviet 62nd Army in Stalingrad against the forces of Generaloberst Friedrich Paulus (the German 6th Army and part of Generaloberst Hermann Hoth's 4th Panzerarmee), Stalin and the Soviet high command were concerned not only with the defeat of this local effort but with the wholesale destruction of the German forces supporting the Stalingrad offensive, and thus reversing the overall course of the war on the Eastern Front up to this time, which had for the most part been characterized by German strategic initiative. Operation 'Uranus' was planned to reverse this trend, and was developed in Moscow from the early part of September 1942 even as the German forces were closing on Stalingrad. Overall co-ordination was entrusted to General Georgi Zhukov, ably backed by Lieutenant General A. M. Vasilevsky and General N. N. Voronov. The Soviet high command appreciated that the weakest points in the Axis salient stretching towards Stalingrad were the flanks, which were held in the west by Colonel General P. Dumitrescu's Romanian 3rd Army and in the south by General C. A. Constantinescu's Romanian 4th Army under the control of Generalfeldmarschall Maximilian Freiherr von Weichs's Army Group 'B' to support the main offensive effort by the German 4th Panzerarmee and 6th Army. The Soviets planned that their vast double enveloping movement would be launched in mid-November to coincide with the Anglo-American landings of Operation 'Torch' and the arrival of the winter's first frosts.

In the north Lieutenant General N. F. Vatutin's South-West Front and Lieutenant General K. K. Rokossovsky's Don Front were to sweep south and north-east from Serafimovich and Kletskaya on the River Don against the Romanian 3rd Army, and in the east the Stalingrad Front was to drive west and north-west from the Sarpa lakes through the junction of the Romanian 4th Army (Romanian VII Corps) and the right wing of the 4th Panzerarmee (Romanian VI Corps). The two thrusts were intended to meet near Kalach on the Don west of Stalingrad, and cut off the 4th Panzerarmee and the 6th Army. The main thrusts were based on the use of substantial mobile forces in the South-West and Stalingrad Fronts, comprising respectively Lieutenant General D. D. Lelyushenko's 1st Guards, Lieutenant General P. L. Romanenko's 5th Tank and Major General I. M. Chistyakov's 21st Armies, and Lieutenant General M. S. Shumilov's 64th, Major General F. I. Tolbukhin's 57th and Major General N. I. Trufanov's 51st Armies. The primary mobile formations of the South-West Front were the 5th Tank Army (I and XXVI Tank Corps, VIII Cavalry Corps and six infantry divisions), III Guards Cavalry Corps and IV Tank Corps, while the mobile formations of the Stalingrad Front were IV and XIII Mechanized Corps, and IV Cavalry Corps. Completing the Soviet line-up was the Don Front, which supported the inner flank of the South-West Front against the German XI and VIII Corps of the 6th

Army with Lieutenant General P. A. Batov's 65th, Major General I. V. Galinin's 24th and Lieutenant General A. S. Zhadov's 66th Armies.

Soviet strength was more than 1,000,000 men, 13,500 guns and mortars, and 100 rocket batteries. The movement of these vast resources through the autumn mud was a formidable logistical undertaking, but the six Soviet air armies allocated to 'Uranus' under the control of General A. A. Novikov were generally successful in preventing German reconnaissance aircraft from discovering too much, even when the Soviets had to build some 500 ferry points between Saratov and Astrakhan to move men, *matériel* and supplies into the assault areas. As the Soviet preparations were completed Zhukov was moved to the Kalinin and West Fronts to supervise the offensive they were to launch as a means of pinning the German forces of Generalfeldmarschall Günther von Kluge's Army Group 'Centre' in that theatre. Vasilevsky remained in the south to co-ordinate the efforts of the South-West, Don and Stalingrad Fronts in 'Uranus'.

The first heavy frost of winter was recorded on 1 November, and from this time the Germans began to worry increasingly about the vulnerability of their position on the Don, especially as no German reinforcements were available except by halting the offensive of Generalfeldmarschall Wilhelm List's Army Group 'A' in the Caucasus. This feeling of Axis insecurity was reinforced by the discovery that Soviet artillery on the north bank of the Don was being strengthened, and that even local air superiority was passing from the 400 aircraft of Generaloberst Wolfram Freiherr von Richthofen's VIII Fliegerkorps of Luftflotte IV to the 1,200 aircraft available to the four Soviet air armies facing VIII Fliegerkorps.

The Soviets launched 'Uranus' at 07.30 on 19 November as the German high command and Hitler were worrying about the development of an air-head and beach-head in Tunisia to oppose the Allied 1st Army moving rapidly east from the 'Torch' landings. The first Soviet forces to move were the 5th Tank Army and 1st Guards Army of the South-West Front, which smashed forward from the Don bridgehead at Serafimovich against the Romanian 3rd Army. The 21st Army also advanced from its bridgehead at Kletskaya some 30 miles to the east with the support of the 65th Army of the Don Front. The Germans wrongly assessed the relative strength of the two initial Soviet moves, and the 14th Panzer Division (6th Army) and Generalleutnant Ferdinand Heim's XLVIII Panzer Corps were at first committed against the Kletskaya advance as the Serafimovich assault made rapid inroads into the defences of the Romanian 3rd Army. XLVIII Panzer Corps was then switched from a north-east to a north-west advance to support the Romanians, but it was too late by the time the corps encountered the 5th Tank Army on 20 November and was pushed back, in the process losing touch with its Romanian armoured division.

By now the nature of the whole strategic threat was apparent to von Weichs, who first ordered the 6th Army to turn round its mobile formations and then its whole effort in preparation for a breakout before the Soviet pincer closed fully. Hitler was furious with von Weichs, and ordered Paulus to continue his offensive against Stalingrad without thought for a breakout. Hitler's only concession was that General Hans Hube's XIV Panzer Corps could co-ordinate the efforts of Paulus's only three armoured formations (14th, 16th and 24th Panzer Divisions) in the westward counteroffensive across the Don in a hopeless attempt to halt the 5th Tank Army, which had advanced some 60 miles to the River Liska (only 20 miles from its objective at Kalach) by 22 November.

On the night of 22/23 November a Soviet *coup-de-main* party took the vital bridge at Kalach in preparation for the arrival of IV and XXVI Tank Corps. On 23 November the five surviving divisions of the encircled Romanian 3rd Army surrendered in the area of Raspopinskaya, and the leading elements of IV Tank Corps met their counterparts of IV Mechanized Corps (of the Stalingrad Front's 51st Army) on the River Karpovka just west of Sovetskiy. The Stalingrad Front's offensive had begun on 20 November and pushed through the junction of the Romanian 4th Army and 4th Panzerarmee without difficulty for its meeting with the South-West Front. The 6th Army was now cut off in

Ursula

Stalingrad, but the Soviet cordon was not yet firm enough to prevent a German breakout, and as the Soviet armies consolidated and expanded their positions Hitler was urged to order the 6th Army's immediate withdrawal. But Reichsmarschall Hermann Goering intervened with the promise that the Luftwaffe could supply all the beleaguered forces' requirements at the rate of 500 tons per day, and Hitler decided that the formations under Paulus should stand and fight where they were. By 30 November the Soviets had completed their offensive with the establishment of a net round the 6th Army, and the formation of defensive positions to check the German counteroffensive (Operation 'Wintergewitter') that would clearly be launched to relieve the Stalingrad garrison.

Ursula Designation of two German offensives against Soviet partisans operating in the region of Rogachev (12/15 February 1943).

U.S. Designation of Indian Ocean convoys (together with a numerical suffix) plying the route from Australia to the Middle East, and inaugurated in January 1940 to bring Australian troops into the Middle East as replacements for British troops required in Europe.

U.T. Designation of US military convoys (together with a numerical suffix) plying the route from the USA to the UK, and inaugurated in August 1943 to ferry US troops across the Atlantic in preparation for Operation 'Overlord'.

Utah Designation of the assault beach on the eastern side of the Cotentin peninsula for Major General Raymond O. Barton's US 4th Infantry Division in Operation 'Overlord' (6 June 1944). Operating as the lead element of Major General J. Lawton Collins's US VII Corps within Lieutenant General Omar N. Bradley's US 1st Army of Field Marshal Sir Bernard Montgomery's 21st Army Group, the 4th Infantry Division was tasked with landing its 8th, 22nd and 12th Infantry Regiments between Les Dunes de Varreville and Pouppeville and advancing inland through the defences of the German 919th Regiment and 6th Parachute Regiment to relieve the US 82nd and 101st Airborne Divisions dropped in the previous night. The object of the landing was to extend the Allied beachhead to the west of the natural barrier formed by the River Vire as a means of facilitating an advance on Cherbourg and its vital port facilities.

Utopia Original version of Operation 'Maurice', the British landings at Andalsnes in central Norway as the southern part of the pincer movement designed to recapture Trondheim. Operation 'Utopia' was a preliminary undertaking in which Royal Navy parties secured the town and its port facilities in advance of the 'Maurice' landings.

V

Valediction Initial Allied plan for a drive to the River Rhine (late 1944), subsequently redefined as Operation 'Veritable'. This operation was planned within the overall strategic concept for the 12th and 21st Army Groups enunciated by General Dwight D. Eisenhower, the Allied supreme commander in Europe, at an inter-Allied military conference held at Brussels on 18 October 1944. Eisenhower's scheme was based on a destruction of the German forces west of the Rhine, followed by wide-front crossings of this river in preparation for a mobile exploitation to the east with early emphasis on the crushing of the Ruhr defences and development into the North German plain. The part allocated to Field Marshal Sir Bernard Montgomery's 21st Army Group was at first north of the Ruhr, and within this sector Montgomery allocated the thrust between the Rivers Maas and Rhine from Nijmegen to Lieutenant General Sir Henry Crerar's Canadian 1st Army as Operation 'Valediction'. The US centre of gravity was later shifted south by the commitment of the US 1st and 3rd Armies to the elimination of the Germans' Operation 'Herbstnebel', and the Ruhr became a 21st Army Group responsibility, so 'Valediction' was recast as 'Veritable'.

Vanguard Initial version (mid-1944) of Operation 'Dracula' for the capture of Rangoon in Burma by amphibious and airborne assault, leading to a northward exploitation as far north as Pegu. This original plan was conceived as an alternative to Operation 'Capital', and was designed to sever the Burma Area Army's main lines of communication (except the roads through Chiengrai and Kengtung) and so force the Japanese to abandon northern and central Burma. Admiral Lord Louis Mountbatten's South-East Asia Command proposed to launch 'Vanguard' in January 1945 at the same time that a cut-back 'Capital' was launched in the north.

Varsity Allied airborne crossing of the River Rhine (24 March 1945) in conjunction with Operation 'Plunder', the assault crossing of this river between Rees and Emmerich by the British 2nd and US 9th Armies. Operation 'Varsity' was planned with considerable skill, for it was appreicated by the 21st Army Group under Field Marshal Viscount Montgomery that the German 1st Parachute Army of General Alfred Schlemm (within Generaloberst Johannes Blaskowitz's Army Group 'H') would expect an Allied airborne assault on the eastern bank of the Rhine to secure an interim bridgehead for the main amphibious crossing. Lieutenant General Lewis H. Brereton's Allied 1st Airborne Army thus decided with Montgomery's support to land its designated formation (Major General Matthew B. Ridgway's XVIII Airborne Corps) in mid-morning, some time after the amphibious crossing had been committed, and comparatively deep in the German rear area (near Hamminkeln and to the east of the Diesfordterwald) so that Major General E. Bols's British 6th Airborne Division and Major General William E. Miley's US 17th Airborne Division could cut the German lines of communication to the amphibious bridgehead (by holding the line of the River Issel just to the east of Hamminkeln and so isolating the battlefield from the

317

intervention of Schlemm's reserve, XLVII Panzer Corps with one Panzer and one Panzergrenadier division) and also take the German defence in rear.

The transport of this substantial force of 21,700 men was undertaken by the US IX Troop Carrier Command, and involved 1,696 powered aircraft and 1,348 gliders. The British 6th Airborne Division departed from 11 airfields in south-east England, and the US 17th Airborne Division was lifted from a complex of 17 airfields inside the rectangle bounded by Orléans, Evreux, Amiens and Reims. The transport fleet was escorted by 889 fighters, and the powerful German Flak defences (710 light and 115 heavy guns) were neutralized by Allied aircraft and artillery so that only 53 aircraft (most of them highly vulnerable Curtiss C-46 Commando twin-engined transports) and 40 gliders were lost.

The landings were made in the sector held by the German 84th Division of LXXXVI Corps, and took the Germans completely by surprise. The British landed in the north, Brigadier James Hill's 3rd Parachute Brigade coming down near Bergen on the eastern side of the Diesfordterwald, Brigadier Nigel Poett's 5th Parachute Brigade just north-west of Hamminkeln, and Brigadier R. H. Bellamy's 6th Air Landing Brigade to the south-west of Hammilkeln. The Americans landed in the south, Colonel Edson Raff's 507th Parachute Infantry Regiment landing close to the eastern bank of the Rhine between Bislich and Wesle, the 513rd Parachute Infantry Regiment to the north-east of Fluren, and the 194th Glider Infantry Regiment to the north of Wesel. The two airborne divisions landed with considerable accuracy and were able to secure all their objectives against slight opposition. By mid-afternoon the two divisions had been relieved by Allied formations advancing from the river bridgehead, and for the relatively high losses of 347 killed and 731 wounded (British 6th Airborne Division) plus 400 killed and 522 wounded (US 17th Airborne Division) the Allied XVIII Airborne Corps took some 3,789 German prisoners and greatly eased the advance from the bridgehead.

Vellum US military mission to Venezuela (1942).

Velvet Allied plan for the air support of the USSR's southern flank with aircraft and personnel moved into the theatre from Persia (1943).

Venerable Recapture of Bordeaux in south-western France by the French (14 April 1945). An important port at the mouth of the River Gironde, Bordeaux had been the headquarters of General Kurt von der Chevallerie's German 1st Army at the time of Operation 'Overlord', and as its forces were drawn north for the Normandy battle and then pulled out to avoid being outflanked by the advance of Lieutenant General Jacob L. Devers 6th Army Group after Operation 'Dragoon', it was ordered to leave a garrison sufficient to hold Bordeaux to the end.

Venezia (Venice) German offensive in the Battle of Gazala (26/27 May 1942). The battle was launched by Generaloberst Erwin Rommel's Panzerarmee Afrika after it had advanced to the Gazala Line in pursuit of Lieutenant General N. M. Ritchie's British 8th Army, which had itself pushed Rommel's German and Italian forces back to El Agheila at the end of December 1941. Reckoning that the Axis forces would be incapable of offensive action for some time to come, Ritchie with the approval of General Sir Claude Auchinleck (Commander-in-Chief Middle East) dispersed his front-line units for refitting, leaving only light forces to keep watch on the El Agheila position. However, the Allied interdiction of Axis supply lines across the Mediterranean by Malta-based air and naval forces had been reduced in capability by severe Axis air raids on the island, and Rommel was thus able to recoup his strength more quickly than the British had anticipated. With the Deutsches Afrika Korps in the van, the Germans and Italians pushed forward again on 21 January 1942, and by 5/6 February had driven the disorganized 8th Army back to the Gazala Line covering the bastion of Tobruk.

The British defensive line consisted of a series of wire-protected minefields, running from the coast just west of Gazala south to Bir Hacheim, and covering powerful defensive 'keeps' each manned by one brigade of Lieutenant General W. H. E. Gott's British

XIII Corps with the tactical object of breaking up any Axis frontal assault. An Axis armoured move round the southern flank of the Gazala Line was clearly possible (such a tactic being one of Rommel's favourite operational strategems), and to this end the armoured formations of Lieutenant General C. W. M. Norrie's British XXX Corps were held in reserve behind the Gazala Line.

With his forces tired by their rapid advance, and once again short of fuel, Rommel could not launch an immediate attack on the Gazala position, and it was May before the Axis commanders could contemplate a resumption of the offensive. Rommel planned to launch an outflanking movement in the south (round the desert flank of the Bir Hacheim 'keep' garrisoned by Général de Brigade J.-P. Koenig's 1st Free French Brigade) with his mobile forces, consisting of the 90th Light Division, the Deutsches Afrika Korps (15th and 21st Panzer Divisions) and the Italian XX Corps (Ariete and Trieste Divisions). To pin the British along their front Rommel allocated Generalleutnant Ludwig Cruewell's extemporized Gruppe Cruewell, consisting of the Italian X Corps (Pavia and Brescia Divisions) and the Italian XXI Corps (Trento and Sabratha Divisions) reinforced with some German units.

Facing this Gruppe Cruewell were the six brigade 'keeps' of Major General D. H. Pienaar's 1st South African Division and Major General W. H. C. Ramsden's British 50th Division of XIII Corps, with the 276 Valentine and Matilda tanks of the 1st and 32nd Army Tank Brigades in support, and farther back to deal with the outflanking development were Major General H. Lumsden's British 1st Armoured Division and Major General F. W. Messervy's British 7th Armoured Division of XXX Corps, these two armoured formations being fronted by the 1st Free French Brigade and the 3rd Indian Motorized Brigade to the south-east of the French. In Tobruk (but part of XIII Corps) were Major General H. B. Klopper's 2nd South African Division and the 9th Indian Brigade. Ritchie had some 125,000 men and 994 tanks, supported by about 320 serviceable aircraft, while Rommel disposed of 113,000 men and 560 tanks, supported by about 500 aircraft.

Gruppe Cruewell started its pinning attack during the afternoon of 26 May, and at 21.00 on the same day Rommel led his mobile forces off to the south-east. The only untoward incident was the loss of the Trieste Division, which turned north-east too soon and blundered into the British 150th Brigade's 'keep' near Sidi Muftah rather than passing round the south of Bir Hacheim. The rest of Rommel's force moved on as planned, and by the morning of 27 May was pushing back the 3rd Indian Motorized Brigade, the British 7th Motorized Brigade and the British 4th Armoured Brigade as it swung north-east towards El Adem and the area south of Tobruk. But as Rommel's force moved across the Sidra Ridge between the 150th Brigade and 201st Guards Brigade it was taken in both flanks by British armour (the 1st Army Tank Brigade in the west, and the 2nd and 22nd Armoured Brigades in the east), losing about one-third of its tanks. Rommel's operational development was also seriously hampered by shortage of fuel, for the German commander had relied on supplies reaching him over the Trigh Capuzzo and the Trigh el Abd, which passed through the 150th Brigade's 'keep', whose existence had been unknown to Axis intelligence at the beginning of Operation 'Venezia'. Rommel was halted for two days, and on 30 May decided to discontinue his advance north in favour of a tactical withdrawal into the Sidi Muftah area, which came to be called 'the Cauldron' for the bloody battles fought here between 30 May and 2 June, when the 150th Brigade was destroyed (allowing the delivery of fuel to the Axis tanks) as Rommel awaited the British armoured counterattack. This materialized on 5/6 June and was easily repulsed by the Axis armour. After a titanic defence at Bir Hacheim the 1st Free French Brigade was forced to pull back on 10/11 June, and on 11 June Rommel smashed his way out of 'the Cauldron' to the south before wheeling north-east and driving off piecemeal British counterattacks. Ritchie had to abandon the Gazala position, and on 18 June the Axis forces surrounded Tobruk, which surrendered on 21 June.

Veracity I Abortive Bomber Command

Veracity II

raid against German naval units in Brest (18 December 1941).

Veracity II Abortive Bomber Command raid against German naval units in Brest (31 December 1941).

Veritable British and Canadian offensive between the Rivers Maas and Rhine (8/21 February 1945). The operation was first schemed as Operation 'Valediction', and was changed to Operation 'Veritable' after a directive to Field Marshal Viscount Montgomery's 21st Army Group by General Dwight D. Eisenhower (Allied supreme commander in Europe) on 31 December. The progress of the Allies against Germany had been delayed by the need to crush the German pocket around Colmar and to deal with Operation 'Herbstnebel' in the Ardennes, and Eisenhower now instructed Montgomery that once the US 1st and 3rd Armies of the US 12th Army Group had advanced from Prum to Bonn and thus reached the Rhine, to the north of these US formations the 21st Army Group, with the US 9th Army under command, would undertake 'Veritable' with the objects of taking the Reichswald region (opening access to Germany from the Netherlands along the corridor between the Maas and Rhine) and advancing to the western bank of the Rhine between Emmerich and Düsseldorf in preparation for Operation 'Plunder', the assault crossing of the Rhine by the 21st Army Group.

Montgomery hoped that he would receive the support of 16 US divisions in 5 corps (13 divisions in 4 corps of the US 9th Army and 3 divisions in 1 corps to be allocated to the British 2nd Army), but signally failed to allow for the fact that Lieutenant General Omar N. Bradley would be unable to release so many divisions while his 12th Army Group was undertaking the offensive from Prum to Bonn ordained in Eisenhower's 31 December directive. At the same time Lieutenant General William H. Simpson was involved in Operation 'Grenade' to push his US 9th Army forward from the region of Geilenkirchen to the Rhine around Düsseldorf. Montgomery was also faced with severe tactical and operational difficulties as the Reichswald was lacking in room for manoeuvre, so Lieutenant General Sir Henry Crerar's Canadian 1st Army (reinforced with Lieutenant General Sir Brian Horrocks's British XXX Corps detached from the British 2nd Army) was tasked with a narrow-front assault on well-prepared German positions held by General Alfred Schlemm's 1st Parachute Army of Generaloberst Johannes Blaskowitz's Army Group 'H'. The approaches to the Reichswald were held by some 10,000 men of the 84th Division, dug in along a 7-mile front west of Grave and Nijmegen and supported by the 7th Parachute Division, with the 116th Panzer and 15th Panzergrenadier Divisions (XLVII Panzer Corps) farther back in mobile reserve.

'Veritable' began with heavy bomber bombardments of the communications leading to the assault area, so isolating the battlefield, and the German defences were then softened up by a massive artillery bombardment by 1,000 guns, this effort being supported by the attacks of Air Marshal Sir Arthur Coningham's 2nd Tactical Air Force. At 10.30 the British XXX Corps moved forward with five divisions (the British 15th, 51st and 53rd Divisions, plus the Canadian 2nd and 3rd Divisions) in the line and another two (the British 43rd and Guards Armoured Divisions) in reserve. In overall terms Horrocks had some 200,000 men and 35,000 vehicles for one of the most difficult battles of the north-west European campaign. The German high command had, despite warnings from Schlemm, not believed that an offensive could be launched in the area, where the spring thaw had just turned the ground to mud, and where the German left was covered by the Reichswald forest and the right by flooded areas.

XXX Corps advanced remorselessly, and by the end of the day the German 84th Division was close to breaking point after losing considerable ground and 1,300 prisoners. By 13 February the Canadian 1st Army had pushed past the Reichswald (where German resistance continued until 16 February, costing the British and Canadians heavy losses) to take Kleve just before the 7th Parachute Division arrived to occupy this ideally located defensive position as the advance guard of XLVII Panzer Corps, which Generalfeldmarschall Gerd von Rundstedt, the German *Oberbefehlshaber West*, had located too far south in the belief that 'Grenade' would offer greater problems than 'Veritable'. On 13 February the British 43rd Division stormed past Kleve towards Udem and Goch, where some of the war's bloodiest fighting was recorded. Reinforced from across the Maas by the British 42nd Division and 11th Armoured Division, XXX Corps and Lieutenant General G. G. Simonds's II Canadian Corps continued to push south against strengthening German resistance as the German 346th Division and Panzer-Lehr Division were committed. Operation 'Veritable' ended on 21 February with the capture of Goch, leaving the next phase of the assault towards the Rhine (Operation 'Blockbuster') to follow on 26 February.

Verrat (treason) German attempt to capture the Greek partisan leader Colonel Napoleon Zervas, commander of the Greek Democratic National Army (EDES).

Vert (green) Plan designed and implemented by the resistance faction within the French railway organization (with the support of the Office of Strategic Services and of the Special Operations Executive) to disrupt the rail network at the time of Operation 'Overlord' to hinder the movement of German reinforcements for the Normandy front (6 June 1944).

Vesuvius French recapture of Corsica (11 September/4 October 1943). It had been decided by the Allied leaders at the Quebec Conference that Sardinia and Corsica should be recaptured only after Italy had left the war and the Allies had established air bases in the area of Rome, but this Allied schedule was perturbed by German decisions, for Operation 'Achse' included the provision that German forces on Sardinia should be evacuated to Corsica in the event of an Italian defection, and that Corsica would then be held by this useful combined strength of the Brigade Reichsführer-SS and one battalion of the 15th Panzergrenadier Division (already in Corsica) plus the 90th Panzergrenadier Division, a fortress brigade and support units (evacuated from Sardinia between 8 and 19 September) under the command of General-leutnant Fridolin von Senger und Etterlin. On Corsica were some 20,000 French resistance fighters and an Italian garrison which suffered a heavy rate of desertion to the resistance in the centre of the island. General d'Armée Henri Giraud, commanding the French forces in the Mediterranean, was worried that the resistance would be overwhelmed by this German strength, and secured permission to reinforce the island forces with French troops from North Africa, the only provision being that the French would have to find their own transport vessels as all Allied capacity was currently involved in Operation 'Avalanche'. Thus Operation 'Vesuvius' used 2 cruisers, 2 destroyers and 1 submarine to ferry some 6,400 troops to Ajaccio between 13 and 27 September. But on 12 September Hitler had ordered that Corsica be abandoned. The evacuation was controlled with meticulous precision by Fregattenkapitän von Liebenstein and the Fliegerführer Corsica, and by 3 October the operation removed all personnel (27,347 Germans and some 1,200 prisoners of war) and considerable stores from the island despite the increasing strength of French resistance attacks with military support.

Victor Overall designation of the American recapture of the southern and central Philippines (1945) within the 'Princeton' plan. The Philippines were intended as the main base area from which the Allies could launch the invasion of the Japanese home islands and so encompass the final defeat of the Japanese empire, and thus the security of the main islands was important to long-term Allied strategy. But it was also decided that Mindanao and the smaller islands lying between Luzon and Mindanao (plus Palawan to the south-east) should be cleared of the scattered garrisons of Lieutenant General Sasaku Suzuki's Japanese 35th Army for additional security and as a means of facilitating the delivery of fuel from Borneo after the capture of its three main oil-producing regions in I Australian Corps' Operation 'Oboe'. The formation allocated responsibility for Operation 'Victor' was Lieutenant General Robert L. Eichelberger's US 8th Army under the overall control of General Douglas MacArthur, with Vice Admiral

Victor I

Thomas C. Kinkaid's US 7th Fleet as its naval and amphibious support element. US plans had initially called for the isolation rather than reduction of these Japanese-held islands (except by Filipino forces), but on 6 February MacArthur ordered Eichelberger to begin 'Victor', and thus modification to the overall strategic plan was accepted by the US chiefs-of-staff on 3 April.

Victor I Reconquest of Panay and Negros Islands in the Visayas group by the US 40th Infantry Division of Lieutenant General Robert L. Eichelberger's US 8th Army (18 March/12 June 1945). After operations to take Masbate and Burias Islands farther to the north with landings on 3 March, the division was landed by the 9th Amphibious Group some 12 miles from Iloilo, the leading city of Panay, on 18 March and was met by Filipino guerrillas, who confirmed that the Japanese defence comprised some 2,750 men covering the approaches to Iloilo. The Americans and Filipinos advanced on Iloilo, which was fired and abandoned by the Japanese on 19 March as they took to the hills in the centre of the island, where Filipino guerrillas harried them for the rest of the war. The 40th Infantry Division landed on the western side of Negros on 29 March and advanced towards the main city, Bacolod, which was defended by most of Lieutenant General Takeshi Kono's 13,000 Japanese troops on the island. By 5 April the Americans had taken Bacolod and its airfield, but it was 4 June before the surviving Japanese were pushed back into the mountains after fierce fighting in the foothills. By this time the 40th Infantry Division's southern drive on the island had been reinforced by a northern movement using the reserve regiment of the Americal Division, which landed at the extreme southern tip of the island on 26 April after moving from Cebu Island. Some 6,000 Japanese survived the attentions of the Filipino guerrilla forces to surrender at the end of the war.

Victor II Reconquest of Cebu and Bohol Islands in the Visayas group by the US Americal Division of Lieutenant General Robert L. Eichelberger's US 8th Army (26 March/20 April 1945). The island was the second most important industrial centre of the Philippines before World War II, and was held in 1945 by Lieutenant General Sasaku Suzuki's Japanese 35th Army headquarters (evacuated to Cebu after the loss of Leyte) with some 14,500 troops. The Americal Division landed to the west of Cebu City on 26 March and discovered the beaches to be heavily mined (the first time such weapons had been used in the Philippines campaign). The Americal Division fought its way into Cebu City on 27 March as the Japanese fell back to prepared positions in the north, and it was not until 18 April that the Americans were able to drive the surviving Japanese into the central mountains. On 10 April Suzuki left the island in an attempt to reach Mindanao and the main strength of the 35th Army. The five small craft were spotted and bombed by US aircraft on 19 April and Suzuki was killed. His staff reached Cagayan in northern Mindanao, and Lieutenant General Gyosaku Morozumi assumed command of the 35th Army in Mindanao. Bohol was cleared by the Americal Division's reserve regiment between 11 and 20 April before it was moved into the southern half of Negros to aid the 40th Infantry Division. The Visayas campaign cost the Americans 835 dead and 2,300 wounded, while the Japanese lost some 10,000 dead and 500 prisoners. About 17,500 Japanese surrendered at the end of the war.

Victor III Reconquest of Palawan, Busuanga and Balabac Islands in the south-east Philippines by units of the US 41st Infantry Division of Lieutenant General Robert L. Eichelberger's US 8th Army (28 February/22 April 1945). The object of this operation was to provide suitable bases for the support of Australian operations in Borneo (Operation 'Oboe') and to open the Sulu Sea to Allied shipping (especially tankers) after the completion of the Australian offensive. Operation 'Victor III' was the first of the 'Victor' components to be launched when the 186th Regimental Combat Team was landed at Puerto Princesa in the middle of Palawan by the 6th Amphibious Group on 28 February. The island was held by some 1,750 Japanese troops, and after some small but hotly contested actions the Japanese survivors were driven into the mountains on 2 March. Busuanga fell to landings on 9 April, and Balabac to landings on 16 April, and the entire group was in American hands by 22 April.

Victor IV Seizure of the Zamboanga peninsula on Mindanao Island by part of the US 41st Infantry Division of Lieutenant General Robert L. Eichelberger's US 8th Army (10/25 March 1945). This long peninsula tipped by the useful port of Zamboanga was held by the 54th Independent Mixed Brigade of Lieutenant General Sosaku Suzuki's 35th Army, and after the landing from ships of the 6th Amphibious Force it took the 41st Infantry Division some two weeks to clear the peninsula and to drive the remnants of the 54th Independent Mixed Brigade into the mountainous interior, where it survived for the rest of the war. The island of Basilan, just south of Zamboanga, was occupied on 10 March, and Tawitawi, only 30 miles from the coast of Borneo, was taken on 2 April. But Jolo in the centre of the Sulu archipelago was garrisoned by some 4,000 Japanese, and it took the 163rd Regimental Combat Team the period between 9 April and the beginning of July to break the resistance.

Victor V Reconquest of Mindanao Island in the southern Philippines by Lieutenant General Robert L. Eichelberger's US 8th Army. Mindanao had been the first objective of General Douglas MacArthur's South-West Pacific Area proposed reconquest of the Philippines, but on 8 September 1944 the US chiefs-of-staff had ordered MacArthur to bypass Mindanao entirely and launch his operation with the invasion of Leyte. So instead of being the first US objective in the Philippines, Mindanao was now the last and potentially one of the most difficult targets for US reconquest as it was defended by Lieutenant General Gyosaku Morozumi's 35th Army of about 43,000 men. The 54th Independent Mixed Brigade was already contained by the US 41st Infantry Division on the Zamboanga peninsula (Operation 'Victor IV'), but Morozumi also had the 100th Division and 32nd Naval Base Force for the defence of Davao, the 74th Regiment at Malaybay in the north centre of the island, and the depleted 30th Division at Cayayan on the northern side of the island. There were also garrisons in the other major towns, but the Japanese strength on the island was somewhat illusory as most of the island's interior apart from the main roads was controlled by 25,000 Filipino guerrillas under Colonel Wendell W. Fertig.

The task of making the first inroads into the Japanese strength was entrusted to Major General Frank C. Sibert's US X Corps, comprising the US 24th Infantry Division from Mindoro and the US 31st Infantry Division from Morotai. X Corps was transported by the 8th Amphibious Group, and on 17 April landed without Japanese opposition at Malabang and Parang in Illana Bay on the island's west coast. Both divisions moved inland with great speed, and the 24th Infantry Division reached Digosa, on the Gulf of Davao to the south of this great port and naval base of Davao, on 27 April after an advance of 115 miles. The division wheeled smartly north-east and stormed into Davao on 3 May as the Japanese garrison pulled back to defensive positions it had prepared on the road north to Malaybay. The 24th Infantry Division moved in pursuit, but could not expel the Japanese from their position until 10 June, whereupon the Japanese pulled back towards Malaybay. The 31st Infantry Division had meanwhile been advancing north-east round the coast towards Cagayan, but on 5 May was halted by strong resistance to the south-west of Cagayan. Accordingly a regimental combat team of the US 40th Infantry Division was landed in Macajalar Bay, to the east of Cagayan, on 10 May and this US pincer forced the 30th Division back from Cagayan towards Malaybay when the 31st and 40th Infantry Divisions met on 23 May.

Further landings were made round the coast of Mindanao (at Luayin on 1 June, on Balut and Sarangani Islands on 3 June, at Cabo San Agustin on 5 June, in Butuan Bay on 23 June and in Sarangani Bay on 12 July) so that the US forces could move inland from a variety of points to split the surviving Japanese defenders into small pockets, and by the end of June the mass of the 35th Army's remnants had been forced into a 20,500-man pocket to the east of Malaybay, where it remained inactive for the rest of the war. A

Viktor

pocket of 2,000 Japanese was contained in the south-east corner of the island by the landing in Sarangani Bay, where MacArthur had intended that the US forces should make their first landing in the Philippines. During the 'Victor' operations the US 8th Army lost 2,556 dead and 9,412 wounded, and Japanese losses are estimated at about 50,000

Viktor (Victor)   German codeword for any Allied landing in the north-east of Italy, in the area of Rimini, after the defection of Italy from the Axis cause.

Vigorous   British supply convoy to Malta from Alexandria (11/16 June 1942). This operation was undertaken at the same time as the 'Harpoon' convoy from Gibraltar, the object being to split the attentions and offensive capabilities of the German and Italian opposition so that the convoys stood a better chance of reaching the beleaguered island (on successive days) with vitally needed supplies. While 'Harpoon' consisted of 6 merchantmen, 'Vigorous' had at its core 11 supply ships, escorted by a force commanded by Rear Admiral Sir Philip Vian and organized by Admiral Sir Henry Harwood, the Commander-in-Chief Mediterranean, with a total of 7 light cruisers, 1 AA cruiser, 26 destroyers, and a number of corvettes, minesweepers and rescue ships. All too evident, however, were the lack of any heavy ships (to deal with any Italian battle-fleet interception) or aircraft-carriers (to deal with Axis reconnaissance or attack aircraft). The old battleship *Centurion* (now used mainly as a radio-controlled target) was allocated to the operation in the vain hope that the Axis forces would be deceived into thinking that there was a battleship among the escort force, but greater reliance was placed on the substantial force of attack aircraft and submarines provided for 'Vigorous'. These should have been more than adequate for the task, but the British lacked reconnaissance aircraft and these attack forces were thus denied the accurate intelligence which would have enabled them to operate effectively against the Italian surface forces. Harwood and Air Chief Marshal Sir Arthur Tedder, the air commander, personally supervised the operation from the headquarters of the naval co-operation No. 201 Group.

'Vigorous' got under way on 11 June with the sailing from Port Said of a diversionary group (4 merchantmen, the AA cruiser *Coventry* and 7 escort destroyers), which was intended to sail as far east as Tobruk before turning back to meet the main convoy. The British hoped that the Italian naval forces would be decoyed south by the diversionary group, then fail to find it and have to turn back for lack of fuel, so leaving the main convoy the chance to make good progress without Axis interference. The main convoy assembled in two parts (at Port Said and Haifa) and joined up with the diversionary convoy off Alexandria on 13 June, the whole convoy then moving east to be joined off Tobruk by Vian's escort (7 cruisers and 17 destroyers).

Axis reconnaissance aircraft discovered the convoy on 12 June and attacks soon developed. One merchantman was damaged on 12 June and sent back to Tobruk, while a straggler was detached to Alexandria but sunk by 40 German aircraft during 14 June. The Axis aircraft kept track of the convoy through the night of 13/14 June, and heavy attacks were launched during 14 June despite the attentions of British land-based fighters. One merchantman was sunk and another damaged by bombers, and during the evening Italian torpedo boats began to close in from the north. Then at 23.15 Vian was informed that Admiral Angelo Iachino had left Taranto (with the 2 modern battleships *Vittorio Veneto* and *Littorio*, 2 heavy cruisers, 2 light cruisers and about 12 destroyers) and could intercept the convoy from about 07.00 on 15 June. Vian secured permission to turn back at 02.00 on 15 June, but was then attacked by the torpedo boats at about 04.00. The cruiser *Newcastle* was sunk and the destroyer *Hasty* so badly damaged that she was abandoned and then sunk by a British destroyer.

At dawn the Italian fleet was some 200 miles north of the convoy, and Vian was once again ordered to make for Malta while Allied aircraft struck at the Italians. The first blood was drawn by Malta-based aircraft, which torpedoed and crippled the heavy cruiser *Trento* (later finished by the British submarine *Umbra*). The British submarines were mean-

324

while struggling to intercept the Italians, and an Egypt-launched air raid developed between 09.00 and 10.00, scoring one bomb and one torpedo hit on the *Littorio*. Virtual chaos now followed in the British camp, for at 09.40 Harwood ordered Vian to turn back once again, then at 12.00 the British commander (having heard the optimistic air reports of damage to the Italian squadron) told Vian to make once more for Malta, and finally at 12.45 Harwood (having heard that the air reports were too hopeful and that air reconnaissance had lost touch with the Italian squadron) left the matter to Vian, who received this signal only at 14.20 after the cruiser *Birmingham* had been badly damaged in an air attack and the destroyer *Airedale* crippled. The destroyer had to be sunk by the surviving British forces, so only a much-reduced escort was available for the convoy of 6 merchantmen, another having been sent back as a straggler.

As Vian was deciding which course to adopt, it was revealed by renewed air reconnaissance that at 14.00 Iachino had reversed course and started his return to Taranto. Harwood now urged Vian to pass through to Malta, but Vian countered with the information that his ships had used two-thirds of their AA ammunition. At 19.39 Harwood ordered the British force to return, especially as the Australian destroyer *Nestor* had been badly damaged, and as Vian struggled back towards Egypt the U-boat *U-205* torpedoed and sank the cruiser *Hermione*, while the crippled *Nestor* had to be sunk. By the evening of 16 June the ships were back at Alexandria. One cruiser, 3 destroyers and 2 merchantmen had been lost, and 'Vigorous' could only be regarded as a severe tactical defeat for the British, who resolved to attempt no further Malta relief convoys from Egypt until their land forces had cleared the African coast and made it possible to provide the ships with permanent land-based air cover.

Violet (i) Plan by the French telephone network in France (with support from the Special Operations Executive and the Office of Strategic Services) to cripple the telephone and telegram system of the country at the time of Operation 'Overlord' to prevent rapid transmission of German reinforcement and movement orders.

(ii) Airborne raid by the Special Allied Airborne Reconnaissance Force to protect Allied prisoners of war near Altengraben in Germmany (25 April 1945).

Vitality Operation by the 2nd Canadian Division and British 52nd Division to reduce the island of South Beveland (24/29 October 1944). This was part of the overall operation by Lieutenant General G. G. Simonds's II Canadian Corps of Lieutenant General Sir Henry Crerar's Canadian 1st Army to ease the opening of the great port at Antwerp by eliminating the German garrisons round the estuary of the River Scheldt and so permitting Allied minesweepers to clear the channel into the port, whose facilities were vitally needed to supply the offensive towards north Germany. Operation 'Vitality' on the northern side of the estuary was undertaken at the same time as the clearance of the Breskens pocket on the southern side, leaving only the clearance of Walcheren Island to complete the whole undertaking. On 27 September Crerar had been invalided to England, so the Canadian 2nd Army was commanded temporarily by Simonds, with Major General Foulkes running II Canadian Corps. 'Vitality' was entrusted to Foulkes's 2nd Canadian Division (now commanded by Brigadier Keefler), and the defence comprised Generalleutnant Wilhelm Däser's 70th Division of General Gustav von Zangen's German 15th Army.

On 2 October the 2nd Canadian Division was in Antwerp, and as the way north through Generaloberst Kurt Student's 1st Parachute Army was cleared by the Polish 1st Armoured Division, the Canadian 4th Armoured Division, the US 104th Infantry Division and the British 49th Division, Keefler began to shift his division towards Woensdrecht at the landward end of the causeway linking South Beveland with the mainland, pushing through the 719th Division at Putte on 5 October and fighting off a determined counterattack by the Kampfgruppe Chill (on 8 October) to take Woensdrecht on 16 October and so isolate the German 70th Division on the Bevelands and Walcheren.

325

Vogelsang

The clearance of the Scheldt estuary and the opening of Antwerp were now of the highest priority, as Allied formations took the brunt of fighting just to the north of the Beveland isthmus, on 23 October the 2nd Canadian Division moved up to its start line for 'Vitality' by 26 October the 4th Canadian Brigade had fought its way forward to Krabbendijke half way along the isthmus and the 6th Canadian Brigade passed through to renew the offensive as the German frontal positions were outflanked by the landing of the 156th Brigade of Major General E. Hakewill-Smith's British 52nd Division, which had been ferried from Terneuzen to the southern shore of South Beveland in tracked assault craft. The 157th Brigade was then ferried onto the island as the German resistance began to crumble in the face of British and Canadian attacks. Effective resistance ceased on 29 October, when the island of North Beveland was also cleared.

Vogelsang (birdsong) Operation undertaken by the German 2nd Panzerarmee against Soviet partisans operating in the region of Bryansk (April/July 1942) and so threatening the lines of communication to Generalfeldmarschall Günther von Kluge's Army Group 'Centre'.

Vulcan Allied 18th Army Group offensive to destroy the Axis Army Group 'Africa' in its Tunisian beach-head (22 April/6 May 1943). Under the command of General the Hon. Sir Harold Alexander, the 18th Army Group (Lieutenant General K. A. N. Anderson's Allied 1st Army and General Sir Bernard Montgomery's British 8th Army) was ordered by the Allied Commander-in-Chief, North African Theatre (General Dwight D. Eisenhower) to complete the destruction of Generaloberst Jürgen von Arnim's Army Group 'Africa' (General Giovanni Messe's 1st Army and General Gustav von Vaerst's 5th Panzerarmee) and so terminate the North African campaign. Alexander issued his orders for Operation 'Vulcan' on 16 April, in them fixing the 1st Army's tasks as the capture of Tunis, co-operation with the US II Corps in the capture of Bizerta and, if necessary, co-operation with the 8th Army for the capture of the Cap Bon peninsula, fixing Lieutenant General Omar N. Bradley's US II Corps' task as the capture of Bizerta, and fixing the 8th Army's tasks as exerting pressure in the south to draw off the Axis 1st Army and an offensive to Hammamet and Tunis to prevent the Axis forces falling back into the Cap Bon peninsula. The operation was to be supported throughout by Air Marshal Sir Arthur Coningham's North-West African Tactical Air Force, with Air Commodore K. B. B. Cross's No. 242 Group (RAF), Colonel Paul L. Williams's US XII Air Support Command and Air Commodore L. F. Sinclair's North-West African Tactical Bomber Force allocated to the 1st Army, and Air Vice Marshal H. Broadhurst's Western Desert Air Force to the 8th Army.

Within this overall scheme, 'Vulcan' demanded that the US II Corps advance in the north to the Garaet Achkel and Mateur as jumping-off points for the capture of Bizerta in 'Strike' (and also push forward on its right flank to cover the left of the 1st Army), that the Allied 1st Army use Lieutenant General C. W. Allfrey's British V Corps and Lieutenant General J. T. Crocker's British IX Corps to destroy the Axis forces blocking the south-western approaches to Tunis between Tebourba and Pont du Fahs (with Général de Corps d'Armée L. M. Koeltz's French XIX Corps moving up to protect the right flank of the British IX Corps), and that the 8th Army pressure the Axis 1st Army between Takrouna and Enfidaville.

The fighting was confused and in places extremely hard, for the Germans had been reinforced, and the Americans were determined to avenge their stinging defeat at Kasserine. However, the strength of the Allies, with overwhelming air support, was too much for the Axis forces, and in the centre von Vaest was forced to give ground steadily if slowly. In the south Montgomery ably fulfilled the task allotted to him, and in the north the US II Corps moved forward with great determination. By 30 April Alexander had come to appreciate that the plan for 'Vulcan' needed revision to accommodate the current situation, and 'Vulcan' was thus revised in its closing stages to become Operation 'Strike' designed to eliminate the Axis forces in the Tunisian beach-head, and this revised second half to 'Vulcan' was launched on 6 May.

W

Wacht am Rhein (Watch on the Rhine) Alternative German designation for Operation 'Herbstnebel'.

Wadham Allied plan for a landing on the Brittany peninsula of western France (1943). This was part of Operation 'Cockade', an Allied plan to tie German forces in France during 1943, with consequent benefits to the development of Allied operations in Italy and Soviet operations on the Eastern Front. 'Cockade' was planned by Lieutenant General Sir Frederick Morgan and the COSSAC staff, and involved an amphibious feint towards France with the object of alerting the Germans and provoking a major air battle in which, it was hoped, the Allies would be able to secure a decisive tactical victory. Of the four separate parts of 'Cockade', 'Wadham' was allotted to the US Army, which planned that the US V Corps should be responsible for the threat against Brest and perhaps other port areas in Brittany, with the added aim of persuading the Germans that US Army strength in the UK was greater than it really was. The other components of 'Cockade' were Operations 'Harlequin', 'Starkey' and 'Tindall'.

Waldrausch (forest fever) German operation against partisan forces in Yugoslavia (1945).

Waldteufel (forest devil) German operation against partisan forces in Yugoslavia (1945).

Waldwinter (forest winter) German operation against Soviet partisans operating in the region between Trudy and Obol to the northwest of Vitebsk (March 1943), and so threatening the rear-area security of Generalfeldmarschall Günther von Kluge's Army Group 'Centre', together with its lines of communication.

Walkurie (Valkyrie) German plan (1942) to mobilize the Reserve Army within Germany, in the event that Allied prisoners of war held in that country mounted a major insurrection, to hold key points in Germany (and especially in Berlin) as the insurrection was quelled; the name was later adopted by the conspirators against Hitler in 1943/1944, who found the concept an ideal way to discuss the methods and means they would use to secure control of Germany once Hitler had been killed in the 'Bomb Plot' attack of 20 July 1944, when in fact Hitler was unharmed by the bomb planted by Oberstleutnant Klaus Graf von Stauffenberg.

Wassermann German early-warning radar.

Watchtower US operation for the recapture of Santa Cruz, Tulagi, Florida and Guadalcanal Islands at the south-eastern end of the Solomons chain (7/9 August 1942). The Japanese had landed in this area on 2 May (as part of the peripheral activity associated with Operation 'MO') to build a seaplane base for scouting flights farther down the Solomons chain and into the lines of communication between the USA and Australia. The Allies were little prepared for offensive action in the middle of 1942, and were not unduly disturbed about the

Japanese seaplane base on Tulagi. However, during June it became clear that the Japanese were preparing an airfield on Guadalcanal just south of Tulagi, and this indicated that the Japanese were considering offensive action in the area, either attacks on Allied convoys bringing men and *matériel* into the South Pacific and South-West Pacific Areas, or further expansion down the Solomons chain.

The Allies had just won their first major strategic victory in the Pacific with the defeat of the Japanese Combined Fleet in the Battle of Midway, and it was now decided to capitalize on this success to check the Japanese in the Solomons. The nearest available forces were the US Marine Corps formations being built up on Espiritu Santo (about 550 miles to the south-east) for the eventual Allied counteroffensive towards New Britain and New Ireland (headquarters of the 8th Area Army and the 4th Fleet responsible for the south-eastern segment of the Japanese outer defence perimeter), and it was decided by the US Joint Chief-of-Staff Committee with the full approval of Admiral Ernest J. King, Commander-in-Chief of the US Fleet, to use Major General Alexander A. Vandegrift's US 1st Marine Division (reinforced to a strength of 19,000 men and using the 2nd Marine Regiment of the 2nd Marine Division instead of its own 7th Marine Regiment, which had been detached for the defence of Samoa) for a counterstroke on Guadalcanal and Tulagi, garrisoned respectively by 1,500 and 2,200 men, most of them construction troops. Operation 'Watchtower' was planned and organized in only one month under the supervision of Vice Admiral Richard H. Ghormley's South Pacific Area using Rear Admiral Richard K. Turner's amphibious forces (15 transports, 8 cruisers and a number of destroyers) escorted by a support force (the aircraft-carriers *Saratoga*, *Enterprise* and *Wasp*, the battleship *North Carolina*, 5 heavy cruisers, 1 light cruiser, 16 destroyers and 3 tankers) commanded by Rear Admiral Frank J. Fletcher who, as senior officer, led the entire 'Watchtower' operation.

The US forces approached Guadalcanal and Tulagi with some trepidation, for the rehearsal landing at Koro in the Fiji Islands had been a complete fiasco. But on 7 August the marines stormed ashore under cover of a powerful ship and air bombardment of the Japanese positions. Tulagi was assaulted by a comparatively small force (one battalion of the 5th Marine Regiment, the 1st Marine Raider Battalion and the 1st Marine Parachute Battalion), while the main weight of the 1st Marine Division landed at Lunga Point on Guadalcanal, to the west of the airfield site. Tulagi was the headquarters for the area, and it took the marines three days of bitter fighting before they had secured this island and its two small neighbours, Gavutu and Tanambogo. By this time the whole of the 2nd Marine Regiment had been committed to Tulagi, for the Guadalcanal operation had gone more smoothly as there were only 150 combat troops on the island. Fortunately for the 1st Marine Division, the Japanese labour troops abandoned all their equipment when they fled on 8 August, so the marines were able to use this captured gear when Fletcher, prompted by the vulnerability of his ships to the violence of the Japanese air attacks that started almost immediately after the landings, pulled out his carrier force and Turner's amphibious ships (together with most of the machines' heavy equipment) on 9 August.

The 1st Marine Division had achieved its objectives in 'Watchtower', and was not left to face the Japanese counterstroke on its own; destroyers brought in additional supplies and men, and US engineers hastily completed the airstrip, now renamed Henderson Field, so that the first supporting fighters and attack aircraft could be flown into Guadalcanal on 20 August, just one day before the reinforced Japanese began to probe into the US perimeter around the beach-head. The Japanese riposte had not been long in coming, therefore, and this set the scene for one of the most vicious campaigns of World War II (together with a protracted and very costly naval campaign) as the two sides fought in ghastly conditions for mastery of Guadalcanal, eventually conceded by the Japanese at the beginning of February 1943.

Waterloo British and Canadian exercise in Kent (summer 1941).

Weary Willy Developed version of 'Aphrodite'.

Weber (weaver) German naval operation against the south-east coast of England (January 1941).

Weiss (white) **(i)** German conquest of Poland (1 September/5 October 1939). This was the operation that sparked off World War II, and gave full notice to her opponents that Germany was indeed a formidable opponent deploying substantial armed forces, centred on fast-moving mobile forces with effective air support, for ruthless operations under very skilled leadership. The Poles were sadly lacking in truly modern weapons, and as their senior commanders had signally failed to appreciate the nature of the tactics the Germans were about to unleash on them, they had thus deployed their forces in large concentrations right up against the German/Polish frontier. This played straight into the hands of the Germans who, under the overall supervision of Generalfeldmarschall Walther von Brauchitsch, had planned deep enveloping thrusts into the Polish rear with aircraft-supported armoured formations in order to divide the Polish forces into pockets which could then be mopped up by the German infantry as the mobile forces pressed on into the Polish heartland. In the north was Generaloberst Fedor von Bock's Army Group 'North', divided by Danzig and the 'Danzig corridor' into two portions. The left flank comprised General Georg von Küchler's 3rd Army (8 infantry divisions in East Prussia) tasked with the destruction of the Polish forces in the 'corridor' and with an advance towards Warsaw and the upper Vistula, and the right flank was General Günther von Kluge's 4th Army (6 infantry divisions and the 1 Panzer and 2 motorized divisions of General Heinz Guderian's XIX Panzer Corps, based in Pomerania) tasked primarily with the destruction of the Polish forces in the 'corridor' and an advance up the lower Vistula. In the west was Generaloberst Gerd von Rundstedt's Army Group 'South' divided into three major groupings. The most northerly of these was General Johannes Blaskowitz's 8th Army (4 infantry divisions and the SS Leibstandarte Adolf Hitler motorized regiment in northern Silesia) tasked with the encirclement of the Polish forces in the region of Kutno and Poznan. In the centre was General Walter von Reichenau's 10th Army (6 infantry, 2 motorized, 3 light and 2 Panzer divisions, including XVI Panzer Corps, in southern Silesia) tasked with driving north-east straight through Wielun and Lodz to Warsaw. And in the south was General Wilhelm List's 14th Army (1 mountain, 6 infantry, 1 light and 2 Panzer divisions, plus the SS Germania motorized regiment, in Slovakia) tasked with an offensive through the Carpathian Mountains to crush the Polish forces around Krakow and Przemysl.

Facing this formidable force were the largely infantry-based Polish forces commanded by Marshal Eduard Smigly-Rydz, most of them much too close to the frontier and thus incapable of manoeuvre once the German penetrations had begun. Facing the German 3rd Army in the north were three groupings (from east to west General Mlot-Fijalkowski's Narew Army of 2 infantry divisions and 2 cavalry brigades, General Skwarczinski's Wyskow Group of 3 infantry divisions, and General Przedrzymirski's Modlin Army of 2 infantry divisions and 2 cavalry brigades. Between the German 3rd and 4th Armies in the 'corridor' was General Bortnowski's Pomeranian Army of 6 infantry divisions and 1 cavalry brigade. Facing the German 8th Army was General Kutrzeba's Poznan Army with 4 infantry divisions and 2 cavalry brigades. Facing the 10th Army was General Rommel's Lodz Army with 4 infantry divisions and 2 cavalry brigades. Facing the German 14th Army were two groupings (in the west General Szylling's Krakow Army of 6 infantry divisions and 1 cavalry brigade, and in the east General Fabryci's Carpathian Army with 2 infantry divisions and 2 mountain brigades). Farther to the rear were two reserve formations, namely General Dab-Biernacki's Prusy Group (6 infantry divisions and 1 cavalry brigade around Piotrkow) and the Pyskor Group (1 infantry division and 1 armoured brigade between Deblin and Brest-Litovsk). In all, some 1,250,000 Germans faced 1,000,000 Poles, but the Germans had 3,200 armoured vehicles and 4,300 guns to the Poles' 600 armoured vehicles and 1,350 guns, and while the Poles could call on some 840 obsolescent aircraft to support their armies, the Germans had 1,930 aircraft allocated to General Albert Kesselring's Luftflotte I (Army Group 'North') and General Alexander Löhr's Luftflotte IV (Army Group 'South').

Despite some hitches by troops little experienced in real warfare, the German offensive in Operation 'Weiss' proceeded much as planned, the inner pincer formed by the 4th and 10th Armies closing on Warsaw (though XIX Panzer Corps was switched from the 4th Army to the 3rd Army's sector for an advance up the River Bug towards Brest-Litovsk), and the outer pincer formed by the 3rd and 14th Armies approaching Brest-Litovsk. The Polish air force fought with the utmost gallantry, but was outclassed technically and in numbers, and the German air formations could thus operate as 'flying artillery' for the German mobile forces. Warsaw held out between 8 and 17 September, but after 17 September the defence crumbled as the German eastward offensive was supplemented by the USSR's westward attack to take most of Poland east of the River Bug. By 5 October it was all over, the Poles having lost 66,000 dead and some 200,000 wounded to the Germans' 10,570 dead, 30,325 wounded and 3,400 missing. About 694,000 Poles surrendered, but large numbers escaped to Romania and thence to France and ultimately the UK. Thus Poland's part in World War II was far from over despite the defeat of the country in 1939.

(ii) Designation of the joint German and Italian offensive against the Yugoslav partisans of Marshal Josep Broz Tito, and known to the Yugoslavs as the Fourth Offensive (20 January/April 1943). The Axis partners in fact launched a series of five offensives as a result of Adolf Hitler's Führerbefehl Nr 47 of 28 December 1942, which established a south-eastern theatre in the Balkans under Generaloberst Alexander Löhr, who was answerable directly to Hitler. In this directive Löhr was ordered to undertake the 'final pacification of the hinterland and destruction of the rebels and bandits of all kinds, in conjunction with the Italian 2nd Army'. Löhr decided that the first step in this programme required the elimination of the partisans in Croatia and Bosnia, and Operation 'Weiss' was initiated to secure this objective.

All went well for the Axis at first, the Germans pushing south from the River Sava into the Grimec Planina as the Italians advanced north from the coast to trap the partisans. Tito and the partisans were forced to pull back into Herzegovina and Montenegro, but then the Axis partnership began to fail, the Italians slowing and preferring to leave matters to their Croat satellite formations. As a result the Axis pincer failed to trap the Yugoslav partisans, who escaped into the valley of the River Neretva and played havoc with the important bauxite mines near Mostar. The Germans and Italians now fell out about the latters' use of the anti-partisan Cetnik movement headed by Colonel Draza Mihailovic. Here matters stagnated, and while the Axis forces attempted to pin down the partisan army in the Neretva valley Tito organized major risings elsewhere in the theatre, the most significant efforts being made in Albania, Serbia, western Croatia, and north of the Sava.

Wellhit Reduction of the Boulogne pocket by the 3rd Canadian Division (17/22 September 1944). This was one of several Channel ports (Le Havre, Boulogne, Calais and Dunkirk) desired by Field Marshal Sir Bernard Montgomery's British 21st Army Group as a means of reducing the Anglo-Canadian troops' reliance on ports such as Cherbourg far to the rear. The reduction of Le Havre was allocated to Lieutenant General J. T. Crocker's British I Corps of the British 2nd Army, while the capture of the other three ports was entrusted to Lieutenant General G. G. Simonds's Canadian II Corps of Lieutenant General Sir Henry Crerar's Canadian 1st Army, using Major General Spry's 3rd Canadian Division as its main offensive formation. The Channel ports had significance to Hitler too, and on 4 September 1944 he ordered General Gustav von Zangen's 15th Army to provide 'fight-to-the-death' garrisons for each of the ports. Boulogne was commanded by Generalleutnant Ferdinand Heim with a mixed collection of 10,000 men and a powerful artillery force. The attack had to wait until ammunition stocks had been built up and specialized armour had been brought up from Le Havre, and the difficult assault began on 17 September with the support of four coastal guns (firing across the English Channel from the North Foreland) and an attack by 800 heavy bombers. But the Germans had prepared excellent defences in depth and the Canadians had to flush out all of the very many prepared positions. Heim eventually surrendered on 22 September.

Werwolf (werewolf) **(i)** Designation of Hitler's headquarters near Vinnitsa (16 July/1 November 1942) for the German summer offensive of 1942 on the Eastern Front.
(ii) German operation against Yugoslav partisans (1945).

Weserübung (Weser crossing) German conquest of Denmark and Norway (9 April/10 June 1940). Hitler and Grossadmiral Erich Raeder, commander-in-chief of the German navy, both desired the conquest of Norway for sound military and economic reasons, and given this primary objective it was natural that Denmark also be taken as the natural means of surface communication with Norway. Raeder wanted Norway as a base for his surface and U-boat fleets, which would then have good access to the Atlantic and the convoy routes on which the UK depended for her very survival. Hitler wanted Norway as a means of exerting pressure on the USSR, of securing the delivery of iron ore from Sweden along the coastal leads of Norway even during the winter freeze of the Baltic, and of preventing British use of Norway as a forward base for attacks on Germany (a fear apparently confirmed by the 'Altmark incident' of 16 February 1940, when a British destroyer boarded the German supply ship *Altmark* in Norwegian territorial waters to rescue prisoners held in the German ship). Hitler's orders were formalized in a *Führerbefehl* of 1 March 1940, which established that General Nikolaus von Falkenhorst would command the operation (initially to be launched on 20 March but later postponed to 9 April), which would be undertaken (with strong naval and air support) by Generalleutnant Kaupisch's **XXXI** Corps (Denmark) and von Falkenhorst's own **XXI** Corps (Norway) comprising 2 mountain and 7 infantry divisions. The 170th and 198th Divisions were earmarked for the occupation of Denmark, where comparatively little resistance was anticipated, and the 2nd and 3rd Gebirgsdivisionen, plus the 69th, 163rd, 181st, 196th and 214th Divisions, were earmarked for the campaign in Norway. Air support was furnished by Generalleutnant Hans Geissler's X Fliegerkorps, which fielded 290 level bombers, 40 dive-bombers, 100 twin- and single-engined fighters, 70 reconnaissance aircraft and, perhaps most important of all, some 500 Junkers Ju 52/3m three-engined transports for supply and delivery of the small airborne forces for the operation. The navy contributed virtually all of its surface fleet, and these warships were supplemented by some 41 troop, weapon and fuel transports.

It was clear right from the start that the best way to undertake 'Weserübung' was to take key points round Norway's long coastline with ship-landed forces (supported in key areas by airborne troops who would land to secure airfields and the like) and then rush in reinforcements to deal with Norwegian opposition before it could be rallied under any sort of able leadership. The primary threat was the Royal Navy, whose overwhelming *matériel* superiority of the German navy threatened the possibility of wholesale destruction of the assault forces even before they reached Norway. The assault force for Norway was divided into five groups, each tasked with the capture of a specific port through which reinforcements could be poured. The five groups were to sail from German ports between 6 and 8 April to arrive off their target ports simultaneously. Responsible for Narvik in the far north was the Gruppe Narvik (10 destroyers) carrying the 139th Gebirgsjägerregiment. Trondheim was allocated to the Gruppe Trondheim (the heavy cruiser *Admiral Hipper* and 4 destroyers) carrying the 138th Gebirgsjägerregiment. The Gruppe Bergen (the light cruisers *Köln* and *Königsberg*, the gunnery training ship *Bremse*, the depot ship *Karl Peters* and 2 torpedo boats) was to lift the advance guard of the 69th Division to Bergen. The Gruppe Kristiansand/Arendal (the light cruiser *Karlsruhe*, the depot ship *Tsingtau* and 3 torpedo boats) ferried the 310th Regiment to Kristiansand and Arendal. Finally in the

Weserübung

south the Gruppe Oslo (the pocket battleship *Lützow*, the heavy cruiser *Blucher*, the light cruiser *Emden* and 3 torpedo boats) shipped the advance guard of the 163rd Division into the Norwegian capital.

The Allies were able to warn the two Scandinavian governments of the impending threat, but neither Denmark or Norway did anything to improve their defence postures, Denmark because she could do little and Norway because she was unwilling to be seen undertaking military preparations. The Germans issued a surrender ultimatum to each country just before the operations were committed, and Denmark's capitulation allowed XXXI Corps to complete its tasks without difficulty. However, Norway's government rejected the German demands and the landings went ahead as planned as the Norwegian forces mobilized under the command of Colonel Otto Ruge, who was immediately promoted to general on his appointment to replace the unfit commander-in-chief. At Narvik Generalleutnant Eduard Dietl's 3rd Gebirgsdivision force was faced by the Norwegian 6th Division, but secured its objectives easily as the division was not mobilized and the city was surrendered by a quisling. At Trondheim the opposition was found by the Norwegian 5th Division, but again the Germans secured their objectives without difficulty. Bergen offered some resistance, for even before the Germans got ashore and into limited action against the Norwegian 4th Division, the light cruiser *Königsberg* was crippled by Norwegian shore batteries and later sunk by dive-bombers of the Fleet Air Arm operating from a British aircraft-carrier. At Kristiansand and Arendal the Norwegian 3rd Division was soon in retreat before the German forces, whose landings had been upset by the torpedoing of the light cruiser *Karlsruhe* by the British submarine *Truant*. In this sector German airborne troops were used to support the amphibious landings, Stavanger and its airfield at Sola being taken by paratroops. But at Oslo the Germans were nearly repulsed even before they got ashore to face the Norwegian 1st and 2nd Divisions, for the assault force under Konteradmiral Oskar Kummetz was heavily shelled by the Norwegian coastal batteries, which sank the heavy cruiser *Blucher*, and shore-launched torpedoes also severely damaged the pocket battleship *Lützow*, which had to turn back to Germany. However, Generalmajor Erwin Engelbrecht managed to get part of his 163rd Division ashore and then to take half of Oslo and the arsenal at Horten, and the German position was stabilized by the arrival at Fornebu airfield of airlifted reinforcements.

The German threat to Norway was dangerous, but was scattered and could have been contained by rapid and concerted action on the part of the Allies. Such action was not forthcoming, though the British Home Fleet under Admiral Sir Charles Forbes tried its best. The battlecruiser *Renown* was already in the area with 4 destroyers, escorting the minelaying forces for Operation 'Wilfred', and Forbes immediately put to sea with the maximum number of vessels he could raise, in all 2 battleships, 1 battle-cruiser, 4 cruisers and 21 destroyers. But this response was ill considered, especially as the cruisers lying at Rosyth to embark troops for Narvik, Trondheim, Bergen and Stavanger were now ordered to offload the troops and sail in support of the Home Fleet, and as the carrier *Furious* was rushed to sea so rapidly she had no time to embark her fighter force. The British were more concerned with intercepting the German battle-cruisers *Scharnhorst* and *Gneisenau* (operating as a detached squadron in the North Sea as a decoy for British naval countermeasures) and other German naval units than in delivering troops to Norway. Yet it was troops that were needed to contain the scattered German effort.

The Germans rushed in reinforcements and began to move out of the ports into the neighbouring country with the object of consolidating their position and linking up, and it was only between 14 and 19 April that the Allies finally began to land troops in Norway. The Allied effort was centred on the capture of Narvik and of Trondheim (the latter in a pincer movement), but little could be achieved against the growing German strength. The Trondheim effort was abandoned on 2 May, and Narvik was evacuated on 8/9 June after the Allies had finally taken this vital city. As the Narvik force was evacuated the British carrier *Glorious* ran into the *Scharnhorst* and *Gneisenau* and was sunk, together with her two escorting destroyers, but the *Scharnhorst* was badly damaged by a torpedo from one of the escorts, and the *Gneisenau* was similarly damaged a few days later. Both ships were out of action for six months, but the Germans were in full control of Norway and Ruge capitulated on 10 June. The Germans had lost 5,636 men killed and missing, while the losses of the Allies were 3,734 (1,869 British, 1,335 Norwegians and 530 of the combined Franco-Polish force).

Westfall (west descent) German codeword to indicate any Allied invasion in France.

Westgoten (West Goths) German codename for the German administrator of home defence units in the west (1944/1945).

Westwall (west wall) Extension to the 'Siegfried Linie' defences ordered by Adolf Hitler in his *Führerbefehl* of 24 August 1944. This decision was spurred by the pace and width of the Allied advance towards Germany, for on 20 August the Allies had poured over the River Seine and one day after the issuing of the *Führerbefehl* were to take Paris. Hitler now placed more reliance in the Nazi party than in the army, and the order was sent to the party organization. The 24 August order called for the construction of a new 'German defensive position in the west' and the call-up of the civil population in four sectors, that between the River Scheldt and Aachen being the responsibility of Gauleiter Grohé, the Reichskommissar of Belgium and northern France (on 7 September an amendment allocated responsibility to Dr Arthur Seyss-Inquardt, the Reichkommissar fro Holland, for the Dutch section from Maastricht to Aachen), that on the River Mosel as far south as the boundary of Gau Moselland and Gau Westmark being the responsibility of Gauleiter Simon, that between the Gau Moselland/Gau Westmark boundary and Saaralben being the responsibility of Gauleiter Bürkel, and that between Saaralben and Belfort being the responsibility of Gauleiter Wagner. Though primary responsibility for the 'Westwall' was thus given to the party, the army was called upon to decide matters of tactical siting, the comparative importance of different sectors and the type of materials to be used. Hitler called for existing fortifications (notably the Maginot Line) to be included in the new line wherever possible, and also ordained that the line should consist of defences in depth, with an uninterrupted anti-tank obstacle and clear fields of fire in front of it. On 29 August Hitler ordered a comparable line to be built along the North Sea coast between Denmark and the Netherlands. The 1 September order modified the party control of various sectors of the 'Westwall' without altering the substance of the preparations ordered on 24 August.

Whale Floating pier for 'Mulberry'.

Whipcord British plan for an invasion of Sicily following the successful conclusion of Operation 'Crusader'.

White City Railway block and fly-in strip for the 2nd Chindit Expedition in Operation 'Thursday'. 'White City' was established by Brigadier J. M. Calvert's 77th Indian Brigade of Major General Orde Wingate's 3rd Indian Division just north of Mawlu on the rail line from Indaw north to Mogaung and Myitkyina. The rail line was cut on 16 March 1944, and the 'White City' position was held with extreme tenacity by the Chindits against counterattacks by the Japanese 24th Independent Mixed Brigade, and was finally abandoned on 9 May.

White Poppy Allied codename for Noumea on New Caledonia Island.

Widewing Headquarters of the Supreme Headquarters, Allied Expeditionary Force, at Bushy Park near London (1943/1944).

Wiesengrund (meadowland) German plan for Generaloberst Eduard Dietl's 20th Febirgsarmee to take the Rybachiy peninsula in the northern USSR. The plan was first mooted in serious form in Hitler's Führerbefehl Nr 37 of 10 October 1941, which called for the occupation of the Rybachiy peninsula 'at a favourable moment' as a prerequisite for the proposed advance on Murmansk. Führerbefehl Nr 44 of 21 July 1942 ordered the indefinite postponement of the operation, with preparations remaining in hand for the reintroduction of 'Wiesengrund' at eight weeks' notice.

Wikinger (Vikings) German destroyer operation over the Dogger Bank (February 1942).

Wildflower Allied codename for the UK.

Wilde Sau (wild sow) (i) German night-fighter operations using single-seat fighters to pick off British nocturnal bomber illuminated from below by German searchlights or fires. This tactic was devised in response to the British introduction of 'Window' to confuse German radar.
(ii) German operation by the 2nd Panzer-armee against Soviet partisans (1943).

Wilfred British minelaying operation in the Norwegian Leads (8/9 April 1940). The operation had been mooted as early as September 1939 as a means of preventing German coastal shipping sailing south in Norwegian territorial waters with iron ore shifted by rail from the Lulea region of Sweden to the ice-free Norwegian ports of Narvik. The Allies wished to prevent the iron traffic to Germany as a high priority, but felt that the implementation of Operation 'Wilfred' might force the Norwegians into the German camp or require the landing of Allied ground forces in Norway to prevent the Norwegians from sweeping the minefields. The latter would be an admirable *casus belli* for the Germans to intervene in Norway. It was finally decided to implement 'Wilfred' on 7/8 April, with three fully-publicized mine-fields to be laid in Norwegian waters and ground forces prepared for rapid delivery to Norway should the situation demand it. On 31 March the light cruiser *Birmingham* sailed with 2 destroyers to deal with German fishing boats off Norway and then to escort the mine-laying force, which had three components, in the form of 2 destroyers to simulate the laying of a field off Bud, the *Teviot Bank* and 4 destroyers to lay a field off Stadtlandet, and 4 minelaying destroyers (with another 4 destroyers as escort) to lay a field in the Vestfjord. Distant protection was afforded by Vice Admiral W. J. Whitworth's Battle-Cruiser Squadron, in the form of the *Renown* escorted by four destroyers, and Operation 'R4' was readied in case the German intervened with landings in Norway. 'Wilfred' was taking place as the Germans launched Operation 'Weserübung', and the British forces soon became involved in the frantic naval effort to intervene with the German operation.

Wilhelm (William) German 6th Army offensive towards Volchansk (10/15 June 1942). Launched in conjunction with the slightly later Operation 'Fridericus II', Operation 'Wilhelm' was undertaken as a preliminary to the 'Blau' offensives by Generalfeldmarschall Fedor von Bock's Army Group 'South', and was designed to eliminate the Soviet 28th Army of Lieutenant General F. Ya. Kostenko's South-West Front in the region of Volchansk, just north-east of Kharkov. The 6th Army under Generaloberst Friedrich Paulus launched 'Wilhelm' on 10 June and in six days pushed the Soviets back some 30 miles.

Winch British fighter reinforcement for Malta (spring 1941). It had at first been thought by the British that the island could not be held against determined Italian (let alone German) attack, but the events of late 1940 and early 1941 had convinced all that the island could not only be held, but also serve most usefully as a base from which British forces could interdict the Italian lines of communication to the Axis forces in North Africa. On 7 March Lieutenant General Sir William Dobbie, lieutenant governor of the island, had urged the need for rapid fighter reinforcements, and steps were soon in hand to bolster the island's defences. Air Chief Marshal Sir Arthur Longmore, commander-in-chief of the RAF in the Middle East, sent six Hawker Hurricanes fitted with drop-tanks from Egypt to Malta on 2 March, and another six on 14 March. A more practical delivery method, however, was flying the fighters off carriers that had collected the fighters at Gibraltar or brought them out from the UK. The first such operation was completed successfully on 3 April, when the *Ark Royal* delivered 12 Hurricanes from a point 400 miles west of Malta. This operation was followed by others in April, May and June whereby 224 fighters were delivered to the island, 109 for local use and the balance for on-shipment to Egypt.

Window Tinfoil strips released by British bombers from August 1943 onwards. These were dropped from the bombers in bundles, which broke up in the air to produce millions of radar echoes on the Germans' screens, so swamping the echoes produced by the bombers and shielding the attacking aircraft from German night-fighters.

Winkelried German extension southwards of the corridor linking the main German positions at Staraya Russa with the pocket at Demyansk held by General W. Graf von Brockdorff-Ahlefeldt's II Corps (August/October 1942) after Hitler expressly forbade any evacuation of the pocket.

Winter Linie (winter line) Designation of the strategic defence line schemed by Generalfeldmarschall Fedor von Bock's Army Group 'Centre' in December 1941 when it became apparent that Operation 'Taifun' had failed and that the German armies were being subjected to a major Soviet winter counteroffensive. The 'Winter Linie' position was some 90 miles to the rear of the Germans' current positions, and ran just to the east of Vyazma through Zubtsov, Gzhatsk and Yukhnov. Generalfeldmarschall Walther von Brauchitsch, commander-in-chief of the German army, thought it advisable to prepare such a fall-back position, and in January 1942 Hitler was forced to permit a general withdrawal to this line in the face of powerful Soviet drives which threatened to cut off major German formations.

Wintergewitter (winter storm) Designation of the relief attempt towards Stalingrad undertaken by the German 4th Panzerarmee (12/23 December 1943). After Hitler had ordered that Generaloberst Friedrich Paulus and his 6th Army should not break out from Stalingrad in the closing stages of the Soviets' Operation 'Uranus', the only way in which the garrison could be saved was the opening of an overland relief corridor, Reichsmarschall Hermann Goering's Luftwaffe air transport operation being patently inadequate. The headquarters of the highly capable 11th Army under Generalfeldmarschall Erich von Manstein were formed into a new Army Group 'Don' to oversee the relief operation, which was named 'Wintergewitter' and entrusted to the stump of the 4th Panzerarmee left outside Stalingrad, Generaloberst Hermann Hoth's renamed Armeegruppe Hoth. The plan was for Hoth to make a concerted thrust with a single Panzer corps (General Friedrich Kirchner's LVII Panzer Corps, consisting initially of the 6th and 232nd Panzer Divisions, but subsequently reinforced with the 17th Panzer Division) not from Nizhne Chirskaya, the point nearest Stalingrad, but from Kotelnikovo farther to the south. Von Manstein's reasoning was that this axis would secure greater tactical surprise, provide LVII Panzer Corps with the best terrain for its advance, and face the weakest of the Soviets armies, namely Major General N. I. Trufanov's 51st Army of Lieutenant General A. I. Eremenko's Stalingrad Front. An advance from Nizhne Chirskaya would have faced the excellent 5th Tank and 5th Shock Armies of Lieutenant General N. F. Vatutin's South-West Front, which had played the most prominent part in the successful implementation of 'Uranus'. The flanks of Armeegruppe Hoth would be protected in the north-west by General Karl Hollidt's Armeegruppe Hollidt, and in the south-east by General C. A. Constantinescu's Romanian 4th Army.

The offensive began on 12 December with the 230 tanks of the 6th and 23rd Panzer Divisions, and with the aid of IV Fliegerkorps at first made good progress through the Soviet 126th and 302nd Rifle Divisions, but in reserve Trufanov had IV and XIII Mechanized Corps, and these began to blunt the speed of the German advance once the German spearheads had crossed the River Aksai. Eremenko also committed IV Cavalry Corps, and the Soviet front was also allocated VII Tank Corps and the 2nd Guards Army from the South-West Front. These strengthened forces finally halted the Germans along the line of the River Myshkova between Kapkinsky and Nizhne Kumsky. By 23 December the Germans were completely at

335

a halt, and von Manstein defied Hitler by ordering Paulus to break out from Stalingrad to the Myshkova. Paulus refused to do so, and the last chance for the German 6th Army to save itself had gone, especially as the Soviets had launched flanking offensives round Armeegruppen Hollidt and Hoth that pushed the Germans back south of Kotelnikovo by 31 December.

Wintermärchen (winter tales) Offensive planned by Generalfeldmarschall Wilhelm List's 'Army Group 'A' for General Italo Gariboldi's Italian 8th Army to launch an offensive against the Soviet bridgehead over the river Don (September 1942).

Winterzauber (winter magic) German operation against Soviet partisans operating in Lithuania (January/February 1943).

Wirbelwind (whirlwind) Operation planned by Generalfeldmarschall Fedor von Bock's Army Group 'B' (June 1942) for an offensive by Generaloberst Maximilian Freiherr von Weichs' 2nd Army and Generaloberst Hermann Hoth's 4th Panzerarmee in the region of Sukhinichi. This concept was overtaken by the 'Blau I' offensive launched by Armeegruppe von Weichs (2nd Army and 2nd Panzerarmee) on 28 June with the object of taking the upper reaches of the River Don as far north as Voronezh to protect the left flank of the German formations advancing south-east towards the Don/Volga landbridge and Stalingrad.

W.N. Designation of UK coastal convoys (together with a numerical suffix) plying the route between the Clyde (later Loch Ewe) and Methil, and inaugurated in July 1940.

Wolfsschanze (wolf's lair) (i) Designation of Hitler's headquarters at Rastenburg in East Prussia.
(ii) Designation of Hitler's headquarters near Reims in France.

Wolfsschlucht I (wolf's den I) Designation of Hitler's headquarters near Givet in France (6 June/25 July 1940).

Wolfsschlucht II (wolf's den II) Designation of Hitler's headquarters near Margival in France for Operation 'Seelowe' (17 June 1940 onwards).

Wolke (cloud) Designation of German reinforcements for Norway (November 1942), ordered by Hitler at the expense of more needy fronts as he remained convinced that Norway was a 'zone of destiny' into which Winston Churchill would inevitably launch a major invasion.

Wolsey SAS airborne intelligence operation near Francieres (26 August 1944).

Wop Designation of the counteroffensive launched by Lieutenant General George S. Patton's US II Corps to retake Gafsa and El Guettar (17 March 1943). These towns had been lost to the Germans in Operation 'Morgenluft'.

Workshop British plan for the capture of Pantelleria Island (1941).

Wowser US 15th Air force strategic/tactical strike against German forces in northern Italy, especially those around Bologna (15 April 1945) in preparation for the breakthrough of Lieutenant General Mark W. Clark's US 5th Army in this sector just north of the 'Gotisch Linie' defences.

W.P. Designation of British coastal convoys (together with a numerical suffix) plying the route from Bristol to Portsmouth, and inaugurated in July 1941.

Wreckage Abortive low-level daylight sweep against Bremen by light bombers of No. 2 Group, RAF Bomber Command (30 June 1941).

Wren US codename for German acoustic-homing torpedoes.

W.S. Designation of military convoys (together with a numerical suffix) plying the route from the UK to the Middle East via the Cape of Good Hope, and inaugurated in June 1940 to end in August 1943.

Wunderland (wonderland) Surface raid

by the German pocket battleship *Admiral Scheer* (16/30 August 1942). The object of this unusual operation was to attack Soviet shipping believed to be using the North-East Passage to ferry men and supplies from Siberia. The *Admiral Scheer* sailed from Narvik on 16 August and passed north of Novaya Zemlya; the only victim the German ship found was a Soviet icebreaker, and the *Admiral Scheer* returned to Narvik on 30 August.

Würzburg German gunlaying, searchlight-control and (for a short time) night-fighter control radar.

Würzlaus German modification of 'Würzburg' in an effort to mitigate the worst effects of 'Window' on the type.

X

X **(i)** Allied codename for Australia.

(ii) Japanese occupation of Christmas Island (31 March/3 April 1942). Lying in the Indian Ocean to the south of Java, this island is a valuable source of phosphate, and in 1942 the island was garrisoned by about 100 British troops. The phosphate workings were shelled and destroyed by the Japanese battleships *Haruna* and *Kongo* on 7 March, and a small occupation force was despatched from Makassar on 25 March under the command of Rear Admiral Kyuji Kubo. The transport ships were escorted by the light cruisers *Natori*, *Nagara* and *Naka*, and by the destroyers *Amatsukaze*, *Minegumo* and *Natsugumo*. The island was bombarded on 31 March as the Japanese troops landed, and the garrison surrendered almost immediately. In the bombardment the flagship *Naka* had been missed by three torpedoes, and on 1 April the US submarine *Seawolf* finally succeeded in hitting her, occasioning damage that caused the Japanese ship to be towed to Singapore. On 3 April the Japanese evacuated Christmas Island as it was unsuitable for the construction of an airstrip.

X.C. Designation of Indian Ocean convoys (together with a numerical suffix) plying the route from the Chagos and Maldive Islands to Colombo, and inaugurated in May 1943.

X.K. Designation of special 'Torch' return convoys (together with a numerical suffix) plying the route from Gibraltar to the UK, and inaugurated in October 1942.

X.T. Designation of Mediterranean local convoys (together with a numerical suffix) plying the route from Alexandria to Tripoli, Libya, and inaugurated in January 1943.

X.T.G. Designation of Mediterranean local convoys (together with a numerical suffix) plying the route from Alexandria to Gibraltar via Tripoli, Libya, and inaugurated in June 1943.

Y

Yokum Allied air support operation for Operation 'Dragoon' (15 August 1944). This operation was undertaken in support of Lieutenant General Alexander M. Patch's US 1st Army by the 2,100 aircraft of Brigadier General Gordon P. Saville's US 12th Air Force, operating from bomber bases in Italy and from 14 specially constructed fighter airfields around Bastia in northern Corsica, and by the 216 aircraft carried on the nine escort carriers of Rear Admiral T. H. Troubridge's command within Vice Admiral H. Kent Hewitt's Western Task Force.

Z

Z Japanese attack on the US Pacific Fleet in Pearl Harbor (7 December 1941). This attack marked the entry of Japan into World War II, and was designed by Admiral Isoroku Yamamoto, commander-in-chief of the Combined Fleet, as a decisive stroke to eliminate Admiral Husband E. Kimmel's US Pacific Fleet at its base on Oahu Island in the Hawaiian group. The attack was planned round the daring use of carrierborne air power, and was intended to provide Japan with the chance to seize the territories she wished and to consolidate round them a defensive perimeter of sufficient strength that when the USA had recovered from the effects of Operation 'Z' it would realise the futility of any counteroffensive across the Pacific and so sue for peace on the basis of the *status quo*.

The force selected for the attack was Vice Admiral Chuichi Nagumo's 1st Air Fleet, comprising the fleet carriers *Akagi*, *Kaga*, *Hiryu*, *Soryu*, *Shokaku* and *Zuikaku*, the light cruiser *Abukuma* and 9 destroyers, supported by the battleships *Hiei* and *Kirishima*, and the heavy cruisers *Tone* and *Chikuma*. There were also 3 submarines for reconnaissance of the approach route for the 1st Air Fleet, 2 destroyers for the operation against Midway Island planned on the return journey, and a fleet train of 8 tankers and supply ships. The 1st Air Fleet assembled in Tankan Bay in the Kurile Islands from 22 November 1941, and began to sail on 26 November, a circuitous northern route being selected to reduce the chances of detection. However, all the signs of a Japanese attack were there, and the news that Japan was about to enter the war was available from messages decoded by the Americans, but nothing was done to safeguard the Pacific Fleet at Pearl Harbor even as Nagumo approached the launch point for his aircraft early in the morning of 7 December. In Pearl Harbor the Pacific Fleet's eight battleships were neatly arranged in rows, and their crews were for the most part enjoying weekend leave.

At 06.00 Nagumo began to launch his first strike force, consisting of 43 Mitsubishi A6M fighters, 51 Aichi D3A dive-bombers and 89 Nakajima B5N bombers (49 carrying 1,600-lb armour-piercing shells modified as bombs and the other 40 carrying torpedoes specially modified for shallow running). Shortly before 08.00 the attack began, the fighters peeling off to strafe airfields and the bombers beginning a decisive blow against Pearl Harbor. Only three of the battleships were not hit, and as the Japanese pulled out at 08.35 the *West Virginia* was sinking, the *Arizona* had settled on the bottom, the *Oklahoma* had capsized, the *Tennessee* was on fire, and the damaged *Nevada* was making for the harbour mouth. But already a second strike force was approaching the harbour, this formation comprising 36 fighters, 54 level bombers and 81 dive-bombers. The pattern was similar to that of the first wave when the attack started at 09.15, and the *Nevada* was forced to beach herself while the *Pennsylvania* was severely damaged.

The Japanese pulled out at 09.45 having lost 9 fighters, 15 dive-bombers and 5 level bombers. American losses were 3 battleships sunk, 1 battleship capsized, 4 battleships severely damaged, 3 light cruisers and 3 destroyers damaged, 65 out of 231 US Army aircraft destroyed, 200 out of 250 US Navy and Marine Corps aircraft destroyed, and some 3,225 Americans killed plus another 1,272 wounded. The Japanese had scored a decisive victory, but this was only of a tactical or perhaps operational nature, the great strategic prizes being missed as the Pacific Fleet's three carriers (*Enterprise*, *Lexington* and *Saratoga*) were absent, and as Nagumo refused his air commanders' pleas for a third strike to eliminate the Pacific Fleet's unprotected oil tank farms and maintenance facilities. But Japan had roused the wrath of the USA, and this industrial giant was to exact a terrible vengeance in the years to come as the Japanese had completely misassessed the American emotional and military capacity for a sustained war.

Zaubeflöte (magic flute) German operation against Soviet partisans operating in the area of Minsk (17/24 April 1943) and so threatening the lines of communication to Generalfeldmarschall Günther von Kluge's Army Group 'Centre'.

Zahme Sau (tame sow) German tactic devised to counter the effects of 'Window' on the radar-controlled night-fighter network. In such attacks the German night-fighters infiltrated the British bomber streams as best they could to destroy targets of opportunity.

Zahnarzt (dentist) German offensive in Alsace and Lorraine (1/20 January 1945). This was an improvised offensive designed to capitalize on the disorder occasioned in the Allied ranks by the need to deal with Operation 'Herbstnebel', and was undertaken by Reichsführer-SS Heinrich Himmler's Army Group 'Oberrhein' against the overextended US 7th Army of Lieutenant General Alexander M. Patch within Lieutenant General Jacob L. Devers's US 6th Army Group. The offensive is otherwise known as Operation 'Nordwind', and resulted in the virtual destruction of General Friedrich Wiese's 19th Army.

Zebra Allied air supply of weapons and other equipment to the French resistance (25 July 1944).

Zeppelin (i) Designation of the headquarters of the Oberkommando des Heeres at Zossen near Berlin.

(ii) German sabotage mission sent to the Moscow area (5 September 1944).

Ziethen German 16th Army operation against Soviet partisans (1943).

Zigeunerbaron (gypsy baron) Operation undertaken by Army Group 'Centre' against Soviet partisans operating near Bryansk (May 1943) and so threatening the army group's rear-area security and lines of communication.

Zinc British commando liaison mission in Czechoslovakia.

Zipper Plan for the capture of Port Swettenham on the north-west coast of Malaya leading to a southward advance on Singapore (October 1945). The plan was devised by Admiral Lord Louis Mountbatten's South-East Asia Command after the receipt on 3 February 1945 of instructions to complete the liberation of Burma as rapidly as possible and then to invade Malaya with the objects of liberating that country and opening the Strait of Malacca. The best course of action appeared to be an overland advance from Burma via Tenasserim and the Kra isthmus, but it was then decided that the process could be speeded by the capture of Phuket Island as a forward base and staging point (Operation 'Roger'), followed by the capture of a beachhead in the Port Swettenham/Port Dickson area of north-west Malaya (Operation 'Zipper') and an advance south towards Singapore (Operation 'Mailfist'). The opposition was found by Field Marshal Count Hisaichi Terauchi's Southern Region command, and more specifically by the Japanese 29th Army in Malaya under the command of General K. Doihara's 7th Area Army. The 29th Army had a total of two divisions (the 46th and 94th) and four independent mixed brigades (the 35th, 36th, 37th and 70th) for the defence of Malaya, the Andaman Islands and the Nicobar Islands. The task facing the 29th Army was thus considerable, and the 7th Area Army thus took over responsibility for the area between Penang and Singapore with the 46th Division,

Zitadelle

this being replaced in the 29th Army by the 37th Division from Indo-China. 'Zipper' therefore faced two divisions and the 70th Independent Mixed Brigade, supported by a tank battalion, in the Kra isthmus region. The Allied landing force for 'Zipper' was Lieutenant General O. L. Roberts's XXXIV Indian Corps (5th, 23rd, 25th and 26th Indian Divisions, 3rd Commando Brigade and one parachute brigade of the British 6th Airborne Division), and though 'Zipper' itself was to use just two divisions and one brigade, the corps' additional forces were to be landed as soon as possible for 'Mailfist'.

The collapse of Japan eventually removed the urgency from 'Zipper', but the operation was undertaken in advance of the original schedule as the best means of getting Allied troops back into Malaya. On 9 September Major General G. N. Wood's 25th Indian Division and Major General D. C. Hawthorn's 23rd Indian Division each landed one brigade (south of Port Swettenham and north of Port Dickson). The landings were extremely difficult as the beaches were far softer than expected, but the forces secured their objectives without undue difficulty as there was no opposition, and troops plus their equipment and vehicles began to come ashore in large numbers for the reoccupation of Malaya.

Zitadelle (citadel) Designation of the German offensive leading to the Battle of Kursk, the greatest armoured engagement of all time (4/12 July 1943). The operation was planned by the German high command under the leadership of Generaloberst Kurt Zeitzler, the chief-of-staff of the Oberkommando des Heeres, in a desperate effort to wrest back from the Soviets the strategic initiative on the Eastern Front, which had passed from the Germans with their catastrophic defeat at Stalingrad in January/February 1943. The operational scenario for Operation 'Zitadelle' was provided by the Soviet and German offensives in the first half of 1943, which had left the Soviets in possession of a vast salient around Kursk (flanked by German re-entrants centred in the north on Orel and in the south on Kharkov), and Hitler determined that this salient would be reduced in 'Zitadelle', which would use Germany's latest armoured fighting vehicles and all available support in what was hoped would be a decisive battle undertaken in the Germans' favourite pincer fashion. The start of the offensive had to be delayed for adequate numbers of these vehicles to reach the front, but this lost time was not compensated by the success of the vehicles, which suffered from mechanical and tactical defects, and also arrived too late for their crews to become fully trained in their deployment.

In the south Generalfeldmarschall Erich von Manstein's Army Group 'South' would launch powerful armoured formations from the region of Belgorod and Kharkov, and in the north Generalfeldmarschall Walter Model's 9th Army of Generalfeldmarschall Günther von Kluge's Army Group 'Centre' would drive south from the region of Orel. The two arms were designed to meet at Kursk and Tim, cutting off the Soviet forces in the salient for subsequent destruction by German infantry forces as the armour exploited to the east. Von Manstein's attacking forces were Generaloberst Hermann Hoth's 4th Panzerarmee and General Werner Kempf's Armeegruppe Kempf. The 4th Panzerarmee deployed General Eugen Ott's LII Corps (3 infantry divisions), General Otto von Knobelsdorff's LXVIII Panzer Corps (1 infantry and 2 Panzer divisions, and the specially strengthened 280-tank Grossdeutschland Panzergrenadier Division) and SS Obergruppenführer Paul Hausser's II SS Panzer Corps (1 infantry division and 3 SS Panzergrenadier divisions). The Armeegruppe Kempf deployed General Hermann Breith's III Panzer Corps (1 infantry and 3 Panzer divisions), General Erhard Raus's Corps Raus (2 infantry divisions) and General Franz Mattenklott's XLII Corps (3 infantry divisions). Von Manstein's reserves amounted to General Walter Nehring's XXIV Panzer Corps (1 Panzer and 1 SS Panzergrenadier division). In all, the Army Group 'South' offensive formations had about 1,000 tanks and 150 assault guns.

The northern arm of the pincer was slightly less formidably constituted, and comprised the 9th Army's XXIII Corps (General Johannes Friessner), XLI Panzer Corps (General Josef Harpe), XLVII Panzer Corps (General Joachim Lemelsen), XLVI Panzer

Corps (General H. Zorn) and XX Corps (General Rudolf Freiherr von Roman). The army reserve was Generalleutnant Hans-Karl Freiherr von Esebeck's Korpsgruppe von Esebeck. In all, Model's 9th Army had 21 divisions, of which 6 were Panzer divisions and 1 a Panzergrenadier division. Model's tank strength was about 900. Air support for 'Zitadelle' was provided by Luftflotte VI's 1. Fliegerdivision (730 aircraft) in the north, and VIII Fliegerkorps (1,100 aircraft) in the south.

The Soviets were expecting the offensive, knew all the vital facts of 'Zitadelle' (as a result of the efforts of Richard Sorge, their able spy in Berlin), and had been given the time to develop their defences in the most meticulous fashion using very large forces designed first to halt the Germans in a battle of attrition, and then to sweep over to the offensive. Under the command of General Georgi Zhukov, the Soviets had thus constructed defences in considerable depth, with 6,000 anti-tank guns and 13,000 other pieces of artillery (plus 1,000 rocket-launchers) in echeloned positions to enfilade the main German axes of advance. Holding the north of the salient was General K. K. Rokossovsky's Central Front with the 48th, 13th, 70th, 65th and 60th Armies, with the 2nd Tank Army in reserve, and holding the south was General N. F. Vatutin's Voronezh Front with the 38th, 40th, 6th Guards and 7th Guards Armies, with the 1st Tank and 69th Armies in reserve. But behind these two formidable groupings was General I. S. Konev's Steppe Front, the theatre reserve with the 5th Guards, 27th, 47th, 53rd and 5th Guards Tank Armies. The Central Front was supported by Lieutenant General S. I. Rudenko's 16th Air Army, the Voronezh Front by Lieutenant General S. A. Krasovsky's 2nd Air Army, and the Steppe Front by Lieutenant General S. K. Goryunov's 5th Air Army, with a total of 3,100 aircraft. The Soviet armour strength was about 3,600 vehicles. Though the Germans did not know it, they stood no chance against an enemy in full possession of the German plans, fully prepared and now equipped with weapons every bit as good as those of the Germans, and available in far larger numbers to troops now well versed in their tactical employment.

The two 'Zitadelle' offensives got under way on 4 July, and succeeded in making only small gains before the depth of the Soviet defences checked them. In the north Model's forces managed to advance about 6 miles before being halted in front of Olkhovatka and Ponyri with dire losses (25,000 dead, plus 200 tanks and 200 aircraft lost), but in the south XLVIII, II SS and III Panzer Corps managed greater success before being slowed drastically after an advance of 25 miles. Again losses were high, Army Group 'South' admitting that 10,000 men had been killed and 350 tanks lost. The threat in the south was clearly the greater of the two, and elements of the Steppe Front (5th Guards, 5th Guard Tank and 53rd Armies) were committed, together with the Voronezh Front's own reserve, to halt the Germans in front of Prokohorovka and Oboyan. Here vast tank battles raged over ideal armour-warfare country before the Germans were completely checked by 12 July.

Totally exhausted by this comprehensive defeat, the Germans were now on the receiving end of massive Soviet counteroffensives, which almost immediately wiped out the Germans' dearly-won gains and then swept the Germans out of their Orel and Kharkov salients to the north and south respectively of the Kursk salient. From this point onwards the Germans were on the strategic defensive on the Eastern Front.

Zitronella (lemon) German naval raid on Spitzbergen (6/8 September 1943). The raid was undertaken by the battleship *Tirpitz*, the battle-cruiser *Scharnhorst* and 10 destroyers, which sailed from Altenfjord on 6 September, bombarded the Allied installations in 7 September and returned to Altenfjord by 8 September.

Z-Plan German pre-war naval construction programme. This plan had its origins in the early 1930s, and was designed against Hitler's assertion that no major military undertakings would be initiated until 1944/1945. The plan called for the construction of a balanced fleet of surface ships and submarines, centred on 13 battleships, 33 cruisers, four aircraft-carriers, a large force of destroyers and some 250 U-boats. At the beginning of World War II this programme was cancelled, Germany's industrial facilities being geared instead to the rapid completion of the battleships *Bismarck* and *Tirpitz*, the cruisers *Prinz Eugen* and *Seydlitz* and the aircraft-carrier *Graf von Zeppelin*, and to the build-up of U-boat construction. In the event neither the *Seydlitz* nor the *Graf von Zeppelin* was completed.

Zwischenspiel (interlude) German reoccupation of Samos in the Aegean (November 1943). The island had been seized by the British in September 1943, but with the loss of other islands in the Aegean to German amphibious and airborne assault, it was decided to evacuate the garrisons on the last islands held by the British, the troops being ferried out of Samos on 19/20 November. The Germans were thus able to bring in their forces unopposed.